WORLD GUIDE TO ENVIRONMENTAL ISSUES AND ORGANIZATIONS

Other recent current affairs and economics titles from Longman Group UK Limited include the following:

Political Scandals and Causes Célèbres since 1945: An International Reference Compendium (1990)

Treaties and Alliances of the World (5th edition), edited by Nicholas Rengger (1990)

Communist and Marxist Parties of the World (2nd edition), edited by Roger East (1990)

Political and Economic Encyclopaedia of Western Europe, edited by CIRCA Ltd (1990)

Youth Movements of The World, by William D. Angel (1990)

Political and Economic Encyclopaedia of the Soviet Union and Eastern Europe, edited by Stephen White (1990)

The European Parliament, by Francis Jacobs and Richard Corbett, with Michael Shackleton (1990)

Anti-Nuclear Movements: A World Survey of Opposition to Nuclear Energy, by Wolfgang Rüdig (1990)

The Broken Mirror: China after Tiananmen, edited by George Hicks (1990)

The British Trade Union Directory, edited and compiled by Wolodymyr Maksymiw (1990)

Employers' Organizations of the World, edited by Martin Upham (1990)

World Development Directory, compiled and edited by Roger East, Miles Smith-Morris and Martin Wright for CIRCA Ltd (1990)

Political and Economic Encyclopaedia of the Pacific, edited by Gerald Segal (1990)

World Directory of Minorities, compiled by the Minority Rights Group (1990)

Religion in Politics, edited by Stuart Mews (1990)

Western European Political Parties: A Comprehensive Guide, edited by Francis Jacobs (1989)

Trade Unions of the World, 1989–90 (2nd edition, 1989)

CPA World Directory of Old Age, compiled by the Centre for Policy on Ageing (1989)

Elections since 1945: a Worldwide Reference Compendium, general editor Ian Gorvin (1989)

Reuters Glossary: International Economic and Financial Terms, edited by the Senior Staff of Reuters Limited (1989)

Political Parties of the World (3rd edition), edited by Alan J. Day (1988)

WORLD GUIDE TO ENVIRONMENTAL ISSUES AND ORGANIZATIONS

Edited by
PETER BRACKLEY

with contributions by the following:
Frans Berkhout, Stewart Boyle, J. C. Farman, James Longhurst, Francis McGowan, Alasdair McIntyre, Gordon MacKerron, Jeffrey McNeely, Andrew Mitchell, Charles T. (Tim) Savin, John Tims, Stephen Trudgill, Brian Walker and Staff of the British Antarctic Survey

Foreword by
Dr Mostafa K. Tolba
Executive Director
United Nations Environment Programme

LONGMAN
CURRENT
AFFAIRS

WORLD GUIDE TO ENVIRONMENTAL ISSUES AND ORGANIZATIONS

Published by Longman Group UK Limited, Westgate House,
The High, Harlow, Essex, CM20 1YR, United Kingdom.
Telephone (0279) 442601
Telex 81491 Padlog
Facsimile (0279) 444501

DPA
DIRECTORY PUBLISHERS ASSOCIATION

Distributed exclusively in the United States and Canada by
Gale Research Company, Book Tower, Detroit, Michigan 48226, USA

ISBN 0-582-06270-5 (Longman)
ISBN 0-8103-8353-5 (Gale)

British Library Cataloguing in Publication Data
World guide to environmental issues and organizations.
1. Environment. Organization
I. Brackley, Peter *1923–*
333.72

ISBN 0-582-06270-5

CONTENTS

About the Authors vii

Foreword xi

Introduction xvii

List of Acronyms xx

PART I. ISSUES

1 Acid Deposition *James W. S. Longhurst* 3

2 The Antarctic *D. J. Drewry, Peter J. Beck, J. A. Heap, R. C. R. Willan, D. W. H. Walton* 24

3 Deforestation *Andrew Mitchell* 42

4 The Greenhouse Effect and Global Warming *Peter Brackley* 52

5 Land Degradation and Desertification *Brian W. Walker* 66

6 The Loss of Biological Diversity *Jeffrey A. McNeely* 79

7 Marine Pollution *Alasdair D. McIntyre* 93

8 Nuclear Power and the Environment *Gordon Mackerron and Frans Berkhout* 106

9 Ozone Depletion: Industrial Halocarbons and their Effect on the Stratospheric Ozone Layer *J. C. Farman* 125

10 Renewable Energy *Francis McGowan* 133

11 Vehicle Emissions *J. M. Tims* 148

12 Water Quality *Stephen Trudgill* 161

13 Other Issues *Peter Brackley* 175

PART II. POLITICS *Stewart Boyle* 181

PART III. CONVENTIONS, REPORTS, DIRECTIVES AND AGREEMENTS *C. T. Savin* 221

PART IV. ORGANIZATIONS

International 256
Regional 294
Government Departments 308
National 314

Bibliography, Further Reading and References 357

Index 367

ABOUT THE AUTHORS

Dr P. Beck is Reader in International History, Faculty of Human Sciences, Kingston Polytechnic.

Dr Frans Berkhout is a Research Fellow at the Science Policy Research Unit at the University of Sussex. He is the author of several publications on radwaste management and nuclear decommissioning, including a book *Radioactive Waste: Technology and Politics* to be published by Routledge in 1990. He gave evidence to the Hinkley Point 'C' Public Inquiry on the economics of the back-end of the nuclear fuel cycle. His current research is on the consequences for nuclear weapons non-proliferation of the expansion of civil plutonium production in Europe and Japan.

Stewart Boyle is currently the Energy and Environment Programme Director at the Association for the Conservation of Energy. He is also joint co-ordinator of the Climate Action Network-UK. He has been involved with environmental pressure groups since 1978, and was National Energy Campaigner for Friends of the Earth from 1984–88. He has written extensively on energy and pollution matters, including *The Greenhouse Effect—A Practical Guide to the World's Changing Climate* (1989), *Solving the Greenhouse Dilemma* (1989) and *Critical Decision—Should Britain buy the PWR*? (1988).

Peter Brackley served with British Petroleum from 1943 to 1982 in various parts of the world including residence in Iran, Aden, USA, and including London posts of General Manager of Worldwide Refining, General Manager of Worldwide Environmental Control and General Manager of Management Consultancy. He has been a member of company boards of directors in the UK, Belgium, The Netherlands, Sweden, Norway, Turkey, and the FRG. He has held the following posts: Chairman, CONCAWE 1976–78; Chairman, Sullom Voe Environmental Advisory Group 1974–76; member of Nature Conservancy Council, Advisory Committee for England 1976–86; Vice-Chairman of environmental sessions of the World Petroleum Congress in Bucharest 1979 and London 1983; Member, IPIECA Executive Committee 1974–77. Currently he is Hon. Treasurer of The Field Studies Council. In addition, Peter Brackley is an Associate fellow of the RIIA, Energy and Environment Programme, and author of their publications (Gower) *Acid Deposition and Vehicle Emissions: European Pressure on Britain* (1987) and *Energy and Environmental Terms: a Glossary* (1988).

Dr A. Clarke is Head of Marine Life Sciences Division, British Antarctic Survey.

Dr D. J. Drewry is Director of the British Antarctic Survey.

Joe Farman, OBE, is with the British Antarctic Survey in Cambridge, part of the Natural Environment Research Council. He first detected and described the "ozone hole" over Antarctica in 1984–85.

Dr J. A. Heap is Head of Polar Regions Section at the Foreign and Commonwealth Office.

James Longhurst is an environmental scientist with nine years' experience in the design and operation of environmental monitoring programmes. He graduated from Plymouth Polytechnic in 1980 and gained his Ph.D. at Birmingham in 1988 on the environmental implications of fossil fuels. He has been director of the Acid Rain Information Centre at Manchester Polytechnic since its creation in 1984 and has published extensively on pollution control and energy utilization as related to the environment. He edited, in 1989, *Acid Deposition: Sources, Effects and Control* for the British Library and is a member of the UK Department of the Environment's Review Group on Acid Rain.

Francis McGowan is a Research Fellow with the Energy Programme at the Science Policy Research Unit, University of Sussex. He is the co-author of *The World Market for Heavy Electrical Equipment* (with Steve Thomas) and *A Single European Market for Energy* (with Jonathan Stern et al.). His research interests include: energy technology assessment, European energy policy, and the electricity supply industry.

Alasdair McIntyre is a graduate in Zoology from Glasgow University and has published some 90 papers on fisheries, marine ecology and pollution. He was Director of Fisheries Research for Scotland from 1983 to 1986, and thereafter Emeritus Professor of Fisheries and Oceanography at the Department of Zoology, Aberdeen University, and a former Chairman of the United Nations Group of Experts on the Scientific Aspects of Marine Pollution (GESAMP) and of the Advisory Committee on Marine Pollution of the International Council for the Exploration of the Sea (ICES).

Gordon MacKerron is a Senior Fellow in the Science Policy Research Unit at the University of Sussex. He has worked for the last 12 years on issues of energy policy and economics, especially nuclear power and most recently on decommissioning. Besides publishing widely in these areas and making frequent radio and television broadcasts, he has also advised a number of agencies on nuclear/electric questions. These include the Monopolies and Mergers Commission, the Electricity Council and the National Audit Office. He also recently gave invited evidence to the House of Commons Select Committee on Energy.

Jeffrey McNeely is Chief Conservation Officer at the International Union for Conservation of Nature and Natural Resources in Switzerland, where he has worked for a decade. Prior to going to IUCN, he lived in Southeast Asia for 12 years, contributing to a wide range of conservation activities for governments, United Nations agencies, and private conservation organizations. He is the author or editor of over 15 books, including *Mammals of Thailand; Wildlife Management in Southeast Asia; Culture and Conservation; Economics and Biological Diversity; People and Protected Areas in the Hindu-Kush Himalaya; National Parks, Conservation and Development; Conserving the World's Biological Diversity;* and *Soul of The Tiger.*

Andrew Mitchell graduated in Zoology from the University of Bristol in 1974. He has 10 years' experience of organizing field research programmes in the tropics, during which he led pioneering studies of the rainforest canopy using aerial walkways. As a broadcaster he has contributed to a number of major series with the BBC and Channel Four on world forests. He is the author of seven books including *The Enchanted Canopy, A Fragile Paradise* and *Vanishing Paradise*, on rainforests. He is Deputy Director of the international research and conservation organization Earthwatch (Europe).

Charles T. (Tim) Savin graduated in Chemistry from London University in 1950 and became a barrister-at-Law in 1962 as a member of Gray's Inn. Following National Service and work as a research and development chemist he joined British Petroleum in 1959. He held a number of posts in that company, including Assistant Manager of the Environmental Control Centre which covered BP's concern and activities, worldwide, to safeguard the environment and to ensure, as far as possible, that its own operations were environmentally sound. He retired in 1988 and now works for the Crown Prosecution Service.

John Tims has worked at the Esso Research Centre, Abingdon since graduating from Oxford University in 1959 with a Honours Degree in Chemistry. During his 30 years in the oil industry he has worked on virtually all petroleum products, but for the last decade has been concerned primarily with transportation fuels and their effects on vehicle performance and emissions.

Dr Mostafa Tolba is Executive Director of the United Nations Environment Programme, based in Nairobi. He led Egypt's delegation to the 1972 Stockholm Conference on the Human Environment which led to the creation of UNEP and soon after he was appointed its deputy director in 1973, moving to his present position in 1976. In leading UNEP, Dr Tolba has applied his belief that environmental decisions are inseparable from socio-political decisions. He has made UNEP an organization which functions largely as a catalyst that informs, assists and spurs governments and others to action. He had extensive experience with various official Egyptian bodies and government appointments and has received decorations from many countries and honours from the academic community around the world, and is the author of some 95 papers on plant diseases, anti-fungal substances and the physiology of micro-organisms, and of more than 200 statements and numerous books and articles on the environment. Dr Tolba contributed the Foreword to the present volume.

Dr Stephen Trudgill is a Reader in the Department of Geography at the University of Sheffield where he specializes in soils and environmental problems. He has travelled widely in the USA, Australia, India and Ethiopia to study environmental problems. He is currently environmental reviewer for *Progress in Physical Geography*, Environment Columnist for *Geography Review* and Chairman of the Scientific and Educational Committee of the Field Studies Council. His books include *Solute Processes* (Wiley, 1986) and *Barriers to a Better Environment* (Belhaven Press, 1990).

Brian Walker, having spent 25 years in the corporate sector, served two terms for 10 years as Director-General of Oxfam, one term as the Director of the Independent Commission on International Humanitarianism Issues in Geneva and one five-year term as President of the International Institute for Environment and Development. Currently, he is the Executive Director of Earthwatch Europe, based in Oxford. He has travelled widely in developing countries and is a regular lecturer, broadcaster and writer on Third World subjects. He is a member of the Editorial Board of the *World Resources Report* and Trustee of the World Food and Peace Commission and of the Oxford Project for Peace Studies.

Dr D. W. H. Walton is Head of the Terrestrial and Freshwater Life Sciences Division, British Antarctic Survey.

Dr R. Willan is a geologist at the British Antarctic Survey.

FOREWORD

Dr Mostafa K. Tolba
Executive Director
United Nations Environment Programme

These are extraordinary times. Suddenly everything seems possible. Cold War seems to be winding down. Conflicts in the developing world appear to be no longer fuelled by great power patronage.

From my vantage point, these are extraordinary times for another reason. From its position as an item rather low on the world agenda we have seen the environment rocket to the forefront of global public concern. However, we still have a formidable task before us—to make peace with nature.

As we continue to waste the natural resources of our planet, new tensions are being created which, unless we as a family of nations mend our ways, will imperil the political stability of the whole world.

The great danger is that we will not see the environmental dimensions behind the new conflicts. And we will seek to resolve disputes through arms—a reaction with a milennial pedigree.

Our notions of what constitutes "security" remain stubbornly narrow. The time has come to recognize the environmental dimension of individual and collective security.

I want to describe UNEP's view of "security". In doing so I shall outline the environmentally-destructive forces which are already undermining collective security. I will seek to show how national, regional and global security are indivisible. And argue that if the world is serious about tackling the environmental crisis with its serious implications on security there is no alternative to global co-operation and the generation of additional resources that goes far beyond anything we see today.

In the past simpler technologies and low population levels contained damage to the environment. These precepts no longer apply. Human economic activities are so vast. Environmental degradation is assuming global dimensions.

Ozone depletion and climate change have served notice that no country can quarantine itself from what happens anywhere in the world. Consideration of these two issues has shown that unwittingly the poor nations have acquired a new power—the power of destruction, over the rich and over themselves.

These tendencies are dangerous for the security of the individual as well as the state. The international diplomacy of the next 50 years could be locked into the chaos and disruption created by the wasting of the natural foundations of the global economy, its grasslands, forests, rivers, seas and air. But action to improve the quality of our environment has vast unifying potential.

Since 1972, since the UN Conference on Environment, we have seen these unifying forces at work. We have seen, for example, how legal treaties have brought nations together. UNEP's regional seas treaties, now involving over 120 states worldwide, have created partnerships among traditional antagonists. UNEP has also helped the nations of the Zambezi River Basin to agree an instrument for its conservation and equitable management. We can reverse the dangerous tendencies of potential conflict, of potential global instability caused by environmental deterioration.

But we need to think about the environmental dimension to security in basically four contexts: national, regional, inter-state and global.

First, within the nation state wastage of resources is creating internal strains and stresses. Each year the world has 90 million more mouths to feed, but 28 million tonnes less soil on which to grow its food. While total global food production is going up, *per capita* production in parts of India and in large areas of Africa is going down. The drift of environmental refugees from the countryside into the slums and shantytowns is an obvious manifestation of how environmental stress can result in social stress. In countries as different as Thailand, Nepal and Mali, deforestation and land degradation has led to open clashes between local people for dwindling resources.

In the Yemen Arab Republic, as time-honoured systems of environmental management break down, there have been civil disturbances as neighbouring communities squabble over the loss of food security.

In Brazil the murder of the rubber tappers' leader, Chico Mendes, was probably a manifestation of civil strife between competing users of the jungle: between those seeking to turn the forest into pasture and the denizens of the forest who exploit its bounty intact.

Second, is the potential for conflict to spill over borders and to involve two or more states. Recently the open clash over desertifying pasture between Senegal and Mauritania made the world's press. In Europe we have already seen how acid rain and North Sea pollution have poisoned relations between states. Chernobyl was a chilling warning that a nuclear accident can involve a whole continent.

Competition over finite freshwater resources is an obvious potential flashpoint. An estimated 40% of the world's population depends for drinking water, irrigation and hydropower on 214 river sy stems shared by two or more countries.

Can Egypt allow nations sharing the watershed of the Nile River to disrupt the lifeblood of its economy—of its very survival? Can Iraq and Syria permit a critical reduction in the flow of the Euphrates? And what will Niger and Nigeria do if planned ambitious barrage and irrigation schemes in nations upstream dry up to the Niger River?

In the case of Central America and Haiti we have already seen how land degradation has forced people to migrate across borders. In their new countries they move into the overcrowded urban areas where new racial and social tensions are created.

Third, is the potential for North/South conflict.

I am talking here about double standards: one for the rich and one for the poor—an attitude that is morally as well as environmentally unjustified. It is reported that in Cubatão, Brazil, multinational corporations have built factories that took advantage of lax local laws. It is also reported that they have helped to make it one of the most polluted places on Earth. And we all know about Bhopal—a name now synonymous with environmental tragedy.

In the aftermath of the anger and passions generated by the export of hazardous wastes to West Africa, African nations have still to agree to the Basel convention that seeks to put an end to uncontrolled disposal and movement of these wastes. A signed and posted warning of how environmental discrimination can engender lasting suspicion and ill-feeling.

And, fourth, is the global dimension. The sum of all the trends I have outlined pose a world threat entirely without precedent. As destructive as a nuclear war, but one made all the more insidious by the stealth with which it destroys the biological wealth of nations.

It is estimated, for example, that tropical forest clearance accounts for the extinction of up to 6,000 species a year. But since only a fraction have been recorded we barely notice their passing. Apart from the losses, the use of these resources itself would raise tensions as developing countries sought compensation for the profits made from new medicines and industrial products derived from their genetic storehouses.

There may be some uncertainties about what is happening to the ozone layer. But what we know for sure is that human activities have already led to its depletion. A depletion that threatens human health and food security.

The drive for economic growth this century may result in a change in the climate—a global warming—on the scale that brought the planet out of its most recent ice age. It took nature 10,000 years to completely alter the ecological face of the Earth, and we are quite possibly facing a change just as large on the timescale of 40 to 60 years.

If only 1% of the world's projected population of six billion by the year 2000 were to be affected by sea level rise induced by global warming that would mean 60 million migrants. Five per cent would produce 300 million. What displacement of populations on this scale will mean for global security scarcely bears thinking about. But think about it we must.

The point is that even if the planet was subject to no threat other than global warming, the case for a new kind of planet-wide co-operation would be overwhelming.

The environment is threatened either because people have too much—or too little. And it is poverty—what Mrs Indira Gandhi once described as the pollution of poverty—that is the most destructive of the two. The rich have the mean to mend their ways; the underprivileged majority of the world's population do not.

If we want to head off the prospect of 21st century eco-wars, the world will have to mobilize not millions, but billions of additional dollars. That is why so much of the environmental debate in this decade will turn on public expenditure decisions taken by all nations. Saving the world is not going to be cheap.

The debate is being fuelled by how the public determines what constitutes "security" and by the way in which the public perceives the nature of the threat to him or herself or to his or her family. After all, so much of the rhetoric of security works at the emotional level of appeals to the need to protect the family and a "way of life" from external threat.

In practice, individual and collective security cannot be segregated. Action is mutually reinforcing. There is not much point in the individual taking action unless the government is responsive. And there is not much point in nations taking steps to conserve energy or protect coasts and rivers unless their neighbours do likewise. No country—no matter how mighty—can protect its own patch of the sky.

What I am implying here is that the debate about environment and security must take place simultaneously on what are, essentially, three levels.

First, the personal level. For most of the world's people, for most of the time security is a strictly local affair—a safe home, a decent standard of living and an ability to take decisions that safeguard the family and community. If a mother feels disempowered to protect her children from lead in the air or toxic substances in the water, then this becomes a matter of her own security. If she believes that the greenhouse effect is likely to alter radically the climate, possibly in her lifetime but certainly in her children's lifetime, then that too becomes an issue of her own security.

Second, is the national level. The first duty of the state is to preserve peace and territorial integrity. These twin aims are achieved through political and military means. But increasingly citizens are demanding that security should be expanded to include their country's environmental quality: clean air, clean water, a secure source of food supply.

Third, is the relatively new concept of global security. The threat from a nuclear war forced us in the post-war period to think in terms of war destroying the whole planet. Human economic activity forces us to think of the environment in the same terms.

Our inheritance from the 19th century, the nation state, is ill-equipped to deal with problems of this magnitude. And this is where the UN and UNEP in particular have a vital role to play. The sovereign state, powerful groupings such as the European Community, cannot deal with these problems unilaterally. Nor is the world ready for a global environmental policeman, even if such a thing was desirable. In current and foreseeable political circumstances, the UN is the only organization in a position to inject equity into the conduct towards the rational use of environmental resources.

Shared resources are vital for development. Traditionally the pattern of their exploitation has been determined by nations with the means and the technology. The UN can play a major role by helping nations to negotiate universally accepted regulations and conventions to ensure equity and sustainability. UNEP—whose annual budget amounts scarcely to the cost of a single wing of a Stealth bomber—is charged with the heavy responsibility of playing a lead role in the negotiation of treaties to address climate change and to protect the planet's species diversity. These will be an acid test of governments' commitment to use shared resources equitably for the lasting benefit of the global community.

The world's nations have not yet demonstrated their readiness to surrender their comparative advantages. But the nature and extent of the environmental crisis and its imperfectly perceived threat to peace are changing the rules, making co-operation and partnership, not confrontation, the only viable course to take.

Recognizing the contribution environmental impoverishment can make to instability is becoming a powerful incentive for a new era of action. There are three issues that must be urgently addressed if this desperately needed era of action is to be ushered in, as follows:

One is the generation of new financial resources. We need levels far beyond anything we have today. We need practical and innovative thinking about revenue-generating methods and market incentives to make the environmental share of the cake bigger. One attractive option is the establishment of user's fees: paying for using environmental resources such as air. Such an intervention in the market mechanism would be needed to ensure prices covered not only energy and raw materials but also the quality of clean air. Fees would be collected by national governments. Part of it would be paid into an international fund to save the Earth.

Such a user's fee fund could be used to assist in the transfer of technology—my second point.

However we approach the problem of environmental security, the question of technology transfer arises. I do not underestimate the formidable nature of this task. We are talking of legal obligations with respect to patents, licences, designs, marks and proprietary rights. The rich nations cannot expect the poor to deny themselves the benefits of ozone layer-depleting technologies or fossil fuel energy or to leap-frog this stage in their industrial development unless the rich nations are prepared to transfer their technology and intellectual property on a concessionary basis. It is a critical issue now being intensively discussed under the Montreal Ozone Layer Protection Accord. It is critical to the extent that it can make or break the next phases in the Protocol negotiations being held to strengthen the Accord planned for London in mid-1990.

It will further have a major impact on the success of negotiations over more complex environmental problems—like climate change and protection of bio-diversity. When we talk about transfer of technology we immediately come to the issues of resources.

And this brings me to my third issue: global environmental protection demands that there should be no conditionality attached to the North–South flow of resources needed to achieve this.

In the biomass-dependant economies, the majority of developing countries, environmental devastation is directly linked to regressive terms of trade, a booming population and to debt. That is why, at the recent Commonwealth Summit, environment was at the top of the agenda; why environment was a major issue in the recent Indian and Brazilian elections; and why the OAU has designated 1991 as the Year of the Environment.

Developing countries have very different perceptions about the causes and cures for their environmental ills. A Brazilian might tell you that land tenure is a most important environmental issue; a West African may say that falling commodity prices is the main culprit. There is a wide gap in perceptions and whatever the rights and wrongs we have to come to terms with this. The worst mistake that could be made is for the rich to apply conditionality to new aid and loans. And to turn environmental protection into a non-tariff barrier.

What I am saying is that financial assistance from the OECD countries is a key element in creating new options, in enlarging the environmental slice of the global cake. A genuine global partnership must be struck with rich and poor which is sensitive to the needs of both. In the last analysis it is for Brazilians to decide if the rainforest is to be preserved. It is for the Indians to decide how desertification is to be stopped.

After two wasted decades, addressing the inequities in the global economy which are among the major causes of environmental deterioration, with its attendant impacts on security will be a formidable and long-term undertaking. And despite all the very welcome pronouncements by political leaders I see very few signs that action on the scale and level required is happening.

I have no patience with those who say that the funds are not available. Approximately four days of global military expenditure—some eight billion dollars—would be enough to pay for five years of the Tropical Forestry Action Plan. Ten per cent of the European Community's agricultural subsidy represents additional UNESCO budget needs over a decade to eliminate illiteracy worldwide.

But even expenditure adjustments on this "wish" list would not be sufficient. Our whole approach to economic development which views environmental resources—clean air, clean water, forest cover, topsoil— as a free good must be reformed. We have to put an end to the separation between economic and ecological priorities and fix unambiguous market values for environmental goods and services.

The environmental crisis in the eastern bloc countries shows that Marx is not environment-friendly. Neither is Adam Smith. Classical liberal economics disregard the value of natural resources and ignore pollution as an externality. These indicators encourage industry and government to deplete resources further and to continue polluting. Too often countries impatient for fast economic growth "mine" their renewable resources and pursue what is essentially ecological deficit financing. In 1988–89 the developing nations transferred $50 billion more to the developed world than they received in new aid and loans. To do so many had to further deplete their natural resources. This is the ecological-deficit financing.

Attention needs to be focused on finding clear-cut values in cost-benefit analysis so that the social as well as productive benefits of environmental protection are clearly calculated. Environmental economics needs to evolve as a rigorous policy tool. Environmentally-sound and sustainable development will remain an elusive goal unless automatic values are built into environmental resources.

Brave and innovative thinking and action are required. Some cherished notions about the sanctity of the free market will have to go by the board. Regulatory incentives, preferential tax rates, rebates, low-interest loans, R&D subsidies for environmentally-friendly products and automatic pollution taxes and—already mentioned—users' fees, are some of the options open to us.

There is no doubt that financing solutions to the global environmental crisis will be the major issue of this decade. It will certainly be a major preoccupation of the UN 1992 Conference on Environment and Development. The establishment of a Global Fund from users' fees cannot be a re-working of Bretton Woods, but a truly global partnership in which all countries contribute and in which all countries have an equal say in resources allocation.

In summary, among the most accessible strategies to deal with environmental problems are: an increase in the flow of resources; debt relief; fair commodity pricing; land reform;

and phasing out of subsidies to developed world agriculture.

Simultaneously, we need to find the additional funds to finance food security for the poor, population control, massive afforestation and desertification control programmes.

This century, no Western democracy has gone to war with another. Why? Surely it is because of a communality of interest which has always been strong enough to overcome inevitable tensions? I believe that by recognizing shared environmental concerns and by working together to overcome shared problems, nations could find a new communality of interest.

The measures I have outlined today are crucial to the peace and security of the world. It is only by making peace with the environment though environmentally-sound development that we can keep the peace among ourselves.

Based on a talk by Dr Tolba at the Royal Institute of International Affairs, London, March 1990.

INTRODUCTION

The "environment" has taken centre stage in the international political debate and the discussion of environmental matters has become increasingly pervasive and strident. World leaders at their summits call for urgent action to preserve the Earth, pressure groups and activists alert the public to particular causes, industrialists are blamed for degrading habitats and scientists strive to unravel complex chemistry. Concerns abound for the future well-being or health of people and nature, for natural resources, climate and ecosystems with, often, scant regard for the knowledge of the detail or science involved. Newspapers, television, radio and the political forums of the world vie with one another in describing the latest stories of ecological or environmental disaster, whether present or predicted. The claim, particularly by politicians, to be "greener" than the next, is widespread and often emotions are roused and information used selectively with an interpretation to bolster a particular point of view.

The approach to environmental issues varies widely between countries. Some, typified by the Federal Republic of Germany, demand early action, long before rigorous scientific proof is available. In the FRG this is embodied in the "Vorsorgeprinzip"—anticipate problems and be prepared. Others, notably the UK, have, in the past, demanded a much higher standard of scientific acceptance although this attitude is moderating and reasonable precaution is more widely endorsed. This different approach can also be described, on the one hand, as allowing the use or practice until some harm is demonstrated, and on the other hand, as preventing or denying the use or practice until it is possible to demonstrate that no harm results. (This latter can be applied to new products but cannot cover the thousands of chemicals and products that have been traditionally used, often for centuries, but which are nevertheless not necessarily without risk.)

A basis for reference is needed, and this volume seeks to describe, factually and in everyday language, the main issues involved, so that users may have a common, agreed starting point for their debate when voicing their particular opinions or proposals.

Dr Mostafa Tolba, Executive Director of UNEP, provides, from his unique position, a broad review, in the Foreword, of the problems facing mankind in the years ahead, the difficult decisions to be made and the changes in attitudes that must, somehow, be achieved.

The topics selected for Part I (Issues) cover the major environmental issues and debates that are common in many parts of the world and which have led or are leading to legislation and control. We invited, to the same brief, experts in the field to give, in their own words and with their own emphasis, an up-to-date picture of the current position with, as necessary, some of the history that brought about the present situation and concern. Policies are reviewed together with the remedial options available, the social implications and alternative strategies. Some details appear in several sections and this repetition is preserved to avoid the need for the reader to switch from one section to another and to maintain a complete and coherent story for each subject.

The subjects have been loosely divided into those with international issues and effects and those issues which are more national. The differentiation is a little indistinct, but in the first are included those matters which arise in many countries and lead to widespread or transboundary pollution or have international implications. With national issues any pollution potential is often local but for other reasons, for example economic or political harmony, often lead to the need for wider accord and agreement.

A separate discussion of population pressures and the consequences of the predicted population growth has been omitted. It is, of course, of wide interest and affects most environmental considerations but, with its heavy political, emotional and religious overtones, it did not seem to fit comfortably in the structure of this reference book although mention is made, as appropriate, in some chapters.

Similarly energy efficiency has not been accorded a distinct section. It is the single, most effective and universal means for alleviating pollution. If energy and resources are used more efficiently less is needed and less pollution or waste results. The possibilities and effects are raised in several chapters.

There are several themes that run through many of the subjects covered. The need, often urgent, for better data and for more scientific research to unravel many of the uncertainties; for better dissemination of information; for a change in attitudes, particularly from the perception that governments must do something to a realization that millions of individuals, all acting in the same direction, can achieve significant change. Several chapters also portray the magnitude of the potential catastrophes that will occur unless something is changed. This is particularly evident, for example, with the current rate of land degradation, more clearly demonstrated today than any perceived climate change or threat of global warming.

Throughout the section the difficulties of achieving change and improvement are apparent. But new findings lead to new theories, even the abandoning of old theories and ideas. New technology, for example genetic engineering, creates new perceptions and possibilities; what is today considered impossible tomorrow becomed plausible. Surprises, too, turn up such as the cause, the damage and consequences of ozone depletion. What, for example, will be shown to be the role of dimethyl sulphide—DMS—in the global environmental effects? Is Gaia mythology or reality?

Part II, on environmental or "green" politics, provides reference to the environmental parties in the major countries in which they are established and active. Most are small in the number of members but have had a significant influence, particularly in Europe, not least in alerting the public to the issues of moment and thereby forcing the larger political parties to adopt policies which reflect the growing concern for environmental care. This has led, in some countries, to the major parties vying for recognition as the most environmentally aware and responsible. The recent political events in Eastern Europe are reflected in the increasing concern and activities in those countries, particularly with the realization of the extent of industrial pollution and environmental degradation.

Environmental concern has led to a large number of meetings, conventions, treaties and agreements to give a framework in which governments and industry have to operate. The most important of these are listed in Part III with details of the results and implications. These are set out under the same subject issues as in Part I.

Part IV provides brief details of the activities and officials of many organizations throughout the world involved in environmental affairs. There are thousands of organizations and millions of individuals active in the environmental field; for example The Environment Council in the UK contacted over 1,000 organizations before compiling their book *Who's Who in the Environment: England*—and there are companion volumes for Scotland, Wales and Northern Ireland. The World Directory of Environmental Organizations, compiled by the California Institute of Public Affairs in co-operation with the Sierra Club and IUCN, lists the addresses of hundreds of bodies around the world. Only a selection can, therefore, be covered here.

Most governments have identified at least one of their departments or ministries as responsible for environmental affairs. The names and addresses of many of these are given, although their precise responsibilities have not been included. Some particular government agencies, for example the FRG's *Umweltbundesamt*, have been described.

The world is full of a confusion of acronyms, and papers and books, including this volume, are peppered with them. A list of many of those met in writings on the environment is included.

For those wanting to know more than can be included in these pages a bibliography provides a reference to other titles and authors for many books, articles and reports about most of the issues covered in this volume.

Finally there is the hope that, with all the attention being given to environmental concerns, by politicians, by the media, the extensive scientific research, the wealth of books, pamphlets, and articles, the campaigns, and above all, by the millions of citizens taking an active interest in the problems and participating in a great variety of organizations, improvements in attitudes and conditions will occur and significant results will be forthcoming.

Peter Brackley

ACRONYMS

ACE American Council on the Environment
ACE Association for the Conservation of Energy* (UK)
ACEEE American Council for an Energy Efficient Economy*
ACF Australian Conservation Foundation*
ACFM Advisory Committee on Fishery Management (of ICES*)
ACMP Advisory Committee on Marine Pollution (of ICES*)
ACOPS Advisory Committee on Pollution of the Sea* (UK)
ACSAD Arab Centre for the Studies of Arid Zones and Dry Lands*
AEA-T AEA Technology*
AERE Atomic Energy Research Establishment (UK)
AES Asian Environment Society*
AGR advanced gas-cooled reactor
AGU Arbeitsgemeinschaft für Umweltfragen e.V.* (FRG)
AIDGAP Aids to Identification of Difficult Groups of Animals and Plants (FSC*)
AIRPLAN Air Pollution Action Network
ALARA as low as reasonably practical (radiation exposure)
AMCEN African Ministerial Conference on the Environment
ANEN African Network of Environmental Non-governmental Organizations*
AONB Area of Outstanding Natural Beauty (UK–CC*)
API American Petroleum Institute
APPEN Asia-Pacific People's Environment Network*
AQS air quality standard
ARIC Acid Rain Information Centre*
ASEAN Association of South-East Asian Nations
ASOC Antarctic and Southern Ocean Coalition*
ASPEI Association of South-Pacific Environmental Institutions
ASTM American Society for Testing Materials
ATCM Antarctic Treaty Consultative Meetings
ATCP Antarctic Treaty Consultative Parties
ATO African Timber Organization*
ATS Antarctic Treaty System
AUMS Aberdeen University Marine Studies Ltd
AURIS Aberdeen University Research and Industrial Services
AWA American Wilderness Alliance
AWL American Wildlands* (formerly AWA)

BAPMoN (GEMS) Background Air Pollution Monitoring Network
BAS British Antarctic Survey (of NERC*)
BAT best available technology
BES British Ecological Society*
BIPE Bureau d'informations et de prévisions économiques
BOD biochemical oxygen demand
B.P. or bp British Pharmocopia

BPEO best practical environmental option
BPM best practical means
BTCY British Trust for Conservation Volunteers*
BTMA best technical means available
BWR boiling water reactor

CABI CAB International*
CACC Central Australian Conservation Council*
CAFE corporate average fuel economy (USA)
CAI International Arctic Committee
CANDU Canadian deuterium-uranium reactor
CAT Centre for Alternative Technology* (UK)
CC Countryside Commission* (UK)
CCAMLR Convention or Commission for the Conservation of Antarctic Marine Living Resources*
CCMC Comité des Constructeurs D'Automobiles du Marché Commun/Committee of Common Market Automobile Constructors*
CCOL Co-ordinating Committee on the Ozone Layer
CCS Countryside Commission for Scotland*
CdF Charbonnages de France
CDSN European Committee for Conservation of Nature and Natural Reources
CEAT Co-ordination Européene des Amis de la Terre
CEED UK Centre for Economic and Environmental Development (also UK-CEED*)
CEFIC Council of European Chemical Manufacturers' Federations*
CEGB Central Electricity Generating Board (UK)
CEIM Conseil International pour l'Exploration de la Mer (also ICES*)
CEMP Centre for Environmental Planning and Management* (UK)
CEQ Council on Environmental Quality* (USA)
CEST Centre for Exploitable Science and Technology
CFCs chlorofluorocarbons
CFR Co-operative Fuel Research
CHP combined heat and power
CIAB Coal Industry Advisory Board
CIDIE Committee of International Development Institutions on the Environment*
CIFA Comité International de recherche et d'étude de Facteurs de l'Ambience (see also ICEF)
CIPRA Commission Internationale pour la Protection des Régions Alpines
CITEPA Centre interprofessionel technique d'études de la pollution atmosphérique
CITES The Washington Convention on International Trade in Endangered Species of Wild Fauna and Flora
CLC International Convention on Civil Liability for Oil Pollution Damage
CMC Conservation Monitoring Centre (now WCMC*)
COBSEA Co-ordinating Body on the Seas of East Africa
COCF Centre for Our Common Future*
COD chemical oxygen demand
CoEnCo Council for Environmental Conservation (now The Environment Council*)
Coline Comité legislatif d'information écologie
COMIDES Dakar Ministerial Conference on Desertification
CONAF Corporación Nacional Foerstal y de Protección de Recursos Naturales Renovables (Chile)
CONCAWE The Oil Companies' International Study Group for Conservation of Clean Air and Water—Europe*, (originally designated Conservation Clean Air and Water—Western Europe)

COSPAR Committee on Space Research
COWAR Committee on Water Research
CPRE Council for the Protection of Rural England*
CPRW Council for the Protection of Rural Wales
CRAMRA Convention on the Regulation of Antarctic Mineral Resource Activities
CRISTAL Contract Regarding a Supplement to Tanker Liability for Oil Pollution
CRP (North Sea) Community Research Project (of NERC*)
CT The Conservation Trust*
CUSEC Canada–US Environment Council

DA-Bern Demokratische Alternative—Bern
DESON Consultative Group for Desertification Control
DoE Department of the Environment
DERV diesel engine road vehicle (diesel fuel in UK)
DOMA Dirección General de Medio Ambiente (Spain)
DGMK Deutsche Gesellschaft für Mineralölwissenschaft und Kohlechemie (FRG)
DMS dimethyl sulphide
DMSP dimethyl sulphonate
DN Danmarks Naturfredningsforening*
DNR Deutscher Naturschutzring e.V-Bunderverband für Umseltschutz

EA Environmental Action
EACN European Air Chemical Network
EAEI Ecology Action Educational Institute
E & P Forum The Oil Companies International Exploration and Production Forum
EC European Community; European Commission
ECE United Nations Economic Commission for Europe* (also UN-ECE)
ECG Ecosystem Conservation Group
ECLA UN Economic Commission for Latin America
ECOSOC United Nations Economic and Social Council
ECY European Conservation Year
EDF Environmental Defense Fund*
EEB European Environmental Bureau*
EEC European Economic Community
EEF European Environment Foundation
EEP Energy and Environment Programme* (at RIIA)
EIA environmental impact assessment
EINECS European Inventory of Existing Commercial Chemical Substances
EIS environmental impact statement
ELC Environment Liaison Centre International
ELR environmental lapse rate
EMEP European Monitoring and Evaluation Programme
EMINWA Environmentally Sound Management of Inland Waters (UNEP*)
ENDS Environmental Data Services Ltd*
EOR enhanced oil recovery
EOS Earth Observing Systems (of NASA)
EPA Environmental Protection Agency* (USA)
EQO environmental quality objective
EQS environmental quality standard
EROS Earth Observation Satellite
ESA environmentally sensitive area
ESCAP Economic and Social Commission for Asia and the Pacific (UN)
ESCWA Economic and Social Commission for Western Asia (UN)

ETSU Energy Technology Support Unit (UK Dept. of Energy)
EURASAP European Association for the Science of Air Pollution*
EURATOM European Atomic Energy Community
EYE European Year of the Environment

FAO Food and Agricultural Organization of the United Nations*
FBA Freshwater Biological Association (of NERC*)
FBC fluidized bed combustion
FEC The Foundation for Environmental Conservation*
FEMAC Fédération d'Amérique des associations non-gouvernementales de conservation
FFSPN La Fédération Française des Sociétés de Protection de la Nature (France Nature Environnment*)
FGD flue-gas desulphurization
FLAJA Federación Latinoamericana de Jóvenes Ambientialistas (Latin American Federation of Young Environmentalists) (Panama)
FoE Friends of the Earth
FOEI Friends of the Earth International*
FSC Field Studies Council*
FUDENA Fundación para la Defensa de la Naturaleza

GCC Co-operative Council for the Arab States of the Gulf*
GCM general circulation model
GEMS Global Environmental Monitoring System
GESAMP Group of Experts on Scientific Aspects of Marine Pollution* (at IMO*)
glc ground level concentration
GOFS Global Ocean Flux Study
GPS Grune Partie der Schweiz (also PES)
GRID Global Resource Information Database (UNEP*)
GVW gross vehicle weight

Habitat UN Centre for Human Settlements (also UNCHS)
H/C hydrocarbons
HELCOM Baltic Marine Environment Protection Committee* (Helsinki Convention)
HFN Fondation—Hellef Fir D'Natur*
HLW high level (radioactive) waste

IAEA International Atomic Energy Agency (UN)
IAHE International Association for Hydrogen Energy
IAU International Astronomical Union
IAWGD Inter-Agency Working Group on Desertification
IAWPRC International Association on Water Pollution and Control*
IBP International Biological Programme
ICBP International Council for Bird Preservation
ICC International Chamber of Commerce*
ICCE International Centre for Conservation Education*
ICEA International Commission for Environmental Assessment
ICEF International Committee for Research and Study of Environmental Factors (see also CIFA)
ICES International Council for the Exploration of the Sea*
ICIDI International Commission on International Development Issues (Brandt Commission)
ICJ International Court of Justice
ICRP International Commission on Radiological Protection

ICS International Chamber of Shipping
ICSEP International Centre for the Solution of Environmental Problems*
ICSU International Council of Scientific Unions*
IDA International Development Association
IEA International Energy Agency* (within OECD*)
IEB International Environment Bureau* (affiliated to ICC*)
IEDS International Environment and Development Service (of WEC*)
IEEP Institute for European Environmental Policy*
IEF International Environment Forum (of WEC*)
IEO Industry and Environment Office (UNEP*)
IES Institution of Environmental Sciences*
IFE Institute of Freshwater Ecology (of NERC*)
IGADD Intergovernmental Authority of Drought and Desertification
IGBP International Geosphere-Biosphere Project
IGO inter-governmental organization
IGU International Geographical Union
IGY International Geophysical Year (1957–58)
IIASA International Institute for Applied Systems Analysis
IIEA International Institute for Environmental Affairs
IIED International Institute for Environment and Development*
IIES International Institute for Environment and Society
IIUG Internationales Institute für Umwelt und Gesellschaft (see WZB*, Berlin)
ILEC International Lake Environment Committee
ILW intermediate level (radioactive) waste
IMCO Inter-Governmental Maritime Consultative Organization (now IMO*)
IMO International Maritime Organization*
INDERENA Instituto Nacional de los Recursos Naturales Renovables y del Ambient (Colombia)
INFOTERRA International Referral System. International Register for Sources of Environmental Information (UNEP)
INPMA Instituto Nacional para la Preservación del Medio Ambiente (Uruguay)
INQUA International Union for Quaternary Research
INTECOL International Association for Ecology*
IOC Intergovernmental Oceanographic Commission (of UNESCO)
IOMAC Indian Ocean Marine Affairs Co-operation
IOPN International Office for the Protection of Nature
IP The Institute of Petroleum
IPCS International Programme on Chemical Study (of WHO*)
IPEE Institut pour une politique Européene de l'Environnement*
IPIECA The International Petroleum Industry Environmental Conservation Association*
IPRE International Professional Association for Environmental Affairs*
IR infra-red
IRM Institute for Resource Management*
IRPTC International Register of Potentially Toxic Chemicals
ISES International Solar Energy Society*
ISSS International Society of Soil Science
ISTF International Society of Tropical Foresters*
ITE Institute of Terrestrial Ecology (of NERC*)
ITOPF International Tanker Owners Pollution Federation*
ITTC International Tropical Timber Council
ITTO International Tropical Timber Organization*
IUAPPA International Union of Air Pollution Prevention Associations*
IUB International Union of Biochemistry
IUBS International Union of Biological Sciences

IUCN International Union for Conservation of Nature and Natural Resources—The World Conservation Union
IUGG International Union of Geodesy and Geophysics
IUGS International Union of Geological Sciences
IUIS International Union of Immunological Studies
IUPAB International Union of Pure and Applied Biophysics
IUPAC International Union of Pure and Applied Chemistry
IUPAP International Union of Pure and Applied Physics
IUPHAR International Union of Pharmacology
IUPN International Union for the Protection of Nature
IUPS International Union of Physiological Sciences
IUTAM International Union of Theoretical and Applied Mechanics
IVEM Institute of Virology and Environmental Microbiology (in NERC*)
IWC International Whaling Commission*
IWRB International Waterfowl and Wetlands Research Bureau*
IYF International Youth Federation for Environmental Studies and Conservation

JEP Joint Energy Programme (now EEP*)
JET Joint European Torus
JMI John Muir Institute for Environmental Studies

LDC less developed country
LDC London Dumping Convention (Convention for the Prevention of Marine Pollution by Dumping of Wastes and Other Matter 1972)
LEAP Less Developed Country Energy Alternatives Planning System
LEEC London Environmental Economics Centre
LGU Liechtensteinishe Gesellschaft für Umweltschutz*
LLMC Convention on Limitation of Liability for Maritime Claims
LLW low level (radioactive) waste
LNG liquefied natural gas
LNVL Letzeburger Natur—a Vulleschutzliga*
LOCA loss of coolant accident (nuclear power)
LPG liquefied petroleum gas
LRTAP Long-Range Transboundary (or Transport of) Air Pollution
LSPN Ligue Suisse pour la Protection de la Nature (also SLNP* and SBN)

MAB (Programme on) Man and the Biosphere* (UNESCO)
MAFF Ministry of Agriculture, Fisheries and Food (UK)
MARPOL International Convention for the Prevention of Pollution from Ships (1973)
MAP Mediterranean Action Plan
MEMAC Marine Emergency Mutual Aid Centre
MEP member of the European Parliament
MEPC Marine Environment Protection Committee
MIAS Marine Information and Advisory Service (of NERC*)
MON motor octane number
MPCU Marine Pollution Control Unit* (of UK Dept. of Transport)
MPE Mouvement Populaire pour l'Environnement (Switzerland)

NAAQS National Ambient Air Quality Standards (USA)
NATURA Fundación Ecuatoriana para la Conservación de la Naturaleza*
NCC Nature Conservancy Council* (UK)
NCE Nordic Council for Ecology*
NCM Nordic Council of Ministers*

NCVO National Council of Voluntary Organizations (UK)
NDP Nuclear Disarmament Party (Australia)
NEA Nuclear Energy Agency (of OECD*)
NEPA National Environmental Policy Act (USA—see CEQ*)
NEPB National Environment Protection Board (also SNV*)
NERC Natural Environment Research Council* (UK)
NGO non-governmental organization
NII Nuclear Installations Inspectorate
NIMBY not in my back yard
NNWS Non-Nuclear Weapons States
NOAA National Oceanic and Atmospheric Administration (USA)
NPT Nuclear Non-Proliferation Treaty (1970)
NRC National Research Council (USA)
NRDC National Research Defense Council* (USA)
NRPB National Radiological Protection Board
NSCA National Society for Clean Air and Environmental Protection*
NSEPB National Swedish Environment Protection Board (also NEPB and SNV*)

OAS Organization of American States*
OAU Organization for African Unity
OCIMF Oil Companies International Marine Forum
ODEFA Organization de défense de l'environnement et de la faune africaine
OECD Organization for Economic Co-operation and Development*
OILPOL International Convention for the Prevention of Pollution of the Sea by Oil (1954)
OIPN l'Office International pour la Protection de la Nature
ÖNB Österreichischer Naturschutzbund*
OPEC Organization of Petroleum Exporting Countries
OPOL Offshore Pollution Liability Agreement
OPRU Oil Pollution Research Unit (now part of FSC* Research Centre)
OSCOM Oslo Commission*
OTEC Ocean thermal energy convention

P&I club Protection and Indemnity club
PACD Plan of Action to Combat Desertification
PAKOE (Panhellenic Centre for Environmental Studies)
PARICOM Paris Commission*
PCV positive crankcase ventilation
PEEM Panel of Experts on Environmental Management for Vector Control
PES Partie Ecologiste Suisse (also GPS)
PFBC pressurized fluidized bed combustion
PIA UK Petroleum Industry Association (also UK-PIA)
PLAGE Uberparteiliche Plattform Gegen Atomgefahren und Zukunftswerkstatt Energie*
PPP polluter pays principle
PWR pressurized water reactor

Ramsar Convention on Wetlands of International Importance especially as Waterfowl Habitat
RCEP Royal Commission on Environmental Pollution* (UK)
RDB Red Data Books (of IUCN*)
RIIA Royal Institute of International Affairs
ROA Regional Office for Africa (UNEP*)
RON research octane number

ROPME Regional Organization for the Protection of the Marine Environment*
RRAG Renewable Resources Assessment Group
RSNC Royal Society for Nature Conservation*
RSP Regional Seas Programme
RSPB Royal Society for the Protection of Birds*

SACEP South Asia Co-operative Environment Programme*
SAGUF Schweizer Arbeitsgemeinschaft für Umweltforschung*
SASREG Southern Africa Sub-regional Environment Group
SBN Schweizerischer Bund für Naturschutz (also SLNP* and LSNP)
SCAR Scientific (previously Special) Committee on Antarctic Research
SCOPE Scientific Committee on Problems of the Environment* (of ICSU*)
SCR selective catalytic reduction (of NOx)
SCRAM The Scottish Campaign to Resist the Atomic Menace
SEMA Secretaria Especial do Meio Ambiente (Brazil)
SERA Socialist Environment and Resources Association (UK)
SEU Socio-Ecological Union* (of the USSR)
SGU Schweizerische Gesellshaft für Umweltschutz*
SHED Sealed Housing for Evaporative Determination
SI Système International d'Unités
SID Society for International Development
SLNP Swiss League for Nature Protection* (also LSNP and SBN)
SMBA Scottish Marine Biological Association (of NERC*)
SNF Swedish Society for the Conservation of Nature
SNPN Société nationale de protection de la nature* (France)
SNR selective non-catalytic reduction (of NOx)
SNSF Sur Nedbórs Virkning på Skog og Fisk (Acid Precipitation Effects on Forests and Fish)
SNV (Swedish Environmental Protection Agency)*
SOTEATG Shetland Oil Terminal Environmental Advisory Group (previously SVEAG)
SPC South Pacific Commission
SPE Société suisse pour la protection de l'environnement (also SGU*)
SPEC South Pacific Bureau for Economic Co-operation
SPEC Society for the Promotion of Environment Conservation
SPP soluble reactive phosphate
SPREP South Pacific Regional Environment Programme*
SSSI site of special scientific interest
SNG substitute natural gas
SPRU Science Policy Research Unit, Sussex University
SVEAG Sullom Voe Environmental Advisory Group (now SOTEAG)

TBT tributyl tin
TFAP Tropical Forest Action Plan
TLV threshold limit value
TMI Three Mile Island
TOES The Other Economic Summit
TOGA Tropical Ocean-Global Atmosphere
TOSCA Toxic Substances Control Act (USA)
TOVALOP Tanker Owners Voluntary Agreement on Liability for Oil Pollution (see ITOPF*)
TÜV Technischer Überwachungsverein
TWC three way converters
TWS The Wilderness Society* (Australia)

UBA Umweltbundesamt*
UKAEA United Kingdom Atomic Energy Authority
UK CEED UK Centre for Economic and Environmental Development*
UNCHS United Nations Centre for Human Settlements (Habitat)
UNCLSO UN Conference on the Law of the Sea (I 1958, II 1960, III 1982) or UN Convention on the Law of the Sea (1982)
UNCOD United Nations Conference on Desertification
UNCTAD United Nations Committee on Trade and Development
UNDP United Nations Development Programme
UN-ECE UN Economic Commission for Europe*
UNEP United Nations Environment Programme*
UNEPCOM USSR Commission for UNEP
UNESCO United Nations Educational, Scientific and Cultural Organization
UNFPA United Nations Population Fund
UNLOSC UN Convention on the Law of the Sea 1982
UKOOA United Kingdom Offshore Operators Association
UKOOG United Kingdom Onshore Operators Group
UK-PIA UK Petroleum Industry Association
UNIDO United Nations Industrial Development Organization
UNSCEAR United Nations Scientific Committee on the Effects of Atomic Radiation (UNEP)
UNSCCUR United Nations Scientific Conference on the Conservation and Utilization of Resources (1947)
USAID United States Agency for International Development
USERC US Environment and Resources Council
UV ultra-violet radiation

VLCC very large crude carrier
VOCs volatile organic compounds

WARMER World Action for Recycling Materials and Energy from Rubbish*
WASWC World Association of Soil and Water Conservation*
WCED World Commission on Environment and Development
WCIP World Climate Impact Studies Programme
WCMC World Conservation Monitoring Centre*
WCS World Conservation Strategy
WEC World Environment Centre*
WHO World Health Organization* (UN)
WICEM World Industry Conference on Environmental Management (ICC*)
WMO World Meteorological Organization
WOCE World Ocean Circulating Experiment
WorldWIDE World Women in Defence of the Environment
WRI World Resources Institute*
WWF World Wide Fund for Nature* (previously World Wildlife Fund)
WZB Wissenschaftszentrum Berlin*

YEE Youth and Environment Europe (Denmark)

*Organizations mentioned in Part IV.

I. ISSUES

1 ACID DEPOSITION

James W. S. Longhurst

Introduction

Acid deposition, more popularly called *acid rain*, is one of the most urgent of our contemporary environmental problems. Effects attributed, at least in part, to acid deposition are reported from most, if not all, industrial nations and an increasing number of developing nations. These effects are to both freshwater and terrestrial components of ecosystems and, increasingly, to economic and culturally important materials.

Whilst there are gaps in knowledge, substantial information is available on the emission of acidifying air pollutants, the transport and transformation processes in the atmosphere, the rate and form of deposition to the earth's surface and the resulting environmental impacts. A broad scientific consensus has now emerged on the major causes and effects, most particularly regarding the role and importance of sulphur and its oxidation products in environmental damage. Sulphur and nitrogen are most clearly implicated in freshwater acidification but the majority of hypotheses concerning the effects on forests include acidic air pollutants as either the primary cause or a major contributory factor to the complex of changes known as forest decline. Many now argue that the new forest damage seen in Europe over the last decade or so would not have occurred either in its present form or to the same extent, had it not been for the presence and severity of acidic air pollutants.

The environmental implications of acid deposition and acidification are the subject of extensive international and national research programmes concerning the local, regional and global sources and effects of sulphur dioxide, oxidized and reduced nitrogen species and volatile organic compounds.

However, the broad relationship between emissions and environmental change is sufficiently well understood to enable national and supra-national control policies to be formulated, such as the European Community Large Combustion Plant Directive or the protocols of the United Nations Economic Commission for Europe (UN–ECE) on emissions of sulphur dioxide or nitrogen oxides and their transboundary fluxes.

The scale and importance of the contemporary acid deposition phenomena tend to suggest that acid deposition is a relatively recent environmental problem. It was, however, first described in 1852 by R. A. Smith working in the city of Manchester, and it was Smith who neologized the term acid rain. At this time, sulphur was clearly the main pollutant and the effects of acid deposition were clearly an urban and near urban phenomenon. Environmental effects attributable to acid deposition either described or hypothesized by Smith included damage to building materials, metalwork, textiles and vegetation. The southern Pennines of England received acid precipitation as a direct consequence of acid emissions in Manchester and other cities and have continued to do so in excess of two hundred years. The combination of dry and wet deposition of sulphur compounds profoundly affected the sphagnum moss communities, leading to species reduction, habitat change, moorland drying and subsequent erosion.

In Victorian times the distribution of pollutants from industrial and urban areas was generally no more than regional in scale, but longer-range transport of pollutants to Norway from the UK is first documented as early as 1881.

Despite a long historical interest in precipitation chemistry only fragmented data of limited quality are available for the period up until the renaissance of interest in the subject of acid deposition. This occurred in the late 1960s and early 1970s when the Swede S. Odens identified a relationship between measurements of acidity and sulphur in rain and the acidification of water and soil. These observations prompted Sweden to present a case study on long-range sulphur pollution to the 1972 UN Conference on the Human Environment, held in Stockholm. From this time research into the causes and effects of acid deposition has been driven by a political impetus as, individually and co-operatively, nations responded to the challenges posed by long-range transport of air pollutants.

One of the most important investigations following the Stockholm conference was the Norwegian SNSF project which began in 1972 (Sur Nedbørs Virkning på Skog og Fisk—acid precipitation effects on forests and fish). Scientific and political interest in the United States was stimulated by observations of the regional distribution of acid precipitation and its significance for terrestrial and aquatic ecosystems in North America. In Europe, in response to growing concern at the conclusions of the Swedish case study and the findings of the SNSF project, the Organization for Economic Co-operation and Development began its review of the long-range transport of air pollution in 1973. Under the auspices of the United Nations the European Monitoring and Evaluation Programme began in 1977 and shortly afterwards the National Atmospheric Deposition Programme became operational in the United States. The US National Acid Precipitation Assessment Programme was established by Congress under the Acid Precipitation Act of 1980. In 1982 Sweden convened an international conference on acid rain and in 1983 the joint UK, Swedish and Norwegian Surface and Water Acidification Programme was proposed. Contemporary scientific understanding of the cause and effect of acid deposition was reviewed at the International Symposium on Acidic Precipitation held at Muskoka, Canada in 1985. More recently UN–ECE has established the International Co-operative Programme to assess the effects of atmospheric pollutants on materials, on forests and on lakes and rivers. The science of acid deposition was reviewed at the Glasgow 1990 conference on acid deposition, the quinquennial successor to Muskoka.

Emissions of acid deposition precursors

The major gaseous precursors of acid deposition are sulphur dioxide (SO_2) and oxides of nitrogen (NO_x), but emissions of ammonia, volatile organic compounds, dusts and hydrochloric acid all influence the acidity of precipitation to one degree or another. These species have both natural and anthropogenic sources. Anthropogenic sources include power generation, refineries, industry, transport and commercial/domestic sources whilst natural sources include biogenic emissions from terrestrial, tidal and oceanic areas and non-biogenic emissions from forest and grassland fires, geothermal activity, lightning, airborne soil particles and water aerosols.

Sulphur Dioxide

Natural emissions are estimated to be in the range 100–1000 million tonnes of SO_2 per year, and anthropogenic emissions 120–160 million tonnes of SO_2 per year, but the estimates are extrapolated from a small number of measurements to the global scale.

Sources of natural emissions are concentrated in tropical areas whereas anthropogenic emission sources are predominantly located in the industrialized northern hemisphere. Some 68% of anthropogenic emissions occur in an area covering less that 10% of the earth's surface. Major source areas of anthropogenic emission include the northern part of England, the Low Countries, the Federal Republic of Germany and Eastern Europe. A large area of high emission density occurs in the eastern United States. Some 75% of all US emissions arise east of the Mississippi river.

In 1987, according to the European Monitoring and Evaluation Programme, Europe is estimated to have emitted some 42,942,000 tonnes of SO_2, an 18% reduction on the 1980 emission. The most recent UK emission estimate is for 1988 when a total of 3,664,000 tonnes of SO_2 were emitted, down 5% from the previous year. Some 71% of this is estimated to arise from power stations, 17% from industrial sources, 4% from the domestic sector, 3% from refineries, 3% from the commercial sector and 1% from road transport. Emissions from large combustion sources, greater than 50MWth and the subject of European Community Directive 88/609, are 84% of total UK emissions.

The location and scale of emissions has changed over time. At the turn of the century emissions were dominated by coal burning for heating and industry but as a consequence of the post-war economic boom, particularly in the 1950s, emissions sharply increased. By 1979 Europe accounted for 44% and North America 24% of global anthropogenic emissions. Since that date utilization of flue gas desulphurization and increased energy efficiency has resulted in decreases in emissions in many of the industrialized countries of the northern hemisphere. However, despite the reductions recorded in the northern hemisphere, global emissions continue to increase.

Oxides of nitrogen

Almost all oxidized nitrogen is released as nitric oxide (NO) which is oxidized, at ambient temperatures, to nitrogen dioxide (NO_2), with the process being accelerated by the presence of volatile organic compounds and ozone. The emission is estimated to be in the range 25–99 million tonnes, expressed as nitrogen, per year. As with SO_2 there are both anthropogenic and natural sources of emission for NO and NO_2. The principal natural sources are biomass burning, lightning, microbial activity, biological processes, ammonia oxidation and stratospheric input. Natural sources may account for some 33% of global emissions although others suggest a rough equivalence between natural and anthropogenic emissions. Anthropogenic sources include high temperature combustion of fossil fuels in power stations and motor transport.

Major source areas are similar to those for SO_2 and in North America and Europe anthropogenic emissions may account for between 75% and 93% of all emissions of NO_x. The 1988 European emission of nitrogen oxides (as NO_2) is estimated at 20,408,000 tonnes. The UK emission in 1988 is 2,480,000 tonnes, a 2% increase on 1987. Road transport is the main source responsible for 45% of UK emissions; of the remainder 32% comes from power stations, 12% from other industrial sources and the balance from a variety of sources including the domestic and commercial sectors and refineries. Emissions from large combustion sources, greater than 50MWth and the subject of European Community Directive 88/609, are 40% of total UK emissions.

Ammonia

Ammonia is the most important neutralizing compound in the atmosphere. Its major sources include animal wastes, fertilizer applications, and industrial emissions. Smaller contributions arise from human respiration, traffic and uncultivated soil. The spatial pattern of ammonia emissions is quite different to that of SO_2 of NO_x, as agricultural areas rather than industrial areas are the dominant sources. European emissions of ammonia are probably 7,000,000 tonnes per year, again expressed as nitrogen. In recent years emissions have increased as a consequence of intensive animal husbandry practices, for example emissions from livestock are estimated to have increased by 50% between 1950 and 1980.

Volatile organic compounds (VOCs)

VOCs include hydrocarbons, oxygenated organics and halogenated organics, and are important in the formation of acidic species in the atmosphere through photochemical generation of oxidizing species. They also react with nitrogen oxides to form ozone. Major emission sources are traffic exhaust, industrial processes and solvents evaporation. Natural sources are also important, particularly forests. The 1988 UK emission of VOCs is estimated at 1,846,000 tonnes, 57% from industrial processes and 30% from road transport. In calculating emissions of VOCs methane is not included.

Transport and deposition

After emission to the atmosphere a pollutant mixes with the receiving air in a manner largely determined by the height of emission and the prevailing weather pattern. High-level emissions such as those from power stations leave the chimney at high velocity. Turbulence in the atmosphere generated by convection and the friction between wind and surface features act to disperse an emission.

Removal from a plume may occur through dry, wet or occult deposition. Dry deposition is absorption directly to a surface or uptake by plants; wet deposition is rain, sleet, snow, or hail; and occult deposition is impaction of cloud water droplets onto vegetation or other surfaces. The term acid deposition is used to encompass all these processes.

Dry deposition can be estimated from the product of ground level concentration and the deposition velocity of the pollutant in question. A deposition velocity is defined as the flux to a surface per unit concentration in air. Measurements have shown that deposition velocities vary from surface to surface, seasonally and diurnally.

Removal by dry deposition is more important for plumes from low-level sources, but such emissions do become well mixed within a few hours and the major part of the emission is transported downwind in the same manner as for high-level sources.

However, if a plume is subjected to rainfall, then removal of precursors such as sulphur dioxide will occur, with the amount removed depending on the amount of sulphur dioxide converted to sulphate. Rates of removal as wet deposition are greater than for dry deposition with the concentration of sulphur in rainwater being determined by the solubility of sulphur dioxide and the acidity of rainwater. As sulphate is a cloud condensation nucleus, wet deposition is a significant removal mechanism. Sulphur dioxide is further oxidized by hydroxyls in the gas phase and by ozone and hydrogen peroxide through aqueous phase reactions.

Nitric oxide is not removed to any degree as dry deposition but is oxidized to nitrogen dioxide, nitrate aerosol or nitric acid. Little aqueous phase oxidation is likely due to the low solubility of nitric oxide and nitrogen dioxide. The conversion of nitrogen dioxide to peroxyacetyl nitrate and subsequent reformation of nitrogen dioxide long distances downwind can be an important reservoir for acidic oxidized nitrogen species. Nitric acid is volatile and will exist in the gas phase in the atmosphere, unlike sulphuric acid which will be present in the fine particle range, less than 0.2 μm. Both acids will react with alkaline materials in the atmosphere such as calcium, magnesium and ammonia, for example, to form ammonium sulphate or ammonium nitrate.

The important oxidizing species, for example ozone, occur naturally but their concentration in the troposphere may be increased by anthropogenic emissions. If there are no competing species nitric oxide will react with ozone to form nitrogen dioxides which, in the presence of sunlight, will decompose to NO and ozone. The reactions are fast and a photostationary state quickly reached so that no more ozone than originally present is produced. However, in the presence of certain VOCs, nitrogen dioxide can be produced without consumption of ozone; thus decomposition of nitrogen dioxide provides a mechanism for ozone production.

In occult deposition, cloud and fog water droplets are deposited onto surfaces by turbulent impact. Recent studies have shown that fog and cloud water may have much higher ionic concentrations than those of precipitation. Depending on location, occult deposition may represent a significant fraction of the total hydrological input to an area, particularly to tops of hills which are in cloud for much of the year. However, occult deposition is of minor significance in the sulphur budget as a whole. The precipitation chemistry at upland sites is further modified by orographic rainfall enhancement mechanisms. The process of seeder-feeder is the most important orographic enhancement mechanism operating in the UK and involves the scavenging of cloud formed as air rises over hills (feeder cloud) by precipitation originating from higher level frontal (seeder) cloud. The process modifies both the intensity and the chemical composition of rainfall.

Deposition monitoring

Wet deposition of acidity and other ions in precipitation can be monitored directly by collection of rainfall. Collectors are carefully designed to minimize the effect of the sampler upon a sample. In most precipitation chemistry networks hydrogen, ammonium, potassium, sodium, calcium, magnesium, zinc, chloride, nitrate, sulphate, and carbonate ions are routinely monitored.

The natural acidity of precipitation is thought to be due to the dissociation of carbon dioxide in rainwater giving rise to a weakly acidic solution of about pH 5.6 (pH is the logarithmic expression of acidity), but some workers consider that natural fluctuations in the sulphur emission cycle can depress the pH of rain to 5.0. The various ions routinely collected have differing sources including combustion, agriculture, terrestrial-derived dusts and sea salts. The latter ions include calcium, sulphate, sodium and chloride and the marine contribution must be calculated to determine the anthropogenic input to precipitation composition.

Measurement of precipitation chemistry is routinely carried out by a number of agencies on a regional, continental or global scale including, for example, the European Air Chemistry Network (EACN), the European Monitoring and Evaluation Programme (EMEP) and the World Meteorological Organization. Patterns of precipitation chemistry show considerable year-to-year variation. Intra-network comparisons are validated by common operating protocols, identical collectors and inter-laboratory comparison exercises.

In the current phase of EMEP, 92 monitoring stations measure precipitation and acid deposition precursors according to a rigorous protocol that ensures comparability of measured data. Gaseous sulphur dioxide, nitrogen dioxide, ozone, nitric acid and ammonia, particulate sulphate, nitrate and ammonium, precipitation amount, concentration of 9 ions and conductivity are all regularly determined. In the period 1984 to 1986 maximum concentrations of aerosol sulphate and non-marine sulphate in EMEP precipitation were found in central-Eastern Europe, with a smaller maximum of aerosol sulphate in western Europe.

Measurements of acidity made during the second phase of EMEP identified a spatial pattern that encompassed the majority of the UK (excluding Northern Ireland, north-west Scotland and south-west Cornwall), southern Scandinavia, northern France, northern Austria, Switzerland and north-eastern Europe within the pH 4.5 isoline. The most acidic precipitation was measured in central Europe and was bound by the pH 4.1 isoline, encompassing northern Belgium, the Federal Republic of Germany, East Germany, eastern Czechoslovakia and Poland.

A recent comparison of North American and European precipitation chemistry measurements made by the Canadian Research and Monitoring Co-ordinating Committee concluded that sulphate and nitrate concentration and wet deposition rates are greater in central Europe, but levels are comparable for wet deposited sulphur in North America, east of the Mississippi and in southern Scandinavia at about 20–40 kg of sulphate per hectare per annum.

In the UK, monitoring of acid deposition on a national basis only began at the start of 1986. Data from the first three years' operation of the monitoring networks broadly confirm previous observations at a smaller number of monitoring stations. The pattern of hydrogen ions shows a clear gradient of increasing concentration from west to east; maximum concentrations of non-marine sulphate and nitrate occurred in the east, particularly south of the Wash; greatest deposition occurred in areas of highest rainfall, particularly parts of Highland Scotland, north Wales, Cumbria and the Pennines, where acid deposition is comparable to areas of southern Scandinavia. The largest concentrations of non-marine sulphate occur in low rainfall easterly air flows and the highest deposition occurs in high rainfall westerly air flows. This spatial pattern of precipitation quality is broadly consistent with the pattern described by EMEP.

The concentration of ions in precipitation shows considerable variation with season, with location of measurement, with type of precipitation and even within precipitation events. The concentration of nitrate in European precipitation is increasing and that of non-marine sulphate decreasing. The highest concentrations are found in places of high emission density. This changing pattern is consistent with observed decreases in sulphur emissions and increases in oxides of nitrogen emission.

Distinct temporal patterns have been observed in emissions of acid deposition precursors and their composition in precipitation and deposition chemistry. In the UK and Europe, emissions of precursor gases are at a maximum in winter and maximum concentrations of sulphate and nitrate are observed in precipitation in spring and early summer. As many different ions exhibit distinct seasonal patterns despite differing sources of origin, a common meteorological explanation is indicated, such as wind direction.

Environmental effects

Air pollution, acid rain and acidification have been implicated in a wide range of environmental effects, particularly damage to forest systems and freshwaters. Some of these are direct effects, others indirect, occurring at the end of a complicated chain of cause and effect. The following section seeks to summarize these effects.

Soil acidification

An understanding of the effects of acid deposition upon soils is a prerequisite to our understanding of effects upon freshwaters as many recently acidified lakes receive most of their water from drainage through, or over, soils.

Soil susceptibility to acidification is related to natural acidity, soil particle size, soil depth, soil moisture, alkalinity production, bedrock geology and local terrain. Soil acidification can arise from either natural or anthropogenic activities, either singularly or in combination. These include: land uses such as agriculture and forestry, natural processes such as microbial respiration, nitrification and decomposition processes and atmospheric deposition of acidifying materials.

Soil acidification decreases the reserves of exchangeable cations, liberates aluminium and heavy metals, disrupts soil decomposition processes, binds phosphate, reducing its availability to plants, and reduces the diversity of soil micro-organisms. Atmospheric deposition also enriches the nitrogen store in soils, possibly leading to nitrogen saturation. Some plants with low nitrogen requirements may be eliminated and for surviving plants other nutrients may become limiting factors. The UK's Terrestrial Effects Review Group has concluded that it has become increasingly evident that acid deposition is accelerating soil acidification and that soil biology changes will result. Such changes will alter plant nutrition and give rise to a changed chemistry in surface and ground waters which in turn may affect the biology of surface waters.

Forest systems

The effect of acid deposition and acidifying air pollutants upon trees is a matter of continuing debate. Air pollutants, including acid deposition, are clearly important in explaining European forest decline but the situation is complex and in many cases the reasons for forest decline are site-specific. There is a continued need for both short-term and long-term monitoring so as to be able to detect any future decline and to determine the effect of emission reductions currently being implemented.

Forest systems have always been subjected to environmental stress; harsh climate, poor nutrition and pathogens have always affected forest productivity. However, since the 1970s an unprecedented decline of forest ecosystems has occurred in Central Europe. Species affected include silver fir, Norway spruce, beech, Scot's pine, larch and oak. Symptoms of decline include yellowing of needles, loss of older needles, crown thinning, growth reduction and growth alteration. Forest decline is particularly severe in coniferous trees in Switzerland, the Netherlands, Czechoslovakia and the Federal Republic of Germany. In the latter more than 50% of the forest area is affected by the decline. Numerous hypotheses have been proposed to account for the decline. Most involve air pollution as a predisposing and/or inciting factor for decline. These include direct attack of air pollutants such as SO_2, ozone, nitrogen oxides or acid mists which can damage the surface of leaves, impair stomata performance, increase water loss in dry weather and enhance nutrient leaching from the leaf surface. Soil acidification due to acid deposition will mobilize aluminium and other metals from the soil, these can affect the fine root systems of a tree and also soil fungi. Other processes include excess nitrogen deposition, epidemics of pathogens, multiple stress and climatic factors.

Data compiled as part of the UN–ECE Forest Damage Survey in Europe for 1987 clearly indicate that the scale of the problem is continental. Comparison of the 1986 results with the 1987 data shows that there has been a slight decrease in the extent of defoliation of conifer forests but an increase in defoliation of broadleaved forests. In most countries air pollution is considered to be the major destabilizing factor affecting forest health. In, for example, Austria, the Federal Republic of Germany, East Germany, Czechoslovakia, the Netherlands, Yugoslavia and Switzerland such pollution is considered the determining factor, and forest management decisions are strongly influenced by air pollution risks. In Bulgaria, Denmark, Hungary, Italy, Sweden and the UK air pollution is regarded as one of the contributing factors for forest damage.

According to the UN–ECE report the overall situation in European forests clearly indicates that further measures to abate air pollution are required.

Surface and groundwater acidification

Only in certain areas are surface and ground waters sensitive to acidification. These are where geological weathering rates are slow and where soils are already naturally acid, dominated by moorland or coniferous vegetation, with variable hydrological characteristics. Such catchments have little ability to neutralize any further increase in acidity. Hence freshwater acidification can arise from natural processes in soils, atmospheric deposition, vegetation cover and land use practices, interacting in complex ways.

Factors influencing the subsequent chemical change in precipitation falling on a catchment include soil buffering capacity, alkalinity production, volume of run-off, size of catchment, and water transfer time. For example, production of organic acids in moorland peat draining to reservoirs will, in the absence of other actions, naturally acidify the water. Changes in agricultural practices such as reductions in the amount of lime applied to upland fields and pasture can reduce calcium availability in watercourses.

Ecological effects are documented for many water courses where damage arises from a changing acidity–alkalinity balance and speciation of toxic metal. In such areas, effects on plankton, invertebrates, benthic fauna, fish and aquatic plants have been described.

Freshwater acidification has been documented in many countries including Norway, Sweden, France, the Federal Republic of Germany, Finland, Canada, the USA and the UK. In the UK, unequivocal acidification of surface waters has been demonstrated over a far wider area of the country than was thought to be the case and palaeoecological evidence from diatom analysis has now defined the extent and the timescale of acidification.

The survival of fish in surface waters is related to the leaching of base elements from the soil; calcium improves fish survival rates whilst aluminium is detrimental. Where sulphate deposition is high and the calcium content of surface waters and soils is low, sulphate ions will mobilize aluminium and other ions from the soil into watercourses. Acid pulses following snow melt waters containing elevated aluminium levels are particularly hazardous to fish.

The effects of acid precipitation on freshwater fish are particularly pronounced in Norway and Sweden. Southern Norway contains some 33,000 km^2 of acidified freshwater systems which are unable to support a normal ecological community. Brown trout and Atlantic salmon are the most affected species and populations of Arctic charr, perch and roach are all seriously at risk in certain areas. It is estimated by the Norwegian government that to restore water quality to lakes and rivers in this area to a level in which fish could survive would cost 250,000,000 NKr per annum. In Sweden, the National Environment Protection Board estimates that 18,000 lakes and 100,000 km of running water have pH values where damage to freshwater organisms can be expected.

The decline of fish populations due to acidic water in Norway started as early as the 1920s, but the most rapid losses occurred during the decade 1960–1970 and by 1978 the population of Atlantic salmon had disappeared from southern Norway. In the same area more than half of the brown trout populations had disappeared by 1985.

Episodic fish kills due to rapid changes in water quality as a result of "acid surges" have severely affected salmon rivers on the west coast of Norway. Most severely affected have been smolts of Atlantic salmon and spawning migrating salmon on returning to acidified home waters.

Large-scale liming exercises to improve acidified water quality by the application of calcium to a lake catchment are now common in areas profoundly affected by acidification, such as Norway and Sweden, and have also been practised on a smaller scale in parts of upland Wales and Scotland.

The environmental effects of a long-term liming programme may, in themselves, be damaging. In Sweden, investigation of the effects of liming clearly demonstrates that application of lime mitigates the direct effect of acidification, but the structure of post-liming fish assemblages appears to be directly related to the pre-liming assemblage. Consequently maintenance of an active fish population will require continued liming and active fisheries management.

The relationship between deposition of sulphur compounds and water acidification is now established, though other factors can play a role. Reduced deposition is necessary if water quality is to be improved for fish. The UK Acid Waters Review Group concluded that a reduction of 90% in 1985 emission levels would be required to return most UK surface waters to near pristine conditions. To maintain water quality at current levels a deposition reduction of 30% will be required. They also note that the response of surface waters to acid deposition reductions will lag behind emission reductions by up to several decades and that some waters will never recover.

Agricultural crops

Most common agricultural crops prefer the soil pH to be higher than six where water uptake can proceed most efficiently, essential nutrients are available, and the concentration of harmful metals, such as aluminium, is low. Deposition of acidity is a contributory source to farmland acidification but the major cause is likely to be agricultural practices, such as the use of ammonium fertilizer and harvesting strategies.

However, air pollutants such as ozone damage crops and reduce yields. Estimates of ozone damage in the USA suggested harvest losses of $2–4 billion (early 1980s prices), equivalent to 4–6% of the crop value. Damage in Sweden is estimated at SKr 60 million per annum. In the UK, the Terrestrial Effects Review Group concluded that there is unlikely to be damage to major agricultural crops in the UK at current rural concentrations of sulphur dioxide and nitrogen oxides, but that summer concentrations of ozone occur in wide areas of southern Britain that are likely to reduce sensitive crop yields. They note that the interaction between pollutant stresses and others, such as pests, can have extremely important influences upon crop yields.

Human health implications

Acid deposition cannot be considered as a toxic substance *per se*, but a consequence of its occurrence is an increased risk of human exposure to air pollutants and toxic metals.

Potential health effects of acid deposition can be divided into direct effects of precursors (air pollutants) and indirect effects such as mobilization of, and increased risk of exposure to, heavy metals in drinking water and foodstuffs.

Direct effects have been extensively studied and reviewed by international and national organizations. Concentrations at which SO_2 and NO_x affect human health have been established and air concentration limits recommended. NO_2 and SO_2 are irritant, acidic gases, potentially damaging to the respiratory tract; they can induce airway resistance and render individuals more susceptible to bronchitis and pneumonia. They may also affect the ability of the lungs to extract oxygen from the air and this effect may be enhanced at times of maximum ventilation such as during exercise.

The European Community has issued directives on guide and limit values for both SO_2 and NO_2. A Limit Value is set to protect human health and a Guide Value to improve the protection of human health and to contribute to the long-term protection of the environment from SO_2, particulate smoke, and NO_2. Limit Values must not be exceeded by 98% of the daily mean values and guide values must not be exceeded by either 50% or 98% of the daily means values.

The World Health Organization recommends a long-term annual daily average for SO_2 of 50 $\mu g\ m^{-3}$. These guidelines are set to ensure human health in extreme circumstances and thus contain a significant protective margin over concentrations known to be deleterious to health.

Swimming in lake waters with a pH of 4.6 does not adversely affect human eyes or skin.

Indirect effects of acid deposition occur as a result of ingestion of contaminated foodstuffs or drinking water. Mobilization of heavy metals by acidified water increases the risk of exposure to contaminated foodstuffs such as freshwater fish, and the consumption of fish from certain acidified lakes is banned in Sweden. Acidified waters that are untreated and used as a drinking water supply, for example from a groundwater well, may corrode copper, lead and cadmium from plumbing systems.

Materials degradation

Observations of the damage acidic air pollutants may cause to materials have been made for some considerable time. R. A. Smith wrote in 1856: "It has often been observed that the stones and bricks of buildings, especially under projecting parts, crumble more readily in large towns where much coal is burnt . . . I was led to attribute this effect to the slow but constant action of acid rain."

Buildings, materials and cultural property are subject to weathering decay under the action of meteorological factors such as precipitation, wind and solar radiation. This is a natural process which acts in the absence of human involvement. However, air pollutants including acid deposition and its precursors can damage or accelerate the ageing of materials and buildings and create secondary effects such as increased expenditure for protective measures, increased cleaning and potentially a diminished utility for the design purpose.

V. Kucera of the Swedish Corrosion Institute provides a simple conceptual model to differentiate the type of damage by acidic air pollutants and their transformation products. According to Kucera, material degradation occurs in two ways, either as atmospheric corrosion or as corrosion in soil/water systems. The former is a direct effect experienced principally at the local level, whilst the latter is an indirect effect experienced at the regional level. Atmospheric corrosion is mainly, but not exclusively, due to dry deposition of pollutants and may affect a range of important technical materials. Corrosion resulting from soil and water acidification is a threat to technical and economically valuable materials such as water pipes, cables, building foundations, steel and cast iron pipes, lead jacketed cables, telecommunication networks and culverts.

One recent estimate from Canada suggests that the 1985 value of construction was C$61 billion (14% of GNP); repair and maintenance was responsible for $11 billion of this total. The OECD has estimated the cost of air pollution damage to buildings in OECD countries to be US$3.5 billion per year.

Paints and coatings are probably the most important and common materials being subjected to deterioration by acid deposition and its precursors, but relatively little is known about the process. Masonry comprises a small part of the built environment but forms the major part of the heritage component, as either buildings or statues. Acid deposition precursors, in particular sulphur dioxide, play a significant role in the deterioration of masonry.

Material degradation is an irreversible cumulative process which can only, at best, be halted either by reduction of the air pollution contribution or by application of some protective coating. There is some evidence to support the view that reducing air pollution levels to those that are below the critical level for biological systems will provide a satisfactory reduction in the rate of material degradation.

Stationary source control

Control over emission of acid deposition precursor gases from a stationary source can be exercised before, during and after combustion.

Control of sulphur dioxide: pre-combustion treatment

Coal cleaning

The sulphur content of coals varies considerably but most of those traded on the world market average about 1%. The average sulphur content in UK coals is 1.6%, of which about 0.8% is organic sulphur. However, some coals, particularly lignites (brown coals), have very high sulphur contents. Generally, coals supplied to power stations are treated at the colliery, based on techniques utilizing gravity separation which reduces the ash content and removes some inorganic sulphur but not the organic fraction. More advanced separation techniques, such as magnetic separation and pneumatic separation, may come into widespread commercial use. It is, however, unrealistic to expect conventional washing techniques of coal to result in anything more than a 10% reduction in SO_2 emissions from coal combustion.

Fuel substitution and blending

Substituting a low sulphur coal or gas for a high sulphur coal is one means of pre-combustion control, but the degree of reduction which can be achieved in this way is limited, as even "low sulphur" coals often have a sulphur content of 1%. Supplies of substitute fuels may be more difficult to obtain and may have to be imported. Blending of high and low sulphur coals to produce a power station fuel of an acceptable sulphur content is an alternative approach.

Control of sulphur dioxide: removal during combustion

Techniques for removal at this stage may be divided into those for use in conventional power stations using pulverized fuel, and those that arise as an integral part of new combustion technologies, such as pressurized fluidized bed combustion (PFBC) or coal gasification.

The direct injection of limestone or lime into the furnace of a coal-fired power station may reduce sulphur emissions by about 35–40%, but requires large amounts of raw material and produces a large volume of waste for disposal.

In fluidized bed combustion, coal is injected into and burnt in a fluidized bed of mineral matter. Pressurizing the bed maximizes the contact of fuel and oxygen, and combustion efficiency can exceed 99%. Some 20–40% of the sulphur in coal is retained in the bed due to the calcium carbonate content of the bed material (compared to 5–10% in conventional plant). The attraction of PFBC is that up to 90% of the sulphur can be retained if dolomite/limestone is added to the bed material. As PFBC operates at lower temperatures than conventional stations, the production of nitrogen oxides is also reduced. PFBC will need large amounts of sorbent, possibly twice that required by flue gas desulphurization to achieve the same SO_2 removal efficiency. Performance of the 90MW PFBC test facility at Grimethorpe indicates that PFBC will give a similar acid emission to that of a conventional power station fitted with both flue gas desulphurization and low NO_x burners, but without loss of generating capacity.

Coal gasification for electricity generation offers improved efficiency for power generation and the potential for significant reductions in gaseous emissions. A number of commercial designs are available to produce fuel gas from coal. In the British Gas slagging gasifier, operated at Westfield, sulphur in the coal feedstock is converted to hydrogen sulphide during gasification. This is highly corrosive to pipework and must, in any case, be removed from the fuel gas. The hydrogen sulphide may then be converted to elemental sulphur or sulphuric acid using existing technology and be offered for sale. Nitrogen and chlorine in the fuel can also be removed before the fuel gas is burnt to generate electricity in a combined power cycle.

Removal of sulphur dioxide: post-combustion

Flue gas desulphurization (FGD) is not a new concept and there are now well over 100 different FGD processes available to control gaseous emissions of sulphur. It was introduced in Britain before World War II when FGD was incorporated into the design of power stations at Battersea, Fulham and, later, at Bankside. Battersea was the first to be commissioned in 1933. These plants were designed to control levels of SO_2 in the air of London. Both Battersea and Bankside used water from the Thames to wash more than 90% of the sulphur from the waste gas. The Fulham plant used a wet spray of lime to remove the sulphur. Operational problems, especially corrosion, were common at all plants, and the discharge of waste water back to the river was always a potential source of pollution. Large quantities of sludge from the Fulham plant were dumped at sea.

The introduction of tall chimneys on new power stations from the late 1950s onwards successfully reduced ground level concentrations of SO_2 to levels below that harmful to human health and thus removed the need for FGD to control urban concentrations of SO_2. However, certain nations required the use of FGD to meet national environmental protection requirements and the original UK work was developed by the US, Japan and the Federal Republic of Germany.

Modern FGD can be divided into two categories; regenerable and non-regenerable, the distinction being made according to what happens to the sorbent after SO_2 has been absorbed. In regenerable systems, after the absorption or absorption reaction, the sorbent is regenerated to release SO_2 and the original sorbent is recycled. The SO_2 is then converted into elemental sulphur, sulphuric acid or liquid SO_2, and sold as a raw material. In non-regenerable systems the sorbent, having reacted with SO_2, either becomes a waste product, or after further treatment can be a useful by-product such as gypsum.

Regenerable systems are less widely used than non-regenerable systems owing partly to their greater complexity and hence increased capital costs. However, environmentally they are more attractive as their waste production and raw material requirements are much smaller as the absorbing agent is regenerated for reuse. The Wellman-Lord is the most widely used regenerative process. In this process, sulphur is absorbed in a solution of sodium sulphite. Either sulphuric acid or sulphur can be produced for sale to the chemical industry and a ready market exists for these products. The reduction in demand for materials, and the sale of products, offsets some of the extra capital costs associated with regenerative systems. Compared with the lime/limestone gypsum process, initial investment is about 20% higher. Despite this economic drawback the process still has the advantages of low raw material requirements, low operational costs, high value product, high SO_2 removal efficiency and low levels of waste.

Non-regenerable systems can be described as wet and dry processes, depending on the form of the sorbent when added to the absorption chamber.

Some wet processes utilize the natural alkalinity of river or sea water to scrub the flue gases (as at Battersea), but effluent disposal can be difficult. The most widely used non-regenerable system is a wet scrubbing system using lime or limestone as the alkaline sorbent; this accounts for about 70% of FGD in the USA. A variant of this system incorporating a forced oxidation stage to produce by-product gypsum is widely used in Europe and Japan and is referred to as the Lime/Limestone Gypsum Process.

In dry processes a slurry of alkali sorbent, usually slaked lime, is injected into the flue gases to form a solid reaction product for landfill.

Control of nitrogen oxides

The formation of NO_x during fuel combustion results from oxygen reacting with nitrogen compounds in the fuel (fuel NO_x) and with nitrogen in the combustion air (thermal NO_x). The relative contributions of fuel NO_x and thermal NO_x depend upon the fuel type and the firing conditions. Coal has an average nitrogen content of 1.5%, oil about 0.3% and in gas the value is negligible. Hence the relative contribution of thermal NO_x to total NO_x emissions from gas fired plant is much greater.

Production of thermal NO_x increases with the intensity of firing, so by controlling combustion conditions and temperatures it is possible to control the amount of NO_x produced. Enough oxygen must be present for complete fuel combustion, but excess air may be controlled or mixing delayed. By delaying the mixing of air and fuel the formation of NO_x is significantly reduced. Low NO_x burners ensure that initial fuel combustion occurs under fuel-rich conditions, (i.e. at a low oxygen concentration), hence gaseous nitrogen products from the fuel are reduced to N_2. Once the initial combustion stage is complete more air is supplied which allows burn-out of the fuel to occur. This technique can be retrofitted to existing power plant.

Flue gas denitrification (FGDN) using selective catalytic reduction (SCR) can be carried out if very high levels of abatement are required, such as in Japan or the Federal Republic of Germany. Ammonia is added to the flue gases as a reducing agent, and the flue gases passed over a vanadium or tungsten oxide catalyst at temperatures of about 300–400°C, where oxidized nitrogen is reduced to nitrogen and water.

Mobile source control

Motor vehicle exhaust is a significant and growing source of air pollutants. The world has witnessed a major growth in the car population from 50 million in 1950 to an estimated 350 million in 1988. The worlds largest car market is the European Community (EC), where in excess of 105 million cars are on the roads.

Production of air pollution in an internal combustion engine

The internal combustion engine converts heat, generated by burning hydrocarbon fuel, into mechanical power. What comes out of a car exhaust depends upon the fuel and the engine. When compressed in the combustion chamber the fuel–air mixture contains hydrocarbons, nitrogen and oxygen from the air, and traces of other compounds present in the fuel. The combustion process is not totally efficient and some of the hydrocarbon fuel is only partially combusted, forming carbon monoxide and water; still other hydrocarbons are caught in the crevices within the engine and do not get combusted at all. These can be emitted from the exhaust as unburned hydrocarbons. During the combustion process the temperature can reach 2,000–2,500°C. At these temperatures, nitrogen and oxygen from the air in the combustion chamber react to form nitrogen oxides.

In the UK during 1988, motor vehicles contributed 45% (1,108,000 tonnes) of nitrogen oxides and 30% (545,000 tonnes) of VOCs emitted in the UK. Diesel engines are also a small contributor to sulphur dioxide emissions, with UK road transport emitting 54,000 tonnes in 1988, 1% of national emissions.

Control systems

As with stationary sources, control of mobile sources may be achieved during or after combustion occurs. The two major techniques available are catalytic systems and lean-burn engines.

Lean-burn engine technology offers improved fuel efficiency and will substantially reduce NO_x emissions under certain driving conditions, particularly at cruising speeds, but some exhaust gas clean-up systems, such as a simple oxidation catalyst, is required if hydrocarbon emissions are to be properly controlled. Lean-burn engines are designed to give an air–fuel ratio of 18:1–21:1 (in a normal engine it is 14.7:1) which will give low NO_x emissions, moderate engine power and good fuel economy. These advantages are at the expense of increased hydrocarbon emissions and attempts are now being made to reduce the number of places in which hydrocarbons can hide without burning in the combustion chamber. The NO_x advantage of lean-burn engines is only found under cruising conditions; as soon as the vehicle accelerates, the extra power demanded from the engine moves the combustion conditions away from lean and results in an increase in the NO_x emission. Thus to operate efficiently under all driving conditions a three-way catalyst is required.

Catalytic converters are the only proven exhaust gas clean-up system to reduce emissions significantly at relatively low expense without unduly affecting vehicle performance and fuel consumption. A catalyst is a substance or group of substances that will accelerate the rate of a chemical reaction without being consumed in the reaction. The most widely used system consists of a cylindrical ceramic body with a honeycomb structure which is chemically treated and coated with platinum group metals (platinum, palladium, rhodium). The honeycomb structure enables a high surface area to be incorporated within a relatively small space which is critical to the durability and reliability of performance. The catalyst is usually incorporated within the exhaust system of the car.

Catalysts have been used extensively since the mid 1970s in both the USA and Japan and have more recently been introduced in Australia and West Germany. Canada, Austria, Switzerland and the Nordic nations also require the use of catalytic converters to meet national emission regulations based upon the most recent US standards. Between 1968 and 1988 the use of catalytic converters enabled US mobile source emissions of hydrocarbons to be reduced by 96%, and nitrogen oxides by 76%, despite a significant increase in both total number of vehicles on the road and miles driven per vehicle.

In 1988 the EC agreed a new set of regulations, Directive 88/76, known as the Luxembourg Agreement, to control motor vehicle emissions of nitrogen oxides, hydrocarbons and carbon monoxide. The agreement laid down emission limits and compliance dates for three car types based upon engine size: large (greater than 2 litres), medium (1.4–2 litres) and small (less than 1.4 litres). These regulations were criticized as only about 10% of cars on the road would be required to have catalysts and the standards imposed were about half those in force in the USA for medium and small cars. Consequently, continued pressure led to the formulation of tougher regulations for smaller cars in 1989, EC Directive 89/458 (affecting engine size less than 1.4 litres). It is expected that the standards agreed will also be applied to medium and large cars. Standards now agreed for small cars are comparable to the existing United States standards which can only be met by the use of catalytic converters to control exhaust emission. A consolidated directive imposing similar standards for all new vehicles and revised test procedures will follow.

Acidification control programmes

International

As emissions of acid deposition precursors will be transported long distances and may fall on other nation states, international agreements are necessary to limit emissions from major sources.

Within the European Community, Directive 88/609 which limited emissions from new and existing large combustion plant, that is power stations and large industrial boilers, was agreed by member states in 1988. Each state has agreed to a community cut in sulphur dioxide emissions based on 1980 emission levels. A 40% cut will be achieved by 1993, a 60% cut by 1998 and a 70% cut by 2003. Tables 1 and 2 identify national obligations under this directive. The debate on emission reductions will be reopened in the early 1990s when the Community examines the success of the directive.

The main forum for co-operation between the governments of east and west Europe and North America on the measurement and abatement of acid deposition is the United Nations Economic Commission for Europe, of which Canada and the United States are members. The UN–ECE Convention on Long Range Transboundary Air Pollution was adopted in 1979 and entered into force in 1983 as the first multilateral treaty to protect the atmospheric environment. Thirty-two parties have ratified this convention which lays down principles and provides a framework for co-operation. Three protocols to the convention provide

Table 1: *Sulphur dioxide emission ceilings and target reductions required by the EC Large Combustion Plant Directive*

Member State	*SO_2 emissions by LCP 1980 '000 tonnes*	*Emission ceiling ('000 tonnes/yr)* 1993	1998	2003	*% red'n over 1980 emissions* 1993	1998	2003
Belgium	530	318	212	159	−40	−60	−70
Denmark	323	213	141	106	−34	−56	−67
France	1910	1146	764	573	−40	−60	−70
Germany	2225	1335	890	668	−40	−60	−70
Greece	303	320	320	320	+6	+6	+6
Ireland	99	124	124	124	+25	+25	+25
Italy	2450	1800	1500	900	−27	−39	−63
Luxembourg	3	1.8	1.5	1.5	−40	−50	−60
Netherlands	299	180	120	90	−40	−60	−70
Portugal	115	232	270	206	+102	+135	+79
Spain	2290	2290	1730	1440	0	−24	−37
UK	3883	3106	2330	1553	−20	−40	−60

Source: Official Journal of the European Communities, No L 336/7, 1988

Table 2: *Nitrogen oxides emission ceilings and target reductions required by the EC Large Combustion Plant Directive*

Member State	*NO_x emissions as NO_2 by LCP 1980 '000 tonnes*	*Emission ceiling ('000 tonnes/yr)* 1993	1998	*% red'n over 1980 emissions* 1993	1988
Belgium	110	88	66	−20	−40
Denmark	124	121	81	−3	−35
France	400	320	240	−20	−40
Germany	870	696	522	−20	−40
Greece	36	70	70	+94	+94
Ireland	28	50	50	+79	+79
Italy	580	570	428	−2	−26
Luxembourg	3	2.4	1.8	−20	−40
Netherlands	122	98	73	−20	−40
Portugal	23	59	64	+157	+178
Spain	366	368	277	+1	−24
UK	1016	864	711	−15	−30

Source: Official Journal of the European Communities, No L 336/7, 1988

the instruments by which emission reductions can be achieved and base-line monitoring carried out. These are;

(a) The protocol on the long-term financing of the co-operative Programme for Monitoring and Evaluation of the Long Range Transmission of Air Pollutants in Europe.
(b) The protocol on the reduction of sulphur emissions or their transboundary fluxes by at least 30%, adopted in Helsinki, July 1985.
(c) The protocol concerning the control of emissions of nitrogen oxides or their transboundary fluxes, signed in Sofia, November 1988.

The 30% protocol has been ratified by 16 nations (see Table 3), and entered into force in September 1987. This protocol, the so called "30% club", aims for a 30% reduction in 1980 sulphur emissions by 1993. Already 10 parties to the protocol have reduced emissions by 30%, all parties have announced a reduction of 50% and four parties reductions of 65% or more. The protocol concerning nitrogen oxides was signed by 25 nations and requires the signatories to ensure that after 1994 emissions do not exceed the 1987 level. A second phase to this protocol will be to ensure the reduction in emissions are consistent with the concepts of critical load and level (see below). Negotiations concerning the second phase will begin in 1990/91 with emission reduction measures required to be in place by the end of 1996.

Twelve UN–ECE member nations who are dissatisfied with the present requirements of the NO_x protocol have formed a 30% NO_x club with the intention of reducing their emissions by 30% by 1998 (see Table 4).

During the early part of the 1990s the UN–ECE will discuss a VOCs protocol and, in due course, an ammonia protocol.

Until recently, emission reductions proposals such as the Large Combustion Plant Directive or the 30% protocol have been essentially political agreements relying upon social and

Table 3: *European members of the 30% Club*

	Date of accession	*Agreement*
Albania	–	–
Austria	Mar 1984	50% by 1993
Belgium	Jun 1984	50% by 1995
Bulgaria	Jun 1984	30% by 1993
Czech.	Sep 1984	30% by 1993
Denmark	Mar 1984	40% by 1995
Finland	Mar 1984	50% by 1993
France	Mar 1984	50% by 1990
GDR	Jun 1984	30% by 1993
FRG	Mar 1984	65% by 1993
Greece	–	–
Hungary	Apr 1985	30% by 1993
Ireland	–	–
Italy	Sep 1984	30% by 1993
Netherlands	Mar 1984	50% by 1995
Norway	Mar 1984	50% by 1994
Poland	–	–
Portugal	–	–
Romania	–	–
Spain	–	–
Sweden	Mar 1984	65% by 1995
Switzerland	Mar 1984	30% by 1993
UK	–	–
USSR	Jun 1984	30% by 1993
Yugoslavia	–	–

Source: UN–ECE, 1987
Note: A dash indicates that a nation has not joined.

Table 4: *Members of the 30% Club for nitrogen oxide reductions*

Austria
Belgium
Denmark
Federal Republic of Germany
Finland
France
Italy
Leichenstein
Netherlands
Norway
Sweden
Switzerland

economic acceptance or the reduction, rather than the capacity of environmental systems to receive deposition. However, a new concept, that of the critical load and critical level, has recently been formulated at the UN–ECE Conference in Geneva, 1988.

A critical load is defined as "*a quantitative estimate of an exposure to one or more pollutants below which significant harmful effects on specified sensitive elements of the environment do not occur according to present knowledge*".

A critical level is defined as "*the concentration(s) of pollutant(s) in the atmosphere above which direct adverse effects on receptors such as plants, ecosystems or materials, may occur according to present knowledge*".

Essentially this defines the environmentally acceptable level or load of pollutant to which an ecosystem or material can be exposed without harmful effect or inducing long-term change in sensitive systems.

Application of the concept of a critical load and level gives some guidance as to the importance of current levels of deposition and the scale of reduction necessary to bring current rates of deposition into line with theoretical critical loads.

Reductions equivalent to 90% of European sulphur emissions and 75% of nitrogen emissions have been suggested on the basis of the critical loads and levels calculations. European environmental pressure groups are calling for these ecological target reductions to supplant the politically derived figures of the 30% protocol. In 1988 these groups affirmed their commitment to large-scale reductions in calling for a 90% cut in sulphur dioxide and nitrogen oxide emissions, a 75% cut in ozone levels and a 90% cut in ammonia emissions with reductions based upon 1980 emissions. Emission reductions of these proportions will, in time, be addressed by the UN–ECE.

National

At the national level, Sweden typifies the response of nations most severely affected by acidification.

In 1988 the Swedish parliament approved the Environmental Protection Board's Action Plan against Air Pollution and Acidification. An impressive range of counter measures to combat both the emission and effect of acid deposition are now in progress; in the period 1987/88 to 1990/91 these actions are costed at SKr 690 million. All actions proposed under the Action Plan are related to the best scientific understanding and to the concepts of a critical loan and a critical level. These actions include:

- (i) reduction in sulphur emissions by 65% between 1980 and 1995;
- (ii) reduction in nitrogen dioxide emission by 30% by 1995;
- (iii) countermeasures against forest soil acidification;
- (iv) improved agricultural practices to reduce use of acidifying fertilizers and limit ammonia emissions;
- (v) improved research and monitoring programmes;
- (vi) reductions in hydrocarbon emissions;
- (vii) measures to reduce traffic growth;
- (viii) more liming of forests, soils, watercourses and groundwater supplies;
- (ix) measures to protect the cultural heritage.

Sweden has already moved beyond the Action Plan in its proposal to reduce national sulphur emissions by 80% of their 1980 level by 2000. Table 5 compares the magnitude of

Table 5: *Proposed sulphur emission reductions 1980–2000*

State	*% reduction*	*Deadline year*	*1980–1987 % reduction*
Sweden	68%	1995	−50%
Sweden	80%	2000	
Austria	70%	1995	−58%
Luxembourg	58%	1990	−45%
Federal Republic of Germany	65%	1993	−36%
Switzerland	57%	1995	−51%
France	50%	1990	−48%
Finland	50%	1993	−44%
Canada	50%	1994	n/a
Norway	50%	1994	−29%
Belgium	50%	1995	−39%
Netherlands	50%	1995	−42%
Italy	30%	1993	−34%
Denmark	50%	1995	−29%
Czechoslovakia	30%	1993	− 6%
East Germany	30%	1993	0
USSR	30%	1993	−20%
UK	30%	1999	−21%
Large Combustion Plant (LCP) sources			
UK	20%	1993	
	40%	1998	
	60%	2003	

Note: in 1988 LCP sources were 84% of UK sulphur dioxide emissions.

the Swedish plans with those of selected other nations. Whilst such actions will significantly reduce the Swedish contribution to acidification they will not, on their own, reduce deposition in Sweden to the target set by the critical load calculations. To do this co-operative international actions are required.

The United Nations Economic Commission for Europe is the forum through which these co-operative actions will occur. Development of the concepts of critical load and level will provide the guidance for both the scientific research agenda and determine the form of future international control programmes.

Conclusion

Significant reductions in acid deposition will only occur through concerted international action. Current agreements such as the UN–ECE protocol requiring a 30% reduction of 1980 sulphur emissions and the European Community Large Combustion Plant Directive have emission reductions set at levels deemed politically acceptable. Approximately half of the signatories of the 30% protocol have moved beyond its narrow requirements in announcing reductions of at least 50% to be achieved by 1993–1995. Whilst this level of emission reductions does not yet reach the levels that adoption of the critical loads and levels would dictate it is, however, a move in the right direction and clearly indicates the concern of severely affected nations to reduce their contributions to an international problem. A reduction in sulphur emissions of as much as 90% has been suggested by environmental groups based on the application of critical loads calculations to enable recovery of systems already acidified.

As the scientific understanding of cause and effect has improved, so attention has focused upon the technologies available to control emissions of acidifying pollutants from both fixed plant and mobile sources. In Western nations, the control of sulphur dioxide emissions from large fossil fuel combustion plants is most advanced. Whilst a number of technologies are available for sulphur dioxide control, their applicability, particularly the engineering problems associated with retrofit activities and the state of their commercial development and cost effectiveness have limited the rapid commercial application of the technology, to date, which many had hoped to see. The exception, however, is the ambitious programme of the Federal Republic of Germany to reduce sulphur and nitrogen oxides emitted from power stations, district heating plant and industrial combustion plant. More than 48,000 MWe of boiler capacity is equipped with flue gas desulphurization (FGD) and and 37,000 MWe of plant are being equipped with DeNOX systems by 1990. The German example clearly illustrates the fact that, given the political will and the economic strength, an ambitious control programme can be quickly implemented over a relatively short period of time.

For bibliography, see p. 357.

Acknowledgement
The author gratefully acknowledges the assistance, advice and encouragement of his colleagues Sue Hare, David Lee, David Raper, Bridget Heath and Tim Jenkins in the Acid Rain Information Centre during the preparation of this contribution.

2 THE ANTARCTIC

D. J. Drewry, P. Beck, A. Clarke, J. A. Heap, D. W. H. Walton, R. Willan

Geographical setting and historical background

Antarctica possesses the most hostile climate on planet Earth yet has become, within the last decade, one of the most challenging areas politically, scientifically and environmentally. This attention is likely to continue into the next century as the natural laboratory conditions of the region play an increasingly important role in the investigation of issues of global environmental relevance such as ozone depletion and climatic warming. Further interest will result as the Antarctic Treaty System evolves to regulate burgeoning interest in renewable and non-renewable resources from the continent and seas, and to control the impacts, some consequential, of heightened activity from scientific research and commercial exploitation.

Geographical setting

The Antarctic constitutes a large, remote region (some 10% of the surface area of the globe) centred around the South Pole. It comprises a continental land mass (Antarctica) of 13,980,000 km^2, covered over all but 2.5% of its area by ice, the surrounding Southern Ocean to the latitude of the Antarctic Convergence at about 55°S, and a large number of peri-Antarctic islands.

The continental area may be divided into three major regions. Lying principally within the Eastern hemisphere but with its western boundary running along the axis of the Transantarctic Mountains is East Antarctica, at about 10,300,000 km^2. This is an old continental shield area and possesses close geological similarities with Australia, India and Southern Africa. To the east of the Transantarctic Mountains is the smaller West Antarctic area (1,970,000 km^2). The ice sheet here masks a landscape much of which is well below sea level but includes substantial upland blocks, including the Ellsworth Mountains where the continent's highest peak is located (Vinson Massif, 5,140 m). Two large floating ice shelves fill major embayments in the Ross and Weddell Seas. The Antarctic Peninsula forms the third, smallest but most diverse region. It is a rugged mountainous panhandle stretching towards South America and with which it has strong geological affinities. Numerous, frequently ice-covered, offshore islands lie adjacent to the Peninsula.

The ice sheet, containing 30,000,000 km^3 forms an immense flattened dome rising to over 4,000 m above sea level in East Antarctica. Its maximum depth is 4,751 m. It receives of the order of 2,500 km^3 snow accumulation per year, which is eventually discharged by ice flow into the Southern Ocean as icebergs. The ice sheet contains an equivalent of 80 m sea level rise.

Climatically, Antarctica is one of the planet's extremes, receiving the lowest amounts of incoming solar radiation. Combined with extreme average height and highly reflecting snow surface, temperatures are the lowest recorded (−89°C at Vostok). High barometric pressure (1030–1040 mb) over the ice sheet and strong pressure gradients across the Southern Ocean generate a characteristic atmospheric and oceanic circulation around the continent and give rise to an extreme wind-wave climate. The inland regions are dominated by strong stable inversions and cold dense air drainage (katabatic winds).

The hostile climate of the continent and its isolation has resulted in a very impoverished biota. The largest terrestrial animal is a small mite, and plants are restricted to mosses and lichens over much of the region. In contrast, the marine environment possesses a considerable abundance of life supported by a constant supply of rich nutrients from upwelling waters. The food web is both complex and long, critically dependent upon zooplankton (especially a Euphausid, krill) but able to sustain the planet's largest animal, the whale.

History of exploration

Antarctica has long been the focus of commercial interests. When Cook first circumnavigated Antarctica in 1774–75 he did not sight land but his reports of fur seals on South Georgia attracted European and North American sealers. Their extended forays led to the discovery of the continent in 1820. In the late 19th century attention returned to the re-stocked fur seal beaches, to elephant seals for oil and in the early 20th century to whaling. This latter activity reached its apotheosis (to some its nadir) in 1938. Thereafter as whale numbers declined the industry shrank, to become virtually moribund by the end of the 1970s.

The Sixth International Geographical Congress of 1895 renewed scientific curiosity in the South Polar Regions. A new period of exploration and research followed, with well-equipped and well-staffed national ventures such as those of de Gerlache, Nordenskjold,

Table 1: *Antarctic treaty parties*

Original Signatories	*Consultative Parties** *Date of signature*
Argentina	1961
Australia	1961
Belgium	1960
Chile	1961
France	1960
Japan	1960
New Zealand	1960
Norway	1960
South Africa	1960
United Kingdom	1960
USA	1960
USSR	1960

**Consultative parties* (ATCPs) — original signatories and states adjudged to perform "substantial research activity" in Antarctica entitled to a decision-making role at Antarctic Treaty consultative meetings.

Table 1: *Contd.*

Additional ATCPs	*Date of becoming ATCP*	*(Date of accession to Treaty)*
Poland	1977	(1961)
Federal Republic of Germany	1981	(1979)
Brazil	1983	(1975)
India	1983	(1983)
Uruguay	1985	(1980)
German Democratic Republic	1987	(1974)
Italy	1987	(1981)
Spain	1988	(1982)
Sweden	1988	(1984)
Finland	1989	(1984)
Peru	1989	(1981)
South Korea	1989	(1986)
*Non-consultative parties***	*Date of accession*	
Czechoslovakia	1962	
Denmark	1965	
Netherlands	1967	
Romania	1971	
Bulgaria	1978	
Papua New Guinea	1981	
Hungary	1984	
Cuba	1984	
Greece	1987	
North Korea	1987	
Austria	1987	
Ecuador	1987	
Canada	1988	
Colombia	1989	

***Non-consultative parties* — accession involves a recognition of the validity of the Antarctic Treaty's principles and entitles a party to observer status at meetings. It is often used as a stepping-stone towards ATCP status.

Charcot, Drygalski, Scott, Shackleton and Mawson. This "heroic age" prior to World War II established knowledge of several large regions of the continent and placed science as the major goal of Antarctic expeditions. Whilst American forays, principally during the 1920s and 1930s, consolidated this activity and introduced aircraft to the continent, it was not until after World War II that Antarctic science came of age. The International Geophysical Year (IGY) in 1957–58 brought 12 nations to the continent simultaneously (see Table 1), set new standards of research and created a unique international collaboration. The IGY established the basis for continuous research of the region and inspired the formalizing of international accord through the Antarctic Treaty of 1959 (ratified in 1961).

Research in the final decade of the 20th century has become increasingly focused, problem-oriented, demanding more sophisticated studies and equipment, frequently on a large scale and necessitating international collaboration. The results of three decades of intensive investigation has established clearly and without ambiguity the integral and in some cases critical role of Antarctica in the functioning and understanding of the natural systems of planet Earth.

The international political status of Antarctica: the Antarctic Treaty System

The changing international polar dimension

Antarctica has moved towards the centre of the international stage during the last decade (a trend which seems likely to continue in the 1990s) through consideration by a range of international organizations, including the United Nations and the Non-Aligned Movement. A series of reports, like those produced by the UN, the European Parliament, and the Brundtland Report, contributed to the impressions of a "continent surrounded by advice".

Antarctic science identified and monitored subsequently the depletion of the earth's ozone layer. This research provided the background for international efforts to limit the use of CFCs (e.g. the 1987 Montreal Protocol) and to investigate climatic change (e.g. the so-called greenhouse effect). Non-governmental organizations (NGOs), principally environmental groups, have identified Antarctica as a major global issue and pressed the benefits accruing from the transformation of the last great wilderness on earth into a world park in which human activities would be strictly regulated and mining, in particular, would be prohibited. The issue has been interpreted as a test of the international community's environmental credentials.

Antarctica's emergence has proved a function also of a growing awareness of its alleged fishing and mining potential; the desire of developing countries to share in its resources and management in accordance with changing political and legal attitudes regarding the introduction of a more open and accountable regime; the inspiration of the 1982 UN Convention on the Law of the Sea.

The Antarctic Treaty

The late 1950s represented a turning-point in the affairs of the region. The IGY and the creation of the Scientific (formerly "Special") Committee on Antarctic Research (SCAR) made significant contributions to the cause of science. The 1959 Antarctic Treaty soon followed, placing the area south of 60°S excluding the high seas under a special inter-governmental regime described by the shorthand term "Antarctic Treaty System" (ATS).

Antarctica became a zone of peace defined by provisions for peaceful use, demilitarization, denuclearization, the shelving of the troublesome sovereignty problem arising from rival territorial claims and inspection. The Antarctic Treaty, representing the only post-1945 agreement for the complete demilitarization of a sizeable geographical region, became a reference point for other regional zones of peace. The IGY experience was extended through the promotion of Antarctica as a continent for science and international scientific collaboration. Henceforth, research data possessing a polar and global significance would prove the region's prime export. Finally, Antarctica is now becoming a special conservation area subject to strict environmental controls.

This regime, having become effective in 1961, may last indefinitely—the preamble mentions the word "forever"—even if it may be reviewed during or after 1991. The Antarctic Treaty does *not* end in 1991, as mistakenly argued by certain commentators.

The history of the regime

The ATS has been characterized by three main trends: the growth of participation, the evolution of the regime's responsibilities, and the increased interest of outsiders in the region.

A prominent development in recent years has been the marked increase in membership of the ATS. The original 12 consultative parties (ATCPs) have been joined by a further 13 governments adjudged to perform "substantial research activity" in Antarctica (see Tables 1 and 2). ATCPs perform the prime decision-making role in the biennial consultative meetings (ATCMs) held by rotation in member states. A further 14 governments, having endorsed the Treaty's principles through accession, are entitled to observer status at meetings, although this form of participation is often used as a stepping-stone to ATCP status. Other governments are moving towards accession. The ATS, though attacked by its critics as an exclusive club composed of only a small proportion of the international community (cf. 159 UN members), comprises the 39 participants, accounting for over 70% of the world's population, includes all the permanent members of the UN Security Council, most European Community states, all the Group of Seven and several major developing states.

Second, the ATS has evolved in a flexible manner designed to accommodate new circumstances and demands as well as to fill perceived gaps through the adoption of recommendations and the conclusion of relevant conventions. Conservation has proved a perennial theme for action, as evidenced by the 1964 Agreed Measures for the Conservation of Antarctic Fauna and Flora, the 1972 Convention for Conservation of Seals, the numerous recommendations adopted on topics like "Man's Impact on the Environment", and the current proposal for a comprehensive environmental protection convention. Resource management is a related concern. The Convention for the Conservation of Antarctic Marine Living Resources (CCAMLR) was concluded in 1980 and became operational in 1982. The CCAMLR regime, guided by expert scientific and technical advice, has regulated fishing according to an innovatory ecosystem approach (e.g. imposition of catch prohibitions), although NGOs favour even stronger controls (for which see later).

During the late 1980s it appeared that the CCAMLR regime would soon be paralleled by a minerals regime based upon the Convention on the Regulation of Antarctic Mineral Resource Activities (CRAMRA), which was opened for signature during 1988–89. The

Table 2: *The Antarctic Treaty System: the growth in membership*

Date	*Consultative parties*	*Non-consultative parties*	*Total parties*
1959	12	0	12
1970	12	4	16
1980	13	9	22
1985	18	14	32
1990 (January)	25	14	39

accompanying controversy about mining and conservation has prompted speculation about a serious divide within the ATS, including a threat to the regime's consensus procedures.

Antarctica's emergence as an international question has owed much to the minerals negotiations, since many of the ATS's critics sought a share in the management and benefits of minerals. The prime forum for debate has been the UN, which has conducted annual discussions on Antarctica since 1983. The initial consensus approach soon broke down, and since 1985 the international community has been divided over Antarctica. On the one hand, the critics, led by Malaysia, have pressed for "collective action under the auspices of the United Nations for an open, accountable and equitable framework for Antarctica for the benefit of mankind as a whole". Their desire to treat Antarctica as the "common heritage of mankind" administered by a new UN-based regime has been reinforced by a demand for the exclusion of the apartheid regime of South Africa from the Antarctic Treaty. By contrast, the ATCPs, though prepared to provide information, have opposed UN interference in the affairs of a region adjudged to be managed by a valid legal regime open to accession by any UN member and have ignored the resulting resolutions.

Looking ahead

The international community remains divided by Antarctica in spite of frequent expressions made at the UN regarding the desirability of a consensus approach. The unbending attitude of the ATCPs, in conjunction with the fact that they include the world's most influential governments, suggests that the critics, though capable of marshalling large majorities at the UN, will make little progress until they recognize the Antarctic realities, including the need to work for change within rather than outside the parameters of the ATS.

In 1991 the ATS celebrates its 30th anniversary. Although a treaty review conference might be convened during or after 1991, the key focus during the early 1990s will be placed upon the fate of CRAMRA, the proposed comprehensive environmental protection convention, and speculation concerning additional management regimes for tourism.

During 1989–90 all of the world's major political leaders, including President Bush of the USA and President Gorbachev of the Soviet Union, acknowledged the importance of Antarctica in environmental matters. Speaking at the UN in November 1989 Margaret Thatcher, the British Prime Minister, acknowledged the crucial role of Antarctic scientists "at the leading edge of research warning us of the greater dangers that lie ahead". In January 1990 President Gorbachev identified Antarctica as a "natural zone of global importance . . . . Our grandchildren will never forgive us if we fail to preserve this phenomenal ecological system".

Scientific activity in Antarctica

Science context

Antarctica has been described as a "continent for science" and a scientific study remains Antarctica's pre-eminent contribution, highly relevant to issues of global debate.

For example, the negative radiation budget of the Antarctic regions is fundamental in driving the global atmospheric regime. The fluctuations and phasing of continental ice sheet volume and sea ice extent provide second order modulating influences on climate and atmospheric circulation on a variety of timescales. The effects of man-induced increases of gases which react to radiation may have fundamental effects in the south polar regions where modelling predicts amplification of temperature changes: the role of the melting of the ice sheet on global sea levels cannot be underplayed. Furthermore, the Southern Ocean possesses an influential though not fully understood role as a major chemical sink, particularly for carbon dioxide (CO_2) for which the estimated uptake is of the order of 30% of that discharged into the atmosphere.

Science in Antarctica covers the very wide range of the life, earth, atmospheric, ocean and medical fields. It includes regional reconnaissance surveys, monitoring programmes (both at a continental scale using satellite systems and at single stations and sites) and problem-oriented research linked to international science priorities.

Earth science

A broad reconnaissance level of geological knowledge of Antarctica has been achieved. Outcrops of rock are restricted to mountain ranges, nunataks and ice-free coastal localities. A major focus of research is understanding the evolution and break-up of Gondwana—the former supercontinent in which South America, Africa, India and Australia were clustered around the central component—Antarctica.

Other important studies are aimed at the geophysical investigations of the rock regions hidden by the ice sheet (over 95% of the continent) and adjacent seas using electromagnetic, magnetic, gravitational and seismic methods. In the Scotia Sea and along the western margin of the Antarctic Peninsula subduction-related processes can be studied in some detail.

The investigation of the dynamics, thermodynamics and stability of the ice sheet is crucial to understanding the response of the ice to, and its role in, climate change and global sea level variations. Furthermore the ice sheet presents unparalleled scope for the study of past climate and environmental conditions extending back to possibly one million years BP[1] from the study of ice cores. The analysis of ice cores also traces the inexorable rise of CO_2 and other gases such as methane and oxides of nitrogen and sulphur since pre-industrial times, some of which contribute to the greenhouse effect.

Marine and Life Science

The Antarctic Circumpolar Current links the flow in the Atlantic, Indian and Pacific Oceans. The Weddell Sea produces very cold ocean bottom water which flows northwards and has a profound influence on biological productivity. Furthermore large areas of the Southern Ocean are subject to seasonal sea ice cover. At a maximum in August and September Antarctic sea ice extends over an area of some 20,000,000 km^2. This breaks back under rising temperatures, swell and wave action to about 3–4,000,000 km^2 in the late summer (February). The presence of sea ice is important in processes of exchange (mass, momentum and energy) between the ocean and the atmosphere—a field of valuable climate-related research.

The Southern Ocean is one of the richest biologically, particularly at the higher trophic levels as witnessed by the large numbers of birds, seals and whales (prior to man-made depletions). This occurs despite the fact that primary production is probably no greater than in other oceanic regions.

---

[1]Technically, geological ages are in years Before the Present (BP)—"present" is taken as 1950.

A central theme of biological research in the Antarctic is the study of systems and processes subject to extreme conditions. This provides information on the adaptations of living organisms to stress and to the changes within their environments, particularly seasonality, day length and temperature in the seas and to moisture availability on land.

The study of biogeochemical cycles in the Southern Ocean will be an area of important development in the 1990s in order to establish the role of this vast region in the uptake of gases by the ocean from the atmosphere, and hence in climate control.

Atmospheric science

Atmospheric research involves understanding the complex interplay of energetic, dynamical and chemical processes using both ground-based and space borne (satellite) instruments. Routine meteorological measurements have been made for many years at Antarctic stations and are important for regional and global forecasting. Due to the sensitivity of high latitudes continued meteorological monitoring and collection of time series records will be essential for the detection of any climate trends.

The most distinctive large-scale feature of the Antarctic atmosphere is the winter stratospheric vortex in which intense cooling creates a circum-Antarctic circulation, to about 50°S, with a cold, dense core over the pole. A strong thermal gradient separates the Antarctic vortex from warmer air to the north intimately associated with physical conditions which control stratospheric chemistry especially ozone depletion. Ozone drawn into the vortex during the winter is photo-chemically destroyed, catalysed by derivatives of man-made CFCs, during the spring in the presence of sunlight.

Antarctica is particularly important in the study of the upper atmosphere—the regions of ionising radiation above the stratosphere (upwards of 20 km). The flow of electrically charged particles emanating from the sun, and known as the solar wind, streams past the Earth and interacts in a complex manner with the Earth's magnetic field. Protons and electrons are directed towards the planet and its ionosphere, along magnetic field lines, leading to auroral displays and atmospheric disturbances and allowing deep-space phenomena to be studied from the ground. An understanding of these plasma processes occurring in the Earth's upper atmosphere is important practically in relation to radio communications and to satellite operations.

Medical science

The personnel on Antarctic Stations present unique opportunities to further certain fields of medical, physiological and psychological research. The population of an Antarctic base is roughly of a single age class, is physically fit, lives in isolation for much of the year, eats the same food and lives within a single confined area.

Medical research exploits these unique characteristics. Studies are undertaken on adaptation and acclimatization and related physiology. Extreme aspects of living medicine can also be pursued. Investigation of human commensal bacteria allow assessment of transmission between individuals, persistence of strains in isolation over the winter, the effects of diet and of re-inoculation in summer.

International organizations of Antarctic science

Scientific work is undertaken by over 20 nations in programmes of varying size, scope and complexity. The Scientific Committee on Antarctic Research (SCAR), an ICSU body, undertakes the international initiation, promotion and co-ordination of national programmes through biennial meetings of delegates and the activities of its Working Groups and Groups of Specialists. Co-ordinated multinational programmes are fostered. Frequent symposia and conferences on Antarctic Science topics are sponsored by SCAR.

ICSU is currently formulating the International Geosphere Biosphere Programmes (IGBP) to study global change. The objectives are to investigate the interdependent physical, chemical and biological processes which regulate the total Earth system. The Antarctic will play an important role in these studies due to the extreme and sensitive nature of its environmental systems. SCAR has developed its plans for the IGBP which will become a major driving force in Antarctic science over the next decade.

Convention on the Conservation of Antarctic Marine Living Resources (CCAMLR)

The Convention on the Conservation of Antarctic Marine Living Resources (CCAMLR) was signed at Canberra in 1980 and entered into force in 1982. It seeks to manage and conserve the Antarctic marine ecosystem and its populations of krill, fish and dependent predators south of the Antarctic Convergence. CCAMLR control extends over an area greater than the Antarctic Treaty by including the waters of South Georgia, the South Sandwich Islands, Kerguelen and Île Crozet.

Negotiations on the Convention began in 1977 and stemmed from increased concerns during the 1970s that unregulated exploitation of fish and krill would result in irreversible damage, not only to exploited target species but also to stocks of seals, seabirds and whales. Between 1969–71, Soviet fishing fleets took 400,000 tonnes of prime Antarctic cod (Notothenia rossii) from the water around South Georgia which has shown little sign of recovery, despite a fishing ban.

Twenty nations, including all seven Antarctic claimants have signed the Convention which also enjoys the participation of the European Community. CCAMLR is operated through a Commission based in Hobart, Australia and financed by contributions from signatory states. A scientific committee and technical working groups provide advice.

The objective of the Convention is the conservation of Antarctic marine living resources. CCAMLR embodies three main conservation elements: (a) no harvested species be fished to below the level of its "greatest net annual increment" or maximum sustainable yield; (b) the ecological relationship between harvested, dependent and related populations must be maintained (and where necessary depleted populations restored to viable levels); and (c) agreements to regulate any fishery must pay due regard to the effect of harvesting, not only on the exploited species but also dependent predators.

In these respects CCAMLR has broken new ground. It extended control to previously regarded international waters and uniquely, regulates exploitation on an ecosystem approach. CCAMLR requires the regulation of marine harvesting to be "pro-active" rather than "reactive" and provides for controls based on the predicted consequences of fishery so ensuring that the maximum sustainable yield is never exceeded.

The Commission, on advice from its Scientific Committee, regulates harvesting through mechanisms standard to other fisheries including the imposition of Total Allowable Catches (TACs), and restrictions or prohibitions within defined areas, on selected species or by specified fishing gear. Recently, the Commission has introduced a widespread monitoring scheme to assess any impact of harvesting on dependent species such as penguins and fur seals.

Despite its obvious successes in restraining and managing marine harvesting in the Southern Ocean, critics emphasize that the system of inspection through international observers is not backed up by effective enforcement and the onus of proof on the impact of any fishery remains with the scientist or environmentalist rather than with the fishing industry.

The Convention on the Regulation of Antarctic Mineral Resource Activities (CRAMRA)

The possibility of a binding and indefinite moratorium banning minerals activity in Antarctica was debated on five occasions between 1972 and 1981. On each occasion the option was opposed by the majority of Antarctic Treaty Consultative Parties (ATCPs). Since the first level of risk to the Antarctic Treaty System would be triggered by prospecting activity, ATCPs considered but failed to achieve agreement on prospecting activity only and negotiations turned to an international agreement to cover all stages of minerals activity. The text of CRAMRA was adopted by a consensus of 33 Antarctic Treaty parties at Wellington on June 2, 1988.

The basic environmental protection provisions of CRAMRA are contained in Article 4. It prohibits all Antarctic minerals activity unless each proposed activity is judged, in advance, to have no significant adverse impact on the Antarctic environment. If, in any given case, it is judged that there is insufficient environmental information to make the required judgement, the activity cannot proceed. It also prohibits mineral resource activity until such time as technology and procedures are available to provide for safe operations and that there exists the capacity to respond effectively to accidents, particularly those with potential environmental effects.

In addition, there is the requirement that no exploration and development activity may take place until a Liability Protocol has been concluded and has entered into force in accordance with the same arrangements covering the entry into force of CRAMRA itself. It is laid down that "Such rules and procedures (elaborated in a Liability Protocol) shall be designed to enhance the protection of the Antarctic environmental and dependent and associated ecosystems".

Entry into force of the Convention depends on all the States, whose ratification or accession is indispensable, taking the necessary constitutional steps. CRAMRA will come into force once 16 of the 20 Consultative parties who participated in the 1988 Wellington meeting have deposited their instruments of ratification or accession. According to the terms of the Convention, those 16 States must include five developing countries and 11 developed countries, amongst which all seven Claimant States (to sovereignty over parts of Antarctica); the USA and USSR must be numbered.

A provision related to CRAMRA is that all States represented at the Wellington Conference should urge their nationals and other States to refrain from Antarctic mineral resource activities pending the timely entry into force of the Convention. The aim of this provision is to encourage the rapid adoption of the Convention so that all stages of Antarctic mineral resource activity shall be definitively prohibited, except in accordance with the Convention's provisions. The understanding underlying the provision, however, is that if any State, whose ratification or accession is required for the Convention's entry into force, fails to ratify or accede—so that the Convention cannot enter into force—then the situation with respect to mineral activity in the Antarctic reverts to the *status quo ante* the beginning of the CRAMRA negotiations.

The mineral resource potential of Antarctica

The scientific press and popular media have fostered erroneously the view that economic mineral deposits, ore deposits and hydrocarbon reservoirs have been found in Antarctica.

Terminology

Mineralized rocks contain elements enriched beyond normal crustal levels. Such rocks occur in all continental and oceanic crust, including Antarctica. A *mineral occurrence* is a locality of rocks with an anomalous mineralogy and geochemistry. Occurrences may be a few millimetres to several kilometres in size and are ubiquitous in all parts of the continental and oceanic crust, including Antarctica. Because of their unusual composition, mineralized rocks are of basic scientific interest.

The term *prospect* is used for a mineral occurrence explored in detail for its economic potential, using geological, geophysical and geochemical mapping, excavation and drilling. Exploration statistics suggest that for any 100 mineral occurrences so investigated, *one* might have economic potential.

Although Antarctic rocks have been mapped and analyzed, this has been mostly on a reconnaissance scale for research on fundamental geological processes. To date, no detailed exploration has occurred, hence no prospects are known.

Mineral deposits are significant volumes of rock whose geology, mineralogy, geochemistry and size allow exploitation (if logistic, technological, economic, political and environmental conditions are favourable). No mineral deposits are known in Antarctica.

Economic deposits are volumes of rock (ore) being extracted, processed and sold at a profit. "Economic" is defined by demand and supply, available technology, global finance and politics. The remoteness, hostile terrain and climate, extensive ice cover and lack of all infrastructure in Antarctica make it the least economic continent to explore and exploit.

The *mineral resource potential* of an area is an estimate of the hypothetical deposits and identified mineral reserves. Assessment requires accurate and detailed geological maps, regional stream sediment geochemistry, detailed airborne geophysics and historical evidence of economic mineralization. None of these data is available in Antarctica. Of the 332,000 km^2 of rock not covered by ice, about 80% has been geologically mapped at a reconnaissance level (c.1:500,000 scale) and possibly 10% in detail (1:50,000 scale or larger).

Known mineral occurrences and geochemical anomalies in Antarctica

An assessment of Antarctica may be attempted by (a) evaluating known mineral occurrences and geochemical anomalies; (b) comparing the known geological composition with similar terrains elsewhere; and (c) by comparison with once contiguous terrains which are known better.

Mineralization has been reported at about 300 localities generally by geologists with little specialist mineralization experience. The Antarctic Peninsula, the region with the most reported occurrences, has 250 localities over an area of 400,000 km^2 (compared to the British Isles with over 4,000 in 241,000 km^2). Most Antarctic localities consist of small outcrops a few centimetres to metres across and for many there is little textural or geochemical evidence for mineralization. Detailed field examination of about 40 localities in the Antarctic Peninsula suggests that two-thirds of reported iron and copper localities are probably innocuous and misleading. Second, although there have been many reports of "porphyry-style mineralization", no confidence can be placed in them. Third, some localities are mineral misidentifications such as galena or sphalerite for hematite.

Elsewhere in Antarctica, the most widely quoted rocks are the iron and coal formations of eastern Antarctica and the Transantarctic Mountains. Although extensive, neither rock type is as pure as identified large iron and coal deposits elsewhere. The "platinum deposits" of the Dufek layered basic intrusion are hypothetical. No platinum-bearing minerals or whole-rock platinum anomalies have yet been reported.

The geological composition of Antarctica

Like other parts of the world, the geological terrains of Antarctica may host a wide variety of geochemically anomalous rocks. However, the available geological maps are not sufficiently detailed to identify their location.

Antarctica and continental reconstructions

The comparison of different regions on geological reconstructions is a popular method of "resource suggestion". Antarctica was once part of a southern hemisphere supercontinent (Gondwana) and shares a common history with Australia, India, southern Africa and South America, all with known mineral resources. Such suggestions are simplistic and state the obvious—that the Antarctic crust is probably as mineralized as the other continents.

On-land and offshore hydrocarbon resources

Hydrocarbon reservoirs occur at depth in the crust. Their discovery therefore always requires expensive exploration. The major tool used, in exploration and assessment, is the seismic survey and requires surveys at 500 m line spacing. The most detailed seismic survey carried out offshore to date (none has been carried out on land) had a line spacing of 100 km. This is inadequate to define hydrocarbon traps.

No oil or gas seeps or potential hydrocarbon-bearing structures are known in the Antarctic. Only two hydrocarbon "shows" are reported from the continental shelf. Both were of biogenic or thermogenic gas at a shallow level in the sedimentary column.

In the absence of data, all published "resource assessments" for Antarctic hydrocarbons are even more hypothetical than for on-land resources. By analogy with other continental margins, the Ross and Weddell Seas might be more prospective than the shelf of east Antarctica. However, sediment starvation during 30 million years of more or less continuous glaciation is not propitious to Antarctic prospectivity.

Conclusion

The Antarctic continent has a small number of mineral occurrences and areas of geochemical anomaly. Although there is no reason to believe that the Antarctic crust is not mineralized or hydrocarbon-bearing to the same extent and variety as similar rocks elsewhere, these rocks remain hypothetical and, for the most part, buried beneath the ice sheet. The general lack of data means that it is not possible to assess the mineral resource potential of Antarctica in the usual way. Its geographic and political situation in the global economy suggests that it has a low potential for economic exploitation.

The living resources of the Southern Ocean

The living resources of the Antarctic region have been exploited since the discovery of fur seals on South Georgia by Captain Cook in 1775. Only the harvesting of whales has been on a scale whereby the Antarctic provided a sustained and significant contribution to world food supplies. The potential of krill and of some fin fish is also considerable but with management regimes agreed internationally it is unlikely that severe over-exploitation, as with fur seals and whales, will re-occur. In this section emphasis is placed on those species under current exploitation.

Seals

The first commercial enterprise in the Antarctic was the fur seal industry followed by the harvesting of elephant seals for oil. Stocks of fur seals were virtually eliminated on South Georgia by 1830, with a million pelts being accrued in 1820–1822 alone. There was a minor revival in 1870 in the South Sandwich and South Shetland Islands. The fur seal population has now recovered to a total of well over 1,000,000.

The elephant seal was taken throughout the later 19th century and the industry continued in a closely controlled manner on South Georgia until 1964 but was never a threat to the species. Other seal species, inhabitants of the high Antarctic seas have sometimes been taken commercially but only in small numbers. The 1972 Convention for the Conservation of Antarctic Seals prohibited the taking of certain seal species and set annual quotas and seasons for others. The activity as a commercial practice is moribund.

Whales

Whaling in the Southern Ocean commenced at the turn of the 20th century, concentrating principally upon the baleen whales, but later included the sperm. The International Whaling Commission (IWC) was established in 1946 to oversee the industry and implement the 1935 International Convention for the Regulation of Whaling. Several species were protected through IWC decisions and a moratorium declared by the UN in 1972 with only the small Minke whale being fished by Japan.

Fin Fish

Potential fin-fish fisheries have been recognized in Antarctic seas since the 19th century but significant commercial-scale exploitation by fleets of freezer-factory trawlers did not begin until the early 1960s. The present fishery is based on demersal populations of nototheniod fish (rock cod, toothfish and icefish) and concentrated over the continental shelves of the peri-Antarctic islands such as South Georgia, Kerguelen, the South Shetland and South Orkney Islands.

Of these, the islands of South Georgia and Kerguelen have been the focus for the Antarctic fisheries and total annual catches of approximately 1,500,000 tonnes and 900,000 tonnes respectively, have been reported. The majority of Antarctic fish grow and mature slowly and have a low relative fecundity, therefore, these fish stocks have a limited ability to resist persistent commercial exploitation. The result of over-exploitation is reflected in the changes in species composition in the catches, a steady reduction in the average size at capture and the decline of targeted species to non-commercial biomass levels. Eventually this has led to the present fishery being based on catches comprising a large proportion of juveniles and species that have been demonstrated to have relatively short life-cycles and faster growth rates such as the icefish, *Champsocephalus gunnari*.

The history of fishing activity and the result on fish populations differs somewhat at the main localities because the fishery at Île Kerguelen was closely monitored and managed from an early stage while that at South Georgia was not controlled until very recently.

The reduction of the fishery at South Georgia to a small proportion of its former size has led the industry to use a diversity of techniques as well as prospecting for alternative species as a means of maintaining a commercial catch at the island. These have included: pelagic trawling for myctophids, demersal fishing on the continental slope, long-line fishing, exploiting "small" species and exploratory squid fishing.

The management policies enforced at Kerguelen have meant that the species composition has remained more stable, spawning populations of adult fish have been protected and the stocks monitored to provide a more consistent fishery. At an early stage, an observer and sampling system was introduced that has resulted in a considerable amount of basic information being accumulated about the population dynamics, biology and migrations of the dominant species at the island.

Since 1981 fisheries in the Southern Ocean have been monitored and regulated by the Commission for the Conservation of Antarctic Living Resources (CCAMLR). Annual scientific evaluation of the reported catches has resulted in the introduction of conservation measures such as quotas, mesh size controls, closed seasons and exclusion from spawning and nursery grounds.

Squid

Major squid fisheries exist in the cool temperate waters of the Southern Ocean around the Falkland Islands and New Zealand and attention is already turning to the cold sub-Antarctic waters further south.

For squid, and other cephalopod species to be suitable for commercial exploitation their flesh must be attractive for the table, in terms of both flavour and texture, and the behaviour of the species must lend itself to harvesting with available fishing gear.

Of 16 species of cephalopod taken by nets and jigs in the Scotia Sea area, about half are suitable. Virtually nothing is known about the schooling behaviour of squid in the sub-Antarctic and Antarctic seas, or about their reactions to commercial fishing gear—trawls, fishing lights and jigs.

Elsewhere, the world's major squid fisheries target two families in particular, the Loliginidae and the Ommastrephidae, partly because of their schooling behaviour and catchability but also because of their creative abundance and good flavour. The loliginids do not penetrate south of the Antarctic Polar Front, but one species of ommastrephid—the red squid, *Martialia hyadesi*—is known to be abundant in the sub-Antarctic Southern Ocean.

It is an important prey item of several vertebrate predators in the Scotia Sea area, notably the grey-headed albatross. At South Georgia during the breeding season, adult grey-heads are estimated to feed some 15,000 tonnes of *Martialia* to their chicks. The species is also consumed by black-browed and wandering albatrosses, elephant seals and probably sperm whales.

Exploratory fishing trials by commercial squid jiggers have taken place in the Scotia Sea and in 1989 commercial quantities of *Martialia hyadesi* were caught at the Antarctic Polar Frontal Zone in the vicinity of South Georgia. This squid is an occasional by-catch of the Falkland Islands squid fishery and is sold, particularly in the far east, for processing into similar products as the Argentine shortfin squid, *Ilex argentinus*, which is the major ommastrephid catch on the Patagonian Shelf. As squid fishing companies seek to expand their operations it seems inevitable that *Martialia hyadesi* in the sub-Antarctic will come under pressure of commercial exploitation.

In view of the rapidity with which squid fisheries tend to develop, and considering the importance of *Martialia hyadesi* in the diet of the Antarctic vertebrate predators, it will be essential that any future fishery for this squid be managed successfully and with due regard to its role in the food chain.

Krill

Euphausid crustacea or krill are sometimes considered to possess the greatest potential for commercial harvesting in the Southern Ocean due to their very high biomass of 125–200 million tonnes and a high protein content. Interest in their harvesting began in the 1960s when trial fishing took place. There are 11 species in Antarctic waters. The most important are *Euphausia superba*, *E. crystallorophias*, *Thysanoessa macrura* and *E. vallentini*.

Krill occur in large concentrations or swarms in the upper 200–300 metres of water around the Antarctic continent in the zone of the divergence. The largest are in the Scotia and Weddell Seas and off Dronning Maud Land. Individual swarms may be up to several kilometres across. Acoustic location methods are used to detect swarms and these techniques are being improved.

Krill are the staple diet of baleen whales, which used to be their greatest single consumer, and many are important to birds and seals. The decline in the population of the former has resulted in increased uptake by these other predators and also the view that there is sufficient excess krill for large-scale harvesting for human consumption. The quantity of krill taken by whales has reduced from 190 to 43,000,000 tonnes annually. It also occupies a key position in the food web of the Southern Ocean so that over-exploitation could have serious implications for other species.

Conservation and environmental management

Conservation legislation

The Antarctic is more nearly pristine than any other sizeable area of the globe and contains unique environments and biological communities of outstanding scientific importance. Conservation is, therefore, as necessary in Antarctica as it is in more populous regions but must be undertaken in a distinctive international framework.

Although the original Antarctic Treaty contains no mention of environmental protection its importance was recognized quickly by the consultative parties. The "Agreed Measures for the Conservation of the Antarctic Fauna and Flora", accepted in 1964, form the basis for all Antarctic conservation on land and ice shelves. They specifically do not apply to the Southern Ocean marine ecosystem.

These agreed measures have four important articles. Article VI prohibits the killing, wounding or capture of any native mammal (except whales) unless authorised specifically by permit. It also allows the designation of Specially Protected Species which, at present, applies to all fur seals of the genus *Arctocephalus* and to the Ross Seal *Ommatophoca rossii*. Article VII requires that harmful interference with native mammals and birds must be minimized. Article VIII defines the category of "Specially Protected Area" (SPA) used to protect unique natural ecosystems or areas of outstanding scientific interest. Finally, Article IX forbids the introduction of non-indigenous species into the Treaty Area except by permit and then only from the groups listed in an annex. The permitted classes of introductions are sledge dogs, domestic animals and plants, laboratory animals and plants (including viruses, yeasts, fungi and bacteria). Any introductions have to be kept under strictly controlled conditions and removed from the Treaty Area or destroyed at the conclusion of the study. All reasonable precautions must be taken to prevent the introduction of disease, including the exclusion of live poultry.

These initial measures were added to at later Treaty meetings. Eight years later the range of categories which could be included as SPAs was extended and a new form of protected area defined—Sites of Special Scientific Interest (SSSI)—was defined to protect from wilful or accidental interference sites at which active scientific work was being undertaken. Such sites could only be designated for a limited period and had to have management plans, in distinct contrast to the original prescription for SPAs where no active management was allowed. In 1989 it was agreed that SPAs did require management plans even if these were simply limitations on access.

At present (1990) there are 16 SPAs and 32 SSSIs. In addition there are over 50 designated Historical Monuments which vary in importance from major relics of Antarctic exploration, to small plaques.

Legislation for the protection of sites continues to evolve, for example multi-use areas zoned for particular activities have been proposed.

Many non-governmental bodies are pressing for the designation of the Antarctic continent as a "World Park". The extent of protection envisaged in these proposals apparently varies from a complete ban on all commercial activities and limited accessibility for scientists to an acceptance of tourism and fishing but a ban on mineral exploitation. The concept at present lacks precise definitions on allowable activities, access, management and funding.

Environmental impact assessment

All human activities in Antarctica cause some impact on the environment.

Antarctic Treaty Recommendation XII-3 accepted the need for environmental impact assessment both for major logistic developments and for certain types of scientific investigations, e.g. offshore seismic survey. In 1987 at the 14th Antarctic Treaty Meeting, Recommendation XIV-2 set out in detail both the sequence of consultations and the contents of the environmental assessment documents required. The EIA must consider the nature and magnitude of the likely changes resulting from the proposed activity, how the effects of the action could be mitigated, and what alternative actions could produce the same end result. On the basis of this assessment a decision is made on whether or not the action should proceed in its original or modified form, why the expected impact is considered acceptable (if the action is to proceed) and what monitoring might be required. The first Comprehensive Environmental Assessment produced under these regulations was for a gravel airstrip at Rothera Point, Adelaide Island in 1989.

Waste disposal

Public attitudes towards the disposal of non-hazardous waste have changed only recently. Until the 1970s it was accepted generally that disposal by land burial, sea dumping or incineration was not only essential but posed little environmental problem. Growing public concern for the global environment has radically changed the view and highlighted problems in Antarctica.

In response to a request from the ATCM XIII, SCAR produced a report reviewing waste disposal for Antarctic ships and stations. Its recommendations were accepted by ATCM XX with virtually no qualifications. In essence these require mandatory removal of plastics, rubber, isotopes, waste hydrocarbons, toxic and harzardous chemicals to outside the Treaty area for specialized disposal, incineration of burnable material only in controlled emission incinerators, treatment of sewage and grey water before discharge, and the removal of as much non-hazardous waste as possible to outside the Treaty area. The wastes specified include both old rubbish dumps and derelict stations.

In general terms all operators are urged to conduct waste audits to reduce waste production, plan for and document waste disposal as part of essential logistic support, report annually on wastes disposed of and train staff in environmentally acceptable routines. Full implementation of the new regulations by all operators should ensure that Antarctica remains the cleanest place on Earth.

Tourism

The first commercial Antarctic tour expedition was in 1958 and although there have been large fluctuations between years in the number of tourists the trend is steadily upwards. At present most of the tour companies are legally registered in the United States and thus subject to the US Antarctic Conservation Act.

Ship-based tours account for most tourism. In 1988 the US tour companies alone carried over 2800 visitors. The expected replacement of two of the present vessels with larger ones by 1993 and an increase in the number of operators, the number of cruises and the length of the tour season (now around 95 days) can only increase substantially the pressure on the areas visited.

Three further sources of tourism must also be considered. The first, sight-seeing flights over the continent, has been suspended since the tragic crash of the Air New Zealand DC10 on Mt Erebus in 1983. Pressure will grow to restart this type of tourism.

The second is the major increase in private expeditions to Antarctica. Every year a larger number of small yachts appear in Antarctic waters. Of special significance here have been the commercial tours supported by aircraft to the Ellsworth Mountains and the South Pole. The Antarctic Treaty Parties agreed not to support materially private expeditions but national interests have ensured that this has not always been adhered to.

Finally there is the prospect of hotel development to provide on-shore facilities for package tours. At present the only "hotel" is run by Chilean authorities on King George Island but proposals have been made by an Australian company for a major development with an associated runway at a site in East Antarctica.

Responsible tourism in collaboration with Antarctic scientists has an important role to play in publicizing the unique character and importance of Antarctica. SCAR has provided a "Visitor's Guide to Antarctica" and the best of the tour companies not only brief their passengers on behaviour but police their activities. More active management of visitors will be necessary which may include the designation of tourist sites, the provision of tourist officers and more rigorous limitations on annual numbers.

Conclusion

It is clear that the Antarctic will maintain a high profile in international affairs and provide major political and scientific challenges during the next decade. The scientific relevance of the region to issues of global importance places a premium on the continuation of high-quality research, co-ordinated internationally. Considerable interest will focus upon resources of the Antarctic, in particular the marine stocks of krill, fish and squid. Management regimes such as CCAMLR will need continued development and more particularly compliance. The hard mineral and hydrocarbon potential of Antarctica is virtually unknown. Regardless of their identification, political decisions driven by environmental considerations may preclude future exploration and exploitation. Negotiation of comprehensive measures for the protection of the Antarctic environment as a possible substitute for CRAMRA is likely to change ineluctably the course of the Antarctic Treaty System.

For bibliography, see pp. 357–358.

3 DEFORESTATION

Andrew Mitchell

Introduction

In a rainforest shortly after dawn the air is filled with an atmosphere as rich as plum cake. It is similar to walking through a huge botanical hothouse filled with mist whilst surrounded by the scent of sweet orchids. In the twilight zone beneath the canopy, beams of light lend shadows to vines and trunks and great walls of leaves giving a sense of creeping through an enormous theatre, behind the scenes. Creeping across the shrubby surfaces, passion flower vines display their exquisite flowers of yellow, purple and violet spikes. Trunks rise up in many forms, some, in areas prone to flooding, stand as if on tiptoe on skeletal roots, others where it is drier are braced with giant buttresses, and still more with huge columns rising, smoothly, directly out of the ground. Small shrubs and bushes crowd the lower layers of the forest. Through them young trees struggle, in their adolescence, upwards through the relative gloom, seeking a place to jostle through a gap in the canopy above. Some 30–40 metres above ground, is the canopy layer of almost interlocking crowns creating a latticework of branches and leaves as complex as any church window. The leaves of each crown do not touch, they merely whisper to each other across a gap, as though preferring to keep each other at arms length. Some species, taller than the rest, break through and spread their giant crowns above the forest soaking up the sun, occasionally carrying great islands of yellow, violet and magenta blooms. These mightiest of trees are known as emergents. This architecture of the forest has kept it largely unexplored and unexploited until this century, for no vehicle has yet been devised which can adequately drive either through it or over it.

Impressions of jungles as inhospitable places filled with fierce tribes and dangerous beasts is largely a legacy of Victorian times when explorers, crazed with malaria, strove to over-glamorize their adventures. Some of their pictures are true. The forest is populated with biting insects, poisonous snakes and spiders, jaguars with lethal jaws, but most are rarely seen and wound from fear not malice. The notion of the forest as an environment to be conquered and controlled is a product of people who do not live in it and who do not recognize the role that these forests play in the world's ecosystem both at a local and global level, and who do not recognize the value of the products such forests can produce whilst they remain *in situ*.

Picking a way along a small path or animal track between giant buttress roots as high as a ten-storey building, each topped with crowns the size of football pitches, is a humbling experience. Some trunks are clear of branches and vegetation for 30 metres, others are thickly clustered with vines, ferns, bromeliads, mosses and lichens. The view of the canopy is obscured by sub-canopy trees, reaching towards the light, criss-crossing the sky with black spaghetti patterns of vines and the fanned beauty of palms. Animals introduce themselves as flashes of light on irridescent butterfly wings or bright reds and yellows on the exquisite plumage as some unidentifiable bird rushes by. A haze of small insects may dance in a light beam or two male butterflies tumble upwards in the shaft of light seeking possession of an airborne territory. Pandemonium occasionally erupts as some unseen creature, perhaps a small deer or a sleeping group of peccaries, is disturbed and makes off through the undergrowth. Then the forest lapses into the varied background hum of insects punctuated with a parrot's unexpected sqwawk or a fleeting cloud of twitters as a hunting party of insect-gleaning birds passes through the canopy overhead.

The nature and location of forests

The term rainforest is to some extent a misnomer. In many so-called rainforests it does not rain for months at a time. These are known as "deciduous" forests and they loose their leaves in the dry season. Some forests appear like jungles but are quite dry. These open dry woodlands may receive less than 100 cm. of rain per year. True "evergreen" rainforests flourish best in lowland tropical areas 10 degrees north and south of the equator, where rainfall is more than 400 cm. annually, the air feels humid and blood-warm. The term "tropical moist forest" covers true rainforest and additionally areas which are still largely evergreen but receive less rain and even experience a limited dry season. Rainforests also occur in temperate regions where precipitation encourages the growth of lush vegetation which outwardly may appear similar to that of tropical forest.

Soils too alter the character of the forest. Where soils are tainted with minerals or are naturally acid, only specialist trees may grow giving the forest a silent quality that is starved of both of plant and animal variety. Despite the apparent richness of the forest, the soil upon which it grows is infertile. Most nutrients are stored in the standing vegetation and not in the soil as in temperate zones. Heavy tropical rains would wash out these nutrients from decaying material which falls to the forest floor were it not for a remarkable association between tree roots and fungal threads which permeate the forest leaf litter. The fungi transfer nutrients rapidly from the thin mulch of leaves on the forest floor to tree roots, gaining sugars in return. The forest survives on relatively little energy input from the sun and efficiently recycles everything it can, so that little is lost as waste to rivers and the soil.

Moving from lowlands to high mountains the forest changes again. An elfin forest of short gnarled trees draped in moss exists in the cool of high mountains. The birds, insects and mammals that live here are quite different from those inhabiting the lofty trees which fill the lowlands of the Amazon basin.

There are still other kinds of rainforest. Those that grow in the mighty *Vareza* of Brazil where each year the Amazon floodwaters spread through mile upon mile of the forest enabling fish to glide between buttressed roots where land animals usually roam. The fish gulp seeds falling from the branches above, so much so that the trees have evolved to rely on them to distribute their offspring.

Forest inhabitants

The world's rainforests are home to the greatest diversity of life in the world. In just one hectare 300 different species of tree may grow. The Malay peninsular, less than half the size of Britain, supports at least 7,900 different species of flowering plants and 2,500 native trees. In the whole of Britain their are 35 native tree species. One rainforest tree may contain more than fifty species of ant alone and 10,000 other species of insects, spiders and mites. The rainforest canopy may contain half of all life on earth. In the last few years the extent of our ignorance has grown as scientists have begun to probe this last biological frontier. So numerous are the discoveries in the last decade that the original estimates of the number of insect species in the world has had to be revised upwards from 1,000,000 to 30,000,000.

Forest loss

These new discoveries make it all the more short-sighted that the rate of destruction of tropical forests has been quickening over the last 10 years despite considerable public outcry in both the developed and developing world where these forests grow. This destruction is not confined to tropical forest alone but also extends to tropical dry forests, as well as temperate woodlands. The Smithsonian Institute estimates about 11,100,000 hectares of tropical forest and woodlands are destroyed each year. In 1987 Brazil lost some 8,000,000 hectares in the burning season which suggests that the 11,100,000 hectare estimate may be as much as 50% too low. Agriculture accounts for some 7,300,000 hectares of tropical closed forest destruction according to FAO and UNEP estimates in 1981. It is likely to be much higher now. In addition to this, 4,400,000 hectares of forest are removed annually by selective logging. A further 3,800,000 hectares of open woodland in the drier tropics are felled each year for fuel wood and agriculture. In little more than a generation, half the world's tropical forests have been destroyed forever.

In the last 30 years Africa has lost 23% of its tropical moist forest. The Ivory Coast has cut some 66% of its forest and woodlands over a similar period and Madagascar has lost 93% of its forest cover. Virtually all Brazil's Atlantic coast moist forest has been destroyed and almost 98% of the tropical dry forest which once covered Central America and Mexico has also been felled.

In recent years, estimates of tropical rainforest destruction have varied widely. Quoted deforestation rates vary depending upon who provided the statistics and which kinds of forest are included. It is often popularly quoted that tropical forests are disappearing at the rate of a hectare every few seconds. Central Park in New York would take about 16 minutes. An area the size of Britain is destroyed in the Brazilian forest burning season each year. In a generation an area the size of India will be wiped out. Unless a new, sustainable way of using these forests can be devised, the world's most accessible forests will be destroyed in less than 20 years. Part of the reason for this is the unreliability of data or the complete lack of it. Many estimates produced are largely dependent upon government departments and local officials, which are notoriously unstandardized, rather than objective recordings of forest cover by satellites, side-looking airborne radar (SLAR), or aerial photography.

Measuring the loss

In the 1960s using satellite technology to monitor the world's forests seemed a revolutionary, if expensive, solution to assessing deforestation. Land resources satellites such as the French SPOT satellite and the US LANDSAT series are able to observe huge areas in a matter of seconds gathering a great volume of information about the landscape below, through multi-spectral scanners, which is then transmitted to ground stations for processing. LANDSAT is able to scan the equivalent area of 5000 aerial photographs taken at a scale of 1:20,000 every 25 seconds. Additionally, such a system can fly over the same area every 2–4 weeks, ideal for monitoring, and the images are cheaper to process per unit area than aerial photographs. Less than 60% of the total area of tropical moist forest has been surveyed since 1970 using any form of remote sensing. Too often thick cloud cover "blinds" the sensors. This can be avoided by using SLAR which can "see" through cloud. The complementary hardware and software for satellite systems has proved too expensive for many countries and, perhaps most importantly, there has been little funding for the crucial field work necessary to "ground truth" the images obtained in space. Satellite images cannot identify individual species of trees or associations of vegetation from space. These must be interpreted with the image on the ground in sample areas and the changes in light spectra seen from space that are represented on the image are then attributed to mangroves, logged areas or pristine lowland forest. This is then scaled up to the huge area the satellite scans.

To do this is time-consuming and labour intensive and in many cases it has not been done. The task is daunting. Vast amounts of data are obtained through satellite-based systems. The new US Earth Observation Satellite EROS, planned for launch in the late 1990s, will produce enough information daily to fill the equivalent of 7 miles of computer floppy discs laid end to end. Entirely new systems of computing and modelling this volume of data are being planned but the data will be useless if equivalent funding is not also made available to send teams of field scientists into the field to interpret representative samples of the images on the ground. To date this kind of input has been sadly lacking.

Brazil has successfully used remote sensing to monitor its forest loss since the early 1970s. At a cost of some $5,000,000 it carried out a comprehensive SLAR survey of Amazonia and, through the National Remote Sensing Programme begun in 1979, it has been able to chart the deforestation of Amazonia relatively accurately. In the state of Rondonia remote sensing proved that the area of destroyed forest trippled from 1,000,000 hectares to 2,700,000 between 1982 and 1985 and clearly linked the deforestation to the introduction of roads in the region. It was this evidence in particular which persuaded the World Bank to alter their funding strategy in the region which, until then, had been indirectly increasing deforestation rates through road development schemes.

Today's forests

Tropical forests are believed to have once covered 1.6 billion hectares of the Earth's surface, an area twice the size of the United States. Since exploitation for farming, cattle ranching, logging, and fuel wood dramatically increased in the last few decades over half has been destroyed. Today forests with a largely closed canopy cover about 21% of the earth's surface. Of those, 43% grow in the tropics. Developed nations contain about 90% of all coniferous forests and developing nations contain 75% of all broad leaved forest. Almost a third of the world's remaining rainforest exists in the Brazilian Amazon alone. West Africa now contains just under a quarter of the world's rainforest. Half of Africa's remaining rainforest is in Zaïre. Asia contains about a quarter of the world's remaining rainforest. Australia is the only Western nation to possess its own tropical rainforest, on the Cape York peninsular. The myriad Pacific Islands harbour some of the world's most endangered tropical forests containing many unique species which have evolved isolated from land. Plantations in the tropics for fuel wood production, watershed protection, and the production of commercial timber or charcoal cover a further 11,500,000 hectares. Today undamaged rainforests cover less than 900 million hectares, 8% of the world's surface, and the area is shrinking rapidly.

Amazonia still contains the world's greatest resources of tropical forest at 357,000,000 hectares. This compares with 792,000,000 hectares of temperate woodlands in the USSR and 459,000,000 hectares in Canada and the USA. The European Community can boast but 43,000,000 hectares having cleared the majority of its once extensive woodlands centuries ago.

Amazonia's extensive forests can give no cause for complacency. Despite all the efforts of conservation groups worldwide and pressure from Western governments, the pace of destruction is quickening. Each year the burning season grows more acute. In the frontier towns the air can grow so thick with smoke, car headlamps must be used in the day and handkerchiefs cover mouths in an atmosphere of perpetual twilight. The forest crackles to the sound of exploding trunks and roasted creatures, and as the stench of death fills the air, eagles, owls and parrots flee across a blackened sky. As pioneer farmers wield chainsaws the timber bleeds the wealth of centuries into the thin soil, and soon it is washed away into already muddy rivers, to clog dams and coastal fishing communities hundreds of kilometres away. With such increasing public outcry, why is this happening?

Reasons for loss

The reasons for rainforest destruction seem almost as varied as the forest itself, Simply put, the most desperate and damaging intrusions are caused by pioneer farmers from outside the forest, who have no land on which to grow crops to feed their children, moving into the forest to create shortlived farms and a mirage of prosperity. At its most complex it is due to the inability of developing nations to meet the crippling interest payments on vast amounts of debt owed to Western banks.

Agricultural destruction

Approximately 8,000,000 hectares of tropical forest are cleared for agriculture each year. Much of this is for shifting cultivation. This is an ancient and potentially productive method of sustainable use of the forest developed over centuries by indigenous Indian peoples. A small area is felled for family or village use and is burned. The ash provides fertility for a few years for a variety of crops and then a new area is chosen, leaving the previously cleared area to regrow for some 20 to 30 years. This form of management requires few people and large areas of forest. Today, increasing population has made this impossible. Old fields are cultivated too often for natural fertility to return. In addition large numbers of pioneer farmers from urban regions outside the forest, who are inexperienced in sustainable slash-and-burn agricultural techniques, have moved into extensive areas of primary forest.

Cash crops grown mainly for export are also responsible for considerable forest loss. In Central America bananas and coffee dominate whilst in Asia it is rubber, oil palm and cacao. In deforested areas of Peru, Bolivia, Colombia, Ecuador and Brazil the growing of cacao to supply the lucrative drug market with cocaine has become an important industry. Cacao thrives on brightly lit eroded hillsides which often remain after forest clearance.

Unequal land distribution

Part of the reason for the influx of poor people into the forested regions of Indonesia and Brazil in particular is due to rising population and unequal land distribution. In Brazil 70% of the population have no land to call their own. In Indonesia over-population on Java has stimulated a Government-inspired redistribution of families to other less crowded islands. Many Governments regard the landless poor, crowded in city fringe slums, as a political embarrassment. The forest is often perceived as a obstacle to development and, in some cases, as a national security risk whilst potentially hostile borders remains unpoliced. Indigenous Indian peoples are not regarded as a good advertisement for a developing nation wishing to present a progressive image to the world. Many governments believe "civilizing" them will offer Indian peoples valuable education and better access to health care. Bringing them into the mainstream of society is a long-term goal. One way to achieve all of these aims has been, through government advertising and incentive schemes, to attract pioneers to the new "Wild West" promising new hope to the landless poor. International lending agencies have been eager to provide the financing for these major resettlement programmes but often without adequate foresight of either the environmental consequences or safeguards for the rights of the indigenous peoples who already live in the lands to be occupied.

The result has been roads which march through Indian lands bringing a tide of destruction by pioneer farmers. The land promised to these pioneers for generations is often overworked or infertile once it is cleared and they have no choice but to move on and cut deeper into the forest. Countries with the highest population growth rates often have the highest deforestation rates. It should also not be forgotten that the majority of these families, and indeed 80% of the people in the developing world, depend upon fuel wood for their primary energy source. The influx of people into the forest inevitably increases the pressure on these forests to provide firewood for cooking.

Cattle ranching

After the failure of agriculture, cattle ranching is a common follow-on activity in Latin America. Land can be bought cheaply, the remaining timber cleared, and cattle reared to supply cheap beef for export. Almost three quarters of Brazil's cleared forest is used for cattle ranching, an area of 2 million hectares is cleared each year for this purpose. Considerable tax incentives helped to encourage the 75% loss of primary forest in Central America between 1950 and 1980. Most of the beef went to America for the fast food industry and for pet foods. Most Latin American beef is now consumed in Latin America and Europe. Cattle ranching is rarely sustainable on cleared forest land. Within 10 years the soil is filled with weeds and degraded by hooves and the cattle ranchers must move on, leaving a barren and wasted desert.

Logging for timber

After petroleum and natural gas, wood ranks as the third most valuable primary commodity traded in the world. In 1985 global trade in wood products was worth approximately $50 billion. In the developed world 20% of timber extraction is for fuel wood and 80% is for industrial use. In the developing world these figures are reversed. Demand from Western Europe and Japan far exceeds the supplies from their own forests hence they import vast amounts of wood products. Developed nations also have the greatest demand for paper pulp. World demand for timber grew by over 50% between 1960 and 1985. There is a growing concern that the world demand for softwood timber may eventually exceed the sustainable supply and this would lead to a sharp rise in timber prices. These predictions are notoriously difficult to make as the balance between natural sources of supply and plantation sources requires complex modelling. In addition, factors such as global warming may increase growth rates to the benefit of countries in higher latitudes where coniferous forests abound, whilst acid rain from industrialized nations may curtail growth in other areas.

After agriculture, logging is the second largest source of rainforest destruction. Tropical forests account for about 30% of all log exports and about 60% of all plywood and veneer exports. Even if the desire to maintain these forests for their remarkable biological diversity falls on deaf ears, Alan Grainger's work, modelling future trends in hardwood exports, makes it clear that current trends will lead to a complete collapse of the world hardwood timber trade by 2020 as these great forests decline. This model also predicts a dramatic shift from Asia being the dominant source of supply, to Latin America. A disappointing aspect of the model is the predicted contribution from plantations. Plantation forestry is often considered as a major long term alternative to supplying world hardwood timber demand. Grainger's model predicts that by the year 2000 less than 2% of hardwood timber exports will be harvested from plantations. Part of the problem is the great length of time that it takes for slow growing hardwoods to reach marketable sizes. Even if extensive plantations were being planted now, which generally speaking they are not, it would be 2020, long after the natural forests will have been destroyed, before plantations could be making significant contributions to world timber markets. If the wholesale destruction of tropical forests through logging is to be lessened there must be far greater emphasis placed on managing existing natural stands of tropical moist forest on a sustainable basis, something which has yet to be proved possible in all but a tiny proportion of cases. Secondly, faster growing varieties of hardwood timber must be cultivated, perhaps through genetically engineered species, and finally, the way in which tropical hardwoods are used in the market place must be changed. Hardwoods are used extensively in the construction industry, in furniture making, even for chopsticks in Japan. Around 40% of world exported tropical hardwoods enter Japan alone. Europe is the second largest consumer, $2 billion worth of tropical timber products enter the USA each year. Indonesia, Malaysia and the Philippines have been the prime suppliers of tropical timber since the 1960s. The majority was exported as raw logs but today more wood is processed into sawn timber and furniture products prior to export, which greatly increases the financial return to the country of origin. Much of the use of tropical timber after it is harvested is extremely wasteful. Selective extraction processes damage much of the forest resulting in ten or more trees felled for every one of value removed. Logging trails cause extensive erosion if put into hillsides that are too steep.

Long-term studies of the effects of selective logging on the regeneration of natural forests have yet to be carried out. Some studies show that there is initially a severe decline in the diversity of wildlife a selectively logged forest contains, but after a number of years, many of the animals seem to return to former or in some cases even greater levels of abundance.

It is likely that the specialist animals reliant upon one or two species of fruit or nut which may vanish from a forest will be the worst affected. It is often these very specialists which are already the most endangered animals in the rainforest.

Mining

Vast quantities of iron ore lie beneath South America's forests. No developing country there can afford to leave them there or to mine them, without financing it through the destruction of their forests. Brazil alone plans to burn 700,000 tonnes of charcoal a year to feed its pig iron smelters deep in the forest. The need for energy to fuel these industries and the towns which support them requires electric power on a massive scale. Around 125 hydroelectric dams are planned in Brazil by the year 2010 which could flood 60,000 hectares of forest and displace the Indians living there. Fortunately the World Bank, which was to approve loans for the dams and other projects, has withheld its support until environmental safeguards are improved, so there are messages of hope.

International debt

Rainforests are inextricably connected to the Third World debt crisis. Through the 1970s and 1980s many countries borrowed extensively to alleviate the burden of raised oil prices, a policy which has left them no option but to exploit their natural resources to keep up with interest payments. The economic success of Brazil is tempered by the fact that it must pay some 40% of its export earnings as interest on foreign loans. So called debt-for-nature swaps, where Western banks write off debt in return for a host country undertaking to protect an area of its rainforest have proved imaginative but complicated. The bank is provided with hard currency by a third party, in some cases a conservation agency. This relieves them of exposure on a debt that is unlikely ever to be repaid. The host country is relieved of a much higher proportion of debt in return for an undertaking to support sustainable development of an area of rainforest to be managed in a partnership with the conservation agency. The complicated nature of arranging these deals has meant that few have actually taken place.

Consequences of destruction

Clearly the loss of species diversity in rainforests in an evolutionary sense is catastrophic. Nothing on this scale has happened since the extinction of the dinosaurs and that took place over many millions of years. Our destruction of the rainforests will have taken less than a century. Many of the effects of this loss are evident far beyond the forests themselves. The steady decline in many migratory song birds in North America and possibly Europe over the last 40 years has been attributed to the loss of their forested wintering grounds in the tropics. A census in Rock Creek Park, Washington D.C. showed that warblers, vireos, thrushes and flycatchers declined from 85% of the total breeding population in 1948 to just 35% in 1985. Many of these rely on the food supplies of the Latin American tropical forests. The case for protection of forests on the basis of diversity alone tends not to convince governments yet it is intriguing that the amount of information contained in one gene of one gnat is greater than all the editions of the Encyclopaedia Brittanica—and few governments would condone the burning of their national libraries. The beauty and ingenuity of tropical orchids or the magnificence of birds of paradise, or a morpho butterfly's wing are nature's art at its finest and once lost, are irreplaceable. Were it suggested that the contents of the Louvre should be burned in the way that rainforests are, the outrage from people, even those who may never have the chance to visit it, would be unimaginable.

It is not only animals and plants that will be lost from the forest but indigenous peoples too. Their lives are rapidly being absorbed into the modern world they are increasingly coming into contact with and this is inevitable. What is sadder is the loss of the knowledge their centuries of forest living has given them. Much of this detail, in particular of the uses, medical and otherwise, of forest plants will vanish in a generation. In Brazil, the 16th century Indian population of about 6,000,000 has dropped to less than 200,000 today.

The loss of forest cover in many countries is resulting in massive soil loss. Sun-baked soil cannot absorb rain effectively, and water swells rivers, washing soil into billion dollar hydro-power projects which silt up within less than a decade, clogging mangroves and coral reefs, thus destroying fisheries, and at worst creating massive floods and attendant loss of life. In the last three decades an estimated 160 million hectares of upland watershed has been grossly degraded in the tropics. It is no surprise that, of the 13 billion tonnes of sediment washed into the ocean by rivers each year, over 50% is from rivers in tropical South America and South East Asia.

Most people are left with a feeling of frustration at these events, but feel either powerless to effect change or, worse, uninvolved. The rainforest touches few Western lives other than through newsprint and television documentaries seen by relatively small and often already committed audiences. Few are aware of the rainforest's contribution to homes, yet each day millions of people use products unknowingly bequeathed to us from them. Coffee, cocoa, rubber, exotic fruits, fine mahogany furniture, hardwood window frames and security doors, cane chairs, even mahogany lavatory seats. In hospitals every day drugs derived from rainforests save lives. *Curare*, a muscle relaxant used by Amerindians to tip their poisoned darts causes wounded monkeys to expire and let go their lofty perch. A derivative enables an anaethetist to control our breathing during surgery. The rosy periwinkle, discovered in Madagascar's forests, is oft quoted for its success in treating Hodgkins disease resulting in 80% remission. The Mexican yam, a rainforest shrub, produced the contraceptive pill. Few can deny the value of these drugs both in billion dollar and critical medical terms, yet barely 1% of rainforest plants have been tested for their value to mankind. A cure for Aids may lie in the next acre of forest to be destroyed.

Tropical forests also bequeath gifts to planet Earth on a global scale. They act as a sponge, absorbing the 100–300 cms of rain that falls on them annually, and delivering clean water to streams and rivers upon which millions of people depend. Most of the water is returned to the atmosphere through leaf surfaces to create billowing white clouds sailing across a green ocean of leaves. This moisture may fall on lands far beyond the forest which otherwise might have no rain. Conversely the burning of tropical forests pollutes the atmosphere with vast amounts of carbon dioxide and so contributes to the greenhouse effect and possible global warming which could grossly alter the earth's climate on a regional and even planetary scale in a generation.

Rainforests have often been described as the lungs of the earth. With plankton, they are our greatest producers of oxygen. Through the process of photosynthesis, each leaf in a rainforest acts like a miniature solar panel, converting the energy of the sun to sugars and in so doing absorbs carbon dioxide from the atmosphere. These forests scrub the air clean of one of the most significant greenhouse gases. However, it will remain unreasonable to dictate terms on their use to countries which own them until Western consumer nations put their own house in order. American automobiles eject as much CO_2 into the atmosphere as the burning of all the Brazilian forests. The changes North America, Japan and Europe have to make are as challenging as those facing Amazonia. In 1985 the Tropical Forestry Action Plan (TFAP) was put forward by the FAO, development agencies and the World Resources Institute as well as other NGO agencies. This plan has yet to see the international funding it needs to adequately carry out its proposals, though it has received wide attention. The International Tropical Timber Organization (ITTO), a cartel of major timber trading bodies with headquarters in Japan, held its first meeting in 1987 and is dedicated to the sustainable use of tropical forests. It is too early yet to say how effective this organization will be but there is no let up in the rate of destruction. History shows that cartels of producers are unlikely to vote in measures that adversely affect the short-term profitability of their industry. Recently plans put forward by Friends of the Earth to create a labelling system to identify wood produced from sustainably managed forests was stalled by the ITTO who claimed it was unworkable. Fortunately, new research is underway to find a way of implementing the scheme.

Altering the market for timber products may be the only way in which a substantial reduction in timber extraction will come about in the short term. Regrettably, science is unlikely to come up with reliable proposals for sustainable cultivation of tropical forests in the short term. Nonetheless, it is vital that the work of science is greatly increased to produce the best evidence possible on which to base current and future decisions and to document the diversity of these forests before it is lost to the world. The influence of plantation forests or genetically engineered fast growth hardwoods is unlikely to be felt in time to provide significant alternative sources of supply. Only a change in the market for ply, pulp wood, and sawn timber will bring about changes in policy fast enough to save the world's tropical forests from complete alteration within two decades and even this will have little effect on the influx of pioneer farmers. Consumers in Japan and Europe are the principal market for much of the loggers' wood, and so the public can influence its use by their buying patterns. Consumers who reject the use of unsustainably grown mahogany, teak, or parana pine in their homes and offices or plywood containing tropical hardwoods, send powerful messages to suppliers which in turn rapidly influence Governments where the forests are grown. The advent of "Green Consumerism" and the growing desire of industry to see sustainable use of resources simply as good business, has not come a moment too soon.

For bibliography, see p. 358.

4 THE GREENHOUSE EFFECT AND GLOBAL WARMING

Peter Brackley

Introduction

The temperature of the earth's atmosphere and surface is influenced by many factors, particularly by the amount of solar energy received and reflected. This is affected by the composition of the atmosphere, the amount of dust and cloud cover and by the amount of snow and ice which reflect more light than soils or vegetation.

Temperatures have varied widely over geological time, encompassing ice ages and periods of widespread tropical conditions. Even over shorter periods significant variations have occurred. For example, over the last few hundred years the temperature during one period, 1400–1800, fell in England by about one degree Fahrenheit (0.6° Celsius), sufficient to change the severity of winter weather to produce Western Europe's "Little Ice Age". The mean global temperature over the last 100 years has increased by about 0.5°C.

Incoming radiation is mainly in the visible and ultra-violet spectrum and this heats the earth's surface which then emits longer wave, infra-red radiation. Air consists of oxygen and nitrogen but also contains a number of other gases in small amounts. All are transparent to visible light but some absorb radiation of other wavelengths, such as those in the infra-red and ultra-violet bands and, therefore, prevent or reduce their passage through the atmosphere, either restricting the path to earth or retaining energy within the earth and its atmosphere. This is somewhat analogous to the behaviour of glass which allows the passage of visible and ultra-violet light but is opaque at some infra-red wavelengths and therefore retains heat in a greenhouse. Hence the popular term "greenhouse effect", indicating the effect of certain gases on the conditions on earth, and the description of "greenhouse gases" to cover those that produce this effect. Any changes that may be brought about are an enhanced greenhouse effect since the earth is probably some 30–40°C warmer than it would be without its present atmosphere and its warming effect. The *Economist* described the atmosphere as a duvet to which more stuffing was being added. The greenhouse effect is not controversial, it is real and keeps the earth warm and habitable.

Over the last one hundred years or so the concentrations of some of the trace gases, notably carbon dioxide, have been rising, mainly due to human activity. They are predicted to continue to increase with rising world population and energy consumption.

There is no irrefutable evidence that the increases so far have had any impact upon the climate or, conversely, whether observed temperature and weather changes and whether recent climatic disasters are abnormal or natural fluctuations. Statistics are very difficult to collect and compare and it is known that other events, such as astronomic and solar cycles and dust emissions from volcano eruptions have an effect on weather. Present scientific opinion suggests a consensus that, if the increases in concentrations of some, if not all, the greenhouse gases do come about, and there is little doubt that this must be so in the immediate future, there will be a rise in average temperature—Global Warming—in the next few decades. This could have dramatic and severe effects upon the world's climate and, in turn, upon agriculture and living conditions and could lead to flooding in many low-lying areas and mass migration.

The scientific uncertainties of the extent of the increases in the concentrations of greenhouse gases and of the changes in temperature and climate that these might bring about lead to major difficulties in developing policies, in taking political decisions and in resisting pressure to mitigate possible, but unsubstantiated impacts. There are many calls for international agreement to limit the emissions of greenhouse gases and extensive research, in many parts of the world, is directed at resolving some of these tantalizing problems.

Some of the details of the gases involved, the consequences of their rising levels and what can be done to limit their increase and the results if the present predictions are borne out, will now be considered.

The gases involved

The main gases contributing to the greenhouse effect are carbon dioxide (CO_2), methane, nitrogen oxides (NO_x), chlorofluorocarbons (CFCs), ozone and water vapour, although UNEP states that there are, overall, some 40 gases contributing to the effect.

Carbon dioxide is produced by the use—oxidation—of organic fuels including foodstuffs, from the decomposition of organic matter and from industrial processes such as cement manufacture. The atmosphere, prior to the industrial revolution, contained about 280 parts per million (ppm) CO_2 (or 0.028%), more or less in equilibrium, for the production from the consumption of food and wood (for fuel) and from decaying vegetation was balanced by uptake in the creation of more biomass by photosynthesis. Once fossil fuels, which represent locked-up stores of carbon derived from CO_2 present millions of years ago, started to be used in significant quantities and forests were cleared, particularly in the Americas, the concentration of CO_2 started climbing and has increased steadily to the present day when it now stands at about 350 ppm. This is not simply a quantitative addition to the air since there are losses of CO_2 in addition to that recycled in growing trees, crops and vegetation. The main sink is dissolution in the seas, but the estimates of the potential capacity for absorption are variable (and today there is 50 times as much CO_2 dissolved in the oceans as exists in the atmosphere). There are many uncertainties in the quantitative understanding of the carbon cycle which, itself, could be affected by changing temperatures. The total worldwide emissions of CO_2 from anthropogenic sources in 1988 were estimated at some 20 billion tonnes whilst the net release from the biosphere was between one eighth and one half of this.

The production from fossil fuels varies with the type and quality of the fuel, but each tonne of coal burnt will release, depending on quality, some 2.5–3.6 tonnes CO_2. Each tonne of crude oil consumed (mainly as products such as motor spirit, diesel fuel etc.) produces about three tonnes and each tonne of natural gas gives 2.7 tonnes CO_2. But these fuels have very different heating potential for unit weight and it is usual to compare emissions based upon the release of heat. On this basis if coal releases one unit of CO_2 for a given heat load then oil would emit three-quarters of one unit and gas only one-half unit. The substitution of gas for coal or oil, in any heating process, will, therefore, reduce CO_2 emissions.

Methane occurs naturally and is known, for example, as marsh gas or firedamp; it is also produced by ruminants, from rice paddy fields and from rubbish tips by anaerobic decomposition of vegetable matter. It is the main component of natural gas and also occurs with other light hydrocarbon gases in association in crude oil reservoirs. It is widely used as a fuel and as a starting point for chemical syntheses. It is transported mainly by pipeline and, after liquefaction (LNG), by ship. The atmospheric concentration is about 2 ppm and is increasing by around 1% per annum. If it continues at its present rate then in 40 years' time its contribution to the greenhouse effect could be as large as that of CO_2 since it is a more effective IR absorbant, although the future contributions of all gases is still very speculative. It is considered that a significant contribution to methane build-up comes from leaks during transport, particularly from inadequate or old pipelines, although other increasing human activities (rubbish, cultivation etc) and an increasing animal population also add to the global rise.

Nitrogen oxides (usually denoted by NO_x since there are several different compounds of nitrogen and oxygen with different molecular formulae and different properties) occur naturally from nitrification and decomposition. They are also produced by nitrogenous fertilizers and during the burning of fossil fuels, mainly by the high temperature oxidation in the flame of atmospheric nitrogen, for example in a motor car engine or furnace. Also, to a much lower extent, from nitrogenous compounds present in the fuel, primarily coal since gas contains none and there are only traces in most crude oils. Nitrogen oxides have an undesirable pollution effect—they contribute to acid rain and smog and take part in the low-level formation of ozone—and also act as a greenhouse gas. Worldwide there is considerably more NO_x from natural sources (estimates vary from 60/40 to 90/10 natural to man-made) but in industrial countries those made by man predominate and emission control limits are in force in many countries.

Chlorofluorocarbons are a group of man-made compounds of carbon and the halogens in wide use in industry. They are very stable, non-flammable and non-toxic and used in refrigeration, plastic foams (in furniture, insulated food cartons etc.), solvents and aerosol propellants. They have been identified as causing destruction of the Earth's protective ozone layer (see Part I, Section 9) and the production and use of some of the family of chemicals is being restricted (see the Montreal Protocol in Part III), with growing pressure for a complete ban. However these compounds also act as greenhouse gases, that is they absorb infra-red radiation, and some of the proposed substitutes for those which damage the ozone layer are still suspect and undesirable because of this.

Ozone plays several roles in the complex chemistry and physics of the atmosphere. It acts as a shield—the ozone layer in the stratosphere—to prevent high levels of ultra-violet radiation reaching the Earth (see Part I, Section 9). It is formed at low level by the interaction of hydrocarbons and nitrogen oxides, particularly from car exhausts, creating pollution and causing damage to vegetation and buildings. Furthermore, by its absorption characteristics, it also contributes to the greenhouse effect.

Finally, heat is retained in the atmosphere and not allowed to escape into space by *water vapour*. The concentration, however, depends upon natural cycles outside human control, although if as a result of man's activities temperatures were to rise then more water would be expected to evaporate. But this, in turn, might lead to greater cloud cover and this to higher albedo or, alternatively, to greater heat retention. The net effect is unclear.

Whilst CO_2 is responsible for about half the greenhouse effects, nevertheless other gases, for example the CFCs, have a disporportionate effect relative to their abundance. This is due to two features; firstly, they absorb more infra-red energy per unit and, secondly, they absorb at wavelengths that are transmitted by CO_2, thereby increasing the range of radiation absorbed. The length of time that each remains in the atmosphere after discharge also affects the ultimate concentration. For example, methane has an average life or residence time of about 11 years, whilst CFCs may survive for 100 years.

The Environmental Protection Agency in the USA estimated the contribution to the effects from greenhouse gases in the 1980s to be some 57% from energy use and production, 17% from CFCs, 14% from agricultural practices, 9% from land use modifications and 3% from other industrial activities. The contributions have, alternatively, been expressed as 50% from CO_2, 18% from methane, 14% from CFCs, 6% from NO_x and 12% from surface ozone etc.

The consumption of fuels is also putting heat into the atmosphere. Each year over 3×10^{20} joules are emitted from fossil fuels and nuclear energy plus a large, unquantified number from biomass (principally wood fuel and forest burning) which, in effect, transforms solar energy by photosynthesis into heat. Large though this is it is only a very small percentage (some 0.03%) of that received directly from the sun. Nevertheless if all this heat from using fossil fuels warmed only the atmosphere, without loss, it would lead to a temperature increase of about 0.6°C in a decade. But heat will exchange with the oceans and land, although the temperature difference will be small and there could be a time lag. Any effect on global temperatures from this source is ignored.

The consequences of increased greenhouse gas concentrations

The magnitude of any change in temperature is uncertain and the prediction of the effects that this might have are variable.

There have been many predictions on the likely temperature rises consequent upon the predicted increase in CO_2 and other greenhouse gases. These are calculated by developing a General Circulation Model—GCM—and the majority of these, and there are over 20 that have been developed mainly from meteorological predictive models, calculate an average steady state temperature rise (that is allowing for the time lag before the full effects are observable) of 1½–4½°C for a doubling of equivalent CO_2 concentration (that is allowing, with appropriate factors, for the other gases in terms of CO_2) compared with pre-industrialization levels. The time taken to reach this level is also debatable but, without drastic intervention, is probably between 30–50 years although the possible feedback mechanisms, such as cloud cover, sea-ice or ocean coupling which could modify this course, are also not well understood or quantified. The GCMs have serious limitations and include a lot of assumptions and guesses in their formulation. Work continues to improve their quality and the quality of the data being used which may narrow or modify the predictions. The report by an IPCC working group (May 1990, see below), based upon the work of some 300 scientists around the world, suggests that there may be a rise of 3°C by the end of the next century, although, in view of the uncertainties surrounding their deliberations, it will take 10–15 years to clarify. (One expert has suggested that there is evidence of an approaching "little ice age" which would offset any warming!) Recent satellite data, incidentally, have shown no global warming in the last decade, but the significance of those measurements is that, for the first time, there is available an accurate means for the measurement of small changes.

If the extent and distribution of any temperature change is uncertain the probable or possible effects are even less clear. The one thing that does seem certain is that, if warming does occur, it will not be uniform and that different parts of the world will be affected to differing degrees. Some models suggest that, for example, the temperatures at the poles will rise more than at the equator. Rainfall patterns will alter and the length of seasons could change leading to differing patterns of agriculture, different crops, different areas being suitable or unsuitable for intensive farming, different desert boundaries. Higher temperatures and more CO_2 could lead to higher rates of bio-synthesis. The frequencies of extreme events could alter. There will, therefore, be changes imposed on human activities and residence with wide sociological repercussions.

Mean sea levels will probably rise, but estimates vary from a few inches to a few feet (although one prediction did suggest a frightening several metres). The rise is due to the melting of the Antarctic and northern ice caps (and there is evidence that glaciers are receding today) and the overall expansion of the oceans which must also rise in temperature if atmospheric temperatures rise, albeit with some lag. Again the extent of both these events is uncertain and unresolved with, for example, in the case of the oceans, the uncertainty being made up of the extent of energy interchange between air and the various layers of the seas—if only the surface is warmed or if ocean currents ensure more general absorption of that energy and the time for this to happen. The results of even a small rise in levels could be catastrophic for many low-lying, inhabited areas of the world—parts of Bangladesh and other major river deltas, and Pacific island states are often quoted as examples—and could inundate important wetland ecosystems. The costs of raising sea-defences to combat this, even in the developed world, would be vast.

Nevertheless with all the uncertainty it is generally considered that a rise in temperature would lead to heavy costs and disruption and would create many more problems than it would solve, partly because the rate of change might be too fast to be accommodated by natural adjustments. Natural eco-systems would be severely disturbed and wild flora and fauna could probably not migrate quickly enough to retain their usual habitat conditions. The earth's temperature has changed in the past over similar, even greater, ranges but it has, as far as can be determined from geological records, taken hundreds of thousands of years, not half a century.

The Toronto Conference on the Changing Atmosphere in June 1988, following other UNEP-sponsored conferences at Villach in 1985, Laxenburg in 1986 and Bellagio in 1987, was attended by some 300 scientists and policy makers from 48 countries. They agreed that there was cause for concern and called on the UN to draw up a "comprehensive global convention" and for a 20% reduction of CO_2 emissions in industrialized countries by 2005 (compared with 1985), although it was not clear that the implications of such a proposal were fully considered. UNEP and WMO later, in November 1988, established three groups of experts—the Intergovernmental Panel on Climate Change—to gather and evaluate: (a) the scientific evidence on global warming; (b) the environmental and agricultural impact of the climatic changes; and (c) to formulate responses to the situation. Its reports are to be presented, debated and acted upon later in 1990. The first group has reported in May 1990 and recommended urgent action on curbing emissions.

The potential problems of the greenhouse effect are now firmly on the political agenda. The theme of the 1989 World Environment Day was designated by UNEP as "Global

Warming—Global Warning". The *New Scientist* said that "Global warming could turn out to be a figment of the imagination, the storms and droughts no more than a minor hiccup. But the risk of ignoring the warnings will be severe". The IPCC group noted that "the complexity of the system means that we cannot rule out surprises".

Steps to limit increases of the greenhouse gases

Increased emissions during the next few years of many of the gases is certain under prevailing conditions and attitudes, for populations are rising and deforestation and the growth in the consumption of fossil fuels continues. If the current use of energy per capita or energy related to GDP in various countries is compared (see Table 1) it is seen that there are vast differences between the developed and developing worlds (and within those categories). Insofar as energy use is an indicator of standard of living, the developing world is trying to catch up with the others.

The increase in demand for energy can, today, most readily be met by the use of fossil fuels and therefore a greater release of CO_2. (Emissions of NO_x and the generation of ozone also follow closely on rising energy consumption.) But all predictions are notoriously difficult and often wrong and estimates of the rise is energy consumption vary widely. Most guesses agree that, unless radical steps are taken to limit energy use, and the IPCC

Table 1: *Energy use in selected countries*

Country	*Pop.* 1	*GDP* 2	*En. use* 3	*CO_2* 4	*En./cap.* 5	*En./GDP* 6	*CO_2/cap.* 7	*CO_2/GDP* 8
France	55	940*	195	100	3.5	0.21	1.8	0.11
FRG	61	1,120	265	190	4.3	0.24	3.1	0.17
Italy	58	810	150	105	2.6	0.19	1.8	0.19
Netherlands	15	220*	75	50	5.0	0.34	3.3	0.23
UK	56	760	210	160	3.7	0.28	2.9	0.21
EC	325	4,520	1,095	740	3.4	0.24	2.3	0.16
East Europe 6	105	1,160	450	400	4.3	0.39	3.8	0.34
India	835	230	210	185	0.3	0.91	0.2	0.80
Brazil	150	310	130	60	0.9	0.42	0.4	0.19
Japan	125	1,850	400	290	3.2	0.22	2.3	0.16
China	1,110	350	730	700	0.7	2.09	0.6	2.00
USA	250	4,850	1,950	1,420	7.8	0.40	5.7	0.29
USSR	290	2,550	1,400	1,005	4.8	0.54	3.6	0.39

Notes: Figures rounded off from OECD data, World Factbook 1989 and BP Statistical Review of World Energy, 1989.
*GNP figures.
1 – population in millions
2 – GDP in \$US $\times 10^9$ at then current exchange rates
3 – energy use in million tonnes oil equivalent (mtoe) for commercially traded fuels only
4 – CO_2 emissions as million tonnes carbon
5 – energy use in tonnes oil equivalent per capita
6 – energy use in tonnes oil equivalent per GDP as in 2
7 – CO_2 emissions in tonnes carbon per capita
8 – CO_2 emissions in tonnes carbon per GDP as in 2

group referred to above has called for an immediate reduction in CO_2 emissions of 60%, global consumption in a "business-as-usual", "do-nothing" world will inevitably rise two- to three-fold in the next 40 years.

The EC Council of Ministers called, in 1986, for an improvement in energy efficiency of 20% by 1995 and their Resolution in 1989 required the Commission to study remedial measures for CO_2 control.

Increases can be mitigated either by emitting less, or by removing what has already been formed, or by changing production processes and systems. Concerning CO_2 the best, most cost effective and quickest reduction, is to use less fuel and to use it more efficiently. There is blatant waste all around from inefficient motors to excessive lighting and poor insulation. In the UK, and in many other similar countries, there was a marked improvement in fuel use following the steep oil price rises of 1974 and 1979, but this was due to economic factors and not for any concern about pollution. The energy efficiency, also labelled energy intensity, that is the amount of energy used per unit of GNP, has improved in the UK by about 2% per annum during the last decade although this is, in part, due to the phasing out of antiquated equipment and heavy, old-fashioned industries. The figure today is a little above the European average, where significant differences show up, but Japan, conscious of the need to import virtually all its fuel, uses over 20% less energy than the UK per unit of GDP.

If indices of emissions of CO_2 per GDP are looked at (see Table 1) rather than those based on energy use, the rankings are very different due to the different primary fuel mixes, particularly that used for electricity generation. France, with its high nuclear energy programme, emits overall 70% of the European average whilst the UK is 30% above. China is over 10 times that average, the USSR two-and-a-half times, the USA nearly double but Japan about the same.

Estimates vary on the extent to which greater efficiency and better design can contribute to a lowering of emissions. Considering the domestic and service sectors, the best refrigerator on the market uses 75% less energy than the average in use and experimental designs use considerably less again; buildings constructed with good insulation use a fraction of the heat required in old ones; improved building regulations have been introduced in the UK in 1990 but are still a long way from Scandinavian practice; the EPA considers that home heating requirements in the USA could be cut by 90% with better insulation and photovoltaics on the roof; a condensing domestic boiler consumes up to 50% less fuel than many conventional boilers for the same heat input to the house; a small combined heat and power (CHP) unit in, say, an hotel or hospital would rapidly (depending on electricity tariffs) pay for itself. The economic advantage applies to all these examples and many others, for they are financially attractive as well as environmentally sound and are available today, but their attractions and consequences are not yet widely realized.

Other possibilities for fuel economy include better lights (for example compact fluorescent rather than incandescent), better controls (particularly to switch off when not required), better design (particularly of buildings), more public transport, more passengers per car, etc. The EPA has recommended, for instance, that new cars should average 50 miles per (US) gallon (mpg), as compared with 26.5 mpg currently in the USA, and France has called for an automobile that runs 100 km on 3 litres of motor spirit (95 mpg). Electrically-driven vehicles are usually thought of as "environmentally friendly" and, indeed, are quiet and do not emit pollutants in crowded streets. But their overall consumption of primary energy, in both construction and operation, is greater than today's cars and, therefore, provides no solution to energy efficiency or to lower CO_2 emissions if the recharging is from fossil-fuelled electricity generation.

The efficiency of electricity generation can also be improved significantly by the introduction of developments such as combined cycle plants, in which gas is first burned in a gas turbine and the exhaust gases are then used in conventional steam generation/turbine, or combined heat and power installations, in which waste heat is used for some useful purpose. The energy efficiency of many manufacturing and production processes could also be improved markedly, although the costs are often a small percentage of the overall costs so that other features have a higher management priority.

In many cases, particularly in the public sector without cost/benefit arguments, there is a disincentive to save fuel by the nature of the accounting, budgeting and taxation systems, for fuel is seen as a revenue item whereas better equipment requires capital expenditure and this requires different justification.

The rate at which equipment can be replaced will vary, but with an economic incentive, in addition to any imposed reasons, such as energy or emission taxes, this should be sooner rather than later. One estimate, by the Association for the Conservation of Energy, suggests that, in the next 15 years, greater efficiency and available remedies could lead to a fall of some 20% in CO_2 discharge in the UK.

The possibility of chemically removing CO_2, once generated, is distant, Research is taking place on processes to remove it from flue gases but there is, today, no commercial process available. This is in distinction to the removal of SO_2 and other pollutants where, incidentally, it should be noted that the technical solutions, for example flue gas desulphurization at power stations or catalytic converters on petrol engines, will marginally increase CO_2 emissions. If success is achieved there will follow massive problems in the use or disposal of the resultant compounds formed from the CO_2, even if useful materials are produced.

Major reafforestation programmes and the cessation of deforestation (see Part I, Section 3) could help remove CO_2 from the atmosphere, but the scale necessary is formidable. As noted earlier, CO_2 does dissolve in sea water and it has been suggested that the amount taken up could be increased significantly by better, contrived mixing of the ocean layers so that the colder, deeper water could be brought to the surface and absorb CO_2 and that already in equilibrium would replace it at lower depths. This would also provide atmospheric cooling, as pointed out by Prof. Sir Fred Hoyle, who also noted that this could store heat for later use. The heat absorption capacity of the oceans could postpone any global warming for a long time. It is unclear, however, how this might be arranged or what it might cost or what it might do to weather patterns and climates if, for example, the Gulf Stream no longer reached Britain's shores.

The third approach is by replacing existing production and electricity generating technologies with ones that do not generate CO_2, particularly by those utilizing the so-called "renewable" energy resources (see Part I, Section 10). Electricity can be generated in a number of ways that do not lead to the emission of CO_2 except, perhaps, for a very small amount used in today's processes during the manufacture of the necessary equipment. The best known and most widely used already are hydroelectric power and nuclear power generation. The scope for increases in hydro- are not widespread and the outlook for additional nuclear is, at best, unclear due to costs, the fear of possible accidents and political pressures. As far as global warming is concerned, however, and ignoring other environmental worries, it does offer the best current alternative to fossil use. The adverse cost differential would be modified if the costs of CO_2 pollution or removal were included in conventional power generation. Even if it were accepted as the right alternative, the practical rate of construction of new facilities is unlikely to match the demand. The sheer size of investment makes it out of reach for many LDCs and the World Bank does not lend for nuclear programmes. Developed countries would also be concerned about the security implications of supplying installations to countries who may turn out to be hostile, irresponsible or simply inept. Nevertheless the International Atomic Energy Agency says that up to 500 new nuclear power stations could be commissioned worldwide between 2001 and 2010 to meet increased demand and combat emissions.

Other renewables in use for electricity generation with no CO_2 emissions are wind power, tidal power and solar energy. In the UK there are applications for wind farms, some of which have been objected to on environmental grounds, although several are in operation in other parts of the world, notably in Denmark and in California. Tidal schemes have been proposed in the Severn estuary and on the Mersey and they, too, have generated opposition. That in the Severn could provide up to some 6% of the national electrical demand and the Mersey scheme, at 660 MW, exceeds the UK government's requirement (in its electricity privatisation measures) for 600 MW from renewable resources by the year 2005. Solar energy for direct electricity generation—photovoltaics—is expensive and only in use for high-technology applications, including space-craft, and in remote locations. Direct solar-space heating, so called "passive solar", also, of course, contributes to lowering the CO_2 discharge by replacing other forms of building heating.

Wider use of bio-mass for heating (including steam for electricity production) is considered not to increase CO_2 concentrations provided replanting, to replace that used, is maintained so that a balance is achieved. The use of land-fill gas, methane, is also increasing not only thereby generating heat but also reducing methane discharge into the atmosphere.

More speculative technologies plan to harness offshore wind and wave power and to tap geothermal heat, but many engineering problems have yet to be solved. A few small-scale schemes are in operation.

Methods to deal with the other greenhouse gases include prevention of use and removal, but those stemming from combustion will also, of course, be best reduced by using less fuel, as for CO_2.

Nitrogen oxides from high temperature combustion in furnaces can be reduced by the improved design of burners and large-scale experiments and installations are progressing and will have to be extended. NO_x can also be removed from flue gases by chemical denitrification processes, Selective Catalytic Reduction (SCR) and Selective Non-catalytic Reduction (SNR), but few installations exist today.

NO_x from vehicles (see Part I, Section 11) can be reduced to nitrogen by a catalytic converter fitted in the exhaust. The use of such equipment is already mandatory in some countries (for example in the USA and Sweden) and every new car licensed in the EC after 1991 must also have one installed (needing unleaded petrol to avoid poisoning of the catalyst). This device will also oxidize any hydrocarbons in the exhaust, thereby limiting the formation of ozone from the reaction between NO_x and these hydrocarbons. A reduction in the hydrocarbons released every time a car is filled with petrol is being addressed and vapour retention facilities are in use in some countries and being introduced in others.

The CFCs pose a greater problem due to their long life so that all those already present in the atmosphere will have an effect for many years to come. The Montreal Protocol, calling for significant reductions in the manufacture of those causing damage to the ozone layer, particularly if the pressure to speed up and intensify the ban is successful, will prevent a worsening of the greenhouse effect from their presence provided, as noted earlier, that the replacements are not only harmless to ozone but also do not absorb infra-red radiation.

The control of methane discharges is difficult. Natural discharges will continue. Rice cultivation and animal husbandry will increase, but accidental loss in the transit of natural gas and the recovery of land-fill gas should improve.

The decade ahead

Much of the equipment that will be in use in 10 years' time is already in place or committed or planned. New designs will have little impact for the turnover rate is low, particularly in the large consumers of energy. Even in private transport any radical new models will not have penetrated the market very far. The predictions for energy consumption suggest that, in a "business-as-usual" world, without attempts or incentives to use less, total CO_2 emissions will rise by some 25–30%.

Some countries, including the UK, have been advocating doing nothing until there is further research and scientific evidence to demonstrate the need for action, but this view seems to be moderating, at least to investigating what can be done and the costs of different options to reduce the threat of global warming, and to calling for, at least, a standstill in emissions.

The Toronto call for a 20% reduction, 2005/1985, in the use of fossil fuel emissions by the industrialized world has been mentioned. The conference agreed that half the reduction could be achieved by increased energy conservation and efficiency and that the remainder would have to come from exploiting alternative energy sources. The results from the IPCC studies will be considered at a major WMO conference in 1990 on world climate when a start could be made, according to Dr Tolba, Executive Director of UNEP, on negotiations for a UN treaty on the prevention of further global warming, for no convention or treaty exists today. A conference in The Hague in March 1989 called for the development within the UN framework of a new authority to: (a) monitor governments' performance in controlling atmospheric pollution; (b) enforce compliance; and (c) compensate countries particularly affected by steps taken to protect the atmosphere. The meeting in Bergen in May 1990 agreed that the "precautionary principle" should be followed, and this reversed the previous position of the UK and the USA, opening the way for some agreement, perhaps at Geneva in the autumn, before scientific uncertainty has been dispelled.

But there are many unresolved questions and difficulties to be overcome before much progress can be made and enormous political will is required to reach international agreement and binding, universal treaties. A comparison has been made with the Montreal Protocol on CFCs which was quickly reached, although not universally accepted, once the scientific uncertainty had been removed and the consequences of ozone depletion appreciated. But the implications of CO_2 control reach much further and deeper into every country's economy and interests. The widespread attention in every medium now focused on global warming as one of the main environmental issues, likely to impose constraints on energy policy in almost every country in the world and particularly in OECD members, bodes well for something being done. It is, also, provoking public and manufacturers' interest in improved design and performance of many items including, for example, motor vehicles.

But it is only recently that the public has appreciated the potential problems and risks and in many eyes it is still seen as something to be tackled by governments rather than by individuals. It has to be perceived by the public that individual effort on the small scale, multiplied millions of times by a country's population, will achieve something. It has yet to be realized that every 100W bulb is responsible for 3 cubic feet of CO_2 being released every hour (with coal-fired power stations) or every car (at 30 mpg) releases over 6 cubic feet of CO_2 every mile. Only if some dramatic development should focus world attention on the need for action, such as happened with the discovery of the ozone hole, can rapid progress be expected. It may be that some societies will see themselves as "losers" if warming occurs and take a firm stand on, and bring pressure to bear for, emission reductions. Similarly, if some natural disasters are seen to be directly caused by warming, only then will political pressure for action increase. There are, however, increasing signs that political leaders are beginning to give voice to the problems, but few seem to appreciate the size of the problems they will face, and countries are beginning to put pressure on those reluctant to take any action.

As suggested above there are many actions, particularly towards improving energy use efficiency, which are beneficial and good in themselves; they are economically attractive and technically possible, and could be taken virtually immediately. These should be implemented nationally without waiting for international accord and would not put a country at a disadvantage relative to its competitors. Stimulus and encouragement will be necessary and better information must be available to provoke interest and to guide choice. Design standards, for example for domestic appliances, are used in some countries and have been proposed for the EC but have been resisted by others, including the UK, as restricting a free market. Once the problem is better appreciated by the public and manufacturers realize that there may be a competitive advantage in marketing efficicient goods, then they will make, and promote vigorously, better products. (Once lead-free motor spirit was put on the market it was the suppliers who encouraged its wider use—even if this was promoted by seeking a return on capital investment.)

Fuel switching, too, could be a national option. The replacement of coal by gas will reduce CO_2 emissions by a half for a given load (but in many countries extensive replacement would create enormous problems for the coal-mining industry and production and distribution problems for the gas industry). Add to the lowering of emissions the attraction that gas can be used in a combined cycle operation (the gas is first burnt in a turbine and the exhaust used for conventional steam raising, thereby raising the overall efficiency from about 35% to 45%) and worthwhile savings are achieved. In the UK there are several planning applications submitted utilizing North Sea gas in this way. But switching to gas is more a palliative and short-term measure than a solution. It will help meet initial reduction targets and provide time for more fundamental solutions to be discovered. Methane is, however, 25 times more effective than CO_2 as a greenhouse gas and therefore gas losses or leaks of 1–2% would offset the advantage of switching from oil.

International agreement on target reductions will not be easy and few nations, acting alone, can have a large enough impact on the problem except as an example to others. If a percentage change is sought, as proposed in Toronto, countries will argue that not all are starting from the same base line. LDCs will not want to be impeded in their growth. Developed countries will be blamed for the present levels of CO_2 due to earlier deforestation and industrialization and be expected to compensate those who come later.

The change in permitted discharges might be expressed in terms of gross emissions of CO_2, or of fuel tonnage, or of emissions per GDP index or per capita. Table 1 shows how these vary, in both absolute terms and in rank, among some countries. These figures are for one given year, but they have changed markedly over the years. This is particularly notably in France where nuclear power now accounts for three-quarters of electricity generation and hydro- a steady 15 million tonnes oil equivalent (mtoe), with the result that CO_2 emissions from power stations have fallen by 70% in the last decade. (This was not prompted by consideration of the greenhouse effect but by the need for France to be less dependent upon imported fuels.) If targets are to be set in terms of reductions the choice of base year for comparison is vitally important and some countries will claim that there should be recognition for their achievements so far.

Emission taxes or carbon taxes have been discussed but are likely to be considered only if most competing nations agree to a common formula, otherwise unfair trading advantages might accrue. The level of taxes would need to be high to influence significantly enough present habits and practices to produce worthwhile reductions. It is also argued that costs from such taxes or other measures, such as the raising of sea defences, could be unduly high if the warming and its effects have been over-estimated or different solutions emerge.

Marketable or tradeable permits have been proposed, based upon one or more of the above indices. One socially based idea uses a per capita limit, since everyone has an equal right to clean air, but Grubb in *Negotiating Targets,* shows the extent of the difficulties and arguments against any of the possible routes.

Some countries have reduced, or plan to reduce, their own CO_2 emissions by "exporting" their heavy industry, including investment abroad to accomplish such a move. Whilst this might mean that the country in question can achieve its target reduction, it would do little for the global scene.

A country's resources, too, must influence the actions it takes, and these resources, both of fossil fuels (see Table 2) and of renewables, are very unevenly distributed. It is difficult to see how China, for example, with its enormous reserves of coal and with its aim of improving living conditions, can avoid burning more coal and, indeed, it plans to increase production substantially. The scope for better utilization and efficiency is, however, widespread.

No amount of reduction in the industrialized world could compensate, however, for a doubling of the discharges of the LDCs, which account, including China, for three-quarters of the world's population and which aspire to improved living conditions. The social and economic problems in halting deforestation and the replanting of areas large enough to have an impact, are formidable. The prospect of drastic population control is yet remote.

Countries, today, could push in the direction of less emission by reviewing their present incentives and tax structures. There is waste in public buildings, hospitals, schools etc. and commercial properties because of the means of financial control, at least in the UK where use is considered a revenue expense and often not subject to Value Added Tax (VAT), whereas means for reduction, for example thermal insulation, are classed as capital expenditure and attract VAT. The same dilemma, or disincentive, often exists between the aims of a landlord and the tenant.

In many cases there is incentive to use more fuel and, in general, the producers of energy promote the use of their products and are encouraged to sell more. Pricing policies usually mean that the greater the use the lower the unit cost and this practice needs review and reconsideration. In the USA some electricity suppliers, for example in California, are paying for customers' higher efficiency equipment since this is more cost effective than constructing additional generating capacity, but this concept is slow in spreading.

Table 2: *Resources of fossil fuels*

Country	*Solid* 1	2	*Oil* 3	4	*Gas* 5	6
France	350	30	0	0	0	0
FRG	60,000	500	0	0	10	18
Netherlands	0	0	0	0	63	33
UK	9,300	100	600	5	21	13
EC	90,000	200	1,000	7	110	23
Japan	1,000	100	0	0	1	20
China	170,000	200	3,100	23	32	65
USA	260,000	350	4,400	10	190	11
USSR	245,000	400	8,000	13	1,500	55

Notes: Figures for 1988, rounded off from OECD data and BP Statistical Review of World Energy
1 – proved reserves in million tonnes
2 – reserves/production ratio, i.e. the number of years at today's production rate
3 – proved reserves in million tonnes
4 – as for 2
5 – proven reserves in trillion (10^{12}) cubic feet
6 – as for 2

Whilst all these possibilities are debated, few, except higher efficiency and, perhaps, fiscal changes, can have much immediate effect this coming decade.

Further ahead

It is possible that the next decade may give a pointer as to whether the greenhouse effect is leading to climate change and global warming with a better understanding of the correlation between them. This may, therefore, change the debate and proposed actions, perhaps to greater concern or complacency. However the best guess today is that, without intervention, equivalent CO_2 levels will rise to double their pre-industrial level of about 280 ppm in the next 40–50 years and that this will lead to global warming of 1½–4½°C. The IPCC working party, as noted earlier, have settled on 3°C for the end of the 21st century. The considerations above for the next decade apply more forcibly to the more distant future.

It is easier to believe that, in the longer term and hopefully before any significant climate change should occur, different behaviour, wiser attitudes, greater scientific research and new inventions or developments will remove the threat. These will help and it is conceivable that some countries, with determined effort, could achieve significant reductions in their CO_2 emissions from the present levels. The UK Energy Technology Support Unit has suggested that a halving of UK CO_2 emissions is "just about achievable" by 2020. It is hard, at present, however, to foresee how worldwide changes can be accomplished great enough to reverse the rise in greenhouse gases and therefore the expectation of global warming, in spite of one group of the IPCC calling for an immediate reduction of 60% in emissions.

Much of the quantity of greenhouse gases present today in the atmosphere is going to remain there for many years and there seems no way in which the position can suddenly be stabilized. There is no easy answer to halt the rise in the concentration of greenhouse gases worldwide and it is difficult to envisage any way of getting to and keeping at an equilibrium level in the near future. Energy use is predicted, on present use patterns and without intervention, to rise by some two-and-a-half times by the year 2030, whereas to stabilize CO_2 atmospheric concentration at the present level it is calculated that emissions must fall to 20–50% of present.

Grubb argues, in *Energy Policies and the Greenhouse Effect,* that the world is simply not prepared for the possible implications of the greenhouse effect: not technologically; not institutionally; not politically; and not intellectually. Known technological advances are largely marginal in overall effect and those of significance, such as CO_2 removal and disposal, nuclear fusion or fast breeding, an hydrogen economy not based on fossil fuels, are speculative. Neither institutions nor treaties yet exist devoted to energy efficiency or the use of renewable energy sources and deep divisions exist in most governments between the providers and users of energy. The political implications of changes in lifestyle, of attitudes to population growth and control, of paying if polluting, of raising taxes, are largely un-addressed whether in the developed or developing worlds. And the intellectual tools for assessing scientific findings, social change, response options and policies are inadequate.

An alternative, therefore, is to learn to adapt to changing climates if the changes and their consequences are as large as some predict. This, inevitably, will involve upheaval but, perhaps, with the attention now devoted to these potential problems, acceptable policies and practices will be found. It is then no longer a scientific problem but a phenomenon which may disrupt peoples and societies on a large scale for which, at the moment, they are ill-prepared. It will require the combined efforts of scientists and sociologists. It will require improved monitoring of change.

It will require new developments in agriculture (for example new crop varieties to withstand different climates, rainfalls, seasons), in renewable energy technologies, in efficient equipment utilizing energy, in traditional process and production industries. But humans are resilient and can adapt to change, even rapid change brought on by political upheavals. The rest of the living world may not be so amenable to disruption caused by man.

Above all, it will require new thinking by those who lead opinion, by those who formulate policies and by those who develop ideas.

For bibliography, see p. 358.

5 LAND DEGRADATION AND DESERTIFICATION

Brian W. Walker

Introduction

During the late 1960s and then increasingly in the '70s, a number of environmental notions began to take root in the public consciousness. By the 1980s such notions had helped to pave the way for the explosive growth of the "green movement". Environmentalism became a powerful moral and political force in Europe and North America. By the end of the decade it had invaded the Soviet bloc countries and many of the oil-rich Arab countries. Increasingly it influences policy decisions in the developing world. Part of this process had their roots in the application of rigorous field science—the "Cinderella" of the sciences. Other parts were speculative, verging on what can only be described as science fiction.

Certain "trigger" words were instrumental to the growth of environmentalism. They included phrases like "the loss of our tropical forests", "ozone depletion", "global warming", "desertification", "loss of bio-diversity", and the like.

Today, each of these areas of environmental change embraces certain common features. The most important is the absence, or unreliability, of baseline data. In some instances this weakness is critical; in others marginal. For example, foresters and plant ecologists do not know how many species there are in the tropical forests—or, for that matter, on the planet itself. A little is known about some five million species, but there are likely to be 30 million or considerably more on planet Earth. On the other hand, scientists know what are the constituent gases which give rise to ozone depletion, although they do not know exactly how they work or interact with each other. A fair estimate can be made of the rate at which they are being generated. Yet scientists do not understand how the global climatic regime works. The models used to predict changes in weather patterns are notoriously inadequate and complex. Weathermen cannot predict the weather 72 hours ahead even though the weather has been dominating everyone's life since homo sapiens began to evolve 5.5 million years ago. The oceans which cover 70% of the planet are largely a mystery in our understanding of their impact on climate.

In considering "desertification", considerable difficulties emerge. It is not so much the absence of base-line data, due to inadequate modelling, the unreliability of figures, the shakiness of illustrative material or of verified case studies—all of which could be corrected if resources allowed for greater inputs so as to achieve improved data collection and analysis.

Rather it is the prior question of whether the phenomenon of desertification, as it is fixed in the public mind, actually exists, or not. As it is popularly conceived, the suspicion is that it does not.

Definitions of desertification

But, first, what is desertification? It is not unreasonable to look for reliable definitions. According to Glantz & Orlousky (*Desertification: Anatomy of a Complex Environmental Process*) scientific literature contains over 100 definitions of desertification. None is wholly satisfactory.

In 1985 the UN's Food & Agricultural Organization defined desertification as "the transformation of arid and semi-arid lands to desert conditions by human exploitation often accelerated by recurrent drought".

In 1988 the Policy Planning & Research Staff of the World Bank (Nelson, R., Working Paper No. 8) defined desertification as "a process of sustained land (soil and vegetation) degradation in arid, semi-arid and dry sub-humid areas, caused at least partly by man. It reduces productive potential", it continued, "to an extent which can neither be readily reversed by removing the cause, nor easily reclaimed without substantial investment". This is a fuller, but more cautious definition. Interestingly, the quotation is preceded by the admission that "to cover our own reluctant use of the word 'desertification', and to start to uncover the issues, [we] are obliged to offer a definition".

The report argues that through the popular press, through articles, books and statements, and sometimes in statements by scientists, the problem of desertification has been "poorly characterized". It points out that an assumption is made that the extent of desertification is well known, whereas "the evidence [for it] is extraordinarily scanty". It justifies the staff's uneasiness by pointing out that "professional agreement amongst scientists and practitioners on the extent, causes and solutions [of desertification] has been over estimated". Then whilst noting that the process of desertification in this or that particular locality may be "a serious problem", it asserts that the "extent of desertification as an irreversible state has probably been exaggerated". Laying to death the popular image of desertification as being represented by the inexorable advance of sand-dunes "down the map"—as has been claimed, at a rate variably put at 5 or 15, or 20, km a year and especially applicable to the Sahel region of Africa—the World Bank prefers instead to emphasize the "more subtle, more complex, pulsating deteriorations, sometimes with reversals, but at least, with substantial periodic remissions, radiating out from centres of excessive population pressure".

The Bank finally notes that "the availability of profitable technologies to combat the problem has been over-estimated because the gap between what is socially profitable and what is perceived as privately profitable has been under-estimated".

Gorse & Steeds, also writing for the World Bank, explain the process of desertification as "the sustained decline of the biological productivity of arid and semi-arid land; the end-result is desert, or skeletal soil that is irrecuperable". This process is now at work in many parts of the West African Sahelian and Sudanian zones (SSZ). Whether desertification is caused mainly by droughts and increased aridity, or by resource abuse by the resident population, is hotly debated. But this debate has little operational consequence, since rainfall patterns cannot as yet be modified nor even predicted, whereas human behaviour can be changed. The desertification problem is, nonetheless, severe, since it is an example of conflict between the public interest in long-term resource use, and private short-term resource abuse. If there is no effective reconciliation between these two interests, the desertification process will continue; while the process can be arrested, the end-result is irreversible.

The normally authoritative World Resources Report (1986–89) does not attempt to define desertification, limiting itself to the following: "Degradation on dry lands (arid, semi-arid and sub-human lands) is called 'desertification', because desert-like conditions appear where none existed before. Desertified dry lands are characterized by low primary productivity (less than 400 kg of dry matter per hectare per year) and poor rain use efficiency (usually less than 1 kg of dry matter produced per hectare per year for each millimetre of rainfall)".

Finally, in 1990, Alan Grainger in his book for *Earthscan,* seems to limit himself to using the 1977 United Nations Conference on Desertification definition which was "the diminution or destruction of the biological potential of the land [which] can lead ultimately to desert-like conditions", and further "an aspect of the widespread deterioration of eco-systems under the combined pressure of adverse and fluctuating climate, and excessive exploitation".

Grainger argues that desertification is a complex phenomenon—which it is—and closes his chapter "What is Desertification?" with the following comments: "Our understanding of desertification is still quite limited, although until now it has been thought of as largely the result of human misuse of the land with overcultivation, overgrazing, deforestation and mismanagement of irrigated cropland leading to the degradation of soil and vegetation. The role of climate has been thought of as mainly catalytic, so that desertification accelerates as drought causes people to overfarm the land to compensate for falling yields. However, the boundary between the roles of climatic variation and human impact is now becoming increasingly blurred. This is especially the case in the Sahel, where it has been suggested that the continuing drought is linked with environmental degradation caused by bad land use. Whether this theory is true or not, there seems to be every likelihood that desertification will be influenced in the future by global climatic changes resulting from the activities of the entire human population. Because of the various lags in the world climatic system there is very little we can do to prevent such changes occurring over at least the next 20 to 30 years, and probably longer. The best way to cope with climatic variability and control desertification in the drylands is therefore to make land uses more sustainable and to alleviate the poverty which is another important underlying cause of the problem."

It is worth noting in passing that desertification is not the same as "deserts". Mabbutt considers deserts have three characteristics. These are said to be "empty of life", "waterless" and "unproductive". They usually receive 25 mm or less of annual rainfall, although some authorities, like Le Houerou, fix the rainfall mean at 100 mm or less.

It is fairly clear from these random but authoritative definitions of desertification that the widespread idea that deserts somehow creep across the map of the world in a steady and inexorable attack on soil and water, turning the landscape into sand-dunes, is inaccurate. Each definition contains important caveats, or reservations which, in the aggregate, undermine the popular concept of desertification.

It appears that that concept is rooted in a small number of anecdotal case histories which surfaced internationally in the late '60s and early '70s to be picked up, repeated and then recirculated in UN and other conferences, and by the media. They lack careful study and rigorous analysis.

It is true that in specific regions as far removed from each other as the dust-bowl prairies of the USA and a Sahelian country like Mauritania, localized transformation characteristic of desertification does take place as human and animal populations exhaust their natural resource base and the wind, rain and sun combine so as to leach, or remove, organic material from the soil, leaving behind desert-like conditions. It is a localized phenomenon. Bio-mass disappears, the productive use of the soil, now largely inert, is rendered impossible, dust-bowls or sand-dunes evolve and creep forward or retreat at the periphery. Human populations traditionally living there are no longer able to do so. In 1982 the UN estimated an annual loss of US$26 billion in agricultural productivity as a result of desertification. Thus, the first, key point is that desertification takes place within the wider context of soil erosion and land degradation. Within that scenario the planet faces a major threat—in the view of many commentators more serious than global warming, or climate change. In arid or semi-arid areas, land degradation and soil erosion can rapidly lead to irreversible desertification. Human populations confronted by that phenomenon face a bleak, if not impossible, future unless they migrate to new territories.

It is wiser, therefore, to consider desertification within the context of the more fundamental challenge of soil erosion and land degradation.

Soil erosion and land degradation

If pressures on a natural resource base by human populations combine with adverse climate conditions they can rapidly deplete the soil base at a rate much faster than that by which nature replaces those losses, that is, creates new soil. Global agricultural land is being degraded at a rate of six million hectares per annum. A further 20 million hectares each year are rendered unprofitable to agriculture. These figures relate to a total cultivated land area of 1,600 million hectares. In the USA, which has had a powerful soil-conscious conservation movement of considerable scientific, agricultural and political strength during the second half of this century, soil losses average 16–18 tonnes per hectare (Napier Ohio State University). This is some two to three times the rate of natural replacement.

John Timmermans, a soil scientist with the Alberta (Canada) Agriculture Department (quoted in the *Edmonton Journal.*, March 16, 1990) has drawn attention to the importance of wind erosion in depleting soil. Successive droughts in 1988 and 1989 increased the potential threat of desertification in Alberta by reducing crops and the amount of erosion-slowing residue left after harvest. "In the long-term it is a serious threat", he said.

Practically all the food consumed by human populations is produced from a topsoil layer of some 200 millimetres in depth. Some 6% of topsoil is lost from all the world's major food producing regions, on average, each year. A worldwide analysis of this process predicts that without remedial long-term action upwards of 50% of these lands will be unproductive within 70 years, that is, by the mid-21st century. It is this rate of regression which suggests that land degradation and soil loss is more important to food security and, therefore, economic and political stability for human populations than, say, predicted climate change, ozone depletion, or freshwater pollution, serious as these issues are.

Soil loss

Writing for the *Earthwatch* magazine (March, 1990), Dr Martin Haigh, a geographer at the Oxford Polytechnic and the European Vice-President of the World Soil and Water Association, explains: "The soil is a living system. Its organic component is the key to its existence and health. Soil micro-organisms produce secretions that hold soil particles as soil crumbs. These aggregates give the soil an open structure, allow the movement of water and air into the soil and hence create a better environment for life. As the life in the soil declines, there is less secreted material to hold the soil crumbs together, and the soil breaks down into fine mineral particles. These particles wash into the rest of the soil, clogging the soil pores and reducing both aeration and water infiltration . . . rainfall either remains near the soil surface in waterlogged hollows or runs off through the soil's upper layers and surface, producing erosion."

Soil loss on the ground is not always obvious. The leaching out of humus, the loss of microscopic life within the soil, the fact that soil crumbs break down more readily when wet, that the density of the soil increases and that, overall, the depth of the soil is not as great as it used to be, may all be taking place year by year without the human communities who depend on that soil realizing what is happening. They do not see the ground disappearing from under their feet.

In Ethiopia, for example, it is estimated that 15% of the content of rivers is soil, washed down from the high central mountain plateau regions. To fly over the estuaries and deltas of any rivers, but especially in the developing world, is to be conscious of the volume of soil being washed off the land to be deposited on the seabed—lost to humanity for ever. A dark brown, black or yellow spume pushes for miles out of the necks of many rivers far into the surrounding oceans.

In the UK, the Soil Association advises that some 40% of soil, especially the ancient soils of East Anglia, are now inert and only keep producing by the application of chemical fertilizers and soil improvers. In Bulgaria, 70–80% of the agricultural land is said to be subject to wind erosion. Norway reports that 10% of its agricultural land is threatened by soil erosion.

In these northern countries, or in developing highland countries like Ethiopia or the Nepalese foothills, the "deserts" produced are not sand deserts, but bare rock and boulders, naked cliffs, stone pavements or the like. Around 70% of Ethiopia's population has lived, hitherto, in the highlands, but at least 50,000 sq km simply are no longer productive. It is estimated that 3.5 billion tonnes of topsoil are being lost each year. Effectively degradation of this kind has exactly the same consequences as desertification in its traditionally understood form—loss of bio-diversity and loss of productivity, leading to the transmigration of entire human populations who must either die or migrate to new living areas.

In Niger over the last 40 years, due to soil degradation, the mono-cropping of pearl millet has resulted in a yield decline from 500 kg per hectare to less than 4 kg per hectare. Throughout Africa as a whole for every 29 trees cut down only one is replanted. The effect of wind, rain and sun on the exposed soil base is little short of disastrous given the poor quality and depth of the soil base of Africa to start with.

Mountainous areas

Mountainous areas are especially fragile and prone to degradation when exposed to large or growing human or animal populations. The degradation of the central highlands of Ethiopia, leading to massive and inevitable soil loss, has all occurred within the space of four decades. It has taken nature millions of years to create the soil and then its cover. Now it is lost, probably for ever. The Himalayan foothills, the Yemeni mountains, the Vietnamese and Javanese mountain areas and those of Central America, all face a mix of human-imposed stress and adverse climate, leading to huge soil losses.

Such districts can support up to 400 people per sq km at best. Yet in many instances the actual population is double the maximum tolerable level. Slope, elevation, soil depth, tree/shrub cover are the main determinants. Historically, mountain people have been able to cling to their fastnesses by dint of the use of varying agricultural techniques. All of these have in commmon two objectives—how to retain the soil (and improve it); how to control rainfall both to benefit crops and to protect the soil.

Gravity determines what happens when heavy rain falls on exposed soil—it is washed (or blown) to the bottom of the mountain and transported in the river system away from the mountain—probably to the sea. Only occasionally, as in the Awash Valley system in Ethiopia, does the soil (now silt) remain in the country.

Contour farming—building trenches, dykes, check dams along the contours of the land, is the main device used by mountain people to retain their soil. Although little capital equipment is needed, most systems are labour-intensive. The North Yemen has developed a system of intricate interconnected walls and stone checks, sometimes enclosing a "field" no larger than an English hearth-rug, but which, in the aggregate, add up to many thousands of hectares of productive land. Many Asian countries like Indonesia and China have developed systems of grassed bunds and banks which fulfill the same purpose. In Colombia the law requires that 4% of the profits from the Upper Magdalena watershed of hydro-electric power companies should be re-invested in conservation management schemes. Part of the company's profits are channelled to mountain farmers to relieve them of their debt as they switch to the use of more sophisticated soil conservation techniques leading to the *sustainable* use of their natural resource base.

Once such systems are in place they need to be maintained regularly. They can be strengthened by reforestation, afforestation, re-seeding grassy slopes, planting the lips of terraces and introducing perennials to help to stabilize the soil. If the latter can produce food, like fruit or nut trees, so much the better. Jordan, for example, has successfully planted and nurtured colonies of fruit trees—almonds, olives, peaches, pomegranates and the like across the Jordan on the West Bank. Israel has had similar success in her so-called "settlement" areas. Gullies can be planted with elephant grass; leguminous plants and forage plants can be used to good effect—serving the double purpose of feeding animals and people as well as stabilizing the soil.

In some of these mountainous areas—like Ethiopia and parts of Central America (Guatemala, Honduras and San Salvador)—there is little dispute as to the seriousness of soil losses and the depletion of the land base. In others, especially the Himalayas, considerable scientific controversy rages as to exactly what has, and is, happening, as human (Nepalese) populations increase and forests are cut down.

It is not possible here to identify all the pros and cons in respect of this major watershed other than to note three key points. First, that the political and economic destinies of the countries comprising the Indian subcontinent are intimately related to the Himalayan watershed. Secondly, until scientists engage in more rigorous and more widespread research it can only be said that findings recently reported for and against massive depletion are likely to be location-specific and not necessarily applicable to the whole region. The region remains highly complex, ecologically speaking. Thirdly, that the *quality* of the Himalayan forests, rather than the hectares/numbers of growing trees, is likely to be the most critical factor. A recent study concludes that only 4.4% of vegetation cover of the region's accessible forest cover is of good quality. All commentators are agreed that severe environmental degradation has taken place in many regions of the Himalayas.

Irrigated croplands

In 1985, some 30% of the world's harvest came from 270 million hectares of irrigated cropland. In China 70% is the figure; in Pakistan, 80%. Egypt's dependence at 98.6% is almost total.

Such irrigated cropland faces three hazards—waterlogging, salinization and alkalinization—as a result of poor water management.

Waterlogging occurs—above or below ground—when excess water cannot escape or drain off. Except for (mainly) rice, which grows in waterlogged soil, most root crops absorb oxygen from the soil and release carbon dioxide into it. If the soil is waterlogged this respiration is impaired or if serious is impossible. In effect, plants "drown".

An even more serious hazard occurs when waterlogging combines with salinization to reduce productivity drastically. In the Euphrates Valley of Syria, for example, the annual crop loss from salinity is set at $300 millions per annum. Salts begin to accumulate on and in soils when standing water is evaporated off to leave their salt content behind. When salts build up or "load" the soil, the root systems of crops cannot function healthily. They die, poisoned.

In alkalinized soils adsorbed sodium accumulates on clay particles. When adsorbed sodium in the soil is high and salinity is low, the clay particles become unstable, cannot cling together and are easily blown away in the wind, or washed away in heavy rain. The nutritional balance in such soil is adversely affected and crops simply fail to grow.

Desertification

It is against this general background of land and soil erosion that the phenomenon of "desertification" can best be considered. Desertification, like wind erosion, salinization or soil washed off the land into the river system by rains, is just one additional form of erosion which results, as the definitions quoted above testify, from a mixture of human interference in ecosystems, leading to a depletion of the natural resource base, compounded by drought, wind and heat factors.

The driving force within the human part of the equation is essentially *poverty*. Poverty tends to lead to the growth of larger populations and a greater assault on already marginalized land as people struggle to survive. Once the essential balance is broken between people and their physical environment, social and economic forces begin to determine the process which leads to the decimation of human populations, through profound suffering. This is called "famine". There is a concomitant loss of bio-diversity and biological productivity whether the disaster is man-made or natural.

But what is a famine—so powerfully associated in people's minds with desertification? The Sudan, the Sahel, Rajasthan in India have all witnessed the classic examples of the drought—desert induced—famine syndrome that grips the public imagination, especially when the television cameras move in to record it. But Peter Walker, in his book on famine early warning systems argues that famine is a process and not an event; that it is rooted not so much in food shortages *per se* but in the social and economic conditions of a community which induce gross deprivation leading to destitution. He re-defines famine, therefore, as a "socio-economic process which causes the accelerated destitution of the most vulnerable, marginal and least powerful groups in a community, to a point where they can no longer, as a group, maintain a sustainable livelihood".

Ultimately, he continues, "the process leads to the inability of the individual to acquire sufficient food to sustain life. This is the phenomenon into which warning systems should key".

Thus desertification may be the setting in which famines occur and certainly desertification plays an important part in pushing communities over a final cliff edge. But the social process is a long one and extremely complex. People have learned how to cope with living in drought prone areas. They know how to live at minimum survival levels for years on end. There are desert plants like the "Mochette" bush in Western Sudan, or the Nara (melon) bush in Namibia, or desert grasses from which thin soups can be made. What finally tips the balance is destitution—poverty. Peter Walker reports that China may once again be facing disaster—"desertification is proceeding at a rate of 60,000 km^2/year. Desertification is on the increase and food production is decreasing". Professor Luo of the Chinese Forestry Ministry blames recent land and ownership reforms. Luo is quoted as noting "the peasant attitudes to the reforms are the key. They do not think the policies will last so why plan for the future? Make as much and spend as much now whilst you can". Until poverty is addressed by governments and the multilateral agencies with some measure of permanent success, famine will continue to haunt the lives of millions of people living in the arid and semi-arid zones of the world. So far, only 10% of African food production has benefited from the "green revolution".

Baseline data

Underlying our understanding of the process of desertification is a paucity of baseline data and information so serious that it is difficult to write authoritatively about the process. It is known that in localized areas, especially the Sahelian belt of Africa, desertification is a fact of life in that desert-like conditions expand and contract. From 1981–1984 the desert moved southwards. In 1985 it moved northwards. In both cases is played havoc with people's lives and, for countries like Mauritania, with whole economies.

It had been assumed that remote sensing devices—satelite technology—which can now monitor the Earth to an image focus of 10 metres, would help people to understand better the desertification process. But there is no panacea. Remote sensing can tell people a great deal—but not everything they need to know. It can indicate when people begin to migrate to escape desertification, ranging further and further afield in their search for food or wages. It cannot explain the years of agonized struggle they put up to resist the corrosive effect induced through increasingly depleted natural resources. Satellites can partly indicate how food crops are dwindling—but not wholly. They can describe the changing periphery of a desertified territory, but even there their images are not wholly reliable. Satellites for example cannot see the infestation of the millet head worm in the ear of an otherwise apparently healthy crop of millet. If the third rains do not arrive to wash out that infestation during the month before harvest, the entire crop is lost. This happened more than once in the Sudan in the early 1980s' drought when famine was rife.

To counter-balance this inadequacy, verification—"ground-truthing"—is needed on the ground. A network of observatories is needed to monitor and measure accurately exactly what is happening in (say) the Sahel, to soil, air, water, wind, temperature, human and animal populations, indeed all ecosystems and the interplay between them, before we can understand and then learn to cope with the science of desertification with any measure of confidence. There is little evidence that national governments or the UN system of agencies, or the multinational banks are willing to undertake this work.

The 1977 UNCOD plan of action listed what needs to be done and how it might be done in the battle against desertification. The international community, which really means the donor nations, have chosen to ignore UNCOD. Nothing fundamentally has been done since the report was published, beyond emergency disaster response. The International Geosphere-Biosphere programme envisages a hundred or so ground-truth observatories strategically placed across the Earth, but none, so far, exists, although Earthwatch has established a pathfinding model at S'Albufera on Majorca which is designed to act as a stimulus and a model to others.

The causes of desertification

Grainger identifies four main direct causes which are likely to lead to desertification. Namely, over-cultivation, over-grazing, deforestation and the mismanagement of irrigated cropland. Whilst traditional forms of agriculture can accelerate the process of desertification, the last half century has seen the growth in the developed world of high energy agriculture and gradually, through donor agencies, the imposition of that model on developing countries. High energy agriculture is based on the use of fossil fuels—for power driven machinery, for the manufacture of fertilizers, pesticides and the like.

The effect of high energy agriculture

The deliberate and planned cutting-down of forests and tree cover in Africa to make way for cash crop plantations has done far more to degrade the natural resource base of that continent than the pressure exerted on that same (local) base by indigenous African communities. Expanding village populations which exhaust their local environment are only the tip of the iceberg. The high energy agricultural model has led to major problems in North America, Western Europe, the USSR and Eastern Europe in respect of soil and land degradation, let alone in the developing world. It is not surprising, therefore, that the use of mechanical devices like disc harrows or tractor-driven ploughs on the fragile soils of Africa have precipitated soil loss through subsequent wind and rain erosion. Again the issue is complex and does not give way to simple or simplistic solutions. The soil in the Sahel, for example, is grossly deficient in phosphorous. The use of phosphate fertilizers—a product of high energy agriculture—can stimulate the root growth of crops allowing the roots to drive deeper into the soil to reach moisture beyond their unaided reach. Yet a return to the traditions of fallow farming and the annual use of organic mulching and fertilizing would do much to restore the lost balance.

The human response

In facing all the hazards arising from land and soil degradation already described, human populations have only three possible responses—massive transmigration as practised in Ethiopia and Java, (or traditionally, but increasingly difficult for obvious political, social and economic reasons, adopting a nomadic or shifting cultivation); or secondly, using techniques to assist the land to recover its productivity through *rehabilitation* or, thirdly, *restoring* degraded wildland to its former glory. Rehabilitation seeks a utilitarian response to degradation—making land productive for human populations; restoration seeks to restore an area's original bio-diversity as it was before humans began to interfere so as to destroy its ecosystems.

Appropriate techniques

Agricultural techniques of intercropping (e.g. acacia albida intercropped with sorghum and millet), alley-cropping, agroforestry and micro water-catchment in Africa and large parts of the arid Indian Sub-Continent are also beginning to play a major part in reversing current trends. It is obvious that experimental success with sand-dune stabilization through the planting of drought-resistant tree seedlings is a priority in the worst affected areas. Tree windbreaks can reduce the velocity of the wind by as much as 50%. Sheltered crops consistently produce higher yields than unsheltered crops.

In Burkina Faso, at Yatenga, Oxfam worked with the local people in the use of small stones to trap scarce rainwater. By using a transparent length of plastic hose-piping half-filled with water they learned how to lay their stone walls (only six inches high) along the contours of the land so that the rainwater could not escape, but could be directed to the crop area. The desert, here, has bloomed successfully. Yatenga now is a show piece.

Social forestry, under which village people plant and own trees outside given forest areas is bound to be part of any long-term strategy for combating desertification. Between 1950 and 1983 China increased its forest area by a spectacular 60% which included the planting and irrigation of a green shelter belt against the Gobi desert, some 1,500 km long and 12 m wide. It took 700,000 peasant farmers to plant it in just two seasons. However, only a centrally controlled bureaucracy can engage in that scale of project. Some commentators point out that the sheer scale of this particular project ensured inadequate post-planting care and maintenance. In any case, tragically in 1987 a large part of the "green belt" was destroyed by fire.

Similarly, Vietnam has mobilized village cadres to replant the defoliated mangroves of the Mekong Delta so as to protect the rice-growing hinterland from desalinization and has begun to manage on a sustainable basis the remaining forest lands also exposed by defoliation to the elements of monsoon rain, drought and wind. Children are encouraged to plant their own trees as they pass certain birthdays. But the task is enormous and Vietnam's own resources are extremely limited. The country needs substantial help from the international community.

Almost 50% of global soil losses occur on the Indian sub-continent and so it is encouraging that some considerable progress has been made through village social forestry schemes, new and carefully planned irrigation schemes, the introduction—or reintroduction—of trees to produce fuel wood, timber for local usage, fruit trees, and fodder species, often supplied free of charge by the local forestry department. Village self-help schemes are being encouraged by government and donor agencies, the early examples being stimulated by non-governmental organizations. These are both indigenous (for example Chipko) and expatriate (for example Oxfam).

But there remains a long way to go. Again, the process is complex. The role of women who often head up families and who, in Africa, are the farmers, is a central one. However, women may have no rights to land tenure, to the more equitable distribution of the benefits of successful social forestry, or knowledge of the techniques for protecting and maintaining forest lots. The accessibility of local markets and means of transporting/selling cut timber, remain daunting. So does the whole process of educating people rapidly in techniques and opportunities of integrating these new forms of social behaviour in a culturally sensitive, and thereby sustainable way. If government provides forest wardens will they be trusted by village people? Can new and reliable land tenure laws be introduced without replacing one set of problems by another? If, as in India, the army provides "free" labour and encouragement how will local communities react? Can governments, whose role is unquestionable, act without corruption and massive waste? The risks and hazards are apparently unending.

Restoring degraded land

The investment needed to rehabilitate such degraded land is substantial as the following guidelines, adapted for the World Resources Report 1988–89 from an FAO report, demonstrate.

In 1988 the International Union for the Conservation of Nature and Natural Resources (IUCN) adopted guidelines for restoring degraded lands, which had been hammered out at a science workshop on restoration ecology held in Varansi, India the previous year.

The guidelines had three principal objects: that international conservation programmes should pay more attention to the issues and threats stemming from soil and land degradation; that international development banks should sympathetically fund pilot projects for restoring such degraded land; and that ecologists should study more carefully the effects of stress and disturbance on ecosystems.

The report recommended the following:

- Critical sites—such as those especially liable to erosion, sources of saline water in the upper reaches of a watershed, or habitats of threatened and endangered species—should be rehabilitated or restored first.
- For the initial revegetation, plants should come from different successional stages to lessen the chances of natural succession being thwarted and to let slow-dispersing species be included.
- Plants that facilitate succession or maintain nutrient and water cycles should be included. Nitrogen-fixers are an important example, as are plants whose roots can penetrate beyond infertile upper soil layers.
- Because socio-economic issues may well decide the success or failure of recovery projects, social scientists should help plan them from the beginning. Local people should also be involved, some of whom may be able to contribute traditional knowledge about local plants and soils.
- Rehabilitation programmes should provide economic benefits to the participants. Incentives are better than sanctions, but if new laws regulating land use are passed, they must be enforced consistently.
- Laws and customs affecting the area under recovery should be reviewed periodically. If they are serving to degrade the environment, the people should be encouraged to change them.
- Tree plantations should be established on degraded lands rather than on undisturbed or otherwise productive tracts.
- As a corollary to recovery projects, protected areas should be set aside to conserve plant and animal wildlife species that may be needed for future rehabilitations or restoration.

Strategy to combat desertification

Ridley Nelson for the World Bank identifies a number of strategies for combating desertification. They are:

(i) Improve baseline data and information for the establishment of *permanent* national systems of land monitoring, e.g. better mapping, quality ground photography, systematic ground-based filmed video tapes, etc.
(ii) Improve technology research in dry areas, e.g. for yield increases, educating local farmers as to successful new techniques.
(iii) Increase systematic research in dry cropping and pastoral areas in farm and pastoral system studies and in the economies and risks of technologies, all to be location-specific. Nelson notes that of 7,000 sorghum species screened for superior results by ICRISAT in Burkina Faso, only nine were good enough to go to on-farm testing and only two of those were judged to be possibly superior.
(iv) Develop small-scale solutions. Because so many variables produce desertification there are no universal or magical blueprints to solve the phenomenon and it follows that small-scale, local solutions rather than huge country-wide solutions offer the best way forward. Land tenure then becomes a central issue in such a participatory, local approach. In such local initiatives, people participation, research and technology, economics, institutions and legislation all have a part to play.
(v) Address the overall policies—including both *enabling* types of incentive policies and the *variable* types of incentive policies, e.g. prices and taxes.
(vi) Consider special strategies which may need to be adopted because of low soil fertility, including population transfer or voluntary migration.
(vii) Understand the delicate balance in poor communities farming dry areas between low-risk, immediate short-term returns so as to survive, and long-term land tenure needs.

All of this argues for a continuing trade-off between varying priorities emerging under each of the strategies identified. Nelson stresses that choices are always there to be made. The strategic question he emphasizes is "what are the social and economic benefits both now, and in the future, from investing in dryland management relative to investing elsewhere".

This brings us full circle. To answer that question in respect of desertified areas calls for hugely improved and rigorously verified knowledge as to the extent and causes of desertification, the kinds of technological and institutional options available for combating desertification, which alternate land tenure systems may be available or may be agreed, what pricing structures are on offer to small-scale, relatively poor farmers, whether people participate in decision-taking, the role played by women in that process, the need for increased institutional pluralism to accommodate differing needs and challenges, the development of effective agricultural extension schemes driven by the real needs of poor farmers working in arid areas, and responding to those needs through effective communications. These are only some of the issues at stake.

It should perhaps be noted that part of the answer to desertification might well be to concentrate on producing more food for human consumption from the oceans of the world which, after all, occupy some 70% of the surface area of the globe. Sea water may also have a role to play in irrigating some plants not hitherto appreciated. Israel, for example, has secured dramatically increased yields from tomato plants by irrigating them with sea water.

One thing, however, is certain, desertification is a complex phenomenon. Scientists, and hence people generally, know far too little about it, let alone how to combat it.

For bibliography, see pp. 358–359.

6 THE LOSS OF BIOLOGICAL DIVERSITY

Jeffrey A. McNeely

Introduction

In seeking ways to conserve biological diversity, it is necessary to have a clear understanding of the major threats which face genes, species, and ecosystems on the ground and in the water. Solutions depend above all on how the problem is defined, and it appears that the **problems facing the conservation of biological diversity have tended to be defined in ways that do not lead to acceptable solutions**.

When the problems are defined in terms of insufficient protected areas, excess poaching, poor law enforcement, land encroachment and illegal trade, possible responses include establishing more protected areas, improving standards of managing species and protected areas, and enacting international legislation controlling trade in endangered species. All of these measures are necessary. But they respond only to part of the problem. Biological diversity will be conserved only partially by protected areas, wildlife management, and international conservation legislation. Fundamental problems lie beyond protected areas in sectors such as agriculture, mining, pollution, settlement patterns, capital flows, and other factors relating to the larger international economy.

This section attempts to define the problems of conserving biological diversity in a more comprehensive way, and one which will lead to more effective solutions being defined. Both problems and solutions are built on economic foundations. Major threats to bio-diversity include:

- Habitat alteration, usually from highly diverse natural ecosystems to far less diverse (often mono-culture) agroecosystems. This is clearly the most important threat, often related to land-use changes on a regional scale which involve great reduction in the area of natural vegetation; such reductions in area—often involving fragmentation of species habitats—inevitably mean reductions in populations of species, with resulting loss in genetic diversity and increase in vulnerability of species and populations to disease, hunting, and random population changes.

- Over-harvesting, the taking of individuals at a higher rate than can be sustained by the natural reproductive capacity of the population being harvested; when species are protected by law, harvesting is called "poaching".

- Chemical pollution, which has been implicated in forest damage in Europe, deformities in birds, and premature births in seals, has become a major concern in virtually all parts of the world. Chemical pollution is complex and all-pervasive. It is expressed in such different forms as: atmospheric pollution with sulphur and nitrogen oxides and with oxidants, directly damaging vegetation and harming fresh waters through the deposition of "acid rain"; excessive use of agricultural chemicals, contaminating watercourses and causing ecological imbalance in wetlands and shallow seas through the run-off of nitrate and phosphate and harming wildlife through the accumulation of persistent pesticides; and the release of many compounds of heavy metals and other toxic substances from industrial sources, with an impact on the life of land, fresh waters, and inshore seas. Such impacts are felt in different places to different extents.

- Climatic change, often related to changing regional vegetation patterns; this problem involves such factors as global carbon dioxide build-up, natural regional effects such as "El nino" and monsoon systems, and local human effects, often involving fire management. Climate change, which appears to be taking place at an exceptionally rapid rate, could have drastic effects on boreal forests, coral reefs, mangroves, and wetlands, as well as change the boundaries of the world's biomes.
- Introduced species, which on some oceanic islands have virtually replaced the native species of plants. Even reasonably well-protected islands such as Galapagos have as many introduced species of plants as native ones. Continental areas are also affected, and introduced species of plants has been identified as one of the most serious threats facing the US national park system. Animals are not immune to such threats; for example, in some of the African Rift Valley lakes, which have remarkably high levels of endemism among fish, introduced species of fish have threatened most native species with extinction. Mongooses, snakes, and other introduced animals can rather quickly lead to the extinction of the native fauna, while introduced herbivores such as goats and even reindeer can extinguish the native flora.
- Increase in human population, accompanying the industrial revolution, global trade, harnessing of fossil fuels, and more effective public health measures. Our species reached a population of one billion at the beginning of the 19th century, reached two billion in the 1920s, and totals over five billion today. Optimists predict that a combination of development, education, the provision of reproductive health services and intelligent self-control will cause the population to level off at around eight to ten billion in the latter part of the next century. A dispassionate external observer must question whether such a population is sustainable, given the degradation in the resource base that has accompanied the current population increase. The danger that the raw forces of nature—drought, flood, famine, strife, and disease—will dominate in at least some regions will certainly continue to place very heavy demands on biological resilience. It is apparent that the longer it takes people to limit their fertility, the more certain it is that misery will prevail.

The above list of major threats is primarily a list of the symptoms rather than a description of the fundamental problems which lead to these threats. While the specifics of the problems will vary from place to place, the main source of all these symptoms can be found in the distribution of costs and benefits of both exploitation and conservation. Those who have reaped the benefits from exploitation have not paid the full costs, and those who have paid most of the costs of conservation (especially opportunity costs) have gained few of the benefits.

Ultimately, the solution is to redress this imbalance through ensuring that exploiters pay the full costs of their exploitation, and that conservers earn more of the benefits of their actions. This requires a more comprehensive perspective on conservation and development, and a more integrated approach to decision making.

The dimensions of the problem

While the various threats to bio-diversity tend to be cumulative in their effects, it is informative to look more closely at the manifestations of these threats on species and habitats (realizing how closely intertwined species are with their habitats). It is important to bear in mind that of the estimated 1.4 million species currently described, only about 400,000 are from tropical habitats—the most species-rich formations on earth; and without understanding the parts of the system, it is difficult to understand the systems themselves. Our ignorance of tropical organisms and ecosystems is vast.

Species

Extinction has been a fact of life since life first emerged from the primordial ooze. The present few million species are the modern-day survivors of the estimated several billion species that have ever existed. All past extinctions have occurred by natural processes, but today humans are overwhelmingly the main cause.

The average duration of a vertebrate species is some five million years. The best current estimates are that on average 900,000 vertebrate species have become extinct every one million years during the last 200 million years, so the average "background rate" of extinction has been very roughly 90 species of vertebrates each century. Norman Myers' *Deforestation Rates in Tropical Forests and their Climatic Implications* suggests a crude estimate for higher plants of about one species becoming extinct every 27 years over the past 400 million years, with the rate increasing in more recent times as the number of species of higher plant has increased. Within the last few hundred years, major waves of human-caused extinctions have washed over oceanic islands, in large part due to the destruction of lowland forests, and to the introduction of mammalian predators and herbivores, diseases and aggressive plants. About 75% of the mammals and birds that have become extinct in recent history were island-dwelling species, and even more island extinctions are likely. Over 10% of the world's species of birds are each confined to a single island. Similarly, the island floras tend to be far more endangered than the continental ones and on several islands (Ascension, Lord Howe, Norfolk, Rodrigues, and St Helena) more than 90% of the endemic vascular plant species are rare, threatened or extinct (see Table 1).

The rapid destruction of the world's most diverse ecosystems, especially in the tropics, has led most experts to conclude that perhaps a quarter of the earth's total biological diversity is at serious risk of extinction during the next 20–30 years. By many indications, the world is already experiencing extinction rates that are of greater scale and impact than at any previous time in the earth's history. More species than ever before are threatened with extinction, with thousands—mostly insects— disappearing each year, many before they are even described. A recent comprehensive review of the world's avifauna concluded that of the globe's 9,000 birds, over 1,000 (11%) were at some risk of extinction, up from just 290 bird species threatened in 1978 (these increases are at least partially due to more complete information becoming available in the past several years).

Table 1: *Status of endemic vascular plant taxa on selected oceanic islands*

Island	*Total*	*Not threatened*	*Insufficiently known*	*Rare, threatened or extinct*
Ascension Island	11	0	1	10 (91%)
Azores	56	14	10	32 (57%)
Canary Islands	612	169	36	407 (67%)
Galapagos	222	89	3	130 (59%)
Juan Fernandez	119	6	17	95 (81%)
Lord Howe Island	78	2	1	75 (96%)
Madeira	129	23	19	87 (67%)
Mauritius	280	31	18	194 (69%)
Norfolk Island	48	1	2	45 (94%)
Rodrigues	55	3	2	50 (91%)
St Helena	49	0	2	47 (96%)
Seychelles*	90	0	1	72 (81%)
Socotra	215	81	2	132 (61%)

* refers to granitic islands only
Source: Davis *et al.*, 1986

The World Conservation Monitoring Centre (WCMC), based in Cambridge, UK, is the major repository of data on threatened species. Using the Red Data Book categories established by IUCN (see Table 2 and Part IV), it has recorded the degree of threat to some 60,000 plants and 2,000 animals. These categories have received some criticism, particularly on the grounds that they can only be used where full data are available on the decline of a species, and on the threats to its survival, throughout its entire range. Such knowledge is available for relatively few taxa. Tony Whitten (*Conservation Biology*), for example, discovered in the course of his work in compiling information on the natural history of Sulawesi (Indonesia) that the Caerulean paradise-flycatcher *(Eutrichomyias rowleyi)* had not been seen in several decades, nor were recent records to be found for many of the endemic species of the fish family *Adrianichtyidae*; at least seven other species of endemic Sulawesi birds had apparently not been observed in over a decade, but had not found their way into Red Data Books. Further, the Red Data Books cannot be expected to deal with the tropical forest invertebrates, of which millions of species are undescribed but are certainly under threat as habitats are cleared out from under them. Jared Diamond *(Conservation Biology)* has pointed out that even the lists that do exist include primarily species known to be threatened and suggests instead that species must be presumed extinct or endangered unless shown to be extant and secure; such a "Green List" might be much shorter than RDB lists. Further, considerable taxonomic issues still remain, and some populations which are now considered subspecies may in fact be full species.

To cope with tropical plants, the IUCN Plant Information Plan proposed the listing of extinction-prone species, defined as species that are confined to endangered vegetation types, as well as of threatened species falling into Red Data Book categories. It also proposed the identification of plant-rich sites for conservation, as a further way of identifying threatened plant diversity. The information in Red Data Books and threatened species

Table 2: *IUCN Categories of threat*

EXTINCT (Ex): Species not definitely located in the wild during the past 50 years (criterion as used by CITES).

ENDANGERED (E): Taxa (species and sub-species) in danger of extinction and whose survival is unlikely if the causal factors continue operating.

Included are taxa whose numbers have been reduced to a critical level or whose habitats have been so drastically reduced that they are deemed to be in immediate danger of extinction. Also included are taxa that are possibly already extinct but have definitely been seen in the wild in the past 50 years.

VULNERABLE (V): Taxa believed likely to move into the "endangered" category in the near future if the causal factors continue operating.

Included are taxa of which most or all the populations are decreasing because of over-exploitation, extensive destruction of habitat or other environmental disturbance; taxa with populations that have been seriously depleted and whose ultimate security has not yet been assured; the taxa with populations that are still abundant but are under threat from severe adverse factors throughout their range.

RARE (R): Taxa with small world populations that are not at present "endangered" or "vulnerable", but are at risk.

These taxa are usually localized within restricted geographical areas or habitats or are thinly scattered over a more extensive range.

INDETERMINATE (I): Taxa *known* to be "endangered", "vulnerable" or "rare" but where there is not enough information to say which of the three categories is appropriate.

Note: In practice, "endangered" and "vulnerable" categories may include, temporarily, taxa whose populations are beginning to recover as a result of remedial action, but whose recovery is insufficient to justify their transfer to another category.

lists should, therefore, be taken as only indicating part of the problem. The full picture is far worse.

Finally, recent work has indicated that the concept of rarity is far more complex than is represented in the Red Data Books. One authority (Rabinowitz *et. al.*) has suggested no less than seven forms of rarity for plants, based on three factors:

- Geographic range: does a species occur over a broad area or is it endemic to a particular small area?
- Habitat specificity: does a species occur in a variety of habitats or is it restricted to one or a few specialized sites?
- Local population size: is a species found in large populations somewhere within its range or does it have small populations wherever it is found?

While these factors are really continuous variables, they can be broken down into the categories in Table 3. In this model, the only set which can be considered common in the ordinary sense are those with wide ranges, many habitats, and large population sizes; all others are rare. Species with narrow distribution, specialized habitat, and small numbers (type G in Table 3) are the ones which are "rare" in the public mind, but species sharing

Table 3: *Forms of rarity*

Geographic distribution	*Wide*		*Narrow*	
Habitat specificity	Broad	Restricted	Broad	Restricted
Local population size:				
Somewhere large	COMMON	RARE (A)	RARE (B)	RARE (C)
Everywhere small	RARE (D)	RARE (E)	RARE (F)	RARE (G)

Source: Rabinowitz *et al.*, 1986

six other combinations of attributes should also be considered rare and deserving of special management attention.

The different forms of rarity have considerable practical relevance for conservation biology, helping to determine the management strategy employed and the priority allocated to certain species. For example, "endemic rarities" of type C in Table 3 might focus on protecting the specific habitat where the species occurs, endemic rarities of type G might call for attempting to reintroduce the species to appropriate habitats elsewhere, and the management strategy for "patchily-distributed rarities" of type E might focus on legal restrictions on trade and direct consumption. Patchily-distributed rarities of type D, which occur in small populations over a wide geographic range in a variety of habitats, are likely to become endangered only in the face of widespread habitat destruction and therefore deserve relatively low priority for management attention. Clearly, the great attention which conservationists pay to endemic species is well justified, as these narrowly-distributed species are easily threatened by habitat destruction or over-exploitation. Conserving habitats remains the most effective way to conserve species, and conservationists concerned with rare species need to consider geographic range, habitat specificity, and local abundance in their assessments.

The very real limitations in the level of current understanding about the concept of rarity and its causes can be increasingly overcome by advances in knowledge and field techniques. In the meantime, the concept of threatened species has been a very effective instrument in promoting conservation of biological diversity. Keeping the limitations in mind, Table 4 presents the current state of knowledge of threatened species, held by WCMC.

Even many animal species which are not in immediate danger of extinction are suffering from declining populations and declining genetic variability. While some wild species—sparrows, starlings, opposums, rats, raccoons, coyotes, white-tailed deer, and other opportunists—are expanding their ranges and populations, far more are suffering catastrophic population crashes. Low populations make species far more vulnerable to disease, climate change, habitat alteration, inbreeding, and many other factors which can threaten their survival. Declining populations also have important implications for development, as reduced populations have less potential for utilization. Where heavy hunting pressures, for example, have reduced populations of game animals to levels far below the carrying capacity of the habitat, the economic benefits of harvesting are much less than they would be with harvesting at a sustainable yield level which maintains the harvested population at the carrying capacity of the habitat.

The planet is also being impoverished by the loss of races and varieties within domes-

Table 4: *Current status of threatened species*

	Ex	*E*	*V*	*R*	*I*	*Total globally threatened taxa*
Plants	384	3325	3022	6749	5598	19077
Fish	23	81	135	83	21	342
Amphibians	2	9	9	20	10	48
Reptiles	21	37	39	41	32	149
Invertebrates	97	221	234	188	614	1318
Birds	113	111	67	122	624	1029
Mammals	83	172	141	37	64	441

Key: Ex = Extinct (post-1600), E = Endangered, V = Vulnerable, R = Rare, I = Indeterminate
Source: Nilssen, 1983; WCMC, 1988

ticated species. The variety of genetic riches inherent in one single species can be seen in the variability manifested in the many races of dogs, cats, cattle, or horses, or the many specialized types of potatoes, apples, or maize developed by breeders. But whole races or cultivars are being lost at a rate that quickly reduces their genetic variability and thus their ability to adapt to climatic change, disease, or other forms of environmental adversity. The remaining cultivated gene pools in the major crop plants such as maize and rice amount to only a fraction of the genetic diversity they harboured only a few decades ago, even though the species themselves are anything but threatened and the various seed banks still retain many of the previously-cultivated forms; but little evolution and adaptation can take place in a seed bank. Thus for biological resources both loss of species and loss of gene reservoirs are significant, and many agriculturalists argue that the loss of genetic diversity among domestic plants and animals looms as an even greater threat to human welfare than does the loss of wild species.

The hidden danger of ever-growing lists of threatened species is that individual recovery efforts are diluted each time a new plant or animal is added to the list. Some have called for greater attention to be given to a more broad-based ecosystem approach aimed at preventing species from becoming endangered, because it is easier and more cost-effective to protect intact, functioning ecosystems with all their species than to initiate emergency conservation measures for one endangered species after another, or to wait until common species become endangered before acting to save them.

On the other hand, the ecosystem approach can sometimes ignore the role of individual species in favour of processes and community organization; therefore, a species-specific approach is required to address the needs of taxa that might not otherwise have been neglected. The Red Data Books have been very important in drawing public attention to the conservation needs of a number of such species.

Habitats

According to one estimate, almost 40% of the net primary terrestrial productivity (associated with plants, algae, and photosynthetic bacteria) is directly consumed, diverted, or wasted as a result of human activities. This estimate provides an excellent indication of how powerful is the ecological influence of humans on our planet. For many centuries, landscapes have been altered and simplified by humans through deforestation, fire and pastoralism.

Tropical moist forests cover only 7% of the Earth's land surface but contain at least half of the Earth's species; and if estimates of the millions of undescribed forest beetles are

Table 5: *Estimates of forest areas and deforestation rates in the tropics*

Country	*Closed forest area (1,000 ha)*	*% deforested per year*
Tropical Africa		
Côte d'Ivoire	4,458	6.5
Nigeria	5,950	5.0
Rwanda	120	2.7
Burundi	26	2.7
Benin	47	2.6
Guinea-Bissau	660	2.6
Liberia	2,000	2.3
Guinea	2,050	1.8
Kenya	1,105	1.7
Madagascar	10,300	1.5
Angola	2,900	1.5
Uganda	765	1.3
Zambia	3,010	1.3
Ghana	1,718	1.3
Mozambique	935	1.1
Sierra Leone	740	0.8
Tanzania	1,440	0.7
Togo	304	0.7
Sudan	650	0.6
Chad	500	0.4
Cameroon	17,920	0.4
Ethiopia	4,350	0.2
Somalia	1,540	0.2
Equatorial Guinea	1,295	0.2
Zaïre	105,750	0.2
Central African Republic	3,590	0.1
Gabon	20,500	0.1
Congo	21,340	0.1
Zimbabwe	200	*
Namibia	*	*
Botswana	*	*
Mali	*	*
Burkina Faso	*	*
Niger	*	*
Senegal	220	*
Malawi	186	*
Gambia	65	*
TOTALS	*216,634*	*0.61*

Table 5: *Cont.*

Country	*Closed forest area (1,000 ha)*	*% deforested per year*
Tropical America		
Paraguay	4,070	4.7
Costa Rica	1,638	4.0
Haiti	48	3.8
El Salvador	141	3.2
Jamaica	67	3.0
Nicaragua	4,496	2.7
Ecuador	14,250	2.4
Honduras	3,797	2.4
Guatemala	4,442	2.0
Colombia	46,400	1.8
Mexico	46,250	1.3
Panama	4,165	0.9
Belize	1,354	0.7
Dominican Republic	629	0.6
Trinidad & Tobago	208	0.4
Peru	69,680	0.4
Brazil	357,480	0.4
Venezuela	31,870	0.4
Bolivia	44,010	0.2
Cuba	1,455	0.1
French Guinea	8,900	*
Surinam	14,830	*
Guyana	18,475	*
TOTALS	*678,655*	*0.6*
Tropical Asia		
Nepal	1,941	4.3
Sri Lanka	1,659	3.5
Thailand	9,235	2.7
Brunei	323	1.5
Malaysia	20,995	1.2
Laos	8,410	1.2
Philippines	9,510	1.0
Bangladesh	927	0.9
Vietnam	8,770	0.7
Indonesia	113,895	0.5
Pakistan	2,185	0.3
Burma	31,941	0.3
Kampuchea	7,548	0.3
India	51,841	0.3
Bhutan	2,100	0.1
Papu New Guinea	34,230	0.1
TOTALS	*305,510*	*0.6*

*No data; in most cases this is where the areas are very small
Source: FAO, 1981. Most other sources consider these figures to be far below actual rates of deforestation.

accurate, they could contain 90% or even more of all species. Some sites are extraordinarily rich; Tim Whitmore counted 233 species of vascular plants in just 100 square meters of a lowland tropical rainforest in Costa Rica, equivalent to about one-sixth the total flora of the British Isles on half the area of a singles tennis court.

Surprisingly, no estimate on the amount of tropical forest remaining has been generally agreed, with figures ranging from 8 million to 12 million sq km. However, it is apparent that deforestation is continuing at a rapid pace, with very conservative estimates suggesting rates as high as 6.5% per year in Côte d'Ivoire and averaging about 0.6% per year (about 6.1 million hectares) for all tropical countries (see Table 5); at this rate, which is a net figure incorporating reforestation and natural regrowth, all tropical forests would be cleared within 177 years. Other figures are much higher. The Brazilian Space Research Institute has reported that forest fires in 1987 destroyed 200,000 sq km of Brazilian forest, including 80,000 sq km of primary rainforest; these figures exceed the FAO figures for the entire world. Norman Myers concludes that some 142,200 sq km of tropical forests were lost in 1989, a level 90% higher than the 1979 figure.

These latter figures are not universally accepted, and indeed estimates of world forest cover and deforestation rates suffer from a surprising lack of firm statistics. Since so much conservation action depends on sound data, and because remote sensing technology is available for providing fairly precise estimates, a global study would seem a very high priority. A systematic assessment of current forests and deforestation rates for the entire tropics could be carried out for about $5 million per year.

Since the information base is so poor, figures on how long it will take for all tropical forest to disappear can only be indicative estimates. The American botanist Peter Raven, for example, suggests that about 48% of the world's plant species occur in or around forest areas that are going to be destroyed over more than 90% of their area during the next 20 years, leading to about a quarter of those species being lost. Further, as deforestation becomes a more severe problem and the accessible forests are exploited, harvesting rates (and income from forestry exports) tend to slow down. Many major tropical timber exporters of the 1960s and 1970s have stopped exporting, and some—such as Thailand—are now even net importers.

But given the projected growth in both human population and economic activity, the rate of deforestation is far more likely to increase than stabilize. The World Commission on Environment and Development concluded that by the end of the century, or shortly thereafter, little old growth tropical moist forest apart from protected areas may remain outside of the Zaïre Basin, the extreme north-east Brazilian Amazonia adjacent to the southern Guianas, western Amazonia, the Guianan tract of forest in northern South America and parts of the island of New Guinea. The accessible forests in these zones are unlikely to survive beyond a few further decades, as world demand for their produce continues to expand. Forests on steep slopes, on the other hand, are quite likely to endure even very dense human populations because of their inaccessibility and their important economic functions in protecting watersheds.

The dimensions of these habitat changes have been assessed for Sub-Saharan Africa and Tropical Asia (see Tables 6 and 7). The implications of these habitat changes for primates in Tropical Asia are summarized in Table 7. In these tables, "original habitat" was determined on the basis of vegetation maps prepared by UNESCO for Africa and tropical Asia. These maps depict the ideal climax vegetation based on climatic, elevation, and edaphic factors, without significant human intervention and usually correspond to the area of the country;

Table 6: *Wildlife habitat loss in Africa South of the Sahara*

Country	*Original wildlife habitat (sq km)*	*Amount remaining (sq km)*	*Habitat loss (%)*
Angola	1,246,700	760,847	39
Benin	115,800	46,320	60
Botswana	585,400	257,576	56
Burkina Faso	273,800	54,760	80
Burundi	25,700	3,589	86
Cameroon	469,400	192,454	59
Central African Republic	623,000	274,120	56
Chad	720,800	172,992	76
Congo	342,000	174,420	49
Côte d'Ivoire	318,000	66,780	79
Djibouti	21,800	11,118	49
Equatorial Guinea	25,000	9,200	63
Ethiopia	1,101,003	30,300	70
Gabon	267,000	173,550	35
Gambia	11,300	1,243	89
Ghana	230,000	46,000	80
Guinea	245,900	73,770	70
Guinea Bissau	36,100	7,942	78
Kenya	569,500	296,140	48
Lesotho	30,400	9,728	68
Liberia	111,400	14,482	87
Madagascar	595,211	148,803	75
Malawi	94,100	40,463	57
Mali	754,100	158,361	79
Mauritania	388,600	73,834	81
Mozambique	783,203	36,776	57
Namibia	823,200	444,528	46
Niger	566,000	127,880	77
Nigeria	919,800	229,950	75
Rwanda	25,100	3,263	87
Senegal	196,200	35,316	82
Sierra Leone	71,700	10,755	85
Somalia	637,700	376,243	41
South Africa	1,236,500	531,695	57
Sudan	1,703,000	510,900	70
Swaziland	17,400	7,656	56
Tanzania	886,200	505,134	43
Togo	56,000	19,040	66
Uganda	193,700	42,614	78
Zaïre	2,335,900	1,051,155	55
Zambia	752,600	534,346	29
Zimbabwe	390,200	171,688	56
TOTAL	20,797,441	8,340,920	65

Note: Data for Mauritania, Mali, Niger, Chad, and Sudan cover only the Sub-Saharan portion of those countries. Islands other than Madagascar are not included.

Source: IUCN/UNEP, 1986b

Table 7: *Wildlife habitat loss in tropical Asia*

Country	*Original wildlife habitat (sq km)*	*Amount remaining (sq km)*	*Habitat loss (%)*
Bangladesh	142,776	8,567	94
Bhutan	34,500	22,770	34
Brunei	5,764	4,381	24
Burma	774,817	225,981	71
China[a]	423,066	164,996	61
Hong Kong	1,066	32	97
India	3,017,009	615,095	80
Indonesia	1,446,433	746,861	49
Japan[b]	320	138	57
Kampuchea	180,879	43,411	76
Laos	236,746	68,656	71
Malaysia & Singapore	356,254	210,190	41
Nepal	117,075	53,855	54
Pakistan	165,900	39,816	76
Philippines	308,211	64,724	79
Sri Lanka	64,700	10,999	83
Taiwan	36,961	10,719	71
Thailand	507,267	130,039	74
Vietnam	332,116	66,423	80
TOTAL	8,169,860	2,487,683	68

Notes:
[a]Tropical portion only (i.e. area south of Yunnan high hills, including the southern coastal strip and the island of Hainan)
[b]Tropical portion only (i.e. southern Ryuku archipelago)
Source: IUCN/UNEP

the estimates of natural habitat remaining were derived from a wide variety of sources of variable accuracy, so the figures should be taken as indicative rather than definitive.

Despite these disclaimers, it is apparent from the figures presented in Tables 6 and 7 that original wildlife habitat has been greatly reduced in virtually all nations in the Old World Tropics; only Angola, Congo, Djibouti, Gabon, Kenya, Namibia, Somalia, Tanzania, and Zambia in Africa, and Bhutan, Brunei, and Malaysia in Asia have lost less than 50% of their wildlife habitat. From the species point of view, habitat losses for South-east Asian primates (which can be taken as reasonable indicators of the other fauna and flora in the region) have been significant (Table 8). But the impacts on species varies considerably; compare the primates from densely-populated Java (Javan Gibbon and Javan Lutong) and Indochina (Francois' Leaf Monkey) with those from sparsely-populated Mentawai islands (Mentawai Gibbon).

If adequate information on the status and value of forest land is available, out of a sense of enlightened self-interest, the governments of the tropical countries will wish to stabilize the area of forest at an amount which enables them to meet national development goals of watershed protection, tourism, firewood, construction, and species conservation.

Table 8: *Range loss and habitat protected for selected primates in South-East Asia*

Species	*Original range (sq km)*	*Remaining range (sq km)*	*(%) loss*	*(%) protected*
Orangutan	553,000	207,000	63	2.1
Siamang	465,110	169,800	63	6.8
Agile gibbon	532,270	184,345	65	3.7
White-handed gibbon	280,700	100,240	64	13.5
Bornean gibbon	395,000	253,000	36	5.1
Mentawai gibbon	6,500	4,500	31	22.9
Javan gibbon	43,274	1,608	96	1.3
Indochinese gibbon	349,330	87,532	75	3.1
Burmese gibbon	168,353	56,378	67	5.1
Pileated gibbon	70,000	11,200	84	9.9
Long-tailed macaque	383,181	123,315	68	3.4
Pig-tailed macaque	1,568,623	481,685	69	4.1
Stump-tailed macaque	1,546,964	556,466	64	3.7
Assamese macaque	802,193	335,002	59	2.5
Rhesus macaque	1,732,270	568,638	67	2.8
Proboscis monkey	29,496	17,750	40	4.1
Snub-nosed langur	29,688	9,060	70	1.5
Douc langur	296,000	72,270	76	3.1
Javan lutong	43,274	1,608	96	1.6
Silvered langur	412,170	169,970	59	3.9
Francois' leaf monkey	97,400	14,106	86	1.2
Phayre's leaf monkey	708,572	193,172	73	3.8

Source: IUCN, 1986

Responsible governments today are constantly seeking ways to ensure that forestry can contribute to the development goals of the nation; the Tropical Forestry Action Plan, prepared by FAO in collaboration with World Bank, UNDP, and World Resources Institute in co-operation with other institutions, specifies the kinds of actions that are required.

But tropical forests are far from the only highly diverse ecosystems. Mediterranean-climate regions (that is, with a cool, wet winter and a hot, dry summer) also have very rich floras with high levels of endemism. For example: the Cape Region of South Africa has about 8,600 species of plants, of which 68% are endemic, California has 5,000 plants (30% endemic), the Mediterranean basin has 25,000 species of plants (about 50% endemic to only one country), and South-west Australia has 3,600 plants (with about 68% endemic to the region). In temperate woodlands soils, species diversity may approach 1,000 species of animals per square metre, with populations exceeding two million individuals. When microfloral communities are added, the numbers are even more impressive.

While wetlands are not noted for high species diversity or endemism (particularly because they tend to be somewhat more ephemeral than most other ecosystems), they do comprise very complex ecosystems and some old lakes display very high diversity indeed. The great lakes of the African Rift Valley each contain more species than any other lakes in the world, with very high levels of endemism. Lake Tanganyika has more than 140 endemic species, Lake Victoria has over 200 endemics, and Lake Malawi has at least 500 endemic species (with nearly as many more estimated to still be described).

Biological diversity in marine ecosystems is also remarkable, and indeed coral reefs are sometimes compared with tropical forests in terms of diversity. Marine ecosystems are far more diverse than terrestrial ones at the higher taxonomic levels. For example, only 11 phyla occur on land (one endemic) while 28 phyla (13 endemic) are found in the seas. Further, filter feeders, especially zooplankton, create extra levels in aquatic food chains that do not exist on land, and the oceans contain far greater diversity in body size—from whales to picoplankton—than is found on land. Consequently, aquatic food webs tend to be more complex than terrestrial ones and aquatic food chains contain more tropic levels. In addition, marine organisms are highly diverse at the genetic level. All of these factors give coastal and marine ecosystems a form of diversity that differs from terrestrial systems, often requiring different approaches to conservation.

Conclusion

Highly diverse ecosystems are found in many parts of the world, and all ecosystems make important contributions to human welfare. Conservation action is required at local, national, and international levels.

At the local level, greater responsibility must be given to the people whose livelihoods require conserving the forests and wildlife resources upon which they depend. This may require giving them forms of ownership or control over their resources, providing training and expertise, and ensuring that government policies promote conservation rather than over-consumption (for example, through economic incentives).

At the national level, protected areas remain the most important conservation tools for conserving natural ecosystems. But effective conservation of these ecosystems is unlikely to come only from direct protection of small samples of them if the remainder are over-exploited. Governments seeking to implement conservation programmes more effectively will need to supplement their protected area programmes with improved policies which deal with other resource management issues having major impacts on management of species and ecosystems. These "non-conservation sectors" such as communications, defence, forestry, energy, and agricultural development, may have a far greater impact on bio-diversity than do the traditional conservation sectors, so they need to be integrated into national conservation programmes.

Finally, since many of the forces causing over-exploitation are international (such as commodities trade, development assistance, tourism, etc.), international co-operation needs to be expanded to ensure that the best available conservation technology is made available to the nations that most need it. A global convention for the conservation of biological diversity would be one means of promoting such co-operation.

For bibliography, see pp. 359–360.

7 MARINE POLLUTION

Alasdair D. McIntyre

Introduction

Pollution is a highly emotive word, and it is useful that some years ago the United Nations Group of Experts on the Scientific Aspects of Marine Pollution (GESAMP) formulated a definition which has been widely accepted and used in the protocols of several international conventions. GESAMP defines marine pollution as "the introduction by Man, directly or indirectly, of substances or energy into the marine environment (including estuaries) resulting in such deleterious effects as harm to living resources, hazards to human health, hindrance to marine activities including fishing, impairment of quality for use of seawater, and reduction of amenities".

Attention may be drawn to two important aspects of this definition. First, it places the responsibility for pollution firmly on the actions of Man, so that natural inputs to the sea, arising for example from underwater techtonic activity, volcanoes or storms, are excluded. Second, it indicates that pollution implies some adverse effect and thus makes an implicit distinction between pollution on the one hand, and what may be called "contamination" on the other. On this view, the input of material by Man which increased the concentration of some substance beyond the existing natural level, but did not result in any adverse effect on the ecosystem, would not be regarded as pollution, a distinction which some find useful.

In considering the definition, it is also worth drawing attention to its wide-ranging nature, including as it does, reference to interference with activities and reduction of amenity, and thus going far beyond simply the immediate effects of chemicals.

This section takes as its starting point the GESAMP definition of marine pollution. It first makes a general examination of the sources of pollution, then considers several of the main categories, and attempts to assess their effects. Finally, it looks at the mechanisms by which pollution of the sea can be controlled.

Sources of marine pollution

Since pollution is generated by human activity it could be expected in its most extreme form to be associated with major aggregations of people and this is found to be the case. The main pollution problems occur along the margins of the seas around large cities and industrial complexes, and in the vicinity of the mouths of large rivers draining highly populated or intensively cultivated areas.

The open sea

The open oceans on the other hand are relatively clean, the main sources of contamination there being from shipping and from the atmosphere. Contamination can be detected along the major shipping routes of the world, with particular emphasis on oil. Surveys of oil slicks and tar balls on the global oceans clearly highlight concentrations especially along the lines of heaviest tanker traffic. As well as oil, ships' domestic discharges, discarded litter and leaching of anti-foulants from paint all contribute to open ocean contamination. Hazardous cargoes other than oil which are transported at sea include sulphur, fertilizers, petrochemicals, caustic soda, acids and various pesticides and weedkillers. All such cargoes represent potential threats to the marine environment as a result of shipwrecks or collisions. In recent years there has been a significant drop in the volume of oil moved by sea as a result of economic and political reactions and in consequence accidental oil spills have declined significantly. A second factor operating in favour of reduced pollution from shipping is the strengthening of international controls, a point referred to in more detail later.

The second source of contaminating inputs to the open ocean, the atmosphere, is more difficult to control. A wide range of materials in soluble or particulate form is transported round the world in the air masses, and much of this eventually ends up in the ocean by wet or dry deposition. The material is derived from industrial emissions, from fuel combustion, from waste disposal, from application of pesticides and from many other activities. It is not easy to obtain exact estimates of the input to the sea from the atmosphere, partly because of the problems of obtaining contamination-free samples of precipitation, and partly because of the difficulty of calculating the net flux at the air-sea interface. In addition, concentrations in the open ocean tend to be so low that very careful chemical analysis is required.

Some pollutants are much more susceptible to atmospheric transport and deposition than others. Among the metals, for example, most of the lead in the open sea enters from the atmosphere, also much of the dissolved cadmium, copper, iron and zinc, and significant quantities of arsenic and nickel. For synthetic organic compounds, the atmosphere accounts for the oceanic input of over 80% of such substances as PCBs and DDT, and for an important part of the polynuclear aromatic hydrocarbons. Of the nutrients, the atmospheric input of nitrogen to the ocean is considerably greater than the net input from rivers, but this does not hold for phosphorus.

The atmospheric contribution is highly diffuse, and even when there is a point source in the open ocean such as from a shipwreck, the rapid dispersion and dilution taking place is such that concentrations are rapidly reduced to very low levels, and in general are well below any level which would be expected to damage living organisms. It may be concluded therefore that while the open sea is contaminated, it is not polluted.

Shelf and coastal waters

In coastal waters, however, sources are multiple and the situation is very different. In addition to the continuing rise in world population, there is an increasing migration to the margins of the seas, and major problems arise from the consequent urbanization and industrialization of the coastal zone. Three-quarters of the world's cities with more than four million people are concentrated along the coasts. The construction of harbours, commercial and industrial installations, hotels and recreational facilities such as marinas means that large stretches of the coast are built over, wetlands drained, and natural habitats lost. In the Mediterranean, for example, 42% of the coast of Spain is now taken up by tourist construction while in the French Riviera and round Alexandria, Athens, Istanbul, Marseilles and Naples 90% of the coast is developed. This pattern is repeated around the world, and in some regions an additional feature is the expansion of mariculture. In

Indonesia almost 30% of the mangrove area was converted to fish ponds or agricultural land in the decade up to 1980 and it is estimated that a further 25% will be lost by the end of the century. In Bangladesh about 18% of the total mangrove area has been denuded for shrimp culture and thousands of acres of mangroves have been lost from the same cause in India. Shrimp culture is also the main driving force for coastal reclamation in the south-east Pacific, where the mangrove forests of Panama are being depleted at a rate of 1% per year, and a similar situation exists in both Ecuador and Colombia.

The loss of wetlands and other coastal habitats has a variety of adverse consequences which must be balanced against the benefits of development. These habitats are an essential component of the shallow water marine ecosystem. They provide feeding and nursery grounds for invertebrates and fish, including many species of commercial importance; turtles need sandy beaches for egg deposition and many marine mammals use coastal areas as haul-out sites in the breeding season. The wetlands not only contribute significantly to the productivity of the shallow waters, they also offer protection, filtering out contaminants from the land and shielding the coast from erosion. The loss of these habitats around the world as a result of human activities must be regarded as pollution in the broadest sense.

It is important also to note that it is not just developments directly at the land-sea interface that can damage the coast. Human activities far back in the hinterland and in the mountains can have repercussions on the shore. This applies in particular to the manipulation of hydrological cycles—the building of dams and the diversion of water for flood control or irrigation. In the 1960s there were many dam-building programmes around the world and up to 55 schemes were completed every year. Since then such activity has increased, and now at least 20% of the freshwater run-off from the continents of Africa and North America originates from impoundments. In Europe and Asia the comparable figure is around 15% while in Australasian and South American regions, although the percentage is lower, it is still significant.

The reduced flow of water following dam construction can have major effects on the salinity regime at the coast, increasing the intrusion of saltwater into estuaries and altering conditions for natural communities along the shore. Severe damage has been reported, for example, to mangrove swamps and rainforests in the deltas of the Niger and the Indus as a result of saltwater intrusion, and in many parts of the world there have been adverse effects on fish and invertebrates which depend on areas of fresh and saltwater mixing for reproduction. In the Black Sea, reduction of brackish water areas as a result of lowered freshwater flow has caused loss of commercial fisheries, and similar problems have been experienced in San Francisco Bay. The flow of nutrients and sediments to the sea is also altered, and this can inhibit fisheries (as off the Nile in the eastern Mediterranean) as well as cause coastal erosion.

Other activities in the hinterland which affect the coast include a range of land-use practices, particularly deforestation which, in contrast to the effects of dams, can result in increased flow of sediments to the coast, again changing the natural characteristics of the region. Off the Philippines, for example, there is a clear correlation between deforestation in the uplands and the death of corals offshore, killed by increased sedimentation of particulate material.

While the issues discussed above may be seen as the general consequences of coastal development, there are other more specific activities which should be considered, in particular the disposal of waste waters, which reach the sea directly from coastal outfalls or indirectly via rivers. Often domestic sewage and industrial effluents are mixed in sewerage systems and are discharged to the sea as municipal waste water. This contains microorganisms, organic matter, nutrients, metals, synthetic organic compounds and petroleum-related components. Such waste water discharges can threaten public health and affect all parts of the marine ecosystem.

As well as direct discharges to the coastal zone, there are disposal operations which involve the dumping at sea of dredged material, industrial wastes and sewage sludges. The dredging of harbours and waterways to keep them navigable is a continuous procedure around the world and every year over 200 million tonnes of dredge spoil are disposed of at sea, representing about 20% of all such material. Some 90% of this is uncontaminated and its main impact is from its bulk, which causes physical smothering. The remainder of the spoil however contains contaminants such as oil, metals, nutrients and organochlorine compounds. This contaminated material must be disposed of with great care, since it will slowly release its absorbed burden, resulting in long-term exposure in the ambient medium. The impact can be reduced by temporary containment or pre-treatment to reduce toxicity and oxygen demand, or by "capping" (placing the material in pits or depressions and sealing it with clean sediment).

Industrial wastes dumped at sea are much less in volume than dredge spoils but they represent a substantially greater problem, because of their toxicity and diversity. They include wastes from the chemical, petrochemical and pharmaceutical industries, from pulp and paper production, from smelters, from the food industry, flue-gas washing and from military activities. In recent years the amounts of industrial waste dumped at sea annually ranged between six million and 17 million tonnes.

Another waste dumped at sea is the sludge arising from the purification treatment of urban sewage. It contains a large amount of organic matter which exerts considerable biological oxygen demand (BOD) in the receiving environment, along with nutrients such as nitrogen and phosphorus, and inert particulate material. If industrial wastes have been mixed with the domestic sewage stream, significant amounts of metals and synthetic organic chemicals may be present. There are strongly conflicting views about the use of the marine environment for sludge disposal. Some maintain that the oceans may be regarded as a resource in the context of waste disposal and that they offer a relatively safe and economically acceptable option. Others argue that the seas should be protected and that sewage sludge can be adequately accommodated by agricultural use and land-fill, with incineration as another viable option. The balance of opinion is currently swinging in favour of land disposal and the United Kingdom, which at present dumps about 11 million wet tonnes of sewage sludge at sea annually, has agreed to phase out this operation.

A specialized form of dumping at sea is incineration. Some organic wastes are environmentally persistent and difficult to dispose of, but can be destroyed by burning. Chlorinated hydrocarbons such as PCBs and some insecticides are in this category and are broken down on incineration to their basic elements, producing a gaseous plume of low pH. Dedicated vessels have been built for incineration at sea and have operated in the North Sea and on an experimental basis in other parts of the world. Scientific studies have concluded that such incineration at sea has little impact on marine ecosystems. The acid deposition is quickly buffered by seawater and as long as the operation is conducted well clear of sea lanes or fishing activities, no public health impact would be expected. Again, however, current opinion comes down in favour of precaution and incineration at sea is likely to be phased out.

Another category of waste which is causing increasing concern is plastics. During the past few decades synthetic compounds have been increasingly replacing natural materials for a wide variety of manufactured goods and the very characteristics which make them attractive, durability and lightness, also make them particularly offensive when discarded in the marine environment. Being almost non-biodegradable they persist for long periods in the sea, where they float and are carried for long distances. Fishing nets, lines and warps, for example, previously made of natural fibre, are now almost entirely supplied in synthetic form. When lost or discarded at sea these float on the surface or, if weighted, drift at mid-depths or sink to the bottom. They persist for years and can continue to operate by a process of "ghost" fishing, entangling and killing marine organisms such as birds, turtles, and mammals as well as fish.

Synthetic materials are now also extensively employed for straps and bands used in packaging and in the yokes for packs of beverage cans. These are often discarded intact into the sea, where they encircle fish and other organisms, tightening as the animals grow and eventually strangling them. There are also many records of plastic materials, in the form of sheeting or as fine particles, ingested by marine animals and interfering, sometimes lethally, with breathing and digestion. In addition to effects on marine organisms, floating plastics can constitute a hazard to shipping, fouling propellers, damaging driveshafts and clogging sea intakes.

Finally, there is a significant amenity impact from these synthetic materials. Plastic debris is found in every sector of the world's oceans, but is most obvious on beaches. A synoptic survey of the Oregon coast recorded 26 tonnes in a three-hour search, mostly polystyrene, plastic food utensils, and plastic bags and bottles. Surveys on UK and New Zealand beaches also showed very high levels of plastic.

While disposal and discarding, as discussed above, contribute directly and immediately to pollution, a number of other human activities cause problems in a more indirect way. This applies in particular to the exploitation of marine resources, and at the present time the most obvious example is the exploitation of offshore oil and gas. This began some 70 years ago, when early efforts were focused in shallow, sheltered water near the shore, and although many wells were drilled, each individual operation was on a relatively small scale and the overall contribution to global oil production was quite small. In the present decade, by contrast, more than one quarter of the world's oil production is from offshore regions, including the east, west and Gulf coasts of the United States; offshore Alaska; the Middle East; the Asia-Pacific region particularly the China Sea; off Latin America, especially Brazil; in the North Sea and off Canada. Several of these regions may be categorized as hostile environments because of storms, strong currents, deep water or ice conditions, and the scale of operation on individual fields may be very large, with concrete production platforms weighing up to 385,000 tonnes.

Pollution from offshore oil exploitation may be categorized under three main headings—spills, operational discharges and interference. Spills and accidents from installations are a continuing problem, with well-head blowouts perhaps the most feared example. Fortunately these have not been frequent, the largest blowouts in recent years being the North Sea EKOFISK incident in 1977, the IXTOC I drilling rig blowout in the Gulf of Mexico in 1979, and that from the FUNIWA 5 rig off the coast of Nigeria in 1980. IXTOC I was the most spectacular, with 400,000 tonnes of oil lost over a six-month perod, and beaches across the Gulf as far away as Texas affected. The EKOFISK blowout, on the other hand, when some 30,000 tonnes of oil escaped over an eight-day period, had no detectable impact on the marine environment.

Operational discharges are a different matter since they are controlled by regulations. In the North Sea, for example, oil in water discharged is limited to a concentration of 40 ppm, a level calculated to protect the environment. The rock fragments derived from drilling (the cuttings) are deposited in the vicinity of the rigs and carry with them residuals of the drilling muds and associated oil. These contaminated cuttings do adversely affect the seabed, changing its physical nature, smothering the benthic communities and contributing toxic chemicals. This effect is however highly localized and is usually restricted to an area of about 3 km round each platform. In the North Sea, it has been calculated that only about 0.1% of the bottom is affected.

The interference aspect of offshore oil operations has perhaps greater impact than direct chemical pollution. The presence of rigs and pipelines creates exclusion zones for ships, while oil-related debris, particularly on the seabed, can seriously disrupt fishing operations. Of great future concern to the fishing industry is the long-term fate of offshore installations. In several parts of the world production platforms are now reaching the end of their useful lives, and decommissioning is underway or projected. Off the south-east coast of the United States, the small easily-moved rigs in shallow water near shore are attractive to fish, and their potential as artificial reefs is recognized. This suggests a possible future for them either *in situ* or after relocation. In the North Sea, on the other hand, the situation is different. The large platforms in deep water are not well placed to function as reefs, and oil industry proposals to topple them *in situ* are looked on unfavourably by fishermen, who see such abandoned structures as potential sources of debris for years to come.

Exploitation of other non-living marine resources, apart from oil, includes such minerals as sand, gravel, shells, heavy metal placers, metalliferous muds, oozes and nodules. Some of these, particularly sand and gravel, are exploited in shallow shelf waters and this can interfere with fishing operations and with the habitats of commercially important species, but operational guidelines agreed in some countries between the fishing and extraction industries help to alleviate problems. Apart from this, mineral exploitation of the sea as at present practised has little impact on the marine environment. Effects are limited to the site and time of the operation and can be reduced by careful planning.

Pollution effects in the sea

The discussion so far has been concerned mainly with sources of pollution in terms of Man's activities, and has recognized that the pathways to the sea are mainly land-based, including direct discharges, run-off and rivers, while the atmosphere and shipping are the main contributors of contaminants to the open ocean.

The next topic is the contaminants themselves, and the effects they produce in the sea. In the account below, sewage, nutrients, petroleum hydrocarbons, metals, synthetic organic compounds, and radionuclides are dealt with.

Sewage

As noted earlier, sewage contains a diverse mixture of components and its high organic and nutrient content can upset the ecological balance, but the focus here is on its load of pathogenic organisms, which constitute a public health risk. Almost all sewage contains pathogens, the numbers per unit volume depending largely on the health of the human population, and are most numerous in countries where water-borne diseases are endemic. While the eggs of parasitic worms, particularly tapeworms, and also cysts of Protozoa may be present, the numerical bulk of the pathogens in sewage are bacterial, viral and fungal agents. There are two main problems, the contamination first of seafood and second of bathing waters. Filter feeding organisms, specially molluscs like oysters and mussels concentrate particulate matter from the seawater which passes over their gills, and can accumulate bacteria and viruses. When eaten raw or only partially cooked, these shellfish can transmit diseases to human consumers. Typhoid, cholera and hepatitis are the most serious, but viral gastro-enteritis may also be passed on in this way. Sewage contamination of seawater at coastal resorts also affects the health of recreational beach users particularly swimmers who ingest water and expose the upper body orifices to the sea. Gastro-intestinal disorders are frequently reported among swimmers. The chances of infection are related to the degree of exposure, which is obviously greater in warmer regions where several hours per day may be spent in the water, and young children are particularly at risk if they paddle in shallow polluted water where sedimented viruses are likely to be resuspended during bathing.

Sewage contamination is a global issue. In the Mediterranean about 50 million people live in coastal cities and there is an influx of 100 million tourists each summer, so that sewage handling facilities are under extreme pressure and beach pollution is widespread. In west and central Africa few of the cities have proper sewerage or treatment plants. In India and Bangladesh most urban wastes are untreated and faecal-transmitted disease is high. Disposal of untreated wastes directly or indirectly to the sea is the general practice in east Asia, and in these areas a high proportion of the population depend on these polluted seas and their products for their livelihood. Most of the large cities in Australia are situated on the coast and beach contamination is extensive. Finally, in central America and in countries like Columbia, Peru and Chile, only a small percentage of the sewage is treated.

Protection of coastal waters requires that sewage should not be discharged in such a way that it can be washed back on to beaches or contaminate shellfish beds or fishing grounds. Treatment of sewage helps considerably, filtration, sedimentation and chlorination progressively removing pathogens, but viruses adsorbed on particles may be particularly resistant. Microbiological control of recreational waters tends to be regulated in terms of the normally non-pathogenic coliform bacteria, which are present in much larger numbers than those organisms which transmit disease and are thus more readily enumerated. The WHO/UNEP guidelines, and also those of the Environmental Protection Agency in the United States use faecal coliforms. However, this is not universally accepted, and some argue that *Enterococcus* counts give a better grading of beaches than faecal coliforms, at least for gastro-intestinal disorders. More research in this field is required.

The control of seafood-associated illnesses is perhaps a little more straightforward. Again, initial contamination should be prevented by adequate control of sewage disposal. In addition, harvesting from polluted grounds should be stopped, and efficient depuration of shellfish should be practised to remove pathogens. Finally consumers should be educated on the hazards of eating raw or partially cooked shellfish.

Nutrients

Nitrates and phosphates in the sea act in the same way as fertilizers on the land, enhancing plant growth. Small-scale addition of these nutrients is beneficial, but oversupply to the sea encourages run-away plant production which upsets the normal ecological balance of the marine communities, resulting in excess growth of macrophytes on the coast and exceptional plankton blooms in shallow waters, a phenomenon known as eutrophication. The blooms themselves can be offensive and damaging to amenities, and when they die off and sink to the bottom, they are broken down by bacteria resulting in de-oxygenation of the water and consequent death of fish and invertebrates. In addition, the plankton blooms may be directly toxic, posing a threat to public health and to the ecosystem in general.

Until quite recently this was regarded as a local problem, but with the increasing inputs around the world of nutrients from sewage and industry, from agriculture and intensive stock rearing, and with the explosive increase of mariculture, it is now recognized that eutrophication is a global issue and that any coastal area may be at risk which has poor water exchange with the open sea and which receives inputs from urban and industrial concentrations or from intensively used agricultural land. Examples of eutrophication are increasing from around the world. The large algal blooms which developed in the spring of 1988 off Sweden and Norway caused massive mortalities of marine plants and animals along a 200 km stretch of coast from the intertidal zone down to 20m depth, resulting in damage to salmon and trout farms estimated at $10 million. In the Southern Bight of the North Sea, which receives the input of large industrialized rivers, nutrients and phytoplankton have been increasing and oxygen deficiency has been detected on the seabed with dead fish and benthic organisms recorded. There are also several reports of the coasts of Germany and the Netherlands becoming covered with layers of slimy white foam up to 2 m thick where decaying algal blooms are washed ashore. In the Mediterranean, signs of eutrophication are found along the coasts particularly in the vicinity of river mouths and urban discharges and extreme effects are found for example in the Northern Adriatic, the Gulf of Lyons, the Lake of Tunis and the Bay of Izmir. In Japan, in many embayments along the central and western Pacific coast, where 72 million people live, the normal nutrient concentrations are greatly exceeded, oxygenation of bottom water is poor, and some species of benthos have declined. These effects pose a threat to the important mariculture industry in Japan. Examples of this sort can be found in many parts of the world, and it is evident that current anthropogenic inputs of nutrients are now at least comparable to those from natural sources. These inputs are related to present population densities in coastal regions and their hinterlands, yet within the next 30 years a near doubling of the human population is projected, with further increases in agriculture and livestock production and in mariculture. Thus anthropogenic input could become several times greater than the natural background and the effect on coastal waters globally could be on a scale at present found only in such enclosed areas as the Baltic and Japan Inland Seas.

Petroleum hydrocarbons

Contamination of the open ocean by oil from operational discharges from shipping has already been referred to and the impacts of offshore drilling briefly discussed. The overall issue of marine pollution from oil may now be considered. It is estimated that around 3.2 million tonnes of oil reach the sea annually as a result of Man's activities, and of this nearly 47% is derived from marine transportation and over 31% from municipal and industrial discharges. The most dramatic inputs arise from tanker accidents. When the *Torrey Canyon* grounded off the British coast in 1967, releasing some 95,000 tonnes of crude oil, almost as much damage was caused by the clean-up procedures, including the use of toxic chemicals, as by the oil itself. Lessons were learnt, and when the largest ever spill took place in 1973, with the loss of 220,000 tonnes of oil from the *Amoco Cadiz* off the coast of France, more effective procedures were available. Today many countries have contingency plans for dealing with oil spills around their coasts. These involve stockpiles of low-toxicity dispersants, the provision of aircraft for spraying, the supply of floating booms for containment, and the establishment of guidelines for action. However, such planning is not in universal operation, and the grounding of the *Exxon Valdez* in Alaska in 1989 will certainly have stimulated further efforts.

These large tanker spills usually take place on or near the coast and the resulting extensive oil slicks destroy seabirds and marine mammals and immense damage is caused to shellfisheries and coastal amenity when the oil is washed ashore. When buried in the sand, hydrocarbons leach out slowly and may be detectable for up to a decade after the event. However, dramatic though these spills are and damaging though they may be to the impacted zone, the global problem arises rather from floating oil which occurs on the shipping lanes and in areas of high oil production. A prime region for such impact is the Middle East. In the Red Sea many kilometres of coast are severely oiled with tar pavements several centimetres thick, blanketing sandy beaches, rocky promontories and mangrove areas. In the Kuwait/Oman area tar weighing as much as 30 kg can be found on a metre-wide stretch of beach between high and low tide. In many places beaches are virtually unusable for any purpose.

When floating oil weathers, the persistent residues form flakes or balls which circulate on the ocean currents and are eventually carried ashore, reducing amenity and threatening tourist industries. Tar is deposited along the west coast of India at a rate of 1,000 tonnes per year and tarballs are found along all the coast of Pakistan, as well as in Indonesia and the Philippines. About 265 million tonnes of oil are transported through the Caribbean every year and as a result of discharges and spills, windward exposed coasts are highly contaminated with tar. Some beaches are severely damaged for recreation and others, for example in Curaçao, Bonaire and Grand Cayman, are totally unusable. Aggregations of tar balls are particularly intense in enclosed seas like the Mediterranean, but even open coasts off countries which import large quantities of oil are affected—the Kuroshio current off Japan for example, is heavily contaminated.

Metals

Although metals released by the actions of Man reach the sea directly via industrial discharges, dumping and mining, and indirectly via rivers and the atmosphere, there is no doubt that these quantities are greatly exceeded by natural inputs of metals from erosion of rocks and from volcanic activity. In the Mediterranean for example, weathering of natural cinnabar deposits in Algeria, Italy, Yugoslavia, Turkey and Spain is thought to account for relatively high levels of mercury found in tuna and some other species of fish, while enhanced levels of cadmium in the brown meat of crabs from the Orkney Islands of Scotland are attributed to geochemical sources.

Because of these accumulations in commercially important species it is desirable that regular monitoring of seafoods for selected metals should continue, but no general threat to the ecosystem is apparent since organisms seem able to adapt to high levels in water and sediments. Current evidence suggests that today metals represent only a minor hazard in the marine environment.

Synthetic organic compounds

The ability of chemists to synthesize new compounds for specific industrial and domestic uses has resulted in the production, often on a large scale, of entirely new substances, including chlorinated hydrocarbon biocides (e.g. DDT), industrial chemicals such as chlorinated biphenyls (PCBs) and organometals such as tributyl tin (TBT). Many of these compounds are stable and not readily biodegradable so are very persistent in the environment. Also, they may be highly toxic, in some cases having been designed as biocides. Finally, since they are not natural substances and have been in existence for quite a short time, organisms have not yet been able to evolve protective responses to them. For all these reasons, synthetic organic compounds can present problems in the environment, and are now widely distributed in the sea.

Chlorinated hydrocarbons, for example, are carried in the atmosphere as well as in water, and are found, usually at very low concentrations, from the poles to the tropics. They can be detected in most species of organisms, including human beings everywhere, and since they are particularly soluble in fat, they tend to accumulate in the fatty tissues of animals and to be magnified up the food chain so that top predators among fish, birds and mammals often carry high body burdens. Of the chlorine bound in fish fat, up to 5% is attributable to known contaminants such as DDT, PCBs, dioxins and chlorophenols but the rest is unaccounted for, and may be low-molecular-weight compounds from pulpmills, aluminium and magnesium smelters and from the burning of chlorine-containing materials. Further research in this field is obviously needed. Chlorinated hydrocarbons can inhibit photosynthesis and movement in plankton and cause a wide range of adverse effects on higher organisms including tumours, liver damage, reproductive failure and birth defects. In recent years, uterine occlusions have been documented in seals in the Baltic and in the Dutch Waddenzee, which prevent the birth of pups. This has been attributed to PCBs and while not fully confirmed, the proposition is supported by experimental work in the Netherlands when PCB-contaminated fish were fed to seals.

Demonstration of the detrimental effects of chlorinated hydrocarbons to non-target organisms has resulted in severe restrictions on their use in many northern industrial countries, some compounds being totally banned. As a result, levels of DDT in fish and shellfish in the USA and Scandinavia have been declining and this applies to a lesser extent to PCBs. For the latter it appears that accumulations in marine sediments may represent a source for years to come. In spite of the restrictions in some regions, global production of chlorinated hydrocarbons is still probably increasing and it must be recognized that biocides contribute significantly to human health and food production in the tropics. In west and central Africa and in south Asia, pesticide use is considerable and is growing. Although in places there is a switch to more readily degradable compounds such as organophosphorus and carbamates, there is still extensive use of organochlorines (DDT, HCH, aldrin, dieldrin, chlordane and pentachlorophenyl).

A more recent introduction to the marine environment is the synthetic organometal TBT. The biocidal properties of organotin compounds were first recognized in the early 1950s, and they have been used as fungicides, bactericides and preservatives for woods, textiles and paper. TBT was introduced in the mid-1960s as an antifouling agent in marine paints for the protection of ships and was so effective that it quickly came into extensive use on commercial and naval vessels, fishing boats and all types of pleasure craft. It was also applied in anti-fouling preparations on net cages in fish farms, and on lobster pots and pounds for keeping fish and shellfish. Laboratory tests suggested that TBT degrades quickly, with a half-life measured in terms of days and it was expected that any side effects of its use would be minimal. However, its impact on non-target organisms began to be noted in the mid-1970s, when it was shown in France that leaching of TBT from anti-fouling paints on pleasure boats berthed in marinas close to shellfish beds was causing serious shell malformations in oysters and a reduction in the natural spat-fall. Similar problems were found in several other countries, and effects on a wide range of organisms, including most of the main marine invertebrate groups and fish, were detected at very low TBT concentrations, in the range of nanogrammes per litre. A marine snail, the common dogwhelk, is particularly sensitive to TBT. At exposure as low as 2.5 nanogrammes per litre this species incurs "imposex" (females develop male characteristics) and populations of dogwhelk in many parts of the British coast are declining. In association with these observations it has been found that the persistence of TBT in the field may be greater than experimental results suggested. In turbid coastal waters and estuaries the half life may be longer because of decreased light penetration and sorption on to particulate matter in the water column and sediments. In addition, it is now known that TBT becomes concentrated at interfaces—on the surface film of the water and on the surface of rocks and beaches, so that organisms may be exposed to relatively high concentrations at these sites.

Public health risks of TBT accumulation in seafood are being investigated but at present no threat to consumers is apparent. However, the impacts on non-target organisms has caused some countries to restrict or prohibit the use of TBT in anti-fouling paints. France has banned TBT-based paints on pleasure craft less than 25m in length (other than those constructed of aluminium) and in 1987 the UK prohibited all use of TBT preparations except those involving low concentrations in copolymer-based paints for use in commercial shipping. Many states in the USA have also adopted restrictions. Monitoring suggests that after restrictions have been imposed, recovery of affected areas may be expected in two to five years.

Radioactive substances

Radioactive substances occur naturally throughout the environment and are present in water, sediments and organisms of the oceans. The natural inputs are from the Earth's crust or from cosmic radiation, but since the 1940s anthropogenic radionuclides have been detectable in ocean waters as a result of nuclear weapon tests in the atmosphere mainly between 1954 and 1962. This has led to worldwide radioactive contamination of the oceans by dry and particularly by wet deposition. The artificial radionuclides produced by such tests include carbon-14, caesium-137, hydrogen-3 (tritium) and strontium-90, as well as plutonium and other transuranic elements. However, because of its widespread dispersal, this atmospheric fallout leads to only low-level ambient concentration and thus to negligible additions to the exposure from natural background.

Apart from weapon testing, a number of other anthropogenic sources contribute to the oceans' radionuclide inventory, but not on a global scale. Accidents at industrial installations are a potential source of radiation to the environment. Major accidents with radionuclide releases took place at Sellafield (Windscale), UK, in 1957; at Chelyabinsk, USSR, in 1957; and at Three-Mile Island in the USA, in 1979. The most recent incident was at Chernobyl, USSR, in 1986 which gave rise to widespread contamination of the environment throughout Europe and to exposure of the population mainly from gamma emitters deposited on the ground and from caesium-137 in dairy and meat products. Less than 7% of the caesium-137 emitted was deposited in the sea, and exposure of people through consumption of seafood was negligible. No effects on marine organisms were detected.

In the past some low-level radioactive wastes have been disposed of by dumping at sea in packaged form. Sites in the Atlantic and Pacific Oceans were used, and in the Gulf of Mexico, but the total amount dumped in this way was much less than that added to the oceans as a result of earlier nuclear weapons testing, and an Expert Panel set up under the London Dumping Convention calculated that any present and future risk to individuals from past ocean dumping of radioactive waste would be extremely small. The practice of dumping low-level radioactive wastes at sea was discontinued as a result of a voluntary moratorium in 1982 and has not so far been resumed.

The main continuing anthropogenic inputs of radioactive material to the sea come from operational discharges of effluents from nuclear reactors and reprocessing plants as well as from disposal of low-level radioactive material from a variety of sources including research and medicine. All these discharges are under strict international control, and are subject to authorisation and rigorous monitoring. In general any enhancement of radionuclides is limited to the vicinity of the discharge site, but in some cases, thanks to the sophisticated analytical techniques now available, the far field distribution can be detected. Thus caesium-137 from Sellafield in the Irish Sea can be traced round the North coast of Scotland and into and around the margins of the North Sea. The levels however are much too low to cause adverse effects and the caesium is regarded as an oceanographic tracer rather than as a pollutant.

The control of marine pollution

The optimum approach to the control of marine pollution is to reduce or, ideally, prevent the input of contaminants to the marine environment. A balanced view, however, will recognize the ocean as a resource in the context of waste disposal but will argue that it should be only one of several options, all of which should be fully evaluated before the decision is made. If, after this process, ocean disposal is selected, it should be conducted within a carefully controlled regime. The site and method of disposal should be selected so as to ensure that there is no public health risk and that impact on the marine environment or interference with other activities is minimal. A monitoring programme should be developed to check that these specifications are adhered to.

While most marine pollution must be dealt with at local or national level, the very nature of the sea with its capacity for widescale dispersal beyond state boundaries also requires an international approach. Fortunately a number of international agreements and treaties are already in force and others are under discussion. In the two decades after 1950 the most obvious marine pollution was that arising from accidental spillages and operational discharges of oil at sea. For that reason a number of multilateral conventions were adopted specifically addressing these problems and such action culminated in the International Convention for the Prevention of Pollution from Ships 1973, as modified by the Protocol of 1978 relating thereto, usually known as MARPOL 73/78. This Convention provides not only for a control system for operational discharges of oil from ships (Annex I) but also covers discharges from ships of noxious liquid substances carried in bulk (Annex

II); harmful substances carried in packaged form, containers and portable tanks (Annex III); sewage (Annex IV) and garbage (Annex V).

A further stimulation to international action on marine pollution was given by the 1972 UN Conference on the Human Environment. During the preparations for this event it was realized that the dumping of wastes from ships would be a relatively easy activity to control and the UN Conference therefore proposed a Convention on the Prevention of Marine Pollution by Dumping of Waste and Other Matter. This Convention (the London Dumping Convention) was adopted in 1972. Also stemming from the UN Convention was the establishment of the United Nations Environment Programme (UNEP) in 1972, which led to the setting up of regional action plans in 12 sea areas round the world by 1989.

Because international agreement on shipping is not too difficult to achieve, control of pollution by waste disposal at sea is well advanced. Unfortunately, the bulk of marine pollution is derived from land-based sources and control of these is a much more intractable problem, not least because of the great diversity of interests involved, including industry, agriculture, and local authorities, and also because of the very considerable costs that adequate control would incur. It is therefore not surprising that conventions on land-based pollution sources are enacted in only a few regions. The Paris Convention of 1974 covers this aspect for the North East Atlantic (including the North Sea) and the Helsinki Convention of 1974 deals with the Baltic Sea in a similar way. Only two of the UNEP's eight Regional Seas Conventions have protocols on the prevention and control of land-based pollution sources—the Athens Protocol (1980) to the Barcelona Convention in the Mediterranean, and the Quito Protocol (1981) to the Lima Convention in the south-east Pacific region. There is clearly scope for extension of such agreements.

In addition to the formal treaties and conventions, public awareness of the need to maintain the quality of the marine environment is being increasingly demonstrated by activities in various parts of the world. A good example is the series of conferences on the Protection of the North Sea. The first of these was held in Bremen in 1984, the second in London in 1987 and the third in the Hague in 1990. More are planned. The conferences aim at an integrated attack on regional problems of the marine environment, and, being arranged at the level of government ministers, they are turning out to be highly effective.

Conclusion

This review of marine pollution points to some clear conclusions. At the present time, as we move into the last decade of the century, the open oceans, although showing detectable signs of Man's activity, are not polluted. The margins of the seas, on the other hand, are under great pressure. Habitats are being lost to coastal development; eutrophication is degrading sheltered coastal regions; pathogens from sewage are contaminating seafood and recreational waters; and synthetic organic compounds are building up in the tropics. Some of the mechanisms for prevention and control of marine pollution are in place but not fully operated, while others remain to be developed. The problems are now well recognized. If international action can be taken at once, an improvement in coastal waters could be seen by the end of the century.

For bibliography, see pp. 360–361.

8 NUCLEAR POWER AND THE ENVIRONMENT

Gordon Mackerron and Frans Berkhout

Introduction

Nuclear power has been haunted by its environmental effects. Perhaps more than any other technology its development has been shaped by caution over the risks it presented. There is a multitude of technical and cultural reasons for this, but perhaps it stems more than anything else from a basic fear of ionizing radiation.

Radiation was perceived to be a health hazard almost as soon as atomic research began at the end of the last century. The danger it posed was silent, odourless and invisible, and its effects were insidious. It led to the development of cancers and was shown to produce genetic mutations in bugs and mice. In this way it was a poison which awakened modern angsts about an incurable disease and a genetic catastrophe. After the atomic bomb, radiation also came to represent the awesome destructive potential of technology.

Pre-eminently, radiation is a pollutant of the Scientific Age. To detect it requires scientific apparatus and expertise; most of it is produced in huge, secretive industries, and its effects on the body happen at the minutest level, damaging atoms and cells in ways which even modern science has not been able to fathom completely. The effects of radiation are expressed as probabilities not facts.

Carrying this baggage of associations, it is not surprising that radiation has often been taken to stand for the perils of modern technology in general. This symbolic role has frequently overshadowed the reality of the hazards of nuclear power, so far as these are understood. By a cruel irony, the images of power and control which were so useful to the birth of nuclear power have been turned against the technology over the last 20 years.

Background radiation is all around us, and although a nuclear power programme raises the *total* exposure to radiation by only a small amount, the world's nuclear industry nevertheless generates enormous amounts of radiation, all of which has to be controlled. Dealing with the waste radioactivity safely is a huge responsibility. The nuclear industry is continually involved in trying to convince enough people that it can discharge this responsibility.

Great efforts have been invested in defining and measuring the health effects of radiation. In this the effects on humans are central, so when we talk about the *environmental* effects of nuclear power we are talking specifically about the effects of radiation on human populations, either directly or through the food chain. It is assumed that in protecting human lives, other life forms will also be protected. Other more minor effects such as the warming of local environments due to waste heat discharges are not considered here.

Strict safety regulations have controlled the development of nuclear technology. Nevertheless, all nuclear facilities do emit some amount of radiation into the general environment. To contain everything is impossible, and since radiation is a natural part of the environment, such an effort might well be illogical.

Controlling the environmental effects of nuclear power has two dimensions—waste management and safety (see below)—and the two merge into each other. Regulatory controls aim to keep the risk of death due to man-made radiation down to what is thought to be an acceptable level.

In spite of all this effort to assure people that nuclear power is safe and responsible, it still suffers from widely-held concern about its risks and dangers. For a set of diverse reasons, nuclear risks are seen by many people as inherently more threatening than other risks faced in everyday life. Attempts have been made to ascribe this to the potential for catastrophic effects, the involuntary nature of nuclear risks, the experience of nuclear accidents, the problems of democratic control of the technology and so on. In places where the economic or strategic benefits of nuclear electricity are widely accepted, as in France for example, then these doubts have little impact. Where the benefits are disputed, or clearly negative (as today in the UK), they become overwhelming.

Ionizing radiation

Atoms are like miniature solar systems. Negatively-charged electrons weighing very little orbit around a much denser nucleus composed of positively-charged protons and neutrons which are without an electrical charge. A chemical element is defined by the fixed number of protons in its nuclei, while the number of neutrons may vary. These different varieties of an element are called isotopes. So, for example, the element uranium has 92 protons in its atomic nuclei, but these may contain anything between 140 and 146 neutrons—uranium-232, uranium-233 and so on.

Some isotopes are perfectly stable. Most are unstable, and are prone to transform themselves by throwing out some of their atomic particles. This transformation, known as decay, takes place in two ways, each unstable nuclide employing only one of these. The first, alpha decay, involves a chunk of two neutrons and two protons being emitted from the atom. The second is the consequence of a transformation, inside the atomic nucleus, of a neutron into a proton. In doing so, one electron is released. This is beta decay. Frequently the emission of particles alone is not sufficient for an excited atom to achieve a new state of relative stability. In these cases a further burst of pure energy is driven off. This is gamma radiation.

All of these atomic transformations come under the general heading of radioactivity, and isotopes which undergo decay are termed radionuclides. Each radionuclide decays at a distinctive and immutable rate. This is generally represented by the half-life, that is the time taken for half of an amount of a radionuclide to decay to another material. An amount of radioactivity, usually shortened to activity, is also defined by the rate at which decays occur in a material. One decay per second is defined as a Bequerel (Bq), after the French chemist. Producing one Gigawatt (GW(e), one million kilowatts) of nuclear electricity will generate some 10^{18} Bq of radioactivity, about 99% of it contained in the nuclear fuel.

Different forms of radiation are emitted at different energies and with varying penetrating power. Consequently their effects on the host material also vary. Alpha particles are large and have little penetrating power, while beta particles, being smaller, may, for example, pass through a sheet of paper, but be stopped by some two centimetres of living tissue. Gamma radiation is extremely penetrative and will pass right through the human body. All of these are ionizing radiations whose main effect is to chemically change matter at an atomic and, in organic matter, a cellular level. Here it may disrupt the process of cell division, or in extreme cases where repair mechanisms are overwhelmed, kill the cell. Because alpha particles cannot penetrate the skin they are a hazard to health only when inhaled or ingested. In contrast, external exposures of beta-gamma radiation are also damaging.

The effects of radiation on the human body are related to *how much* energy is deposited into the tissue (the absorbed dose) and *where*, since some organs are more sensitive than others. When estimating the effect of a dose of radiation on tissue a number of things have to be taken into account. First, the potential of different radiations (alpha, beta-gamma, neutrons) to do damage must be allowed for. Alpha particles, for example, are normally taken to be 20 times more damaging than beta particles. The dose equivalent, expressed in Sieverts, is the absorbed dose weighted to take into account these variations.

A second consideration is the vulnerability of different organs to ionizing radiation. A given dose of radiation is more likely to cause a fatal cancer in a lung than in the thyroid, for example, although the reproductive organs, the gonads, are the most sensitive of all.

The effects of radiation on humans have been the subject of investigation for almost 100 years. This scientific work has grown enormously since World War II. Its results have been synthesized into a unique, internationally-respected set of radiation protection standards based on the recommendations of the International Commission on Radiological Protection (ICRP). Radiobiology is a notoriously difficult and inexact science, and the great effort at achieving an international standardization of protection measures through the ICRP has been essential for giving assurance about the use of nuclear materials in whatever application.

At high, rapidly delivered doses, radiation may damage organs and cause death. Such exposures are generally associated with unique events such as a nuclear explosion or a major accident. Normally radiological protection is concerned with the effects of relatively small doses absorbed over long periods of time. These may give rise to leukemia or cancers (somatic effects) over decades, or lead to genetic or chromosomal damage which can be passed on to subsequent generations. Somatic effects are thought to occur at lower doses than genetic effects so it is these which are kept in mind when regulations are drawn up.

Interpreting precise causal chains in the development of radiation-induced cancers has proved to be impossible, mainly because they cannot be separated from the many other risks to which human beings are exposed. Laboratory animals have also not proved a sufficient substitute. Instead, the revealed effects in whole populations have been used to draw up risk factors which correlate radiation doses with health effects.

Such research has, however, been faced with a basic methodological problem. The main sources of data on human exposures come from instances where groups of people have been exposed to sufficiently high doses for their eventual effects to be statistically measurable, such as the bomb survivors at Hiroshima and Nagasaki. Usually these doses have been higher than those received from natural background radiation, or from sources such as the nuclear weapons tests or nuclear power. A number of assumptions have therefore had to be made about the effects of small doses of radiation. First it is assumed that all doses, however small, have the potential to cause somatic damage. The second, and more contentious assumption is that there is a linear relationship between dose and the risk of a somatic effect (i.e. each unit of radiation increases the risk by a fixed amount).

From these assumptions and the dose-effect relationships derived from epidemiological data, the ICRP has sought to recommend permissible levels of radiation exposure under controlled circumstances. At first these levels were set for occupational exposures in atomic research or the nuclear industry, but limits for public exposure have existed since 1953. Historically the limits have fallen. For example, the basic occupational dose limit recommended by the ICRP as long ago as 1934 was 700 milliSieverts (mSv) per year. After successive reductions, in 1987 a new limit of 15 mSv per year was recommended for occupational exposure, a decrease by a factor of nearly 50. For the general public the principal dose limit was reduced in 1985 to 1 mSv per year. Limits of exposure from man-made sources of between 0.3 and 1 mSv per year have been adopted by most countries.

Dose limits represent levels of risk which are deemed by the ICRP and national regulatory authorities to be "acceptable". This is a notion which many people feel uncomfortable with, principally because risk is not a concept which fits easily into our understanding, except in special cases like betting or financial investment. Nevertheless, the risk of injury or disease does apply to many of our everyday activities, and through a study of these it is possible to assess what, on average, people regard as an acceptable risk. Of course, risk factors are never truly equivalent because they take place in different contexts. The risk attached to flying a hang glider is not readily comparable with the risk of death due to exposure to radiation. In the first case the risks are voluntary and easily understandable, in the latter they are involuntary and obscure. Furthermore, there is no simple, single dividing line to distinguish between risk levels which are acceptable and those which are clearly unacceptable, but rather a broad range within which a dose limit is set. In general a risk of death in any one year of about one in a million is taken to be the limit of what is acceptable for public exposure to radiation from man-made sources.

The inhalation of gaseous radon and its short-lived decay products is the principal mechanism of exposure to radiation for most people. Radon occurs naturally, seeping out of the earth particularly in areas of granite and other igneous rocks. Recent evidence shows that the risk of contracting lung cancer from this source is greater than previously thought. In Britain the limits on exposure to radon in dwellings were revised in early 1990. The action level—the point at which measures must be taken to lower the concentration of the gas—was halved to 200 Bq per cubic metre, which compares with an average concentration in Britain of 20 Bq per cubic metre. The new level is equivalent to an exposure of 10 mSv per year.

The nuclear fuel cycle

Harnessing nuclear energy requires an extensive infrastructure of integrated facilities, which starts with the mining of uranium ore and will eventually end with the disposal of radioactive wastes. In between, several transformations take place and these are represented in Figure 1.

Nuclear power is produced by exploiting the energy of atomic fission. Fission is the splitting of atomic nuclei, and a fissile atom is one which can be split under the conditions prevailing inside a nuclear reactor. It is achieved when a neutron is absorbed by a fissile atom making it unstable, so that it disintegrates into two fragments of more or less equal size. During this disintegration heat and other radiation is liberated, together with a number of neutrons which may in turn cause fission, and so on in a chain. In today's commercial

Figure 1: *Nuclear fuel processing cycle*

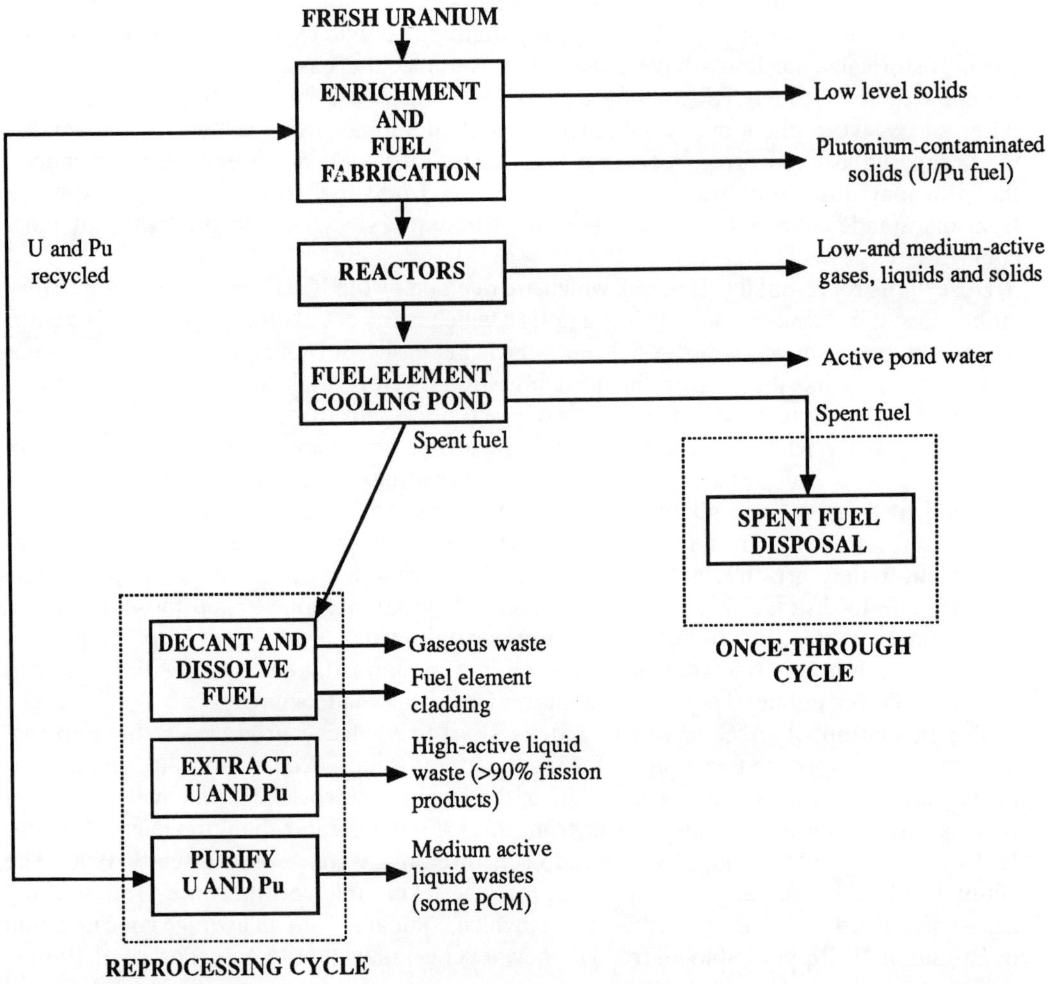

reactors these fissions take place at relatively low temperatures with neutrons slowed by a moderator. These are thermal reactors, and include Magnox, Advanced Gas-cooled Reactors (AGR), Boiling Water Reactors (BWR) and Pressurized Water Reactors (PWR). Fast reactors in which fission is achieved at high temperatures and neutron speeds and without a moderator are still at the development stage.

The mineral used in all of today's commercial reactors is uranium. Only one uranium isotope, uranium-235, is fissile, and it forms just 0.7% of the naturally occurring ore. Most of the ore is composed of uranium-238 which, while radioactive, is not fissile. In order for fission to take place continually and controllably in most operating reactors, the proportion of uranium-235 in nuclear fuel has to be raised to between 2 and 4%. This process is known as enrichment.

Nuclear fuel rods composed of enriched uranium are placed in the reactor where they become irradiated with neutrons. After three to five years the fuel is depleted and must be replaced. The spent fuel is removed from the reactor and put into storage, normally under water, to allow it to cool. Spent fuel contains unused uranium, plutonium which may also be used to fuel nuclear reactors, and an amalgam of fission waste products.

Reprocessing and once-through

The decision about how to deal with the spent fuel is crucial to the fuel cycle's environmental consequences. The simplest option is to regard the spent fuel as a waste to be further cooled, and eventually disposed of. This so-called "once-through" option is presently preferred in the USA, Canada and Sweden.

Alternatively, and this has been the dominant view since the 1950s, the uranium and plutonium can be retrieved from the fuel for recycling in either thermal or fast reactors. In thermal reactors the fissile plutonium-239 can be substituted for uranium-235. The main source of energy in fast reactors is plutonium which is "bred" from the other uranium isotope—uranium-238. By utilizing this otherwise redundant material the principle is that fast reactors provide a more efficient way of using uranium. Recycling can be portrayed as environmentally and strategically prudent because valuable resources are conserved. This model of nuclear development is now undergoing major review. Commercial fast reactors have not been built because the costs of construction are high compared to thermal reactors and because enriched uranium has remained cheap. Nowhere is commercialization expected before about 2030.

Retrieval of uranium and plutonium is by a technique of chemical separation called reprocessing. Radioactive wastes separated in reprocessing are mostly set aside for packaging and disposal, although a small proportion is discharged straight into the environment. Of all the spent fuel produced by commercial reactors by the year 2000, some 25% is expected to be reprocessed.

The environmental differences between the once-through and reprocessing fuel cycles have been the subject of much dispute over the years. It used to be assumed that since plutonium is a toxic and long-lived substance (plutonium-239 has a half-life of nearly 25,000 years), there would be long-term advantages in extracting it from the wastes to be disposed. Furthermore, the volume of high-level waste produced in reprocessing is only some 5% of the original spent fuel. Reprocessing was therefore seen as a step in waste management.

Experience has shown that this assumption may well have been incorrect. When spent fuel is reprocessed it is dissolved. The solution produced is then subjected to a succession of solvent extraction steps. Not only are the radioactive materials more difficult to control in a fluid state than when they were fixed in the spent fuel, but each treatment stage yields new volumes of more dilute radioactive waste. Not only does reprocessing present new safety risks, it also greatly increases the complexity and scale of radioactive waste management. Moreover, the advantages of extracting most of the plutonium from the high-level waste stream are less persuasive now that more is known about the performance of radioactive waste repositories (see below).

The scale of the nuclear industry

The civil industry

Nuclear power is now a significant but far from dominating technology for the generation of electricity (for all practical purposes electricity is its sole civilian use). By 1989, nuclear reactors generated around 17% of the world's electricity. Within this average there are wide variations: France generates 70% of all its electricity from nuclear power, followed by Belgium at 65%, Hungary at 49%, and Sweden and South Korea, both with 47%. Nearer the average the USA and UK both have a 20% nuclear share, while the Soviet Union comes in at 13%. A significant number of industrialized countries have no nuclear generation, including Italy, Norway, Denmark, Austria and Australia, while among developing countries there is some capacity in Taiwan, India, Pakistan, China, Brazil, Argentina and Mexico.

In terms of absolute size of the nuclear sector, the USA is the world's leader, with 107 Gigawatts (GW): this is equivalent to roughly 100 large modern reactors. The USA has some 30% of the world's nuclear capacity of 338 GW (439 reactors), followed by France with 55 GW, USSR with 37 GW, Japan 29 GW, Germany 26 GW and the UK with 15 GW. Much the predominant type of plant in use is the pressurized water reactor (PWR), which accounts for 62% of all operating reactors and an even higher proportion (77%) of those under construction. The boiling water reactor (22%) is the next most commonly used, while the fast breeder reactor—with its potential for eventually breeding its own fuel—accounts for less than 1% of all capacity.

The heyday for nuclear investment in the civilian sector was the early 1970s, when on average 20–30 GW per year was ordered around the world. The boom was shortlived, however: by the early 1980s, the rate of investment had declined to around 10 GW/year, and by the late 1980s, only 3–4 GW/year (four or five reactors) were being ordered. This decline in the popularity of nuclear power as a new energy source has had a number of sources: saturation in Belgium and France; low levels of ordering of new plant of all types in many countries; escalating levels of construction and other nuclear costs; and specific political problems in a number of countries (much of it pre-dating the Chernobyl accident), including Sweden and Italy. The limited activity in the current world market for nuclear power is largely confined to the Pacific Rim, where Korea and Japan are the main actors.

For many years it was thought that there would be steady and even exponential growth in the use of civilian nuclear power. However the sharp reduction in the rate of ordering new plant in the past decade means that growth in the 1990s (and probably beyond) will be relatively limited. A total of 101 reactors (88 GW) are presently under construction, but some—especially in eastern Europe—will be abandoned before completion. Given the very low level of new investment and the fact that many of the earliest reactors are now approaching retirement, it is unlikely that world capacity by 2000 will grow, from a 1989 level of 338 GW, to more than 400 GW.

Nuclear power is supported by a complex array of fuel cycle facilities, most of which suffer from severe excess capacity as a result of the unexpected decline in the ordering of new reactors. Uranium mining capacity is of the order of 75,000 tonnes annually, against a demand of around 45,000 tonnes. Production is concentrated in the USA, USSR, Australia, Canada, Namibia and Gabon, though smaller quantities are available from many other countries.

The two most important processing activities—for reasons of expense and military sensitivity—are the enrichment of uranium and the reprocessing of spent fuel. These services are available on a much more geographically restricted basis, partly because it has been an objective of the nuclear weapons states to restrict access to these technologies. Uranium enrichment is carried out in at least 12 countries, but the USA, USSR and France are dominant: adding in the UK, these four countries account for more than 95% of world capacity. Civil reprocessing services are available in only five countries. France and the UK are the dominant actors while Germany, Japan and the USSR have relatively small-scale facilities. Outside the industrialized world, India has substantial reprocessing capacity and plans more. Generally, enrichment and reprocessing are subject to the same over-capacity problem that afflicts the uranium mining industry.

The military fuel cycle

The military fuel cycle is virtually identical to the civil cycle, the main difference being that military reactors are not loaded with enriched uranium, but with natural uranium ore. Irradiation of natural uranium produces plutonium with a high proportion of the isotope plutonium-239, the main bomb material. Enriched uranium is also used in nuclear warheads.

There are currently five acknowledged Nuclear Weapons States: the US the USSR, France, the UK, and China. Three other countries; India, Israel, and South Africa, are generally assumed to possess nuclear weapons, but have never publically confirmed this. Pakistan, Argentina and Brazil (and possibly one or two others) are thought to be close to producing nuclear weapons.

The largest research, development, testing and production capabilities for nuclear weapons lie in the USA and the USSR. The USA maintains three laboratories (Sandia, Lawrence Livermore and Los Alamos), three major materials production sites (Hanford, Oak Ridge and Savannah River), and one main warhead factory (Amarrillo) among others. Testing is carried out at the Camp Mercury site in Nevada.

Weapons research, testing and production in the USSR include a wide range of plants and sites, the main ones being the Kurchatov Institute in Moscow, Kyshtym and Semipalatinsk. In Britain there are three research and production centres: Aldermaston, Burghfield, and Llanishen near Cardiff. Materials production is carried out in reactors at Windscale and Chapelcross and spent fuel from these facilities is reprocessed at Sellafield. French research and production is located at Saclay, Grenoble, Marcoule (plutonium and tritium) and Pierrelatte (enrichment). Testing is done in the Pacific at Mururoa Atoll.

Controlling radioactivity

Each step of the nuclear fuel cycle generates waste materials which contain radioactivity (see Figure 1). The control of these wastes is one of the main tasks of operators of nuclear facilities since almost all of them are toxic enough to come under regulatory control. In industrial countries with nuclear power, the majority of radioactive wastes (80–90%) arise in the nuclear fuel cycle, except perhaps in the USA and the USSR which have very extensive nuclear weapons programmes. Medical, research and industrial users of nuclear materials produce the rest.

Radioactive wastes are an extremely variegated group of materials. Usually they contain a mixture of radionuclides, each with distinct chemical behaviours and toxicities. Indeed there has been a persistent problem with their definition. Several attempts to standardize definitions have foundered, and each country has adopted different conventions. Even more confusingly, several classification systems may compete with each other in one country. The labels used in public discussion are usually generic, referring to a variety of waste characteristics—activity, longevity and disposal route, for instance, as in the British classification: low-, intermediate-, and high-level waste (LLW, ILW, HLW respectively). During the 1980s, in those countries which have made provision for waste disposal, classification schemes have tended to refer more to a planned disposal route, based on the technical criteria for acceptance at waste repositories. Germany is the most extreme example of this.

The main distinction in all these schemes lies between heat-generating waste—either spent fuel or high level waste produced in reprocessing—and non-heat generating wastes, which comprise nearly all the rest. A secondary division, which cuts across the first, is that between wastes containing long-lived alpha-emitters (usually plutonium), and beta-gamma emitters. Dealing with alpha wastes is generally considered more difficult because of the greater health hazards they pose if ingested. Lastly, the phase of the waste—whether it is a gas, a liquid, a sludge, or a solid—will be critical to the management strategies chosen.

Another common ambiguity in the language of radwaste management is the conflation of the words "storage" and "disposal". For simplicity, the term storage should be used for a management step which foresees some further handling of a waste, while disposal means the placing of wastes in a place where further human intervention is not anticipated. Typically, solid wastes are not disposed of as they arise, but are chemically treated, fixed in a solid matrix like cement or glass, and packaged, before being disposed of to engineered repositories.

Principles of waste management

There are two extreme approaches to dealing with any waste. Either it can be discharged straight into the general environment without any intermediate processing steps, or it can be retained at the production site and stored there securely. The first has been called "dilute and disperse" because it depends on the ability of the environment to absorb a pollutant and then to spread it thinly enough so that its effect on people is negligible. The second, given the name "concentrate and contain", assumes the opposite. It supposes that the pollutant cannot be placed into the environment because it will pose an unacceptable hazard to life. Although radioactive wastes have the unique property of decaying through time, the longevity of some of the most significant radiotoxics would logically mean an almost indefinite storage of wastes under human surveillance. Such a prospect is not without its problems.

In essence the difference between the two approaches is that one involves the relinquishment of human control, while the other seeks to prolong or intensify control. Since the idea of perpetual human control is perhaps not credible, it is generally assumed that active management will, at some point, be given up. The question then becomes one of setting the conditions under which control could be given up, preferably in an orderly way. This is both a technical and political problem. Techniques of disposal must be developed, together with methods of scientific evaluation, but all of this effort is finally directed towards a social need, that is, the generally-felt desire to be assured that the future consequences of disposal will be acceptably small. No final proof will be available of long-term safety; only well-informed, systematic speculation—a speculation which is never freed from its social role of persuasion.

Historically, radioactive waste management practice has tended to move away from dilution and towards containment. In early nuclear weapons projects in the USA, all wastes were disposed of more or less directly into the environment, including high-level wastes. In densely-populated Europe there was more caution after the war because of a basic apprehension about the hazards of radiation, particularly its genetic effects. Discharges of liquid and gaseous waste streams were kept down, often by the simple expedient of delay tanks which allowed the bulk of the short-lived activity to decay. For many solid wastes, a policy of storage evolved. Britain, France and the Soviet Union are the only countries which have consistently had disposal routes available for low-level wastes.

Gradually a set of principles have evolved in radiological protection which have been applied to waste management. In 1977 these were set out by the ICRP as

(i) *justification:* the use of ionizing radiation should always produce a net benefit;
(ii) *optimization:* exposures to radiation should be kept *as low as reasonably achievable* (ALARA), economic and social factors being taken into account;
(iii) *dose limitation:* doses to individuals should not exceed recommended dose limits.

The first principle is traditionally met by claiming that the production of electricity or nuclear weapons creates a self-evident benefit. The third is basically an undertaking which flows from the concept of critical groups. These are identifiable parts of a population most exposed to radiation released from a nuclear facility (e.g. shellfish eaters in coastal areas near reprocessing plants which discharge radiation into the sea). Resources will be most efficiently employed by focusing on ways of reducing the exposure of these groups. This fact, that some groups are much more highly exposed to radiation from nuclear activities due to where or how they live, is often lost in generalized portrayals of the risks of nuclear power.

The second principle, optimization, is the most complex, and has the most profound impact on waste management. It suggests that the nuclear fuel cycle and waste management should be arranged so as to minimize its health effects. The objective of optimization is a kind of environmental "efficiency" where, according to the state of knowledge and technology, and the availability of resources, the lowest environmental cost is sought for nuclear power. And as in the wider economy the key aspects of the drive to efficiency is a reduction of waste (waste minimization) and a control of costs (increased control of activity through technical intervention).

Optimization has many specific effects in the details of nuclear facility design and operation, but its main effect has been in promoting a systemic view of radwaste management. In particular, it has led to the notion of a waste life-cycle (the series of storage and handling steps which a waste undergoes between production and eventual disposal). Under an optimization regime, all the possible treatment, packaging and disposal scenarios applicable to a waste stream are investigated, and the best one from the point of view of environmental protection is chosen. This is no small task since the nuclear fuel cycle produces a great variety of wastes, especially if it includes reprocessing. In Germany, for example, some 300 solid waste streams have been identified, and each allocated conditioning, packaging and disposal paths.

Regulating liquid and gaseous wastes

Some wastes, large in volume, but containing only a small proportion of total fuel cycle activity (in the UK less than 0.05% of the alpha emitters and less than 0.0002% of the beta-gamma emitters produced annually by the nuclear industry), are routinely discharged by all nuclear facilities, under specified conditions. At reactors these are mainly short-lived beta-gamma effluents, while at reprocessing facilities they include a component of the alpha activity liberated in the dissolution of spent fuel.

Setting limits on the discharge of radioactivity requires estimates of the exposures of critical groups. To do this there must be a good knowledge of the environmental pathways by which human populations will be exposed to it. Ideally, each radionuclide should be tracked through the local ecology. This model must then be integrated with models of how nuclides are metabolized, and of the dosimetry of the affected organs, to give a picture of the risks represented by that discharge. All of these models are now well established, although uncertainties inevitably persist, principally knowledge about the transmission and concentration of radioactivity in the biosphere.

In general, limiting the risks associated with reactor discharges has been easily achievable. In most countries exposures to critical groups around power reactors have been kept well below 1% of the recommended dose limits. Controlling the liquid discharges from reprocessing plants, however, has been one of the most difficult waste management problems of the nuclear industry. Perhaps the most graphic example of this is the British Sellafield plant. Although discharges were generally under control during the 1960s, they climbed steeply during the first half of the 1970s as activities at the plant expanded without adequate investment in effluent control being made. By 1975 liquid discharges of alpha emitters was estimated to be giving doses to local critical groups of about 4 mSv per year, 80% of the ICRP recommended dose limit current in those days. Although defended as being still within the limits, this level of discharges was widely seen as excessive and dangerous, not least to the nuclear industry's image as a clean technology. Over the next 10 years, Sellafield attracted the unenviable reputation of being the most polluting nuclear facility in the world, and political pressure forced the operator (British Nuclear Fuels) to invest heavily in cleaning up its effluents. Today discharges have been dramatically reduced, but at the cost of producing large new sources of solid wastes for disposal.

Dealing with solid wastes

Most of the radioactivity produced in the fuel cycle will be contained and disposed of as a solid. In comparison with most other industrial processes the volume of wastes produced is small. Operational wastes from a PWR, for instance, amount to about 20 cubic metres (cu. m) of ILW and 170 cu. m of LLW per year. Reprocessing spent fuel is the main source of wastes. Reprocessing the annual fuel discharges from a large PWR produces about 4 cu. m of HLW, 40 cu. m of ILW and 200 cu. m of LLW.

The technology of radwaste disposal has developed markedly over the past 15 years, with one option coming to be preferred over the others—geologic disposal on land. Shallow burial of low-level wastes has been practised in many countries since the 1950s with mixed results, and there is now a drift towards deep disposal of all but the least active wastes. Alternatives such as shooting long-lived material into space and burial in the polar ice-sheets attracted little support. Another, involving the neutron bombardment of long-lived isotopes to fission them into short-lived products has recently attracted renewed interest in Japan, although it has been written off as too expensive in other countries. Sea disposal is also no longer a viable alternative because of a *de facto* international embargo on the practice.

The basic concept for geologic repositories accepted around the world stems from a

Swedish proposal developed in the late 1970s. This is the so-called multi-barrier concept in which onion-like layers are placed between the waste and those who will receive doses of radiation from it far into the future. Total physical containment is impossible over the 10,000 years or more that nuclear wastes will present a discernable hazard. It is predicted that natural processes, or some catastrophic event like an earthquake, will inevitably lead to the leakage of some radioactivity out of the repository. Multiple barriers including both engineered features (the wasteform, the package) and natural features (the bedrock in which the repository is situated, the biosphere at the surface) are designed to inhibit the process so that doses to critical groups in the future will be negligible. Repository siting and design is the art of balancing the interplay between the man-made and natural barriers with the objective of enhancing those chemical and hydrological conditions which will limit corrosion and dispersion of activity away from the repository. Careful siting is also the main way of reducing the likelihood of catastrophic or unintended events.

Since it is impossible to do a full-scale test of how a repository will behave, an alternative way of predicting its performance has been developed. Mathematical models exist which attempt to simulate the evolution of critical variables in the repository (the near-field) and the geologic (the far-field) environments as they affect the release and transmission of radioactivity. These are partly based on laboratory and field experiments, but much of it is informed guesswork. For instance, in characterizing a site for a repository, boreholes must be sunk to gather geological data. The greater the number of holes bored the better will be the information to feed into the model, but the more perforated will become the rock mass. More serious is the question of how chemical, physical and hydrological conditions will themselves develop due to climatic and geologic change.

Performance assessments pose difficult theoretical, methodological and data problems which have only been partially solved. While it is possible to build a simple probabilistic model with "conservative" assumptions (i.e. assumptions which overstate the risk of hazard), it has been found that these models are highly sensitive to changes in parameter values. More complex deterministic models have therefore been developed on which sensitivity analysis can be done to explore a range of release scenarios as the repository environment evolves.

All of this endeavour would come to nothing if there was not an attempt to match the results of these computer models with reality. Increasingly this is being done in underground field laboratories in which assessment techniques are tested. The Stripa mine in Sweden is the best known of these, although a lab also exists in Germany, and further ones are planned in France, Japan and the USA. The results of models can also be compared in a process called validation as a way of finding strengths and weaknesses.

Finally it is possible to look at natural analogues of radwaste repositories. Analogues can be found for each component of the repository, but the best known complete example is the Oklo uranium ore deposit in Gabon, Africa. Spontaneous chain reactions took place in several "reactor zones" at Oklo about 2000 million years ago, and the migration of nuclides away from these reactors has been studied. This shows that dispersion over a distance of only a few metres has occurred. While analogues are good exemplars, they cannot be seen as definitive proof that a repository will be safe. Each case is unique.

Alternatives

Disposal is not the only way. It is sometimes argued that the uncertainties of radiobiology, radioecology and repository performance assessment are such that disposal is irresponsible. The argument goes that the future will inevitably produce new and better knowledge and technologies. The demonstrable hazard of some current disposal practices suggest that what we are doing today will in turn be found wanting. Most important, public confidence cannot be built around irretrievable radwaste disposal schemes. An alternative means of storage is therefore proposed.

There are two main objections to this. First, to store high-level waste until it had returned to the radioactivity of the original uranium would take of the order of 10,000 years. To guarantee that human society can endure for that long is optimistic. Second, the risks associated with keeping the material at the surface for so long are likely to be greater than if the wastes were disposed of in a repository under controlled conditions. A commitment to disposal is therefore the international norm.

The notion of retrievability attempts to fill the middle ground in this debate. It states that even after a repository has been finally sealed, the choice of opening and evacuating it should be retained. There is clearly a tension between safety and this kind of accessibility, but retrievability is taken seriously in several countries.

Nuclear accidents and their consequences

The fear of serious accidents at nuclear power plants has always been one of the principal concerns about the technology. This fear is understandable enough: an individual nuclear plant contains a vast store of radioactive material. Even though, contrary to some public fears, a reactor cannot explode like a nuclear bomb, the release of radioactivity to the environment can kill large numbers of people, both immediately and in the future, and—as Chernobyl showed—contaminate large areas of land for long periods.

Because of this enormous potential harm, the designers of nuclear plant have been dominated by the need to provide multiple defences to prevent such radioactive releases to the environment—defences which are intended to mitigate the effects of human error that inevitably accompanies any complex human activity.

Two particular characteristics of the design of reactors intensify the problem of isolating radioactivity from the biosphere. First, in most reactor systems, but especially in the most common PWR type, there is the need to operate the core under high pressures (up to 150 atmospheres), necessitating a pressure vessel of high integrity. Secondly, there is the need, in order to keep the cost of reactor cores manageably low, to operate at fairly high "power density". This simply means that reactors are designed to produce high levels of heat per unit volume per period of time, and leads to the need to have an efficient heat removal system which is backed up by rapid emergency responses if primary cooling is lost. Different reactors offer different levels of challenge to designers in making the finished product acceptably safe: PWRs operate at high pressure and fairly high power density, while fast breeders have exceptionally high power density but need no pressurization at all. There have been intense debates about the merits of "inherent" and "engineered" safety in reactor design. It is not, however, possible to argue convincingly that any particular current reactor type offers clear safety advantages over others, although claims to this effect are often made for gas-cooled and heavy water reactors.

Designers try to defend reactors against radioactive releases in two main ways: first there is the prevention of serious malfunctions which might trigger or accumulate in accident-creating sequences; second there is the provision of strong and usually multiple barriers (i.e. both primary and secondary containments) so that even if accidents do take place, the chances of radioactivity reaching the biosphere are made as tiny as possible.

In the important and primary area of prevention, early design attention (up to the mid-1970s) was heavily focused on the most catastrophic forms of accident that might take place—the major loss of coolant accident (LOCA). In this sequence, core coolant is lost and cannot be replaced, the core overheats and melts, containment is breached and radioactivity is released to the environment. While it is natural that the most serious consequences should receive prime attention, concentration on the large LOCA involved two main omissions: first little attention was paid to the more minor and individually harmless malfunctions which might combine to produce more serious events; secondly, accident sequences were seen as purely technical phenomena, it being generally (if implicitly) assumed that technical systems would prove "fail safe" in the face of human error.

The major accident at Three Mile Island in 1979 helped modify these biases. Broadly what caused the accident was the accumulation of many individually small malfunctions and errors, which cumulatively had a potentially disastrous result (though in the end the level of radioactive releases to the atmosphere was small and did not clearly damage physical health). The particular errors or malfunctions included: valves that had been wrongly left closed during maintenance, preventing the operation of emergency feedwater; a relief valve that stuck open, leaving a hole in the primary cooling system, and which thus allowed over-heating in the core of the reactor; the iodine filters, as a matter of routine, were left running continuously, which reduced their design filtering capacity when they were needed; no mechanisms existed, when shifts changed, to check systematically on the status of the plant.

While operator and maintenance error played a part in the Three Mile Island accident, so, too, did a number of "latent" failures (e.g. the iodine filter problem, the shift change issue) which were traceable to broader managerial failure. While the TMI accident stimulated much new work on human error and its mitigation (in contrast to earlier concentration on technical failures) the latent and managerial issues have tended to receive less attention than the more obvious issue of immediate operator error.

This need to give attention to the whole social and technical *system* in nuclear safety is well illustrated in the Chernobyl accident in 1986. As is well known, Chernobyl was an accident with very large consequences for human life and health, in the short and long term, as well as leaving a very large area of land in a dangerously contaminated condition. The immediate fatalities were over 30, but the eventual toll will be much higher, including some tens of thousands of long-term cancers induced by radiation.

At Chernobyl there was no component failure of any kind. There was however a combination of managerial, design and operational failures. The start of the accident was a test designed to discover whether a safety system could be operated in a different mode. The emergency core cooling system was deliberately disabled and not reconnected at any point. The operators then failed to hold power at sufficiently high level (the reactor design is unstable at low power levels), and as things became more unstable and unfamiliar, they stripped the reactor of most of its remaining defences, including most of the control rods.

While the catalogue of errors and violations was a particularly sorry one, all the individual element of the accident have been found in other countries. The avoidance of future Chernobyls undoubtedly depends on attention to the whole social and managerial system of nuclear power, as well as its details, whether of component design and interaction or of detailed operation.

While the broad managerial and socio-technical issues apply to all reactor systems, rather different *technical* issues are raised in the safety of the two advanced reactor designs—the fast breeder and the fusion reactor. Breeders have very compact cores and need particularly efficient cooling. In liquid metal-cooled fast reactors close attention must be paid to avoiding sodium/water interactions, and in normal operation (unlike the great majority of current reactor designs) the plant is not in a state of maximum reactivity. In other words the rate of fission reaction can, in principle, increase, during abnormal conditions.

These characteristics of breeders pose major safety design challenges. Fusion power, by contrast, has been much supported in the past on grounds that it would be environmentally clean. However the cleanliness of fusion depended on the use of a fuel cycle that involved only the virtually harmless isotope deuterium. But all remotely practical schemes for fusion require the additional use of tritium, which is radioactive and poses some difficulties of control. In addition, because of the high neutron flux in a fusion reactor, the structure becomes highly irradiated, posing special problems for decommissioning.

On balance fusion is likely to pose fewer safety problems than conventional reactors, but it will produce large amounts of radioactivity, and fusion reactor accidents could result in serious radioactive releases. Support for fusion cannot therefore be based on the idea that it is much "cleaner" than existing nuclear technology.

Decommissioning nuclear facilities

What is to be done once the operating life of nuclear power plant is over? The term decommissioning is used to describe whatever is then done, whether this involves clearance to greenfield site, or the less radical strategy of long-term or indefinite entombment. In practice, virtually all operators of nuclear plants and their governments anticipate that decommissioning will mean a return to greenfield site rather than indefinite entombment. Most expect to move to complete dismantling as early as practically feasible (within 20 years or so of plant closure), though in Britain delays of 100 years or more are officially contemplated.

Until recently decommissioning has been a hypothetical, future issue: commercial sized reactors had not reached the end of their lives and there was little public attention paid to the issue of what should be done at the point of shutdown. This is now rapidly changing. In the late 1980s commercial reactors began to shut in France and Britain for reasons of old age, and in the USA for regulatory and political reasons. In the 1990s there will be many more nuclear plant closures as the stock of reactors ages, and by the early years of the next century very large numbers of reactors will be closing.

Decommissioning has environmental implications because the cores of nuclear reactors remain radioactive for long periods after the end of plant operation, while other parts of the plant may be contaminated to a lesser degree. The operations involved in decommissioning can be classified along two dimensions: by type of operation, and by stage.

Type of operation

Essentially decommissioning as conventionally defined includes two major types of operation

(i) *On-site engineering.* These are the various processes, some more or less conventional demolition, others much more difficult and involving complex remote-handling machinery, required to dismantle the various items of plant on a nuclear site.

(ii) *Off-site disposal.* While some parts of a nuclear plant can be disposed of conventionally, there are also very large volumes of structural material which constitute low level radioactive waste, and much smaller volumes which are at intermediate level. The disposal of these materials is subject to exactly the same constraints and policy decisions as the disposal of radioactive waste in general (see above). However the sheer volume of material involved makes disposal of decommissioning waste an important issue: as a rule of thumb the volume of radioactive waste created by decommissioning is about twice as much as that created by reactor operation and reprocessing the fuel a reactor uses through its entire lifetime of 30 or so years.

Excluded from most definitions of decommissioning operations are the removal and disposal of the fuel that remains in the core at closedown. This is simply treated as part of the question of the disposal of used fuel.

Stages of decommissioning

Conventionally decommissioning is divided into three stages. They are broadly sequential, though they can in principle overlap:

Stage 1. This is simply the defuelling of the reactor (the fuel contains the bulk of the radioactivity in the core) plus limited sealing operations.

Stage 2. This involves the demolition of all the more-or-less uncontaminated structures outside the nuclear core, in some cases following a decontamination process to ensure that the resultant material can be disposed of without restriction. If Stage 3 is to be delayed, Stage 2 may also involve a more thorough sealing of all the penetrations into the reactor core.

Stage 3. This stage, generally expected to be significantly the most expensive of the three, is also the one that some countries expect to delay. It involves the dismantling and disposing of all remaining structures including the radioactive reactor vessel. It is now expected that much of the core, constituting mainly LLW, will have to be cut into small pieces and then boxed or drummed before being taken to radioactive waste depositories. Some releases of radioactivity may accompany Stage 3.

Early designers of nuclear reactors paid little attention to the question of how to carry out decommissioning operations, and current expectations are that full decommissioning—return to greenfield conditions—will prove a costly exercise. The minimum level of cost expected is $100 million per commercial reactor, a more typical level is around $300 million, and for particularly problematic reactors (for instance the British Magnox gas-cooled reactors) the official expectation is that the cost will be of the order of $500 million. These expected cost levels have in recent years been escalating much more rapidly than general price levels.

A large part of the uncertainty about the costs of decommissioning stems from the fact the world has little practical experience of fully carrying it out. Only very small and relatively lightly irradiated reactors have yet completed Stage 3 (the largest, Elk River in the USA, is, at 22 MW, up to 50 times smaller than the typical commercial sized unit). No start has yet been made on Stage 3 for any of the larger plants. The difficulty of predicting precisely what will be involved in Stage 3 (and therefore accurately predicting its cost) is made all the more difficult by the fact that the radiological standards applying both to worker exposure during dismantling, and to radioactive waste disposal in general, are continually becoming more stringent. Consequently, the complexity and cost of decommissioning is increasing, and is, incidentally, rendering more doubtful the supposed advantages (especially allowing more human access to the core) of delaying Stage 3.

Despite such problems, the nuclear industry argues that it is already technically capable of safely decommissioning reactors to Stage 3. However a good deal of detailed development work (as well as some research) is needed to make such possibilities fully practical, as well as to keep up with increasingly stringent regulatory requirements about maximum radioactive exposures.

A large technical effort is now under way to develop practical and improved decommissioning technology. Specific areas include improvements to remote handling technology, chemical decontamination of piping and components, improved methods for waste treatment and improved measurement techniques to allow more accurate segregation of waste streams.

In addition there are a number of major decommissioning projects on small reactors, all intending to complete Stage 3, and from which it is hoped to learn lessons of general or at least wider applicability. The most important of these projects are at Windscale in the UK (a 32 MW prototype reactor: completion expected around 1994), Shippingport in the USA (68 MW) and Niederaichbach (106 MW) in Germany.

Now that commercial-sized reactors are beginning in the 1990s to come off line, decommissioning is likely to become an increasingly real environmental issue. While it is widely intended to move towards full decommissioning and a return to greenfield conditions as rapidly as possible, this may well be frustrated in many countries by the very large consequent volumes of low-level radioactive waste that will be created—unless more countries enjoy greater success than in recent years in creating more or larger waste repositories.

Nuclear proliferation and international security

The exploitation of the energy of the atom began with the Bomb. This is a legacy which post-war nuclear planners of civilian programmes, beginning with President Eisenhower who heralded the "peaceful atom" in 1953, have tried to put behind them. They have not always been successful because the technology of civil nuclear power is basically no different from that of the military fuel cycle.

To build a nuclear weapon two things are needed: a bomb design and a quantity of fissile material (either plutonium or highly enriched uranium). The design is a problem of experimental physics, but plutonium is, as we have seen, an unavoidable product in the irradiation of uranium nuclear fuel. The main difference between an electricity-producing reactor and one which is producing plutonium for bombs is that the fuel is kept in the reactor for longer in the former. Civil reactor fuel is thereby "polluted" with a higher proportion of neutron-absorbing plutonium isotopes which make it more difficult, though not impossible, to build a reliable weapon.

It is held as more or less self-evident in the Western world that the spread of nuclear weapons would not be a good thing for peace in the world. Not everyone agrees with this, especially in those countries who would like to possess such a weapon. They argue that if the established Nuclear Weapons States (the USA, the USSR, the UK, France, China) are justified in having nuclear deterrents, then as mature members of the international community with their own strategic interests to defend, they too should be allowed to have them. This view has some force, but it is held by only a minority of governments.

Elsewhere the peaceful use of nuclear power is assured by the Nuclear Non-Proliferation Treaty (NPT) of 1970 which 141 countries have now ratified. Under this treaty, Non-Nuclear Weapons States (NNWS) pledge not to develop the Bomb and submit their civil nuclear activities to international scrutiny through a system of nuclear safeguards. In return they are assured of access to technology and nuclear material, while the NWS agree to pursue nuclear disarmament. This last promise has only started to be honoured in the last two years.

So far the NPT has worked well, although weaknesses remain. What horizontal proliferation there has been since its inception (to countries like India, Pakistan, Israel and South Africa), has occurred outside the treaty, and there has been little progress in getting these countries, together with other important absentees such as France and China, to join. Second, large parts of the civil fuel cycle in NWS party to the treaty still lie outside NPT safeguards. Lastly there is a question of whether the NNWS parties will find that the steps towards disarmament so far taken by the Superpowers are sufficient within the terms of the treaty, and whether this issue could complicate the fourth Review conference in 1990, and the Renewal conference in 1995.

The environmental consequences of nuclear war

Certainly the most catastrophic imaginable effects of nuclear technology would be a full-scale nuclear confrontation. The debate over the environmental consequences of nuclear war have been important in the arcane debate over nuclear strategy, with one side claiming that such a war would be "winnable" and the other holding that nuclear war would amount to a holocaust from which developed human societies could not recover.

Nuclear war would have four types of environmental effect. The first would be blast in the immediate area of an explosion. The second, assuming the war occurred in the Northern hemisphere, would affect up to about 30% of mid-latitude areas with prompt fallout. This would deliver radiation doses approaching or exceeding lethal levels. On an intermediate timescale more widespread fallout would cause further millions of cancers and birth defects among the survivors of a war. During the early 1980s another effect—the "nuclear winter"—was postulated. Carl Sagan and others argued that soot, smoke and dust from fires following a nuclear war could darken and cool the earth's atmosphere with devastating global biological consequences. Full-scale nuclear war would mean, under these circumstances, the end of life on earth. The "nuclear winter" debate still rumbles on, even though in these times of détente and reconciliation it has lost some of its charge.

Conclusion

Such are the passions unleashed by nuclear power that it is difficult, and more likely impossible, to reach a consensus about the objective environmental safety of the complex array of nuclear technologies. There is little doubt that the nuclear industry, partly as a result of these strong feelings, must meet a level of safe operation to which no other human activity is subject.

In the late 1980s, when fossil fuel prices fell precipitously, and many nuclear costs escalated, it began to seem likely that as an active energy source, nuclear power might be on the way out—though leaving a substantial environmental legacy for many future generations. Now that global warming has become an issue, the nuclear industry is hopeful of a major revival, gambling on the idea that environmental consciousness will bifurcate, rejecting fossil fuels and embracing "cleaner" nuclear power. If the revival does take place, then the safety record of the industry will almost certainly need to improve further—a Chernobyl-level accident in the West would prove fatal to further expansion.

For bibliography, see p. 361.

9 OZONE DEPLETION

Industrial halocarbons and their effect on the stratospheric ozone layer

J. C. Farman

Introduction

Ozone is the only constituent of the atmosphere present in sufficient quantity to serve as an effective screen against solar ultraviolet radiation; this radiation can adversely affect many living organisms, including man, and a wide range of materials. The abundance of ozone is determined by the net effect of the photochemical processes which produce and destroy it, and of atmospheric transport. The recognition that the main processes of destruction were catalytic cycles, involving constituents present in only trace proportions, led to an awareness that the abundance of ozone could be substantially altered by human activities. There is now no doubt that this has occurred. The continued release of industrially produced halocarbons has caused severe damage to the stratospheric ozone layer. Because of the long atmospheric lifetimes of many of these halocarbons, the damage will continue for many years after releases of these halocarbons have been stopped.

Ironically, man has also shown his ability to create ozone in substantial quantity at ground level, perhaps most notably in the photochemical smog of Los Angeles. The ozone is produced by sunlight following the accumulation of oxides of nitrogen, derived mainly from internal combustion engines, and from large power generators working on fossil fuel. Unfortunately, a large abundance of ozone at ground level is harmful to human health, and damaging to many plants and materials. It cannot be used to compensate for the destruction of stratospheric ozone.

Damage to the stratospheric ozone layer

The first clear sign of damage to the ozone layer was the Antarctic ozone "hole". This very severe seasonal depletion at high latitudes and at moderate altitudes was completely unforeseen. The effects of chlorine had been predicted to occur mainly in low latitudes and at altitudes above 30 km, in the region where the ozone concentration is controlled largely by photochemistry, and where the response time to chemical change is very short, i.e. hours or less. Prior to the discovery of the ozone "hole", it had been thought that chemically-driven changes in early spring over Antarctica would be very slow; the lifetime of ozone there was thought to be many years.

In 1987, and again in 1989, half of the ozone column over Antarctica was destroyed in six weeks, from late August to early October, spring months in the Southern Hemisphere. Profiles of the ozone layer, obtained from balloon-borne instruments, showed that the destruction took place over a limited range of altitudes, between 12 and 22 km. In this layer, which over Antarctica normally contains about one-half of the total ozone column, destruction was almost complete; over 95% of the ozone was removed.

Successive American expeditions to McMurdo Station in Antarctica in 1986 and 1987 using ground-based instruments capable of measuring many different minor constituents produced much evidence to support the view that the formation of the ozone "hole" was caused largely by chemical processes. This conclusion was strongly reinforced when, in August and September 1987, American aircraft carrying many instruments flew into and below the ozone "hole". The abundance of the chlorine monoxide radical at the altitudes where ozone destruction was observed was found to be over 100 times that predicted by current models of the atmosphere. At such concentrations, catalytic cycles whose significance had previously been discounted come into play. Unlike the classical catalytic chlorine cycle, these other cycles do not require the presence of oxygen atoms, and so can drive rapid ozone destruction in the lower stratosphere. The rate-limiting reactions are the self-reaction of chlorine monoxide to form a dimer (combination of two radicals), and the reaction between chlorine monoxide and bromine monoxide. Although the concentration of bromine monoxide is very low (less than one-fiftieth of that of chlorine monoxide), this last reaction nevertheless may account for between 20 and 30% of the ozone destruction.

The processes which lead to such a large abundance of chlorine monoxide have been identified. At very low temperatures nitric acid vapour condenses into particles composed initially of almost pure nitric acid trihydrate. If the temperature drops still further, these particles can grow by the condensation of water. Chemical reactions between substances which are mutually inert as gases take place rapidly on the surfaces of these particles. The net effect of these reactions is that gaseous chlorine compounds which can be readily photolysed are produced from the more stable inorganic chlorine compounds (largely, hydrochloric acid and chlorine nitrate), whilst oxides of nitrogen are converted into nitric acid which remains trapped in the particles. The denitrification and dehydration of an air parcel induced by the formation and growth of these particles, now referred to in bulk as polar stratospheric clouds, may be irreversible if the particles grow to such a size that they can fall rapidly. These processes can occur in darkness. Subsequent exposure to sunlight of air parcels in which these processes have taken place, leads to rapid accumulation of chlorine monoxide.

The spectacular nature of the ozone "hole" is a consequence of the wind structure at high latitudes in winter. An intense whirlpool of westerly winds develops, with a very cold centre. The winds are so strong that the centre of this vortex is effectively isolated from the surrounding air. Once formed, the ozone "hole" persists (in 1987 and 1989, almost until mid-summer) until the vortex is broken down, by a combination of radiative and dynamical forcing. However, it is important to realize that ozone destruction can take place outside this isolated air-mass, indeed on any trajectory which passes through temperatures low enough to initiate the formation of polar stratospheric cloud particles. The chemistry, so to speak, knows nothing about the subsequent motion of the air-mass, whether it is to be confined in the isolated cold centre, or to be transported to lower latitudes. Once the chemical composition has been perturbed, enhanced abundance of chlorine monoxide can persist for many days. The dimer of chlorine monoxide is thermally unstable, so if the air-parcel subsequently warms that catalytic cycle becomes ineffective. However, the bromine cycle remains very efficient.

Recently it was recognized that there has been a decline in the amount of ozone in winter over northern mid-latitudes for at least the last 10 years. The loss is most marked over North America and over Europe, amounting in January to some 8% relative to the amounts recorded in 1969. The cause of this loss has not yet been identified with certainty. However, it is now known that in winter the composition of the Arctic stratosphere can undergo changes similar to those which precede ozone loss over Antarctica, and it must be regarded as highly likely that the ozone loss is driven by the chlorine/bromine cycle in air parcels whose trajectories have skirted the Arctic winter vortex. If this is correct, the losses can be expected to increase rapidly through the next decade.

Sources of stratospheric chlorine and bromine

To destroy ozone in the stratosphere, chlorine and bromine must be present as radicals, that is, in atomic form or bound in small active inorganic molecules. The radicals are produced there by photochemical reactions involving so-called reservoir gases; less active inorganic compounds, into which the radicals retreat during darkness. In the case of chlorine, the reservoirs are mainly hydrochloric acid and chlorine nitrate, as indicated in the preceding section. However, these inorganic compounds are highly soluble in water, and if released at the earth's surface would be rapidly washed out of the atmosphere by rain. Very little of the released material would get to the stratosphere, except possibly in very large explosions or in volcanic eruptions. In fact, halogens are most effectively transported to the stratosphere when they are organically bound, in inert molecules such as the halocarbons (CFCs, halons, etc.). The halogens are released, as radicals, mainly by the action of ultraviolet light, when the halocarbons get above the ozone layer. However, this direct production of radicals from the CFCs is now only a small fraction of the total production of radicals. The continued release of CFCs has built large abundances of the reservoir gases.

The potential of a halogen to destroy ozone is determined by the ease with which the active radicals can be released from these reservoirs. The main reservoir for fluorine is hydrogen fluoride. As a gas this is so strongly bonded that fluorine presents little apparent threat to the ozone layer. It may be remarked that prior to the large-scale manufacture of CFCs there was practically no hydrogen fluoride in the stratosphere. The present abundance confirms that the only processes which remove substantial quantities of the CFCs from the atmosphere are photolysis and oxidation in the stratosphere. The hydrogen/chlorine bond in hydrochloric acid is less strong, and the hydrogen/bromine bond is yet weaker. Thus, on an atom-for-atom basis, bromine is much more likely, about 30 times so, to be found in the form of active radicals than chlorine.

The natural, or background abundances of chlorine and bromine in the stratosphere are derived predominantly from two halocarbons, methyl chloride and methyl bromide. Both are now also produced industrially, but at rates which are thought not to exceed 10% of the natural production. However, starting in the early 1900s with carbon tetrachloride, industry has produced a wide range of halocarbons (the CFCs, methyl chloroform, the halons, and the HCFCs), which for all practical purposes may be regarded as new constituents of the atmosphere. Between 1960 and 1985, some 20,000,000 tonnes of fully halogenated halocarbons (CFCs and carbon tetrachloride) were released into the atmosphere. The rate at which these substances are removed from the atmosphere is so slow that fully one-third of that amount will remain in the atmosphere at the end of the next century (2100 AD). While, as discussed in a later section, it has now been agreed internationally to phase out the production of these substances through the next decade, the releases between 1985 and 2000 are likely to exceed 12,000,000 tonnes.

The CFCs are very safe to handle, they are non-toxic and non-flammable. CFC-11 and CFC-12 were introduced initially mainly for use in refrigerating equipment, in which they replaced more dangerous substances, and as aerosol propellants. A wide variety of applications have since been developed. At present the refrigeration, air-conditioning, and heat-pump industries represent about 25% of global consumption of CFCs, of which 5 to 8% is used for food preservation, with about 1% being used in domestic refrigerators. A further 25% is used in foam production. Solvent uses of CFC-113 in the electronics and precision engineering industries, and in metal and dry cleaning applications, represents about 16% of global consumption. The balance is made up by use as aerosol propellants, in sterilisation, and in food freezing.

The industrial halocarbons containing bromine, chiefly halon 1211 and halon 1301, are used almost exclusively by the fire protection industry. Halon 1211 is used in portable fire extinguishers; halon 1301 is used in total flooding applications, such as protecting art collections and museums, large computer installations, and communication centres.

History of chlorine and bromine loading of the lower atmosphere

The quantities of most concern for ozone depletion are the abundances of chlorine and bromine in the stratosphere. Unfortunately the information available is relatively recent, and remains sparse. The simplest relevant parameters are the abundances of chlorine and bromine held in the lower atmosphere in halocarbons which have long enough atmospheric lifetimes to carry the halogens to the stratosphere. These abundances are referred to as the chlorine and bromine loadings. Historical loadings can be inferred from industrial records. For the last decade there have been careful systematic measurements.

The natural background loadings are thought to have been about 0.6 ppbv (parts per billion by volume; one billion is one thousand-million) of chlorine and 15 pptv (parts per trillion; one trillion is one million-million) of bromine, although there is much uncertainty in the case of bromine. These loadings refer notionally to about 1900. By 1970 the atmospheric chlorine loading was about 1.4 ppbv, today it is about 3.6 ppbv. Growth was very rapid from 1970 to 1975, slackened slightly from 1976 to 1982, and then quickened again in response to growth in the use of halocarbons, to settle to an almost steady rise of 0.12 ppbv per year.

In the last five years the loading has increased by 0.6 ppbv, an amount equal to the natural loading of the atmosphere. Five-sixths of the loading is now carried by man-made halocarbons, two-thirds residing in halocarbons with atmospheric lifetimes in excess of 50 years. Even should there be no further releases, the man-made chlorine loading will exceed the loading from natural sources for at least another 110 years (see Table 1).

Two industrial halocarbons are actually produced in much greater quantity than CFCs, but have very short lifetimes (less than four months), and do not appear to be accumulating in the atmosphere. These are the ethylene derivatives, vinyl chloride, $CHClCCl_2$, and perchloroethene, CCl_2CCl_2.

Halons were first marketed in 1975. Releases since then have raised the bromine loading to about 20 pptv, 30% higher than the natural loading.

There is a time lag of several years between the release of halocarbons at the earth's surface, and the involvement of the halogens derived from them in ozone destruction in the lower stratosphere at high latitudes. Hence the full effects of today's loadings are yet

Table 1: *The contributions to chlorine loading in 1985 and 1990*

	ppbv of chlorine	
	1985	*1990*
CFC-11	0.660	0.858
CFC-12	0.750	0.962
CFC-113	0.090	0.170
Carbon tetrachloride	0.400	0.428
Methyl chloroform	0.390	0.479
HCFC-22	0.080	0.103
Methyl chloride (natural)	0.600	0.600
Total	2.970	3.600

to be felt. Moreover, since the loadings have been increasing for many years, the damage now seen is the result of loadings much lower than those which now exist. In retrospect, it appears that damage was occurring in both Antarctica and the northern hemisphere in the early and mid'-70s when the chlorine loading was between 1.5 and 2.0 ppbv, and the bromine loading was near the background level. It must be assumed that depletion will continue to appear until the loadings return to these levels. It is not sufficient to merely stabilize the loadings. Policies must be devised which allow the loadings to fall from their present unprecedented values as quickly as possible.

International regulation of halocarbons: the Montreal Protocol on substances which deplete the ozone layer

Concern that the continued large-scale release of chlorofluorocarbons could lead to substantial depletion of stratospheric ozone first arose in 1974. Seminal papers by Cicerone and Stolarski, and by Rowland and Molina, identified the key issues, and lively debate ensued. Some countries took action. The use of CFCs as aerosol propellants was banned in the United States, in Canada, and in Scandinavia. Japan and most European countries declined to take action, arguing that the scientific case was not proven. Even in the countries which did take action, the effect on overall release rates was slight, as new applications and markets were developing rapidly.

It became clear that regulation would be effective only if agreed internationally. The United Nations Environment Programme (UNEP) assumed responsibility for leading negotiations in 1979. It proved to be impossible to get general assent to regulatory measures. However UNEP did succeed in getting support for the Vienna Convention to Protect the Ozone Layer, which was formally adopted on March 22, 1985. In effect, this was a simple statement of intent, a recognition that there might indeed be a global problem. However, attempts to proceed beyond this statement of intent continued to founder.

The breakthrough came at a meeting in Montreal in September 1987, when at last a Protocol on Substances which Deplete the Ozone Layer was adopted. In retrospect, considering what was already known from Antarctica, and the high probability that much stronger evidence would be made public later that same month (as, indeed, it was), the proposed controls were absurdly weak.

The projected cuts would slow down the rates at which the CFCs and halons were accumulating in the atmosphere, but would nevertheless allow their abundances to increase indefinitely. Of more lasting significance than the control measures themselves was the provision for review of the control measures. Article 6 of the Protocol stipulated that "Beginning in 1990, and at least every four years thereafter, the Parties shall assess the control measures . . . on the basis of all available scientific, environmental, technical and economic information . . .".

To become effective the Protocol had to be ratified by at least 11 countries, representing at least two-thirds of the estimated global consumption of the controlled substances in 1986. The target date for the entry into force of the Protocol was set as Jan. 1, 1989, and this was duly achieved. By that date 34 governments had ratified the Protocol. The review procedure was implemented at once. Four assessment panels were set up, and their reports became available in the last quarter of 1989. A total of 136 scientists from 25 countries took part in the preparation and review of the report of the Ozone Scientific Assessment Panel. Forty-eight scientists from 17 countries took part in the preparation and review of the report of the Environmental Effects Panel. Twenty-four experts from 12 countries prepared the report of the Economic Assessment Panel, and their conclusions were reviewed by 25 experts from 18 countries. The Technology Review Panel Report was a summary of five detailed Technical Options Reports, dealing separately with Refrigeration, Air Conditioning and Heat Pumps, with Rigid and Flexible Foams, with Electronic, Degreasing and Dry Cleaning Solvents, with Aerosols, Sterilants and Miscellaneous Uses of CFCs, and with Halon Fire Extinguishing Agents. A total of 110 experts from 22 countries helped to compile these reports.

All this material was presented to the second meeting of the Parties to the Montreal Protocol, held in London from June 21 to 29, 1990. By then, the number of countries ratifying the Protocol had increased to 59, with the European Communities as an additional international signatory. Some 40 other countries attended the meeting as observers. In contrast to the meeting in Montreal, when many of those attending would not accept that action was necessary, there was little discussion on the science of ozone depletion. No one contested the view that halocarbons were damaging the ozone layer. The discussion concerned timetables, temporary solutions, and development aid. The key decisions were to phase out the production of the fully halogenated CFCs and halons by the end of the century, to extend greatly the list of controlled substances, and to set up a fund to help developing countries to comply with the controls.

The substances controlled under the revised Protocol are listed in two Annexes, A and B. The meeting was unable to reach agreement on control of HCFCs, but decided to create a new category of "transitional substances", and enjoined countries to make only "prudent and responsible use" of them. The lists are as follows:

Annex A controlled substances (as agreed in Montreal, 1987)

Group I	CFCs 11, 12, 113, 114 and 115
Group II	halons 1211, 1301, and 2402

Annex B controlled substances (added in London, 1990)

Group I	CFCs 13, 111, 112, 211, 212, 213, 214, 215, 216, and 217
Group II	carbon tetrachloride
Group III	methyl chloroform (1,1,1-trichloroethane)

Note: all isomers of Group I substances are included.

Annex C transitional substances (added in London, 1990)
33 derivatives of methane, ethane and propane are listed.

The old and new control measures are shown in Table 2.

Reactions to the revised Protocol have been mixed. Some have hailed it as a great step forward; to others, it seems that more desirable goals have been fixed, but that there is considerable reluctance to move towards them. Indeed, in the short term the revised Protocol actually defers action. For, remembering that the freeze to the consumption levels of 1986 should by now have been completed, no further action is now stipulated until 1995. This caused some concern at the meeting itself, and delegates from 13 countries signed a declaration to take more rapid action. It is difficult to see why the majority of countries cannot do the same. There are no outstanding technical or economic problems. Indeed, the Assessment Panels Report described the first 50% reduction as a relatively easy first step, which "will require modest new investment capital, will incur little or no net cost, will result in some business disruption, and will require very little abandonment of capital".

Such views are clearly accepted in Sweden, where much stricter regulation is already in force, and in West Germany, which came to the meeting having just placed very strict proposals before its Parliament. The German cabinet is recommending to phase out the controlled substances by 1995, and the restriction of HCFC-22 (the only HCFC used in substantial amounts at present) pending phasing out of that chemical by 2000.

The establishment of the development aid fund has been warmly welcomed. The Indian and Chinese delegates announced that they would recommend that their governments should sign the Protocol. It had been widely stated that the Protocol would be worthless if it did not include these two nations, with the world's biggest populations and the fastest growing CFC industries.

The most sensitive area of discussion at the meeting seems to have been the question of HCFCs. Industry's view has always been that these short-lived compounds are necessary—for a limited period—to help speed up the withdrawal of the long-lived CFCs and halons. However, it is clear that substitution of CFCs by HCFCs in other than modest proportions (which depends on the lifetime of the particular HCFC used) could throw away much of the benefit gained by cutting CFCs. Substantial releases of HCFCs could

Table 2: *How the Montreal controls were tightened (percentage cuts)*

	Montreal 1987			*London 1990*				
Annex/Group	*1989–90*	*1993–94*	*1998–99*	*1993*	*1995*	*1997*	*2000*	*2005*
A/I	Freeze[a]	20	50		50	85	100[b]	
A/II	Freeze[a]				50		100[c]	
B/1		Not controlled		20	50	85	100	
B/II		Not controlled		Freeze[a]	85		100	
B/III		Not controlled		Freeze[a]			30	100
C		Not controlled			Not controlled[d]			

a "Freeze" means at level of year preceding conference, 1986 (Montreal), 1989 (London)
b 10–year grace for developing countries
c Except for essential safety uses
d Call for "prudent and responsible use"

both increase the peak chlorine loading, and sustain unprecedented levels of stratospheric chlorine for many years. In the event, the negotiators produced a compromise. The compounds have been listed in Annex C of the Protocol, but left uncontrolled. Industry has been exhorted to use them "prudently and responsibly", and in particular, not to use them where safer alternatives are already available. Statistics of production and use will be compiled, with a view to further negotiations.

The interval permitted between meetings was originally set at four years, but the conference agreed to meet again in 1992. Some have seen this as a sign that further progress is not far away, and that differences over HCFC policy can be resolved. Let us hope so. Success in this field could be the spur needed to counter other environmental threats.

For bibliography, see pp. 361–362.

10 RENEWABLE ENERGY

Francis McGowan

Introduction

The increased awareness of the environmental consequences of energy technology choices has presented a major challenge to both the energy supplier and consumer as well as to policy makers. With most conventional sources of energy (the fossil fuels—coal, gas and oil—and nuclear power) inflicting damage upon the environment, or posing a potential threat to it, greater attention is being paid to those sources of energy supply commonly referred to as "renewable", those sources which utilize the forces of nature, (sun, water, wave and wind) or which consume resources which can be rapidly replaced (such as waste or certain agricultural products). Because they have, for the most part, much less significant effects on the environment than any of the conventional sources, they are now being taken more seriously as a means of harnessing energy, and more particularly producing electricity, than they have been hitherto.

While the idea of "renewable" energy resources is relatively new, the use of those sources is not. Solar energy is of course the key to the functioning of the planet and of humanity. Conscious exploitation of renewable resources started with the use of wood for fire, and it remains the main source of energy in the developing world, and the harnessing of the wind for traction and transport.[1] More recently, renewable energy has been used for electricity production through hydroelectricity for more than 100 years and through geothermal and wind, for most of the last century.

The encouragement of renewables as an explicit component of energy balances over the last 20 years has been motivated by a coincidence of two concerns: the oil crises of the 1970s and the worry that these were manifestations of a fundamental fossil fuel supply problem on the one hand; and, fears over the development of the principal non-fossil fuel technology—nuclear power—on the other.

Since then anxiety over the supply position of fossil fuels has largely faded, though there are still worries over how existing reserves of oil, coal and gas can provide energy to a rapidly expanding world population much beyond the middle of the next century. Indeed, the collapse of fossil fuel prices in the mid 1980s largely neutralized many of the 1970s fears on supply and reversed some of the measures adopted to reduce fossil fuel consumption, including renewables, at least in those assessments where cost concerns predominated.

Instead, it has been with regard to the environment that concern over energy choices has grown, and the debate on renewables redirected. Nuclear power remains for many a source of concern, in the light of the Three Mile Island and Chernobyl accidents and

[1]For example, see Braudel (1985) for an account of energy use in the period 1400–1700.

the intractability of radioactive waste disposal. These fears have been compounded by a realization that the economics of nuclear power were also problematic.

More important has been the realization that fossil fuels were themselves contributing to major environmental problems. Worries that carbon dioxide emissions from coal, oil and gas (amongst other emissions) were contributing to a "greenhouse effect", or climatic change, were first voiced in the 1970s and subsequently, but with more scientific support, in the late 1980s. The potential consequences of this phenomenon could have a massive impact on the world's climate and habitats. Its prominence in the current debate has overshadowed another issue, that of acid rain (caused largely by sulphur dioxide emissions from coal and oil burning), which had become politically sensitive in the 1980s. Whereas the control of such emissions was open to technical solutions, the problem of carbon dioxide was, in most assessments, not.

In tackling this new environmental agenda, the task for policy makers and those pressing for changes in policy, has been to determine how to stem the rising emission levels of greenhouse gases, given the level of energy demand in developed countries and the rapid growth in the developing world. They have had to consider how the energy balance can be reshaped to allow for continued growth and economic well-being without jeopardizing the global ecological balance. The principle "solution" to the greenhouse problem has been a mix of greater energy efficiency and fuel substitution policies away from carbon emitting energy sources and towards those, like renewables, which would provide energy at a much lower environmental price.

The concerns over environmental degradation have undoubtedly revived the prospects for renewable energy. Yet for the most part, the potential of this resource is not reflected in current energy balances or in most official forecasts of future energy supply.

This section seeks to review the development of and prospects for renewable energy. What are the renewable energy technologies? How far have they already been integrated into developed and developing countries' energy systems? How much scope is there for future growth and what are the obstacles to achieving this? Can they change the profile of energy supply and limit environmental damage or do they have their own environmental problems?

The renewable technologies[2]

Renewable technologies are often broadly defined as those which utilize natural forces to produce energy or which exploit readily replaceable resources with the minimum environmental impact. Some argue that all renewables are ultimately solar-derived, but, while technically correct, such an all-embracing definition offers little illumination. Renewable energy technologies can be divided between those which primarily produce or provide energy which is used directly as heat or light and those which convert energy into electricity. They can be distinguished by the apparent natural force or resource which they utilize. This latter option is the one used here, with some indication given of whether or not they can be used for electricity production.

---

[2]This section is based largely on the analysis provided by the International Energy Agency's report (1987) on renewable energy and the discussion of renewable resources in Eden *et al.* (1982) and Goldemberg *et al.* (1988).

Water

Water offers a range of renewable energy options, particularly for the production of electricity. As noted, hydro-electricity is one of the most developed renewable resources and is based on the established use of water for motive power. The energy of running water can be converted into mechanical energy and via a turbine into electrical energy (it is this use which currently predominates). How much energy is obtained depends on the mass of water available and the height through which it moves. Electricity can be obtained by placing turbines along a river and catching the run of the water. Larger supplies can be exploited by damming a source of water and channelling the store for electricity production. The scale of hydroelectricity generation can thus vary from units providing a few kilowatts of power to massive power plant with capacities of thousands of megawatts.

While these technologies are well developed, other forms of water-based energy are less so. These rely either on the gravitational effects on water (through tide or wave) or on the difference in temperatures within large masses of water.

Tidal power is not a new idea—tide mills existed in the Middle Ages—but it is only recently that they have become considered as a potential source of electricity production. To exploit this resource, a barrage has to be built across a bay or estuary and the tide forced to flow through turbines to generate electricity.

Wave power converts the motion of waves into electricity by a number of techniques. Some use a mechanical connection between a device on the water's surface and a pivot to convert the up-and-down motion of the wave into electricity. Others use the variations of water head to produce pressure driving an air turbine to generate power. Most systems now under review are for systems which use close-to-shore plant though more ambitious offshore technologies have also been investigated.

Ocean Thermal Energy Conversion (OTEC) technologies, first suggested in the 1880s, seek to exploit the potentially large differences in temperature between the surface layers of the ocean and those in deeper waters. A pump takes a fluid with a low boiling point from these cool low depths to the higher and warmer levels where the fluid evaporates to drive a turbine and generate electricity. The cycle then returns the fluid down the circuit to condense and the process is repeated.

Wind

Wind has been harnessed for sea transport for some millenia and for mechanical purposes in windmills for many centuries. Using the wind to produce electricity, by using its drag force, dates back to the early 20th century. However, it fell into disuse as rural electrification developed and the price of other fuels fell. It has only been since the 1970s that interest in the technology has revived. Now wind generators rely on the aerodynamic lift across propellers or blades, using gears to optimize how much energy can be converted to electricity in a turbine. The generators themselves can either be land or off-shore based.

Solar

Solar energy sources can be distinguished between those which are designed to provide non-electrical energy and those aimed at producing electricity. The former can be further classified into technologies which actively collect energy, for example to heat water for domestic purposes, and those which passively utilize heat and light through the design and architecture of buildings. The electricity technologies comprise those which involve concentrating solar heat to raise steam and drive a turbine and those which convert solar radiation into electricity directly through photovoltaic cells. This latter option is increasingly considered in tandem with the production of hydrogen for energy purposes: the electricity produced by solar power could be used for the manufacturing of hydrogen which could in turn be used as a clean fuel for transportation.

Biomass

Biomass is a term used to cover a wide range of potential resources which have in common their origins in rather different renewable sources: the wastes and residues from nature and civilization on the one hand and the harnessing of rapidly replaceable plant life on the other. Thus while they utilize finite resources, those resources can be "renewably" generated, through the cycle of waste by-products or through crops (as opposed to the much longer time-horizons for the replacement of conventional fossil fuels).

The means of exploiting such fuels cover a variety of forms. In the case of industrial or refuse-based biomass, the residues can be formed into waste-derived fuels directly or indirectly in the course of recycling. If they are dumped, the gases given off in land fill sites can be harnessed as a boiler fuel as well. Natural wastes can be exploited in similar ways. In both cases, biotechnologies may help speed the process of energy production from such sources. The cultivating of crops or forests specifically for energy production is another possibility, building on the traditional gathering of wood for fuels (a continuing feature of energy use in developing countries).

Geothermal

Like biomass, geothermal technologies, which use the heat of the earth for energy production are not strictly renewable: moreover, whereas biomass sources can in most cases be rapidly replaced, replacement of geothermal resources on their current scale is not feasible. Although there is considerable potential for exploiting geothermal power, specific pockets are effectively finite, only replenishable in the very long run. Geothermal sources can be broadly distinguished between hydrothermal technologies (where the earth releases hot water or steam) and hot dry rocks where a potential source of heat is identified and water channeled through it to produce hot water or steam. In a number of projects the energy is used to produce electricity.

The various renewables offer scope for exploitation at relatively small scales and in larger projects, and most have the potential to be developed incrementally, allowing the user to acquire experience in their operation before large-scale commitment of resources and investment. The degree of development varies widely, with some well established and in operation (such as Hydro and Wind) while others have yet to be fully researched and developed (such as Ocean Thermal). The scale of investment also differs with some, such as tidal, necessitating very large financial commitment.

Renewables in energy supply

What is the role of renewable energy in global energy balances? Figures from the International Energy Agency, which do not cover the traditional energy usage still prevalent in developing and some Socialist Bloc countries, give some idea of the role of renewables in energy markets.[3]

Overall, renewables contributed 463 million tonnes oil equivalent (mtoe) to a total world primary energy demand in commercially traded fuel of 7654 mtoe, approximately 6% (estimates which take more account of traditional resources suggest that renewables account for 15% of primary energy needs).[4] The developed countries were responsible for 255 mtoe, 60% of global renewable production and 6% of their own requirements. The developing countries contributed about 122 mtoe (excluding for example fuel wood), 25% of total renewables and 9% of their own needs. The countries of the Socialist Bloc contributed 85 mtoe, 15% of renewable supply and only 4% of their requirements.

Developed countries

For developed countries, renewable energy use is focused primarily on hydroelectricity and, in certain countries, geothermal power. For the OECD countries, hydroelectricity accounts for 20% of electricity capacity and 20% of production, and in some countries, such as Austria, Canada, Norway, Sweden and Switzerland, more than 40% of electricity is produced from this source. As a large-scale resource, much of the major hydro sites have been exploited in the developed countries with the exception of Canada and Scandinavia. Small-scale hydro appears to have considerable potential in a number of countries, thanks to developments in turbine technologies and electronic control systems. Geothermal accounts for less than 1% of capacity and of production (though there is also a substantial amount of heat only capacity). Although it is a mature technology in many countries, such as Iceland, Italy, Japan and New Zealand, there is still potential growth. Moreover, a number of countries (including the UK) are researching into "hot rock" technologies.

Other renewable technologies contribute much less to energy balances. While their role is increasing in many countries, they start from almost nil and their overall share is minimal. With one or two exceptions, therefore, indications of the use of renewables are not statistically significant, even if the fact of specific developments might point to future development.

Of all those technologies, probably wind is the most developed. Technologies have now advanced to produce individual wind plants in excess of 1MW and there are numerous wind farms of several machines across the developed world. In Denmark, there has been a major energy policy commitment to wind power (see below). In the UK experimental island installations are operating and wind farms have been designed by electricity companies, some of whose estimates suggest that, in the right locations, their costs were competitive with those of conventional technologies.

Biomass, whether agricultural or waste-based, is also developing as a commercial fuel for heat and for electricity production. In Europe and the USA a number of utilities or local authorities have constructed plant to burn refuse. Use of gas from waste sites is also being developed in the UK for the production of power. Agricultural residues are also being exploited and some countries, notably Sweden, have been developing energy forest programmes. In many cases, the energy is produced for local consumption, so its real contribution may be greater than the apparently low levels reported by most countries.

---

[3]See IEA (1989).
[4]See Goldemberg.

Wave and tidal power are for the most part unexploited technologies. Wave power projects have generally been very small scale and are largely used for decentralized electricity requirements (e.g. navigational buoys). There are some well developed pilot projects on wave power in Norway and the UK, however. Tidal barrages have scarcely got beyond the pilot project stage, the major exception being the La Rance tidal station in France, built in the 1960s and with a capacity of 240 MW.

Solar power is also relatively undeveloped. While the integration of passive solar concepts into new buildings is gaining ground, measurement of its impact is complicated by the fact that it saves energy which would otherwise be produced for heat or light. Active solar technologies are not well developed while photovoltaics remain unattractive except in circumstances where solar cells are used in limited applications (such as calculators). Other renewable technologies remain largely untried.

In what was the Socialist Bloc, renewable capabilities are almost totally focused on hydroelectric plant, though some countries like Hungary have developed geothermal power, while there also remains widespread use of traditional wood fuels in rural areas. In some countries, notably the Soviet Union, there have been pilot projects for other renewables, notably solar power, but these have generally not achieved even the limited integration and take-up experienced in the capitalist world.

Developing countries

Developing countries' renewables are split between hydro and biomass fuels with a few countries, notably Mexico and the Phillipines, operating geothermal power stations.

Electricity systems are often dominated by hydroelectric capacity (for example the Itaipu dam in Brazil, and the Guri dam in Venezuela). Other technologies such as solar have also been attempted, in some cases as a technique for providing electricity in remote areas where it has been particularly well developed in applications such as telecommunications, agriculture and medical refrigerators in Africa. Wind is largely untried but wave and to a lesser extent tidal have been developed for a number of countries. Biomass is being exploited on a major scale in some countries, the most radical experiment being the alcohol-from-sugar fuel programme in Brazil. This project has however run into major problems, in the wake of the collapse of oil prices in 1986, the discovery of oil in Brazil and the reduction in subsidies to the domestic sugar industry.[5]

Biomass is far more significant in the traditional sector which itself remains a major source of energy in many countries: estimates suggest that for most developing countries, between 40–50% of total energy needs are still met by biomass through firewood and to a lesser extent plant residues and animal wastes. In some poorer countries these resources account for 80% of total energy use.

Research activity

Aside from this traditional role, and the well developed presence of hydroelectricity, renewables contribute only a minute share of total energy supply. If this is because they are relatively undeveloped, then a guide to the future use of renewables might be found in national research budgets. How high do they figure in national energy research

---

[5]See the *Economist*, March 10, 1990.

programmes? Consistent indicators across time and countries are only available for the developed market economies.[6] It appears likely that the bulk of research is conducted in these countries, although a number of developing and Socialist Bloc countries conduct their own energy R & D programmes which may give a high priority to renewables (at least in the developing countries). Moreover, they may participate in research programmes sponsored by international organizations such as the UN agencies.

Moreover, most data, such as that used here, concern only public sector commitments and do not take any account of private R & D expenditure. It is likely to be on a smaller scale given that most of the technologies are pre-competitive and unlikely to gain much favour in private industrial companies. The bulk of their R & D will be focused on specific projects which are closer to market than many renewables are perceived to be. Nonetheless, renewables have, in the past, been a target for venture capital projects and have been developed, notably in the sphere of photovoltaics, while many of the large engineering and energy companies have devoted their own resources to the technologies (again photovoltaics have been a key concern).

Renewable energy R & D occupies a relatively small part of overall public sector budgets for energy research and development. In the 1970s it constituted about 7% of total developed-country government R & D. By 1980, this had risen to over 10%, but the share quickly slipped back to around 7%, where it has stabilized. The share of renewables must be seen in the context of the trend for overall R & D budgets (see Table 1). Again there was an absolute rise in the amount devoted to energy research up to 1980, but from then on the funds have declined in real terms.

The renewables have been dwarfed by the outlays required in both conventional and advanced nuclear technologies and even by fossil fuel research requirements. In part this reflects the rather small financial requirements of such research in its initial stages, but arguably it reflects a bias towards other types of research in both government and the energy industries.

The balance of funds for renewables has remained consistent overall, though some technologies, such as ocean thermal have not been able to sustain the commitment to research in the form of a steady stream of financial resources. Others such as wind, biomass and photovoltaics have been more successful in sustaining, in some cases, their share of funding, reflecting the perceived prospects of these technologies.

This overall pattern of energy R & D funding masks variations between countries and

Table 1: *Energy Research and Development and the Role of Renewables in the Developed Countries (US$ 1988)*

	1977	*1980*	*1987*
Renewables R & D	820	1601	495
Total energy R & D	9014	12471	7343

Source: IEA (1989).
Note: Excludes France.

[6] See IEA (1989).

over time. National commitments to renewable research naturally vary widely both in terms of the relative importance of the sector in their research efforts and the overall amount they allocate. Countries such as Belgium, Canada and the UK devote less than 6% to renewables, while those which have focused on the sector in their research include Greece with 62%, Spain with 34%, Portugal with 26% and Sweden with 21%. The relative commitment of specific countries should moreover be considered in the context of absolute contributions. Greece's relatively high R & D commitment is equivalent to only $5,000,000 for renewables, while those of the UK and USA are worth $21,500,000 and $124,000,000 respectively.

Within Europe, a substantial element of research is carried out within EC programmes. The EC has paid considerable attention to the sector for a mixture of supply security, environmental and industrial policy reasons. For example, a number of renewables projects were supported in less developed Community member states as part of a regional development programme. However, this attention has not necessarily been matched by financial resources. In 1987, renewables accounted for only 9.5% of EC grants for energy projects. The Community has restated its support of the sector in its new programme, *Thermie*, though the finance available will remain much lower than for other energy resources.

Why do renewable energy resources not receive a larger share of R & D funds? One answer is that in a competitive market for energy research budgets, renewables have failed to convince, relative to the established technologies or to those nuclear options which have an articulate and influential lobby. Since these projects are often extremely capital intensive, they have tended to obtain the bulk of the available scarce finances.

The potential for renewables, and obstacles to their development

Renewables play only a minor role in energy supply and research programmes. Yet, in theory, they have considerable potential particularly in view of growing concern over greenhouse gas emissions from fossil fuels. In an ideal world it is possible to envisage radical improvements (i.e. reductions) in the cost profiles of these technologies and large increases in energy prices from conventional sources; in such conditions, renewables could meet practically all energy requirements. However, such a scenario demands not only a leap in the competitiveness of most renewables but also a leap in faith or imagination. Assessments based on more realistic scenarios of costs and price balances and a relatively short time horizon indicate a correspondingly modest but nonetheless significant contribution from renewables.

Assessments conducted for the European Commission suggest that renewables could contribute 100 mtoe by 2010, or 14% of total EC energy demand.[7] This would largely be achieved by an increase in wind and biomass resources, raising by nearly 30 mtoe their contribution to energy balances. The EC's official assessment is less optimistic, seeing non-hydro renewables increasing by little more than 4 mtoe.[8] Other assessments indicate a similar range of shares, globally. One study suggests that renewables could contribute

---

[7]Palz (1989).

[8]See Commission of the European Communities (1990) *Energy for a New Century—the European Perspective* (Brussels: Commission of the European Communities).

20% of primary energy requirements by the next century, while the IEA's figures suggest that renewables would rise from 465 mtoe to 743 mtoe by early next century, maintaining its share at 6% of requirements.[9]

National potential for renewables varies widely, hingeing on the commitment of politicians and governments and the availability of resources or incentives. In the UK, renewables have been estimated by some as able to meet over one third of current electricity demand, though government estimates suggest a much more limited role. Spain sees a rise in consumption of non-hydro renewables from 3% to 6% by the early 1990s. Often these national prospects depend on specific technologies in particular countries. American assessments suggest that wind power would provide up to 5–6% of its total electricity requirements. Such figures appear plausible in countries such as Denmark, where wind power has been actively encouraged and appropriate wind conditions are available. In those countries with major tidal resources, barrages could provide between 15 and 20% of power plant capacity via one or two projects.

The gap between the potential of renewables and their actual use and prospects is large. Even in terms of research and development, one indicator of future use, albeit an imperfect one, there appears to be less than full commitment. Why is this? What are the factors which constrain the resources devoted to the innovation of renewables and impede the widespread diffusion of existing technologies?

The factors which shape how far renewables are taken up fall into four broad and interrelated categories. One is the technical development of the technologies—how viable and developed are they? Some are practically untried and for the rest, aside from one or two, none has been in operation very long and their reliability has yet to be fully tested. The economic context within which renewables have to operate is also important. It is not only the costs of developing the renewables which affect their prospects but also their competitiveness vis-à-vis other means of producing fuels. The third factor is the acceptability of the developments: are people prepared to see renewable technologies in their back yard? Finally, the institutional context can play a major role in shaping renewable prospects. How far do the structures of the energy industries and their practices help or hinder the development of renewables? How far do government's own actions affect the prospects for these fuels?

The relative newness of renewables inevitably places a question mark over the technical viability of many options. How far can they be transferred from the drawing board to full-scale commercialization? There may be lack of clarity regarding how such renewables can be integrated technically into existing systems. Such uncertainties colour perceptions of the technologies and inhibit decisions to invest in the sector. Moreover, in many cases, it is by no means clear that the renewables will cost as little to build, or operate as well as might initially be claimed. There is a risk that the construction of renewables may incur higher costs than predicted (particularly in large-scale projects such as hydro plant and tidal barrages which might follow other engineering projects and fall victim to time overruns and soaring budgets), adding to the burden of capital repayments. Furthermore, there is the possibility of failure of equipment and higher maintenance requirements, which will not only raise the costs of the technology but also lose potential revenue by rendering

---

[9]See Besant Jones (1989) for a critical account of renewables' role in future energy balances, particularly for developing countries.

the plant less available than was initially planned, requiring expensive reserve capacity. There might also be an overestimation of how far the renewable sources themselves will be available (e.g. wind speed, solar availability) and an underestimation of the damage which natural forces might do (e.g. corrosion). It might be suggested that enthusiasts and supporters of renewables risk "appraisal optimism", a problem associated with the adherents of many other new technologies across the industrial spectrum. Their views are marked by a decidedly glowing vision of the technology's potential and an inadequate consideration of the problems which might affect the technology.

The construction and operating costs of renewables and their reliability relate to the broader question of the overall economics of the technologies. This is, in many accounts, the most difficult barrier which the renewables face. The main objection to most renewable energy projects, particularly those producing electricity, is that they are not cheap enough. As long as there are lower cost methods of obtaining power from conventional fossil fuel and nuclear plants so long as pollution costs are not included, renewables will not develop. The credence of this view was heightened by the developments in 1986 when oil prices and energy prices in general collapsed, leaving a number of energy projects, including many in the renewables area, far less economic than had been anticipated.

Another problem for renewables on a large scale in the discount rate which is used to assess their feasibility. For example, the proposed Severn Tidal Barrage which is estimated to cost £8.3 billion, would produce electricity at 3.4 pence/kilowatt hour, competitive with coal power. However such a price is based on an assumption that the discount rate was set at 5%, a common rate in the UK public sector. If the rate were 10% then the price would rise to 7p/kwh.

Moreover, as long as the costs of renewables remain high then there is little incentive to expend resources on their development. There is, in effect, a vicious circle at work. The economics of renewables often discourage the granting of R & D resources to the sector. The current low level of R & D means that the renewables are not sufficiently cheap to compete with other sources. So the renewables are seen as too costly to deserve resources. Another variant of this problem is that many technologies remain too costly because they cannot benefit from scale economies in production. They cannot be produced on a large enough scale until there is the demand for them and there is no demand for them until the costs come down.

While these are not impossible cycles to break, economic attractiveness does not guarantee take-up. Some renewables are sufficiently low cost to attract capital and to receive the engineering and expertise to develop them into full scale technologies competitive with existing fossil fuels. An example of this is wind. In 1988, the then-publicly owned British electricity producer, the Central Electricity Generating Board, in evidence to an inquiry into the construction of a nuclear power station, accepted that in many circumstances wind is broadly competitive with most sources of conventional production of electricity.[10] Yet the actual application of renewables may fall well short of the potential.

Another constraint is that of the practical acceptability of renewables. In many cases the potential of a renewable is constrained by the fact that siting the plant would be difficult in many locations which would otherwise be suitable. A number of resources may require large amounts of land to produce significant amounts of power (e.g. wind or solar). There

---

[10] Goddard (1988).

may also be significant environmental problems which may prompt local opposition in much the same way as a large conventional power station would.

If a technology is apparently reliable and proven in rigorous engineering tests, if it is seen as effectively economically competitive and if it does not appear to incur local opposition in being developed, there is still a further hurdle to overcome. How will the energy industry and policy community react to renewables and how will their structures and conduct affect its potential?

Undoubtedly, government action is a key factor, critical at the point of allocating R & D budgets, funding promotional projects and implementing policies which encourage their take up. In doing this, of course, government departments will face competing claims on their resources and on their time. Unless therefore there is a sufficient momentum behind the promotion of renewables, it is unlikely to gain more attention than a share of R & D. This will be particularly the case where governments adhere to the conventional wisdom of the technical and economic status of renewables.

Allied to this problem of government action or inaction is the attitude of the energy industries themselves. Questions of economics and technical feasibility will be one factor in companies' attitudes, particularly for utilities. However, given the importance of energy to the economy and the complexities of the industry, it is to be expected that key suppliers will adopt a modest approach rather than a radical, innovative strategy. In particular, utility industries have historically sought to achieve most reliable supply and cheapest costs. The main means for that goal have been the pursuit of scale economies in conventional and nuclear technologies. The focus of their research and investment, and in their relationship with governments and suppliers will be along this trajectory: the risks which have been taken have been ones which aim to extend this approach rather than make any break with it. In this context, the option of renewables has not been very high on the agenda. Such technologies which often imply decentralized organizational structures may not be well suited to these utilities' approaches although the influence of this factor will vary from country to country, and with the different structures and preferences of the sector and, particularly in the UK, with privatization.

Needless to say, such companies, if not well disposed to adopting renewable technologies themselves, are not very enthusiastic about providing facilities to non-utility suppliers of these resources. Where renewables suppliers have sought to gain access to public markets they have encountered problems. In many cases, governments have obliged utilities to offer terms, though the success of such measures have depended on how far the government has been prepared to oblige the utility and what mechanisms it has used (quotas or guaranteed purchase rates). In some cases, utilities are able to use their strong information advantages regarding the relative costs of different parts of the system against the independents' sale of renewables effectively to neutralize their contribution to national energy supply. It was for this reason that the EC suggested that member state electricity utilities publish special terms for purchasing power from renewable resources.

These problems exist for developed and for developing countries, though the balance may differ. For instance it is possible that the decentralized character of some renewables may be more suited in countries without a full infrastructure. However such plans are often rejected by the developing countries themselves, which see such proposals as denying them the prospect of a fully integrated energy system and of confining them to a lower level of economic development.

While the balance of factors and the justifications behind certain actions may vary, it appears that a pivotal role is played by the policy makers. The differences in national constraints to renewables owe less to the respective economics vis-à-vis other energy sources or to the development of their technical and siting potential than to the attitudes of government and the policy milieu within which the energy industries operate. Every country has some relatively economic renewables potential. Exploiting that potential depends in the final analysis on the attitude and approach of governments. Almost every country has a policy for renewables either specifically geared towards their development or within the context of a broader energy strategy. Most programmes aim to provide assistance to R & D promotion, etc, but the approaches and the "commitment" vary widely. Other aspects of energy policy can affect prospects, for example access to grids and fiscal treatment of investment. To illustrate the differences, two European countries, the UK and Denmark are examined.

Policies for renewables

The UK's approach to renewable energy has varied over time and with the priorities of different governments, as well as with the evolution of the technologies concerned. From the 1970s to the early 1980s, much of the research in the UK, as elsewhere, was devoted to assessing the technical potential of renewable energy resources. Subsequently, research shifted to a more applied phase as different technologies were tried out, and small scale pilot projects established.

In the last five years, the policy has increasingly been conducted in the context of a very radical shift in energy policy. As part of its overall programme of deregulation and privatization (and also in response to the shortcomings of previous policies), the Thatcher government has developed an energy policy based on market forces. For the most part energy policy had been hitherto based on a presumption of market failure in the sector and the need to intervene. In the 1980s, the balance of the programme shifted, and while the government was not afraid to intervene in specific cases, the thrust of policy had radically changed.

The change of policy has been most clearly seen in the government's programme of privatization and the introduction of legislation designed to encourage competition in the gas and electricity supply networks. Its main impact on renewables has been in the changes to the programme of research and development. In 1988, the government made it clear that its support of renewables research would be wound down over the 1990s and private industry would have to play an increasing role in their development.

The government defined technologies in three ways. Those which were economically attractive (where a technology was seen as likely to make a cost effective contribution to energy supplies at its existing stage of development), would be left to private industry, and government help would be focused on promoting them and increasing awareness of them. Technologies in this area included biomass and passive solar. Those which were classified as "long shots" (where deployment would only be cost effective if there were a dramatic improvement in costs or a dramatic increase in fuel prices), were to be abandoned by the government. These included active solar heating, off-shore wave energy, photovoltaics, etc. The focus would therefore be on those which were promising, but uncertain where there was scope for competitiveness if costs were marginally improved or energy prices rose slightly in real terms: wind and some wave technologies were the main options in this area.

Actual use of renewables has been shaped by attitudes of the energy industry. They have offered some support for renewables but rarely have fostered development. They have instead preferred to look to conventional fossil fuel or nuclear technologies as the focus for power generation.

A major fillip to renewables was to have been given by the government's plans to privatize the electricity industry. As part of its programme, the government sought to protect the nuclear power sector from the full force of competition, given its high costs. It justified this on the grounds that nuclear was a strategic asset that maintained diversity of supply. The government extended the protection to the renewable sector. As a result, renewable sources of energy (up to a maximum capacity of 600 MW or just over 1% of total capacity), were to be encouraged by the receipt of a price premium for the electricity they produced, roughly double what average prices would be. In response the government received nearly 300 proposals equivalent to 2000 MW. Such plans were subsequently thrown into uncertainty by a revision in the policy. The placing of an eight-year time limit on the premium, as required by the EC, has jeopardized a number of the proposed schemes. Moreover, there were worries that the task of privatising the electricity industry would prevail and special terms would be given to the companies to be privatized to the disadvantage of others including the independent renewable suppliers.

Denmark offers a contrasting perspective on how renewables development can work. The country has successfully encouraged the use of renewables in energy balances. The key to this has been the country's interventionist energy policy, a response to its serious problems during the 1970s oil crises. At that time Denmark was a major importer of oil and felt the supply and price shocks particularly hard. The energy policies of the time and ever since have sought to develop their own resources and aside from a little oil and gas, this has meant renewables.

As a follow up, the government has obliged utilities to agree to incorporate significant renewable technologies into their capacity balance. In 1986 they agreed to build 100 MW of wind power plant (in addition to an existing 100 MW). The programme has already exceeded expectations in the field of wind energy: over 250 MW of wind capacity is now in place, about 3% of capacity. The utilities also agreed to a programme of investment in 450 MW of plant using biomass resources.

The programme of support for renewables has been intensified by the development in 1990 of a new energy policy. "Energy 2000" is aimed primarily at improving the environmental content of energy policy. As part of this, further development of wind energy (including off-shore plants) is called for and expanded research efforts in the fields of solar energy and biomass are envisaged.

Throughout the last 15 years, and particularly in the new programme, Danish energy policy has been backed by a policy of maintaining high energy prices, through taxation. This has made renewable options more competitive than they are in other parts of Europe. The attractiveness of renewables has been further enhanced by the favourable terms on which private suppliers can set up and sell to the electricity industry.

The programme is aimed as much at providing opportunities for Danish manufacturers in developing capabilities in this sector as for providing a more secure and benign energy future. It has been criticized as raising costs of energy to uncompetitive levels. Others suggest that what has been implemented will have to be taken up by other developed countries as environmental concerns grow in importance.

Renewables and the environment

Despite their differences, it is noteworthy that both UK and Danish policies have focused on renewables in the light of environmental pressures. The issue of global warming has undoubtedly been the catalyst here though, for environmentalists, there has been a much wider concern with this sustainability of existing development models and the role of renewables in reshaping the energy trajectory.

Certainly, the role of renewables in containing environmental degradation is a valuable one, probably vital. For the most part, energy produced by renewables offsets or displaces that which would otherwise be produced by fossil fuels. Already the existing levels of hydro power in the EC mean that 150 million tonnes of carbon are not emitted. Given the rate of growth in global energy demand, that role is likely to be initially one of containing the incremental growth in energy demands. A vigorous programme of renewables development, one targeted at developed countries and at developing countries could potentially contain growth in the emission of greenhouse gases. Such prospects have to be set against the existing record, however. Correspondingly, the contribution of renewables to containing environmental degradation will be low in the short and medium term, unless vigorously promoted and supported.

In any case there are those who consider that renewable technologies may not be entirely benign environmentally. There are a number of aspects of renewables development which may create environmental problems. These cover the spectrum of concerns which are loosely classified as "environmental", ranging from amenity issues such as siting, land use and impact on neighbouring habitats (raised at the local level), through issues such as air pollution (generally raised at a national or transfrontier level), to the truly global issues of global warming and ozone depletion. Renewables have consequences in all three respects.

Almost a defining characteristic of renewables is the need for space. While the land hunger of resources such as solar and wind power remain only a potential problem, they are a current and pressing problem in the case of hydroelectricity. In developed countries, most potential sources have been declared "out of bounds" while in developing countries, the many hydro sources which have been exploited or which remain have involved, or will require, the displacement of tens or even hundreds of thousands of people and the loss of millions of acres of land, with their flora and fauna. Smaller hydro projects may also create conflicts between the developments and local agriculture and other needs. There are in addition major problems for nature and wildlife in the area, problems also anticipated in the development of other hydro resources, notably tidal power.

In addition to the land problem, there are a number of pollution problems. Wind projects, aside from siting problems, have noise and electromagnetic fields problems. Photovoltaics may use chemicals which require treatment. Both geothermal and biomass may create residues which are harmful and need to be disposed of.

Biomass resources contribute to greenhouse emissions although to some extent these are offset by displacing the inevitable emission of greenhouse gases from decomposing plant life. In developing countries, demand for firewood is a contributory factor to air pollution and deforestation, but it has a relatively small impact compared with agro-industrial use and depletion of the resources.

However, these environmental problems have to be placed in perspective. Many biomass techniques may control greenhouse emissions better than conventional fossil fuel resources.

Hydro projects have to be designed carefully, but a number of the problems can be overcome. Technologies such as wind will undoubtedly be improved, becoming less noisy and reducing electromagnetic interference.

One final environmental consequence stems from the fact that manufacturing renewable equipment almost inevitably entails the emission of greenhouse gases. In an energy economy where conventional fuels dominate, it is virtually certain that the energy used in manufacturing components for renewable energy production equipment is derived from fossil fuels. However, this is true for all energy technologies, and when the lifecycle of the technologies is considered, most renewables will make no further contribution to the greenhouse effect. Therefore the ratio of total energy produced to greenhouse gases emitted across the life cycle of the technology is minute for renewables such as wind, wave, solar and so forth.

The role of renewables in global commercial energy balances falls well short of what is possible and, if environmental issues are to be tackled, what is necessary. There is massive potential for renewable energy in both developed and developing countries, much of it viable economically. For the most part these fuels have a better environmental impact than conventional sources of fuels: hydro, solar, wind and wave have practically no impact in terms of degrading atmospheric quality, and, although they may have other undesirable consequences, they can be managed and minimized in all but the most extreme cases. Biomass may be more of a problem, especially in its traditional use: potentially however, this too can be controlled.

The image of renewables as technologies ranking behind the conventional energy sources has been a barrier to their development. However, they need not be regarded as inappropriate for modern industrial economies. They are likely to have just as many local and national economic benefits as those more established energy resources have. The renewable technologies are varied, utilizing a variety of manufacturing and engineering techniques and, in most cases, requiring substantial research commitments. Although they seek to exploit freely available resources, the investment costs are relatively high. Many are exploiting developments in computing, microelectronics, materials science and biotechnology in both their design and manufacture. With one or two exceptions, however, they are technologies which can be developed incrementally and modestly (in contrast to the experience in conventional energy technologies).

A programme of support for renewables can be reconciled with the goals of a modern economy and the structures and practices of the existing energy industries. They do not necessitate the transformation of society which "sustainable development" models (favoured by some environmentalists) imply. Indeed, given the difficulties in achieving such major changes in economic and social structures, it may be that the more modest contribution of renewables to the prevailing economic and energy systems would be more attainable. Whichever economic future is adopted, however, they are likely to be only one aspect of policies aiming to tackle environmental problems. Other options, such as cleaner fossil fuel technologies and, above all, a more robust programme on energy efficiency will also be important.

For bibliography, see pp. 362–363.

11 VEHICLE EMISSIONS

J. M. Tims

Contribution of vehicles to air pollution

Across the globe the usage of motor vehicles has increased enormously since World War II. It is estimated that between the years 1950 and 1990 the world car population has risen tenfold, from around 40 million to 400 million, and it is forecast to reach 536 million in the year 2000. One consequence of this has been a growth in the importance of motor vehicles as a source of atmospheric pollution.

Although more than 98% of a car's exhaust is composed of water, oxygen, nitrogen and carbon dioxide, the volumes produced are so great that the remaining 2% normally considered as pollutants are highly significant. In Europe, for example, some 90% of the man-made emissions of carbon monoxide, together with 30–40% of the nitrogen oxides and 40% of hydrocarbons are believed to originate from motor vehicles. Although vehicle emissions of sulphur oxides and particulate matter constitute only a small factor of total emissions from all sources, they tend to be concentrated in urban areas, where exposure of human populations is greatest. Until comparatively recently the air pollution problems associated with motor vehicles were considered local in nature. However, over the last 20 years evidence has been accumulated that some of the effects may occur over long distances and over long periods of time. The ramifications then become regional or even global as well as local.

Sources of vehicle emissions

There are basically two ways in which emission of pollutants arises from motor vehicles. Much the greater part (some 65–70%) is formed during combustion of the fuel (gasoline, diesel or LPG) in the engine and is emitted from the exhaust pipe. The main polluting components of exhaust gas are carbon monoxide, nitrogen oxides, hydrocarbons, particulate material including lead compounds, and oxides of sulphur.

The other source of pollutant is evaporation of the fuel (predominantly gasoline) during and after operation of cars, and during refuelling. The pollutant emitted from this source is almost entirely light hydrocarbons.

Carbon monoxide is formed in the internal combustion engine by incomplete combustion of the fuel. Much of the technical development by vehicle makers has been aimed at maximizing conversion of the fuel, both in the engine itself and by after treatment of the exhaust into CO_2. This has until recently been considered harmless, but CO_2 is now believed to contribute to global warming, and may itself need to be controlled. Diesel engines produce less carbon monoxide than gasoline engines since the combustion takes place in the presence of excess air.

Nitrogen oxides, mainly NO and NO_2, are created in the high temperatures of the combustion process mainly by reaction of the nitrogen and oxygen of the air present. They play a role in the phenomenon of acid rain as well as being irritating to the respiratory tract in humans as components of photochemical smog.

Hydrocarbons emerging from the tailpipe are to a large extent fuel components passing through the combustion chamber unburnt. However, transformation of hydrocarbons from one chemical species to another does take place as shown by the presence in exhaust gas of hydrocarbon compounds which are not present in the ingoing fuel. These exhaust hydrocarbons together with those escaping to the atmosphere by fuel evaporation play a vital role in production by photochemical oxidation of ozone, through reaction with nitrogen oxides in the presence of sunlight. In an uncontrolled car, hydrocarbons can also be emitted from the crankcase. These emissions are mainly lubricating oil mist and unburnt fuel from blowby past the pistons.

Sulphur is present at concentrations up to 0.2% in gasoline and up to 1% (though more typically in the range 0.2–0.5%) in diesel fuel. During combustion of the fuel this sulphur is converted to sulphur dioxide and trioxide, which are respiratory irritants and also affect crop growth and erosion of buildings.

Particulate emissions are a product mainly of the diesel engine. They are composed of soot and unburnt lubricating oil together with lesser proportions of unburnt fuel, sulphates and wear debris. Their significance is due to the possibility that they may be carcinogenic when inhaled. Amongst the particulate emissions from gasoline engines running on leaded gasolines are inorganic lead compounds arising from combustion of lead alkyls used as antiknock additives. Gasoline engines running on unleaded fuel produce very few particulate emissions.

Techniques for controlling vehicle emissions

The automobile industry has developed a range of technologies designed to meet actual and prospective emissions limits from crankcase, tailpipe and fuel system of motor vehicles. This section reviews the more important of these.

Control of crankcase emissions

Potential crankcase emissions arise from blowby past piston rings in an uncontrolled car. They are predominantly hydrocarbons in the form of lubricating oil mist and unburnt fuel/air mixture. Unless controlled, these emissions escape to the atmosphere through the road draught tube or the crankcase ventilation cap.

Crankcase emissions can be completely controlled by positive crankcase ventilation (PCV) systems, which prevent the escape of blowby gases. The PCV system works by eliminating the road draft tube and providing means for circulating air through the crankcase. The circulated air and blowby gases are drawn into the intake manifold while the engine is running, and are carried into the combustion chamber where they are burned with the intake fuel/air mixture.

Control of tailpipe emissions

The composition of these products of in-cylinder combustion is described above. Until recently control of tailpipe emissions has focused on the gaseous compounds, carbon monoxide, hydrocarbon and nitrogen oxides, and a repertoire of control methods appropriate to legislative controls of varying severities has been developed. Of these the simplest is engine modification which actually affects the composition of the exhaust gas formed in the cylinder. The amounts of carbon monoxide hydrocarbons and nitrogen oxides formed in a spark ignition engine depends primarily on air-fuel ratio, compression ratio, spark timing, load factor and rate of exhaust gas recycle. Air/fuel ratio has a complex affect on gaseous emissions and a compromise must be sought. At high air/fuel ratios (lean mixtures) and maximum fuel economy, carbon monoxide and hydrocarbon emissions are low but nitrogen oxides are high. At low air/fuel ratios (rich mixtures) and maximum power, carbon monoxide and hydrocarbons are high but nitrogen oxides are low. There is no air/fuel ratio at which CO, HC and NO_x are all low. Increasing compression ratio gives improved economy, but increases hydrocarbon and nitrogen oxide emissions by increasing peak flame temperature. With the advent of emissions control, retarded spark timing became a common control technique. Retarding the spark lowers peak flame temperature and lowers engine efficiency, the exhaust gases are hotter and post-cylinder oxidation of carbon monoxide and hydrocarbons takes place. Load factor (intake manifold pressure) has little effect on carbon monoxide or hydrocarbons, but increases nitrogen oxides at higher levels.

Exhaust gas recycle, achieved either by external recirculation or high valve overlap, lowers peak combustion temperature and lowers nitrogen oxide formation.

The extreme case of engine modification was reached with the so-called "lean-burn" engine designs of the mid 1980s. These designs run with very lean mixtures and high compression ratios to achieve maximum economy. This is achieved by injecting very precisely controlled amounts of fuel into the manifold and providing a high degree of swirl within the combustion space to enhance complete combustion. These designs with their excellent fuel economy and low CO and NO_x looked promising as a means of meeting European emission standards originally envisaged for the 1990s. However, the adoption of severe US-type standards by Europe for 1993 onwards seems virtually to have sealed the fate of lean-burn designs for the longer term. Since preventing pollutants from being formed is beyond foreseen technology we are left only with the prospect of cure.

The alternative route to controlling exhaust emissions through combustion is to clean up the combustion products in the exhaust system itself. This is done by fitting a catalyst converter in the exhaust system close to the exhaust manifold. The first and simplest type of converter was the "oxidation catalyst". This consists of ceramic substrate, either pelleted or monolithic, impregnated with small amounts of platinum and other noble metals and packed into a metal canister in the exhaust system. When so placed these catalysts are capable of oxidizing a large part of the carbon monoxide and hydrocarbon in the exhaust to carbon dioxide and water, given conditions of high enough temperature and sufficient oxygen. Oxidation catalysts can be used in tandem with "lean-burn" or other engine modification designs to control emissions up to quite severe levels, but not those in place in USA and Japan since the mid 1980s, and scheduled for Europe by 1993 (see Tables 1, 2 and 3). The only technology capable of achieving these limits is the three-way catalyst. Here the air/fuel ratio is maintained as close as possible to stoichiometric. The exhaust gas then contains an almost perfect balance of oxidizing and reducing components, which, when passed over a suitable catalyst, react with each other, leaving only small residues of carbon monoxide, hydrocarbons and nitrogen oxides in the treated exhaust. Stoichiometric control of air/fuel mixture over a wide range of driving conditions is beyond the scope of conventional carburettors, and it has been found necessary to employ oxygen sensors in the exhaust gas to provide a feedback signal to a fuel metering device. This is the so-called closed-loop three-way catalyst system. It is reckoned to control exhaust by 95% or better and is expected to remain the basic means of exhaust emissions control into the future. All exhaust catalysts, whether of the oxidation type or the three-way type, require exclusive use of unleaded petrol, since lead acts as a poison to the catalysts and eventually renders them inoperative.

Particulate emissions other than lead are important mainly for diesel engines, which have relatively low gaseous emissions. Current US particulate limits can be met by careful engine control, but limits foreseen for the future may require the use of particulate traps in the exhaust system. Although no particulate trap has yet been fully proven in service they will probably consist of ceramic honeycomb filters with a catalyst coating which physically filters out particulates. Diesel engines produce relatively large amounts of particulates and the filters will soon be clogged. They must then burn off the deposited material with the aid of externally-provided heating and an air pump. This may be necessary after as little as 300 km, which is acceptable for city centre buses, but could cause severe problems on long-distance haulage vehicles.

Control of evaporative emissions

Evaporative emissions can be considerably reduced by relatively simple mechanical modification of fuel systems, such as using pressurized fuel tanks with pressure relief valves, sealing leaks, venting the carburettor float bowl into the air-cleaner and venting fuel tanks into the crankcase. some of these techniques were adequate to meet US standards in 1970–71, but they were not sufficient as the limits were progressively tightened in later years. The technique universally adopted to meet more severe limits employs canisters filled with activated carbon, to which all external fuel system vents are connected. Any hydrocarbon vapours generated by hot soak or diurnal temperature changes are thus absorbed by the carbon and retained in the canister, which must be large enough to absorb some 30–40 grams of hydrocarbon vapour, and is usually of 1–2 litres volume. The carbon is purged of hydrocarbons during normal driving by drawing air back through the canister and into the engine where it is burnt. Based on the experience gained in the USA since the early 1970s, and later in Japan and Australia, small carbon canisters represent well proven and effective technology. Estimates of the efficiency of these devices range from 75% to 90% depending on such factors as canister sizing, ambient temperature etc. Enlarged versions of the carbon canister technology have also been shown as an effective method to control vehicle running losses and refuelling losses. Refuelling losses are controlled by connecting the carbon canister to the fuel tank by a large bore vent line. During the refuelling operation displaced vapour is absorbed in the canister and, as with the small canister, is regenerated by passage of air and burnt in the engine when operating. The volume of the enlarged canister is in the region of 5 litres. The enlarged canister has demonstrated 97% efficiency and offers an attractive alternative to restrictions on gasoline volatility or Stage 2 equipment at service stations (see below).

Legislation on vehicle emissions

The United States was the first country to recognize the contribution of road transport to atmospheric pollution and the first to take serious measures to control it. Action was centred on California, where air pollution was worst, and to this day legislation in California has been more severe than that obtaining in the remaining 49 states. Other countries have to a greater or lesser extent followed the general trends set in the USA, and the history of vehicle emissions legislation is therefore heavily oriented towards what has happened in that country.

Crankcase emissions are no longer a matter of concern, with all vehicles in the developed world having adopted positive crankcase ventilation devices. Legislation covering this is normally covered by statutes dealing with exhaust emissions and will not be dealt with separately here. Evaporative emissions controls and legislation have pursued somewhat different courses and will be detailed separately in the following sections.

Exhaust emissions legislation—USA

Concerns about the role of the motor vehicle as a source of air pollution first arose in southern California in the late 1940s because of the smog problem in the Los Angeles basin. In 1947 the state of California put in place basic legislation authorizing local jurisdictions to handle specific control problems which were, however, not identified by origin. When other sources of pollutants were gradually reduced without any significant improvement in Los Angeles smog it became clear that motor vehicles were a major contributor. It was not until 1959, when crankcase blowby was first identified as a major source of emissions, that pressure on the motor industry resulted in positive action. In 1961 the manufacturers voluntarily installed positive crankcase ventilation devices on all new cars sold in California. Subsequently the state government made the fitting of these devices to all new cars mandatory starting with 1964 model year. Meanwhile, a report of the US Surgeon General to Congress summarized known information relevant to vehicle emissions, including methods of control, and in 1963 pressure for action resulted in the Clean Air Act, which directed the Department of Health, Education and Welfare to encourage development of emissions control technology and appointed a liaison committee to make contact with industry. A major stride was taken in 1965, when the Clean Air Act was amended to provide the Health, Education and Welfare Secretary with authority to set and enforce national standards limiting gaseous emissions from new vehicles. In the following year Federal Standards for crankcase emissions and carbon monoxide and hydrocarbon exhaust emissions, together with procedures for compliance with the standards were adopted, applying to all 1968 model year cars and light duty vans. The limits were achievable by engine modifications such as control of combustion and ignition timing.

The Clean Air Act Amendments of 1970 marked a change in Federal pollution control policy. A two-level structure for air pollution control was set up. First, the Environmental Protection Agency (EPA), which took over responsibility from HEW, was mandated to establish national ambient air quality standards (NAAQS) which would protect public health with a margin of safety. The standards were to be nationally uniform and to be expressed in terms of maximum concentration of pollutant in ambient air which poses no threat to public health. Under this mandate EPA soon set standards for carbon monoxide, hydrocarbons, ozone, nitrogen oxides, particulates and sulphur dioxide. The second part of the amendments announced the setting up of limits on emission of pollutants from individual sources at levels which would allow NAAQS to be achieved. Accordingly, EPA defined separate standards for automobiles, light duty trucks, heavy duty trucks and motor cycles. The standards for automobiles required 90% reduction in carbon monoxide and hydrocarbons by 1975 against a 1970 base, and 90% reduction in nitrogen oxides by 1976. These standards were translated by EPA into 0.41 g/mile hydrocarbons, 3.4 g/mile carbon monoxide and 0.4 g/mile nitrogen oxides. The amendment was more lenient towards trucks, buses and motor cycles in not requiring specific percentage reductions. These automobile targets were generally reckoned to be beyond existing technical capabilities of the industry and were designed to force the pace of technical development. Provision was made for EPA to authorize delays in implementing the target dates by one year if it was considered that technology to meet the standards was genuinely not available. In the event a whole series of delays took place both through the inability of motor manufacturers to meet the targets and also as a result of further amendments to the Clean Air Act triggered by energy conservation concerns in the wake of the 1974 Arab oil embargo. By April 1975 the original 1975/1976 target dates had been delayed till 1978. Although the motor industry had by mid-1976 made substantial progress in developing catalyst technology it was clearly not going to be able to meet the 1978 standards. Congress was therefore obliged to amend the Clean Air Act yet again, delaying the 0.41 g/mile hydrocarbon requirement till 1980, delaying the 3.4 g/mile carbon monoxide to 1981 and delaying a relaxed nitrogen oxides standard of 1.0 g/mile also to 1981. The same amendments required 90% reductions in hydrocarbons and carbon monoxide, compared with uncontrolled vehicles from heavy duty trucks by 1983 and 75% reduction in nitrogen oxides by 1985. They also instructed EPA to set particulate standards, but without specifying numbers.

Since 1981 there has been no change in Federal limits for gaseous exhaust emissions from cars, although allowable particulate emissions were reduced from 0.6 to 0.2 g/mile in 1988. There have been further reductions in limits for light duty and heavy duty trucks, although the stringent reductions in hydrocarbons and CO were deferred until 1987. Diesel particulate standards have also been introduced for heavy duty trucks, and exceptionally severe limits were proposed for such vehicles operating in urban areas from 1990. It is virtually certain that diesel particulate traps will be needed to meet these limits. Throughout the history of ever more severe Federal standards, California has had its own limits, usually well in advance of the Federal situation, and this seems likely to continue into the future.

Table 1: *US Federal gaseous exhaust emissions standards for automobiles since 1968*

	Standard (gram/mile)			*Percentage reduction from uncontrolled vehicles*		
Model year	*HC*	*CO*	*NO_x*	*HC*	*CO*	*NO_x*
Uncontrolled (pre-1968)	8.2	90.0	4.0	–	–	–
1968–1969	5.9	50.8	–	32	44	–
1970–1971	3.9	33.3	–	53	63	–
1972	3.0	28.0	–	63	69	–
1973–1974	3.0	28.0	3.1	63	69	22
1975–1976	1.5	15.0	3.1	83	82	22
1977–1979	1.5	15.0	2.0	83	82	50
1980	0.41	7.0	1.0	95	92	75
1981	0.41	3.4	1.0	95	96	75

At the time of writing there are proposals for yet further amendments to the Clean Air Act reducing emissions from automobiles to 0.25 g/mile hydrocarbon and 0.4 g/mile nitrogen oxides in 1995, and there has been speculation that these limits could be halved again in 2003.

Since the late 1970s US emission limits for gasoline powered automobiles have been achievable only by use of catalytic exhaust reactors, and today virtually all such vehicles are fitted with closed loop three-way converters (TWC). At the present time US standards apply over the "useful life of the vehicle", which for passenger cars is defined as 50,000 miles or five years. Consequently catalytic systems have to be certificated over 50,000-mile duration tests. There are now proposals that durability testing should also be carried out at 120,000 miles, albeit with some increase in permitted levels of emissions. This recognizes that emission levels from new cars are perhaps approaching the point of diminishing returns and that continued limitation over a greater part of the life of older cars is more rewarding in terms of atmospheric pollutant burden.

Exhaust emissions legislation—Japan

Japan has been second only to the USA in the severity and promptness of its automotive emission legislation, although comparisons of severity are difficult because of large differences in test methods. Automotive emissions were first controlled in 1966, with a 3% limit on carbon monoxide by the Japanese 4-mode test, and in 1969 this was reduced to 2.5%. In 1971 hydrocarbons and nitrogen oxides were brought under control, and in March 1972 control was extended to particulate emissions including diesel smoke.

The next phase in automotive emissions control became effective in 1973, with separate standards set for two categories, namely (i) passenger cars, light trucks and light buses, and (ii) heavy duty trucks and buses. Category (i) was also divided into three separate engine types, which were (a) gasoline 4-stroke and rotary, (b) liquefied petroleum gas (LPG), and (c) gasoline 2-stroke. Emissions levels of carbon monoxide hydrocarbons and nitrogen oxides were specified for each class when tested on a new 10-mode cycle. For category (ii), vehicles emissions of carbon monoxide, hydrocarbons and nitrogen oxides were specified in a 6-mode test run on a bench engine. Plans for further reductions in limits planned for 1975 and 1976 were postponed because of the inability of existing technology to meet them, and interim limits were set for 1976 and 1977. The degree of control called for is demonstrated by the fact that, compared with uncontrolled 1966 vehicles, the standards current in April 1975 called for 95% reduction in CO and 96% reduction in hydrocarbons. By April 1978 a requirement for 92% nitrogen oxides reduction compared with the uncontrolled case was in place. Since this time further reductions in nitrogen oxides from diesel vehicles have taken place (1986/87 and 1989). The main standards at the present time are as shown in Table 2.

Exhaust emissions legislation—Europe

Regulation of vehicle emissions came relatively late to Europe and, at least initially, in moderate severity compared with the USA and Japan. The regulations were until 1989 formulated by the United Nations Economic Commission for Europe (UN–ECE) through one of its technical advisory bodies (GRPE). It was open to signatories to the ECE agreement to adopt these regulations, but they were not mandatory. In complying with the UN–ECE regulations signatories undertook to accept imported vehicles meeting the

Table 2: *Japanese exhaust emissions standards for passenger cars (10-mode test)*

Vehicle type	*Exhaust emissions g/km*		
	CO	*HC*	*NO_x*
Gasoline/LPG	2.70	0.62	0.98 (<1.25 tonnes) 1.26 (>1.25 tonnes)
Diesel	2.70	0.39	0.48

appropriate regulation or amendment. The following countries are currently signatories: Belgium, Czechoslovakia, Denmark, Finland, France, East Germany, West Germany, Holland, Hong Kong, Hungary, Israel, Ireland, Italy, Luxembourg, Poland, Romania, Singapore, Spain, United Kingdom, USSR and Yugoslavia. Notable absentees are Austria, Norway, Sweden and Switzerland, which have revoked their agreement to accord with ECE regulations and have adopted US standards for passenger cars, although not necessarily the most recent standards. Since 1987 there has been a further division in Europe, with the EC countries through the Commission issuing standards with directive status, which are binding on the 12 Member States.

During the 1970s and early 1980s EC member states generally adopted exhaust emissions regulations identical with UN–ECE proposals. The original UN–ECE Regulation 15 was published in 1970 and adopted widely by UN–ECE signatories in 1971/2. It specified limits on crankcase emissions and carbon monoxide at idle, together with carbon monoxide and hydrocarbon exhaust emission limits in a defined dynamometer drive cycle, for gasoline powered vehicles up to 3.5 tonnes gross vehicle weight. The carbon monoxide and hydrocarbon limits varied according to car weight in order to impose an equal burden of control on all car types. These standards typically gave 30% reductions in carbon monoxide and 20% reductions in hydrocarbons compared with uncontrolled cars of the same weight class. A first amendment (ECE 15/01) coming into effect in 1975 called for further reductions in carbon monoxide and hydrocarbons, and a second amendment (ECE 15/02) in 1976 instituted for the first time limits on nitrogen oxides. These limits were mild compared with contemporary limits in the USA and Japan and were relatively easily met by modification of ignition and fuelling systems. Amendment ECE 15/03 coming into force in 1979 demanded further moderate reductions in CO, hydrocarbons and nitrogen oxides, and the fourth amendment ECE 15/04 included diesel passenger cars for the first time, with a further reduced CO limit and a combined hydrocarbons plus nitrogen oxides limit. This recognized the rapid growth in importance of diesel cars as a result of fuel economy pressures ensuing from the 1974 Arab oil embargo. The combined HC + NO_x limit was set up to avoid penalising the diesel car with its relatively high natural nitrogen oxides emission. The progress of European standards for a typical medium-weight car is shown in Table 3.

In 1987 the EC ceased to rely on UN–ECE proposals and issued its own requirements for vehicles below 3.5 tonnes GVW in the form of a directive. This differed from Regulation 15 and its amendments in being mandatory for the member states of the Community, by now increased to 12 by the accession of Spain, Portugal and Greece. The directive dispensed with separate vehicle weight classes and replaced it with three engine displacement categories, those below 1.4 litres capacity, those greater than 1.4 litres but less than 2 litres capacity,

Table 3: *European exhaust emissions standards 1971–1984 (medium-weight car)*

Regulation		*Emissions (g/test)*(1)			*% reduction*		
		CO	*HC*	NO_x	*CO*	*HC*	NO_x
Uncontrolled		200	12.0	–	–	–	–
ECE 15 (1971)	70/220/EEC	134	9.4	–	33	22	–
ECE 15/01 (1975)	74/121/EEC	107	8.0	–	47	33	–
ECE 15/02 (1976)	77/102/EEC	107	8.0	12.0	47	33	–
ECE 15/03 (1979)	78/665/EEC	87	7.1	10.2	57	42	15
ECE 15/04 (1984)	83/351/EEC	67	$HC+NO_x$ = 20.5		66	$HC+NO_x$ = 43	

and those greater than 2 litres capacity. Each class took its own limits for carbon monoxide, hydrocarbons plus nitrogen oxides and nitrogen oxides alone, and implementation dates also varied from October 1989 for all new cars with engines greater than 2 litres capacity to October 1993 for all new cars with engines in the range 1.4 to 2 litres. Cars smaller than 1.4 litres were assigned moderate interim limits pending agreement being reached on a second stage to be implemented in October 1993. In the event this class of car was assigned the same limit as cars in the range 1.4 to 2 litres. The general approach behind the directive was to achieve a reduction in atmospheric pollution from vehicles equivalent to that achieved in the USA, but with a European test cycle and limits. The directive in fact allowed certification of cars with engines larger than 1.4 litres, on the basis of US Federal 1983 test and limits, as an alternative. Relatively the most severe limits were imposed on gasoline cars with engines larger than 2 litres, which could only be met by vehicles fitted with 3-way catalytic converters. It was intended that the limits on intermediate size cars could be met by "lean-burn" engine designs with enhanced fuel economy which were beginning to enter service, although some models would undoubtedly have required a simple oxidation catalyst to dispose of unburnt hydrocarbons. In view of the difficulty of applying catalytic converters to diesel cars, diesels larger than 2 litres were assigned the same limits as gasoline cars of 1.4 to 2 litre engine capacity.

The provisions of this directive were felt by some countries to be insufficiently stringent, and in these countries financial incentives were offered to people buying cars fitted with catalysts, even though they might not be required by the directive. In the event the directive seems likely to have only a short life. In January 1990 the Commission of the EC issued a new draft vehicle emissions directive scheduled to come into force in July 1992 for new models and December 1992 for all new cars. It sets single carbon monoxide and hydrocarbon plus nitrogen oxides limits of 2.72 g/km and 0.97 g/km respectively for cars of all engine sizes and fuel types, using an expanded test cycle which includes a high speed mode. These limits are based on performance of the best available technology (3-way closed-loop catalytic converters) and are considered by the Commission to be as severe as those in the USA. They effectively seal the fate of the lean-burn engine approach to exhaust emissions control. The draft directive also includes limits for evaporative emissions and for particulate emissions from diesel passenger cars. Allowances of 16% for gaseous emissions and 25% for particulates are to be allowed for conformity of production. It excludes light commercial vehicles smaller than 3.5 tonnes GVW on the basis that these vehicles tend to have poorer power to weight ratios and higher emissions than passenger cars. A new directive covering this class of vehicle is planned. The passenger car directive is envisaged as remaining valid for at least five years after adoption so as to provide a measure of stability to manufacturers.

Exhaust emissions regulations for heavy duty vehicles are in an early stage of development, but can be expected to be covered by directives in the next five years. UN–ECE Regulation 49 limiting gaseous emissions and Regulation 24 covering smoke emissions have been in existence for a good few years, but they were not mandatory and have been adopted by few countries. However, EC countries are now obliged to adopt the following limits for new models since April 1988 and for all production from October 1990; carbon monoxide 11.2 g/kWh, hydrocarbon 2.4 g/kWh, nitrogen oxides 14.4 g/kWh. These limits are not unduly restrictive.

Austria, Norway, Sweden and Switzerland, which are not members of the EC and have revoked their agreement to accord with UN–ECE Regulations, have all adopted US Federal Standards for passenger car emissions. At the present time, Austria, Norway and Sweden apply US 1983 limits and Switzerland 1987 limits for passenger cars. It may well be that with the intensification of EC restrictions these countries will choose to fall into line with the rest of Europe.

Legislation on lead emissions

Lead compounds are present in the exhaust of gasoline vehicles running on leaded fuels in the form of particles of lead halides, oxyhalides, oxides and sulphate. The function of lead compounds in gasoline is primarily to improve the antiknock performance, but it also provides lubrication between exhaust valves and non-hardened valve seats. Lead levels in commercial gasolines up until the late 1960s were universally in the region of 0.8 g/litre. However, at that time questions began to be asked, particularly in the USA, about the possible health hazards associated with the presence of lead in the environment, to which motor cars were a large contributor. Secondly, in 1970 it began to be understood that foreseen US exhaust emissions legislation were likely to require catalytic exhaust converters, and that lead compounds acted as poisons to these catalysts. With these issues in the wind, in February 1972 EPA proposed regulations providing for the general availability of one grade of unleaded gasoline and a phased reduction of the lead content of leaded grades, both commencing in 1974. The phased reduction in lead content of leaded gasoline was scheduled to drop from maximum average Pb content over all grades of 1.7 g/US gal in 1975 to 0.5 g/US gal in 1979. Subsequently further reductions took permitted lead levels down to 0.1 g/gal (0.026 g/litre) from Jan. 1, 1986. This is considered to be the lowest level of lead which will allow continued operation of older US engines. A system of "lead banking" was in operation until 1987, whereby companies using less lead than their legal maximum prior to Jan. 1, 1986 could bank their lead rights and then use them after 1986. These lead rights could also be exchanged or traded between companies. This lead banking system was withdrawn by recent EPA legislation.

Phasedown of lead levels commenced in Europe in 1972 and was based purely on health considerations since gaseous emissions regulations in force at the time did not require catalytic converters and unleaded fuel. However, Europe during the 1970s was preoccupied by the energy crisis and the pace of lead reduction was therefore slowed down due to the potential loss of octane capacity. Consensus about the effect of lead on human health began to be voiced in the UK and Germany in 1969. In 1970 the UK government's Chief Medical Officer advised that lead in air should not be allowed to rise above current levels, and a phased reduction to 0.4 g/litre was announced. Germany, as part of comprehensive Protection of the Environment legislation, passed a Lead Law requiring a reduction in the lead content of gasoline from the existing 0.6 g/litre to 0.4 g/litre from January 1st 1972, and to 0.15 g/litre from January 1st 1976. After months of debate, in 1978 the EC Commission published a directive requiring Member States to set maximum lead limits not greater than 0.4 g/litre and not lower than 0.15 g/litre from 1981. By 1986 all Western European countries except France, Italy, Spain and Portugal had reduced the lead limit to 0.15 g/litre maximum. Meanwhile, pressure from Germany for severe legislation to control possible effects of automotive emissions on forest die-back led to demands for unleaded gasoline, to make possible the use of catalytic converters. The EC responded by issuing a directive in 1985 which required that unleaded gasoline of a defined quality must be made available throughout the Community by October 1989. In the event the oil industry made unleaded gasoline available in most parts of Europe well before this date, and at the time of writing sales of unleaded gasoline are nearing 50% of total gasoline off-take in a number of countries. The implementation of the latest automotive exhaust emissions directive has made it certain that all new cars will require catalytic converters by October 1993 and will hence have to run exclusively on unleaded fuel. This in effect means that sales of leaded fuel will rapidly diminish as the catalyst cars dominate the population and the problem of lead emissions from vehicles will be brought to a natural end.

Legislation on evaporative emissions

Vehicle emissions in the form of evaporated fuel contribute some 9–12% of total man-made emissions of volatile organic compounds into the atmosphere in developed countries. Of this some 2% arises from fuel vapour loss during refuelling. Emissions from this source have generally been regarded, particularly in Europe, as less important than exhaust emissions, not only because of their smaller volume, but also because of their lower reactivity in photochemical transformations leading to smog formation. Compared with exhaust emissions the composition of evaporative emissions is relatively uncomplicated consisting at least 90% of light hydrocarbons. Nevertheless the USA and Japan have legislation in place and Europe is in the process of introducing legislation to control them.

Evaporative emissions legislation—USA

The United States was the first country to put into practice legislation controls on evaporative emissions, first under the 1970 Clean Air Act and then through amendments to it. Under this Act Stage 1 controls at marketing terminals and service stations became mandatory, and the 1971 amendments also required the fitting of on-board vehicle controls to prevent losses from the vehicle itself. The device used to achieve this was the carbon canister (qv). This collects only diurnal and hot soak losses, which are the only evaporative emissions controlled by law. Under subsequent amendments the standard has been successively tightened until at the present time it is estimated that there has been a 66% reduction in evaporative emissions since 1971. Despite this the ground level ozone problem is still severe, with up to 100 zones containing 100 million inhabitants failing to comply with NAAQS. The attention of legislators is now focused on evaporative "running" losses, on refuelling losses and on improvements in service effectiveness of the small carbon canister. Running losses are emissions of VOCs released during vehicle operation from locations other than the tailpipe or crankcase. Most of the running losses come from evaporation of fuel from the fuel tank, whose temperature tends to increase while the vehicle is running. This results from hot air from the engine compartment being swept under the car, from hot road surface, from proximity of the exhaust pipe and from gasoline recirculation in the case of fuel injected cars. A proposed EPA regulation would require the installation on new vehicles of enlarged carbon canisters capable of recovering diurnal, hot soak and running losses. Technology for achieving this has been demonstrated.

Refuelling emissions are the other source of evaporative hydrocarbon loss which are amenable to control. They arise by displacement of fuel vapour already in the vehicle fuel tank by fresh fuel being pumped into the tank. They can be controlled either by the so-called Stage II system fitted to the dispensing pump or by an enlarged version of the on-board carbon canister used for collecting other evaporative losses. In a Stage II vapour recovery system the vapour displaced from the vehicle fuel tank during refuelling is prevented from escaping to atmosphere by a flexible rubber vapour seal fitted round the filler nozzle, which forms a vapour tight seal between the nozzle and the vehicle filler pipe. This is connected by hose to the underground tank, and displaced vapour from the vehicle is fed back to the underground tank. It is generally reckoned that these devices have efficiencies in the range 66–85%. Besides involving substantial investment at the service station, customers find Stage II systems difficult to operate. In the USA Stage II systems are currently in place in California, New Jersey, Washington DC and St Louis as part of state plans to achieve NAAQS.

The second method of control is the fitting of large carbon canisters to vehicles. Studies on these devices by EPA and CONCAWE have indicated that better than 90% efficiencies are consistently achievable with large carbon canisters. There have been objections to the use of large canisters on the grounds of fire risk during collision, but it is probable that such risk could be eliminated by careful siting of the devices.

In an effort to further reduce evaporative emissions from vehicles and refuelling systems, in summer 1989 EPA issued a regulation limiting the volatility of gasoline for the hottest summer months (May–September), when 96% of ozone violations take place. In most areas maximum Reid Vapour Pressure was reduced to 10.5 psi (720 milibars) from 11.5 psi and in the hottest regions to 9 psi (620 millibars) from 10 psi. EPA estimated that this would reduce emissions by some 13%. At the same time the expected requirement to fit the enlarged canister on 1990 model year cars was postponed. It is expected that the Clean Air Act will be further amended sometime during 1990 and that it will require on-board controls with 95% recovery efficiency, with a three-year lead time.

Evaporative emissions legislation—rest of the world

Japan has had evaporative emissions regulations requiring carbon canisters since 1972. The regulations are based on a test method entirely different from that used in the USA and cannot easily be compared in severity with US Federal regulations. since 1979 some larger Japanese conurbations have required the fitting of Stage I type vapour recovery systems at marketing terminals and service stations, but to date there is no indication of an intention to control re-fuelling losses.

Up to the present time there has been no European legislation on evaporative emissions, since photochemical oxidant has not been viewed as a major concern. However, the draft Consolidated Vehicle Emissions Directive issued in January 1990 calls for the fitting of small carbon canisters to all cars from 1993 model year to meet a 2 g/test limit in the SHED test (Sealed Housing for Evaporative Determination). This test, like that in the USA, is required to cover only diurnal and hot soak losses, but the reference fuel and test conditions are different from those in the USA. It is anticipated that in the future the directive will be extended to cover running losses and refuelling losses. There is currently dispute between oil and motor industries about the best way to achieve this, with the oil industry promoting the fitting of enlarged carbon canisters and the motor industry calling for tighter controls on gasoline volatility. It is generally accepted that reduction of gasoline volatility would have a more rapid effect on evaporative losses, but that on-board canisters would have a larger effect in the end and would be less costly for the consumer. In the current climate of uncertainty about the outcome a few motor manufacturers are voluntarily fitting enlarged canisters to some of their models, and Stage II controls at service stations have begun to appear in Germany, Switzerland and some parts of Scandinavia.

Future prospects

Scope for further reducing emissions from conventional cars using conventional fuels must eventually reach the point where improvement achieved no longer justifies the cost of doing so. At this point other approaches must be identified. One such approach which seems likely to bear dividends is that of ensuring that cars which meet specific emissions limits when new continue to do so throughout their working lives. The potential value of this approach is illustrated by a recent Dutch government study based on random sampling of 1,200 cars up to three years old, which showed that only 35% met all the appropriate emissions standards. After retuning 85% of them met the standards. Ensuring continued compliance with "as new" standards would most naturally be achieved through annual inspection along the lines already in existence in a number of countries for road-worthiness. Such a system would place the onus of compliance on the car owner, who will have to pay for inspection and maintenance of emissions control equipment. It therefore represents a change from the current situation where the cost of implementing vehicle emissions legislation has fallen mainly on the vehicle manufacturer through the requirement to certificate new models.

Alternative routes to reduced emissions are via alternative propulsion units or alternative fuels, or both. The scope for alternative types of engine such as the Stirling engine, the gas turbine or the steam engine have already been explored. None seems able in their present state of development to match the spark ignition and compression ignition engine in terms of balance between flexibility, performance and emissions. Although much further development on these units is to be expected, it seems likely that use of alternative fuels is a more immediate prospect. Of these, methanol seems currently the most favoured. Indeed, President Bush's 1989 proposals for amendments to the Clean Air Act envisage having methanol-powered cars in the nine most smog-laden cities of the USA beginning in 1995. Methanol not only produces less CO and hydrocarbon in exhaust than gasoline, but is also less volatile than gasoline and is likely to contribute less to photochemical smog through fugitive emissions during refuelling and running losses. It is, however, very toxic and there are concerns about the aldehydes produced during combustion. Ultimately the ideal fuel is perhaps hydrogen, producing as it does water vapour as its main combustion product, but this is a prospect only for the 21st century.

For bibliography, see p. 363.

12 WATER QUALITY

Stephen Trudgill

Introduction

Freshwater use doubled globally between 1940 and 1980 and is expected to double again by the year 2000. About two thirds of this is used in agriculture and some 80 nations now face water shortages. In California, for instance, where much is supplied by aqueducts from the Sierra Nevada mountains and the population, and therefore water demand, is rising rapidly, shortages are imminent and attention is directed at the subsidized water in use, often wastefully, for irrigation. Irrigation, too, is blamed for the catastrophic decline in both quantity and quality of the waters flowing into the Aral Sea in the USSR which is now only a fraction the size it was a few years ago. Underground aquifers, for example in the western USA, in North Africa and in Saudi Arabia, are being rapidly depleted or exploited; 70% of the European Community's drinking water is extracted from underground sources.

This scenario underlines the need for the careful husbandry of water resources, but in many cases, it is not just the quantity of water which is important, but also the quality. Pollution of water courses, lakes and ground water is widespread, particularly in the Third World, where other, more pressing economic and social problems demand attention ahead of what is often a multitude of small discharges of harmful chemicals and sewage. Many rivers flow through more than one country and there is a lack of agreement between them of remedial measures for mutual benefit, often dictated by the costs of clean-up. Even with water resources confined to one country there is gross contamination. The China News Agency reported that at least 80% of China's rivers and lakes were polluted. They reported billions of tonnes of untreated sewage being discharged—40% into the Yangtze river! The UN (WHO) declared as an ambition and goal that all peoples in the world should have access to wholesome water by the end of the 1980s (but the deadline has slipped). But how is quality determined? This section describes the methods and attributes by which water quality is measured and judged.

Water quality is concerned with substances present in water either in solution or as particles. These, together with water temperature and flow rate, can have substantial effects on water as a medium for plant and animal life. There is also interest in the effects of water quality on human health, whether it is being used for drinking or for washing or bathing purposes: water can be a vector for pathogenic organisms which cause diseases and debilitation. There are four main areas of concern to scientists, engineers and politicians interested in water quality:

(i) specification of the substances present;
(ii) the provision of adequate data;
(iii) specification of sources and their control;
(iv) specification and enforcement of safe limits for potable water.

Water quality specification

The substances involved in water quality include inorganic and organic substances in solution (solutes), sediments suspended in the water body and solutes attached to sediments; also involved are heavy metals, pesticides, acidity, oxygen and organisms. Table 1 lists the main variables involved.

The exact specification of the substances present and the reliability of analytical methods can pose substantial problems. Analytical methods have improved markedly in recent years, but scientists will only find what they are analyzing for; additional substances may,

Table 1: *Water quality*

I. Water quality variables		
Temperature	Chlorophyll "a"	Dissolved oxygen
pH	Transparency	Suspended sediment
Electrical conductivity	Coliforms	
Total dissolved solids	Total Organic Carbon	

II. Nutrient elements/compounds essential or useful to life, but if present in high concentrations, can have deleterious effects on life		
Nitrate	Ammonium	Copper*
Phosphate	Sodium	Boron*
Calcium	Sulphate	Iron*
Magnesium	Silica	Zinc*
Potassium	Chloride	Manganese*

*Useful only as trace element.

III. Heavy metals and other elements/compounds generally regarded as not useful or undesirable	
Arsenic	PCBs
Cadmium	Benzene
Chromium	Cyanide
Lead	Pesticides/herbicides:
Mercury	Total organochlorine compounds
Manganese	Dieldrin
Selenium	Aldrin
Hydrogen sulphide	DDT
Nitrite	Simazine
	others

IV. Substances added during water treatment
Fluoride
Chlorine

sometimes, be present and can be missed by routine analysis. Very small concentrations of hazardous substances may be present in only trace quantities at the limits of instrumental detection. The variety of organic chemicals present in industrial effluent can be difficult to analyze adequately without specialized equipment—which may not be widely available. Field instrumentation for water quality study may also be less reliable than laboratory methods of analysis, yet some water quality indices can change during transport from the field to the laboratory. Specific water quality variables are discussed in turn below.

Temperature

Many life processes are temperature related, especially in the presence of adequate moisture and nutrients. Within the range of about 4°C to 20°C, increasing temperature generally leads to increasing metabolic activity. Thermal pollution can be an issue, where, for example warm water from power stations leads to increased productivity of aquatic life and changes in species composition. The issue is usually couched in terms of any changes in species diversity being undesirable.

pH

pH is a measure of acidity or alkalinity where pH is a logarithmic transformation of the hydrogen ion (H^+) concentration:

$$\mathrm{pH} = -\log_{10}[\mathrm{H}^+]$$

where [] is used to indicate concentration, thus:

$$0.0000001 \text{ g } 1^{-1} [\mathrm{H}^+] + \mathrm{pH}\ 7.$$

As H^+ concentrations increase, the pH value drops, so:

$$0.001 \text{ g } 1^{-1} [\mathrm{H}^+] = \mathrm{pH}\ 3$$

and so on, lower pH values thus indicating greater acidity. A value of pH 7 indicates neutrality, where $[H^+]$ and $[OH^-]$ are balanced, with values below 7 indicating acidity and above 7 indicating alkalinity. As the pH scale is logarithmic, each unit is a tenfold difference, thus pH 5 is ten times more acid than pH 6.

Under natural systems, pH values as low as 2 are rare and the values do not commonly exceed 11. Rainfall equilibriated with atmospheric concentrations of carbon dioxide (O.03%) has a pH of 5.6, the acidity being derived from carbonic acid (H_2CO_3) formed from water and CO_2 which then rapidly dissociates to yield H^+ and hydrogen carbonate:

$$CO_2 + H_2O \rightarrow H_2CO_3 \rightarrow H^+ + HCO_3-$$

Other sources of acidity can include nitric acid and sulphuric acid, formed by the combination with water of nitrogen oxide and sulphur dioxide gases, derived from volcanic or bacterial sources or from the burning of fossil fuels in automobile engines and power stations. These can give rise to pH values lower than 5.6, a phenomenon commonly referred to as *acid rain*. This term implies that much of the acidity is in solution, but acid particulate matter may form a significant proportion of acid deposition.

The impact of acid deposition on water quality depends substantially on the pathway of deposition and the chemical properties of the receiving medium. The pathway may be direct onto a water body or via intervening vegetation and soil systems. Further acidity may be added from living and dead vegetation matter as organic acids. If the pathway includes a soil body, an important property is the one of *buffering*. This term implies, in general, that the acidity can be controlled or offset by chemical reactions in the soil; the processes can also involve the buffering effects of water bodies which are not already acid. The reactions involve bases which accept H^+, such as CO_3^{2-}, as can be illustrated by the reduction of acidity using lime ($CaCO_3$):

$$CaCO_3 \rightarrow Ca^{2+} + CO_3^{2-}$$

$$H^+ + CO_3^{2-} \rightarrow HCO_3^-$$

Thus, the dissociation of lime in water produces carbonate which accepts H^+, yielding calcium and hydrogen carbonate in solution. Rocks, soils and water bodies can vary considerably in their ability to buffer acidity, and weakly buffered systems, with few bases, are susceptible to rapid acidification. Conversely, strongly buffered systems can receive high amounts of acid deposition and show few changes in water quality.

pH values in the region of 5.5–7.5 are generally thought of as desirable. Below this range, aquatic life may progressively decrease, especially as many substances regarded as toxic or damaging in high concentrations, such as aluminium, are more soluble at lower pH values. Extreme alkalinity can also be damaging, especially when associated with high concentrations of salts which can be disruptive of cell processes involving water balance.

Electrical conductivity and total dissolved solids

As the total amount of solutes (dissolved material) in water increases, it exhibits a greater ability to conduct an electrical current. This ability is related to the amount of solutes present as dissociated ions which have an electrical charge, for example sodium chloride dissociates in water to produce charged sodium and chloride ions:

$$NaCl \rightarrow Na^+ + Cl^-$$

The presence of charged ionic chemical species in solution makes the solution conductive to an electrical current. Electrical conductivity can therefore be used as a general indicator of the total dissolved solids in solution. It is especially valued as an indicator of the suitability of water for irrigation, where high concentrations of salts are undesirable as evaporation subsequent to irrigation will tend to leave the salts behind in the soil where they will hinder plant growth. Conductivity is expressed in microsiemens (μS, = micromhos) per cm. Water of a conductivity above 2250 $\mu S\ cm^{-1}$ is generally regarded as unsuitable for irrigation, with $< 750\ \mu S\ cm^{-1}$ being preferred.

Total dissolved solids can also be assessed by weighing the residue present after a filtered sample has been evaporated to dryness. This can be expressed as mg residue per litre of water.

Chlorophyll "a"

Levels of extractable chlorophyll in water samples are used as an indicator of the presence of algae. Several types of chlorophyll occur in plants but quantitatively the most important is known as chlorophyll "a". This is measured on an acetone extract using a spectrophotometer and repeated measurements can be used to indicate fluctuations in algal populations.

Transparency

The transparency of a water body is related to the presence of organisms and sediments. It can be used to indicate relative algal populations and sediment concentrations. It can be measured by the depth at which a standard disc is visible from the surface.

Coliforms

Coliform counts include estimates of pathogenic bacteria, especially *Escherichia coli* associated with sewage sources. Such counts, together with other pathenogenic organisms, can be used to indicate any health hazard from sewage contamination for drinking and bathing waters.

Total organic carbon

This indicates the amount of organic matter in the water from a number of sources, including natural organic mater from leaves and soils. It can be used to indicate where water is being derived from sources rich in organic matter, whether natural or contaminated from a source such as organic manures.

Dissolved oxygen

As well as the need for dissolved oxygen to be present to allow aquatic organisms to breathe, oxygen is also used in the decay process of organic matter whereby organic carbon (C) is oxidized to produce carbon dioxide (CO_2). Parallel measurements often taken are of biological oxygen demand (BOD) and chemical oxygen demand (COD), used to indicate the amount of oxygen needed to decompose, or oxidize, organic matter loadings in streams. This is a useful indicator of the capacity of an aquatic system to be loaded with additional organic matter. If the load is too great, oxygen deficiency, or *anoxia*, can lead to the loss of aquatic animal life.

Suspended sediment

This can be readily measured by filtering a sample of known volume and weighing the dried residue retained on the filter paper. The suspended sediment can be of inorganic sediment, derived, for example from river bank or soil erosion, or of organic matter from leaf, soil or sewage sources.

In either case, there can be considerable amounts of nutrients, heavy metals or other substances adsorbed onto (attached by a positive charge onto negatively charged surfaces) or incorporated into the sediments. This amount can be much greater, or as least as significant as, the amounts of the substances in true solution. This is especially true of nitrogen and phosphorus compounds present in organic suspended sediments and of phosphorus compounds absorbed onto inorganic sediments.

Nutrients

Of those listed in Table 1, many are essential for plant growth, but if present in high concentrations, they can have undesirable consequences. Each element or compound has an optimum concentration, below which they are said to be deficient and above which they tend to be toxic.

For compounds such as nitrate, ammonia, phosphate and sulphate the concentrations of the substances can be expressed as mg l^{-1} of that substance itself, or of the nitrogen, phosphorus or sulphur part of that compound. Care has to be taken when comparing data as to which of these is being used:

Nitrate (NO_3^-)	× .2258	= Nitrate–nitrogen (NO_3-N)
Ammonium (NH_4^+)*	× .7777	= Ammonium–nitrogen (NH_4-N)
Phosphate (PO_4^{2-})	× .3263	= Phosphate–phosphorus (PO_4-P)
Sulphate (SO_4^{2-})	× .3340	= Sulphate–sulphur (SO_4-S)

*as distinct from ammonia (gas), NH_3

Nitrate and phosphate are both essential elements but can cause nutrient enrichment, a process known as *eutrophication*, when additional increments are derived from agriculture, sewage or soil erosion. Such enrichment can lead to prolific plant growth—of both macrophytes and smaller algae—which can choke and smother waterways. This, in itself may be a problem in obstructing passage of water craft and in blocking the access of sunlight to the aquatic ecosystem in the waters below. A further problem, and often a more severe one, occurs when the vegetation decays because a blanket of rotting vegetation smothers bottom-dwelling organisms and uses up oxygen in the decay process. This process may be minimized by harvesting the vegetation for use as a green manure on agricultural and horticultural land, or tackled more fundamentally by nutrient source control.

Phosphate is strongly adsorbed onto sediments and thus is often present in higher quantities in this form than in the soluble form, known as soluble reactive phosphate (SRP). Sediment-associated phosphate is largely derived from the erosion of agricultural soils whereas SRP is more readily available from sewage. SRP can, however, be released from sediments in aquatic ecosystems, especially under low pH and anaerobic conditions.

High nitrate levels (above 50 mg l^{-1} NO_3 = 11.3 mg l^{-1} NO_3-N) are also implicated in the incidence of methaemoglobinaemia (blue babies) and stomach cancer. The medical evidence for the former is well established but incidence is rare where high nitrate waters are treated by denitrification and/or bottled water is used for infants. The evidence for nitrate causing stomach cancer is more equivocal: nitrosamines are known to be carcinogenic but the links between nitrates in drinking water and the formation of nitrosamines are not entirely clear. Areas exist with high stomach cancer and low nitrate in drinking water and vice versa; equally nitrate levels in food, rather than water may be involved.

Calcium, magnesium and potassium are all useful plant nutrients and rarely give rise to environmental problems. They can be augmented in soils by liming (calcium and magnesium) and the addition of fertilizers (potassium). As positively charged cations, they are strongly held in the soil on the surfaces of clays and organic matter compounds which have a net negative charge. As both calcium and magnesium are often present as carbonates in solid form, they provide bases in solution which are useful in offsetting acidity. In carbonate rich waters, some precipitation can occur by degassing of carbon dioxide, which can cause obstructions of pipes in severe cases:

$$Ca^{2+} + 2HCO_3^- \rightarrow CaCO_3 + H_2O + CO_2$$

The same process occurs in "hard" water, which is that rich in such carbonates, when it is boiled, leading to the furring of kettles. There is some evidence that "hard" water may be associated with cardio-vascular diseases.

Ammonium is used by many plants as a nutrient, especially under acid terrestrial systems. It may be readily oxidized to form nitrate under aerobic conditions.

Sodium and chloride are not widely recognized as important plant nutrients, though there may be some response to their addition if they are lacking. They can be major contributors to electrical conductivity (see above) and if present in large quantities can be deleterious to plant and animal life not adapted to saline conditions.

Sulphur is a plant nutrient and there is some evidence that sulphur in acid rain may have a benefit in this context. The main problem arises from acid sulphate soils where sulphur bearing shales and other sediments, both inorganic and organic, are oxidized (through drainage, for example). Here, oxidation of sulphur compounds or minerals (like pyrites, FeS_2) may yield sulphuric acid (H_2SO_4) and sulphate compounds (e.g. ferrous sulphate) in amounts damaging to aquatic life. This can also be a problem in acid mine drainage.

Silica is a constituent of some plants, and especially of diatoms in aquatic ecosystems. It can be present in a number of compounds in solutions and also as a colloid. It is not normally considered as a hazard.

Copper, boron, manganese, iron and zinc are all important trace elements which, if deficient can impair growth. However, the relevant amounts are usually measured in microgrammes per litre ($\mu g l^{-1}$) rather than mg l^{-1}. Above these levels they become toxic, though iron-rich waters can be tolerated more than the others. Many of these increase in solubility as acidity increases. Iron deficiency can occur in alkaline situations as iron is less soluble in the ferric (Iron III) form present under these conditions. Both iron and manganese are more soluble under reducing conditions (including low oxygen and acid conditions), resulting in high concentrations which may be damaging.

Heavy metals and other elements/compounds generally regarded as not useful or undesirable

The remainder of the substances listed in Table 1 are inimicable to life or have no life-support function. They can normally be tolerated only in very small quantities, though some organisms may be adapted to tolerate their presence at higher quantities (for example, some plants exhibit a degree of lead tolerance and some bacteria can use pesticides and herbicides as a substrate). The effects may be of changes in species composition, sub-lethal effects, cumulative lethal effects in the long term or toxic. Some, such as lead and aluminium, occur naturally in geological strata, and many of these are more soluble under acid conditions. These may be added to by the discharge of industrial processing effluent, mineral extraction or waste disposal. Others, including hydrogen sulphide and nitrite may form naturally in anaerobic conditions in wetlands.

Others are largely man-made, including a spectrum of industrial processing effluents. Some may occur naturally in very low concentrations (like benzene, derived from coal), but the major sources of concern are man-made. Many of them may be complex organic molecules which are difficult to identify unless appropriate analytical equipment is available.

Pesticides and herbicides can be derived from agricultural sources, especially the more mobile, water soluble ones. The chief concern is with the more persistent substances where non-lethal doses may accumulate in food chains to levels which are eventually damaging especially in predators at the top of the food chain, including man.

Adequate data

The provision of adequate data is difficult, especially in view of the fact that water quality can not only vary markedly over space but also widely over time. Characterization of water quality in terms of frequency distributions, average and extreme values can be difficult, especially where conditions of water flow vary widely from day to day. This is especially true during floods when hazardous substances can be mobilized into the water cycle under transient conditions, but yet go undetected by routine sampling if the sampling strategy is not frequent enough.

The problem is illustrated in Figure 1. This considers a substance dissolved in a stream which has a maximum acceptable concentration (MAC) of 4 mg l^{-1}. The top diagram shows its actual fluctuation in concentration, with three storm peaks and a final gradual rise. The MAC is exceeded for 32% of the time. However, a sampling scheme, shown by the dots in the centre diagram may miss the peaks. While this indicates that three peaks existed, the levels indicate only a 1 mg l^{-1} excess rather than the actual peaks of 2, 3 and nearly 4 mg l^{-1}. The later gradual rise, is however, indicated. The MAC time drops to 24%. In the lower diagram, a less frequent sampling scheme only picks up a marginal MAC of the first peak and indicates safe levels for the latter two peaks which it completely misses. The later rise is indicated, but the high concentrations, which may have deleterious consequences for aquatic life or be unacceptable for human consumption, are not evident. In other words, any sustained rise will be picked up by an infrequent sampling scheme, but such a scheme is inadequate for indicated transient peaks which may nevertheless have important consequences.

A further problem can arise where average values are used. For example, the median values change from 4 to 3.3 to 3.2. from the upper diagram downwards. The latter two do not give cause for concern, though the first may indicate that the concentration is close to unacceptable. However, the actual situation is that the MAC is exceeded for about one third of the time.

Policy enforcement can therefore be less than adequate if the data base is inadequate. It is unfortunate that situations can arise when it can be concluded that water is safe when in fact it is not. Careful scrutiny of any data base is therefore essential and sampling regimes have to be based on a time interval that is more frequent than the time span of fluctuations in concentration: in practice, the only way to judge this is to sample at an interval which is at least daily but, more reliably, hourly. This endeavour is however, expensive and many successful schemes note that most water quality indices are more stable at low flows and only change rapidly during storm events. Quite often, therefore, only daily samples are taken under stable, low flow conditions and float trigger switches activate automatic water samplers to sample hourly, or even more frequently, as water level rises during storm events.

An interesting development in this area is the use of indicator organisms in fresh water. Some organisms are intolerant of various forms of pollution, even to transient peaks of concentration. Thus, they will tend to be absent from fresh water bodies affected by peaks in pollutant concentrations. The advantage of this approach is that it does not require expensive programmes of monitoring, sampling and laboratory analyses and it does not rely on automated equipment, which can break down, nor even on methods of continuous water quality monitoring, such as ion selective electrodes wired to recording charts, which again can break down and also suffer from calibration drift. Pilot tests of water quality using indicator organisms have already shown high degrees of correlation between the organisms and water quality. For example, in streams in Wales, UK, high levels of acidity have been indicated by the absence of the Dipper (*Cinclus cinclus*), a

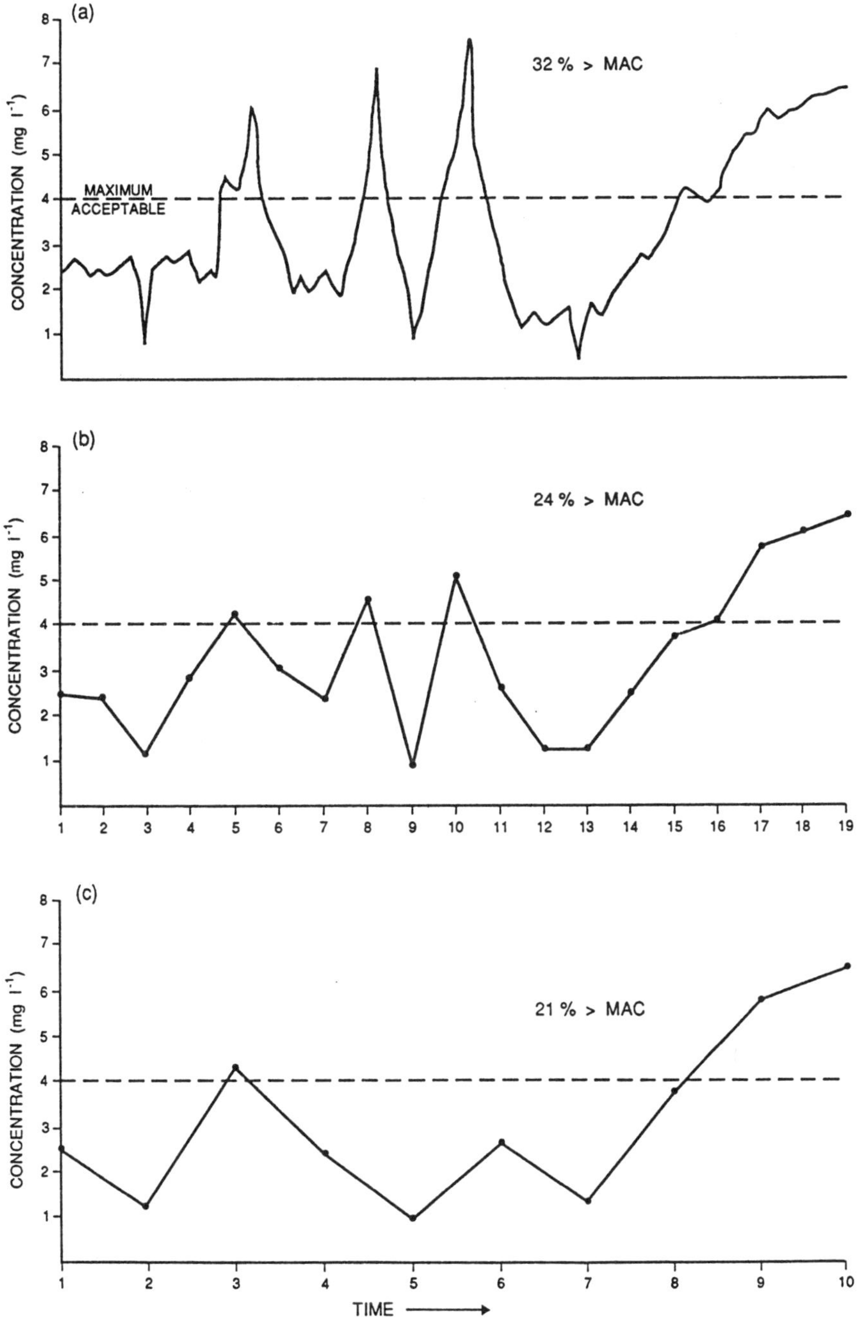

Figure 1: The assessment of water quality and the enforcement of control depend upon the adequacy of the database. Schematic diagrams of (a) actual fluctuations in water quality for a substance of Maximum Admissable Concentration (MAC) of 4 mg l^{-1}; *(b) data graph plotted for the same data from frequent sampling; (c) data graph plotted with infrequent sampling.*

bird which feeds on aquatic invertebrates which decline in numbers as acidity increases. A disadvantage of the method, however, is that reasons other than water quality can affect the distribution of organisms and a lack of organisms is not necessarily an indicator of the presence of specific pollutants or of their source. It also needs training in species identification and careful survey, especially where conclusions may be drawn from lack of observations of particular species—absence of evidence is not the same as evidence of absence. It is however, a very useful approach in bringing attention to problem areas and can lead to further investigation of a more specific nature.

One of the more successful approaches is to predict the diversity of organisms that should occur given the nature of a stream in relation to its environment. For example, characteristic assemblages are to be expected in upland, nutrient poor streams and in lowland, nutrient-rich streams. Based on observations of unpolluted sites, the type of community that should occur is predicted and then a comparison of observed values at a particular site with predicted values for that type of site provides an environmental quality index: the greater the difference, the more the site is polluted. This gives an index which does not need to investigate the detailed mechanisms involved in the relationships between water quality criteria and biotic response and is not reliant on chemical monitoring. It is especially useful where complex interacting mixtures of chemicals are involved. In addition, a useful approach can be to predict water quality from hydrological behaviour.

Solute and sediment concentrations can vary characteristically with flow conditions. Monitoring of water levels in streams throughout rainfall events can be undertaken and drawn up on a chart termed a hydrograph. This can be produced automatically with a pen placed on a revolving chart recorder, the pen being attached to a float mechanism in contact with the water. As the water rises, a gear mechanism allows the pen to draw a scale chart of water level changes. Plotting of water quality data on the same time basis frequently shows that sediment concentration peaks as the hydrograph rises as sediment sources are mobilized during a storm. The supplies of sediment often then become exhausted and suspended sediment concentrations drop.

Dissolved solutes may rise and fall as the water level and flow rate rise and fall, showing that the situation is *transport controlled*. Here, there is adequate supply of solute from whatever source and the movement of the solute is controlled by flow rate. Alternatively, the solute may show a drop in concentration, i.e. a dilution, during the hydrograph rise, indicating that the situation is *supply limited*. Here, the amount moved is controlled by the amount of solute available. These variations in response underline the need for an adequate sampling programme stressed above.

In addition, expression of solute movement in terms of concentrations alone does not give the whole picture. It may well be that even with dilution of a solute, that is a decrease in concentration expressed in mg l^{-1}, there may be so many litres of high flow, that the net loss, even at dilution, is greater than at lower flows with higher concentrations. Thus, overall losses and movements are usually expressed in terms of *load*. This is the concentration multiplied by the discharge:

$$\underset{\text{CONCENTRATION}}{\text{mg l}^{-1}} \quad \times \quad \underset{\text{DISCHARGE}}{\text{l s}^{-1}} \quad = \quad \underset{\text{LOAD}}{\text{mg s}^{-1}}$$

Thus, for example, C 20 × D 10 = L 200, but at higher flows with a lower concentration, C 10 × D 50 = L 500.

Load calculations are not normally relevant where frequency distributions and peak concentrations which exceed maximum acceptable concentrations are of interest. However, load calculations are very useful where attempting to budget for the relative contributions from different sources over time. For example, concentrations of nutrients from a point source, like a sewage treatmenι works, may be very high but the flow may be low, giving a low overall annual load to an overall catchment, whereas low concentrations from a diffuse source, say agricultural runoff, may involve a much higher combined flow, giving a higher net load per year. Thus, for the overall load inputs to the catchment outflow, the agricultural source may have a higher percentage load input, calculated in kg a^{-1}, than the sewage input.

Sources and control

Specification of sources and their control forms an important topic. Unless the sources of water pollution are clearly known, there is little chance of effective pollution control measures being taken. A particular difficulty lies in the trans-boundary nature of many sources, especially where rivers pass through many countries, with downstream effects passed on from one country to the next. A special problem is the specification of the possible multiple sources for ocean pollution which may involve many countries. Although for most substances suitable water treatment technologies exist, it is obviously easier and cheaper in the long run to tackle any pollution at source, rather than take remedial measures once an undesirable substance is present in water.

In particular, the separation of natural sources and anthropogenic sources is important. A second consideration is pinpointing the man-made sources and a third involves the pathways of solute transport and any associated transformations or changes.

Natural sources are mainly atmospheric inputs and from the weathering which takes place in rocks and soils. Atmospheric inputs can arrive in solution in rain, including dissolved gases and particles, or they involve dry deposition of particulate material. Much of the sources for these involve windblown dust and solutes derived from sea water entrained in wind from spray from breaking waves. Weathering of minerals forms a major input. These sources are the chief contributors to total dissolved solids and electrical conductivity as well as the major nutrients specified in Table 1. (See also the discussions on loss of land).

Anthropogenic inputs involve either the acceleration or increase of the natural inputs or the introduction of new substances. In the first case, the two sources have to be differentiated, in the second, the challenge is often one of identifying the substance and its sources.

Sources are easier to identify if they are point sources, such as effluent pipes, than if they are non-point diffuse sources, such as drainage from agricultural land. In the former, it is relatively easy to sample above and below a discharge point and to identify those substances present below the point but not above it. With more diffuse sources, it is often a matter of making a series of observations downstream and assessing incremental inputs from fields and other contributing areas. Diffuse inputs from groundwater can also be difficult to assess where the transit times of any pollutants in the bedrock may be long—a problem may then appear at a groundwater source in relation to some inputs some years earlier. Equally, transformations, such as decomposition and adsorption with the bedrock, can substantially alter the relationships between inputs and outputs. Problems, too, have arisen with previously dumped wastes. In the Federal Republic of Germany, old wartime dumps of chemicals, often long forgotten, have leaked and contaminated ground water and the much publicized illnesses stemming from the Love Creek dump in the USA have led to speculation on the extent of other dormant hazards which one day might erupt.

Downstream transformations also have to be evaluated. Many substances can be changed in their progression through water bodies, especially, for example, nitrogen compounds. Nitrate may be released from suspended organic material or be lost as gaseous nitrogen, especially in wetlands. Other substances, especially heavy metals, may be adsorbed onto sediments and then be released if sediment disturbance occurs. In this case, the source may not be immediately apparent as it may not relate to current inputs but to prior depositional events.

The transition from freshwater through estuarine to marine systems may also influence water quality, especially through suspended sediment flocculation (coagulation) in salt water. In addition, many marine pollutants can have a terrestrial origin, nitrate and phosphate levels being high in offshore waters receiving estuarine inputs, for example. Heavy metal concentrations can also be high where estuarine sedimentation is occurring from a polluted river source. These inputs have to be differentiated from point sources of effluents and also from direct deposition or dumping at sea.

Safe limits

A further difficulty may lie in the specification and enforcement of safe limits for potable water. In particular, there may be long-term cumulative effects which can occur even though instantaneous levels recorded may be regarded as safe. In addition, water may not be the only source of a substance and intake through other sources, such as food and airborne particles, may also be involved. This is true, for example for lead and nitrate, where there is concern over levels in water, but also inputs in food and from other sources. Given these difficulties, enforcement may be challenged when there is some doubt over the effects, though it is clear that where there is doubt, legislation about acceptable levels should err on the side of caution. However, those bodies or institutions implicated in the proposal of costly control measures often play upon any doubt as a reason for avoiding the implementation of control measures. In addition, given the multiple source of many substances, it is clear that organizations should take an overall view of possible sources and not just water. However, the remit of many authorities is often partial and concerned with either water or food or air pollution. Integrated pollution control is a crucial factor in progress.

In particular, attention has to be paid to the severity of any adverse effects on populations exposed to pollutants, and whether this is direct, through drinking water, or indirect via food chains or other exposure. Also important is the persistence of a substance in the environment. Many organic substances degrade or disperse over time, but others, such as heavy metals, do not. Setting standards for water quality also has to consider the frequency and magnitude of exposure and the existence of any vulnerable receptors, be they in the natural environment or human.

Nevertheless, in spite of the difficulties and different priorities, standards have been set, notably for Europe, by the European Commission in their Directives. Their Directives on Detergents (73/404, 73/405, 82/242, 82/243) followed the growing use of hard detergents which did not break down in sewage treatment and led to unpleasant foaming and impaired oxygenation and photosynthesis. The composition of detergents has changed as a result. Directive 75/440 was to ensure that surface water abstracted for use as drinking water reached certain standards and had adequate treatment and the subsequent Directive 79/869 recommended methods and frequency of measuring quality parameters. Directive 80/778 laid down standards for drinking water quality for 60 parameters in six different categories, together with the frequency and methods of analysis. Directive 78/659 was a little different in that it laid down the quality of fresh water needed to protect fish life and 79/923, similarly, for shellfish. The quality of bathing waters, Directive 76/160, has received notoriety, particularly for alleged non-compliance in the UK. Directive 76/464 aims at the elimination or reduction of pollution of inland, coastal and territorial waters by specified dangerous substances, and Directive 80/68 prohibits or regulates discharges of dangerous substances which might pollute underground water sources. Not all Directives are fully met and, of course, in many other parts of the world, for example in eastern Europe, either no such specifications are yet adopted or are ignored.

Future needs

It is clear that inadequate data bases is one of the greatest limiting factors in (a) specifying situations needing attention and (b) bringing about effective controls. It is also clear that advanced analytical equipment is often needed, especially where man-made organic compounds are involved. In addition, it is insufficient to specify the separate levels and effects of individual water quality parameters—the synergistic effects of interacting pollutants needs to be borne in mind as well as the multiplicity of possible sources other than water.

Identification of sources is crucial to water quality control programmes. The relationship between industrial processes and water quality is a critical one where costing of pollution control within the manufacturing process is a major focus of concern. Sewage treatment is also critical, both in terms of the quality of the effluent and the disposal of sewage sludge on land—which may then be re-mobilized into the aquatic system if emplacement is not adequately engineered. The movement of organic material from the land to waterways can place severe strains on the ability of the water to provide adequate oxygen to decompose the material—a caution that applies equally to organic farming as to sewage sludge disposal.

The relationship between land use and water quality is also a crucial one, especially where sediment yields, organic loadings and nutrient loadings are concerned. This needs to be adequately modelled in order to minimize any deleterious impact of land use change to water quality.

A particular need is the formulation and implementation of pollution control measures. To be effective, they must be based on sound scientific knowledge of sources and effects but implementation represents a major global challenge. In the developed world there is increasing public concern and, therefore, political interest in water purity. There is increasing media attention, with television pictures graphically pointing out polluted discharges into rivers and waterways. There are pressure groups, with their increasing membership and finances, sampling, professionally analyzing and publicizing effluent discharges. Thus there is hope that resources will be allocated, or demanded from those responsible for the pollution, to clear up the existing bad practices and to prevent any new threats.

In the developing world, however, there are problems of increasing populations with the inevitable increase in material to be discharged, both directly and from the demands for more material comfort. With the lack of resources to combat both the present and the potential harmful effluents, with other social and economic ills, the outlook for a cleaner Yangtze or Ganges or even for urban sanitation to reduce the spread of disease through contaminated water supplies is distant without massive input from the developed nations. The scale of aid needed, however, seems vast and in competition with that needed for other environmental problems of potential global warming, land degradation and health.

For bibliography, see pp. 363–364.

13 OTHER ISSUES

Peter Brackley

There are a number of environmental topics which, although not in quite the same category as those already described, do give cause for concern, and of which a brief mention must be made.

Waste disposal and recycling

The handling of waste of all sorts generates problems, both national and international, and reference has been made in earlier chapters to the disposal of radioactive materials (Section 8) with all the attendant difficulties and arguments, and to the contamination of rivers and seas (Sections 7, 12). One of the problems is the description of types of waste. "Toxic" waste is, by definition, poisonous although the level of toxicity may be argued. But there is disagreement over what constitutes "hazardous" waste and this hinders the drafting of treaties and even the keeping of statistics, inadequate at the best of times. Most hazardous waste, however defined, is generated in the developed countries and there has been pressure to export it, especially to developing countries where its treatment may be cheap but often inadequate. West African states seemed particularly involved. However recent publicity and the extended journeys of some ships carrying cargoes of waste such as the *Karen B* or the disappearance of some drums containing toxic waste from Seveso, has prompted international concern, and legislation within the EC on transboundary shipments has been strengthened.

In May 1988 the Organization of African Unity (OAU) resolved that member countries would "refrain from" accepting shipments of toxic waste and the following month the Economic Community of West African States declared it a criminal offence (even, in some places, leading to the death penalty) for anyone to import such waste. In 1989 a treaty, with stronger provisions and arranged by UNEP, was signed although there is still the fear that many poor nations may feel under pressure to earn foreign currency by allowing their territory to become the dumping ground for other nations' rubbish. The growing practice of transporting toxic waste to Eastern Europe, for example to East Germany and Romania, may well be affected by recent political upheavals there. The incineration of toxic wastes at sea has been widely criticized and has virtually ceased. On-shore, high temperature processing facilities for hazardous wastes have been constructed but still produce an ash containing some toxic residues for disposal and generate much local opposition.

The dumping of wastes at sea and the disposal into rivers and therefore, eventually, into the sea are increasingly under control and being eliminated as described in earlier sections. But whilst important Northern rivers tend to be covered by treaties Southern waters are governed by fewer, or no, agreements and river water disputes are growing in the Third World. But environmental concerns over rivers and seas still rank low in the list of priorities in the Third World where governments are facing more immediately pressing economic and social problems.

The performance of countries varies greatly in the recovery and recycling of everyday items of waste such as metal cans and bottles (where care must be taken to ensure that the recycling does not require more energy and resources than making new). There are schemes, and a few installations, to extract heat direct by the combustion of domestic rubbish but this is often only considered or justified if tips are not available. Where they are, methane will be generated and may be recovered for use for heating and steam raising. But such landfill sites, although now lined with impermeable materials, do carry a risk of soil and ground water contamination from leaks. Love Creek in the USA and old wartime chemical stocks in Germany provide dramatic cases of severe pollution, leading to illness, from dumps long forgotten or ignored.

Third World development

The issue of population growth was mentioned in the Introduction as being outside the scope of this book. But the predicted increases, particularly in the Third World, together with the ambitions for improvement in living standards, will lead, on present evidence and technologies, to higher consumption, particularly of energy, and therefore more pollution. Debt-ridden countries especially in Africa, but also in South America, tend to over-use soils and to over-cut forests to increase exports and repay debts and to capitalize on their indigenous resources. This means that they subsidize exports by assuming the environmental costs themselves and slowly destroy their agricultural resource base. The dire consequences of this loss and degradation of productive land have been described in Section 5.

Some countries, for example Brazil and Nigeria, fear that growing environmental concern in the developed world may lead to "environmental conditionality", that is that aid and debt relief will be conditional upon, say, conserving tropical forests and other ecosystems. This would prevent them developing their own territories and economies and they seek compensation from countries already developed. Some "debt-for-nature" swaps have taken place for example, in Bolivia, in the Philippines and in Ecuador to preserve parts of the Galapagos Islands. An agreement, for US $3,000,000 was made between Costa Rica and the WWF, but in relation to total debts these possibilities are small. Brazil has recently changed its stance and will now consider "debt-for-nature" deals related to its rain forest. "Debt-for-Development" swaps are also being arranged.

The growing feeling, as described in the Foreword, is that conditionality cannot be accepted and that better means for technology transfer from the developed to the developing world, with fewer strings attached and at lower cost, must be found.

In 1988, the World Bank changed its criteria for funding to include environmental considerations. Existing projects are being examined to identify and rectify environmental problems caused by them. Criticism has been especially directed at some road construction and dam developments which have led to the destruction of large areas of rain forest, with severe implications for the local environment, indigenous peoples and even of the wider global environment. Proposals for agenda items for the 1992 UN Conference on Environment and Development include the establishment of an international "green financing facility" which would use money saved from arms cutbacks to fund environmental projects in the Third World.

Health

Environmental or Occupational Health provides a new discipline of medical practice, principally concerned with the working environment and with local effects on populations from nearby industrial or other activity. Much progress has been made in the last few decades in identifying hazardous or damaging operations and materials and in correcting processes and procedures to prevent harm. Industrial diseases such as silicosis and asbestosis and the effects of toxic fumes from heavy metals, particularly lead and mercury, led to early controls on workplace conditions, and have been followed by the recognition that there are many chemicals which, even in modest concentrations, can be not only unpleasant but harmful.

The campaigns for the removal of lead in motor gasoline were, at times, based upon the harm to human health from lead in the air or on roadside vegetation from exhaust fumes. (The need for the removal of lead was also to enable the introduction of catalytic converters, which remove other harmful emissions, for the chemicals in these devices are poisoned by lead as described in Section 11.) High lead levels in blood are known to cause brain malfunctioning, particularly in children, and although there are other sources of lead ingestion, such as old water pipes and paint, unleaded fuel is now widely available.

Permitted exposure levels for many chemicals are contained in legislation in many countries and these are reviewed and extended and lowered from time to time as new evidence of effects becomes known. In many countries extensive testing of new chemicals must now be undertaken before being marketed.

The most widely used group of potentially dangerous chemicals are those used in agriculture due, in part, to the frequent absence or impossibility of control at the point of use. The damage to waterways and the seas from run-off containing fertilisers and the dispersal of pesticide residues has been described in Sections 7 and 12. A recent World Bank report gave details of the pollution entering the Mediterranean, including 550 tonnes per annum of agricultural chemical residues and there was much publicity for the algal blooms in the Adriatic. Some commercial pesticide products that have been used in the past are now prohibited in many countries but the concern is that they are often still widely used, particularly in the developing world. India has reported much human illness deriving from excessive use of pest control chemicals, often because those dispensing them cannot read the precautions and dosage rates on the labels. There is, too, in some countries, a flourishing trade in banned products. In others the benefits, in pest control and improved yields (or reduced losses), are considered to outweigh the risks.

Ignorance or carelessness also leads to tragedies involving dangerous substances. In September 1987 radioactive caesium chloride powder, found in a dump in Goiana, Brazil from a cylinder stolen from a hospital radiotherapy unit and sold for scrap, was handled casually by children and others ignorant of its dangers. The death toll of four did not take account of longer-term effects of exposure of others and from the pollution of the area. Similarly chemical discharges at places such as Bhopal, with over 2,500 deaths, and from the Sandoz chemical company is Basle, Switzerland which contaminated the Rhine with mercury and phosphorus, and many other lesser incidents lead to extensive pollution and hazard.

Noise and vibration

Noise is another health problem. In Britain local government is responsible for many environmental and health matters and the Royal Commission on the Environment in its 10th Report, in 1984, stated that local authorities received more complaints about noise than on any other environmental topic. Legislation in many countries lays down the permitted maximum levels of noise at workplaces and for equipment, particularly vehicles and even lawnmowers, and compensation is sometimes payable for excessive noise disturbance, for example near aerodromes, or for hearing damage. Ear protection is now available and in common use.

Lower frequency vibrations are now also recognized as causing damage. For example in 1985 white finger disease, or the hand-arm vibration syndrome—HAVS—was added to Britain's list of prescribed industrial diseases and is caused by the use of tools such as chainsaws or pneumatic handtools such as chipping hammers, without protective damping.

Environmental disasters

There are a number of recent disasters, accidents or incidents, connected with environmental issues or concerns whose names or locations have become part of the language. Some have had significant influence on the progress and subsequent direction of research and control legislation. One cumulative effect has been to erode public confidence in technical competence and to lead to much more questioning of "progress".

Amoco Cadiz, 1978. A very large crude oil tanker (VLCC) wrecked on the coast of Brittany, Northern France, released over 200,000 tonnes of crude oil affecting some 200 km of coastline.

Bhopal, 1984. The Indian city where a major explosion occurred, killing over 2,500 people, due to the release of a toxic gas, methyl-iso cyanate, from a chemical plant.

Chernobyl, 1986. The site, in the USSR near Kiev in the Ukraine, of a nuclear power generator disaster which destroyed one of four identical 1000MW reactors, and spread radioactive materials over vast distances (even as far as Wales where, four years later, there are still controls on affected sheep).

Exxon Valdez, 1989. The grounded and holed crude oil tanker caused extensive oil pollution and damage to coastlines, wildlife and habitats in Alaska, particularly in Prince William Sound.

Ixtoc 1, 1979. An exploratory oil well in the Gulf of Mexico from which a massive oil release occurred causing widespread pollution and consequential damage to beaches, wildlife and commercial fisheries.

Lake Nyos, 1986. The lake in Cameroon, West Africa, that released vast quantities of carbon dioxide in a cloud which killed, mainly by asphyxiation, over 1,700 people.

Minamata, 1959. The town and bay in Japan which was the location for the worst recorded poisoning by fish contaminated by methyl mercury, formed in the Bay from mercury discharged over several years by a chemical factory. Many people died or were incapacitated.

Rainbow Warrior, 1985. A ship, owned by Greenpeace which was sunk by French government agents in Auckland harbour, New Zealand, to prevent its use in protest against French nuclear weapons testing in the Pacific.

Sandoz, 1986. The Swiss chemical company at whose Basle warehouse a fire occurred that led to a major spillage of pesticides into the river Rhine. Hundreds of thousands of fish died and emergency action had to be taken to safeguard municipal water supplies.

Seveso, 1976. The village near Milan in northern Italy where a factory discharged large quantities of dioxins which caused major skin problems for the people in the neighbourhood. This led to world-wide interest in these chemicals, their occurrence, toxicity and exposure levels and, in some places, particularly in West Germany, to extreme limits for control being imposed. It also led to the EC considering major accident hazards and requiring member states to set up safety plans, emergency plans, training, information, tests, surveys etc.

Three Mile Island, 1979. The site of a nuclear power station near Harrisburg, Pennsylvania where a serious accident occurred leading to the release of radioactive materials and severe damage to the reactor core.

Torrey Canyon, 1967. The crude oil tanker wrecked on the Seven Stones off the Isles of Scilly to give the first large scale experience of oil pollution in Europe. Little was known at the time on the effects and how to deal with the incident. The RAF attempted to bomb the hulk and to set it on fire and dispersants, more toxic than the oil itself, led to damage over hundreds of miles of coastline. The accident led to research and the establishment of proper equipment and contingency plans to deal with future spills.

Windscale, 1957. Now renamed Sellafield. The site in Cumbria, north-west England of the first plutonium-producing nuclear reactor in 1952 which was shut down in 1957 following a serious fire which released radioactive materials.

There are other, longer term environmental disasters of which one of the most publicized is that affecting the Aral Sea, an inland sea in Kazakhstan/Uzbekistan in the USSR which has diminished to a fraction of its former size due to the use, for irrigation, of river water previously flowing into the sea.

Loss of amenity

More difficult judgements arise in the loss of amenity or visual intrusion for these are individual perceptions rather than pollution subject to scientific measurement. Developments of almost any kind, whether they be industrial expansion, leisure activities or even renewable energy projects, generate opposition, particularly in crowded conditions. Loss of amenity or access to open spaces and wilderness, restrictions on behaviour, for example on hunting and shooting, are differently perceived and accorded different priorities in different countries. In Germany the damage to forests, where they hold a particular place in folklore and custom, generated countrywide alarm. In Sweden the loss of wilderness from hydroelectric schemes meant that the present generation could not pass on the land to their children in the same state as they had inherited it which they felt was their bounden duty. In Britain the uprooting of hedgerows, which changed the face of the countryside, was widely condemned. All led to strong public reaction against change or damage to the environment. Visual intrusion of power lines, roadways, wind farms, barrages, let alone new industrial complexes or new towns, is resisted and resented but difficult to quantify.

These problems usually generate local opposition, often with exaggerated hyperbole (and led to the acronym NIMBY—"not in my back yard"), but the same sort of activities can lead to much wider concern if wildlife habitats, wetlands or wilderness are involved. The threat to, say, waders from reclaiming estuarine mudflats can lead to widespread objection far from the scene. International agreements, such as the Ramsar Convention, protect some of the more important sites and reserves, particularly those used by migrating waterfowl. The possible opening up of the interior of Alaska is a national issue, although few Americans visit the State. The continuing loss of part of the Amazonian rain forests is an international issue.

There are many large organizations, particularly in the USA, dedicated to protecting wildlife and their habitats and to leaving the remote wildernesses and untouched lands in their pristine state.

Gaia

Finally mention must be made of the theory, developed by James Lovelock FRS, that the earth exhibits the behaviour of a living creature or superorganism. He gave it a mythical name—"Gaia" the Earth goddess of ancient Greece. The idea was at first totally rejected by many scientists but has led to extensive debate and a large conference (in March 1988 organized by the American Geophysical Union). The basis is that, whereas existing theories held that plants and animals evolve on, but are distinct from an inanimate planet, Lovelock showed that the Earth, its rocks, oceans and atmosphere and all living creatures are part of one great organism, evolving over the vast span of geological time. He states that "Gaia theory forces a planetary perspective. It is the health of the planet that matters, not that of some individual species of organisms. This is where Gaia and the environmental movements, which are concerned first with the health of people, part company."

Hope

The hope then is that, with all the problems confronting the peoples of the world, as outlined in this and the earlier sections, the growing awareness of the conflicting interests and potential disasters will lead to some solutions. Many scientists are engaged in research on environmental problems, many politicians are realizing that something has to be done, consumers are demanding products free of environmental effects both in production and use, and many millions of individuals, through innumerable organizations, some of which are listed in Part 4, are demanding attention and action so that sustainable development may be achieved.

For bibliography, see p. 364.

II. POLITICS

STEWART BOYLE

Introduction

"No single ideological formulation could possibly corral such a rich variety of experience and feeling, and still preserve the independence and authenticity of everyone's protest". (Theodore Roszak writing about the green movement) (Porritt, 1984).

In June 1989, 36 Green politicians were elected to the European Parliament.[1] Their election, linked to significant gains made by the British Labour Party, allowed a "red–green" (socialist–environmental) grouping within the European parliament to take the overall majority away from conservative groups for the first time. The result, which included a 14.5% vote for the Greens in the UK (see Table 1), was a further sign that, 17 years after the first Green party was formed, Green politics had become a force to take note of.[2]

Since the first Green was elected to a national parliament in Switzerland in 1979, Green politics has taken root in most Western European and Scandinavian countries. Nearly 20 countries have Green politicians in national parliaments. This trend is continuing; in 1989, the Miljopariet de Grona became the first new Party to enter the Swedish parliament for 70 years, polling 5.6% of the votes and winning 20 seats.

Many of the politicians actively involved in the momentous political changes in Eastern Europe in 1989 and 1990 cut their teeth on environmental struggles, and East Germany elected Green MPs. Many other East European political parties contained a high proportion of environmental activists; one estimate suggests that 15–20% of those elected have strong environmental credentials.

Green political parties are also to be found in most of the rest of the world, especially Australasia and North America, although the political system in the latter makes it extremely difficult to achieve success in the voting booth.

The influence of Green politicians and Green parties has been invariably out of proportion to their actual membership or votes won. They have been particularly effective through influencing the policies of other political parties, though in many countries, the environmental pressure groups have arguably been more influential in this process, particularly where voting systems hinder small parties. Despite many attempts by the media and the conventional political parties to describe and define them to the public, their varied and sometimes confusing policies, tactics and support base, defy conventional political labels.

Green parties appear to thrive under voting systems such as proportional representation,

---

[1]The term Green used in describing politicians has no simple definition (see sections below on "Who are the Greens?"), but is commonly used in this chapter when referring to members of formal Green parties rather than environmentally inclined politicians in conventional parties.

[2]Several of the MEPs were not acknowledged by fellow Green MEPs as belonging to a Green Party (see footnotes in Table 1).

Table 1: *European Parliament elections: Green parties' support*

	1979		*1984*		*1989*	
State	*Seats*	%	*Seats*	%	*Seats*	%
Belgium	0	3.4	2	8.2	3	13.9
Denmark	4	21.0*	4	20.8*	4	16.5*
France	0	4.4	0	3.4	9	10.6
Federal Republic of Germany	0	3.2	7	8.2	8	8.4
Greece			0	nil	0	nil
Ireland	0	nil	0	0.5	1	3.3
Italy	0	nil	0	nil	5	6.2
Luxembourg	0	6.1	0	1.0	0	10.4
Netherlands	0	5.0	2	5.6*	2	7.0*
Portugal			1	3.0		
Spain			3	6.0		
UK	0	0.7	0	0.5	0	14.5

*Denmark's group is the anti-European Community federation of parties. Although having many ecological policies, it is not fully accepted as a Green party by other Greens. The Dutch Green Party has only recently been accepted as a Green party due to its strong leftist leanings.

The total in the Rainbow group in 1984 was 20: in 1989 it had 39 seats (including some leftist MPs from Italy).

which allow seats in parliament with a low percentage of the vote, and in particular where funding to assist political campaigns is available. In countries such as the USA and UK, where a simple majority voting system exists, the opposite is the case.

The Greens' influence is closely related to general concern over specific environmental and peace issues within a country. Their future role is likely to depend on a number of key factors. These include the general state of the environment and public concern about it; the performance of both the country's economy and the ruling political parties in dealing with it and the environment; the extent to which other political parties are able to convince the electorate of their green credentials; and critically, whether Greens can organize themselves without the self-destructive splintering into new groups and ideologies which has characterized their first 17 years.

The early days of Green politics

On May 3, 1972, the world's first Green party was formed at a conference in Wellington, New Zealand. Called the Values Party, its formation was based on concern over environmental issues such as the 1969 campaign to save Manapouri Lake in the South Island from a hydro-electric scheme which led to the formation of an Environmental Defence Society, and the rapid spread of environmental activism to university campuses. In the run-up to the November 1972 general election, a "Blueprint for New Zealand" was launched, outlining the Party's manifesto. In the event, it obtained just 2% of the national vote. Subsequently it was to be dogged by internal organizational problems (a recurring theme in many other Green parties worldwide), and the difficulties in maintaining any momentum in a "simple majority" electoral system which makes it very hard for new parties to gain representation.

At its annual conference in 1973, the Party resolved not to have a national office. The result was a collapse of local groups and any semblance of organization. Although some coherence was restored by the 1975 national election, and some 5% of the votes were gained, (just short of the support which allowed the German Greens to enter their national parliament for the first time), thereafter it was downhill all the way. In 1978, the vote dropped to 2.4% and the Party currently exists only in name. As one European Green has remarked, almost by way of an epitaph, "perhaps the Values Party arrived on the political scene before its time, unable to sustain its initial momentum without the support of the global green movement" (Parkin, 1989).

UK Greens formed the People Party in 1973. Over the next 17 years, its name changed first to the Ecology Party and then to the Green Party. Battling once again against a simple majority voting system, success proved elusive until the European parliamentary elections in 1989. As one Belgian Green stated in 1984, "it is a matter of astonishment that a Green party exists in Britain at all" (Spretnak and Capra, 1985).

The first breakthrough for European Green politicians came with the 1979 European Parliamentary elections. Although none of the Green parties gained any seats in that election, they were able to introduce their political ideas to a much wider public for the first time. Most European Green parties were formed in the following six years. Table 1 charts the growing electoral success in Europe from that period through until the most recent election.

The greatest electoral success and impact of green politics has undoubtedly been in West Germany. The Green Party grew from a strong tradition of citizens initiatives against environmentally and socially damaging projects, and stimulated by proposals to site nuclear Cruise and Polaris missiles in the country. Local Green parties in Lower Saxony, Hamburg, Hesse, North-Rhine-Westphalia, and Baden-Wurttemberg were formed in the period 1978–79. Die Grünen (the Greens) was founded on March 16–17, 1979 in Frankfurt, and was able to contest the European parliamentary elections in June 1979.

Based on an alliance of peace and environmental campaigners, more conservative nature protection groups, and far left activists, Die Grünen has always been a party in tension (see section on the German Greens below). When asked "what is the glue that holds the Green Party together?", one Green state legislator in Lower Saxony, Helmut Lippelt, responded with a simple word: "success!".

Die Grünen entered regional (Länder) parliaments for the first time in Bremen in October 1979. Further electoral success came in Baden-Wurttemberg in March 1980. Berlin in May 1981, Lower Saxony in March 1982, Hesse in September 1982, and Hamburg in December 1982. It was in the national elections of January 1983 however, with 5.6% of the vote, that Die Grünen entered national politics with a vengeance. They have maintained and increased support from the original 28 MPs to 42 today, and have been something of an inspiration to other Green parties around the world.

Although figures are not available for at least a third of the Green parties in existence worldwide, it is likely that membership totals less than 150,000. For the 80,000 known members, over 60% are West German. Despite the low membership, their influence has been considerable in a number of countries. The percentage of the vote received has so far reached a high of 14.5% in the European parliamentary elections, 8.3% in national elections, 10.6% in regional or state elections, and greater than 30% in some local municipalities where concern over environmental issues has been particularly high. More than any other factor, they have brought environmental issues into the election process.

Who are the Greens and what do they want?

> "Putting the Earth first in our personal life and our politics does suggest a new set of values and practices that is considerably different from today's dominant ethos" (Parkin, 1989).

Definitions

To better understand the basis of Green politics, some definitions are required. The word 'ecology' comes from the Greek *oikos* "home" or "habitat", and *logos* "subject of study". Ecology is defined in different ways by different ecologists, but it essentially means looking at, and studying all the relationships and interactions between living things and their environment.

Many early British and North American ecologists saw ecology as an approach rather than a discipline. This was true of those who formed the British Ecological Society in 1913, and the American Society shortly afterwards. Barrington Moore, first president of the American Ecological Society, argued in 1919 that ecology was the science of synthesis, and that such a science was clearly essential if we were to understand the functioning of the world as a whole. Full development of such a science has not occurred however, and ecology as taught in colleges has tended to become a very reductionistic and highly specialized discipline.

Environmentalism

This is a very broad term, linking the range of individuals and groups concerned about the protection of the environment. Jonathon Porritt, Director of UK Friends of the Earth from 1984–90, and a Green Party member, has suggested that there are three varieties of environmentalists. First are the conservationists or traditionalists, who lay great emphasis on the restoration of order and authority. They don't want to change society as such, they prefer to work with current structures and the law, and want to conserve the best bits of society that might otherwise disappear due to industrialism. At the other end of the scale are radical, libertarian environmentalists. They support small-scale, self-sufficient communities as a means of escaping from the hierarchical pressures of contemporary industry. They are opposed to the present industrial system, and totally reject the idea that the present crisis can be solved by technological fixes. A fundamental change in values is thus sought.

Somewhere in between, and according to Porritt "certainly in a majority", are the reformists who are deeply concerned about a whole range of environmental issues. They tend to support the dominant social paradigms, and have conventional middle-class concerns and interests (Parkin, 1989).

Environmental organizations reflecting these three varieties include conservation bodies such as Stichtung Natuur et Milieu (Netherlands) and the Royal Society for the Protection of Birds (UK); the range of Green political parties; and finally, a large number of environmental pressure groups such as Greenpeace, Friends of the Earth, Bund (West

Germany), Lego Ambiente (Italy), Environmental Defense Fund (US), and the Polish Ecological Club.

Recently there has been a growing tendency to draw a clearer distinction between environmentalism and ecology. Murray Bookchin, the American eco-anarchist, accuses environmentalists of being guilty of a "managerial approach to the natural world", that merely helps existing authorities to do their job better, and simply papers over all the cracks of an unworkable system.

The roots of the Green movement

Holmes has pointed out that the roots of the 1970s' Green movement are quite complex. He suggests that far from being "a Green species of socialists . . . the Green movement is as much a social and spiritual phenomenon as a political one" (Holmes 1987). He points to three roots: (a) the socialist leaning **radicalism** of the 1960s which had run its course, but led to feminism and environmentalism; (b) the **personal growth** movements which grew from the "hippy" culture of the late 1960s, and which are based on the "primacy of the individual's search for happiness and spiritual development"; and (c) **new religions**. He stresses the importance of "holistic" thinking in much of Green activism and politics, an approach which is based on the "assumption that society's problems cannot be solved one by one, but must be tackled through a complete change of direction, and indeed a general spiritual renewal". Indeed, he concludes that "it is important to understand that Green politics implies not just a spring-cleaning of the planet, but a thorough-going revolution . . . (non-violent, of course) in the way society is organized and the way people behave towards each other and towards the earth".

The French Greens coined the phrase: "Europe will be Green or not at all". Though the "limits of growth" arguments put forward by the Club of Rome in the early 1970s have been heavily criticized, an underlying concern over the unsustainability of current trends is pervasive amongst most Greens. Holmes has suggested that their rather gloomy world view can be best described as "creative pessimism". This is in contrast to the "unrealistic optimism" of many who want to believe that the environment is in safe hands with the government and business.

The four principles

There is no single definition of what constitutes a Green individual or a Green party. At the Offenbach Congress which formerly set up Die Grünen in 1979, it seemed almost impossible to agree even broad principles amongst the diverse and argumentative factions. August Haussleiter, a founder member of Die Grünen who, at the age of 82, is still editor of their weekly newspaper, recalled: "although agreement seemed impossible, I took a piece of paper and wrote four words on it: ecology, social responsibility, grass roots democracy, and non-violence. Then I called Gruhl (leader of the Conservatives) and Reents (leader of the Left), into the room where the journalists were and said "sign". We then went back into the convention hall and announced, we have a programme".

Holistic thinking is a basic philosophy also frequently mentioned by Greens, as is decentralization, which is closely linked to "grass roots democracy". The need for integration, or holism, which links up seemingly disparate trends, issues and views, is a key idea pervading much of Green thinking. Holistic thinking tries to get to the heart of why things happen, and to understand the philosophical and social paradigms which lead to environmental destruction, poverty and violence. It follows through the consequences of decisions; it looks at life cycles, not just the short-term consequences; and it concentrates heavily on the role of individuals and consequences of all their actions. Above all, it emphasizes the need for individual responsibility in one's actions.

Porritt has expanded on some of these very general themes by developing his 14 "minimum criteria for being Green" (see Table 2). These range from "a reverence for the Earth and for all its creatures", to "harmony between people of every race, colour and creed".

Deep ecology

Ecology has several meanings within Green politics. Most can be understood in the context of "deep ecology", a concept that has grown in recent years. As Spretnak and Capra note: "far more than protecting or repairing the *status quo*, which is generally the goal of environmentalism, "deep ecology" encompasses the study of nature's subtle web of interrelated processes and the application of that study to our interactions with nature and among ourselves. The teachings of deep ecology, include implications for our politics, our economy, our social structures, our educational system, our health care, our cultural expressions, and our spirituality".

Deep ecologists such as John Seed "question the fundamental premises and values of contemporary civilization . . . nothing short of a total revolution in consciousness will be of lasting use in preserving the life-support systems of our planet" (Seed *et al*, 1988). Deep ecologists view humans as a "plain member" of the biotic community and not the "crown of creation". A small number of "deep Greens" formed the "Earth First" movement in the early 1980s. This is particularly active in California and Australia, where it carries out direct actions "on behalf of the planet". These include "spiking" trees with long nails in order to make them useless for loggers, and burying people up to their necks in roads to prevent machinery entering a reserve. One of its founders, Dave Foreman, has been quoted as saying "the human race could go extinct, and I, for one, would not shed any

Table 2: *List of criteria for being Green*

A reverence for the Earth and for all its creatures.
A willingness to share the world's wealth among all its peoples.
Prosperity to be achieved through sustainable alternatives to the rat-race of economic growth.
Lasting security to be achieved through non-nuclear defence strategies and considerably reduced arms spending.
A rejection of materialism and the destrustive values of industrialism.
A recognition of the rights of future generations in our use of all resources.
An emphasis on socially useful, personally rewarding work, enhanced by human-scale technology.
Protection of the environment as a precondition of a healthy society.
An emphasis on personal growth and spiritual development.
Respect for the gentler side of human nature.
Open, participatory democracy at every level of society.
Recognition of the crucial importance of significant reductions in population levels.
Harmony between people of every race, colour and creed.
A non-nuclear, low-energy strategy, based on conservation, greater efficiency and renewable sources.
An emphasis on self-reliance and decentralized communities.

Source: Porritt, 1984.

tears", but few take such an extreme view. Though somewhat anarchic in organization, its adherents (there are no members as such) possibly run to several thousand. Their presence may grow if environmentalists sense a worsening crisis in the global environment.

Seed, Spretnak and others highlight the key difference in the two views on human relationships with other species. Most human beings have an anthropocentric (man-centred) ethic, the deep ecologists have a biocentric (nature-centred) ethic (Fenton, 1987).

Some Greens have gone to great lengths to explain the difference between the two approaches, called by some "deep ecology" and "shallow ecology" (Schwartz and Schwartz, 1987). Walter and Dorothy Schwartz give a range of definitions and examples based on the pioneering work by Norwegian Arne Naess, who first coined the term "deep ecology". They contrast 'shallow ecology', which, for example, assumes that "natural diversity is valuable as a resource for us", against "deep ecology", which assumes that "natural diversity has its own intrinsic value" (see Table 3).

Greens hence support the development of appropriate technology as it encourages an interdependence with the earth. This would include "soft" energy production, such as solar power, that works with cycles and flows of the sun, wind and water, as against using capital stocks of finite fossil fuels, and regenerative agriculture that replenishes the soil and incorporates natural means of pest control. Broader ecological thinking also leads to "social ecology" which is the perception of societal structures in human interactions as an intricate web of dynamic systems. This is in contrast to conventional Western cultural thinking, which views our bodies, the body politic, and the natural world as "hierarchically arranged aggregates of discrete components". Hence "social ecology" is a systems view which looks at the world in terms of relationships and integration.

Table 3: *Two branches of Green ethics*

Shallow ecology	Deep ecology
Natural diversity is valuable as a resource for us.	Natural diversity has its own intrinsic value.
It is nonsense to talk about value except as value for mankind.	Equating "value" with value for humans reveals a social prejudice.
Plant species should be saved because of their value as genetic reserves for human agriculture and medicine.	Plant species should be saved because of their intrinsic value.
Pollution should be decreased if it threatens economic growth.	Decrease of pollution has priority over economic growth.
Third World population growth threatens ecological equilibrium.	World population at present level threatens eco-systems, but the population and behaviour of industrial states does so more than others. Human population today is exessive.
"Resource" means resource for humans.	'Resource' means resource for living beings.
People will not tolerate a broad decrease in their standard of living.	People should not tolerate a broad decrease in the quality of life but in the standard of living in over-developed countries.

Social responsibility

The second of the four pillars of Green thinking, "social responsibility", is understood to mean social justice and an assurance that the poor and the working class will not get hurt by programmes to restructure the economy and consumer society in ecological ways. This is strongly influenced by the German Greens, where the concept of a social contract between communities, the trade unions, and industry was developed in the course of rebuilding the German economy in the 1950s and '60s. Radical-left Greens tend to interpret "social responsibility" as a code word for democratic marxism. Indeed, this has led to many of the battles within the West German Greens and other parties in the UK and the Netherlands. The transition in society from a "consuming" to a "consumer" society has been identified as a problem for Green politics, and is the subject of much study.

Grass-roots democracy

The third pillar—"grass roots democracy"—was heavily inspired by West Germany citizen movements during the 1970s. It is also linked closely to the strong support for decentralization of political and economic power. As Die Grünen's federal programme stated in the mid-1980s, "grass roots-democratic politics means an increased realization of decentralized, direct democracy . . . We start from the belief that the decisions of the grass roots levels must, in principle, be given priority" (Spretnak and Capra, 1985). On occasion, this has led to intense arguments within Green parties, (particularly those with political representation), over whether to maintain strong national bodies or to devolve all authority to the local level.

The themes of grass roots democracy and decentralization have also led to conflicts over the role of "leaders" or "personalities" in the Green parties. In France, the overt political ambitions of Brice Lalonde, former Green Party presidential candidate and now Socialist Minister for the Environment, led to a great mistrust of strong leaders. In the UK, though wary of "leaders", the Party took a pragmatic view and allowed a number of speakers to present their views to the media in 1989. These included TV broadcaster David Icke, Sara Parkin, and Jean Lambert. Conscious of the need to present a professional image, rather than the "brown bread and sandals" hippy so beloved of some sections of the UK media, these speakers, with wide experience of dealing with the media, presented a smart and "reasonable" face to the public.

The extreme decentralists are called "fourth worlders", who believe in returning to small village communities. Porritt and others have rejected these notions as "ludicrously nostalgic" and the proponents as "manic minisculists".

Non-violence

The fourth pillar, "non violence", means to the Greens the cessation of both personal violence and of the violence and oppression imposed by the state and its institutions. For these reasons, the Greens support the concept of self-determination for individuals and groups, peace education in schools, and a non-exploitative economic system in which employee-owned and controlled businesses replace huge multinational operations. One of the best-known Greens, Petra Kelly, expresses the centrality of this principle when she says, "non-violence is the essential ingredient in an ecological society".

The impact of the above principles and other Green criteria on specific policies is discussed briefly below.

Green policies

"I would be hard put even now to say what our ideology is. Our politics seem to be a fairly simple mixture oi pragmatism and idealism, common sense and vision" (Porritt, 1984).

On the basis of the manifestos provided by some of the major European Green parties, in particular the West German, Swedish, French and UK Green parties, plus discussions with a number of Greens worldwide, Green principles appear to be reflected on specific policies as follows:

Economics

Greens argue that instead of recognizing the economy as just one aspect of a wider ecological and social system, most economists tend to isolate it and describe it in terms of highly unrealistic models. Basic concepts such as Gross National Product (GNP) and productivity are defined in a narrow way, without considering this wider social and ecological context. Even the economist David Pearce, who is advisor to the UK Government and believes in calculating the value of environment and including the costs of environmental pollution and resource usage in economic analysis, makes this mistake, say the Greens. Green politicians hence try to include consideration of the environment in every decision made by a society. It should, they argue, be at the forefront of all investments, the development of new institutions, and the use of resources.

Green politicians are also opposed to growth in its many current guises. Porritt argues that "sustainability and industrialism are mutually exclusive" and that we cannot "grow our way out of unemployment". Indeed, he argues that "unemployment can actually be caused by economic growth . . . conventional economics has all but collapsed, its theoretical basis now bankrupt, its practices quite unable to handle the unfamiliar problems that the world now faces". Porritt also argues for an economic system where "working and producing things to meet people's needs *directly* rather than working and producing things to make enough money to meet people's needs *indirectly*" should prevail. Multinational companies are hence a favourite hate subject of the Greens.

Contrary to the view of Greens as the "no-growth Party", most Greens acknowledge that there will always continue to be some economic growth. This will take place in certain sectors of the economy in the industrialized world, and in the Third World, where "there will have to be substantial economic growth for some time, though with much greater discrimination as regards the nature and quality of that growth."

Greens throughout OECD countries argue for a move away from income tax to resource taxation, which will discourage excessive consumption of resources and "put a brake on polluting activities". This, for example, would include an energy tax on fossil and nuclear fuels, and a nitrate tax on fertilisers.

Die Grünen's federal programme states: "we are for an economic system orientated towards the vital requirements of people and of future generations, towards the preservation of nature, and the judicious handling of natural resources . . . a society where attention to Nature's life cycles, the development and use of technology, and the relationship between production and consumption becomes the business of all of those concerned. An economy founded on ecological principles does not mean renouncing a qualify of life; it means people supporting those products that fulfil their needs and are compatible with the natural environment".

The UK Greens emphasize the need for an "integrated, self-sufficient sustainable economy" (UK Green Party, 1989). This would be an economy which: (a) *integrates* the primary-producing *and* manufacturing sectors; (b) which is based upon largely *self-sufficient* units; and (c) which would be *sustainable* because of the emphasis of conserving primary resources (food, energy, minerals, etc.) and recycling. The ultimate aim "is the achievement of a steady-state economy, based on stock rather than flow economics, where wealth is assessed from what we have instead of how quickly we use it" (Wall, 1980). The Greens recognize that the transition period may be difficult, though they are rather vague about how to build up the sustainable and largely informal economy as fast as possible, which has "a very high degree of integration and self-sufficiency". International trade is to be restrained by agreements, through tariff barriers and quotas, in order to encourage greater self-sufficiency.

Green politicians are in favour of qualitative rather than quantitative growth that entails environmental destruction. They would also use alternative economic indicators to GNP which, according to Derek Wall, would "define human worth in terms of . . . human and ecological health and happiness".

The Greens would dismantle life-threatening industries, above all the nuclear weapons industries, and reorientate production towards ecologically and socially necessary products. They would attempt to control and reverse the situation where "billions of pounds are spent on trinkets and TVs, and used to feed domestic pets instead of people" (Wall, 1980). They would support ecological investments like energy efficiency, recycling, water management, agriculture, housing and public transport. They would also respond to the current high rate of unemployment in many industrialized nations through redistributing the available work by shortening workers' hours and re-hiring unemployed workers. In line with the concern over human scale and the size of organizations, they would also support self-managed, co-operative enterprises in which those involved in the production process are able to decide themselves what is produced, as well as how and where it is produced.

The Green parties are *not* opposed to private ownership, and they would propose new economic structures by developing grassroots networks of individuals and organizations, as well as alternative banking organizations for example. They would also attempt to restrict advertising and other means of encouraging material wealth and aggrandisement.

Work

Green parties worldwide share the view that full employment will not return. Indeed, increasing productivity *and* full employment can only lead to substantial economic growth, a heavy use of resources and extensive pollution. Greens argue that a new work ethic should be developed. This includes an emphasis upon shorter hours, flexible and more varied work patterns, a major growth in the self-employed and the so-called "unofficial economy", work sharing, early retirement, and a wide range of new jobs. Swedish Greens have specifically called for a two-hour reduction in the working week. These would be generated from the "greening" of the inner cities, a "back to the land" movement, resource saving (recycling, energy conservation, etc.), and new financial institutions catering to local needs. The guaranteed "basic income" would provide a subsistence existence, which would be supplemented by the many new jobs generated, particularly those "directly concerned with improving the quality of the environment".

Nuclear weapons and peace

Many Greens gained some of their early campaigning experience against nuclear weapons. New defence strategies hence form a major plank of their manifestos. They would divert a substantial proportion of the US$1 trillion dollars spent annually around the world on weapons, and up to 50% of government research and development (R+D) finance spent on defence projects. This would include dismantling the world stockpile of nuclear arms, and encouraging the move towards a purely defensive "citizens" army rather in the mode of the Swiss. As Kelly has stated: "every neighbourhood will have to know how to conduct resistance and become subversive".

Social issues

The Greens believe in the 'self-determination' of every human being, but are rather short on details on how people will live in an ecological non-exploitative society. They tend instead to develop Green responses to a number of specific issues such as health care, education, technology and women's rights.

Health care would be switched away from a very mechanical and reactive system, with its heavy emphasis upon machinery and drugs, to preventive medicine, with full scope for alternative treatments such as acupuncture, psychotherapy, dietary advice and other healing methods. Abortion would be a choice for women.

Green politicians tend to support a minimum social wage, which would replace the complicated "means tested" series of social benefits that currently exist in many Western countries. Their argument is that most people tend to procure a basic minimum wage by one method or another, whether this be through crime, working, begging, the black economy, or a combination of these. The UK Green Party advocates a Basic Income Scheme (BIS) replacing most welfare benefits. This would mean that basic needs would be guaranteed unconditionally, but that there would be competition for anything else over and above that level of subsistence. The scheme would obviously remove work as an obligation, but as Porritt asserts: "would re-instate the work incentive taken away by the welfare state" by removing the poverty trap.

The Third World

Green politicians write and talk a great deal about relationships between the industrialized world and Third World countries. Die Grünen argue that in an economic system with the so-called "international division of labour", industry and agriculture of Third World countries are controlled by foreign aid and by credits from international banks, so that production is primarily orientated towards the needs of industrial countries. They are forced to sell their commodity goods cheaply to buy expensive industrial products in return, which leads to massive indebtedness. To pay their debts, Third World countries have to further increase their exports, which is possible only by paying starvation wages. At the same time, their purchasing power keeps decreasing, as "massive poverty becomes the foundation of an economy totally orientated towards foreign countries" (Cooper 1988).

Petra Kelly has described the over-production and consumption in the West, followed by the dumping of highly poisonous waste in developing countries as "garbage imperialism" (Kelly, 1990). Greens thus tend to support efforts leading to a lessening of the Third World dependence on the world market, with some radical Greens even favouring Third World countries decoupling from the Northern industrial trading market.

Technology

Green politicians argue that technology is political rather than objective, and that there must be democratic control of many technologies. The general approach is to set up watchdog committees and a major reorientation of research and development policies and investments. Wall criticizes those such as Bahro who talk of abolishing railways, telephones and the microchip and states that: "technology should be used carefully, not thrown away" (Wall, 1980).

Population

This has been a problematical area for Green politicians. On the one hand there are greater than 5 billion people on the planet, with projections of 10 to 12 billion by the second half of the next century. This clearly leads to immense pressures on resources and the biosphere. On the other hand, population control, particularly in the Third World, has connotations of genetic imperialism and interference in people's lives. Though Greens frequently point out the disparity of the use of resources between the First and Third Worlds, reducing the birth rate and overall population levels is a theme at many conferences and discussions. Fearful of the media backlash, the UK Green Party modified a proposed population policy, which initially suggested target reduction figures for the UK of 15–20 million (25–40%) to a rather vague reference of the need to reduce population levels (UK Green Party, 1989).

"Deep Greens" have no such quibbles, and talk of returning one third of the land area to wilderness where no development is allowed, and where massive reductions in population are essential.

Green party voters

> "Greens are a kind of popular army, with a function comparable to that of the antibodies generated to restore normal conditions in a diseased biological organism". (Aurelio Peccei, founder of the Club of Rome).

Green party supporters tend to be in the 20–45 year-old age group, although support does exist in older age groups. According to one survey, they are younger and more middle class than the electorate as a whole and they contain a high percentage of women (*The Independent*, July 7, 1989). Many of the original Green politicians and their supporters tend to have been influenced by a range of books and writers such as: *Limits to Growth*, Schumacher's *Small is Beautiful*, a range of publications by Ivan Illich, and *Blueprint for Survival*, all of which were widely translated throughout the world.

Opposition politicians have tried hard to define Green politics and its supporters in conventional terms. The West German CDU, as well as other conservative groups around the world, have likened Green parties to a water melon: "green on the outside but red in the centre". One of the early German Greens, Herbert Gruhl, author of *A Planet is Plundered*, and formerly a CDU politician in the Bundestag, created the slogan "we are neither left nor right, we are in front". Though Green politicians include a number of disaffected socialists or leftist individuals, Green parties so far have managed to attract a growing number of voters who can't be categorized in this way.

Holmes notes that "environmentalism grew out of the post-1968 disillusionment with politics in general and socialist politics in particular; it is not another form of socialist politics, but a substitute for, or escape from, politics as conventionally understood". Indeed, he has described Green politicians and many of their supporters as "socialism's lost generation". Wall, though a UK marxist Green who believes "Green politics to be inevitably left of centre", is heavily critical of dogmatic marxism, describing it as "a form of Victorian New Ageism—the workers show no more sign of spontaneous uprising than the harmonic convergences at Glastonbury and other sacred sites do of coming together to save us. Marxism has for many become a new form of mysticism, a new slice of pie in the sky to be served up tomorrow" (Wall, 1980). The rightwards movement of socialist parties to become more centralist "social democrats" has been, in part, a reflection of the loss of this support, and the need to capture voters from other political parties. As Holmes concludes, "the Green view of the world is so radically different from that of conventional political parties that it cannot be understood or usefully described in the terms usually used to define political standpoints".

Confusion over Green voters and the wider "Green movement" reflects its huge diversity. As Porritt has questioned, "whether all this teeming greenery constitutes as yet a fully paid up 'movement' is anybody's guess. Mine is that it doesn't, for the simple reason that for many of the thousands of people involved in Green activities, the separate concerns they have still matter more than the sharing of a common Green perspective" (Porritt, 1984).

The influence of Green parties on politics in general

> "You are quite right of course, but it's political suicide to say so". Denis Healey (former UK Labour Party spokesman responding to Green Party policy proposals from Sara Parkin) (Parkin, 1989).

The influence of Green politics is hard to measure accurately. One would need to screen out a range of additional factors first. For example, in some countries, the role of environmental pressure groups has arguably been much more important in increasing public awareness and hence changing the policies of political parties, than the presence of Green Parties. Also, throughout the past 15 years, clear signs of environmental degradation and a series of disasters have been occurring, thus providing a backdrop of anxiety and disorder.

It is clearly impossible to separate out fully these factors and quantify the Greens political influence with any accuracy. However, their influence can best be seen by a) the growing plagiarism of Green Party policies by others; b) the extent to which the other political parties view the Greens as a threat and specifically criticize them (always a clear sign that an opponent has been taken seriously); and c) the stance taken by individual, regional and national governments where Green politicians hold the balance of power or are a sufficiently important minority party to have influenced the political debate.

In countries such as the UK, the USA, the Netherlands and Denmark, it is arguable that environmental groups in general have been much more important in raising public concern than Green politics as such. In the UK for example, there is very little formal contact between pressure groups and the Green Party, and until recently, voting levels were so low as to make little impact on the national political scene. However, and to counter-balance this view, the near 15% of the vote obtained by the UK Green Party in the 1989 European parliamentary election, has encouraged a wave of responses from the other political parties. This has included political speeches critical of the Green Party, internal briefings, as well as a major increase in the profile given to Green issues by these political parties and their leaders.

The manifestos and policy statements of the conventional parties are now littered with terms, (and at least some of the policies), which were the sole preserve of Green Party manifestos until several years ago. So much so that, in 1986 the UK Green Party co-chair claimed in a press release that the Labour Party has plagiarized her own Party's manifesto by subsuming virtually everything as part of their policy statement.

In line with growing concerns over the impact of environmental issues on business, UBS Phillips and Drew, a major international investment house, refer frequently to the influence of Green politics in their report "Investing in a Green Europe" (UBS Phillips and Drew, 1989). They suggest that the good showing of the Green parties in the European elections is based on "the upsurge in support for environmentally sensitive policies". This in turn, is based on a greater awareness of part of the public on some of the problems of unfettered economic expansion, and the sustained economic growth for recent years which "tends to make both public and government behave more openly to ideas which include the quality of life generally". They further add that: "a cynic may feel that many governments are only now responding because they wish to steal the clothes of 'fringe' parties before further embarrassment at national elections".

Some of the criticisms from the mainstream political parties have been quite vitriolic. They range from the sarcastic, such as German SPD defence spokesman Egon Bahr who argues that: "the Greens ask interesting questions—but they do not give interesting answers", to the out-and-out hostile, such as that by the UK Prime Minister Margaret Thatcher, in describing them as "airy fairy environmentalists" (Thatcher, 1990).

In parliaments where Greens have representation, they tend to be very active. Though always a very small group, they ask many questions, court publicity in the media, and often propose a disproportionate amount of the legislation in parliamentary sessions. In some cities, the German Greens hold public hearings on the budget to which they invite numerous citizens groups and the press. In some Länder such as Baden-Wurttemberg, the Greens have been successful in getting a certain amount of legislation passed. Although at first ignored, or even derided, by the other West German politicians in their first few years in Parliament, increased support for Die Grünen has led to them being taken very seriously indeed. Many of the socialist parties have taken on a number of their policies, and are actively courting the Green vote. As Porritt has suggested "the left would like nothing more than to co-opt the growing support for the Green Party as a way of winning back much of its lost votes".

Country by country assessment of Green political parties[3]

Federal Republic of Germany

Viewed from the outside, the German Green Party has seemed almost continuously riven by feuds. Splits between the left and the right, and the "fundis" and the "realos", much of this conducted in a full glare of publicity, have occurred. Add to this the major public

---

[3]I am heavily indebted to Sara Parkin for the writing of this section. Her book *Green Parties: An International Guide* is an excellent source.

criticisms of well-known personalities (such as Petra Kelly and Rudolf Bahro) by their own party members, and it would appear that the public has supported the Greens almost despite their public antics. Had much of this taken place within any of the conventional political parties, it would undoubtedly have destroyed them. Though disputes within socialist parties are common, much takes place within closed doors. Die Grünen had 44 seats in the German *Bundestag* from a total of 519 after the January 1987 federal elections, eight in the European Parliament, as well as representation in all but one of the 11 regional Länder.

There have been a number of conditions that led to the success of the German Green Party. Since the late 1960s, and in response to very high levels of pollution in the country, a large number of Burgerinitiatiren (Citizens Initiatives) were set up around the country. Campaigns on local pollution issues, such as water pollution, acid rain and dying forests, toxic waste and the siting of nuclear power stations, gradually moved to issues of broader and more national concern. From this well organized support, grew the various strands of the formation of the Green Party. From 1977 onwards, Green candidates began to stand in local elections in order to back up the extra-parliamentary efforts of the citizens' campaigns.

The Green Party was certainly helped in its early stages by the high quality of some of its individual leaders. These included Petra Kelly, a peace activist and inspiring speaker, Rudolf Bahro, an economist and exiled dissident from East Germany, Gert Bastian, a retired NATO general, Herbert Gruhl, a former CDU politician, and Rudi Dutschke, a brilliant organizer in the 1968 student disturbances in France. Another factor leading to the rapid take-off of the Green Party, was the major focus after 1979 provided by the decision of the Social Democratic Party (SPD) government to allow the siting of Cruise and Polaris missiles in the country. A series of massive demonstrations and acts of civil disobedience helped to focus public attention on some of the main concerns of the emerging political party.

It is clear that a crucial element in the success of the Greens has been the distinctive West German electoral system. In particular, its heavy emphasis on the decentralized Länder, the proportional voting system which allows representation once 5% of the votes have been taken, and most of all, the giving of funds for every vote gained, have helped the growth of the Party enormously. It is the last reason that allowed the economically run campaign of the Greens to make a major profit (US$1,600,000 in 1979), which in turn allowed the funding of a national and local Green Party organization. A final ingredient in the Green Party success was the failure of the SPD to respond to voters' concern over nuclear weapons and environmental issues. There was hence a sizeable floating vote dissatisfied with what the current political parties had on offer.

The Green Party used a number of innovative tactics and strategies during its election campaigns. In 1983, for example, as well as some striking TV spots and colourful posters, their most popular initiative was the "Green Caterpillar". Based on well-known rock and new-wave musicians, this was a rather anarchic, but fun, roadshow which allowed short speeches from Green politicians, poked fun at the other political parties, and engaged many young people in politics who had never been involved before.

Some of the Green Party posters were also striking. In Hesse for example, the lion which is the state symbol, was shown having stepped down from its ferocious, medieval pose to become a smiling cat, lounging contently on the grass before the green hills. The slogan underneath was: "Let Hesse Become Green". The famous Green Party sunflower which has been used by many other Green parties around the world, originated in West Germany.

The Party has also used a number of well-known scientists in their political broadcasts. These included Professor Hoimar von Ditfurth, a widely respected ecologist who hosted a national TV broadcast programme about science. The majority of their political campaigns were run at a fraction of the cost of those from the mainstream political parties, leading to large profits on each occasion.

After the first regional success in the Bremen Länder in 1979, seats were picked up in virtually all of the remaining *Länder* over the following six years. At a national level, six years of steady improvement, amidst fighting between different factions of the party, led to the breakthrough into the national parliament in 1983. The Green Party, currently has seats in 10 of the 11 *Länder*, with votes ranging between 5.9% and 10.2%, and had 44 delegates out of a total of 519 elected to the *Bunderstag* after the federal elections of Jan. 25, 1987.

The Greens have gradually moved from being a vociferous but minority Party to one occupying the balance of power. On a number of occasions, particularly in Hesse, Hamburg and Berlin, Greens have entered into either power-sharing with, or tolerance of, an SPD government. This has not been easy for the Party, particularly when one of them, Joschka Fisher was Minister for energy and environment in Hesse from 1985–87. Although this has required compromises from the SPD, it has also required some major compromises from a hard line Green Party position. In Berlin, where there are few "fundis" in the Party, 12% of the vote was obtained, reaching up to 25% in certain parts of the city. The Party's prolonged opposition to development plans, which envisaged pulling down many older apartments and putting up high-rise dwellings, has been successful, and all of the other parties now support this position. They now work co-operatively with the SPD on an issue-by-issue basis.

One critic of the Greens has stated that: "two Greens, two opinions". This reflects the continuing conflicts and resulting pressures between the left and right orientated factions of the Party, as well as the "realos" and the "fundis". In addition, due to the obsession of avoiding central hierarchies and abhorrence of "the cult of personality", there have been disagreements over the rule requiring successful candidates to stand down for substitutes only half way through their parliamentary term. Add to this the fact that Green politicians have been under intense pressure because of their very success, and it is small wonder that major disagreements have occurred.

"Fundis" are particularly noticeable on the state and national committees and elected bodies. Although present in the parliamentary groups, they are in a minority. Their basic philosophy is that the Party must continue to criticize industrial society heavily, avoid any compromises whatsoever, and refuse coalitions unless these are on its own terms. Rudolf Bahro and Petra Kelly are among the better-known fundamentalists. Kelly has recently stated: "there is more and more a move towards joining established power at the top instead of transforming that established power we once rejected so clearly . . . this development toward becoming a so-called Green, middle-of-the-road party (pro-European Community, pro-NATO) has made me very sad" (Kelly, 1990).

"Realos" argue that the rapid disintegration of ecological systems, and the developing global crisis, requires action even within the existing power structures. They think that to maintain rigid attitudes towards politics would condemn the party to be always on the sidelines, while powerful and vested interests continue to destroy the environment. "Realos" would accept the responsibility in setting out to clean up polluted areas, and acknowledge that the time has come to start providing some answers. The "realos" best known speakers in the late 1980s were Joschka Fisher and Otto Schily, a lawyer famous for supporting civil liberties in the 1970s. Schily formally joined the SPD in 1989. These "realos" have been recently questioning the Green Party's commitments to take West Germany out of NATO, and want the Green Party to seek coalitions with the SPD in order to keep them moving leftwards rather than seeking coalitions with the right of centre liberals (MPP). They are likely to gain the upper hand if Hesse SPD need the Greens to form a working majority in 1990.

Green Party spokesman Jorgen Meyer feels that the "realo–fundi" debate has run its course. There is now a much greater acceptance of coalition politics, he argues, particularly as a means of responding to the rise of extreme right-wing parties. Wall agrees, and notes that "despite some bitter battles, the Party has its motto: "Einheit in der Vielfalt" or unity in diversity" (Wall, 1980). Jan Bonkaerts, an environmental scientist from Berlin disagrees. He feels that a more likely scenario is for the "fundis" to split and join with the East German radical Greens.

A number of people with a long background in left-wing politics were absorbed into Die Grünen during the 1970s. They brought valuable political experience to the Party. As one Green MP has stated: "from a practical point of view, the chief lesson for the ecologists was organizing—how to organize a conference, a demonstration, or a boycott. A great deal was learned in this area, they (the left) also emphasized the role of capital in environmental destruction" (Kelly, 1990). However, the presence of marxists who had split from the Communist League has led to the development of factionalism within the Party and intense arguments. Petra Kelly and others have criticized the left. She has stated that: "The former communists became critical of Marx, left their tradition and came to us—but never really left behind their loyalty to that group. In times of crisis it is stronger than their loyalty to the Greens, and it is sometimes brutal". Thomas Ebermann and Raiener Trampert, who are both from Hamburg and former Communist League members, are two of the main spokespeople of the left.

The future for Die Grünen looks quite bright, particularly as their roots in local communities are quite deep, but moving beyond the 10–15% vote will be very difficult. They will also need to attract voters in their 20s in order to sustain their current group of activists. Internal conflicts still simmer. Petra Kelly remains an MP, but was forced out as a spokesperson and spends most of her time on international work. A 10th anniversary celebration for the Party had gone well until a furious row erupted at the final press conference. The political gaffs are becoming less frequent, though Juter Ditmass's apparent condoning of terrorism as a response to "state terrorism" in late 1989, suggested that the party's propensity for self-destruction in full public view remains. Kelly has concluded that: "our Party has not yet solved the problem of how to deal with committed, energetic and credible personalities: each time an individual stands out as committed, working very hard for the party and receiving much support, there is envy, jealousy and constant attacks for the work one does" (Kelly, 1990).

Austria

Energy issues have been the prime triggers of Green politics. In particular—the nuclear reactor at Zwentendorf, which was cancelled three months before the accident at Three Mile Island, USA, in March 1979, and the building of a huge hydroelectric dam across the Danube at Hainburg, have generated support for Greens. The United Greens of Austria was founded on Dec. 2, 1982, mainly from groups who had taken part in campaigning against nuclear power. An additional alternative list was earlier founded by a range of ecological, feminist, peace and Third World activists. Neither party won any seats, but their votes did contribute to the ruling Socialist Party losing its overall majority.

The Greens won their first success in a provincial election in October 1984, when a "Green List" in Vorarlberg polled 14% and won four seats on the 36 seat council. In May 1986, Freda Meissner-Blau polled 5.5% in the first round of the presidential elections against Kurt Waldheim. This success led to the two Green lists and others coming together as the Green Alternative in September 1986. The radioactive fallout from Chernobyl had a major political impact in Austria (and in other countries such as Italy, Sweden and Poland), and support grew. The Greens won 4.8% of the vote and eight seats in the November 1986 national elections.

A number of splits in the Party have occurred since then, with negative effects on the overall vote. The "Green Alternative" is, according to the Party itself, a coalition of "moderate ecologists, former leftist Socialist Party members, peace activists, eurocommunists and other formal radical leftists as well as anti-nuclear activists and critical Christians". Parkin has suggested that the "strains of so many people with different interests and objectives even trying to work as one, are beginning to show".

Belgium

Due to the linguistic divide in Belgium, there are two Green parties—Agalev in Flanders, and Ecolo in Wallonia. They are the only political grouping to span the divide in Belgium and Agalev started from a catholic-inspired lifestyle movement, and Ecolo from a group within one of the Wallonian parties that was concerned with democratic structures. Both groups work closely together. In 1981, the first Green politicians were elected to the national parliament after obtaining a vote of 3.9%. Support has grown steadily since then, with particularly strong support in Antwerp, Brabant, and Flanders. In June 1984, Paul Staes, an environmental journalist, was elected to the European parliament with a vote of 7.08%. In the December 1987 national elections, Agalev obtained six seats and 4.5% of the vote in the lower house and five seats in the Senate. Meanwhile in Wallonia, Ecolo obtained a seat in the European parliament in 1984 with 9.9% of the vote. On a vote of 6.5% for the national parliament, it obtained five seats in the lower chamber and three seats in the Senate.

Internal problems have dogged the party since this time, particularly over the question of "professionalizing" the party's executive. Several of their leading members have resigned as a result of the party's failure to move in this direction. Worse was to follow, as the Party agreed to work with the Liberals in the Wallonia regional assembly. A large number of Green MPs and other major supporters resigned in response, with a consequent major haemorrhage in the finances of the party. The vote of Ecolo has held up remarkably well despite all these troubles, and both they and Agalev expect an expansion of support of 10–12% in future elections. In the 1989 European elections they polled 13.9% to win three seats.

Denmark

Denmark has no civil nuclear power, as a result of a concerted eight-year campaign by the OOA anti-nuclear organization—originators of the "Nuclear Power? No thanks!" slogan and a smiling sun logo. In addition, although Denmark is a member of NATO and committed to providing "facilities" in the event of hostilities, no nuclear weapons or foreign bases are officially sited in Denmark. The relatively minor impact of the formal Green Party in Denmark is in part a reflection of the high prominence given to environmental issues by most of the other political parties. The Green Party entered into coalition with a number of anti-European Community parties for the 1989 European and 1990 national elections, but failed to get any of their nominations elected. Though these other parties have an environmental emphasis, they are not accepted as Green by other European Greens.

The Greens were officially founded on Oct. 16, 1983, but so far have failed to elect politicians to either national or European parliaments. Most Greens lay the blame for the lack of any significant impact so far on the "Revolt From The Centre" movement. This grew out of the publication of a book of the same title by physicist Niels I. Meyer, K Helveg Petersen, a liberal government minister between 1967–70, and Villy Sorensen, a philosopher.

Published in 1978, *Revolt from the Centre* caused a long and heated debate in Denmark, and described the authors' vision of a "human ecological sustainable society". Unfortunately, the promise and excitement generated by the book and subsequent debate has not been translated into political activity. Of the authors, Petersen and Sorensen withdrew due to ill health and age, and Meyer, a well-known figure in Denmark argued against the development of a Green Party. Many Greens feel that he has staked out the intellectual ground for Green ideas but regret that he failed to follow through due to jealousy in guarding these ideas for himself. The Danish Greens have also suffered from poor organization and general confusion over their objectives.

Notwithstanding the lack of an obvious political niche, it is likely that Green politicians will enter national politics during the next five to six years, keeping Denmark in the vanguard of environmental protection in Europe.

France

French Greens have had a troubled history. This has included major splits in their grouping, and the eventual election of a former Green as a socialist environment minister in 1988. The Greens have had a long history, and first tested the electoral waters in the French general elections of March 1973. The group, Ecologie et Survie, ran on the theme of "halte à l'expansion" and the candidate, Henri Jenn, obtained 3.7% of the votes. In April 1974, René Dumont, an internationally known agronomist, was supported by a number of environmental groups during the snap presidential election. He drew 1.3% of the votes. In 1976, a local by-election in Paris was fought by Brice Lalonde, president of the French Friends of the Earth. He achieved 6.5% of the vote on the first ballot. Encouraged by this result, a coalition of groups was formed to support candidates in all of the districts of Paris and many other areas. The diverse range of personalities and strategies launched by different groups were to be problematical, and was to dominate the movement in France for the next decade.

The 1977 elections saw the Greens obtain an average of 10.13% of the vote in Paris and a vote of 13.8% in one district. Following these results, the coalition of groups broke up, arguments broke out between the provincial and the Paris groups, especially over the rather overt personal ambitions of Lalonde.

Despite these arguments, Lalonde was selected as presidential candidate in 1981 and scored 3.9%, with more than one million votes. For the first time the Greens held the balance of votes between the blocks of right- and left-wing parties, and were courted by both sides before the next round. Various promises were made by Socialist leader Francois Mitterrand, including his intention to have a moratorium on the nuclear power programme. In the event, few of these promises were kept. Things rapidly fell apart for the Greens afterwards with a series of new groupings forming and dissolving almost at random.

Bad results followed in the 1984 European and March 1986 national elections. Though the Greens managed to improve their organizational ability to poll 3.8% of the presidential election votes in 1988 for Antoine Waechter, President Mitterrand's decision to immediately dissolve parliament and call new elections proved a disaster for them. Brice Lalonde was suddenly announced as the Secretary of State for the Environment by Prime Minister Michel Rocard. Reactions amongst the Greens, in seeing a man still popularly perceived as "monsieur ecology", holding a junior post in a pro-nuclear, highly technocratic and very unecological government, were mostly of dismay and depression. Despite all this, growing concern by the French electorate over the environment led to Green politicians entering the European parliament for the first time in 1989 with 11% of the national vote. In 1989, the Greens also doubled their tally of municipal councillors to 1,369, and achieved votes higher than 20% in some cities, particularly in the Alsace region.

The profile of environmental issues in France has been heightened by President Mitterrand government's decision to pick up the Green banner. The G-7 meeting in Paris in July 1989 included a major environmental statement heavily influenced by the French. At the same time, a major budget increase for the tiny Environment Ministry was announced.

Though the socialist-led government is clearly attempting to drape the Green mantle around itself, the French business response has somewhat undermined this. A number of senior industrialists have been openly dismissive of the Green lobby, including the chemicals company Rhone-Poulenc, Europe's second largest producer of phosphates, and Peugeot. Jacques Calvet, president of Peugeot, has responded to concerns over acid rain from car emissions by stating: "why are trees growing healthily along motorways, when they are suffering at the top of mountains?".

Antoine Waechter, though a rather conservative and uncharismatic politician, has brought an important "air of respectability and stability to the Party after the divisive ambitions of Lalonde", according to one French Green who requested anonymity. Good organization and the building up of Party lists with well-known individuals from minority groups, as well as ecologists, lay behind their European success.

The future progress of the French Greens will be heavily dependent on the extent to which the government responds to and acts on growing environmental concerns, and whether they themselves can avoid damaging splits and arguments in future. The simple majority voting system in national elections will be a major impediment. In contrast to virtually all other Green parties in Europe, the French groups have not focussed on nuclear power as an issue.

Italy

Green politics in Italy emerged mainly from opposition to nuclear power. A key starting date was 1975, when the government published a national energy plan proposing a programme of 20 nuclear reactors by 1985 and a further 22–42 reactors by 1990. A campaign co-ordinated by the Radical Party led to the formation of Friends of the Earth and several other groups. Money from elections was pumped into the anti-nuclear campaign. Rosa Phillipina, a former member of the Radical Party, has been involved in Friends of the Earth since the beginning, and became a Green member of the European Parliament in 1984. Other members of the Greens included disenchanted communists and socialists. Green local politicians were formally elected for the first time in northern Italy in 1978. As the number of local election successes grew, a co-ordinated set of "Liste Verdi" was gradually developed in the run up to national elections in 1987. With 2.5% of the vote, 13 Green politicians were elected.

There is no official Green Party as such in Italy, simply a federation of lists put together for electoral purposes. Indeed, the national organization exists simply for administrative purposes, such as handling the monies due to parties contesting elections and, since 1987, for co-ordinating the activities of local lists. "Liste Verdi" have stimulated other political parties to bring in a large number of environmentalists to their own lists.

On entering parliament, the Radical Party and other Greens including the "Rainbow Greens", ploughed about 40% of the reimbursement they received from the near 1,000,000 votes to campaign for a referendum on nuclear power. The result in 1988 was a clear "no" to nuclear power, and the cancellation of the government's large nuclear programme. This result has had a major impact in the rest of Europe and has moved the European Community's 12 members to be in almost equal balance between nuclear and non-nuclear countries.

The low entry point for small parties and the funding available, are two characteristics of the Italian political system which have allowed the Green lists to achieve such rapid success. Of the 13 Radical party MPs, four have now linked with another four left-wing MPs to join the "Rainbow Greens".

The Netherlands

In common with Denmark, a strong Green Party has been slow in developing. Due to the long tradition of environmental and anti-nuclear activism, many of the other political parties have absorbed certain environmental issues into their programmes. Die Groenen was officially formed in December 1983, and contested the 1984 European elections. A combination of in-fighting and a lack of substance in their election manifesto drew a mere 1.3% of the votes cast. However, the Green Progressive Accord, a grouping of four small leftist parties with a green tinge, which also fought the elections, managed to obtain 5.6% of the vote and two seats in the European parliament. They were not initially accepted however by the other Green parties. In 1989, the Green Platform, or Rainbow Coalition, (as the Accord had now become), increased its vote to 7% in the European elections.

The official Green Party is now working more closely with the Platform, who were recently accepted into the European co-ordination group for Green parties. In the 1989 national elections, six MPs were elected.

Sweden

Though formed in September 1981, Miljopartiet de Grona, failed to make an electoral impact until the September 1988 national elections. Initially stimulated by the strong anti-nuclear movement in Sweden, the Party ended up being squeezed by the two principal political blocks, the Social Democrats and the Liberals, in a succession of closely fought elections. In addition, the Swedish electorate has a high level of knowledge and understanding of environmental issues, and the Party has struggled to achieve strong media interest.

In 1987 however, two events helped to change this. Firstly, the body in charge of assuring the political impartiality of radic and television ruled that the Party had been discriminated against during the 1985 election campaign. Even more important, the main Swedish polling agency started to list the Party as a separate choice on polling question forms. In 1988, as a result of higher media profile and heightening public concern about the environment, the Party polled 5.6% of the vote in the national election. This gave them 20 seats, to become the first new party to enter the Swedish parliament for 70 years. They also did well in the simultaneously held local elections, being represented in all of the local councils and holding the balance of power on seven of them. Though not holding the balance of power in the national parliament, their presence will undoubtedly move Sweden further along an environmental path, and their future prospects look quite bright.

Switzerland

The Swiss electoral system, which is heavily based on the autonomy of "cantons" and "communes" (regions and districts), allows relatively easy access for new parties such as the Greens. At a local level in 1971–72, a coalition grew up around opposition to the motorway being built along the shores of Lake Neuchatel. In 1972, the coalition won 18% of the vote and eight seats. As a result, much of the road was re-routed underground. This "Mouvement Populaire pour l'Environnement" (MPE), has subsequently seen several splits and re-fusions and has lost some of the seats. In the area of Baud, Greens won 5.6% of the vote in 1973, increasing this to 8.2% in 1977.

In 1979, Daniel Brelaz became the first Green in the world to be elected to a national parliament, with 6.5% of the vote. Following this, there was a gradual increase in seats won at local level, but the coming together of the various Green factions of the national Party was not easy. A series of painful negotiations and meetings in 1983 led to the Greens going it alone from the Demokratische Alternative-Bern (DA-Bern). The five criteria adopted at the meeting in Geneva to guide their platform were "long-term", "quality", "humanism", "anti-technocracy", "decentralization".

Five separate groupings came together at this time, to be joined in turn by a further eight. The grouping changed its name to Grune Partei der Schweiz/le Partei Ecologiste Suisse (GPS/PES) in May 1986. In the 1983 national elections the grouping won three seats, to be increased to nine seats by the 1987 elections. At a local level, more than 15% of councillors are Greens in Swiss cities such as Geneva.

The future looks quite bright for the Swiss Greens. A key question for them will be whether the greater than 50% of potential voters who don't vote at all in elections, can be mobilized around Green ideas and issues.

United Kingdom

The UK Green Party was set up originally as the People Party in 1973. It changed its name in 1975 to the Ecology Party, and its colours from coral and turquoise to green. It then became the Green Party in 1987. It has been dogged by the British electoral system since its inception. The simple majority voting system, makes it extremely difficult for new parties, particularly in national elections, to make any substantial impact.

The Party first contested national elections in 1974 when five candidates won 1.8% of the vote in their constituencies (and less than 0.05% nationally), with a high of 3.9% in one seat. In the snap general election called in October 1974 however, the four candidates won only 0.7% of the vote. This was followed in turn by a growing coolness of environmental pressure groups to the Party, and a splitting away of some of the leftist members to join the Socialist Environment and Resources Association (SERA) with a view to influencing the Labour Party.

During the late 1970s, environmental concerns in the United Kingdom grew, particularly around issues such as nuclear power and wildlife protection. Friends of the Earth and SCRAM (the Scottish Campaign to Resist the Atomic Menace) held demonstrations, attended a number of public inquiries, and gained growing influence and members, if not immediate success.

In 1979, 53 Green candidates were fielded in the national elections, winning 1.5% of the vote in these seats (less than 0.1% nationally), and greater than 2% in some places. The real breakthrough for this election was the Party's appearance on TV and radio party political broadcasts, and the subsequent increase in public exposure. Membership shot up to 5,000 in the months following the election, and the Party gained some grim satisfaction at least from the Liberal Party's unabashed adoption of their own slogan—"the real alternative". A central office was established in London in 1980.

Voting results in local and national elections over the next seven years were patchy. At the 1983 general elections, the Green Party vote was squeezed to 1% in the constituencies they fought, with only four candidates gaining more than 2%. At a local level, several seats were won on town Parish councils. In the 1985 county council elections, 248 candidates obtained 4.4% of the votes where they stood, and a number of councillors were elected in the West Country, bringing the total on local and parish councils and affiliates up to 55.

Though continuing to generate new organizations, such as The Other Economic Summit (TOES), who have helped to develop a stronger economic basis for Green policies, the departure of one of their co-chairs, Jonathon Porritt, to Friends of the Earth in 1984, led to some loss of momentum over the following years. In 1987 for example, the general election vote was still only 1.4%, less than in 1979. Lack of experience in some of the senior posts in the Party has led to some splits, as some members argued for greater centralization and professionalism amongst the Party in order for them to be taken seriously.

In September 1988 however, amidst rapidly growing public concern over environmental issues, Prime Minister Margaret Thatcher made her first environmental speech to the Royal Society. In the aftermath, Green issues leapt to the top of the political agenda, fuelled by rapidly growing concerns over seal deaths in the North Sea, toxic waste dumping, water pollution, nuclear waste dumping, and global warming. In June 1989, at the European elections, where the ruling Conservatives ran a lucklustre campaign, the Green Party achieved a remarkable 14.5% of the total vote, the highest amongst Green Parties in Europe. Support ran as high as 25% in several constituencies.

Appearing as a separate choice on public opinion polls subsequent to this has lead to the maintenance of the Green Party in the public eye. In the 12 months following the European election breakthrough, the vote has settled down to between 4–6%, often greater than the Social and Liberal Democrats. A Labour Party analysis of the result indicated that 53% of 18–35 year olds would be tempted to vote for a Green Party in future.

However, a bad result in the first by-election to follow the European elections, with only 2% of the vote being won, was a painful reminder to the Party of the fickleness of the electorate, and that in the UK's electoral system, the vote of small parties can get badly squeezed. It also put pressure on leading Party organisers to select better candidates in such instances, and to present their policies with greater professionalism.

The Party's future progress will be heavily determined by any changes to the current electoral system towards proportional representation in future. The extent to which both the Labour and Conservative parties take on the Green mantle, and convince voters that their concerns can be best answered by them will also be crucial. Current party membership is over 18,000 and the Party holds the balance of power in just one city council, Stroud in Gloucestershire. The future emphasis of the Party will, according to spokesperson Jean Lambert, be on providing "practical solutions to problems, achieving greater professionalism, and pointing out the connections between local problems and wider issues".

Ireland

Though founded in 1981, it has made little impact, obtaining no higher than 2.3% of the vote in one district. The lack of real personalities within the party appears to have limited the amount of public exposure required to put the Party's wider political ideas forward.

Norway

They are not yet formally constituted, but obtained up to 8% of the vote in local elections and seem likely to gain significant support in future years.

Australia

Despite a long tradition of environmental activism, such as the land rights campaigns for Aborigines, and pioneering work with trade unions in the evolution of green bans (i.e. banning certain types of development) in the late 1970s, the Greens have not quite managed to take off in political terms. There are however a number of Green independents sitting in the Tasmanian parliament and holding the balance of power, which grew out of the eventually successful campaign to prevent the damming of the Franklin river for a controversial hydroelectric plant. At a national level, the Nuclear Disarmament Party (NDP), which was set up in 1984, has managed to gain several Senate seats and achieved 6.8% of the vote. However, in the aftermath of a Socialists Workers Party takeover in 1985, two of their main personalities, rock singer Pete Garrett and social activist Jo Valentine, walked out. Valentine currently holds a seat in Senate as an independent. The Greens are currently going through a period of introspection, and it is uncertain whether a true Green Party will emerge in future years.

USA

Although a great deal of the philosophical writing inspiring Greens worldwide has originated from American authors, the American political system is not conducive to the emergence of small new parties. Though there have been interesting initiatives by Tom Hayden's campaign for economic democracy in 1976, and the Citizens Party in 1980, Green politics has made only minimal impact in the country, at least at a national level. Recent attempts to stimulate new Green political thinking have ranged from the "Earth First!"

movement, which is involved in direct action to protect the environment, the bio-regionalist movement, which is centred on deep ecological philosophy within the biotic community, and the "Committees of Correspondence" initiated in 1984. The Committee held their first conference in July 1987 when 1,500 participants rallied to the theme of "Building a Green movement".

In contrast, membership of environmental organizations stands at more than 15 million, and many groups have become politically adept on Capitol Hill. The groups range from the mass membership Greenpeace and National Wildlife Federation, the Sierra Club, with grassroots "chapters" in most areas of the country, and the legally orientated National Resources Defense Council. They had some success in preventing the worst excesses of the Reagan Administration. Indeed, they were influential in deposing former President Reagan's first Interior Secretary of State, James Watt, who wanted to open up wilderness areas for mining. They have also been influential at a State level in pushing forward legislation on recycling, air pollution, waste incineration, nuclear power and oil exploration. Many of the groups actively support particular politicians with helpers and resources during elections, a practice rare in Europe.

The League of Conservation Voters ranks Congressmen and Senators on their environmental record, as an attempt at influencing voters. This has proved a successful tactic during elections, particularly if a local issue brings environment to the fore during a state election. Membership is burgeoning amongst environmental groups, and the 1990 "Earth Day" celebrations involved millions of Americans, though the political focus was blurred. At a national level, the groups have had much less success in convincing either of the two political parties to take up environment as a key election issue. The groups are facing an increasingly sophisticated business community, who have set up a number of "front" organizations to argue against strong regulation to protect the environment.

Japan

There are no formal Green Parties in Japan, and the political system is dominated by factions within the ruling Liberal Democratic Party. The main opposition party, the Socialists, have raised some environmental issues, and are prepared to call a halt to further nuclear expansion, but until recently have not been effective in getting their message across. Environmental pressure has been most visible and active within local groups opposing nuclear plants, airports and motorways, plus women's consumer groups, particularly those working within co-operative purchasing groups. Planning delays for new "green field" sites to build nuclear or fossil fuel stations are now extensive. At a national level, WWF, Greenpeace and Friends of the Earth have small offices, but they have not been particularly effective to date.

Assessments as to the reason why environmental activism is at such a low level in Japan, in contrast to the large level of destruction wrought both domestically and overseas by Japanese business, suggest two possible reasons. The first is the long history the Japanese people have in fighting nature in order to gain a living from the soil. A mountainous series of islands, which suffer from tornados, tidal waves, and earthquakes, has led to a people who regard nature as something to be controlled and subdued. Another suggestion is that the Japanese institutional structure within businesses and other organizations means that few people take personal responsibility for their own actions.

Whatever the reason, as the world's most successful economy which is pumping billions of yen into projects all over the world which are impacting on the environment, Japan is an important country. It may see rapid growth in environmental awareness as its population travel around the world and come increasingly under Western influences, and as pressure from the world community grows.

Eastern Europe—ecoglasnost and revolution

Over the past few years, and particularly in response to Gorbachev's "perestroika", the full extent of environmental destruction in Eastern Europe has started to be understood. A heavy emphasis upon rapid industrialization, particularly in the metal, chemicals and mining industries, with little or no controls on pollution, has left large areas of Eastern Europe scarred. Low efficiencies in energy use and production have led to the irony of high energy use, costs and excess pollution, but low comfort and service levels for the people.

In Hungary, pollution has been officially costed at $270 million per annum, which is 1.6% of GNP. This mainly covers medical bills, corrosion and acidified soils, and the true cost is likely to be higher. In the Soviet Union, the Aral Sea has lost 60% of its water, and near Rostov, excessive pesticides use has caused 50% increases in lung cancer, 30% in stomach cancer and a 55–60% rise in birth defects in the past five years alone. A local dissident was quoted as saying that "chemical warfare has been declared against us" (Perera, 1988).

In Poland, air pollution is now reaping a grim harvest, as local cancer and lung disease rates soar. Childhood leukaemia rates are now 10 times greater than those in the West; cancer rates in the whole of Poland are five times greater. In both Poland and East Germany, more than 50% of forests are exhibiting serious decline due to acid emissions from power stations and the steel industry.

Eastern European economies are now in the throes of rapid change, as they move from centrally-controlled, planned economies, to market-led economies. They currently show a number of common characteristics; being based upon heavy industry, utilizing old and very inefficient technology, with little in the way of air and water pollution controls in place. Domination by the economic and planning ministries and a narrow view of "growth" which has little regard for the environmental consequences, has led to a situation where scientists, academics and activists have increasingly found themselves "in a state of war" with their own ministries who are meant to protect them.

Environmental activism has been an important breeding ground for many of the politicians prominent in the popular movements which overturned most of the communist governments in 1989–1990. Czech President Vaclar Havel specialized in environmental issues within the dissident group Charter 77. Ecological protests were one of the few areas to be deemed non-political and generally tolerated up to certain limits in the mid- to late 1980s. The Ecoglasnost movement in Bulgaria for example, attracted large crowds—a precursor to the huge demonstrations which finally toppled the Communist Party regime. The Danube Circle attracted crowds of up to 150,000 in Budapest in 1988 to stop a huge dam across the river.

The "success" of the environmental movements can be gauged by the abandonment of many proposed developments. Since Chernobyl, eight nuclear plants have been abandoned or delayed in the Soviet Union. In a single week in early 1989, BBC monitoring of East European broadcasts revealed that work had stopped on two new nuclear power stations, and the management of an existing one was under review; one major hydroelectric project had been abandoned and another severely cut back; and there were complaints about pollution from a shale oil-fired power station in Estonia.

In Hungary, the Danube Circle, a movement of ecologists, academics and the general public, succeeded in halting a huge dam across the river Danube after a 10 year campaign. This was a remarkable victory, based initially on the efforts of one biologist, Janos Vargha, who lost his job after publishing a critique of the government's plans, and was treated as a state dissident. Once he uncovered data that showed major safety and ecological risks to Budapest, a signature campaign grew throughout the country. It culminated in 150,000 people marching to the river in 1988. Though owing large sums of money to the Austrians who funded most of the project in return for cheap electricity, the dam was cancelled in early 1990.

In Poland, a grassroots peace and ecology movement: "Freedom and Peace", successfully defeated plans for toxic and radioactive waste dumps in the north of the country.

Despite widespread popular sympathy for these environmental protests, political success in recent open elections has appeared limited. Amongst the hundreds of new MPs elected to national parliaments in free elections held in Poland, East Germany and Hungary in 1989/1990, only eight East German MPs are officially Greens. Though many of the other MPs elected have a green tinge, chaotic organization and a feeling that economic problems were paramount, led to the poor results. In fact the performance of so-called Green parties is misleading. According to Enika Bollobas, a former teacher and dissident, now the Hungarian ambassador to Washington, "the real environmental activists joined the main political parties or took up official posts in the new governments. Opportunists, who had not taken part in the struggles against the government, saw that Green was a popular colour which allowed free travel to the West. They formed or joined these new parties but the public were not fooled in the elections". She estimates that around 15–20% of Hungarian MPs are very positive on environmental issues. Many of them were formerly environmental activists.

The state of Eastern European economies has certainly loomed large in the minds of politicians and the electorate in recent times. One East German Green has suggested that the people were "too obsessed with buying goods from the West to worry about pollution". Long-time environmental activists within the plethora of new Green parties talk of infiltration by former communists. Szusa Beres, a Danube Circle activist, told the Guardian's Walter Schwarz of deep splits in the Hungarian Green Party. "We find the other side's methods and mentality unacceptable" (Perera, 1988). Poor organization was another factor. Many of the Green Parties have so far failed to communicate their message to an electorate hungry for economic change and Western materialism. Schwarz notes that "the old revolutionary eco-movements have had to dirty their hands in party politics: they have become involved with fledgling Green parties and they have not enjoyed the experience".

For some environmental activists, political change has brought a meteoric rise in fortunes. Many now find themselves running government agencies and ministries. Simona Bouzpovva, a founding member of the Czech Green Circle, now works for the Czech environment ministry. In Poland, in the pre-election "round table" talks between all political parties, the environmental groups were offered control of the Environment Ministry, though without any budget.

A major investment and technology crisis is affecting the ability of East European economies to change towards a more efficient and cleaner future. In Poland for example,

Government subsidies, particularly to the coal industry, were soaking up 16% of GDP in 1989. The extent to which environmental criteria will prevail in the huge loans being promised from a wide range of investment banks, will be crucial. The dangers of using outdated Western technology are all too evident. The European Bank for Reconstruction and Development, for example, has been specifically set up to reconstruct Eastern Europe but less than 10% of the official budget of $8.2 billion has so far been earmarked specifically for environmental projects. The Greens throughout Europe are as one in arguing for advanced technology rather than old Western technology as being essential in cleaning up the environment.

It is difficult to predict the future for Green parties in Eastern Europe. Much will depend on the apparent progress of new governments in curing economic as well as environmental ills. A rapid growth in contacts between environmental groups throughout Europe and North America is now certain however. Friends of the Earth International have affiliates from Poland, East Germany and the Soviet Union. Greenpeace International now have offices in most of the East European countries. The Natural Resources Defense Council have formal links with the USSR Academy of Sciences, as do other research and scientific groups from the USA. The UK Panos Institute opened a small Hungarian office in 1990, run by Janos Vargha, a founder member of the Danube Circle. Access to data (glasnost has so far only had limited success in releasing pollution and health data) will undoubtably fuel the growth of both environmental groups and Green parties, as the full extent of environmental degradation becomes better known.

The future of Green politics

> "An ounce of practice is worth a ton of theory", Fritz Schumacher.

> "There is enough evidence already that indicates that we can't simply go on as we are. The fact alone is reason enough to show quite clearly that the recent dramatic growth and interest in the environment is not destined to be a passing fad" (Christopher Patten, Secretary of State for the Environment, in a speech to the CBI national conference, Nov. 20, 1989).

It seems clear that the environment will continue to be a major issue within world politics. International investment house UBS Phillips and Drew identify the issues of global warming, acid rain, the ozone layer, nuclear power, water pollution, and waste treatment and disposal, as ones which loom large over the next three decades. They conclude that: "no sector of industry is left untouched by the Green issues" (UBS Phillips and Drew, 1989). Holmes agrees, and suggests that: "from the industry viewpoint, this means dispensing with the ideas that environmentalism is a) a temporary phenomenon, or b) an anti-capitalist conspiracy" (Holmes, 1987). Opinion polls throughout the European Community show a high level of awareness on a broad range of environmental issues. For example, in a 1989 opinion poll carried out for the European Community, 78% of Europeans believed that Green issues were very important, a higher figure than that for battling against unemployment, poverty, and the Third World (European Commission, 1990).

Green consumerism has also entered the supermarkets of Europe and North America, in line with revealing discussions over the quality of life. Set against the backdrop of a series of major environmental disasters over the past 10 years, membership of environmental organizations has burgeoned. Such disasters include three major nuclear accidents such as Chernobyl, the Exxon Valdez oil spill, Bhopal, algae blooms in the Adriatic and Baltic, seal deaths in the North Sea, vivid evidence of tropical forest destruction, the discovery of a major hole in the ozone layer in 1986, serious smog in many cities, and the continuing destruction of trees and other ecosystems due to acid rain. The international membership of organizations such as Greenpeace, the World Wide Fund for Nature, and Friends of the Earth has more than tripled over the past four years. Greenpeace membership now stands at more than 4,000,000, for WWF it is greater than 3,000,000 and Friends of the Earth probably in excess of 700,000. Membership of wildlife groups is certainly in excess of 30,000,000 worldwide.

In the UK, it is predicted that the combined membership of all of the so-called Green organizations will overtake membership of trade unions in early 1991. In this context, the question arises as to whether Green political parties will thrive and increase representational power, or the conventional political parties will simply take on board a number of their policies in order to convince the electorate that they are environmentally friendly. As Holmes has asked, will the electorate opt for a simple "spring cleaning of the planet" or a more radical change in society and development?

Parkin has suggested that 1989 was a "watershed" in the development of Greens in Europe. Many more people are now aware of the presence of Green Parties, and a sizeable minority are either sympathetic to or are voting for the parties at a local, regional, national and European level. Will Green parties capitalize on these trends or will it be the conventional political parties and environmental groups?

Answers to the above questions depend on the answers to a number of other questions. Firstly, do Green voters really know what they are voting for? UBS Phillips and Drew suggest: "the upsurge in support of the Greens is undeniable, but we may wonder whether many of their supporters really knew what they were voting for". And when Green voters do, will they continue to vote for them? It is clear that to some extent a vote for the Green parties has been a protest vote, without those voting knowing the details of the party manifestos.

Conservative and Social Democratic politicians have picked out what, in their view, are the more extreme aspects of Green Party policies, such as population control, legalizing cannabis or the "no-growth" economy, to suggest to the electorate that they should think again. Green parties have clearly influenced the other political parties to the extent to which their policies, or at least bits of them, have been absorbed. Previous references have been made to possible plagiarism of Green ideas and policies. There will clearly be an attempt by the mainstream parties to present themselves as the party most likely to look after the environment. With their greater resources and access to media, this may lead to voters' confusion and a possible falling away of the Green vote. In coalitions, where they have an opportunity to bring some of their policies into reality, voters may start to see them as a practical vehicle for change.

Another key question on the future of Green parties is the extent to which they can avoid the very damaging splits in their parties, and improve their organizational ability in order to be more effective. Porritt has noted that: "these very damaging internal divisions take up a great deal of their time". Parkin has always argued for the need "for Greens to come to terms with the dynamics of power and to transmit Green ideas more clearly and more widely than ever before". "Unity in Diversity" may be a convenient slogan, but the reality is often more acrimonious and counter-productive.

There is a paradox that Green Parties tend to flourish in rich economies. As one newspaper has noted: "the Green movement has flourished in rich countries, where people can afford to worry about Green matters, and have the political and economic means to express their concern. In these countries, democratic pressure has been applied for more stringent controls on pollution, and Green consumers are demanding environmentally sound products to buy. It is in poorer countries, whether in Eastern Europe or the Third World, that corners are more likely to be cut, leading to much worse pollution; or where funds are too short to remedy the situation" *The Independent*, July 7, 1989).

For the Green parties to thrive, there needs to be clear signs that governments are unable to cope adequately with the environmental problems facing the world. There will need to be a backdrop of deterioration of the environment, probably linked to signs that the economy is not flourishing. In an economy which is in decline however, voters tend not to take risks with unknown politicians and groups. They also tend to cut back on spending and activities which are not immediately related to the provision of basic needs, including membership and support of environmental and Green groups.

One commentator has suggested that "perhaps this environmental awareness and concern will continue for the next two or three years, but it could easily fade" (Wall, 1980). UBS Phillips and Drew suggests that as the implications of Green Party policies "begin to sink in, we believe that it is likely that Green support will fade". Other evidence suggest that, in West Germany at least, there is a greater than 50% probability that the Greens will become a well established party in the Bundestag (Spretnak and Capra, 1985). The same study has also suggested that although they have taken votes from left-of-centre parties in the past, the "Greens will win many votes from right wing parties in the future as the supporters' concern over local and national environmental issues grows". Greens take some of the above problems very seriously indeed, and are conscious that they can no longer rely simply on support because they are new, and in the words of the UK Green Party slogan, Green in contrast to the "grey" of current political parties.

Parkin has recently tried to analyze some of the above problems. She has stated that "the urgency of the human predicament demands a strategy more profound than an increased couple of percentage points at the polls every four or five years, and the spectre of remaining a ghetto for the 10% protest vote looms large" (Parkin, 1989). She has issued a challenge to Green parties in order for them to become "a relevant political force into the next century, never mind fulfil the objective of the Green revolution". She has suggested that Greens need to recognize where their strongest opposition lies and to confront them directly with the policies that clearly differentiate between them and the Greens. This would apply to both left-wing and right-wing political parties. She is particularly concerned over "kitsch greenery acting as camouflage" and urges Greens to go on a major political offensive against those parties and industries which are not truly environmental.

She suggests that Greens ought to play to a number of strategic strengths. These include the need to put environment at the centre of all their policies and relate issues such as the economy, unemployment, energy and transport for example to this, rather than simply making environmental comments about these issues. She suggests that Greens engage and mobilize their biggest supporters, namely women and the young.

A third strategic strength is the extent to which Green parties can shift the political debate from a left/right one, to a green/non-green one. Parkin is heavily critical of those Green parties that are squeamish about taking power. She notes: "only by becoming experts in the nature and dynamics of power can Greens hope to redistribute it in ways that do not have undesirable side-effects". She castigates some of her fellow Greens for their "naive approach to organization", although she is vague about how to improve on this, suggesting that some aspects of the systems theory would fulfil the apparently incompatible demands for strength and flexibility, power and accountability, style and efficiency. Coalition politics is clearly the basis of future development.

Wall has tried to address honestly the major problems faced by any incoming Green government. Though clearly siding with the "fundis" of the Green parties, he admits to the dilemma whereby: "either Greens stand by their principles, losing direct influence and being accused . . . of supporting Conservative politicians through default, or they enter into reformist alliances with Social Democrats eager to "gobble them up like spinach" (Wall, 1980). His solution is a rather implausible mixture of consumer pressure, "imploding capitalism", alternative investment, workers' power, changing commodity prices to help the South, and self-sufficient local economic enterprises. He also urges the use of cybernetics theory such as the tactic of pinpointing the weaknesses in systems which allow an unstoppable positive feedback which in turn rapidly changes the whole system itself.

The overriding impression gained from talking to Green Party activists and reading their histories is one of sheer surprise about the extent to which a sizeable and growing minority of the electorate have supported them, almost despite their schisms, arguments and well-documented antics. They are a genuinely unique voice in world politics, combining a mixture of protest, philosophy and pragmatism in addressing some of the major threats facing the planet. Whether Greens will sweep to political power in the next few decades is impossible to say. Some of the critical factors have been discussed above. They can certainly improve their chances through better political strategies and organization. The state of the environment itself and the extent to which the other political parties modify their policies will be paramount however. In that sense, even if Green parties fail to progress from vociferous minorities to controlling governments, they will already have had a major impact on world politics.

For bibliography, see pp. 364–365.

APPENDIX 1: GREEN PARTY CONTACTS WORLDWIDE

AUSTRALIA

Green Electoral Movement
Address: c/o Andrew Allison, 22 West Street, Torrensville 5031, South Australia

Nuclear Disarmament Party
Address: Box 414, Canberra City 2601 ACT
Tel: (61) 62 866686

Rainbow Alliance
Address: PO Box 494, South Brisbane 4101 Queensland

Vallentine Peace Group
Address: Parliament House, Canberra 2600 ACT
Tel: (61) 62 721211
Contact: Senator Jo Vallentine

Tasmanian Wilderness Society
Address: 130 Davey Street, Hobart 7000, Tasmania
Tel: (61) 2 349366

AUSTRIA

Die Grune Alternative
Address: Millergasse 440/9, 1060 Vienna
Tel: (43) 222 5979182

Parlamentsklub der Grunen
Address: Dr Karl Rennerring 3, 1017 Vienna
Tel: (43) 222 4804691

BELGIUM

Agalev
Address: Tweekerkenstr 78, 1050 Brussels
Tel: (32) 2 2306666

Agalev Parliamentary Group
Address: Palais des Nations, Rue de la Loi, 1000 Brussels
Tel: (32) 2 5199418/19 (Chamber); (32) 2 5158679 (Senate)

Ecolo
Address: 26 rue Basse Marcelle, Namur
Tel: (32) 81 227871

Ecolo Parliamentary Group
Address: Rue de la Sablonnière 9, 1000 Brussels
Tel: (32) 2 2183035

BRAZIL

Partido Verde
Address: Rua Dr Francisco Muratori, Lapa-Rio de Janeiro

CANADA

Parti Vert du Canada
Green Party of Canada
Address: c/o 831 Commercial Drive, Vancouver East, British Columbia V5L 3W6
Tel: (1) 604 2548165

Parti Vert du Quebec
Green Party of Quebec
Address: 1206 due Mont-Royal Avenue, Montreal, Quebec H2G 1Y1
Tel: (1) 514 5261700

Green Party Political Association of British Columbia
Address: c/o 831 Commercial Drive, Vancouver East, British Columbia V5L 3W6
Tel: (1) 604 2548165

The Ontario Greens
Address: PO Box 1912, Brantford, Ontario N3T 5W5
Tel: (1) 416 6988207

DENMARK

De Gronne
Address: Voonporten 14–108, 1220 Albertslund
Tel: (45) 2 642037

FINLAND

Vihrea Liitto Green Union
Address: Latinen Papinkatu 2–4, 00530 Helsinki
Tel: (358) 0 7011613

Vihrea (Green parliamentary group)
Address: Eduskunta, 00102 Helsinki 10
Tel: (358) 0 432 ext 3273/3271

FRANCE

Les Verts
Address: 90 rue Vergniaud, 75013 Paris
Tel: (33) 1 45899911

FEDERAL REPUBLIC OF GERMANY

Die Grunen
Address: Colmanstrasse 36, 5300 Bonn
Tel: (49) 228 692021/2

Die Grunen im Bundestag
Address: Bundeshaus, 5300 Bonn 1
Tel: (49) 228 16 7213 (press office)

GREECE

Ecological Club and FOW Greece
Address: 7 Anapafseos Street, 11636 Athens

Panhellenic Centre for Environmental Studies (PAKOE) (independent research)
Address: 7 Soufliuo Street, Ampelokipi, 11527 Athens
Tel: (30) 1 7770198/7752050

HUNGARY

Duna Kor
Danube Circle
Address: Bosckai út 31, 1113 Budapest
Tel: (36) 1 661583

Panos Institute
Address: Frankel Leó út 102–104.IV.40, 1023 Budapest

ICELAND

Kvennalissstinn (Women's Alliance)
Address: Hotel Vik, Vallarstraeti 4, Reykjavik
Tel: (354) 1 651250

Men's Green Party
Address: Skolavoroustigur 42, Reykjavik 101

INDIA

Chipko Information Centre
Address: P.O. Silyara via Ghansali, Tehri-Garhwal, U.P. 249155

IRELAND

Comhaontas Glas
Address: 5a Upper Fownes Street, Dublin 2
Tel: (353) 1 771436

ITALY

Federazione delle Liste Verdi
Address: via Panisperna 237, 00184 Rome
Tel: (39) 6 4820852/3/4

Gruppo Parlamentare Verde
Address: via Uffici del Vicario 21, 00186 Rome
Tel: (39) 6 67179837/6717507

JAPAN

Midori Green Party
Address: 6–42–12 Asakusa, Daito-Ku, Tokyo

Seikatsu Club
Address: 2–26–17 Miyasaka, Setagaya-ku, Tokyo 112
Tel: (81) 3 7060031

KENYA

The Green Belt Movement
Address: c/o National Council of Women of Kenya, Moi Avenue, PO Box 67545, Nairobi

LUXEMBOURG

Dei Greng Alternativ
Address: Boîte Postale 2711, 1027 Luxembourg
Tel: (352) 490049

NETHERLANDS

De Groenen
Address: Postbus 3244, 1001 AA Amsterdam
Tel: (31) 20 996418

De Groenen—Green Amsterdam
Address: Henri Dunant Straat 31, 1066 HV Amsterdam
Tel: (31) 20 179543
Contact: Aga Veltman (co-ordinating secretary)

NEW ZEALAND

Values, Green Party of Aotearoa
Address: Mekaweka Valley, Waimamaku, South Hokianga
Tel: (64) South Hokianga 529
Contact: Janine McVeagh (international secretary)

NORWAY

Alternativ Framitid
(Alternative Future Project)
Address: Hausmannsgt 27, 0182 Oslo 1

Framtiden i vare hender
(Future In Our Hands)
Address: P.O. Box 73 Ankertorget, 0133 Oslo 1
Tel: (47) 2 697650

De Gronne
(Oslo and Akershus Greens)
Address: Rosenkrantzgate 18, 0160 Oslo 1
Tel: (47) 2 425512

POLAND

Polski Klub Ekologiczny
(Polish Ecological Club)
Address: Palac "Pod Baranami", Rynek G1 27, 31010 Krakow
Tel: (48) 12 221884

Wolnosc i Pokoj
(Freedom and Peace)
Address: c/o Tomasz Wacko, ul. Gersona 7/10, Wroclaw 51–664

PORTUGAL

Movimento Democrático Portugues
Address: R. Coelho da Rocha 27, 1200 Lisbon
Tel: (351) 1 662303

Os Verdes
Address: Av. Torre de Belem 8–A, 1400 Lisbon
Tel: (351) 1 617046

Partido Popular Monárquico
Address: Largo zu Picardeiro 9, 1200 Lisbon
Tel: (351) 1 366587

SPAIN

Confederación de los Verdes
Address: c/o Los Verdes Alternativos, Apartado de Correos 52135, 28080 Madrid
Tel: (34) 1 4685147

Los Verdes
Address: c/o Pilar de Zaragoza 83, 28028 Madrid
Tel: (34) 1 2567952

SWEDEN

Miljopartiet de Grona
Address: Box 15264 (letters); Urvadersgrand 11 (visits), 104 65 Stockholm
Tel: (46) 8 4111351

SWITZERLAND

Der Grune Parteio
Parti Ecologiste Suisse
Address: Postfach 1441, 3001 Bern
Tel: (41) 31 619959

UNITED KINGDOM

The Green Party
Address: 10 Station Parade, Balham High Road, London SW12 9AZ
Tel: (44) 81 6730045/6/7

UNITED STATES OF AMERICA

Green Committees of Correspondence Clearinghouse
Address: P.O. Box 30208, Kansas City, Missouri 64112
Tel: (1) 816 9319366

Earth First!
Address: P.O. Box 30208, Kansas City, Missouri 64112
Tel: (1) 816 9319366

Institute for Social Ecology
Address: P.O. Box 384, Rochester, Vermont 05767

North American Bioregional Project
Address: HCR3 Box 3, Brixey, Missouri 65618
Tel: (1) 417 6794773

Joint declaration of the European Green parties

As the 20th century approaches its end, the Green movement is offering real hope for the future. This it does by aiming to return power to the citizen, to make it clear that a better way of life need not depend on a higher standard of living, to restore the balance between the human race and the rest of nature, radically to re-think relations between the rich and poor peoples of the world and to defend the cause of peace.

Green politics are a fact of life in more and more European countries. In order better to fulfil the aspirations of an increasing number of their citizens, the Green parties have decided to work together closely, at an international level, for the ecological aims they already pursue at the local, regional and national levels. We intend to extend this co-operation to Green movements in both Eastern Europe and other continents.

The elections to the European Parliament in June 1984 will offer an opportunity to stop those who, in pursuit of continued economic and industrial growth, are undermining the basis of life itself, either by supporting pollution and other damage, or by encouraging war. These tendencies are to be found in all traditional parties, whether they claim to be of the left, the centre or the right. The millions of citizens who already share an ecological viewpoint know that such tendencies will be removed only if there is a fundamental change of mind by everyone concerned.

We in the Green movement believe that Europe should no longer be governed, or misgoverned, by central authorities. The diversity of its cultures, of its peoples and regions is one of Europe's greatest assets, to be conserved and developed for the benefit of every European; true sovereignty can only come from a federal structure which takes that diversity into account. Such a structure, which should ultimately consist of regions rather than nation states, must also be established in a way that respects the dignity and responsibility of all citizens: political, social and economic decisions must be taken by those who have to bear the consequences of them. A truly democratic Europe will be made possible only through decentralization of institutions, constant dialogue between citizens and those making decisions at various levels, open discussion of problems, free access to all official documents and files, referenda at the will of the people, and the granting of the vote to immigrants, which is a matter of particular importance in elections to the European Parliament.

We in the Green movement do not want a Europe whose governments are heavily involved in the accumulation of weapons while every year millions of people are dying of hunger and poverty. Indeed, the terrifying gap between those who have too little and those who have more than they know to do with is one of the most likely causes of a future war, and the evening up of living standards must be a priority in the struggle for peace.

In the light of this we must radically transform and diversify our agricultural policies which are currently heavily subsidized and based on industrial methods which exploit animal and plant life, and instead promote nutritional self-sufficiency both for our own regions and for those of the Third World.

Therefore continuing research into ecological and nutritional adaptation on our planet constitutes a main aim of the Green movement's peace strategy.

In conjunction with this, the Green movement advocates civilian-based, non-violent defence, rather than the traditional concept of armed defence. We also call for a stop to the arms trade, for an independent European defence strategy and for a unilateral first step towards multilateral disarmament.

The Green movement is opposed to any growth based on soaring energy production in industrialized countries since this brings intolerable pressure to bear on the environment. Moreover, excessive consumption leads to a depletion of the energy resources of the planet at the expense of Third World countries. We oppose the use of nuclear energy, as an expensive, outdated, inhuman and extremely dangerous technology that creates environmental problems persisting for thousands of years. Instead, we wish to see an energy policy which is based on real needs, promotes energy conservation, rational use of energy and the use of locally produced renewable resources.

The Green movement rejects an economy based primarily on productivity, on the concentrated means of production, on irreversible environmental damage (partly due to uncontrolled waste disposal), on the creation of artificial needs, on the prevention of self-fulfilling activities, and on the accentuation of inequalities between continents, regions and social groups thereby leading to widespread unemployment. We wish to break totally from the liberal capitalism of the West and the state capitalism of the East, and want a third path which is compatible with an ecological society. We favour regenerating the economy from the bottom up, making it human and sustainable, creating a system of community-based self-reliance, giving priority to respect of the ecosystems. We want positive discrimination in favour of human-scale economic activity producing socially useful, lasting and environmentally compatible products which meet the real needs of society. We favour human-scale organized businesses, involving the participation of workers, consumers and those living in the immediate vicinity. We are in favour of a significant reduction in working hours, work-sharing, and a general redistribution of income and resources.

This declaration marks the creation of a European Green Co-ordination, the members of which hereby underline their commitment to co-operate closely within this framework and to pool aims and means thus creating a genuine Green international.

Jan. 23, 1984, Brussels, Belgium

APPENDIX 2: THE "PARIS DECLARATION"

Our common commitment for a new Europe, neutral and decentralized, with autonomous regions, each conserving their own cultural independence, is based on the following points:

We are opposed to the stationing of nuclear weapons in East and West Europe, we are for total disarmament and for the dissolution of the power blocs and the military blocs.

We are for environmental policies that uncompromisingly respect the ecological balance; we are against pollution of the air, water and earth, and we are against the concreting of nature and the countryside.

We are for the equality of women in all sectors of social life.

We demand measures against unemployment and the reduction of social welfare, which, whether in the interest of the workers or the consumers, must be not only at an economic level but also at a social and work level.

Policies with regards to the Third World must be based on equal relations with the people of the Third World. We are for a reorganization of economic relations between Europe and the Third World, and for a closer co-operation between solidarity movements and Third World movements in Europe.

We are for the free expression of the fundamental rights of the people, one of the conditions most important to bring us to an emancipated, ecological society.

We recommend an ecological form of agriculture and we wish to preserve jobs in the smaller and middle-sized agriculture businesses.

The Technical Alliance

The following political groups

Ecolo and Agalev (Belgium)
Die Grünen (Federal Republic of Germany)
Les Verts Europe—Ecologie (France)
Comhaontas Glas (Eire)
Dei Greng Alternative (Luxembourg)
CPN, Groene Partij Nederland, PSP, PPR (Netherlands)
De Europese Groenen (Netherlands)
Ecology Party (United Kingdom)

sign a declaration for a technical alliance for the European elections of June 1984, so conforming with the regulations of the European Parliament for the purpose of the funds destined for reimbursement of the expenses of political groups who have taken part in the European elections of 1984 as published in the Official Journal of the European Community of 29 October 1983, no. C 293/1.

April 28, 1984

III. CONVENTIONS, REPORTS, DIRECTIVES AND AGREEMENTS

C. T. SAVIN

Introduction

In the second half of the 20th century there has been an increasing awareness of interdependence on the part of Earth's inhabitants. With this has come increased consciousness of the importance of the environment in which all on this planet live, work, and have their being. At the same time, there is a developing appreciation of the harm which can be done to this environment by thoughtless or reckless activities and by the introduction of materials which are inimical to it to a greater or lesser degree.

These problems are recognized by individual states and national legislation has increasingly been used to regulate and control such activities and materials within the more developed states. This legislation has been recognized for the good that it brings to the national state and its environment. However there is a growing understanding of the adverse consequences of actions by individuals and states on their neighbours as well as on the environment at large.

It is recognized that national legislation has helped in combatting some of the worst effects of man's activities in each state. It has therefore been natural to hope that similar legal initiatives could be developed internationally. This has been expressed most publicly and concretely through the Stockholm Conference on the Human Environment of 1972. This resulted in the Stockholm Declaration on the Environment and immediately thereafter in the establishment of UNEP, the United Nations Environment Programme. Certainly there has been in recent years no lack of International and Regional Treaties, Conventions, Reports, Directives, and Agreements purporting to deal with the environment. An outline of the most important of these will be found on the following pages categorized, as far as possible, under the 13 headings of Part I of this Guide.

Before proceeding to this detail, it may be useful however to say something on the nature and effect of international instruments at large.

Any law broadly allows things to happen or places constraints on happenings. National law relates to individual citizens whether private or corporate. By contrast, international law reflects essentially relationships between sovereign states. Such law can be categorized as either private or public law.

Private international law is concerned primarily with determining the law governing transactions between individuals. Thus one could have a contract made in Paris between an Englishman and a Dutchman for a project to be carried out in Saudi Arabia. The question to be determined is: what law governs the operation of that contract?

However, the environmental arrangements considered here fall within the realm of public international law which governs relationships between states, either bilaterally, universally or on a regional basis.

National law is formulated by a law-making body. For example in the United Kingdom this is basically Parliament. Such law is applied by courts and tribunals operating under and applying these laws. Supporting these structures, are systems for enforcing these laws in the last resort.

On the other hand, international law has no corresponding law making body. Even a resolution of the General Assembly of the United Nations has merely persuasive effect: it is not legally binding. International law is supported by no system of courts. The International Court of Justice for example based at The Hague is only operative when both parties to a dispute accept its jurisdiction. It follows that there is no enforcement agency for international law.

Under national law, individuals must essentially obey the law which has been created for them. Under international law, individual states themselves create the law and then have discretion to obey it or not. Thus each formal signature on the agreement must be ratified by the national parliament of each signatory country before it can accede to the treaty in question. This process may take many years. It is usually provided that such agreements do not become operative before a minimum of ratifications has been received. Therefore it is important when considering the scope and effect of international proceedings to check which countries have made formal accession and have thus agreed to be covered by the relevant legislation and further whether sufficient accessions have been received to bring the agreement concerned into force.

In the circumstances, it is reasonable to ask why states should subscribe to international arrangements which will clearly impose often onerous obligations upon them. Frequently of course benefits will be seen. For example, powers may be given to intervene directly in maritime accidents which might result in pollution of a state's coastline. Again, a state could have a direct interest in reducing atmospheric pollution which can only be achieved by all states accepting emission discharge limits. In this context, an international agreement can establish a defined framework within which conflicts and disputes in the area in question can be resolved. If agreed by both parties, it could even be taken to the International Court of Justice. However, probably the major factor driving forward such agreements is the realization of new scientific evidence and the establishment of a widespread consensus that action is required: for example the fact of the depletion of the ozone layer and its causes.

In these initiatives, the advent and effect of a persistent vocal and informed public opinion plays a large part in modern democracies in influencing individual governments. Environmental pressure groups such as Greenpeace and Friends of the Earth also play an important part in raising public awareness of perceived environmental problems.

In the field of international law, the environment has become the third major topic of concern to emerge joining the hitherto predominant security and economic issues. Until now, the environment has also been a relatively neutral topic in which all states may contribute irrespective of their political or ideological views. This may be seen in the way that the 1975 Helsinki Accord has developed its environmental scope when recently little progress has been possible in the human rights area. In this respect, the developing environmental organizations both governmental and non-governmental have played increasing parts as UNEP, IMO, IUCN and the like demonstrate. This is counterparted regionally in groupings such as the Organization of American States and the Organization for African Unity. This regional dimension is perhaps taken to its highest extent in the case of the European Economic Community. This is in the forefront of developing systems and regulations for harmonization of the environmental practices of its member states and keeping the ability to a certain extent to see that these are carried out.

International environmental agreements might be said to have started with those between neighbouring states on shared waters: for example USA, Mexico and Canada; the Indian sub-continent; and European river conventions. These initially largely related to the equitable sharing and development of resources. After World War II environmental issues gave rise to increasing concerns, prompted initially by marine pollution problems. These latter arose out of the transport of ever larger cargoes of oil between producing and consuming states. The alleged impact of acid rain on forests and inland waters added to these concerns and culminated in the great Conference on the Environment and the ensuing Stockholm Convention in 1972. Large numbers of international and regional treaties, conventions, reports, directives and agreements are now extant. Their development is perhaps less rapid than the idealists had hoped both because of the difficulty of reaching scientific consensus on any particular issue and, arising partly out of this, the balancing of short-term costs against the long-term benefits. With few exceptions most countries are wary of spending too much too soon where the immediate benefits are difficult to demonstrate and the longer-term effects cannot be shown beyond reasonable doubt. A further problem exists with less developed countries who often lack the necessary resources, whether technical or financial, to play their full part. Frequently, they also perceive conflict between the environment and their urgent need for economic development.

As one considers in further detail some of the current agreements, it is reasonable to ask if greater priority should now be given to the more effective integration and operation of such agreements before embarking upon further legislative initiatives.

United Nations

The post-World War II framework of international relations was established by the United Nations Charter of 1945. With all its imperfections it is subscribed to by virtually all the nations of the world. At the same time it is drafted in sufficiently wide terms to accommodate a variety of environmental initiatives and a range of bodies that have a bearing on the environment e.g. UNCTAD, ECOSOC and the Regional Economic Commissions, UNDP, ICJ, FAO, UNESCO, WHO, IDA, IMO, UNIDO, IAEA and, more specifically, UNEP. *The United Nations Charter* was signed on June 26, 1945 at the end of the San Francisco Conference and entered into force on Oct. 24, 1945.

Under *Article 1*, the objectives of the United Nations are set out *inter alia* as the achievement of "international co-operation in solving international problems of an economic, social, cultural or humanitarian character, . . ." and further "to be a centre for harmonizing the actions of nations in the attainment of these common ends".

Under *Article 2*, the United Nations and its members, in pursuit of the purposes in Article 1, are enjoined to act "in accordance with the following principles:

(1) The organization is based on the principle of the sovereign equality of all its members;

(2) All members shall fulfil in good faith the obligations assumed by them in accordance with the Charter".

Following mounting concern for the environment, led particularly by the Scandinavian countries and Canada, a *Declaration on the Human Environment* was approved at the conclusion of the Stockholm Conference June 5–16, 1972.

It had been preceded by an International Biological Programme 1964–74 which itself had arisen out of the International Geophysical Year 1957–58.

This Declaration is the base document by which the importance of the natural environment was formally recognized by the nations of the world in the overall pattern of economic and social development. Out of it the United Nations Environmental Programme, UNEP, was born.

Thus the importance of preserving and improving the quality of the environment for future generations is highlighted in association with man's fundamental rights to freedom, equality, and adequate conditions of life. In this connection, the special needs and requirements of the developing countries were recognized. This was important to them as they had initially been reluctant to participate fearing that the developed nations concerns and resources could overbear these countries' own very real and pressing economic and financial needs.

The importance of the planning process in developing and safeguarding of natural resources was stressed together with the need to take into account wildlife and habitat considerations. The requirements to control the discharge into the environment of toxic and other pollutants was also recognized together with the need for combatting marine pollution. The role of national institutions in guarding environmental quality was also recognized.

The importance of science and technology in developing a better environment was accepted as was the importance of the mass media in developing informed public opinion on these topics.

On the other hand, the needs of developing countries for economic and social advancement were accepted. Care for the environment must help and not hinder this process. This is a constant theme in the environmental dialogue and certainly means support, both financial and technical, is needed from more developed countries to cater for these concerns. Differing stages of the national development must be understood and appreciated.

However in any consideration of international documents, the Declaration set out principles of most immediate concern:

"(21) States have, in accordance with the *Charter of the United Nations* and the principles of international law, the sovereign right to exploit their own resources pursuant to their own environmental policies, and the responsibility to ensure that activities within their jurisdiction or control do not cause damage to the environment of other states or of areas beyond the limits of national jurisdiction.

"(22) States shall co-operate to develop further the international law regarding liability and compensation for the victims of pollution and other environmental damage caused by activities within the jurisdiction or control of such states to areas beyond their jurisdiction.

"(23) Without prejudice to such criteria as may be agreed upon by the international community, or to the standards which will have to be determined nationally, it will be essential in all cases to consider the systems of values prevailing in each country, and the extent of the applicability of standards which are valid for the most advanced countries but which may be inappropriate and of unwarranted social cost for the developing countries.

"(24) International matters concerning the protection and improvement of the environment should be handled in a co-operative spirit by all countries, big or small, on an equal footing. Co-operation through multilateral or bilateral arrangements or other appropriate means is essential to effectively control, prevent, reduce and eliminate adverse environmental effects resulting from activities conducted in all spheres, in such a way that due account is taken of the sovereignty and interest of all states.

"(25) States shall ensure that international organisations play a co-ordinated, efficient and dynamic role for the protection and improvement of the environment."

Further to the Stockholm Declaration, the Vancouver Declaration on Human Settlements arose out of a UN Conference on Human Settlements in Vancouver (Canada)) from May 31 – June 11, 1976. Altogether not supported by many of the more developed countries for other reasons, it did affirm the importance of the protection of environmental resources "upon which life itself depends."

A UNESCO UNEP intergovernmental conference at Tbilisi in October 1977 brought forth a *Declaration of the Importance of Environmental Education* in the overall appreciation of this worldwide concern.

The studies and preparation for the Stockholm Conference together with its aftermath provided impetus for a more integrated and co-ordinated international approach to the problem of the environment. It has been gradually borne in on the electorates of the world that their quality of life both short term and in the more distant future depends on the success in preventing further environmental deterioration and in redressing the unbalanced approach of former times. Nowhere have these concerns been more publicly expressed than in North America and in Western Europe. Here the individual national programmes have been reinforced by the activities of such bodies as OECD and the UN's ECE and in the case of the European Economic Community by a succession of action programmes initiated by the Paris Declaration of 1972. The fact that the environment is common to all is perhaps most apparent in these areas and does not have to be subordinated to the pressing needs of social and economic development or even survival.

The unifying nature of international environmental concern is further emphasized by the environmental initiatives arising out of the 1975 Helsinki accord on security and co-operation in Europe. Genuine East–West progress has been made in the environmental area when progress in the human rights and other areas have proved more difficult.

The following pages attempt to list and say something of the major agreements, treaties and the like set out under the headings of Part I. As noted earlier there is no lack of such instruments. It cannot be doubted that these have helped improve the environment. To what extent this has happened because of these agreements must be a greater question of debate.

Before producing further agreements, some would argue the case for securing the performance of the present arrangements not least by subsequent ratification of the widely publicised initial signatories. Then assessing how such agreements might be implemented more fully and vigorously.

1. Acid deposition

An early recognition of the problems of atmospheric pollution was achieved by the 1941 arbitration in the Trail Smelter case. This adjudicated that fumes from a Canadian smelter were causing injury in neighbouring US territory of Washington necessitating compensation. It established that "no State has the right . . . to cause injury by fumes in or to the territory of another . . .". This was a concrete example of the old common law principle *sic utere tuo ut alienum non laedas* — 'so use your property as not to injure your neighbour's'.

The perceivable impact of acid rain on northern forests and lakes was a key factor in the launching of the Stockholm Conference in 1972. The principal components of this acidification are sulphur dioxide, derived from the sulphur content of fuels, and nitrogen oxides, an inescapable product of combustion processes. As it is easier to remove sulphur from fuels or from combustion gases than to eliminate oxides of nitrogen from combustion products, it is not surprising that the majority of legislation in this area has been devoted to the sulphur aspect — a clear example of legislative enthusiasm being matched to technological capability.

A seminal work here was a 1971 Swedish government study *Air Pollution across National Boundaries — the Impact of Sulphur in Air and Precipitation*. This was coupled with the growing realization that airspace was common to all and, for example, the problems of Western Europe and North America could not be effectively tackled in isolation by individual national initiatives.

In 1975, the EC established a reciprocal exchange of information and data from networks and individual stations measuring air pollution levels across the Community. In 1982 its scope was extended from monitoring sulphur dioxide and smoke to include also nitrogen oxides, heavy metal particles, carbon monoxide (CO) and ozone.

A major initiative, largely arising out of the Helsinki Accord of 1975, came however in 1979 when a meeting under ECE auspices in Geneva adopted a *Convention and Resolution on Long-Range Transboundary Air Pollution*.

This obliged signatory states to "develop without undue delay policies and strategies . . . as a means of combatting the discharge of air pollutants". Signatories further undertook to make full exchange of information on environmental protection technology.

Under the Convention an executive body was established to carry out a co-operative programme for monitoring and evaluating the long-range transmission of air pollutants in Europe.

In 1985, these generalities were made more specific by a protocol to the convention signed in Helsinki. Countries agreed to reduce sulphur emissions and their transboundary fluxes by at least 30% of the 1980 levels by 1993. Some countries voluntarily increased their reduction commitment to 40–65%.

On Nov. 1, 1988 a further protocol signed in Sofia agreed a reduction in nitrogen oxides emissions to 1987 levels by 1994. Twelve countries pledged a specific 30% reduction by 1998 at the latest.

These initiatives prompted a July 1985 bilateral agreement between Finland and USSR to monitor and reduce air pollution.

Similarly, on March 19, 1986 a plan was agreed between Canada and the United States whereby the US wind-borne pollution into Canada from mid-Western power plants and factories would be fought by a five year project to develop methods of reducing sulphur dioxide (SO_2) and nitrogen oxides (NO_2) emissions particularly from coal-burning plants. This pollution had long been a source of concern between the two countries.

The EC was at the forefront in adopting practical measures. Thus a 1980 Directive was agreed on air quality limit values and guide values for sulphur dioxide and suspended particles (smoke). This established mandatory air quality standards for these materials in order to protect human health and the environment.

This was counterparted in 1985 by a corresponding *Directive on Air Quality Standards for Nitrogen Dioxide*. It must be said that these standards counterparted the *US National Ambient Air Quality Standards* first issued in 1971.

A 1975 *Directive on the Sulphur Content of Gas Oil* was superseded in 1987 by an amended version which provided for a maximum sulphur content of 0.3% with a lower limit of 0.2% in specific circumstances particularly where damage to the environment or the national heritage was feared to result from the use of the higher sulphur levels.

In implementing the 1979 *Convention on Long Range Trans-Boundary Air Pollution*, the EC adopted a directive in 1988 to develop plans to reduce the level of annual emissions of sulphur dioxide and nitrogen oxides from existing large scale combustion plants e.g. power stations. It was foreseen that sulphur dioxide emissions would be cut by 50% across the Community by the year 2003. Under this directive, it was further agreed that new plants being built with a capacity in excess of 400MW would have an upper level for SO_2 emissions.

Acid deposition has been a particular problem of the heavy industrial plants in Eastern Europe. In August 1987, an *Environmental Co-operation Agreement* was signed between West Germany and Czechoslovakia. In September of that year, a similar agreement was concluded between East and West Germany, now of course one nation. In March 1988 an environmental protection protocol was signed between Czechoslovakia, East Germany and Poland.

Other agreements relating to acid deposition may be found under the headings of Deforestation and Vehicle Emissions in Part I.

Principle Agreements relating to acid depositions:

(a) EEC Decision establishing a reciprocal exchange of information and data from networks and individual stations measuring air pollution. Decision 82/459 OJL 210, 19.7.82.

The original 1975 Decision relating only to sulphur dioxide and particles was extended to include most common air pollutants by this 1982 Decision directive.

(b) EEC Directive on approximation of the laws of member states relating to the sulphur content of certain liquid fuels. Directive 87/219 OJL 91, 3.4.87.

The initial 1975 Directive regulated the sulphur content of gas oil (principally domestic heating and cooking oils and DERV). This was replaced by this 1987 Directive setting an upper sulphur limit for such oils at 0.3% reducing to 0.2% when used in particularly sensitive areas. Limits to be met by Jan. 1, 1989.

(c) *ECE Convention on Long-Range Trans-Boundary Pollution*:

(i) subscribed to by the USA, Canada and most European states in Geneva Nov. 13, 1979 and coming into force March 16, 1983;

(ii) On July 19, 1985 in Helsinki a protocol was signed on July 8, 1985 targeting a 30% reduction on 1980 sulphur emissions: and

(iii) On Nov. 1, 1988 in Sofia a further protocol was signed providing for a reduction to 1987 NO_x emission levels by 1994.

(d) (i) *EC Directive on Air Quality Limit Values and Guide Values for Sulphur Dioxide and Suspended Particulates. Directive 80/779 OJL 229, 30.8.80.*

Limit values for these products were to be met if possible by April 1, 1983 and in any event by April 1, 1993.

(ii) EC Directive on Air Quality Standards for Nitrogen Dioxide. Directive 85/203 OJL 87, 27.3.85.

(e) *Canada–US Agreement on "acid rain"* on March 19, 1986 to combat the long-term Canadian problem caused primarily by wind-borne pollution from US power plants and factories.

(f) *EC Directive on Limitation of Emissions of certain Pollutants into the air from Large Combustion Plants*. Directive 88/609 OJL 2336/1, 24.11.88.

This provides for the preparation of progressive reduction plans in respect of SO_2 and NO_x emissions. New plants to be constructed in excess of 400MW capacity have to ensure the achievement of a sulphur dioxide maximum emission limit.

2. Antarctica

From the 19th century onwards, the Developed Countries staked claims to portions of Antarctica as part of the high colonial era. As technology advanced however it began to be seen as one of the world's last remaining untouched areas and, as such, an important baseline for research into developments on this planet — particularly environmental. Coincidentally, Antarctica was also perceived to be a convenient and readily exploitable resource base.

This has resulted in a series of agreements attempting to guard against these later developments.

Arising out of a 12-country Scientific Committee for Antarctica Research, was the 1959 Antarctic Treaty which came into force in June 1961. The original signatories were Argentina, Australia, Belgium, Chile, France, Japan, New Zealand, Norway, South Africa, USSR, United Kingdom and USA. The principal provisions of the treaty were:-

(a) Antarctica would be used for peaceful purposes only;
(b) Freedom of scientific investigation would be maintained including exchange of scientific information and personnel;
(c) There would be no new claims to territorial sovereignty whilst the treaty was in force; and
(d) nuclear explosions and radioactive waste disposal were prohibited.

At a 1979 meeting of the treaty signatories, it was agreed to:-

(a) maintain voluntary restraint in exploration and exploitation of minerals (oil and gas);
(b) draft a convention for the regulation of fishing; and
(c) co-operate in telecommunications, developing tourism guidelines, and study the impact of various measures on the environment.

A 1972 agreement provided for the protection of seals in the Antarctic whilst a *Convention on the Conservation of Antarctic Living Resources*, particularly krill, was adopted in 1980. This provided for the establishment of an international commission in Hobart, Australia, to supervize the preservation of marine life, to study the food chain of Antarctic fish and bird life and to recommend measures to protect the species.

Principal Agreements relating to Antarctica

(i) *Convention on Peaceful, International, Scientific Co-operation in Antarctica*. Washington (USA). Dec. 1, 1959. In force June 23, 1961;
(ii) *Agreement on Protection of Seals in the Antarctic*, Feb. 11, 1972. In force March 11, 1978; and
(iii) *Convention on Conservation of Antarctic Marine Living Resources*. Canberra (Australia), May 20, 1980. In force April 7, 1981.

3. Deforestation

Loss of tropical forest is of particular environmental concern. Most of these forests are poor in nutrients and their clearance for agriculture is rarely successful. Erosion frequently ensues with resultant silting of water courses. Other problems are aggravated — the greenhouse effect is enhanced and further loss in biological diversity occurs.

This is one area where the conflict between the short-term benefits for the individual state contrast most starkly with the longer term consequences for that country and the world community. Developing countries therefore have been hostile to those more developed countries perceived to be interfering with the national sovereignty of the states concerned. In consequence, such international agreements as exist are primarily concerned with securing economic benefits to the host countries.

Thus the African Timber Organization was established in 1975 to help African states secure better returns on their timber. The South East Asia Lumber Producers Association, founded one year earlier, is likewise concerned with similar matters.

The International Tropical Timber Agreement of November 1983 under UNCTAD auspices was likewise concerned with securing better returns for the Developing Countries. It provided for the International Tropical Timber Organization which was formed November 1984. In addition to maximizing returns, its other main aim was to promote the expansion of international trade in tropical timber.

More hopefully as concern has grown, a Tropical Forestry Action Plan has been drawn up by the World Resources Institute (WRI) supported by the World Bank, FAO and UNDP. This seeks to achieve a balance between the harvesting and replanting of tropical rain forests by the year 2000.

In February 1986, an International Conference on the Protection of Forests (the Silva Conference) took place in Paris. It had two principal topics: the deforestation in Africa because of increasing firewood use; and the forest damage in Europe attributed to atmospheric pollution. One positive outcome was the pledging of US $8,000 million over five years by Developed Countries to help reafforestation in developing countries.

Within the EC, a 1986 regulation was promulgated to establish an inventory and monitoring network against which to measure periodical assessments of forest damage within the community on a scientific basis.

Other related agreements will be found in Part I, especially in the contributions on acid deposition, greenhouse effect and global warming, land degradation and desertification, renewable resources and vehicle emissions.

International agreement on deforestation

(a) *EC Regulation on the Protection of the Community's Forests against Atmospheric Pollution*, OJL 326 Nov. 21, 1986.

4. Greenhouse effect and global warming

The so called "greenhouse" effect is said to be brought about by gases which allow the sun's rays to penetrate the atmosphere and warm the earth whilst trapping the resultant heat radiation within that atmosphere. The principal gas involved is CO_2 with support from other gases such as nitrogen oxides, chlorofluorocarbons (CFCs) and methane. CFCs of course have an additional effect as detailed under the contribution entitled Ozone Depletion in Part I.

Whilst to date no agreements specifically relating to this overall phenomenon have been drafted, all agreements relating to the reduction of the gases in the atmosphere must have beneficial effects. Examples of these will be found under the headings of Acid Deposition, Land Degradation and Desertification, Ozone Depletion, Forest Loss, Renewable Resources and Vehicle Emissions (see Part I).

An international conference of scientists and policy makers in Toronto on June 27–30, 1988 called on the UN to prepare a "comprehensive global convention" for the protection of the atmosphere.

Subsequently in Geneva, Nov. 9–11, 1988 a meeting under UNEP/WMO (World Meteorological Organization) auspices agreed to set up three working groups, the Intergovernmental Panels on Climate Change. These were (a) to assess the scientific evidence on global warming; (b) to assess the agricultural and environmental impact of the climate changes; and (c) to formulate responses to the situation disclosed. Conclusions were to be ready by mid-1990 and have highlighted the CFC problem.

On March 11, 1989 a conference in the Hague called for a UN-based institutional authority (a) to monitor governments' performance in controlling atmospheric pollution; (b) to enforce compliance through the International Court of Justice; and (c) to compensate countries particularly affected by steps to protect the atmosphere. Would that it could happen! It would transform the approach to international legislation. Needless to say such recommendations will not be adopted.

5. Land degradation and desertification

Desertification clearly cannot be considered independently of climatic changes. To a considerable extent however, desertification is a consequence of man's activities in destroying natural habitats designed to resist the encroachment of desert or prevention of soil erosion. Land degradation is an inevitable result. Amongst these activities must be considered over-use of the area because of population pressures and agricultural systems which do not adequately reflect the complexities of the region's ecology. Other factors such as global warming, water quality, deforestation, and loss of biological diversity cannot be ignored and the whole is aggravated by the poverty of the majority of the regions where the problems are most acute. By and large, what needs to be done is known. To be effective however united efforts by all concerned are required, coupled with a massive injection of resources. To date these have been sadly lacking.

Internationally, a UN Conference on Desertification was held in Nairobi under UNEP auspices, on Aug. 29 – Sept. 9, 1977. A plan of action to halt the spread of deserts by the year 2000 was unanimously adopted.

It called for:

(a) efficient planning, development and management of water resources;
(b) improvement of degraded rangelands and the introduction of suitable systems of rangeland, livestock and wildlife management;
(c) soil conservation and the improvement, prevention or control of waterlogging, salinization or alkalinization of irrigated lands;
(d) improved irrigation systems; and
(e) improvement of social and economic conditions of people dependent on irrigation culture.

National and regional initiatives were called for as a means of achieving these aims.

Nonetheless, desertification continues to increase together with famine and deaths as well as displacement of affected persons.

In 1984, a four-year Drought and Desertification Control Programme for the Sahel was announced by the Permanent Inter-State Committee on Drought Control in the Sahel (the African countries concerned) together with UNDP and the UN Sudano–Sahelian Office.

In February 1985, a Conference on Drought and Desertification in East Africa resulted in the setting up of the Intergovernmental Authority on Drought and Development.

Later that year in Cairo, a programme for African co-operation was agreed to prevent environmental degradation; to help Africa become self-sufficient in food and energy; and to achieve a balance between resources and population.

The real concerns were again stressed at the 1989 meeting of UNEP's Governing Council in Nairobi. Prior to this gathering, however, the UN Director-General encouraged the meeting of African Environment Ministers to start implementing the 1985 Cairo Action Programme.

There have been no international agreements specifically addressing the problems of land degradation and desertification. As noted however there have been a variety of such initiatives addressing contributory factors.

6. Loss of biological diversity

Biological diversity is daily being reduced throughout the world. In part, it is due to excessive takes of endangered species. The largest contributing factors however are the pressure on habitat and related ecosystems brought about by development needs, pressing and otherwise, with the widespread population increase particularly in developing countries. Loss of biological diversity is also accelerated by other factors such as acid deposition, marine pollution, land degradation and desertification, forest loss and waste disposal.

Many agreements have been set up relating to fishing in marine environments throughout the world. These are primarily concerned with study and research of particular marine organisms — especially fish — with a view to developing strategies to maximise the ongoing sustainable takes of particular species. Thus, there are fishing commissions for most of the major areas of the world as well as for specific types such as tuna, halibut and salmon.

In 1911, a convention was signed for the preservation and protection of fur seals. Early legislation related to the usefulness of wild life to man exemplified in the 1902 *Paris Convention for the Protection of Birds Useful to Agriculture*. Essentially countries of Western Europe subscribed to it. A further *Convention for the Protection of Birds* was signed in Paris in October 1950.

North and South America gave a more general lead in October 1940 when the member states of the Pan-American Union adopted a *Convention on Nature Protection and Wild Life Preservation in the Western Hemisphere*.

One of the earliest agreements to protect animals was signed in London to protect whales. An agreement immediately after World War II provided for the establishment of the International Whaling Commission. This meets once a year and member governments have now voted for a moratorium on commercial whaling — nevertheless the temptation for certain countries still remains: for example, Japan and Norway, which is vocal in expressing environmental concerns which directly affect its social and economic well-being.

An interim convention was signed in 1957 by the countries of the North Pacific in respect of the conservation of fur seals. This, following the 1911 convention, is expressed however in terms of obtaining the maximum sustainable productivity of fur seal herds allied with programmes of research into the behaviour and lifestyle of these animals.

Polar bears were protected by convention in 1973. This broadly forbade their killing and required contracting parties to protect their ecosystems.

In 1971, an international meeting in Iran agreed a convention recognizing the importance of wetlands, particularly as wildfowl habitat. Under its aegis, protection has been extended to well over 200 sites covering in excess of 6,000,000 hectares. Under this agreement Denmark and the Netherlands further undertook to co-operate in the conservation of the Wadden Zee adjoining their coasts.

Another important international agreement was reached in 1973. In Washington in that year a convention was signed virtually eliminating legitimate commercial trade in endangered species of wild flora and fauna.

In 1976, the Council of Europe drew up an *Ecological Charter for the Mountains of Northern Europe*.

Despite the provisions of the 1950 Convention, indiscriminate slaughter of birds continued. Following widespread outcry against the hunting and killing of migrating birds — particularly in Southern Europe — the EC agreed in 1979 on a Directive on the Conservation of Wild Birds. This sought to control the hunting and killing of birds. In particular for 74 (later increased to 114) vulnerable species it required member states to provide a diversity and area of habitats in order to ensure the maintenance of these endangered populations. Despite the best efforts of legislators however, a 1990 referendum in Italy could not muster the necessary quorum to confirm a ban on the shooting of birds in that country.

Taking up this biological diversity theme on a broader basis, was a Convention on the Conservation of European Wild Life and Natural Habitats later in 1979. It provided for the protection of 119 plant species and 400 species of fauna threatened with extinction together with, to a lesser degree, protection for other species.

Also that year there was a wider convention on the conservation of migrating species of wild animals.

Although not a formal agreement, a World Conservation Strategy was launched in March 1980 under the auspices of IUCN, WWF and UNEP. One aspect was particularly concerned with species extinction.

Regionally, arising out of the *Barcelona Convention on Pollution and the Mediterranean Sea* an action plan has been agreed to harmonize activities to ensure continuous development of the ecology of the Mediterranean region. At Cannes in 1981, it was agreed to establish a regional centre in Tunis to monitor a network of specially protected reserves to help to preserve plants and animals threatened in the Mediterranean area. Specified animals included the monk seal and the marine turtle. However it was found that around 500 species of Mediterranean fish were declining rapidly due to the pollution of the grass beds providing food, shelter and habitat for these fish. In 1982, a fourth protocol envisaged the establishment of some 100 protected marine areas to conserve endangered species; halt the spread of pollution; and to enhance tourism.

The 1983 *Cartagena (Caribbean) Convention* also developed an action plan and contained projects for the protection of coral reefs, mangroves, tropical forests, and endangered species such as turtles and parrots.

Action on biological diversity was enhanced and encouraged by the *US Endangered*

Species Act of 1973 which set out to establish a recovery plan for 425 threatened species and is regarded as a model of its kind.

International agreements relating to loss of biological diversity

(a) *Convention on Nature Protection and Wildlife Preservation in the Western Hemisphere.* Pan-American Union Oct. 12, 1940. In force May 1, 1942;
(b) *Convention for the Regulation of Whaling.* Washington Dec. 2, 1946;
(c) *Interim Convention on the Conservation of the North Pacific Fur Seal.* Washington Feb. 9, 1957. In force Oct. 14, 1957;
(d) *Convention on Wetlands of International Importance Especially as Wildfowl Habitat.* Ramsar (Iran) Feb. 2, 1971. In force Dec. 21, 1975;
(e) *Convention on International Trade in Endangered Species of Wild Flora and Fauna* (CITES). Washington March 3, 1973. In force July 1, 1975;
(f) *Agreement on Conservation of Polar Bears.* Oslo Nov. 15. 1973. In force May 26, 1976;
(g) *EC Directive on Conservation of Wild Birds* 79/409 OJL 103 April 25, 1979.
(h) *Convention on the Conservation of European Wildlife and Natural Habitats*, Berne Sept. 19, 1979. In force June 1, 1982; and
(i) *Convention on the Conservation of Migratory Species of Wild Animals.* Bonn, June 23, 1979. In force Nov. 1, 1983.

7. Marine pollution

Initially, international agreements relating to the sea were largely concerned with ownership and sharing of its resources, particularly fish stocks.

After World War II however there was increasing concern at the perceived growth in oil-based pollution associated particularly with the increase in size and number of tankers. These were engaged in the transportation of crude oil and products largely between the oil producing countries and the consumer nations. Such pollution arose in a number of ways the most notable being from accidents; inadvertent oil spills, and discharges; and marine disasters such as that of the *Torrey Canyon* which ran aground off Land's End, England in March 1967 with an associated marine discharge of crude oil. The other principal factor was that of washing out oil tanks at sea together with the discharges from the bilges. These took place from tanker and non-tanker ships alike and were frequently heavily oil-contaminated.

Agreements were increasingly developed in post-war years to deal with these problems. An interesting aspect here was the part played by international organizations and by multinational corporations such as the major oil companies.

Following these oil-based agreements, there were more controversial developments in other marine pollutant discharges. The problem from land-based discharges has also been recognised increasingly: particularly relating to domestic sewage. It presents major difficulties in the light of increasing urbanization in the newly developing countries of the world.

In considering water pollution, the contribution on Water Quality should also be read. The main body concerned with marine matters is the International Maritime Organization

(IMO), formerly the International Maritime Consultative Organization (IMCO). This was established under a convention approved in Geneva on March 16, 1948 at an international maritime conference called by ECOSOC.

The convention established the IMO as a consultative and advisory body. It became a UN specialized agency in 1959. Under its aegis a number of environmental agreements have been developed and in 1973 a Maritime Environment Committee was established.

The first such agreement (OILPOL) was signed in London in 1954 — an *International Convention for the Prevention of Pollution of the Sea by Oil*. This banned the discharge of crude, fuel, diesel and lubricating oils in certain specified zones. It came into force in 1958 for tankers and in 1961 for dry cargo ships.

A pioneering agreement — *Tanker Owners' Voluntary Agreement Concerning Liability for Oil Pollution* (TOVALOP) came into operation in 1969. It was signed not by governments or international organizations but by major oil companies to make compensation for the costs of clean-up and limitation of damage in the event of oil spills. In 1971, building on the earlier agreement, a *Contract Regarding an Interim Supplement to Tanker Liability for Oil Pollution* (CRISTAL) was signed. It became a strict liability, that is undertaking compensation irrespective of fault, subject to maximum limits, and it supplemented the provisions of TOVALOP.

International governmental legislation came increasingly into play however. Prompted by the *Torrey Canyon* disaster, an international convention relating to intervention on the high seas in cases of oil pollution casualties was adopted under IMO auspices in 1969 and came into force in 1975. This recognized the right to coastal states to take measures to protect their own interests when an oil casualty occurred on the high seas which gave rise to grave and imminent threats from pollution. These provisions were extended in 1973 to non-oil pollution incidents and came into force in 1983.

At the same 1969 Brussels Conference, an *International Convention on Civil Liability for Oil Pollution* (CLC) was adopted which made tanker owners strictly liable for oil pollution damage caused by escape of oil. This came into force in 1975 and provided that all ships carrying more than 2,000 tonnes of oil in bulk should be insured against their stipulated maximum Convention liability. It also gave the plaintiff power to sue the insurer direct without the need to sue the ship owner. By a further protocol in May 1984, liability was extended to smaller vessels and the Convention's scope extended to cover the territorial waters and Exclusive Economic Zone of each contracting state.

Also in Brussels, a *Convention on the Establishment of an International Fund for Compensation for Oil Pollution Damage* was signed in 1971 and came into force in 1978. This was essentially a "top up" agreement to CLC to provide for those massive incidents where the liability under CLC would not be sufficient to meet the costs arising. The fund was organized by the payment of a levy based on the crude and fuel oil received into the territories of each contracting state. A 1976 protocol signed in Bonn extended coverage to non-oil substances. It further enabled states to take preventive action outside their territorial waters when faced with threats of massive pollution.

In November 1972, a *Convention on the Prevention of Marine Pollution by Dumping* was adopted at a London conference. The principal aim of this convention was to prevent the indiscriminate disposal at sea of waste materials and chemicals by prohibiting the dumping of certain materials and making others subject to licence. It came into force in 1975. Under it the dumping of high-level radioactive waste was prohibited and low-level activity material only allowed under certain conditions.

A further London conference in 1973 adopted a *Convention for the Prevention of Pollution from Ships* (MARPOL). This was to supersede OILPOL. When it came into operation in 1983 it formed part of the 1982 *UN Law of the Sea*. MARPOL did not deal with marine dumping — covered by the 1972 Convention — nor did it deal with the release of harmful substances arising from the development of mineral seabed resources (also dealt with under the *UN Law of the Sea*).

MARPOL aimed at preventing pollution of the sea by oil and other noxious substances which might be discharged operationally. It was also designed to minimize the quantities of oil which would be released in the case of marine collisions or strandings from ships including fixed or floating platforms. MARPOL also designated the Mediterranean, Baltic, Red, and Black Seas together with the Gulf area as special areas, in which oil discharge was virtually prohibited. These areas were particularly sensitive as they had small tidal action. This Convention also contained special provision for the control of pollution from more than 400 noxious substances as well as for sewage and garbage disposal. A 1978 protocol, also in force in 1983, laid down that a ship could only be cleared to operate after surveys and the issuing of an International Oil Pollution Prevention Certificate.

The *UN Convention on the Law of the Sea* (UNCLOS) was signed at Montego Bay in 1982. In addition to incorporating MARPOL, general rules and principles were set out for the control of marine pollution from land-based sources. Signatories were also enabled to extend territorial waters to 12 miles from shore together with a 200-mile Exclusive Economic Zone stretching to 350 miles in the case of a continental shelf. These provisions of themselves should enable the states concerned to exercise more effective pollution control over their adjoining waters.

In parallel with these global marine conventions, a series of regional seas programmes have been developed, many under UNEP auspices.

Thus in 1969, an agreement was signed in Bonn for co-operation in dealing with the pollution of the North Sea by oil. This covered all North Sea coastline states. It required member governments to request ships and aircraft to report major oil slicks and to circulate reports on the presence, extent and movements of such slicks. On request they further agreed to assist other countries in disposing of oil threatening their coasts. Zones of responsibility for each country were also agreed. In 1983, the agreed co-operation was extended to cover pollution from other harmful substances.

At Copenhagen in 1971, the Scandinavian countries subscribed to a marine co-operation agreement which replaced an earlier 1967 agreement and took into account their obligations under the Bonn agreement.

In early 1972, a *Convention for the Prevention of Marine Pollution by Dumping from Ships and Aircraft* was signed in Oslo. This anticipated the IMO Convention later that year and related only to the waters of the North East Atlantic.

In 1974, in Helsinki, all Baltic States signed a *Convention on the Protection of the Marine Environment of the Baltic Sea Area*. It came into force in 1980 and the MARPOL provisions relating to pollution from ships were followed closely. Under it the Baltic Sea had been declared a "special area" whereby oil discharges were subsequently prohibited. However, this Convention goes much further in that it was the first to deal with pollution from all sources, whether airborne, waterborne, landward or otherwise. Land-based pollution, e.g. sewage, agricultural materials and riverborne pollutants is to be controlled. Sixteen specific substance groups e.g. PCBs, DDT, were identified specifically for control and minimization.

This comprehensive agreement had been preceded by a series of bilateral/multilateral arrangements between the individual states on the Baltic Sea.

A further agreement relating to the North East Atlantic was the 1974 *Paris Convention for the Prevention of Marine Pollution from Land-based Sources*. The Convention provides for the elimination of pollution from substances in the so called "black" list e.g. mercury, cadmium, organic phosphorous compounds together with the strict limitation of pollution from substances in the "grey" list e.g. zinc, copper and lead compounds, and ammonia.

In 1976, the EC adopted a *Directive on Pollution caused by Certain Dangerous Substances discharged into the Aquatic Environment of the Community*. This attempts to co-ordinate the provisions of the Paris Convention and the inland waters, Rhine and Strasbourg (draft) Conventions. In this context, it relates not only to territorial waters and inland coastal waters but to ground and surface waters also.

In 1984 in Bremen, the environmental ministers of states bordering the North Sea agreed to develop further North Sea anti-pollution measures. This included reinforcing existing surveillance measures on ships and their discharges, reducing sewage discharge from rivers; trying to reduce the dumping of radioactive waste, and intensifying research on the impact of air pollution on the sea.

The countries adjoining the Mediterranean are at more diverse stages of development than the North Sea group. Under UNEP's auspices at Barcelona in 1975, an action plan for the protection of the Mediterranean was agreed by virtually all affected states. In 1976 this resulted in the Barcelona Convention with protocols thereto which came into force in 1983. The Convention provided that signatories would take all measures to prevent sea pollution by dumping from ships and aircraft, by exploitation of the continental shelf and sea bed or by land-based sources. The first protocol banned the dumping of toxic substances at sea from ships and aircraft (reference MARPOL) and contained a "black" list of prohibited substances with a list of restricted substances for which a special permit was required. The second protocol provided for co-ordinated action in the event of oil spills and for the establishment of a regional headquarters in Malta to direct such operations. An earlier 1974 agreement had been for the protection of the Adriatic Sea between Italy and Yugoslavia.

As a result of UNEP initiative, a *Kuwait Regional Convention* in respect of the Gulf area was agreed in 1978 and entered into force in 1979. Under this, the states of the area undertook to fight against pollution caused by discharge from ships or the dumping of waste and other matter from ships and aircraft as well as from land-based discharges. A protocol signed at the same time also called upon the states to co-operate in protecting the coastline from oil and other materials arising from marine emergencies. The Action Plan, amongst other things, resulted in the establishment of the Marine Emergency Mutual Aid Centre in co-operation with the Regional Seas Activity Programme of UNEP.

In 1982 another UNEP-inspired conference resulted in the *Jeddah Convention for the Conservation of the Red Sea and Gulf of Aden Environment*.

Before this in 1951 the *Abidjan Convention for Co-operation in the Protection and Development of the Marine and Coastal Environment of the West and Central African Region* had been signed together with a *Protocol on Co-operation in Combatting Pollution in Cases of Emergency*. These came into force in 1984 and covered the West African coastal region from Mauritania to Namibia.

The associated Action Plan provided amongst other things for the assessment of oil and land-based pollution and for the establishment of facilities for inspection of tankers before deballasting. A *Protocol on Co-operation in Pollution Emergencies* was also agreed as well as giving states' naval vessels the "right of hot pursuit" of oil tankers who cleared their tanks in West African coastal waters — a major problem of the area.

In 1981, also under the UNEP programme, a fund was established for the prevention of pollution in the Malacca Strait. At a subsequent meeting in Manila, an action plan was drawn up for the protection and development of the marine environment and coastal areas in the S.E. Asian region.

Another convention under the same programme was the 1981 *Lima Convention for the Protection of the Marine Environment and Coastal Aras of the South-East Pacific* together with an *Agreement on Regional Co-operation in Combatting Pollution of the South-East Pacific by Hydrocarbons and Other Harmful Substances in Cases of Emergency.*

In 1983 the *Cartagena (Colombia) Convention for the Protection and Development of the Marine Environment of the Wider Caribbean* was signed. This arose out of an action plan drafted in Managua (Nicaragua) under the sponsorship of UNEP and the UN Economic Commission for Latin America (ECLA).

Finally, under UNEP's Regional Seas Programme, in 1985 an agreement was signed in Nairobi by East African states to prevent and reduce pollution in the Indian Ocean. A feature of the agreement was the participation of the EC to help finance a joint organization to monitor any threat to the sea in the area, particularly arising from the tanker traffic between the Gulf and Europe.

Inland water pollution

Before the World War II, there were numbers of agreements relating to rivers crossing national boundaries. In the main these related to navigation and the apportionment of waters as for instance between the USA and Mexico in respect of the Colorado and Rio Grande rivers. In Europe there was a convention signed in Barcelona in 1921 on navigable waterways of international concern.

However, arising out of the 1941 arbitration award under the *Boundary Waters Treaty* 1909 between Canada and USA, came one of the earliest assertions of environmental principle as noted already in the Acid Deposition contribution. This was the Trail Smelter case which asserted that "no state has the right . . . to cause injury by fumes in or to the territories of another . . .".

The river Rhine has long been the subject of water supply and management agreement based on the *Mannheim Convention on Navigation* of 1868. An international commission was established in 1950 and a convention, signed by all Rhine riparian states in 1963, came into force in 1965. The commission is responsible for research on the extent and origin of the river's pollution. By protocols of 1976 a long-term plan was introduced for the underground storage of salt from potash mines in Alsace which had long been a source of Rhine pollution. Also covered were precautions against the thermal pollution of the Rhine by nuclear power stations and against chemical pollution. It is perhaps pertinent to mention that none of these provisions was able to prevent widespread mercury and chemical pollution of the Rhine in 1986 as a result of a fire in a Swiss chemical factory.

At a lesser degree of intensity, the protection of the rivers Moselle and Saar are also covered by international commissions.

Meantime, within the framework of the Council of Europe, a *European Convention for the Protection of International Watercourses against Pollution* is being developed to be known as the *Strasbourg Convention.*

In order to ensure consistency between the somewhat varying provisions of the Paris and Barcelona Conventions and the draft *Strasbourg Directive*, the EC in 1976 agreed a *directive on pollution caused by certain Dangerous Substances Discharged into the Aquatic Environment of the Community*. As in the other conventions a "black" list I of substances has been drawn up which in due course members states will eliminate as a source of pollution. Meantime, signatories will use the "grey" list II as a basis of reducing pollution from those substances. This is to be achieved largely by observing limit values which emissions of the listed substances will not exceed.

Principal Agreements relating to marine/inland water pollution

International

(a) *Convention establishing the International Marine Consulative Organization* (IMCO), Geneva, March 6, 1948. Came into force March 17, 1958 and became UN specialized agency Jan. 13, 1959. Became International Maritime Organization (IMO) on May 22, 1982;
(b) *Tanker Owners Voluntary Agreement concerning Liability for Oil Pollution* (TOVALOP). Jan. 7, 1969, in force Oct. 6, 1969;
(c) *International Convention relating to Intervention on the High Seas in cases of Oil Pollution Casualties*. Brussels, Nov. 29, 1969. In force May 6, 1975. Protocol Nov. 2, 1973 in force March 30, 1983 extending provisions to non-oil pollution incidents;
(d) *International Convention on Civil Liability for Oil Pollution Damage* (CLC). Brussels Nov. 29, 1969. In force May 6, 1975. Protocol Nov. 19, 1976. In force April 8, 1981. Further protocol signed May 1984;
(e) *Contract Regarding an Interim Supplement to Tanker Liability for Oil Pollution* (CRISTAL). 1971. In force 1978 supplementing TOVALOP;
(f) *International Convention on Establishment of International Fund for Compensation for Oil Pollution Damage*, Brussels, Dec. 18, 1971. In force Oct. 16, 1978 supplementing CLC. Protocol, Bonn, Dec. 19, 1976. Further protocol May 1984;
(g) *International Convention on Prevention of Marine Pollution by Dumping*, London, Nov. 13, 1972. In force Aug. 30, 1975;
(h) *International Convention for the Prevention of Pollution from Ships* (MARPOL), London, Nov. 2, 1973. Protocol, Feb. 17, 1978. Both in force Oct. 2, 1983; and
(i) *UN Convention on the Law of the Sea* (UNCLOS) Montego Bay, Dec. 10, 1982.

Regional

(a) *Agreement for Co-operation in dealing with Pollution of North Sea by Oil*, Bonn, June 9, 1969. In force Nov. 28, 1970. Protocol, Sept. 13, 1983, extending to other harmful substances.
(b) *Convention for Prevention of Marine Pollution by Dumping from Ships and Aircraft*, Oslo, Feb. 15, 1972. In force April 7, 1974. List of dangerous substances covering water of North East Atlantic amended March 2, 1983;
(c) *Convention on the Protection of the Marine Environment of the Baltic Sea Area*, Helsinki, March 22, 1974. In force May 3, 1980;
(d) *Convention for Prevention of Marine Pollution from Land-based Sources*, Paris, June 4, 1974. In force May 6, 1978 relating to waters of North East Atlantic;
(e) *Convention for the Protection of the Mediterranean Sea against Pollution*, Barcelona, Feb. 16, 1976 together with these which entered force on February, 1978:

(i) *Protocol regarding Co-operation in Combatting Pollution of the Mediterranean Sea by Oil and Other Harmful Substances in Cases of Emergency*; and
(ii) *Protocol regarding Protection of the Mediterranean Sea against Dumping from Ships and Aircraft*;
(iii) *Protocol regarding Protection of Mediterranean from Pollution from Land-based Sources*, Athens May 17, 1980. In force June 17, 1983;
(f) *EC Directive on Pollution caused by Certain Dangerous Substances Discharged into the Aquatic Environment of the Community*. Signed May 4, 1976. Takes into account requirements of Paris and Rhine Conventions and (draft) Strasbourg Convention;
(g) *Kuwait Regional Convention for the Protection of the Gulf Marine Environment*, together with:
(i) *Protocol for Co-operation to Protect the Coastline arising out of Marine Emergencies resulting from the Threats and Effects of Pollution due to the Presence of Oil and Other Harmful Substances*; and
(ii) *Action Plan including the Establishment of a Marine Emergency Aid Centre*. Agreed April 24, 1978. In force June 30, 1979;
(h) *Jeddah Convention for the Conservation of the Red Sea and Gulf of Aden Environment*, signed Feb. 14 1982, together with *Protocol concerning Regional Co-operation in Combatting Marine Pollution by Oil and Other Harmful Substances in Cases of Emergency;*
(i) Memorandum of Understanding for the Prevention of Pollution in the Malacca Strait. Signed Feb. 11, 1981;
(j) *Action Plan for the Protection of Marine Environment in the South-East Asia Region*. Signed Feb. 11, 1981;
(k) *Abidjan Convention for Co-operation in the Protection and Development of the Marine and Coastal Environment of the West and Central Africa Region*, with: *Protocol on Co-operation in Combatting Pollution in Case of Emergency*. Both signed on March 23, 1981. In force Aug. 5, 1984;
(l) *Lima Convention for the Protection of the Marine Environment and Coastal Areas of the South-East Pacific*; together with *Agreement on Regional Co-operation in Combatting Pollution of the South-East Pacific by Hydrocarbons and Other Harmful Substances in Cases of Emergency*. Both signed Nov. 12, 1981;
(m) *Cartagena Convention for the Protection and Development of the Marine Environment of the Wider Caribbean Area* signed Mar. 24, 1983;
(n) *Agreement for Joint Action to Reduce and Prevent Pollution in the Indian Ocean*, Nairobi, June 21, 1985; and
(o) (i) *Convention for the Protection of the Rhine against Pollution* April 29, 1963. In force May 1, 1965;
(ii) *Convention for Protection of the Rhine against Chemical Pollution* Dec. 3, 1976. In force Feb. 1, 1979, and
(iii) *Convention for Protection of the Rhine against Pollution by Chloride*, 3rd December, 1976. In force 5th July, 1985.

8. Nuclear issues

Since World War II, nuclear issues have figured largely in public and political debates. To a large extent these have been based on the morality of nuclear weapons. Increasingly discussion has centred however on whether it is sensible and prudent to make use of nuclear reactions even for peaceful purposes particularly in the generation of power. These concerns have looked at the problems of controlling nuclear emissions — particularly in the event of accident — and dealing with the inevitable radioactive waste when the time comes for the facility's disposal. What must not be overlooked however, is the positive contribution that can be played by nuclear plants to the problems of global warming, acid deposition, and renewable resources.

This nuclear interest has generated a host of international agreements. For the purpose of this guide however the aspects principally considered are the inadvertent discharge of radioactivity into the environment and the disposal of nuclear waste.

The International Atomic Energy Agency was founded under UN auspices in July 1957. Although not specifically environmental in nature, the IAEA statute dealt with broad categories that would include the environment amongst many other matters.

Thus it was "to encourage and assist research on and the development of atomic energy for peaceful purposes . . ." and to "foster the exchange of scientific and technical information" on such purposes.

Under this statute, for example, a laboratory has been established in Monaco for the study of marine radioactivity and other forms of marine pollution. Other initiatives include an International Nuclear Information System and a Nuclear Data Section.

To attempt to minimize the release of radioactivity into the environment a Nuclear Test Ban Treaty was signed in Moscow in August 1963. This provided for the banning of all such tests except those held underground.

Inspired by IAEA, a *Treaty on the Non-Proliferation of Nuclear Weapons* was adopted by the UN General Assembly in June 1968. This attempted to restrict the spread of nuclear weapons and to limit and eventually to eliminate the testing of such devices. This had been preceded by a *Treaty for the Prohibition of Nuclear Weapons in Latin America* signed in Mexico in February 1967.

Also under IAEA auspices, a *Convention on Early Notification of a Nuclear Accident* was signed in Vienna in September 1986 in the immediate aftermath of the Chernobyl disaster. This established an early warning system for all incidents with potential trans-boundary consequences. Governments are required to notify all essential details to the government of those states likely to be affected, either directly or through the IAEA.

In parallel and at the same time was also signed a *Convention on Assistance in the case of a Nuclear Accident or Radiological Emergency*. This provides a framework whereby governments notify IAEA of experts, equipment and materials which could be made available internationally in the event of such emergencies.

In parallel with the IAEA, the European Agency was initiated in December 1957 and was absorbed into the OECD structure when this was founded in September 1961. At that time, it became the Nuclear Energy Agency. A growing aspect of its work is the safety and regulatory aspects of nuclear energy including the development of uniform standards governing safety and health protection.

At the regional level, the European Atomic Energy Community (Euratom) came into being in 1957 in parallel with the EEC. Its objectives include the establishment of a code of standards relating to personal safety against dangers resulting from ionizing radiation. Under this, the EC has developed a Radioactive Waste Programme.

As the disposal of radioactive waste caused increasing international concern, a resolution, at a meeting of the Organization for African Unity in Addis Ababa in May 1988, pledged

African governments to refrain from accepting the dumping of toxic and radioactive waste from developed countries.

Showing the dislike of nuclear testing in the Pacific area and reflecting the strongly held antinuclear views of the New Zealand government, was the *Rarotonga declaration* of March 1982. This stated that "the storage and release of nuclear wastes in the Pacific regional environment shall be prevented" and that "the testing of nuclear devices against the wishes of the people shall not be permitted".

International Agreements on nuclear Issues

(a) *International Atomic Authority* (IAEA) — United Nations Assembly, New York, Oct. 26, 1956. In force July 29, 1957;
(b) *European Atomic Energy Community* (EURATOM) *Treaty*, March 1957. In force Jan. 1, 1958. Merged with EEC and ECSC July 1, 1967;
(c) *Nuclear Energy Agency* (NEA) *Statute*. Adopted in OEEC Dec. 20, 1957. In force Feb. 1, 1958. Taken over by OECD, May 1972;
(d) *Nuclear Test Ban Treaty*, Moscow, Aug. 5, 1963. In force Oct. 10, 1963;
(e) *Treaty on Non-Proliferation of Nuclear Weapons*. Signed July 1, 1968. In force March 5, 1970;
(f) *Treaty on Natural Resources and the Environment of the South Pacific*. Rarotonga, March 1982. In force December 1986;
(g) *Conventions on Early Notification of a Nuclear Accident*. Vienna, Sept. 26, 1986. In force Oct. 27, 1986; and
(h) *Convention on Assistance in the Case of a Nuclear Accident or Radiological Emergency*. Vienna, Sept. 26, 1986. In force Oct. 27, 1986.

9. Ozone depletion

Scientists have, and are still, worried about the reduction of the ozone layer above the earth. A hole in the layer above Antarctica has also developed each Spring. This reduction is viewed with alarm and is believed to have been brought about by chemical pollutants in the atmosphere. Chief among these are chlorofluorocarbons (CFCs). By themselves, they are harmless to humans. Once released into the atmosphere however they break down and react with the ozone layer causing its depletion. Because of their typically neutral behaviour, CFCs have been used increasingly as refrigeration agents, as well as in aerosols, foam plastics and the electronics industry.

First hypotheses in 1974 that CFCs impacted on the ozone layer were somewhat tentative. However, the USA began to ban non-essential use as aerosol propellants in 1976. In May 1978, the EC adopted a resolution calling for a limitation on CFC production. This was followed by an inter-governmental meeting in 1978 in Munich which recommended precautionary measures to reduce global CFC releases.

In 1985, concerned states signed a *Convention for the Protection of the Ozone Layer*. Under this, signatories agreed to take relevant measures to protect human health and the environment against adverse modification of the ozone layer.

A 1987 Protocol to the Convention provided for the halving of CFC consumption by the year 2000.

In 1988, a joint report by WHO and the US National Aeronautics and Space Administration (NASA) confirmed the gravity of the problem.

In February 1989, EC Environment ministers agreed to ban all CFCs by 2000 with an 85% reduction to be made "as soon as possible". Australia, Canada and the USA made similar unilateral commitments to coincide with the conference "Saving the Ozone Layer" held in London in March 1989.

A further conference in Helsinki in May 1989, including the signatories to the 1987 protocol, issued a declaration of intent to stop CFC production and use completely by 2000. Although not a formal agreement, this was an explicit commitment. It was further agreed that a working group would be established to consider different ways to help Third World countries to produce alternatives to CFCs including "adequate international funding mechanisms which do not exclude the possibility of an international fund".

A review in London in 1990 of the 1987 Montreal Protocol produced agreement on the establishment of a US$240 million fund provided by the developed world to assist the Third World to minimise and eliminate their use of CFCs. Meantime, the 50% reduction target has now become a complete phase-out by the year 2000. Indeed, a group of 13 nations led by Australia, Canada and the Scandinavian countries has undertaken to achieve this objective by 1997.

Meantime, manufacturers, ICI and Dupont, announced plans to cease production and make an alternative material. Ominously however, they warned of the high cost of implementing a worldwide ban.

International agreement on ozone depletion

(a) *Convention for the Protection of the Ozone Layer*, Vienna, March 22, 1985 followed by Protocol, Montreal, Sept. 16, 1987. In force Jan. 1, 1989.

10. Renewable resources

Admirable though the concept of renewable resources is, legislation in the area of renewable resources is essentially national in character. This assumes that the phrase relates to alternatives to conventional energy resources. Thus subsidised experiment and fiscal advantages, including taxation differentials, have to date been determined solely by national governments as in the Brazil and US "gasahol" initiatives. There seems little prospect of economically viable developments in this field in the foreseeable future. Clearly other environmental issues impact on the scene particularly where biomass accumulation is concerned. In this connection the reader is referred to the essays on the Greenhouse Effect and Global Warming, Acid Deposition, Land Degradation and Desertification, Ozone Depletion, Deforestation, Nuclear Issues and Loss of Biological Diversity.

In the light of the foregoing, it is not surprising that there has been no international legislation, although the EC has undertaken studies, as a contribution to understanding of this topic.

11. Vehicle Emissions

The burning of hydrocarbon fuels and their additives in motor vehicles gives rise to a range of potentially harmful emissions. In addition to unburnt hydrocarbons, the principal pollutants concerned are carbon monoxide, nitrogen oxides, sulphur dioxide, lead and suspended particles. In particular climatic conditions, hydrocarbons and nitrogen oxides can give rise to the "smog" phenomenon which is of much concern in particular conurbations.

Sulphur dioxide is perhaps the easiest of these pollutants to control by eliminating or restricting the sulphur content of fuels as for example set out in the essay on acid deposition. However control of emission standards is a complex interaction between fuel quality and engine modification. The time required to achieve the desired scale of emission reduction is of necessity considerable.

The air pollution problem first manifested itself overtly in California, USA, giving rise to the Federal Motor Vehicle Central Programme which, beginning in 1966, has set out progressively stricter vehicle emission standards for new production vehicles. In some states indeed this has led to mandatory periodic inspection and maintenance for vehicles before registration renewal. Catalytic converters have been an essential part of this regime to reduce unburnt hydrocarbons and carbon monoxide. In turn, this has meant the elimination of lead from gasolines, as lead is a catalyst poison. Vapour recovery nozzles at filling stations have also played an important part in reducing hydrocarbon emissions.

ECE, which includes USA and Canada, has developed a series of regulations including those on emissions to air. An overall framework has been developed within an ECE agreement of 1958. This provided for the adoption of uniform conditions of approval and reciprocal recognition of approval for motor vehicles and equipment and parts. Although these regulations are not binding they have been followed progressively by the EC in issuing successive directives. From 1970 onwards these have related to gaseous emissions from positive ignition engines of motor vehicles. These have set out maximum emission limits for carbon monoxide, unburnt hydrocarbons and nitrogen oxides. Directives relating to diesel engined vehicles and diesel driven tractors have also been enacted including standards relating to particle emissions. These standards are not necessarily mandatory but vehicles conforming to them cannot be refused approval on air pollution grounds within any member state of the EC.

Methods of improving the octane numbers of gasolines have included the addition of organic lead compounds and of cyclic aromatic hydrocarbons, particularly benzene. These give rise to potentially toxic emissions and have also been the subject of legislation, particularly in the USA and EC.

Within the EC, there was an initial directive in 1977 to determine blood lead levels across the Community. Lead can be absorbed by the human body, of course, from a variety of sources other than lead in gasoline. Other frequently quoted sources, other than lead emissions from metal smelters, include lead paints, lead water pipes and "pica" cosmetics, particularly in the case of Asian families. Two campaigns were envisaged. These proved useful in establishing figures for an overall lead burden within the Community. On average, excessive lead levels were not found. In addition to determining a base line figure, the surveys were useful in highlighting particular localities where higher than normal figures were occurring because of local factors — not, it should be said, because of the incidence of lead in gasoline.

In 1982, an EC directive was agreed setting out an annual average mean concentration of lead in air within the Community. To assist in this objective, a series of lead in gasoline directives has been enacted. In 1978, a directive set out maximum lead contents ranging from 0.4g/litre (premium grade) to 0.15g/litre (regular grade). In 1985, a further directive asked member states to reduce maximum levels to 0.15 g/litre as soon as possible and to ensure the availability and balanced distribution of unleaded premium grade gasoline throughout the member states by October 1989. This directive further provided that the benzene content of all gasolines should not exceed 5% by volume by that date.

As noted above, in addition to its contribution to the lead burden in the environment, lead in gasoline also acts to poison the catalysts of catalytic converters. These converters will be increasingly used to minimize hydrocarbon and carbon monoxide emissions.

International agreements relating to vehicle emissions

(a) *ECE Agreement on the Adoption of Uniform Conditions of Approval and Reciprocal Recognition of Approval for Motor Vehicle Equipment and Parts*. 1958;
(b) *EC Directive 77/312 on Biological Screening of the Population for Lead*. Agreed March 31, 1977. In operation March 31, 1978. OJL 105 28.04.77;
(c) *EC Directive 82/884 on a Limit for Lead in the Air*. Agreed Dec. 9, 1982. In effect Dec. 9, 1984. OJL 378 31.12.82;
(d) *EC Directive 85/210 on the approximation of the Laws of the Member States concerning the Lead Content of Petrol*. Agreed March 26, 1985. In operation Jan. 1, 1986. OJL 96 03.04.85;
(e) *EC Directive 72/306 on the Approximation of Laws of the Member States relating to the Measures to be Taken Against the Emission of Pollutants from Diesel Engines for Use in Vehicles*. OJL 190 20.8.72;
(f) *EC Directive 77/537 on the Approximation of Laws of the Member States relating to the Measures to be Taken against the Emission of Pollutants from Diesel Engines for Use in Wheeled Agricultural or Forestry Tractors*. OJL 220 29.8.77; and
(g) *EC Directive 83/351 Amendment to the Directive on the Approximation of the Laws of the Member States relating to Measures to be Taken against Air Pollution by Gas from Positive Ignition Engines of Motor Vehicles*. Original Directive 1970. This amendment July 1983. OJL 197 20.7.83.

12. Water Quality

Beyond the prevention of pollution of water, is the more positive concept of provision of a quality of water sufficiently pure for Man's needs for drinking, bathing, sanitation, and food production.

This concern was crystallized by a UN Water Conference held at Mar del Plata, Argentina, March 14–25, 1977. This followed preparatory work by the UN Committee on Natural Resources established in 1970.

Among the conference's many recommendations were:

(a) calling on national governments to provide all people with water of safe quality and adequate quantity and with basic sanitary facilities, according priority to the poor and less privileged;
(b) an action programme for agricultural water use aimed at improving and extending irrigation and rain-fed agriculture;
(c) the development of economic measures of reusing and recycling water, together with economic incentives to use efficiently and to treat wastes at their source; and
(d) each country to formulate a national water policy.

Other topics bearing on this theme include Acid Deposition, Marine Pollution, Deforestation and Loss of Biological Diversity.

This 1977 Conference had been preceded by a *European Water Charter* agreed at Strasbourg in May 1968. The USA with its own geographical constraints was active early in this area. The *Federal Water Pollution Act* of 1972 was amended by the 1977 *Water Act*. The objects of this legislation were to achieve fishable and swimmable water by 1983 and, ultimately, to eliminate pollutant discharge into the country's waterways. With these in mind, guidelines were developed to determine water quality criteria according to use - fishing, swimming, irrigation or industrial cooling. A system of effluent standards and discharge permits was also established.

The EC has also striven to improve the quality of the Community waters by a series of directives. The first directive related to the quality required of surface water intended for the abstraction of drinking water. Its purpose was twofold: to ensure that the surface water abstracted for use as drinking water achieved particular standards and was given adequate treatment before being put into the public supply and thereby to improve rivers or other surface waters used as sources of drinking water. Associated with this directive was a 1979 edict recommending methods of measuring the parameters for surface water quality and setting the frequencies for such measurements.

Following these initiatives was a 1980 directive setting out standards for the quality of water intended for drinking or for use in food and drink manufacture and designed to protect human health as well as thereby improving the environment. These standards were a response to the mounting concern at the increased reuse of waste water for potable supply coupled with the increasing number of new organic and other trace substances entering such supplies. These standards were based on the 1970 WHO drinking water standards.

In 1976, a Bathing Water Directive was agreed. This provided that bathing water quality be maintained, or raised, over time both to protect public health and for amenity reasons. This was to be achieved by ensuring that sewage is not present or has been adequately diluted or destroyed. The Commission, through a series of actions in the European Court of Justice is now seeking to ensure that member states execute the promised improvements in bathing beaches promised 15 years ago.

In 1978, a directive was issued relating to the quality of fresh waters needing protection or improvement in order to support fish life. This sets out two categories of water, one for salmon and trout and the other for coarse fish.

In 1977, a directive was approved establishing a common procedure for the exchange of information on the quality of surface fresh water in the Community. Initially providing for annual reports, this was amended in 1986 to a three-yearly basis. The Commission had not the resources to cope with more frequent reporting.

In 1979, the concept was extended to a directive on the quality required for shellfish waters. This required designation of coastal and brackish waters which need protection or improvement to support shellfish life.

A directive on the protection of groundwater against pollution caused by certain dangerous substances was agreed in 1980. This was designed to protect underground sources from which the bulk of the community's drinking water derives. A prohibited list of substances was drawn up, which were to be prevented from entering ground waters, whilst a second list was of substances whose introduction was to be limited so as to avoid pollution. These lists were similar to but not identical to those of the *Paris Convention*.

With the passage of time, it is becoming clearer that this series of directives has been of value to a greater extent than initially foreseen. They have enabled agencies to press for resources from cash constrained governments whilst at the same time providing opportunities for environmentalists and others to pressure those agencies to meet the designated standards and objectives.

International agreements on water quality

(a) *Recommendations of UN Water Conference*, Mar del Plata, March 14–25, 1977;
(b) *EC Directive 75/440 relating to the Quality Required of Surface Water intended for the Abstraction of Drinking Water in Member States*. Compliance June 18, 1977. OJL 194, 25.7.75;
(c) *EC Directive 76/160 concerning the Quality of Bathing Water*. Compliance Dec. 10, 1977. OJL 31 5.2.76;
(d) *EC Decision 77/795* (OJL 334 24.12.77) *amended by 84/422* (OJL 239 5.9.84) *establishing a Common Procedure for the Exchange of Information on the Quality of Surface Fresh Water in the Community*;
(e) *EC Directive 78/659 on the Quality of Fresh Water Needing Protection or Improvement in order to Support Fish Life*. Compliance July 20, 1980, OJL 222 14.8.78;
(f) *EC Directive 79/869 concerning the Methods of Measurement and Frequency of Sampling and Analysis of Surface Water intended for the Abstraction of Drinking Water in Member States*. Compliance Oct. 11, 1981. OJL 271 29.10.79;
(g) *EC Directive 79/823 on the Quality required for Shellfish Waters*. Compliance Nov. 5, 1981. OJL 281 10.11.79;
(h) *EC Directive 80/778 relating to the Quality of Water intended for Human Consumption*. Compliance July 17, 1982. OJL 229 30.8.80; and
(i) *EC Directive 80/68 on the Protection of Groundwater against Pollution caused by Certain Dangerous Substances*. OJL 20 26.1.80.

13. Others including toxic and hazardous waste

In considering this section of environmental legislation, it is necessary to bear in mind the difficulty of defining unambiguously the terms "toxic" and "hazardous" which can vary according to the criteria used. In fact the number of truly international agreements in this sector is small but there is extensive regional legislation as well as the trend setting US initiatives. It is helpful to consider this legislation in two broad categories. Firstly, those dealing specifically with the disposal of wastes and those relating to the possible discharge into the environment of potentially toxic and hazardous materials.

When considering this general topic the contributions particularly relating to Marine Pollution, Vehicle Emissions, Nuclear Issues and Water Quality should also be taken into consideration.

The principal US legislation in this field has been the 1976 Resource Conservation Act and the Toxic Substance Control Act (TOSCA). As a result, firms or individuals using, handling or transporting such materials have to obtain permits for their handling. Dumping of such materials can only occur in specially designed, regulated and monitored land disposal sites—primarly to avoid contamination of ground water and the discharge of noxious substances into the environment.

The EC also has much legislation in both categories. An early initiative was a 1975 directive on the disposal of waste oils. This relates to all waste oils — not merely lubricating. A duty is placed on states to ensure that the collection and disposal of such oils causes no avoidable damage to man and his environment.

A wider directive on waste was signed in 1975. This sets out a broad framework for the Community within which more detailed directives may be set. It is also based on the "Polluter Pays Principle". The cost of disposing of such waste has to be borne by the holder of the waste or by previous holders or producers of such waste. Within this framework, two specific directives have been enacted relating to polychlorinated biphenyls (PCBs) and terphenyls, and toxic waste. The 1976 directive relates to the control of the disposal and regeneration of PCBs without harm to either human health or the environment. This followed a 1973 OECD decision requiring member states to regulate the use and disposal of PCBs in the light of a number of fatal incidents in Japan involving these materials.

The 1978 *Toxic Wastes Directive* provides that such wastes may only be stored, treated and/or deposited by authorized undertakings. "Toxic and dangerous" waste is here defined as "any waste containing or contaminated by the substance or materials listed . . . of such a nature, in such quantities or in such concentration as to constitute a risk to health or the environment".

These latter provisions were extended in 1984 to the supervision and control of transfrontier shipments. Provision was made for a system of controls and regulations for movement of hazardous wastes across frontiers from collection to disposal. Movements covered relate to both those within and in and out of the Community and should ensure that disposal of such materials is undertaken in a controlled and responsible manner. Following a UNEP initiative on the problem of Third World countries and a 1975 OECD Conference, a 1984 amendment to the Directive provided that export of such waste should not be allowed unless there was proof that the importing country had agreed to the shipment and was able to dispose of such waste adequately.

A more specific directive relates to the waste disposal problems of the titanium dioxide industry. An Italian plant had caused problems in the Mediterranean with it notorious "red mud" causing problems for nearby Corsica. The 1978 Directive required that member states ensure that titanium dioxide is disposed of without endangering human health or harming the environment.

In 1985, the waste concept was extended further to cover containers of liquids for human consumption. This requires member states to draw up programmes for reducing the tonnage and volume of containers in waste for disposal. Sealed containers for all liquids for human consumption are covered although barrels and casks are excluded.

In 1989 in Basle regulation of the international transport and disposal of hazardous products was initiated with agreement in a convention covering this problem and initially signed by 34 countries.

Turning to the second category, the potential discharge of toxic and hazardous materials into the environment, agreement was reached within OECD in 1973 for controls on the use of toxic chemicals employed in a variety of industrial processes and products.

A series of EC directives has been produced relating to the composition and testing of detergents. The basic 1973 directive prohibited largely the marketing of detergents within the Community where the average level of bio-degradability of the surfactants is less than 90%. This was essentially to counteract the widespread phenomenon at that time of foaming of rivers. This was not only unsightly but it also materially impaired the effectiveness of sewage treatment processes. The resultant encouragement of detergent bio-degradability has virtually removed that foaming problem from the Community's rivers. This EC legislation followed a 1970 OECD agreement in the same area.

Two important series of EC directives have been those relating to the *Marketing and Use of Certain Dangerous Substances and Preparations* and to *the Packaging and Labelling of Dangerous Substances*. These parallel the US legislative developments in this field quoted earlier.

The 1976 directive was a general framework for bans or restrictions on the marketing and use of dangerous substances. An annexe listed the materials subject to restrictions — PCBs, polychlorinated terphenyls (PCTs) and vinyl chloride monomer (VCM). Subsequent directives added to the list and expanded the restrictions covering, amongst others, trichloro-ethylene, tetrachloro-ethylene, carbon tetrachloride, benzene, and asbestos in various consumer applications.

Directives were introduced in 1978 and 1979 prohibiting and restricting the use of certain pesticides and laying down regulations for the classification, purchasing and labelling of those that are marketed. A series of directives have also been introduced laying down the maximum pesticide residues allowable on fruit, vegetables and cereals as well as on foodstuffs of animal origin.

Clearly related to the marketing and use directives within the EC is a series of directives dealing nominally with the approximation of laws, regulations and administrative provisions relating to the classification, packaging and labelling of dangerous substances. This was the principal thrust of the parent 1967 directive and five subsequent amending directives. The sixth amendment in 1979 however marked a fundamental development. In addition to consolidating the previous enactments, it introduced a classification of "dangerous to the environment". More fundamentally however it introduced a scheme of prior notification of tests made for potential hazards before a substance is marketed. Development of this sixth amendment was related to a 1974 OECD recommendation on the assessment of the potential environmental effects of chemicals. Latterly it was also heavily influenced by the enactment of TOSCA in the USA. Essentially the EC Commission was to draw up a *European Inventory of Existing Commercial Chemical Substances (EINECS)* of substances marketed within the Community before Sept. 18, 1981. Thereafter lists have to be maintained of all new substances notified to the Commission together with relevant data and classification.

The notorious "Seveso incident" in Italy in 1976 gave rise to the *Major Accidents Hazards Directive* of 1982. This places a general duty on manufacturers using a wide range of processes to prevent major accidents and to limit their consequences for man and the environment. At the same time there is a general duty to report major accidents. Specific duties are placed on manufacturers at such plants. They must produce a safety report and an on-site emergency plan. At the same time a competent authority must produce an off-site emergency plan. The public in the neighbourhood must then be informed of the safety measures and the correct behaviour to adopt in the event of an accident.

An EC directive of 1987 on the *Prevention and Reduction of Environmental Pollution by Asbestos* sets an interesting precedent. This supplements the control over asbestos set out in other directives and uniquely attempts in one directive to set pollution controls for a single substance in the three environmental media.

In modern life, noise and vibration are increasingly seen as environmental pollutants. Much national legislation has accordingly been devoted to controlling noise and vibration levels within individual countries. For mobile sources, particularly motor vehicles and aircraft, international standards have been established to attempt to ensure that minimum criteria are met when the source concerned crosses national boundaries. Within the EC these standards have formed the basis of non-discretionary legislation. Initially these were agreed as removing obstacles to trade within the Community. They have increasingly come to be seen however as aids to a quieter environment.

Thus for cars, buses and lorries a Community directive of 1970 derived largely from the ECE non-mandatory Regulation 9. This established noise limits under which vehicles concerned could not be banned on grounds relating to the permissible sound level or exhaust system. The criteria and methods of test have been increasingly tightened in successive directives of 1973, 1977, 1981 and 1984.

As regards aircraft, a 1980 EC directive set out to implement the non-mandatory noise standards adopted by the International Civil Aviation Organization (ICAO). An amending directive was agreed in 1983 and under it EC member states are not to permit the operation of civil subsonic jet aeroplanes which are registered outside member states and which do not comply with the ICAO standards.

Other EC noise directives have developed standards for motorcycles, tractors and construction plant as well as items of a more domestic nature including lawnmowers and household appliances.

International agreements relating to other environmental matters

(a) *OECD Decision on Regulating Use and Disposal of PCBs* 1973;
(b) *EC Directive 75/439 on the disposal of Waste Oils* OJL 194 25.7.75. Amended by 87/101 on OJL 42 12.2.87;
(c) *EC Directive 75/442 on Waste*. OJL 194 25.7.75;
(d) *EC Directive 76/403 on the Disposal of Polychlorinated Biphenyls and Polychlorinated Terphenyls*. OJL 108 26.4.76;
(e) *EC Directive 78/319.8 on Toxic and Dangerous Waste*. OJL 843 31.3.78;
(f) *EC Directive 78/176 on Waste from Titanium Dioxide Industry* OJL 54 25.2.78. Amended by 83.29 OJL 32 3.2.83;
(g) *EC Directive 84/631 on Transfrontier Shipment of Toxic Waste*. OJL 326 31.12.84. Amended by 86/279 OJL 181 4.7.86;
(h) *EC Directive 85/339 on Containers of Liquids for Human Consumption*. OJL 176 6.7.85;
(i) *Convention on International Transport and Disposal of Hazardous Wastes*, Basle, March 23, 1989;
(j) *OECD Agreement on Controls on the Use of Toxic Chemicals employed in a variety of Industrial Processes and Products,* February 1973;
(k) *EC Directive 73/404 on Detergents*. OJL 347, 17.12.73. Amended by 82/242 L109, 22.4.82; and 86/94 L80 25.3.86;
(l) *EC Directive 76/769 relating to Restrictions in the Marketing and use of Certain Dangerous Substances and Preparations*. OJL 262, 27.9.76. Formal compliance Feb. 3, 1978. Seven subsequent Amendments, 79/663, 82/806, 82/828, 83/264, 83/478, 85/467 and 85/610;
(m) (i) *EC Directive 76/895 on the fixing of Maximum Levels for Pesticide Residues in and on Fruit and Vegetables*. OJL 340, 19.12.76. Amended by 80/428, 81/36 and 82/528;
(ii) *EC Directive 86/362 on the Fixing of Maximum Levels for Pesticide Levels in or on Cereals*. OJL 221, 7.8.86;

(iii) *EC Directive 86/363 on the Fixing of Maximum Levels for Pesticide Residues in and on Foodstuffs of Animal Origin*. OJL 221 7.8.86;
(n) (i) *EC Directive 79/117 Prohibiting the Placing on the Market and use of Plant Protection Products Containing Certain Substances*. OJL 33, 8.2.79. Amended by 83/131, 85/298, 86/214, 86/355 and 87/181;
(ii) *EC Directive 78/631 on the Approximation of the Laws of the Member States relating to the Classification, Packaging and Labelling of Dangerous Substances (pesticides)*. OJL 296 29.7.78. Amended by 81/187 and 84/291;
(o) *EC Directive 79/831 being the Sixth Amendment to Directive 67/548 on the Approximation of the Laws, Regulations and Administrative Provisions Relating to the Classification, Packaging and Labelling of Dangerous Substances*. (N.B. This directive incorporates also the substantive parts of the parent and five subsequent amending directives). OJL 259 15.10.79;
(p) *EC Directive 82/501 on the Major Accident Hazards of Certain Industrial Activities*. OJL 230 8.5.82. Amended by 87/216 OJL 85, 2.3.87;
(q) *EC Directive 87/217 on the Prevention and Reduction of Environmental Pollution by Asbestos* OJL 85, 28.3.87.
(r) *Convention on International Civil Aviation*, Chicago, December 1944
(s) *EC Directive 70/157 relating to the Permissible Sound Level and Exhaust Systems of Motor Vehicles*. OJL 42 23.2.70 and amended by Directives 73/350, 77/212, 81/334, 84/372, 84/424
(t) *EC Directive 80/51 relating to the Limitation of Noise Emissions from Subsonic Aircraft*. OJL 18 24.1.80 as amended by Directive 83/206. OJL 117 4.5.83.

IV. ORGANIZATIONS

Introduction

This part provides some details of some of the many organizations and institutions involved today in aspects of environmental activity or concern. Most of the information is based upon data provided by the organization concerned and it is presented in four groupings each in alphabetical order of title. The first includes international bodies and agencies, the second those concerned with regional activities, the third provides the government departments responsible for environmental affairs and the fourth lists national bodies, albeit often with international interests or contacts. Political "green" parties have not been included but are listed in Part II. Similarly commercial undertakings, with one or two minor exceptions, are omitted although many membership and other organizations have some commercial activity, usually to provide additional funds for their work.

Whilst every effort has been made to ensure accuracy no responsibility or liability can be accepted for any errors or omissions, nor of any applied acceptance, recognition or endorsement of any activities.

INTERNATIONAL

Bureau of the Convention on Wetlands of International Importance Especially as Waterfowl Habitat (Ramsar Convention Bureau)

Telephone. 022 64 91 14 *Fax.* 022 64 46 15 *Telex.* 41 96 24 IUCN CH
Address. Avenue du Mont-Blanc, CH-1196 Gland, Switzerland
Officials. Daniel B. Navid (Secretary-General)

The Convention, signed at Ramsar, Iran in February 1971 and which entered into force in December 1975 (see Part III), provides the framework for international co-operation for the conservation of wetland habitats. Its broad objectives are to stem the loss of wetlands and to ensure their conservation. The Bureau, established in 1987 and administered by IUCN in co-operation with IWRB, provides a permanent structure for administrative, scientific and technical support on behalf of the 52 contracting countries (two other countries are about to join).

The triennial Conference of the participants sets the programme and budget, which in 1990 is approximately SFr 750,000. Priorities for action include: wise use, conservation and management of listed sites; development assistance and international co-operation for shared resources and share species; and training of wetland personnel.

The Bureau issues an annual report, providing information on the implementation of the Convention, the monitoring work and a listing of the 463 designated sites (covering about 30 million hectares). It also produces a newsletter, proceedings and a Convention Brochure.

Its annual income comes from the contracting parties for the core funding and from other contributions for specific projects.

The Bureau also has an office in the UK at Slimbridge, Gloucester GL2 7BX.

CAB International (CABI)

Telephone. 0491 32111 *Fax.* 0491 33508 *Telex.* 847964 (COMAGG G)
Address. Wallingford, Oxon OX10 8DE, UK
Officials. Don Mentz (Director General)

CABI started in 1928 as the Commonwealth Agricultural Bureaux although its earliest constituent part, the Bureau of Entomology, goes back to 1913. Membership was confined to governments within the Commonwealth but in 1985 the 29 members adopted a new constitution with membership open to any interested government. This action was motivated by a recognition that the services provided are used by countries all over the world. Journals and other information services are sold throughout the world and the biosystematic institutes provide identifications to more than 60 non-Commonwealth countries.

CAB International is an intergovernmental body which provides information, scientific and development services on agriculture and related disciplines throughout the world.

The Information Services provide access to the world's largest database on research in agriculture, forestry etc., including relevant social sciences and aspects of human medicine.

The Scientific Services include four professional institutes:

The Institute of Entomology, 56 Queens Gate, London SW7 5JR
The Mycological Institute, Ferry Lane, Kew, Richmond TW9 3AF
The Institute of Parasitology, 395A Hatfield Road, St Albans, Herts AL4 0XU
The Institute of Biological Control, Silwood Park, Buckhurst Road, Ascot, Berks SL5 7TA, with stations in Trinidad, Switzerland, India, Kenya, Pakistan and Malaysia.

The first three are centres of excellence for research and the identification of organisms of agricultural and economic importance, handling some 40,000 specimens each year. All are among the largest institutions of their kind in the world and offer worldwide experience and expertise.

CABI has extensive publications of books, abstracts, journals, databases and news sheets, dictionaries and works of reference. (Catalogues are available from the above address.)

It has an annual expenditure of around £11 million, 80% of which comes from sales of printed and machine-readable information services.

Centre for Alternative Technology (CAT)

Telephone. 0654 702400
Address. Machynlleth, Powys SY20 9AZ, Wales, UK
Officials. Roger Kelly (Director); Dr Robert Todd (Technical Director)

The Centre, founded in 1973 and opened to the public in 1975, demonstrates and promotes sustainable technologies and ways of living including renewable energy sources, energy conservation, organic growing etc. It provides working displays of a wide range of up-to-the-minute "alternative technologies", claimed to be the only one of its kind in Europe, and visited by some 60,000 people a year. It provides, in addition to the display, an information service and consultancy.

There is also a supporters movement—Alternative Technology Association—with about 2,000 members which campaigns for the adoption of alternative technology ideas, promotes the Centre's work and raises funds, mounts exhibits in libraries, shows, festivals, etc., gives talks and meets in local groups.

The Centre arranges residential weekend courses, courses tailor-made for schools and colleges and development courses designed for people about to go to work in developing countries.

The Centre markets a wide range of practical equipment and devices that are "environment friendly" and publishes many information sheets, resource lists, do-it-yourself plans, project resource booklets for schools and technical papers. It has recently commenced publishing a newsletter, *Clean Slate*.

The Centre, along with Quarry Trading Ltd. (handling sales, including an educational publication *Green Teacher*) and Dulas Engineering Ltd. (providing consultancy and design) are the "Quarry Group" owned by a holding charity. The largest contribution to income comes from visitors (37.5% in 1988–89), courses (24%) and from grants and donations from nearly 40 organizations, trusts and companies. The Centre's income in 1988 was £243,000.

Centre for Environmental Management and Planning (CEMP)

Telephone. 0224 272482 *Fax.* 0224 487658 *Telex.* 73458
Address. Auris Business Centre, 23 St Machar Drive, Aberdeen AB2 1RY, UK
Officials. Prof. G. M. Dunnet (Chairman)

Established to provide a service, based in Aberdeen University and a part of the Aberdeen University Research and Industrial Services (AURIS), encompassing research, consultancy, training, conferences and information on a wide variety of environmental issues throughout the world.

Centre for Our Common Future (COCF)

Telephone. 22 732 71 17 *Fax.* 22 738 50 46 *Telex.* 27910
Address. Palais Wilson, 52 rue des Paquis, 1201 Geneva, Switzerland
Officials. Warren H. Lindner (Executive Director)

The Centre is a small, totally independent charitable organization, set up in 1988 following the publication of the final report of the UN World Commission on Environment and Development under the title *Our Common Future*, known as the *Brundtland Report* after Mrs Gor Harlem Brundtland, the then Prime Minister of Norway, who chaired the Commission.

Our Common Future is about the politics of the future. It lays down principles on which the world must be managed—sustainable development—if life itself is to survive and flourish into the foreseeable future. It is a political consensus document, the outcome of an exhaustive process and research, consultation, analysis and argument conducted by an international Commission of 21 scientists and politicians.

The Centre serves as an information exchange on activities taking place globally in keeping with the concept of sustainable development. It promotes the recommendations and vision of the World Commission and encourages global activity towards their implementation. It has a staff of five persons, 150 working partners (environment, development, media, trade union, youth, scientific, academic, industrial, intergovernmental and international organizations from 60 countries) and over 3,000 correspondees.

The Centre co-sponsors conferences; produces different language versions of the Commission's Report and guides to that report; and is mobilizing the independent sector in the preparations up to and following the 1992 World Conference on Environment and Development.

It publishes a quarterly newsletter the *Brundtland Review*, together with *A Guide to Sustainable Development, Food 2000, Industry 2000, Energy 2000* and, in May 1990, *Signs of Hope* by Linda Starke, about the world's new-found environmentalism.

Its annual budget is about SwF800,000 which comes from MacArthur and Carnegie Foundations, the Governments of Norway, Sweden, Denmark, Finland, Spain and Portugal, the City of Geneva and the Gro Harlem Brundtland Environment Foundation.

Club of Rome

Formed in 1968 and with a small but widespread membership from some 40 countries. It has attempted a global approach to environmental problems and tried to establish, with detailed computer programmes, the inter-relationship and interactions of political, social and environmental issues, particularly the long-term perspectives. It is most remembered for its sponsorship of the report *The Limits to Growth* published in 1972 which predicted that, on the then consumptions there would soon be shortages of most basic resources although many of the assumptions were later shown to be doubtful when the oil price rises of the 1970s occurred. In 1974 it published *Mankind at the Turning Point* and *Beyond the Age of Waste* in 1978.

Comité International de Recherche et d'Etude de Facteurs de l'Ambience (CIFA/ICEF)
(International Committee for research and study of Environmental Factors)

Telephone. 2 311497
Address. CIFA, Av. F. D. Roosevelt 50, B-1050 Bruxelles, Belgium
Officials. E. P. Wedler (President) (Freie Univ. Berlin, Inst. für Meteorologie, Dietrich-Schäfer-Weg 6–10, D-1000 Berlin 41); Dr Giuseppe Bonacina (Secretary-General) (Via Cenisio 49, I-20154 Milano, Italy)

The Committee was formed in September 1969 and now has some 40 members.

It organizes, on an international level, interdisciplinary co-operation in research and scientific study of environmental factors which are the origin of fluctuating phenomena in exact, natural and human sciences.

It holds a triennial General Assembly (next in 1993) and publishes *CIFA News* twice a year.

Committee of International Development Institutions on the Environment (CIDIE)

Telephone. 254 2 333930 *Telex.* 22068 unep ke
Address. PO Box 30552, Nairobi, Kenya

The Committee was established in 1980 to facilitate the integration of environmental concern into the development process. Its members include: African Development Bank, Arab Bank for Economic Development in Africa, Asian Development Bank, Caribbean Development Bank, Central American Bank for Economic Integration, EC, European

Investment Bank, Inter-American Development Bank, International Fund for Agricultural Development, Nordic Investment Bank, OAS, UNEP, World Bank.

Annual meetings focus on different matters of concern, such as desertification or the use of pesticides. CIDIE also provides an exchange of information and technical co-operation.

Earthwatch

Telephone. 617 926 8200 *Fax.* 617 926 8532 *Telex.* 5106006452
Address. PO Box 403, 680 Mt. Auburn Street, Watertown, MA 02272, USA
Officials. Brian A. Rosborough (President)

Founded in 1971 Earthwatch is a non-profit, international company of citizens and scientists working to sustain the world's environment, to monitor global change, to conserve endangered species and habitats, to explore the vast heritage of the people and to foster world health and international co-operation. It aims to improve human understanding of the planet, the diversity of its inhabitants and the processes that affect the quality of life on Earth. It is non-confrontational. It aims to act as a bridge between science and the community by enabling willing adults to join scientists in the field and act as their assistants. It has a worldwide membership of 55,000 and is sending approximately 3,300 volunteers (ranging in age from 16 to 85) in 1990 to work with scientists around the world.

It currently sponsors 120 projects in 46 countries and 27 states. Projects are year-round and each volunteer pays a share of the costs to cover field work, accommodation and lodging. These expeditions cover, amongst others, 12 projects dealing with rain forest conservation and ecology, 28 projects on art and archaeology, 14 projects on geosciences, 41 projects on life sciences, 21 projects on marine studies and four projects on social sciences. Since the start over 23,000 EarthCorps volunteers have contributed over US$15,000,000 to search for solutions to important problems of the world. Earthwatch's affiliate, The Centre for Field Research, receives over 400 proposals each year from scholars who need the help of volunteers. The Centre, with its academic advisory board, is responsible for peer review, screening and selection of projects for Earthwatch support.

It publishes *Earthwatch* magazine six times a year, available to members at $25 yearly. This gives wide coverage (136 pages in February 1990 edition) on many items of topical interest. An annual *President's Report* details the projects and activities of the year.

Money is raised through grants provided by foundations and corporations, particularly the National Geographic Society and the World Wide Fund for Nature. The bulk however (84%) comes from subscribers and volunteers who share the cost and labours of field research. The overall, worldwide, budget amounts to US$6,500,000 a year. Earthwatch hopes to provide scholarships and financial aid to over 300 teachers and students to enable them to join expeditions in 1990.

Other centres are:

Earthwatch California
861 Via de la Paz, Suite G, Pacific Palisades, CA 90272

Earthwatch Europe
Belsyre Court, 57 Woodstock Road, Oxford OX2 6HU, UK. *Telephone.* 0865 311600 *Fax.* 0865 311383; *Officials.* E. Max Nicholson (Chairman); Brian W. Walker (Director); Andrew W. Mitchell (Deputy Director)

Earthwatch Australia
Suite 3, Level 2, 283 George Street, Sydney 2000, Australia.

There are also offices in Boston, Massachussetts, and in Moscow.

Energy and Environment Programme, Royal Institute of International Affairs (EEP/RIIA)

Telephone. 071 930 2233 *Fax.* 071 835 3593
Address. Chatham House, 10 St James's Square, London SW1Y 4LE, UK
Officials. Jonathan Stern (Head of Programme); Silvan Robinson, CBE (Chairman of Steering Committee)

The Programme was established in 1981 (originally as the Energy Programme which was extended to include environmental topics in 1987) at the Royal Institute which was founded in 1926. The Royal Institute is an independent, self-governing body which exists to further the study and understanding of all aspects of international affairs through lectures, discussions, conferences, research, library facilities and publications. It has a number of research programmes providing in-depth analysis in accessible form of policy issues relevant to British and worldwide interests. The EEP aims to inform and stimulate the debate and to influence governments and industry on the political, strategic and economic aspects of domestic and international energy and environmental policy issues.

In pursuit of these aims the Energy and Environment Programme researches and publishes independent studies and provides a forum for debate. Recent publications include *The Greenhouse Effect: Negotiating Targets; The Greenhouse Effect: Issues for Policy Makers; Acid Depositions and Vehicle Emissions;* and (forthcoming) *Energy Policies and the Greenhouse Effect* and *Environmental Issues in International Relations: the Next 25 Years*. (A full list of publications is available from the above address.)

The programme is financed by contributions from British Coal; British Gas; British Petroleum; British Steel; Chuba Electric Power Co.; Department of Energy (UK); ELF UK; Eastern Electricity; Esso; Commission of the EC; Japan National Oil Corporation; Kuwait Petroleum; Office of Gas Supply; National Energy Administration, Sweden; National Power; Petróleos de Venezuela; Petroleum Economics; PowerGen; Sedgwick Energy; Shell; Statoil; Tokyo Electric Power Co.; UKAEA.

The annual cost of the Programme is about £150,000.

Food and Agriculture Organization of the UN (FAO)

Telephone. 39–6 57971 *Telex.* 610181 FAO 1 *Fax.* 57973152, 5782610
Address. Via delle Terme di Caracalla, 00100 Rome, Italy
Officials. Edouard Saouma (Director-General)

The FAO was founded at a conference in Quebec, Canada on Oct. 16 1945 following a UN conference on Food and Agriculture at Hot Springs, Virginia in 1943, which established a commission to plan the Organization. It now has 158 member nations.

FAO aims to increase production of agriculture, forestry and fisheries and to improve the standard of living of those engaged in these activities. It provides member nations with technical assistance, information and policy advice and a neutral forum for specialist conferences.

Currently its technical assistance is mostly in agriculture with a quarter of field work aimed at crop production. Other important areas include rural development (16%), natural resources (14%), forestry (12%), livestock (11%) and fisheries development (9%). Increased activities and resources are to be focused on policy advice, biotechnology, agricultural data development, crop and weather monitoring, crop protection, aquaculture and the Tropical Forestry Action Plan.

FAO publish a number of yearbooks covering the state of food and agriculture, production, trade, fertilizer, forest products, fishery statistics, commodity review and outlook. It also publishes a quarterly *Plant Protection Bulletin, Food Outlook* monthly, and periodically a *Bulletin of Statistics*.

It co-operates with other international organizations especially within the UN family and is currently (1990) preparing an international accord on the biodiversity of the planet in co-operation with UNEP for presentation at the 1992 UN Conference on the Environment and Development. It has an Environment and Energy Programmes Co-ordinating Centre and environmental concerns are a major component of all the Organization's field work. FAO, jointly with WHO, is working for food safety through its Food Standards Programme. The joint FAO/IEAE Division is exploring nuclear and biotechnologies for safe, environmentally-friendly solutions to agricultural problems.

The FAO has a budget of US$570 million (1990–91 biennium). Its regular programme is financed by its members on a scale of contributions established by the Conference, the supreme governing body which meets biennially and is composed of all member nations. Its field programme is funded by the UN development programme (48.5% in 1989), trust funds from donor countries or financing institutions (44.6%) and FAO's Technical Co-operation Programme out of regular budgetary funds (6.9%).

Foundation for Environmental Conservation (FEC)

Telephone. 022 798 2383 *Fax.* 022 798 2344
Address. 7 Chemin Taverney, 1218 Grand-Saconnex, Geneva, Switzerland
Officials. Dr Nicholas Polunin (President); Dr F. K. Hare (Hon. Secretary)

Founded in 1975 by the IUCN and WWF with Dr Polunin who had been active in related fields for some years.

It exists to foster pertinent conferences, particularly the International Conferences on Environmental Future, to sponsor the Baer-Huxley Memorial Lectures and to organize workshops on environmental causes of concern.

The Foundation publishes, quarterly, *Environmental Conservation*, an international journal founded in 1974, a series of monographs and the *Cambridge Studies in Environmental Policy*.

Its finances are based upon a contribution from its publications, donations and sponsorship of the various conferences. For example the Fourth International Conference on Environmental Future, in 1990, will be supported by the Hungarian Academy of Sciences, UNFPA, IUCN, WWF, UNEP, Japan Shipbuilders and others.

Friends of the Earth International (FOEI)

Telephone. 071 490 1555 *Fax.* 071 490 0881
Address. 26–28 Underwood Street, London N1 7JQ, UK
Other centres. In 33 countries, worldwide, see below, and several associate members.
Officials. John Hontelez (Chairman); Charles Secrett (UK) (Treasurer); Julia Langer (Canada); Jim Barnes (USA); Patricia Gay (Argentina); Chee Yoke Ling (SAM); Theo Anderson (Ghana) (Committee members)

FOEI was founded in 1971 and now has members groups in 33 countries around the world. FOEI is a UN accredited non-governmental organization and has observer status at the FAO, the IMO, the IWC, the ITTO and the Ramsar Convention and consultative status at UNESCO.

The International secretariat, in London, plays a crucial role in facilitating information exchange, joint campaigning and fund raising. It publishes *FOE-Link*, the FOEI newsletter, it administers a small travel fund to help Southern members participate in Annual Meetings and other events and services the FOEI Executive Committee, elected at the Annual Meeting of members.

Each country member group is autonomous, with its own operating methods, legal structure and funding base. Each is bound in a common cause—the conservation, restoration and rational use of the Earth's resources.

FOEI groups are increasingly co-ordinating their activities at the international level through campaigns led by national members groups elected at the Annual Meeting. These lead groups co-ordinate political lobbying, citizen action initiatives and the flow of information throughout the FOEI network. Current international projects include global warming, tropical rainforests, marine conservation, nuclear power, air pollution and East–West co-operation.

The member groups each have their own campaigns and priorities and many have become respected sources of information and assessment. For example, in the UK they regularly give evidence to parliamentary Select Committees. There are a large number of publications available—reports, pamphlets, analyses, information and action packs, briefings etc., (catalogues are available from the offices).

Members and offices of FOEI:

European Co-ordination
Co-ordination Europèene Des Amis de la Terre (CEAT), 29 Rue Blanche, 1050 Bruxelles, Belgium.

Argentina
Amigos de la Tierra, Casilla, Correo Central no. 3560, c.p. 1000, Buenos Aires.

Australia
Friends of the Earth, Chain Reaction Co-operative, PO Box 530E, Melbourne, Victoria.

Austria
Friends of the Earth, Reinlgasse no. 34–28, 1140 Vienna.

Bangladesh
IEDS-FOE Bangladesh, PO Box no. 4222, Dhaka 1000.

Belgium
Les Amis de la Terre, Place de la Vingeanne, 5158 Dave.

Brazil
ADFG-Amigos da Terra, Rua Miguel Tostes 694, 90,000 Porto Alegre.

Canada
Friends of the Earth/Les Amis de la Terre, 251 Laurier Ave. W, Suite 701, Ottawa, Ontario K1P 5J6.

Cyprus
Friends of the Earth, Maroni, Larnaca District.

Denmark
NOAH International, Studiestraede 24, DK1455 Copenhagen.

Ecuador
Tierra Viva, PO Box 1891, Cuenca.

Estonia (USSR)
Estonian Green Movement, 8 Veski Street, Tartu 202400, Estonia SSR.

France
Les Amis de la Terre, 15 Rue Gambey, 75011 Paris.

Ghana
Friends of the Earth, PO Box 3794, Accra.

Hong Kong
Friends of the Earth, One Earth Centre, 61 Wyndham Street M/F.

Indonesia
WAHLI, J1. Penjernihan 1/15, Kompleks Keuangan, Pejompongan, Jakarta Pusat, 10210.

Ireland
Earthwatch, Harbour View, Bantry, County Cork.

Italy
Amici della Terra, Via del Sudario 35, 00186 Rome.

Japan
Chikyu no Tomo, 501 Shinwa Building, 9–17 Sakuragaoka, Shibuya-ku, Tokyo 150.

Malaysia
Sahabat Alam Malaysia, 43 Salween Road, 10050 Pulao Penang.

The Netherlands
Vereniging Milieudefensie, PO Box 19199, 1000 6D Amsterdam. *Telephone.* 31 20 221366 *Fax.* 31 20 275 287.

New Zealand
Friends of the Earth, PO Box 39-065, Auckland-West. *Telephone.* 064 04 3034 319

Nicaragua
ABEN, Casa Ricardo Morales Aviles, lc abajo 3 1/2c al Sur, Managua.

Papua New Guinea
Friends of the Earth, PO Box 4028, Boroko.

Poland
Polski Klub Ekologiczny, Ul. Garbarska no. 9, 31.131 Krakow.

Portugal
Amigos da Terra, Rua Pinheiro Chagas 28, 2 Dto., 1000 Lisboa.

Scotland
Friends of the Earth, 15 Windsor Street, Edinburgh EH1 5LA.

Spain
Fed. de Amigos de la Tierra, Avda Betanzos 55.11.1, 28029 Madrid.

Sweden
Jordens Vanner, Fjallgatan 23A, S-116 45 Stockholm.

Switzerland
Heinzpeter Studer, Engelgasse 12a, CH9000 St. Gallen.

Tanzania
Tanzania Environmental Society, PO Box 1309, Dar er Salaam.

United Kingdom
Friends of the Earth, 26–28 Underwood Street, London N1 7JQ. *Telephone.* 071 490 1555.

United States
Friends of the Earth, 218 D Street, SE, Washington, DC 20003. *Telephone.* 202 544 2600. *Fax.* 202 543 4710. *Telex.* 62949875ESL.

Uruguay
Ruben Perdomo, Millan 4115 cc 15229, Montevideo.

Affiliates:
International Rivers Network, 300 Broadway, Suite 28, San Francisco, CA 94133 USA.

Rainforest Information Centre, PO Box 368, Lismore 2480, Australia.

Rainforest Action Network, 301 Broadway, Suite A, San Francisco CA 94133, USA.

Werkgroep Noordzee Foundation, Vossinstraat 20–111, 1071 AD Amsterdam, The Netherlands.

Greenpeace International

Address. Keizersgracht 176, 1016 W Amsterdam, The Netherlands

The movement was founded in North America in 1971. It is an international, independent environmental pressure group which acts against abuse to the natural world. It has offices in 20 countries and a worldwide membership of over 3,000,000 supporters.

Greenpeace tackles the threat to wildlife from direct killing, pollution and habitat loss and the first action was a protest voyage into the nuclear test site at Amchitka in the Aleutian Islands. The testing was cancelled a year later and the island is now a bird sanctuary. It continues to face the major dangers caused by the production and release into the environment of radioactive material and the threat of nuclear war. It acts against the disposal of toxic wastes into rivers and seas and the release of pollutants into the atmosphere. Greenpeace campaigns are uncompromising and based upon what is best for the environment to protect it from harmful human interference. They specialize in non-violent, direct action protests and claim a number of spectacular successes over the years.

Its present campaigns are concerned with, among others, the following topics:

air pollution—acid rain, ozone depletion, greenhouse effect;
wildlife—commercial whaling, seal culling, dolphin kills;
preservation of Antarctica;
nuclear—power, reprocessing waste;
disarmament—nuclear testing, weapons at sea;
toxic pollution;
river and sea pollution; and
the waste trade.

A magazine *Greenpeace News* is published along with campaign briefings and occasional campaign reports. The organization is financed by voluntary contributions from the public and members and from the sale of merchandise.

There are now Greenpeace organizations in many countries, for example:

Greenpeace Australia, Private Bag 6, 134 Broadway, Sydney NSW 2007.
Greenpeace Austria, Mariahilfer Gurtel 32, A-1060 Vienna.
Greenpeace Belgium, Waversesteenweg 335, B-1040 Brussels. *Telephone.* 02 512 30 10.
Greenpeace Canada, 578 Bloor Street West, Toronto M6G 1K1.
Greenpeace Costa Rica, Apartado 230, Centro Colon, San José.
Greenpeace Denmark, Thomas Laubsgade 11–13, DK-2100 Copenhagen 0.
Greenpeace Germany, Vorsetzen 53, D–2000 Hamburg 11.
Greenpeace Ireland, 29 Lower Baggot Street, Dublin 2.
Greenpeace Italy, 28 Viale Manlio Gelsomini, I-00153 Rome.
Greenpeace Luxembourg, B.P. 229, L-4003 Esch/Alzette.
Greenpeace Netherlands, Damrak 83, NL-1012 LN Amsterdam.
Greenpeace New Zealand, Private Bag, Wellesley Street, Auckland, and also at 240 Hobson Street, Auckland. *Telephone.* 9 776 128 *Fax.* 9 3032676.
Greenpeace Norway, St Olavsgt. 11, Postboks 6803, St Olavs Plass, N-0130 Oslo 1.
Greenpeace Spain, Rodriguez San Pedro 58, 4 piso, E-28015 Madrid.
Greenpeace Sweden, Box 7183, S-402 34 Gothenburg.
Greenpeace Switzerland, Mullerstrasse 37, Postfach 4927, CH-8022 Zurich.
Greenpeace UK Ltd. 30–31 Islington Green, London N1 8XE. *Telephone.* 071 354 5100. *Fax.* 071 359 4062. *Telex.* 25245 GPEACE G.
Greenpeace USA, 1611 Connecticut Avenue, NW, Washington, DC 20009.

Group of Experts on Scientific Aspects of Marine Pollution (GESAMP)

Telephone. 071 735 7611 *Fax.* 071 587 3210
Address. c/o International Maritime Organization, 4 Albert Embankment, London SE1 7SR, UK
Officials. Professor H. L. Windom (Chairman); D. Calamari (Vice-Chairman)

GESAMP was formed in 1969 to serve as a mechanism for encouraging co-ordination, collaboration and harmonization of activities related to marine pollution of common interest to the sponsoring bodies. These bodies, initially, were four:

Inter-governmental Maritime Consultative Organization (now International Maritime Organization—IMO);
Food and Agricultural Organization (FAO);
UN Educational, Scientific and Cultural Organization (UNESCO);
World Meteorological Organization (WMO);

but were subsequently joined by four others:

World Health Organization (WHO),
International Atomic Energy Agency (IAEA),
United Nations (UN),
United Nations Environment Programme (UNEP).

GESAMP is a multi-disciplinary body of independent experts whose terms of reference are (a) to provide advice relating to scientific aspects of marine pollution:

(i) to the sponsoring organizations and to the Intergovernmental Oceanographic Commission (IOC) on specific questions referred to it;
(ii) to the other organizations of the UN system and to member states of the UN organizations on particular problems referred to it through the sponsoring organization; and
(iii) to the executive heads of one or more of the sponsoring organizations on such other specific questions within its competence;

and (b) to prepare periodic reviews of the state of the marine environment as regards marine pollution and to identify problem areas requiring special attention.

Its secretariat consists of an administration secretary supported by eight technical secretaries, one from each of the sponsoring organizations.

Over 30 GESAMP working groups have been formed to consider and report on items of concern, usually to its annual meeting. In this way it has minimized the duplication of effort of UN agencies seeking information of matters of marine pollution. It expects this work to continue.

GESAMP has published nearly 40 reports on subjects such as the evaluation of natural transport pathways of contaminants, including thermal discharges, and the biological effects of marine pollution and has organized studies, for example, of pollution dispersion models.

Further details are available in a booklet, to be published by GESAMP in late 1990, entitled *Two Decades of Accomplishments*.

Institute for Resource Management (IRM)

Telephone. 801 322 0530 *Fax.* 801 328 3457
Address. 19, Exchange Place, Salt Lake City, Utah 84111, USA
Officials. Robert Redford (Founder/Chairman); Howard Allen (Chairman); Terrell J. Minger (President and CEO); Paul Parker (Vice-President); Robert E. Gipson (Secretary/Treasurer)

The Institute was founded in 1981 to provide a catalyst for local, national and international environmental problem solving. It provides a forum where leaders of industry, science, government and the environmental community can discuss areas of conflict and find solutions to defined problems. It encourages involvement on a local and international level so that the public may be informed about environmental choices that they make, thereby creating a constituency for political and corporate action.

The underlying objective of the Institute is to improve both the skills of decision makers and the decision making process by: (a) providing new opportunities for communication and collaborative problem solving. It will stimulate action in those areas of consensus and promote dialogue and understanding in areas of conflict and disagreement; and (b) providing information concerning natural resource issues to the general public and those responsible for the development of public policy. Through the media, films and publications, the Institute hopes to initiate new approaches to current problems and identify emerging resource issues.

It is currently involved in the "Southern California Clean Air Project", in the US–USSR research and demonstration project to "Assess the Impacts on Northern Forests" and in the US–USSR "International Education Curriculum for Global Warming" and a variety of consulting services.

It has published "Search for Common Ground" in the Harvard Business Review (May–June 1987) and "Greenhouse/Glasnost: The climate change" is in preparation.

The IRM's programmes have been financed by donations from participating industries and the continuing support of foundations committed to finding new approaches to sustainable development. Its annual expenditure is US$860,000 and it is sponsored by a Board of Trustees.

International Association for Ecology (INTECOL)

Telephone. 1 404 542 2968
Address. c/o Institute of Ecology, University of Georgia, Athens, GA 20602, USA

Established in 1967 as the International Organization of Professional Ecologists to foster international communication between ecologists and to represent professional scientific ecology to intergovernmental bodies such as UNEP, UNESCO and the World Bank. It has individual members but is mainly an umbrella organization for over 30 national and regional societies and seven international societies concerned with various disciplines of ecology.

The Association has working groups concerned with: agroecology; aquatic primary productivity; ecological futures; evolutionary ecology of mammals, granivorous birds; physiological ecology; plankton ecology; tropical ecology; urban ecology and wetlands.

It arranges conferences and workshops and publishes INTECOL Newsletter, bimonthly and various bulletins, books and reports.

International Association on Water Pollution Research and Control (IAWPRC)

Telephone. 071 222 3848 *Fax.* 071 233 1197
Address. 1 Queen Anne's Gate, London SW1H 9BT, UK
Officials. Prof. P. Harremoes (Denmark) (President); Prof. P. Grau (Czechoslovakia); Dr S. A. S. Almeida (Brazil) (Vice-Presidents); A. Milburn (Executive Director)

The Association developed out of the international conferences on Water Pollution Research held in London in 1962 and in Tokyo in 1964. It was formally established in June 1965 as an independent, non-profit, non-governmental organization and registered in the UK as a charity. It now has 2,600 members, including scientists, engineers, managers and administrators, from the water pollution control industry. Corporate membership covers consultants, manufacturers, research institutes and water utilities and national members are affiliated through existing national bodies.

The Association organizes a biennial conference and exhibition as the major meeting for its members and committees. Up to 20 regional and specialised conferences are held each year in various parts of the world.

It publishes two journals—*Water Research* and *Waste Science and Technology*, a magazine *Water Quality International* and scientific and technical reports. The *IAWPRC Yearbook* gives full details of its activities, its membership and committee listings.

Its annual budget is £500,000 which is met by membership subscriptions and from the sale of publications.

International Centre for Conservation Education (ICCE)

Telephone. 04515 777/549 *Fax.* 04515 705
Address. Greenfield House, Guiting Power, Glos. GL54 5TZ, UK
Officials. Mark Boulton (Director); Prof. Charles Taylor; Prof. John Smith; Lady Medawar; Mark Gibbs; John Lewis; John West; Mrs P. Koechlin-Smythe (Advisory Council)

ICCE aims to promote greater understanding of conservation and the environment and stresses the importance of sustainable development. It offers consultancy and advisory services on all aspects of preparation and management of national conservation education programmes; provides specialized training for conservation educators; produces audio-visual programmes for use by schools and conservation bodies on major and current educational topics (the catalogue is available free of charge); administers an environmental photolibrary.

The consultancy services provide education, information and interpretation, especially for those in the developing countries, with a broad overview coupled with practical proposals based on field experience and specialized technical knowledge. Training, too, is directed at those educators working in developing countries, including Uganda, Zambia, Swaziland, Kenya, Senegal, The Philippines, Nigeria and Egypt. It has produced a series of audio-visual resource packs for secondary schools on behalf of the Association for Science Education.

The Centre is financed primarily through the activities of its subsidiary trading company Conservation Education Services Ltd (CES Ltd), but has in the past received some funding from the World Wide Fund for Nature in addition to grants and donations, particularly from trusts. Its income in 1988 was about £223,000.

International Center for the Solution of Environmental Problems (ICSEP)

Telephone. 713 527 8711 *Fax.* 713 527 8025
Address. 535 Lovett Boulevard, Houston, Texas 77006, USA
Officials. Dr Joseph L. Goldman (Technical Director)

ICSEP grew out of common ideas shared by six persons attending the NATO conference in 1973 on Technology Transfer and the 1974 Tropical Meteorology Conference. It was established in 1975 as a non-profit organization, centred in Houston but worldwide in scope. It has more than 20 affiliated scientists, engineers, economists and other professionals from all over the world.

The Centre conducts research and projects for city planners, land developers, engineering and architectural firms, the petroleum and chemical industries, the construction industry and government agencies. A great proportion of the work deals with weather-related agricultural problems, including the relationship of weather and agriculture to the increasing urbanization of the planet.

Its income varies and comes mainly from clients.

International Chamber of Commerce (ICC)

Telephone. 33 1 45 62 34 56 *Fax.* 33 1 42 25 86 63 *Telex.* 650 770
Address. 38 Cours Albert 1er F-75008 Paris, France
Officials. Peter Wallenburg (Sweden) (President); Joseph E. Connor (USA) (Vice-President); Hugh Faulkner (Canada) (Secretary-General); Nigel Blackburn (Director)

The ICC is a non-governmental organization serving world business. It has members in 110 countries which cover many business organizations including many internationals. There are national committees or councils in 58 countries.

It set up in 1978 a Commission on the Environment (present chairman: Helmut Sihler) to promulgate sound environmental policies for industry and to encourage and help their input to national and international projects and organizations. The Commission provides the means for businessmen to meet and discuss and exchange views and information on current environmental issues and developments. It represents business interests with UNEP and other international agencies concerned with environmental issues. It formulates positions and possible policies on issues, particularly on technical matters.

It organized (with UNEP) the World Industry Conference on Environmental Management (WICEM) in 1984 which was attended by over 500 participants from 70 countries. Plans are well advanced for WICEM II to take place in Rotterdam from 10–12 April 1991. The programme for this envisages seven major topics for working sessions on: (a) making market forces work to improve the environment; (b) how can we ensure that the expansion of world trade is a positive factor for the environment?; (c) which business sectors will thrive under the sustainable development ethic, and what can be done about the declining sectors?; (d) tools of environmental management; (e) improving the environmental credibility of industry; (f) prospects and limits of new technologies and more widespread diffusion of existing environmentally sound technology and (g) redefining the industrial role in solving environmental problems.

It publishes *Environmental Factsheets*, guidelines, updates and many pamphlets. It participates, on behalf of industry and business, at many gatherings, conferences and exhibitions. It issued ICC Environmental Guidelines for World Industry, first in 1974 and revised in 1981, 1986 and 1990. It is published in English, French, Dutch, German, Portuguese and Spanish.

The ICC also includes the International Environment Bureau (*vide infra*).

The UK Council is based at Centre Point, 103 New Oxford Street, London WC1A 1QB. *Telephone.* 071 240 5558 *Fax.* 071 836 5223 *Telex.* 21332

International Council for the Exploration of the Sea (ICES)
(Conseil International pour l'Exploration de la Mer—CEIM)

Telephone. 33 15 42 25 *Fax.* 33 93 42 15 *Telex.* 22498 ices dk
Address. Palaegade 2–4, DK-1261 Copenhagen K, Denmark
Officials. Jakob Jakobsson (Iceland) (President); Dr Emory D. Anderson (Ireland) (General Secretary)

The Council was founded in Copenhagen in 1902 by Denmark, Finland, Germany, The Netherlands, Norway, Sweden, Russia and the United Kingdom, whose contract establishing ICES was renewed every five years. This was replaced in July 1968 by the 1964 Convention for the International Council for the Exploration of the Sea with membership open to any state upon approval by three-quarters of the member states. It now has 18 member countries, the additions being Belgium, Canada, France, the GDR and the FRG separately, Iceland, Ireland, Poland, Portugal, Spain and the United States of America.

It exists to promote and co-ordinate international investigations of the marine environment and its living resources in the North Atlantic and adjacent seas and to publish or otherwise disseminate the results of this research, including the provision of scientific information and advice to national governments and fishery management and pollution control commissions.

It has various advisory and consultative committees including one on fishery management (ACFM), on marine pollution (ACMP) established in 1972 and sub-committees on hydrography, marine environmental quality, biological oceanography and on demersal, pelagic and Baltic fish. It is also concerned with work on fish capture, detection and searching techniques, design and operation of fishing gear, mariculture including investigations relating to the culture of marine organisms, transplantation and the introduction of new species, shellfish, anadromous and catadromous fish and marine mammals. It promotes and co-ordinates research in the fields of fisheries, oceanography and marine pollution in member countries by means of these subject and area committees and about 75 working or study groups on specific problems. It co-sponsors, with the Oslo and Paris Commissions, the North Sea Task Force.

The Council publishes the ICES journal of marine science *Journal du Conseil, Rapports et Procès-Verbaux des Réunions* and co-operative research reports, *Bulletin Statistique*, oceanographic data lists and inventories, plankton identification leaflets, fish and shellfish disease identification leaflets, techniques in marine environmental sciences, abstracts and the ICES/CIEM newsletter.

Its annual budget is DKr 13 million, met by member countries (80%) and by contributions from organizations with which the Council works.

International Council of Scientific Unions (ICSU)

Telephone. 33 1 4525 0329 *Fax.* 33 1 4288 9431 *Telex.* 630553 F
Address. 51 Boulevard de Montmorency, 75016 Paris, France
Officials. Prof. M. G. K. Menon (India) (President); Prof. W. E. Gordon (USA) (Vice-President); Prof. Sir John Kendrew (UK) (past President); Prof. J. W. M. La Rivière (Netherlands) (Secretary-General); Prof. K. Thurau (FRG) (Treasurer); Mrs J. Marton-Lefevre (Executive Secretary); M. T. L. Millward (Assistant Executive Secretary)

The Council was founded in 1931 as an international non-profit organization and successor to the International Research Council. Its members now consist of 20 international scientific unions, 76 national and 26 scientific associates. It exists to promote international scientific activity in the different branches of science and their applications for the benefit of humanity and to address, through the diversity of its membership, international interdisciplinary issues. Through its membership it is in touch with hundreds of thousands of scientists world-wide and is increasingly being called upon to act as spokesman for the world scientific community and as an adviser in matters ranging from ethics to the environment.

It co-ordinates major international interdisciplinary research programmes such as the international geosphere–biosphere programme and the world climate research programme. In the past it initiated the International Geophysical Year (1957–8) and the International Biological Programme (1964–74). It organizes interdisciplinary committees on biotechnology, genetics, antarctic research, problems of the environment, data, space research etc. and provides a means for discussing common concerns and services to members in such fields as the free circulation of scientists, ethics, the teaching of science and the use of science and technology for development.

The Council acts as a focus for the exchange of ideas, the communication of scientific information and the development of scientific standards. Scientific conferences, congresses and symposia are organized all round the world—the total in excess of 600 a year, and a wide range of newsletters, handbooks, learned journals and proceedings of meetings is published. It publishes a comprehensive *Year Book* and the quarterly newsletter—*Science International*.

The Council maintains close working relations with a number of intergovernmental and non-governmental organizations, in particular with UNESCO, in co-operation with which a number of international programmes have been launched and are being run, and with WMO.

The annual budget is US$15,000,000 which money is raised from membership dues, grants, foundations and support from UNESCO and other UN organizations.

International Energy Agency (IEA)

Telephone. 45 24 94 40 *Fax.* 45 24 99 88 *Telex.* 630 190
Address. 2 rue André Pascal, 75775 Cedex, Paris 16, France
Officials. Mrs Helga Stecy (Executive Director); John F. Ferriter (Deputy Executive Director)

The IEA, founded in 1974 as an autonomous body within the OECD, is the energy forum for 21 countries. Its objective is to maintain and improve the energy security of its member countries by: (a) maintaining co-operative systems for coping with oil supply disruptions; (b) strengthening the world's energy supply and demand structure by increasing the efficiency of energy use, diversifying energy supply sources and developing alternative energy sources; (c) assisting the integration of environmental and energy policies; (d) encouraging international collaboration in energy research and development; (e) operating an information system on the international oil market and other sources of energy; and (f) sharing energy expertise and experience with non-member countries and international organizations.

International Environmental Bureau (IEB)

Telephone. 22 786 5111 *Fax.* 22 736 0336
Address. 61 Route de Chene, 1208 Geneva, Switzerland
Officials. D. M. Roderick (Chairman); W. K. Wenger (Executive Director); A. E. Fry (Director)

The Bureau was founded in May 1986 as a specialist division of the International Chamber of Commerce. Its annual budget is US$500,000 and some 30 US and European corporations form its membership.

It publishes a bimonthly newsletter and reports and supplies information, mainly relating to industrial matters, on request to companies, governmental agencies and others.

International Institute for Environment and Development (IIED)

Telephone. 071 388 2117 *Fax.* 071 388 2826 *Telex.* 261681 EASCAN G

Address. 3 Endsleigh Street, London WC1H ODD, UK
Officials. Richard Sandbrook (Executive Director)

The Institute assists and advises governmental and private organizations concerned with the links between environment and development. It is concerned to promote the wise use of natural resources through sustainable development, particularly in the Third World.

It was formed in 1971 by Barbara Ward, Maurice Strong and Robert O. Anderson as a platform for persuading governments, the multilateral agencies and the NGOs of the nature of sustainable development and the critical importance of rigorous research in its pursuit. During the last 20 years it has established itself as a leading non-governmental organization devoted to understanding and coping with environmental problems of the late 20th century. From its inception the Institute has recognized that, almost without exception, these problems are common to the entire planet and supersede political boundaries.

The Institute's policy researchers specialize in such areas as sustainable agriculture, tropical forestry, Third World housing issues and environmental economics. IIED advises decision makers and aims to raise public awareness of these crucial issues through research, information and publishing.

The Institute is seeking economically sound means by which people may be protected from the worst effects of acid rain, global warming, sea-level rise and ozone depletion. Recent projects have dealt with forestry and land use, particularly in working through the international agents, the International Tropical Timber Organization (ITTO) which, in its membership, covers 95% of the trade, and the Tropical Forest Action Plan (TFAP), the initiative of the FAO and the World Resources Institute. It is also concerned with energy from trees, still the main source of fuel for much of the developing world.

The Institute has trained many people in agricultural development, again particularly for the LDCs, where many are still short of food. Its Sustainable Agricultural Programme has, in the last year, conducted workshops in the UK, USA, Sweden, Norway, the Netherlands and Switzerland and carried out fieldwork in countries such as the Sudan and Zimbabwe, often in collaboration with other organizations such as the Aga Khan Rural Support Programme in India.

Africa's drylands, home to millions of people, are being studied in several programmes, funded by UNEP, the Norwegian Ministry of Development Co-operation and Band Aid.

The Institute's Human Settlements Programme is concerned with urban problems and poverty in the Third World, particularly through IIED-America Latina in South America.

It has established, in a joint venture with University College, London, the London Environmental Economics Centre (LEEC) to demonstrate that conservation can be in the financial interests of a nation. Marine resources have been studied by the Renewable Resources Assessment Group (RRAG) based at Imperial College in London.

A recent successful and prominent activity has been in publishing through the Institute's subsidiary Earthscan Publications Ltd. with many new titles, related to environmental topics and concerns.

The Institute's European office also publishes regularly a bulletin—*Perspectives*—and the Human Settlements Programme has recently launched a new journal called *Environment and Urbanisation* which aims to provide for Third World researchers, teachers, activists and professionals a journal in which to write about their work and present ideas, to debate issues and to inform others. The Drylands Programme publishes a quarterly bulletin—*Haramata*—in which reports, in recent issues, have covered new ways to control locusts, helping Sahelian countries to monitor changes in their pasture resources by low cost means and suggestions from Sahelian NGOs as to ways to strengthen their own competence and organization.

The Institute is financially supported by governments and their agencies, international agencies, foundations and corporations. In the year it receives grants and contributions totalling some £2,300,000.

Other centres are:

IIED America Latina
Piso 6, Cuerpo A, Avenue Corrientes 2835, (1193) Buenos Aires, Argentina.
Telephone. (1) 961 3050.

WRI/CIDE
7th Floor, 1709 New York Avenue NW, Washington DC, 20006, USA. *Telephone.* (202) 638 6300.

International Maritime Organization (IMO)
Telephone. 071 735 7611 *Fax.* 071 587 3210 *Telex.* 23588
Address. 4 Albert Embankment, London SE1 7SR, UK
Officials. W. A. O'Neil (Canada) (Secretary-General)

The Convention establishing the Organization was adopted on March 6, 1948 by the UN Maritime Conference. The Convention, then known as the Convention on the Inter-Governmental Maritime Consultative Organization, entered into force on March 17, 1958 and the new Organization (IMCO) was inaugurated on Jan. 6, 1959. The name was changed to the International Maritime Organization on May 22, 1982. It is concerned with: (a) safety at sea; (b) prevention of pollution from ships; and (c) the facilitation of maritime transport.

The Organization has 134 Member States who meet biennially as the Assembly, its governing body. It approves the work programme and budget and elects a Council, composed of 32 member states, to act as the executive organ of IMO. There are four main committees consisting of all member States. The highest technical body of the Organization is the Maritime Safety Committee which has 10 sub-committees dealing with different aspects of safety such as the carriage of dangerous goods, fire protection, training etc. The Legal Committee was set up after the Torrey Canyon disaster in 1967. The Marine Environment Protection Committee is concerned with the prevention and control of pollution from ships, and the Technical Co-operation Committee acts as the executing or co-operating agency in the technical field. Its programme, which is designed to help governments implement the requirements of IMO conventions and other instruments, included some 80 projects. The largest (in 1988) was the World Maritime University with a total budget for the year of US$5,400,000.

The IMO has concluded agreements of co-operation with 32 intergovernmental organizations and there are 44 non-governmental organizations in consultative status with IMO.

The IMO has drawn up and promoted the adoption of 29 conventions and protocols which are binding legal instruments and, upon entry into force, their requirements must be implemented by all States which are party to it. In addition the IMO also adopts numerous non-treaty instruments such as codes and recommendations which, although not mandatory, members are expected to implement their provisions.

It publishes many books, proceedings, conventions, pamphlets codes etc. (a catalogue is available from the above address).

The IMO is financed by member states and its annual budget amounts to about £12,000,000.

International Petroleum Industry Environmental Conservation Association (IPIECA)

Telephone. 071 248 3447/8 *Fax.* 071 489 9067

Address. 1, College Hill, London EC4R 2RA, UK
Officials. Dr D. F. Rijkels (Chairman); John S. Lemlin (Executive Secretary)

IPIECA was formed in 1974, following the creation of UNEP after the 1972 UN Conference on the Human Environment at Stockholm, by BP, Esso (now Exxon), Mobil and Shell to be the point of contact between the international petroleum industry and that new organization. It now has 28 members, including companies and national or international technical associations, and provides the accepted focus for the development of oil industry opinions on global environmental issues; an acknowledged important source of international consensus on the defined key global environmental issues; and a recognized, competent participant in the discussions of environmental sciences and their communication to international centres of opinion.

At present it is concerned with global climate change; oil spill response; environmental health, waste minimization; and environmental communications.

It has published *Management of Oil Spill Response* and *Organizations for Environmental Management of the Petroleum Industry*.

It is funded by a levy on members and has an annual budget of about £250,000.

International Professional Association for Environmental Affairs (IPRE)

Telephone. 2 513 60 85 *Fax.* 2 514 33 86

Address. 31, rue Montoyer, Boîte 1, B-1040 Bruxelles, Belgium
Officials. W. J. Cairns (President); Dr J. S. Harding (Vice-President/Treasurer); Dr R. E. van Essche (Vice-President/General Secretary)

IPRE was established in Brussels in May 1976 under the name of "International Association of Environmental Co-ordinators". To reflect more accurately the role of the Association, the name was changed in 1982 to the present one. It has 175 members drawn from all countries of Western Europe and from other continents.

Its objectives are: (a) to organize gatherings during which important environmental problems can be discussed in the broadest possible way; (b) to bring together people who devote a significant part of their working time to environmental problems; and (c) by organizing these meetings and by the publication of the proceedings, to contribute to an awareness of the complexity of environmental problems and to contribute to a balanced and unemotional solution to these problems.

A symposium on "The Integration of Environmental Control Policy into Strategic Corporate Management" was held in Brussels in April 1990 and another meeting is planned in October in the Federal Republic of Germany.

It has published the proceedings of 31 symposia and issues a Newsletter to members.

Its costs are met by membership fees.

International Society of Tropical Foresters (ISTF)

Telephone. 301 897 8720 *Fax.* 301 897 3690

Address. 5400 Grosvenor Lane, Bethesda, MD 20814, USA
Officials. Warren T. Doolittle (President); Frederick Owino (Vice President and regional director for Africa); Khubchand Tejwani (Secretary and regional director for Asia); Ronnie de Camino V (Regional director for Latin America); Bjorn Lundgren (Treasurer and director at large); S. Dennis Richardson; Jeffrey Burley (Directors at large).

Honorary vice-presidents have been appointed in more than 60 countries.

The Society was formed in 1950 and now has about 2,000 members in 116 countries.

Its aims include the transfer of technology and science to those persons and organizations concerned with the management, protection and wise use of tropical forests.

It holds conferences, workshops and symposia, run in co-operation with other organizations. It is concerned to promote the establishment of country and regional chapters.

It publishes a quarterly *ISTF News* and a Spanish edition *ISTF Noticias* and works closely with the Society of American Foresters and the US Department of Agriculture-Forest Service.

Its annual budget of about US$30,000 is met by membership dues, contributions and grants.

International Solar Energy Society (ISES)

Telephone. 61 3 571 7557 *Fax.* 61 3 563 5173 *Telex.* AA154087 CITVIC
Address. PO Box 124, Caulfield East, Victoria 3145, Australia
Officials. D. Lorriman (Canada) (President); W. Read (Australia) (Secretary/Treasurer); P. Bilston (Administrative Secretary)

The ISES is a worldwide, non-profit organization dedicated to: (a) the advancement of the utilization of solar energy; (b) fostering science and technology relating to the applications of solar energy; (c) encouraging research and development; (d) promoting education; and (e) gathering, compiling and disseminating information in these fields.

It was founded in Phoenix, Arizona, USA in December 1954 and now has nearly 4,000 members whose subscriptions provide its source of funds.

It holds an international biennial congress and publishes, monthly, *Solar Energy Journal* and, quarterly, *Sunworld Magazine* and a newsletter. The national sections hold many specialized conferences and publish the proceedings. Recent UK meetings have covered:

> Energy Policy and the Environment (C56) in 1989 which explores the policy options and the technologies available to the UK over the next few years to allow the energy services needed by society to be provided at the least financial and environmental cost. Regional, national and international options are covered and the role of independent power producers in the UK energy supply.
>
> Housing for the Elderly: Energy and Comfort (C55) in 1989, emphasising the importance of energy savings in buildings with the growing demand for elderly people and the escalating concern with the environment.
>
> Daylighting Buildings (C54) in 1989 dealt with energy savings, solar gains and the optimization of systems.
>
> Solar Electricity for Development (C53) in 1989 gave the current status, recent advances and future prospects of photovoltaic systems in developing countries. This included rural electrification, water supply, health care and food production.
>
> Low Head Hydro-Electricity (C52) in 1988.
>
> Solar Optical Materials (C51) in 1988.
>
> Biomass for Energy and Chemicals in Europe: Industry and Agriculture (C50) in 1987,

and many others, available, with a catalogue, from the UK address: UK – ISES, King's College, Kensington, Atkins Building South (128), Campden Hill Road, London W8 7AH. *Telephone.* 071 938 2919.

International Tanker Owners Pollution Federation Ltd. (ITOPF)

Telephone. 071 621 1255 or (24 hrs) 042 691 4112 *Fax.* 071 621 1783 or 071 626 5913 *Telex.* 887514 TOVALOP G
Address. Staple Hall, Stonehouse Court, 87–90 Houndsditch, London EC3A 7AX, UK
Officials. Peter John Goulandris (Chairman); Dr Ian C. White (Managing Director)

ITOPF was established in 1968 as a non-profit making service organization for the principal purpose of administering the Tanker Owners Voluntary Agreement concerning Liability for Oil Pollution (TOVALOP) and its companion voluntary industry agreement CRISTAL (Contract Regarding a Supplement to Tanker Liability for Oil Pollution). These were set up as a result of the determination of tanker and oil industries, respectively, after the Torrey Canyon incident in 1967, to take constructive action both to encourage prompt and effective clean-up and to assure adequate and timely compensation to those affected by spills.

The Federation also gives great emphasis to the provision of technical services in the fields of: response to oil spills; damage assessment and analysis of claims; contingency planning and advisory work; and training and information.

During the past 10 years the Federation's staff have attended some 150 incidents around the world. It publishes a number of booklets and technical information papers and a newsletter and training videos.

Its turnover (1990–91) is about £950,000 met from dues based upon members registered tanker tonnage. These are set for 1990–91 at 0.5 of a UK penny per grt and this applies to some 6,200 ships.

International Tropical Timber Organization (ITTO)

Telephone. 81 45 671 7045 *Fax.* 81 45 671 7007 *Telex.* 3822480 itto j
Address. Sangyo Boeki Centre Building, 2 Yamashita-cho, Naka-ku, Yokohama 231, Japan

The Organization was founded in 1985 and is controlled by the International Tropical Timber Council (ITTC) which meets annually. Its members are the governments of 41 countries. It provides a framework for co-operation and consultation between tropical timber producing and consuming countries.

It also promotes research and development in forest management and wood use and encourages development of national policies aimed at sustainable utilization of tropical forests and their genetic resources.

International Union of Air Pollution Prevention Associations (IUAPPA)

Telephone. 0273 26313 *Fax.* 0273 735802
Address. 136 North Street, Brighton BN1 1RG, UK
Officials. Air Commodore John Langston (Director-General)

The Union was formed in 1964 and now has 28 members and observers representing 30 countries.

It aims to promote public education, worldwide, in all matters relating to the value and importance of clean air and methods and consequences of air pollution control. This is achieved by: (a) convening World Congresses on air quality every three years; (b) exchanging information about air pollution legislation and control techniques; (c) using uniform terminology; (d) encouraging the use of uniform monitoring and measuring methods; and (e) liaising with other national and international scientific, technical and control organizations.

The Union publishes a newsletter, a *Members' Handbook,* the *World Congress Proceedings* and *Clean-Air around the World-Air Pollution Control in 14 Countries.* It maintains contacts with the UN and OECD, the EEC, UITA and representatives of ministers, local government, professional bodies and industry in many countries.

IUAPPA is funded by annual subscriptions from members (other non-contributing affiliates have the status of observers).

International Waterfowl and Wetlands Research Bureau (IWRB)
Telephone. 0453 840634 *Fax.* 0453 890827 *Telex.* 437145 WWFG

Address. Slimbridge, Gloucester GL2 7BX, UK
Officials. Dr James H. Patterson (President); Dr Michael E. Moser (Director)

The Bureau was founded in 1954 as an independent non-governmental organization. It is governed by an Executive Board which comprises delegates from almost 40 member countries and co-ordinators of 17 Research Groups.

The goal of the IWRB is to contribute to the conservation of migratory waterfowl and their wetlands habitats through the stimulation of international co-operation in the fields of monitoring, research and conservation action. The detailed objectives are achieved through catalytic activities including the co-ordination of international monitoring programmes and research projects, the organizing of symposia, workshops and training courses, and the production and dissemination of publications. It also played an instrumental role in the creation of the Ramsar Convention (see Part III) and hosts a section of the Ramsar Bureau to which it provides technical support.

It is organized in three divisions;

Waterfowl, which co-ordinates studies of the status and trends of waterfowl populations worldwide and promotes research into their ecological requirements and population dynamics;

Wetland, which aims to promote the conservation of wetlands through activities including monitoring the status of wetlands; researching the functions, values and management of wetlands; holding on-site wetland workshops and training courses to promote awareness and activity among staff of national conservation agencies; urging governments to safeguard threatened wetlands; organizing workshops, conferences and publications that will further co-ordinate wetland research and conservation activities; and

Finance and Administration, to provide efficient and cost-effective support and to handle information and publicity matters.

The Bureau collaborates closely with other international and national organizations involved in wetland and waterfowl conservation, notably the Bureau of the Ramsar Convention, the Asian Wetland Bureau, IUCN, WWF and others.

It publishes a regular *IWRB* News, a number of books on specific topics and areas and some posters (details are available from the above address).

The Bureau has an annual expenditure of £200,000 met by member countries and contributor organizations.

International Whaling Commission (IWC)

Telephone. 0223 233971 *Fax.* 0223 232876
Address. The Red House, Station Road, Histon, Cambridge CB4 4NP, UK
Officials. S. Irberger (Sweden) (Chairman); Dr L. A. Fleischer (Mexico) (Vice-Chairman); Dr R. Gambell (Secretary)

The IWC was set up under the International Convention for the Regulation of Whaling signed in Washington, DC in December 1946. This Convention was concluded in order to provide for the proper conservation of whale stocks and thus make possible the orderly development of the whaling industry. Membership is open to any country in the world by formally adhering to the 1946 Convention. At present there are 37 countries in membership (although the Solomon Islands are withdrawing in 1990).

The main duty of the Commission is to keep under review and revise as necessary the measures laid down in the Schedule to the Convention governing the conduct of whaling. These measures (a) provide for the complete protection of certain species of whales; (b) designate specified ocean areas as whale sanctuaries; (c) set the maximum catches on whales which may be taken in one season; (d) prescribe open and closed seasons and areas for whaling; (e) fix size limits above and below which certain species of whales may not be killed; (f) prohibit the capture of suckling calves and female whales accompanied by calves; and (g) require the compilation of catch reports and other statistical and biological records.

The Commission also encourages, co-ordinates and funds research on whales and promotes studies into related matters such as humaneness of the killing operations and the management of aboriginal subsistence whaling. This last category applies to and is permitted from Denmark (Greenland), St Vincent and the Grenadines, the USSR (Siberia) and the USA (Alaska).

The Commission holds an annual meeting, usually in June, and has three committees—Scientific, Technical, Finance and Administration—to assist its work. The Commission decided in 1982 that there should be a pause in commercial whaling from 1985–6 and a comprehensive assessment of the effects of this decision on whale stocks would be undertaken by 1990 when modification of the zero catch limits will be considered. There are major research programmes in hand, including some by member countries, into whale stocks, sampling of whales caught under special permits and sponsorship of a second International Decade of Cetacean Research currently concentrating on sightings surveys of the Antarctic minke whale stocks.

The Commission publishes an Annual Report and special issues, for example bibliographies and specific scientific studies, statistics and regulations.

International Youth Federation for Environmental Studies and Conservation (IYF)

Address. Klostermolle, Klostermollevej 48, DK-8660 Skanderborg, Denmark

The Federation was founded in 1956 under the auspices of the IUCN. It is a federation of regional, national and local youth organizations concerned with the study and conservation of the environment and has some 130 member organizations in 54 countries. It has two regional groups: the Federación Latinoamericana de Jóvenes Ambientalistas, FLAJA (the Latin American Federation of Young Environmentalists) in Panama and Youth and Environment Europe (YEE) in Denmark.

It is interested in environment/development problems and in many topical issues such as tropical forests, pesticides, marine pollution and acid rain.

It has published a number of reports, including an international survey *Youth in Environmental Action in 1987,* booklets and a member magazine.

IUCN—The World Conservation Union (IUCN)

Telephone. 022 64 91 14 *Fax.* 022 64 29 26 *Telex.* 419605 IUCN CH
Address. World Conservation Centre, Avenue du Mont-Blanc, 1196 Gland, Switzerland
Officials. HRH The Duke of Edinburgh (Patron); Dr M. S. Swaminathan (President); Dr Martin W. Holdgate (Director-General)

IUCN is a union of sovereign states, government agencies and non-governmental organizations concerned with the initiation and promotion of scientifically-based action that will ensure the perpetuation of man's natural environment. It is an independent, international organization which has consultative status with ECOSOC and several specialized agencies of the UN. It maintains close working relationships with many inter-governmental organizations, especially UNESCO, FAO and UNEP with which it forms the "Ecosystems Conservation Group". It also maintains close working relations with the World Wide Fund for Nature (WWF). It has 648 members drawn from 119 countries of the world.

Its mission is to provide international leadership for the conservation and management of living resources, and its objectives are to: (a) evaluate the status and trends in usage of renewable natural resources and the policies concerning their management; (b) analyze the obstacles to more effective management of renewable natural resources and to recommend ways and means of overcoming these obstacles; (c) promote action designed to implement more effective conservation of renewable natural resources; (d) generate an increased awareness of the inter relationships between conservation, long-term survival and human well-being; and (e) report to the conservation constituency (IUCN members and the various networks) on the above.

IUCN undertakes seven general activities: (a) it provides advice and expertise to governments, inter-governmental bodies and institutions concerning the conservation of nature and natural resources and advises on national and regional policies of conservation and assists in their execution by establishing co-operative programmes with other international agencies; it manages networks of scientists, conservation organizations and technical experts and uses these networks to formulate policies, strategies and programmes; (b) it manages and publishes information, including gathering, integrating and synthesizing data from a wide variety of sources; (c) it assists conservation institutions to enhance their capacity to manage their resources effectively, within the framework of the "World Conservation Strategy" (see below), and fostering increased efforts to train conservation professionals, field staff and decision-makers; (d) it promotes conservation action through working with members and collaborating with institutions in designing, screening, marketing, implementing and monitoring action-orientated field projects; (e) it provides technical support to conservation treaties, conventions and agreements, including World Heritage, CITES, Wetlands, Migratory Species, Regional Seas, CCAMLR and others; and (f) it promotes research and new techniques relating to the conservation of nature and natural resources and facilitating their application and transfer to the local level.

Its organization includes a General Assembly which meets triennially to determine policy and its broad programme; a Council, elected by the general Assembly, to review, annually, the execution of the programme; the Bureau, elected from Council, to act between meetings; and six Commissions, bodies of volunteer experts including over 3,000 scientists and professionals, covering ecology, environmental education and training, environmental policy, law and administration, national parks and protected areas and species survival.

IUCN regularly publishes reports and other books on important conservation issues. Essential information resulting from IUCN's programme has been published in key source documents such as:

> The *World Conservation Strategy* which is designed to help advance the achievement of sustainable development through the conservation of living resources. It was prepared with the advice, co-operation and financial assistance of UNEP and WWF in collaboration with the FAO and UNESCO. It was launched in March 1980 in over 30 nations and has since been endorsed by numerous world leaders, the UN, many governments (many of whom have responded with their own dependent strategy), and international institutions;
>
> the *Red Data Books* which describe the world's threatened species of mammals, amphibians, reptiles, invertebrates, plants and swallow-tailed butterflies. The first *Red List of Threatened Animals* was published in 1986 and is updated each year;
>
> the *United Nations List of National Parks and Protected Areas* which lists national parks, nature reserves, World Heritage sites and biosphere reserves worldwide;
>
> the IUCN *Bulletin,* the news journal of the Union which keeps members and supporters informed of current activities and other international news.

There are many other publications and a catalogue is available on request.

Apart from membership dues, which constitute the basic source of unrestricted funds, IUCN raises voluntary unrestricted contributions from governments, foundations and the WWF. Programme and project restricted funds are received from governments, UN agencies—particularly UNEP—WWF (which originally was set up to fund IUCN), foundations and the private sector. In 1989 IUCN's overall budget was over SFr 24,000,000.

OECD—Environment Committee (OECD)

Telephone. 45 24 82 00 *Fax.* 45 24 78 76 *Telex.* 620160 F
Address. 2 Rue André Pascal, 75016 Paris, France
Officials. Jean-Claude Paye (OECD Secretary General); Bill Long (Director for the Environment)

The OECD, created in 1960 as a continuation of the OEEC created in 1948 with the aid of the Marshall Plan, is, in the words of its Secretary-General, "not a supranational organization but a place where policy makers can meet and discuss their problems, where governments can compare their points of view and experiences". Member countries number 24 and one other, Yugoslavia, has a special status.

Its Environment Committee was formed in 1970 and has made a number of specific recommendations and decisions on the economic, legal and scientific aspects of environmental management. The well-known "polluter pays principle"—PPP—originated in OECD and has been accepted by all member countries, as has the concept of "prevention is better than cure".

The Committee is: (a) examining common problems related to environmental management and proposing effective means of preventing, minimizing or solving them, taking into account economic and other relevant factors; (b) encouraging the harmonization of environmental policies in member countries; (c) proposing policy options to prevent or minimize conflicts that could arise between member countries in the use of shared environmental resources or as a result of national environmental policies; reviewing, assessing and consulting on environmental measures taken or proposed by member countries; (d) assessing trends in environmental quality and improving the information base for environmental and natural resource management policies; and (e) giving special attention to ways and means by which member countries can contribute to environmental improvement and better management of natural resources in countries outside the OECD region.

The main pillars of the environment programme are economics of sustainable development; energy and environment; technology and environment; environmental health and safety (for example with chemicals); and co-operation with non-OECD countries.

The Environmental Directorate which services the Environmental Committee composed of high level government officials, is only one component of the OECD Secretariat but, due to requests from the highest political levels for greater integration of environmental policies with other sectoral policies, environmental matters are being given increasing attention in other Directorates such as the Economic and Statistics Department, the Development Co-operation, Agriculture and Trade Directorates and the OECD's International Energy Agency, Nuclear Energy Agency and Development Centre. The Environmental Directorate works closely with many other international bodies, particularly those of the UN and the European Community and much of its work, for example on vehicle emissions, has been the basis for Community Directives.

OECD publishes many books, codes, pamphlets etc. There are some 120 new titles each year and many of these relate to environmental topics including specialized subjects and a widely-used periodic assessment of the state of the environment in member countries. (Full details are available from the OECD Publications Service at the above address.)

The OECD is funded by contributions from its 24 member countries.

OECD—Nuclear Energy Agency (OECD/NEA)

Telephone. 33 1 45248200 *Fax.* 33 1 45249624 *Telex.* 630 668 AEN/NEA
Address. 38 Boulevard Suchet, 75016 Paris, France
Official. Dr Kunihiko Uematsu (Director-General)

The OECD Nuclear Energy Agency (NEA) was established in 1957 under the name of the OECD European Nuclear Energy Agency. It received its present designation in April 1972 when Japan became its first non-European full member. Membership today consists of all European member countries of the OECD as well as Australia, Canada, Japan and the United States, totalling 23. The Commission of the European Communities takes part in the work of the Agency.

The primary objective of NEA is to promote co-operation among the governments of its participating countries in furthering the development of nuclear power as a safe, environmentally acceptable and economic energy source. (Nuclear power contributes about 24% to total electricity production in the OECD members and the nuclear capacity at 250GWe represents 16% of generating capacity.)

The current role of the NEA is to: (a) encourage harmonization of national regulatory policies and practices with particular reference to the safety of nuclear installations, protection of man against ionizing radiation, preservation of the environment, radioactive waste management, and nuclear third party liability and insurance; (b) assess the contribution of nuclear power to the overall energy supply by keeping under review the technical and economic aspects of nuclear power growth and forecasting demand and supply for the different phases of the nuclear power cycle; and (c) set up international research and development programmes and joint undertakings.

The Agency organizes technical committees to undertake specialized studies and promotes research projects, particularly relating to waste management and disposal. Many workshops and specialist meetings and symposia are held each year. It works closely with the IAEA and government agencies in member countries.

It publishes an Annual Report and a newsletter, twice a year, and many papers on specific topics related to its role. In 1978 it founded the NEA Data Bank, located in Saclay, France whose role covered the collecting, testing and distribution of computer programmes over the whole range of Agency activities, but for data it was limited to the narrow, though essential and prolific, field of neutronics. Gradually, however it has been able to take on new projects and new forms of co-operation with the nuclear safety and waste management divisions of the Agency.

The Agency is funded by member governments and its budget (in 1988) was FFr 58,000,000.

Programme on Man and the Biosphere (MAB)

Telephone. 45 68 40 68 *Fax.* 45 67 16 90 *Telex.* 204461 Paris
Address. MAB Secretariat, Division of Ecological Sciences, UNESCO, 7, place de Fontenoy, 75700 Paris, France

The MAB programme, formed in 1971, is a nationally based, international programme of research, training, demonstration and information diffusion aimed at providing the scientific basis and the trained personnel needed to deal with problems relative to rational utilization and conservation of resources and resource systems and to human settlements.

It emphasizes research for solving problems. It thus involves research by multi-disciplinary teams on the interactions between ecological and social systems; field training; and the application of a systems approach to understanding the relationships between natural and human components of development and environmental management.

MAB is a decentralized intergovernmental scientific programme with field projects and training activities in over 100 countries.

The MAB national committees are composed of scientists with a diversity of disciplines and now exist in more than 100 of UNESCO's member countries. These, in turn, keep the International Co-ordinating Council, composed of 30 elected member states of UNESCO, and the International Secretariat informed of their programmes and membership.

Originally some 13, later 14 research project areas were identified, but by the late 1970s effort was concentrated on six main areas: coastal areas and islands; humid and sub-humid tropics; arid and semi-arid zones; temperate and cold zones; urban systems; and biosphere reserves. By the mid 1980s the Council considered that it was necessary to establish an independent, expert advisory panel to review the scientific programme. There are now four new research orientations within MAB for the 1990s. These are: ecosystem functioning under different intensities of human impact; management and restoration of human-impacted resources; human investments and resource use; and human response to environmental stress.

MAB is also concerned with Biosphere Reserves. These are protected areas of representative terrestrial and coastal environments which have been internationally recognized under the Programme for their value in conservation and in providing the scientific knowledge, skills and human values to support sustainable development. The reserves should help to strengthen the conservation of biological diversity, genetic resources and ecosystems.

The Programme publishes technical notes and reports and a series of books are being launched. (A catalogue is available in English and French.) The UNESCO in-house quarterly, published in English, French, Spanish, Chinese and Russian, includes the *Bulletin* of MAB.

Scientific Committee on Problems of the Environment (SCOPE)

Telephone. 33 1 45 25 04 98 *Fax.* 33 1 42 88 94 31 *Telex.* 630 553 F ICSU
Address. 51 bd de Montmorency, 75016 Paris, France
Officials. Prof. F. di Castri (France) (President); Academician M. V. Ivanov (USSR), Prof. C. R. Krishna Murti (India) (Vice Presidents); Dr T. E. Lovejoy (USA) (Treasurer); Prof. J. W. B. Stewart (Canada) (Secretary-General)

The Scientific Committee on Problems of the Environment, one of the interdisciplinary scientific committees of the International Council of Scientific Unions (ICSU), is an international non-governmental, non-profit organization established in 1969 with the objectives of: (a) advancing knowledge of the influence of humans on their environment, as well as the effects of these environmental changes upon people, their health and their welfare—with particular attention to those influences and effects which are either global or shared by several nations; and (b) serving as a non-governmental interdisciplinary and international council of scientists as a source of advice for the benefit of governments and intergovernmental and non-governmental bodies with respect to environmental problems.

SCOPE has 35 adhering national bodies and 20 ICSU international bodies (see below).

SCOPE seeks to synthesize environmental information from diverse fields, identifying knowledge gaps and disseminating the results. The main emphasis is currently on the problem areas of: bio-geochemical cycles; ecotoxicology; genetically designed organisms in the environment; subsiding coastal areas; global change; groundwater contamination; and the use of scientific information towards sustainable development.

It is considering the feasibility of further projects concerned with: (a) the potential environmental effect on biological processes, especially on non-human targets, of an increase in UV radiation consequent upon a depletion of the ozone layer; (b) the potential impact on human health of global climate change induced by anthropogenic activities; and (c) the loss of bio-diversity and genetic resources.

It has published over three dozen papers and books in its own series in addition to various collaborative works, particularly with the Man and Biosphere Programme, and with its member committees.

SCOPE's income is derived from member dues, about US$100,000, subventions and grants ($300,000) and from contracts ($300,000). It estimates that services, travel etc. met by its adhering bodies amounts to about another $300,000 per year.

SCOPE adhering bodies are in:

Argentina: Consejo Nacional de Investigaciones Cientificas y Tecnicas, Conicet.
Australia: Australian Academy of Sciences.
Austria: Die Osterreichische Akademie der Wissenschaften.
Belgium: Academie Royale de Belgique/Kononklijke Academie voor Wetenschappen van Belgie.
Bulgaria: Bulgarian Academy of Sciences.
Canada: National Research Council of Canada.
China, Beijing: China Association for Science and Technology.
Taipei: Academia Sinica.
Czechoslovakia: Ceskoslonenske Akademie VED.
Denmark: Ministry of the Environment.
Egypt: Academy of Scientific Research and Technology.
FRG: Deutsche Forschungsgemeinschaft.
Finland: Finnish Academy of Sciences.
France: Académie des Sciences.
GDR: Akademie der Wissenschaften der D.D.R.
Ghana: Ghana Academy of Arts and Sciences.
Hungary: Magyar Tudomanyos Akademia.
India: (Distinguished Scientist Dr T. N. Khoshoo.).
Israel: The Israel Academy of Science and Humanities.
Italy: Consiglio Nazionale delle Ricerche.
Japan: Science Council of Japan.
The Netherlands: Koninklijke Nederlandse Akademie van Wetenschappen.
New Zealand: The Royal Society of New Zealand.
Nigeria: Nigerian Academy of Science.
Norway: Det Norske Videnskaps-Akademi.
Philippines: National Research Council of the Philippines.
Poland: Polska Akademia Nauk.
South Africa: Council for Scientific and Industrial Research.
Spain: Consejo Superior de Investigaciones Científicas.
Sweden: The Royal Swedish Academy of Sciences.
Switzerland: Swiss National Academy of Sciences.
Thailand: National Research Council of Thailand.

USSR: Academy of Sciences of the USSR.
UK: The Royal Society.
USA: National Academy of Sciences—National Research Council.

International bodies adhering to SCOPE: ICSU; COSPAR; COWAR; IAU; IGU; IIASA; INQUA; ISSS; IUB; IUBS; IUGG; IUGS; IUIS; IUPAB; IUPAC; IUPAP; IUPHAR; IUPS; IUTAM; SCAR.

United Nations Environment Programme (UNEP)

Telephone. 254 2 333930 or 254 2 52000 *Fax.* 254 2 520711 *Telex.* 22068 Or 22173 C:UNITERRA
Address. P.O. Box 30552, Nairobi, Kenya
Officials. Dr Mostafa K. Tolba (Executive Director)

UNEP was established in 1972 following the UN Conference on the Human Environment held in Stockholm that year. Its role is to co-ordinate, catalyze and stimulate environmental action, primarily within the UN organization. It works to "identify gaps where nothing or little is being done and to stimulate and catalyze the necessary action; and to pinpoint overlaps in the UN system's efforts to protect and improve the environment and to seek to co-ordinate those efforts both inside and outside the system".

It has specific programmes on: environment and development; environmental awareness; Earthwatch; oceans; water; terrestrial ecosystems; arid and semi-arid lands' ecosystems and desertification control; health and human settlements; the arms race and the environment. Its programme also includes the Global Environment Monitoring Systems (GEMS), which furnishes a rigorous scientific basis for environmental management by providing reliable information from its global monitoring networks, and the Global Resource Information Database (GRID), a major data management arm of GEMS. GEMS also undertakes the Background Air Pollution Monitoring Network (BAPMON), measuring atmospheric carbon dioxide, and other greenhouse gases as well as precipitation chemistry, and the Evaluation of long-range Transmission of Air Pollutants in Europe (EMEP). INFOTERRA, a worldwide network with national focal points in 137 countries, assists organizations and individuals in obtaining technical, scientific and decision-orientated information on the environment.

The United Nations itself has a six-year environment programme 1990–95, details of which are available from UNEP. This programme cuts across the entire UN system and involves many individual agencies in its implementation and covers thirteen areas of concern, each with subdivisions:

atmosphere: composition, processes and pollution: climate and climate change;
water: water resources and freshwater ecosystems; drinking water supplies and sanitation;
terrestrial ecosystems: soils; arid lands and desertification; tropical forest and woodland ecosystems; temperate and cold zone ecosystems; mountain and highland ecosystems; biological diversity and protected areas; microbial resources and related biotechnologies, agricultural lands and agrochemicals;
coastal and island systems: management and rehabilitation;
oceans: regional marine environments; global marine environment; living marine resources;

lithosphere: mineral resources and disaster mitigation;
human settlements and the environment: human settlements planning and management; community preparedness for natural and man-made disasters;
health and welfare: hazards of pollution; environmental aspects of communicable disease; the working environment;
energy, industry and transportation: energy and environment; industry and environment; transportation;
peace, security and environment: environmental impacts and consequences;
environmental assessment: scientific and technical information for environmental impact assessments; monitoring and environmental data/assessment, UN system;
environmental management measures: environmental aspects of development planning and co-operation; environmental law and institutions;
environmental awareness: environmental education and training; public information (increasing public awareness of policy issues).

UNEP co-ordinates the environmental activities of all the UN Agencies and works to win the co-operation and participation of governments, the international scientific and professional communities and non-governmental organizations.

UNEP publishes a bi-monthly magazine *UNEP News,* several other periodicals related to specific programmes, briefs, newsletters, particularly about regional activities and numerous guidelines, reports books and papers and a regular magazine *Industry and Environment.* (Listings are given in its Annual Report.)

UNEP is funded from the UN and its annual expenditure amounts to about US$36,500,000.

It has established regional, information and other offices around the world:

Regional Office for Africa is at the headquarters in Nairobi.

Regional Office for Asia and the Pacific, ESCAP
Rajadamnern Avenue, Bangkok 10200, Thailand. *Telephone.* 66 2 829161 200
Telex. 82392 th *Cable.* UNITERRA

Regional Office for Latin America
Edificio Naciones Unidas, Presidente Mazaryk 29, Apartado Postal 6-718, Mexico 5, DD, Mexico. *Telephone.* 52 5 2501555 *Cable.* CEPAL

Regional Office for West Asia
P.O. Box 10880, Manama, Bahrain. *Telephone.* 973 27 60 72 *Telex.* 7457 unep bn *Cable.* UNEPROWA

Regional Office for Europe
Pavillons du Petit-Saconnex, 16, avenue Jean Trembley CH-1209 Geneva, Switzerland. *Telephone.* 22 798 84 00 *Cable.* UNITERRA

Regional Co-ordinating Unit (Caribbean)
14–21 Port Royal Street, Kingston, Jamaica. *Telephone.* 1 809 92 29 269 *Telex.* 2340 unlos ja

Co-ordinating Unit for the Mediterranean Action Plan
Leoforos Vassileos Konstantinou 48, Athens 501/1, Greece. *Telephone.* 30 1 72 44 536 *Telex.* 222 611 medugr.

New York Liaison Office
Room DC2-0816, New York, NY 10017, USA. *Telephone.* 212 963 8138
Cable. UNATIONS

Washington Liaison Office
1889 F Street, NW, Washington, DC 20006, USA.
Telephone. 202 289 8456 *Telex.* 89–606 uninfocen wsh

Industry and Environment Office
Tour Mirabeau. 39–43 Quai André Citoem, 75739 Paris, France.
Telephone. 331 45 78 4310

Secretariat of the UN Scientific Committee on the Effects of Atomic Radiation (UNSCEAR)
Vienna International Centre, PO Box 500, A-1400 Vienna, Austria.
Telephone. 43 222 26310 *Cable.* UNATIONS

Secretariat for the Convention on International Trade in Endangered Species of Wild Fauna and Flora (UNEP/CITES)
6 rue de Maupas, Case Postale 78, CH-1000 Lausanne 9, Switzerland.
Telephone. 41 21 20 00 81 *Telex.* 24584 ctes ch.

Wissenschaftszentrum Berlin (WZB)
(Internationales Institut für Umwelt und Gesellschaft)
(International Institute for Environment and Safety)

Telephone. 49 30 25 49 1 0
Address. Reichpietschufer 50, D-1000 Berlin 30, Federal Republic of Germany

The Institute, founded in 1969, focuses on four research areas: environmental monitoring and assessment; environmental impacts and environmental behaviour; evaluation of environmental policies; and evaluation of selected policy areas from environmental perspectives. It considers the problems and options of preventative environmental policies at national and international levels.

World Action for Recycling Materials and Energy from Rubbish (WARMER)
Telephone. 0892 24626 *Fax.* 0892 25287
Address. 83 Mount Ephraim, Royal Tunbridge Wells, Kent TN4 8BS, UK
Official. Mrs M. Thurgood (Editor)

The Warmer campaign, founded in 1984, is totally independent of commercial vested interests. It is devoted to a safer and healthier environment and acts as a worldwide information service to encourage recycling of materials and energy from post-consumer waste.

It publishes the *WARMER* bulleting four times a year which is circulated, free, to 100,000 readers in 70 countries.

The campaign is sponsored by the World Resources Foundation, a registered British charity.

World Association of Soil and Water Conservation (WASWC)

Telephone. 515 289 2331 *Fax.* 515 289 1227
Address. 7515 Northeast Ankeny Road, Ankeny, Iowa 50021-9764, USA
Officials. Dr Rattan Lal (Agronomy Department, The Ohio State University, 2021 Coffey Road, Columbus Ohio 43210-1086) (President); Wm C. Moldenhauer (317 Marvin Ave., Volga SD 57071) (Executive Secretary)

The Association was formed in August 1982 and now has 700 members. It exists to encourage the wise use and conservation of soil and water resources through the identification of problems and their solution by the scientific and professional communities and the education of policy makers to the dangers of misuse of these resources.

It helps conduct workshops concerning the use of steep lands for agriculture and agroforestry with maximum production and minimal erosions and water run-off. The results of these workshops are published as reference books and guidelines manuals. The first workshop was held in San Juan, Puerto Rico in 1987 and the proceedings have been published. The second was in Taichung, Taiwan in March 1989 and is due for publication in 1990. Further workshops are scheduled in 1991 in Solo, Indonesia and Nairobi, Kenya.

A quarterly newsletter is published and two books—*Conservation Farming on Steep Lands* and *Land Husbandry: A Framework for Soil and Water Conservation* have been produced.

The annual expenditure of about US$20,000 is met by members dues and donations with sponsorship of individual projects. The Soil and Water Conservation Society supplies support staff and secretarial time and editorial assistance.

World Conservation Monitoring Centre (WCMC)

Telephone. 0223 277314 *Fax.* 0223 277136 *Telex.* 817036
Address. 219c Huntingdon Road, Cambridge CB3 0DL, UK
Officials. Rudolph Agnew (Chairman); Dr Robin Pellew (Director)

The Centre was founded in 1982 as the Conservation Monitoring Centre but was renamed in 1987 when the three partners in the World Conservation Strategy, IUCN, UNEP and WWF agreed to support, jointly, the restructuring and development of the IUCN Conservation Monitoring Centre, so that it could fulfil effectively its role as the focal point for information on the world's biological diversity. It is registered in the UK as a company limited by guarantee and has applied for charitable status.

It has some 50 staff and is responsible for publishing the *Red Data Books* (see IUCN), and has produced directories of national parks and information on bio-diversity.

It is sponsored by IUCN, UNEP and WWF.

World Environment Center (WEC)

Telephone. 212 683 4700 *Fax.* 212 683 5053 *Telex.* 261290 Envirocent
Address. 419 Park Avenue South, Suite 1404, New York NY 10016, USA
Officials. Antony G. Marcil (President and CEO); Dr Betsy Ancker-Johnson (Chairman)

The World Environment Centre, established in 1974 with initial support from UNEP, is an independent, non-profit, non-advocacy organization that contributes to sustainable development by strengthening the management of environmental, health and safety practices worldwide. It acts as a liaison between government and industry and its activities are almost entirely restricted to working with these two groups. Consequently WEC is not a source of public information.

The WEC establishes partnerships among industry, government, non-governmental and international organizations and serves as a bridge for them to exchange information and expertise. It provides technical assistance and volunteer experts to developing countries.

Among its programmes are the International Environment Forum (IEF) and the International Environment and Development Service (IEDS). The first consists of a group of 52 major US, Canadian and European multinational corporations which meets quarterly to discuss, off-the-record, environmental and resource management issues with senior policy makers from around the world. They arrange workshops and produce reports on particular countries. The IEDS provides assistance to rapidly industrializing countries, currently in the Near East, Asia and the Pacific, completing more than 70 missions in 1989.

WEC has established a Gold Medal for International Corporate Environmental Achievement to give recognition to innovative corporate programmes and projects. Recipients include 3M in 1985, Exxon in 1986, du Pont in 1987 BP in 1988, Dow Chemical in 1989 and IBM in 1990.

Several publications on environmental topics are available to eligible countries.

It has an annual budget of over US$1,000,000 contributed by US agencies, industry, the World Bank and development programmes.

World Health Organization, Division of Environmental Health (WHO/EHE)

Telephone. 791 21 11 *Fax.* 791 07 46 *Telex.* 415416 OMS
Address. Avenue Appia, CH-1211 Geneva 27, Switzerland
Officials. Dr Hiroshi NaKajima (Director–General–WHO); Dr W Kreisel (Director, EH Division); Dr D. B. Warner (Manager, Community Water Supply & Sanitation Unit); Dr F. Kaferstein (Manager, Food Safety Unit); Dr M. Mercier (Manager, International Programme on Chemical Safety); G. Ozolins (Manager, Prevention of Environmental Pollution Unit).

The aim of the Programme is to protect and promote human health through national, community, family and personal measures for the prevention and control of conditions and factors in the environment that adversely affect human health. The function of the Division and its four units is: (a) the world-wide co-ordination of environmental health matters on behalf of WHO's constituencies; (b) the central organization of global and inter-regional programmes; the collation, analysis, synthesis and dissemination of valid information on environmental health matters; and (c) the support of regional offices.

Its current activities include: (a) support to the sustainable extension of water supplies and sanitation facilities and monitoring of progress; (b) prevention of health hazards associated with food contamination and participation in elaboration of food standards; (c) constituting on executing agency for the International Programme on Chemical Safety (IPCS); (d) support to Member States in the development of national programmes for control of environmental health hazards including air quality, water quality, radiation monitoring, human exposure to pollutants and environmental epidemiology; and (e) promotion of human health through measures to improve living conditions and to mitigate the adverse environmental and health impacts of socio-economic development actions.

WHO combines with many other UN agencies, bilateral agencies and non-governmental organizations. It chose Environment and Health as the theme for World Health Day, April 7, 1990, with the slogan "Our Planet — Our Health, Think Globally—Act Locally".

WHO publishes *World Health* a monthly journal of general interest, and the *Bulletin of the World Health Organization,* a semi-annual scientific journal. Many publications stem from the work of the Division including environmental health criteria, health and safety guides, chemical safety cards, medical guides, monographs, training documents etc. (Lists available from the Unit's Documentation Centre at the above address.)

WHO has 166 Member States and an annual budget of some US$650 million of which the Environmental Health Division's share is about US$10,000,000 being met from WHO regular budget, funds from other UN agencies and support agencies.

World Resources Institute (WRI)

Telephone. 202 638 6300 *Fax.* 202 638 0036 *Telex.* 64414 WRI WASH
Address. 1709 New York Avenue, NW, Washington, DC 20006, USA
Officials. James Gustave Speth (President); Jessica Tuchman Mathews (Vice-President); Mohamed El-Ashry (Vice-President for Research and Policy Affairs); Alan Brewster (Vice-President for Administration and Finance); Wallace Brown (Secretary-Treasurer)

WRI, founded in 1982, is an independent research and policy institute. It was formed to help governments, environmental and development organizations and private business address a fundamental question: How can societies meet basic human needs and nurture economic growth without undermining the natural resource base and environmental integrity?

It currently focuses on four broad areas: forests and biological diversity; energy, climate and pollution; economics, technology and institutions; and resource and environmental information. It augments policy recommendations with field services and technical support for groups working in natural resource management.

Its publications include: *The Greenhouse Trap, Solar Hydrogen; Moving Beyond Fossil Fuels, Keep Options Alive; The Scientific Basis for the Conservation of Biodiversity;* and *Air Pollution's Toll on Forests and Crops.* A complimentary *Publication Catalog* is available from the above address.

It has recently merged with IIED-North America and they are now referred to as WRI's Centre for International Development and Environment. This Centre provides services for developing countries in the sustainable management of natural resources. It carries out programmes in six areas: natural resources management strategies and assessments; natural resource data, biological diversity and sustainable agriculture; forestry and land use; NGO support services; and "From the Ground Up"—analysis and dissemination of example of villages managing their resources in an exemplary way.

WRI's annual expenditure (1990) is US$8,200,000 which is met by private foundations, the UN and governmental agencies, corporations and concerned individuals.

World Wide Fund for Nature WWF

Telephone. 22 649 111 *Fax.* 22 643 239
Address. World Conservation Centre, Avenue du Mont-Blanc, CH-1196 Gland, Switzerland
Officials. HRH The Duke of Edinburgh (President); Charles de Haes (Director General)

The WWF, founded in 1961 as the World Wildlife Fund originally to help fund the work of the IUCN, aims to conserve nature and ecological processes by: (a) preserving genetic, species and ecosystem diversity; (b) ensuring that the use of renewable resources is sustainable both now and in the longer term; and (c) promoting actions to reduce pollution and wasteful exploitation and consumption. It now has more than 3,700,000 members, including those within its family of 28 national organizations.

Its current work includes the conservation and rehabilitation of forests and woodlands, the conservation and revitalization of wetlands and coasts and the preservation of biological diversity.

The Fund publishes a number of books, many of which are free, and may be obtained from the International Information and Education Division at the above address. It produces *WWF News* for members and an *Annual Review*.

Its annual expenditure (in 1988 for the whole family of affiliated and associated national organizations) was SFr 195 million. This is met by individuals (70%), earned income (e.g. trading, royalties, sponsorship, investments) (16%), corporate contributions, governments grants, trusts and foundations etc.

The UK branch was founded in 1961 by Sir Peter Scott and now has 1,200,000 supporters.

World Wide Fund for Nature–UK, WWF-UK
Panda House, Weyside Park, Godalming, Surrey GU8 1XR. *Telephone.* 0483 426444 *Fax.* 0483 426409 *Telex.* 859602. HRH Princess Alexandra (President); Martin Laing (Chairman)

REGIONAL

African NGOs Environment Network (ANEN)

Telephone. 28138 *Fax.* 335108 *Telex.* 25331ANEN KE
Address. P.O. Box 53844, Nairobi, Kenya
Officials. Jimoh Omo-Fadaka (Nigeria) (Executive Chairman); Mazide N'Diaye (Senegal) (Vice-Chairman); Simon Muchiru (Kenya) (Executive Director)

ANEN is an African network of indigenous Environment and Development NGOs and grassroot community groups. It was founded in 1982 by 21 representatives of African NGOs and nine African nations gathered in Nairobi for the UNEP's 10th anniversary. They were concerned that environmental problems affecting Africa transcended national boundaries and were associated with lack of development or arose because of the process of development itself. They realized that poverty and the failure to satisfy basic human needs left many African people with no option but to inflict damage or destruction on the environment and natural resource base. It currently has over 530 member organizations in 45 African nations.

Its long term objectives are to: (a) promote environmentally sound, culturally accepted, economically feasible, sustainable community-based development; (b) strengthen the capacity and technical competence of indigenous African NGOs and community groups; and (c) promote and facilitate participation and the involvement of the local people, particularly women and youth, in environment and development work and issues.

It collects, analyzes and disseminates information and data; it provides advice and training on the development and management of eco-development projects and research; prepares and produces development education and environmental awareness materials for use by policy makers and others; and builds links between members and their governments, UN Agencies and other international organizations.

It publishes *ECOAFRICA,* a bimonthly, bilingual (French and English) magazine and prepares and produces audio-visual materials, information kits, press and feature articles, press briefings and organizes workshops for journalists. It also publishes issue and case study reports and papers, directories and Action guides.

Its annual budget is around US$500,000.

African Timber Organization (ATO)

Telephone. 241 73 29 28
Address. B.P. 1077 Libreville, Gabon

The Organization's members are the governments of 12 African countries who co-operate in forestry management and marketing. It is concerned with technological and industrial research, particularly on unknown and little-known tree species, and with policies of reafforestation and environmental management.

African Wildlife Foundation

Telephone. 202 265 8393 *Fax.* 202 265 2361
Address. 1717 Massachusetts Avenue, NW, Washington, DC 20036, USA
Officials. J. H. Hemingway, Jr. (Chairman); Paul T. Schindler (President); Diana E. McMeekin (Vice-President)

The Foundation was incorporated in March 1961 and now has a membership of some 50,000.

It exists to promote wildlife conservation in Africa, particularly at the moment in Kenya and Tanzania.

It publishes *Wildlife News* quarterly and works closely with WWF, the National Wildlife Federation and Conservation International.

It has an annual budget of US$4,200,000 met by individuals, a private foundation and a Federal grant.

Antarctic and Southern Ocean Coalition (ASOC)

Telephone. 2002 544 2600; 202 328 0103 *Fax.* 202 328 4518
Address. 218 D Street, SE, Washington, DC 20003, USA
Officials. Lyn Goldsworthy (Executive Secretary); James N. Barnes (General Counsel)

The Coalition, started in 1978, now has in membership 200 organizations in 35 countries. Its purpose is the protection of Antarctica, mainly under the title of "The Antarctica Project", founded in 1982. This covers monitoring by informing and by lobbying in both domestic and international forums. Its programme holds governments legally, politically and morally accountable for their stewardship of the Antarctic region.

Under the ASOC umbrella the Project publishes critiques, lobbies internationally and presents ecologically sound alternatives for management of the region. The Coalition produces, roughly three times a year, an international newspaper *ECO* which reports information on what is happening behind the scenes. It makes available the text of documents otherwise inaccessible to environmental organizations, scholars and the press.

It conducts policy research and legal analysis and presents testimony and policy proposals to governments. It prepares articles, books, slideshows, videos and posters suitable for educational and advocacy purposes. A publications list, covering over 100 items, is available from the above address. Intergovernmental and scientific meetings are regularly attended and it is assisting IUCN in preparing the Antarctic Conservation Strategy.

Its annual expenditure is some $50,000 which is met by individual subscriptions and from foundations.

Arab Centre for the Studies of Arid Zones and Dry Lands (ACSAD)

Telephone. 755713 *Telex.* 412697 ACSAD SY
Address. P.O. Box 2440, Damascus, Syria
Officials. Dr Mohamed El-Khash (Director-General); Nuri Rohuma (Assistant Director-General)

The Centre was founded in 1971 by the League of Arab States and now has 17 Arab States in membership, each with a representative on the board of directors.

It is an intergovernmental autonomous organization whose main objectives include regional programmes and studies related to arid zones such as water resources, soils, plants and animal production as well as training Arab technicians. It currently has 12 projects and eight programmes relating to those arid zone subjects plus agro-meterology.

ACSAD issues annual technical reports and various papers and reports relating to the results of specific projects. It publishes a periodical *Water and Agriculture in Arab Arid Zones* and a newsletter *Camel.* It maintains data bases on water resources, agro-meteorology and bibliography.

Its annual budget of about US$4,000,000 is met by contributions from its member states.

Arctic Institute of North America

Telephone. 1 403 220 7515
Address. University Library Tower, 2500 University Drive, NW, Calgary, Alberta T2N 1N4, Canada

The Institute is a research organization with some 2,500 individual members. It acquires, interprets and disseminates knowledge of the polar regions including their natural resources and their environmental concerns.

Asia–Pacific People's Environment Network (APPEN)

Telephone. 376930
Address. c/o Sahabat Alam Malaysia, 43 Salween Road, 10050 Penang, Malaysia

The Network, founded in 1983, brings together NGOs and individuals in the region to collect and disseminate information on environmental issues. It organizes local communities who may be affected by environmental problems and it provides education on environmental and occupational health issues. It is particularly concerned with tropical rain forests.

It publishes newsletters, reports and papers and the *APPEN News Service* every two weeks.

Asian Ecological Society

Telephone. 04 359 0249 *Fax.* 04 359 0991
Address. Box 843, Biology Department, Tunghai University, Taichung, Taiwan 40704, Republic of China
Official. Dr Jun-yi Lin (President)

The Society was formed in 1978 and now has 120 members. Its aims are to: (a) mobilize and encourage Asian scientists to take more interest in basic research on their native ecosystems; (b) amass baseline ecological information of the natural environment in each country, so that short- and long-term environmental changes can be detected; and (c) supply ecological information to government agencies for decision-making in matters pertaining to the environment, or where impact on the local environment should be considered.

It encourages students and professors of ecology to organize into a cohesive group that can exert pressure on the government for a better funding for ecological research.

It used to publish the *Journal of Asian Ecology* and has issued a *Catalogue of Taiwanese Dragonflies*.

It is funded by members and by donations and is sponsored by seven universities from Taiwan, the Philippines, Hong Kong, India, Korea and Indonesia.

Asian Environment Society (AES)

Address. 8 Darya Ganj, New Delhi 110002, India

Founded in 1972 to provide a forum for the discussion of environmental problems in Asia. Its members include 60 organizations as well as individuals, in 11 countries.

Baltic Marine Environment Protection Committee (Helsinki Commission) (HELCOM)

Telephone. 358 90 602 366 *Fax.* 358 90 644 577 *Telex.* 125105 hlcom
Address. Mannerheimintie 12 A, SF-00100 Helsinki 10, Finland

The Commission was established in 1974 to protect the marine environment of the Baltic Sea from all types of pollution. Its members are the governments of Denmark, Finland, FRG, GDR, Poland, Sweden and the USSR.

Commission for the Conservation of Antarctic Marine Living Resources (CCAMLR)

Telephone. 002 31 0366 *Fax.* 002 23 2714 *Telex.* AA 57236
Address. 25 Old Wharf, Hobart, Tasmania 7000, Australia
Official. Dr Darry L. Powell (Executive Secretary)

The commission is an intergovernmental organization established by the international Convention on the Conservation of Antarctic Marine Living Resources, 1980. It, assisted by the Scientific Committee also established under the Convention, is responsible for developing measures necessary for the regulation of harvesting and for the conservation, including rational use, of marine life of the Southern Ocean surrounding Antarctica.

The negotiation of the Convention was initiated by the Antarctic Treaty Consultative Parties following reports of scientific studies expressing concern that unregulated fishing of Antarctic species, especially krill, could result in irreversible damage to the populations of other species in the Antarctic ecosystem. It came into force in April 1982 and there are now 21 countries as members of the Commission.

The Commission works for the conservation and rational use of marine living resources including fish, molluscs, crustaceans and all other species of living organisms including birds. It facilitates research; compiles data; disseminates information; identifies conservation needs; analyzes the effectiveness of conservation measures; formulates, adopts and revises conservation measures; and implements a system of observation and inspection.

The Commission publishes reports of its Annual Meetings and of the Scientific Committee, selected scientific papers, basic documents (relating to the Convention), conservation measures and details of members' activities. It works closely with other international bodies such as the FAO, IUCN, IWC etc.

The annual budget amount to about A$1,100,000 which is met by member countries' contributions.

Committee of Common Market Automobile Constructors
(Comité des Constructeurs d'Automobiles du Marché Commun—CCMC)

Telephone. 32 2 513 58 48 *Fax.* 32 2 514 00 58 *Telex.* 26308
Address. 5, Square de Meeûs, Boîte 7, 1040 Brussels, Belgium
Officials. R. Levy (President); F. Perrin-Pelletier (Secretary-General)

The Committee was established in 1972 with the object of achieving, within the EC, uniformity of technical regulations concerning motor vehicles, in particular in matters of vehicle safety and environmental protection. Membership is open to all motor vehicle manufacturers and, at the moment comprises twelve, situated in France: PSA Group, RNUR; in Germany: BMW, Daimler-Benz, Man, Porsche and Volksvagen; in the UK: Rover Group, Rolls-Royce Motor Cars; in Italy: Fiat; and in the Netherlands: DAF and Volvo B.V.

Its main discussions are with the European Commission and, more recently, with the European Parliament. It has also developed its relations with the other Community institutions such as the Council, the Economic and Social Committee and the Permanent Representatives of the Member States.

It collaborates with the Liaison Committee of the automobile industry of the countries of the European Communities, also located in Brussels, which represents the trade associations of the EC motor industry.

Conseil Européen des Fédérations de l'Industries Chimique (CEFIC)
(European Council of Chemical Manufacturers' Federations)

Telephone. 640 20 95 *Fax.* 640 19 81 *Telex.* 62444
Address. Avenue Louise 250, bte 71, B-1050 Bruxelles, Belgium

Cefic, a non-profit organization, was formed in 1972 and now has as members the national Chemical Federations of 15 European countries and represents the interests of companies in various sectors of the chemical industry.

It covers, on behalf of its members, issues such as the environment, health and safety, transport and distribution of chemicals, energy and raw material supplies, international trade, and information and statistical surveys. It is particularly concerned with proposed and pending EC legislation and the Commission's work.

Co-operative Council for the Arab States of the Gulf (GCC)

Telephone. 966 1 4827777 *Fax.* 966 1 4829089 *Telex.* 203635 tawini sj
Address. P.O. Box 7153 Riyadh 11462, Saudi Arabia

The Council provided co-operation among its member states: Bahrain, Kuwait, Oman, Qatar, Saudi Arabia and the United Arab Emirates. The heads of state approved, in 1985, the *General Policies and Principles of Environmental Protection for GCC States*, and this led to an environmental action plan which covered six topics: a survey of the environmental problems of each state, the laws, research, education, training and the organizations in the region. Studies and surveys have covered radiation protection, environmental assessment, industrial air pollution and toxic substances.

Council of Europe

Telephone. 44 88 61 49 61 *Telex.* 870 943
Address. BP 431 R, F-67006 Strasbourg Cedex, France

The Council, established in 1949, consists of the representatives of 21 Western European countries. One of its permanent steering committees is the European Committee for the Conservation of Nature and Natural Resources. This, in turn, has committees devoted to: Planning and Management of the Natural Environment; Conservation of Wildlife and Natural Habitats; Protected Areas; Environmental Education and Training.

The Council administers the Berne Convention (1979) on the Conservation of European Wildlife and Natural Habitats, and has established the European Network of Biogenetic Reserves.

The Council publishes a journal *Naturopa* and a newsletter as well as reports and handbooks.

European Association for the Science of Air Pollution (EURASAP)

Telephone. 071 589 5111 *Fax.* 071 584 7596 *Telex.* 929484 IMPCOL G
Address. c/o Dr H M. ApSimon, Air Pollution Group, Mechanical Engineering Dept. Imperial College, London SW7 2AZ, UK
Officials. Prof. A. Eliassen (Norway) (President); Prof. E. Meszaros (Hungary), Dr J. Pruchnicki (Poland) (Vice-Presidents); Dr Helen M. ApSimon (UK) (Chairman); Dr P Bessemoulin (France) (Secretary)

EURASAP was formed in 1986 to advance education and knowledge in air pollution science and its applications. It brings together in conference scientists throughout Europe actively working in the relevant disciplines and encourages and assists theoretical and experimental research. It promotes the exchange of scientists and arranges exhibitions, meetings, lectures, seminars and training courses. Membership may be either individual or corporate and currently has reached about 220.

The Association holds about three meetings or workshops a year on selected topics: in 1990 at Utrecht, The Netherlands on cloud chemistry and wet deposition; in Budapest, Hungary on monitoring requirements in and around human settlements and in Krakow, Poland on the application of sodar and lidar techniques in air pollution monitoring.

It publishes a regular newsletter and collaborates with other international bodies.

Its annual budget amounts to about £3,000 raised from subscriptions.

European Environmental Bureau (EEB)

Telephone. 32 2 647 01 99
Address. Luxemburgstraat 20, B-1040 Brussels, Belgium

Founded in 1974 following an initiative of the (US) Sierra Club and the International Institute for Environment and Development to bring together environmental non-government organizations in the member states of the European Community in order to exchange experience and information. It now has over 100 members in the 12 EC countries and concentrates on environmental policy, and education, nature protection, pollution control, land use planning, transportation, energy and agriculture and the environmental aspects of European relations with developing countries.

It publishes an annual report and *RISED* bimonthly.

Institute for European Environment Policy (IEEP)

Telephone. 228 7290050 *Telex.* 886 885 fec d
Address. Aloys-Schulte Strasse 6, D-5300 Bonn, Federal Republic of Germany

The IEEP was founded in Bonn in 1976 by the European Cultural Foundation (Amsterdam) to provide an independent body for the analysis of environmental policies in Europe. It seeks to increase the awareness of the European dimension of environmental protection and to advance European policy making. There is emphasis on the study of EC environmental policy, including implementation, air and water pollution, nature conservation, impact assessment, major accident hazards, agriculture, waste, cross-media (integrated) pollution control, international policy developments with a European dimension including climate change, environmental law and East-West co-operation in Europe. It is currently engaged in a number of research projects on some of these policy areas.

It has published a number of books, particularly on policy issues (included in the bibliography). It publishes a bimonthly newsletter *The Environment in Europe* (separate editions in English, French and German) an Annual Report and policy reports.

Its income is derived from the Foundation for European Environmental Policy (Amsterdam), the WWF and from commissioned research for government departments, the European Commission etc.

It also has offices in Paris, Brussels and London:

IEEP, Paris. 55 rue de Varenne, F-75007, Paris, France.

IEEP, London. 3 Endsleigh Street, London WC1H 0DD, UK.
Telephone. 071 388 2117 *Fax.* 071 388 2826 *Telex.* 261681. Opened in 1980.
Official. Nigel Haigh (Director).

Nordic Council for Ecology (NCE)

Telephone. 46 46 148188 *Fax.* 46 46 104716
Address. Ecology Building, Lund University, S-223 62 Lund, Sweden
Officials. Prof. Petur Jonasson (University of Copenhagen, Denmark) (Chairman); Dr Pehr H. Enckell (Secretary)

The Council was established in 1964 as a joint Nordic organization and now has five members (and five deputies). Its purpose is to support joint research (courses, seminars, fellowships and symposia) in ecology in the Nordic countries.

It publishes a newsletter *Nordecol.* and works with the Nordic Society "Oikos".

Its annual expenditure of about SwK 600,000 comes from the Nordic Council of Ministers via its sponsor the Nordic Cultural Budget.

Nordic Council of Ministers (NCM)

Telephone. 45 33114711 *Fax.* 45 33114711 *Telex.* 15544 nordmr dK
Address. Store Strandstraede 18, DK-1255, Copenhagen K, Denmark
Official. Fridjov Clemet (Secretary-General)

The NCM, founded in 1971, is the means for co-operation at governmental level of the five sovereign Nordic states of Denmark, Finland, Iceland, Norway and Sweden, as well as the self-governing areas of the Faroe Islands, Greenland and the Aaland Islands. These cover some 22,000,000 people with a common cultural background and the same political values. Through co-operation, it claims, better results are achieved than by independent efforts.

The Secretariat, serving the Council, is divided into five specialist divisions, one of which includes concern with energy and the environment.

The overall budget of the NCM is DK 700 million.

Oil Companies' European Organization for Environmental Health and Protection (CONCAWE)

Telephone. 32 2 2203111 *Fax.* 32 2 2194646 *Telex.* 20308
Address. Madouplein 1, B-1030 Brussels, Belgium
Officials. Klaus Kohlhase (Chairman); Dr M. T. Westaway (Chairman of Executive Committee)

CONCAWE (the name coming from the original title—Conservation of Clean Air and Water in Western Europe) was founded in 1963 by six international oil companies and now has in membership 36 companies operating in Europe. These represent 90% of the refining capacity in Western Europe together with downstream oil operations in all 19 OECD countries in Europe.

The scope of CONCAWE's activities has expanded beyond the original air and water remit to include consumer and employee health protection and safety.

The justification for CONCAWE is based on the conviction that decision-makers who have access to sound technical and economic analyses and understand them, will enact more effective laws and regulations and make other decisions which will benefit society at large, including industry. It believes that cost-benefit analysis of environmental control measures is a prerequisite to ensure rational use of society's resources and that this must be based on sound scientific, technical and economic data. CONCAWE's task is to generate these data and make them available to the appropriate authorities. In its Fourth Environmental Action Programme the European Community recognizes that industry generates the wealth which, amongst other things, makes possible investments to improve the environment and stresses the need to consult closely with industry in developing legislation.

CONCAWE is, therefore, a source of expert information and it is an outstanding example of a successful industry organization devoted to doing something about environmental problems. Its analyses are based on the collective expertise of its member companies and their employees who include not only chemists and engineers, but also physicians, toxicologists, ecologists, hygienists and safety experts. More than 200 member company experts work on an *adhoc* basis in the various committees and task forces.

CONCAWE publishes many expert technical reports (catalogues of the reports and of special interest reports are available from the above address). The subjects covered in the index to current reports include; air protection (listing 19 titles and a further seven of special interest); automotive fuels and emission (nine titles plus nine specials); water and soil protection (eight plus six); oil pipelines (two); oil spill clean-up technology (11 and two); petroleum products—handling and use (nine and 19); health (10 and 18); noise (four plus seven); major hazards management (seven and one); and general reports, annual reports etc. Among the most recent, in 1990, are *VOC Emissions from Gasoline Distribution and Service Stations in Western Europe—Control Technology and Cost-Effectiveness* and *Closing the Gasoline System—Control of Gasoline Emissions from the Distribution System and Vehicles*.

CONCAWE's annual budget is some BFr 135 million, including a research budget of some BFr 20,000,000, met by members, but the members' main contribution is the time and expertise of the 200 company experts who participate, as noted above, in the management groups, study groups and task forces set up for specific investigations and projects.

Organization of American States (OAS)

Telephone. 1 202 789 3000
Address. 17th Street and Constitution Avenue, NW, Washington DC 20006, USA

OAS, founded in 1890, claims to be the oldest regional organization in the world. It covers political, social and cultural co-operation among its 31 member countries. It is concerned with the environment and natural resources which are dealt with through the Inter-Secretarial Committee on the Human Environment which first met in 1972. Its regional development programmes and projects include environmental assessments and it sponsors research related to environmental protection.

It publishes a number of guidelines including *Minimal Conflict; Guidelines for Planning the Development of American Humid Tropical Environments* and *Environmental Quality and River Basin Development: A Model for Integrated Analysis and Planning.*

Oslo Commission (OSCOM)

Telephone. 071 242 9927 *Fax.* 071 831 7427 *Telex.* 21185 BOSPAR G
Address. New Court, 48, Carey Street, London WC2A 2JE, UK
Officials. Claire Nihoul (Secretary); Hans-Georg Neuhoff (First Deputy Secretary); Stig Borgvang (Second Deputy Secretary)

The Commission was set up under the Convention for the Prevention of Marine Pollution by Dumping from Ships and Aircraft, Oslo 1974, and now works jointly with the Paris Commission set up under the Convention for the Prevention of Marine Pollution from Land-based Sources, Paris 1978. A total of 13 European countries have signed the Oslo Convention and 12 have signed the Paris Convention.

The Commissions carry out programmes to assess the state of the marine environment and formulate policy to eliminate or reduce existing pollution and prevent further contamination of coastal waters and the open sea. The Commissions adopt appropriate measures to implement these policies and assess their effectiveness on the basis of reports on their implementation and on the results of monitoring, thus adapting their policies and introducing new measures as appropriate.

Apart from meeting at yearly intervals, the Commissions have established a number of working groups to deal with specific issues. These included: Working Group on Oil Pollution; Industrial Sectors Working Group; Joint Monitoring Group; Standing Advisory Committee for Scientific Advice; Technical Working Group; and North Sea Task Force. They work with all intergovernmental organizations dealing with the issues of marine pollution and its prevention. At the Second International Conference on the Protection of the North Sea in London in November 1987, ministers invited the Oslo and Paris

Commissions to address a number of issues related to the input of dangerous substances via rivers, nutrients, atmospheric pollutants, dumping and incineration at sea, offshore installations and radioactive wastes. A report giving an account of this work and the results achieved is being published in 1990 for review at the Third International Conference on the Protection of the North Sea in the Hague in 1990.

The Commissions publish a number of books and the annual reports give detailed information of current activities, recommendations, reports etc.

The annual budget of the Commissions amounts to about £400,000 and is met by funds supplied by the governments who are Contracting Parties to the Conventions.

Paris Commission (PARCOM)

Telephone. 071 242 9927 *Fax.* 071 831 7427 *Telex.* 21185 BOSPAR G
Address. New Court, 48, Carey Street London WC2A 2JE, UK
Officials. Claire Nihoul (Secretary); Hans-Georg Neuhoff (First Deputy Secretary); Stig Borgvang (Second Deputy Secretary)

The Commission, set up under the Convention for the Prevention of Marine Pollution from Land-Based Sources, Paris 1978, now works jointly with the Oslo Commission.

Further details are available from the "Oslo Commission" (see above).

Red Latinoamericana de ONGs Ambientalistas
(Latin American Network of Environmental NGOs)

Address. c/o Grupa Investigación y Conservación, CIPFE, Casillo Correo 13125, 11700 Montevideo, Uruguay

The Network was founded in 1985 for the exchange of information on environmental issues and for joint activities among its 22 member organizations in 12 countries. It supports the endorsement of national and international laws, and receives funding from CIPFE, Montevideo.

Regional Organization for the Protection of the Marine Environment (ROPME)

Address. P.O. Box 26388, 13124 Safat, Kuwait
Officials. Dr Abdul Rahman Al-Awadi (Acting Executive Secretary); Dr Badria Al-Awadi (Co-ordinator, Tech. & Admin.)

ROPME was established in July 1979 with the Secretariat being established in January 1982. The members are the states of Bahrain, Iran, Iraq, Kuwait, Oman, Qatar, Saudi Arabia and the United Arab Emirates, and the objective is the protection of the marine environment of the region, defined as the water body surrounded by the eight members and called the "Sea Area".

The Marine Emergency Mutual Aid Centre (MEMAC) was established in Bahrain in August 1982.

The Council consists of representatives, at ministerial level, of all the members, and meets every two years with a rotating chairmanship. It delegates its authority to an Executive Committee consisting of representatives of Bahrain, Iran, Iraq, Kuwait and Saudi Arabia and this meets, normally, twice each year. The Council member for Kuwait is also chairman of the Executive Committee and Acting Executive secretary of ROPME.

The Council's judicial commission, composed of experts from the member states, has been responsible for five legal instruments as follows:

Kuwait Regional Convention for Co-operation on the Protection of the Marine Environment from Pollution, April 1978

Action Plan for the Protection and Development of the Marine Environment and the Coastal Areas, April 1978

Protocol concerning Regional Co-operation in Combating Pollution by Oil and Other Harmful Substances in Cases of Emergency, April 1978

Protocol concerning Marine Pollution resulting from Exploration and Exploitation of the Continental Shelf, March 1989, which entered into force on 17 February 1990

Protocol for the Protection of the Marine Environment against Pollution from Land-based Sources, February 1990.

Secretariat for the Protection of the Mediterranean Sea

Telephone. 34 3 217 16 95 *Telex.* 54 519
Address. Placa Lesseps 1, E-08023 Barcelona, Spain

The Secretariat, established in 1983, organizes periodic inter-municipal conferences against the contamination of the Mediterranean amongst its members who are representatives of municipalities in the 13 countries of Africa, Asia and Europe bordering the Mediterranean Sea.

It seeks to protect the sea from pollution etc. by information exchange and action amongst its members.

South Asia Co-operative Environment Programme (SACEP)

Telephone. 589369
Address. P.O. Box 1070, Colombo 5, Sri Lanka

The Programme, founded in 1983, promotes co-operation among countries of South Asia in environmental protection and management with individual countries acting as liaison centres for specific issues.

The members are the governments of Afghanistan, Bangladesh, Bhutan, India, the Maldives, Pakistan and Sri Lanka.

South Pacific Regional Environment Programme (SPREP)

Telephone. 687 26 20 00 *Fax.* 687 26 38 18 *Telex.* SOPACOM 3139 NM
Address. SPREP, South Pacific Commission, BP D5, Noumea, New Caledonia

SPREP works on behalf of 22 Island Governments and Administrations of the South Pacific Region to help them to maintain their shared environment. It also receives support from the other South Pacific Commission member countries, namely Australia, New Zealand, France, the USA and the UK.

It was formed in 1978 with the support of the international bodies in the South Pacific (SPC, SPEC and ESCAP) and UNEP, and organized the Conference on the Human Environment in the South Pacific which took place in Rarotonga, Cook Islands in 1982. At this inaugural conference SPREP's Action Plan for future activities was produced. This is reviewed at biennial intergovernment meetings with the region's member governments playing a very active role in their Environment Programme.

The Action Plan identifies some 60 aspects of environmental assessment, management and law and SPREP is responsible to its member governments and administrations for the overall technical co-ordination and continuous supervision of the implementation of the plan. It will: (a) identify experts and institutions with the specific skills required to assist Pacific Island governments in solving their environmental problems; (b) ensure that monitoring of the state of the environment is continually underway to enable the early detection of problems; (c) facilitate environmental information exchange among experts, institutions, governments and the community; (d) develop and increase regional expertise especially through training programmes in environmental management skills; and (e) provide the secretariat for two important environmental treaties in the South Pacific: the Convention for the Protection of the Natural Resources and Environment of the South Pacific Region and the Convention for the Conservation of Nature in the South Pacific Region.

Activities include: coastal water quality monitoring; protected areas and species conservation; the management of natural resources, environmental education and training; water quality projects; waste management and pollution control; and environmental planning and administration.

SPREP publishes a newsletter, environmental education materials and occasional papers. It is funded by contributions from member countries and from funding agencies.

United Nations Economic Commission for Europe (UN-ECE)

Telephone. 22 734 60 11 *Fax.* 22 734 98 25
Address. Palais Des Nations, 8–14 Avenue de la Paix, 1211 Geneva 10, Switzerland
Official. Gerald Hinteregger (Executive Secretary)

The Commission, established in 1947, has served as the only permanent intergovernmental forum for regional multilateral economic co-operation among the countries of Europe, both East and West, and North America, and now has 34 countries in membership. Its activities cover a wide spectrum, including environmental matters, and one of its principal subsidiary bodies is the "Senior Advisers to ECE Governments on Environmental and Water Problems". As early as 1975 all main ECE subsidiary bodies were required to take environmental aspects into account in their work across different economic sectors.

The Secretariat services the 1979 Convention on Long-Range Transboundary Air Pollution and its two protocols for sulphur oxides (the "Helsinki Protocol") and nitrogen oxides (the "Sofia Protocol") emissions control. A new protocol for reduction of hydrocarbons and their transboundary fluxes is under preparation. It has many programmes on air and water pollution, industrial accidents, environmental impact assessment, low-waste technology and waste management and flora and fauna and their habitats. Its early work on vehicle emissions has been the basis for the EC's Directives over the last 20 years (see Part I, Section 11).

In 1988 ECE endorsed a set of principles regarding co-operation in the field of transboundary waters. These address issues regarding control and prevention of transboundary water pollution, as well as flood management in transboundary waters and, more particularly, pollution control of hazardous substances; mitigation and control of accidental pollution; warning and alarm systems to counteract such pollution; mutual information exchange regarding measures taken to reduce or eliminate causes of pollution and floods; and mutual assistance on an agreed basis.

The Commission publishes extensively in English, French and Russian languages, both general bulletins and surveys and series on particular subjects such as energy, environment, agriculture and timber, industry and technology, statistics and transport. (Listings appear each month and are available from the above address.)

The Commission is funded as part of the UN budget.

GOVERNMENT DEPARTMENTS

Many governments have established, in the last few years, departments with responsibility for matters such as those described in Parts I and III. The following list indicates the principal ministry, department or agency concerned in the major countries of the world. In many countries other departments, such as those concerned with Agriculture, Forestry, Foreign Affairs etc., also have responsibilities and influence.

Algeria	Agence National pour le Protection de l'Environnement BP 154, El-Annaser
Argentina	Secretaria General de la Presidencia, Subsecretaria de Politica Ambiental Corrientes 1302, 1er Piso, 1043 Buenos Aires
Australia	Department of the Arts, Sport, the Environment, Tourism and Territories GPO Box 1252 Canberra, ACT 2601 (the state governments also have environmental responsibilities)
Austria	Unweltbundesamt Ministry of Environment, Youth and the Family, Biberstrasse 11, A-1010, Vienna
Bahrain	Environment Protection Committee (EPC) PO Box 26090, Manama also Environmental Protection Technical Secretariat, Manama
Bangladesh	Department of Environment Pollution Control 6/11/F Lalmatia Housing Estate, Satmasjid Road, Dhaka-7
Belgium	Ministère de la Région Wallone, Direction Générale des Resources Naturelles et de l'Environnement, Namu (for the French speaking region); Ministerie van de Vlaamse Gemeenschap, Administratie voor Ruimtelijke Ordening en Leefmilieu, Brussels (for the Flemish speaking region)
Bermuda	Ministry of the Environment Government Administration Building, 30 Parliament Street, Hamilton HM12
Bolivia	Comisión del Medio Ambiente y Recursos Naturales La Paz
Brazil	Ministerio de Habatacao, Urbanismo e Leio Ambiente- Secretaria Especial do Meio Ambiente (SEMA) SEPN, Av. W3 Norte—Q.510, Ed. Cidade de Cabo Frio, Brasilia DF 70.750

Bulgaria	State Committee for Environmental Protection ul. Triaditza 2, Sofia Komitet za Opazvane na Prirodnata Sreda ul. Vladimar Pontonov, 67 100 Sofia
Canada	Department of the Environment Ottawa, Ontario K1A 1G2
Chile	Corporación Nacional Forestal y de Protección de Recursos Naturales Renovables (CONAF) (part of the Ministry of Agriculture) Avenida Bulnes 285, Oficina 501, Santiago
China	Ministry of Urban and Rural Construction and Environmental Protection Baiwanzhuang, Beijing
Colombia	Instituto Nacional de los Recursos Naturales Renovables y del Ambiente (INDERENA) Ministry of Agriculture, Apartado Aéreo 13458, Bogotá
Czechoslovakia	Federal Ministry of Technological Development and Investments Department of the Environment, Slezska 9, CS-120 29 Prague The Czech and Slovak republic governments also have Ministries involved in environmental affairs
Denmark	Miljoestyrelsen Strandgade 29, DK-1401 Copenhagen K
Ecuador	Consejo Nacional de Desarrollo (CONADE), Programa de Recursos Naturales y Medio Ambiente Quito
Egypt	Environmental Affairs Agency Cabinet of Ministers, Kasr Al-Aini Street, Cairo
El Salvador	Comité Nacional de Protección del Medio Ambiente c/o Ministerio de Planificación, San Salvador
Finland	Ministry of the Environment Ratakatu 3, PO Box 399, SF-00531 Helsinki
France	Ministère de l'Environnement et du Cadre de Vie 14 boulevard du General-Leclerc, F-92524 Neully-sur-Seine
(East) Germany	Ministerium für Umweltschutz und Wasserwirtschaft DDR-1020 Berlin
(West) Germany	Bundesministerium für Umwelt, Naturschutz und Reaktorsicherheit Ableitung N, Postfach 120629, D-5300 Bonn 1 (the 10 Länder, State, governments also have environmental responsibilities)
Ghana	Environment Protection Council PO Box M326, Ministries' Post Office, Accra
Greece	Ministry of Physical Planning, Housing and the Environment—Environment Directorate Pouliou 8, GR-115 23 Athens

Guatemala	Comisión Nacional del Medio Ambiente Presidencia de la República, 9a Avenida entre 14y 15, Zona 1, Oficino no. 10 Edificio Antigua Corte Suprema, Guatemala
Hong Kong	Environment Protection Department Sincere Building, 17th Floor, 173 Des Voeux Road, Central Hong Kong
Hungary	Ministry for Environment and Water Management Fö-u. 46-50, Pf 351, H-1011 Budapest
Iceland	Nature Conservation Council Hverfisgötu 26, ISL-101 Reykjavik
India	Ministry of Environment and Forests B-Block, Paryvaran Bhavan, CGO Complex, Lodi Road, New Delhi 110003
Indonesia	Ministry of State for Population and Environment Jalan Merdeka Barat no. 15, 13th Floor, Jakarta
Iran	Department of the Environment Ostad Nejat-Ollahi, Avenue no. 187, PO Box 4565-15875, Teheran
Iraq	Higher Council for Environmental Protection and Improvement c/o Ministry of Health, PO Box 423, Baghdad
Ireland	Department of the Environment Custom House, Dublin 1
Israel	Environmental Protection Service Ministry of the Interior, PO Box 6158, Jerusalem 91061
Italy	Ministry of the Environment Piazza Venezia 11, 1-00187 Rome
Japan	Environment Agency of Japan 1-2-2 Kasumigaseki, Chiyoda-ku, Tokyo 100
Jordan	Ministry of Municipal and Rural Affairs and the Environment Department of the Environment, PO Box 35206, Amman
Kenya	Ministry of Environment and Natural Resources PO Box 67839, Nairobi
(South) Korea	Environment Administration 17-16 Sincheondong, Songpa-gu, Seoul 134-240
Kuwait	Environment Protection Council PO Box 24885, 13104 Safat
Libya	National Committee for the Protection of the Environment Tripoli
Liechtenstein	Ministry of Agriculture, Forestry and Environment FL-9490 Vaduz
Luxembourg	Ministère de l'Environnement et des Eaux et Forets 51 rue de Prague, Luxembourg-Ville

Malaysia	Ministry of Science, Technology and the Environment 14th Floor, Wisma Sime Darby, Jalan Raja Laut, 50662 Kuala Lumpur
Malta	Environment Division Department of Health, Valletta
Mexico	Secretaría de Desarrollo Urbano y Ecología (SEDUE) Avenida Constituyentes 947, Edificio B, PB, Mexico City
Nepal	National Commission for Conservation of Natural Resources Babarmahal, Kathmandu
The Netherlands	Department for Nature Conservation, Environmental Protection and Wildlife Management Ministerie van Landbouw en Visserij, Postbus 20401, NL-200 EK The Hague
New Zealand	Ministry for the Environment PO Box 10362, Wellington
Nicaragua	Instituto Nicaragüense de Recursos Naturales y del Ambiente (IRENA) Apartado 5123, Managua
Nigeria	Environmental Planning and Protection Division Federal Ministry of Works and Housing, P M B 12698 Lagos
Norway	Royal Ministry of Environment Myngtaten 2, Postboks 8013-Dep., N-0030 Oslo 1
Oman	Council for the Conservation of Environment and Water Resources PO Box 5575, Ruwi
Pakistan	Environment and Urban Affairs Division Ministry of Housing and Works, Block B, Pakistan Secretariat, Islamabad
Panama	Ministerio de Planificación y Política Económica, Comisión Nacional del Medio Ambiente Apartado 2694, Zona 3, Panama
Papua New Guinea	Department of Environment and Conservation Central Government Buildings, Waigani, PO Box 6601, Boroko
Paraguay	Servicio Nacional de Saneamiento Ambiental (SENASA) Mariscal Estigarribiy Tacuary 796, Asunción
Peru	Ministerio de Agricultura, Dirección General Forestal y de Fauna (DGFF) Natalio Sánchez 220, 3er piso, Lima 11
Philippines	Department of the Environment and Natural Resources Quezon Avenue, Diliman, Quezon City 1100
Poland	Ministerstwo Ochrony Srodowiska i Zasobow Naturalnych ul. Wawelska 52-54, PL-02-067 Warsaw
Portugal	Secretaria de Estado do Ambiente e dos Recursos Naturals Rua do Seculo, 51-20, P-1200 Lisbon

Qatar	Environmental Protection Committee c/o Ministry of Public Health, PO Box 42 Doha
Romania	National Council for Environmental Protection Piata Victoriei 1, Bucharest
Saudi Arabia	Meteorology and Environmental Protection Administration (MEPA) PO Box 1358, Jeddah
Singapore	Ministry of the Environment Princess House, Alexandra Road, Singapore 0315
South Africa	Department of Environmental Affairs Private Bag X447, Pretoria 0001
Spain	Ministerio de Obras Públicas y Urbanismo-Dirección General de Medio Ambiente (DGMA) Paseo de la Castellana 67, E-28071 Madrid
Sri Lanka	Central Environmental Authority Maligawatte New Town, Colombo 10
Sweden	National Swedish Environment Protection Board PO Box 1302, S-171 25 Solna
Switzerland	Bundesamt für Umweltschutz/Office Fédéral de la Protection de l'Environnement CH-3003 Bern
Syria	Environmental Protection Agency Government House, Damascus
Taiwan	Environmental Protection Agency Taipei
Tanzania	National Environment Protection Council Ministry of Lands, Housing and Urban Development, PO Box 20671, Dar es Salaam
Thailand	National Environment Board Soi Prachasumpun 4, Rama Vl Road, Bangkok 10400
Tunisia	Ministère de l'Agriculture et de l'Environnement 30 rue Alain Savary, Tunis
Turkey	Prime Ministry, General Directorate of Environment Atatürk Bulvari 143, Bakanliklar, Ankara
USSR	State Committee for Environmental Protection 11 Nezhdanovoy ul., Moscow
United Arab Emirates	Higher Environmental Committee c/o Ministry of Health, PO Box 1853, Dubai
UK	Department of the Environment 2 Marsham Street, London SW1P 3EB
USA	Environment Protection Agency (EPA) Washington DC 20460

Uruguay	Instituto Nacional para la Preservación del Medio Ambiente (INPMA) Ministerio de Educación y Cultura, Reconquista 535, piso 8, Montevideo
Venezuela	Ministerio de Ambiente y de los Recursos Naturales Renovables Torra Norte, Centro Simón Bolivar, Caracas
Yugoslavia	Savez za Zastitu Covekoves Sredine 2 boulevar Lenjina, YU-11000 Belgrade

NATIONAL

Acid Rain Information Centre (ARIC)

Telephone. 061 228 6171 ext 2421 *Fax.* 061 236 7383
Address. Department of Environmental and Geographical Studies, Manchester Polytechnic, Chester Street, Manchester M1 5GD, UK
Official. Dr J. W. S. Longhurst (Director)

The Centre was set up in September 1984 as a non-profit organization to bring together research, abatement, education and public information activities on acid deposition.

It is particularly active in monitoring and survey work in the Greater Manchester area, but undertakes a national public information programme, and provides advice to local authorities on acid abatement techniques. It arranges conferences.

It publishes a number of reports, teaching packs, directories and pamphlets, and an Annual Report.

Originally it was funded by the local authority but is now supported by a number of organizations, the Department of the Environment, and National Power, and generates income from consultancy and from publications. Its annual budget is about £100,000.

Advisory Committee on Pollution of the Sea (ACOPS)

Telephone. 071 499 0704 *Fax.* 071 493 3092 *Telex.* 261681 Eascan
Address. 57 Duke Street, Grosvenor Square, London W1M 5DH, UK
Other centres. 85 ave Pierre Larousse, 92240 Malakoff, Paris, France.
Telephone. 1 47 46 10 12
Officials. Lord Callaghan of Cardiff (President); Rear Admiral M. L. Stacey (Vice-President, UK); Lord Clinton-Davies (Chairman); J. Wardley-Smith (Vice-Chairman); Douglas Jack (Hon. Treasurer); Dr Victor Sebek (Executive Secretary)

The Committee was set up first in 1952 by James Callaghan. It now has some 40 corporate members and 40 individuals in membership. Its aims are to: (a) promote preservation of the seas from pollution from human activities; (b) promote and conduct research into causes and effects of pollution of the seas including research into the means whereby the injurious effects of such pollution may be affected or reduced, and to publicize and comment on such research; and (c) advance public education by the study of the impact of human activities, especially extractive and manufacturing industries and transport, on the natural resources of the sea.

It is currently preparing for the 1991 Conference on land-based pollution.

It publishes a Yearbook, biennially, (1989/90 in preparation) and an annual survey of oil pollution round the UK coastline.

It has an annual budget of around £70,000, which is met by government grants, local authority contributions, sales of the Yearbooks and conferences and contract work.

AEA Technology: Environment and Energy (AEA-T/AEA-E&E)

Telephone. 0235 821111 *Fax.* 0235 43 2910 *Telex.* 83135 ATOMHA G
Address. Harwell Site, Didcot, Oxon, OX11 0SA, UK
Official. Dr J. Rae (Chief Executive)

AEA Technology is the trading name of the research and laboratory activities of the United Kingdom Atomic Energy Authority, founded in 1954, and Environment and Energy is one of its operating units. AEA-T as a whole has 10,000 employees and an annual budget of some £400 million. It is sponsored by the UK Department of Energy in the sense that the Secretary of State is accountable for it to Parliament, but its funds are generated by a wide range of contracts from customers in government, industry and overseas.

It is Europe's largest contract R&D organization and provides consultancy and R&D technical services in nuclear and non-nuclear science and technology. Specifically it deals with: waste management and disposal; chemical analysis; environmental pollution research and modelling; combustion processes; radiological protection; integrated pollution control; and energy technology assessment.

Alliance to Save Energy

Telephone. 202 857 0666 *Fax.* 202 331 9588
Address. 1725 K Street NW, Suite 914, Washington, DC 20006-1401, USA
Officials. Senator Timothy Wirth (Chairman of the Board); Senator John Heinz (Co-Chairman); James L. Wolf (Executive Director)

The Alliance was formed in 1977 to promote the efficient use of energy. It is a non-profit coalition of government, environmental, consumer and business leaders dedicated to its cause.

It conducts research and pilot projects to stimulate investment in energy efficiency and uses its experience in these activities to formulate policy initiatives and conduct educational programmes. Its programmes focus on five policy areas most affected by energy efficiency: the environment; affordable housing; competitiveness; national security; and economic development. It works with other organizations with similar goals both in the USA and internationally.

Alliance publications cover a wide range including, recently, *Making Residential Weatherization Programs more Cost-Effective* and *Energy Saving Opportunities for Non-Profit Organizations*.

It has an annual budget of US$800,000 coming from restricted and unrestricted grants.

American Council for an Energy-Efficient Economy (ACEEE/ACE^3)

Telephone. 202 429 8873 *Fax.* 202 429 2248
Address. 1001 Connecticut Avenue NW, No. 535, Washington, DC 20036, USA
Officials. Prof. Arthur Rosenfeld (President); Prof. Robert Socolow (Chairman); Dr Carl Blumstein (Secretary/Treasurer); Prof. Marc Ross (Technical Director)

The ACEEE is a non-profit organization dedicated to advancing energy-conserving technologies and policies. It conducts research, analysis, advocacy and information dissemination, and it organizes conferences.

It is not a membership organization, but it does send out notices of publications, conferences and other activities to individuals on the mailing list.

The ACEEE specifically: (a) advises governments and utilities on techniques for improving energy efficiency; (b) researches and prepares in-depth studies of energy-efficient technologies, policies and related issues; (c) organizes conferences for researchers, practitioners and policy makers; and (d) publishes and distributes books, conference proceedings and reports. (Its publication catalogue is available from the above address.)

It is conducting projects in Energy Efficiency and the Environment; Utilities; Transportation; Buildings; Appliances, Lighting and Equipment; Conservation Research and Development; Energy Efficiency in Developing Countries.

The Council is supported by a broad range of foundations, governmental organizations, research institutes, utilities and corporations.

American Wildlands (AWL)

Telephone. 303 771 0380 *Fax.* 303 694 9047
Address. 7500 E. Arapahoe Road, Suite 355, Englewood, CO 80112, USA
Other centres. Northern Rockies Office, 127 W. Main, Suite 1, Bozeman, MT 59715. *Telephone.* 406 586 4522
Officials. Sally A. Ranney (President); W. Mitchell (Vice-President); Andrew Wiessner (Secretary-Treasurer)

American Wildlands, formerly American Wilderness Alliance, founded in 1977 with the name changed in September 1989, is a national, non-profit conservation, education and recreation organization. It is dedicated to protecting bio-diversity and promoting the prudent management of wildland resources including wildlife, wilderness, wetlands, watersheds, free-flowing rivers and fisheries. It now has 3,500 members.

Its programmes focus largely on the interior western states of the USA and Alaska where 92% of America's public wildlands and resources are located. It carries out research and monitoring, particularly concerning forest management, river conservation schemes and wilderness protection. A recent major initiative is the "Recreation-Conservation Connection", building upon the growing interest and participation in outdoor recreation. Special projects involve a wildland resources research programme aimed at defining the economic benefits of pristine watersheds and the watershed rehabilitation project.

International involvements have been primarily focused on African wildlife including management issues and stopping the poaching of elephants.

AWL publishes a quarterly newsletter *It's Time to go Wild*, *On the Wild Side* (a quarterly newsletter of the Northern Rockies Office Timber Management Reform Program), *Wild America Magazine* and trip catalogues, an Annual Report and research reports.

Its annual budget is US$350,000 coming from foundations, corporations, individuals and membership subscriptions ($25 per annum).

Arbeitsgemeinschaft fur Umweltfragen e.V. (AGU)
(Study Group for Environmental Questions)

Telephone. 0228 37 50 05
Address. Matthias-Grunewald-Strasse 1-3, 5300 Bonn 2, Federal Republic of Germany
Officials. Dr Benno Weimann (Chairman); Arnim Schmulling (Manager)

The Group was formed in 1970 in Bonn by the initiative of the legislative and the executive branches. It now has 375 members consisting of institutions, government agencies and environmental organizations (over 40%), commercial companies (nearly 20%) and individuals.

It has published some 40 reports and papers on specific topics.

Asociación pro Conservación de la Pesca Deportiva Costarricense
(Costa Rican Sport Fishing Conservation Association)

Telephone. 506 20 1160 *Fax.* 506 31 5987
Address. Apartado 3089-1000, San José, Costa Rica
Officials. Carlos Barrantes (President); Murray Silberman (Executive Director)

The Association was formed in 1988 and now has about 20 companies as members. It aims for the conservation of species important to the sport fishing industry in central America. It produces educational programmes and pamphlets and holds public meetings. It expects to start publishing a bulletin later in 1990.

Its main battle is against the indiscriminate use of pesticides, gill netters and long liners.

It has a budget of US$100,000 coming from dues, donations and sales of small items such as T-shirts etc.

Association for Conservation of Energy (ACE)

Telephone. 071 935 1495 *Fax.* 071 935 8346
Address. 9 Sherlock Mews, London W1M 3RH, UK
Officials. W. N. Adsetts, OBE (Chairman); Andrew Warren (Director)

The ACE was formed in 1981 by a number of companies concerned with energy and conservation equipment, including Bayer UK Ltd., BPB UK Ltd., BP Energy, Danfoss Ltd., Dow Construction Products, Drayton Controls, Encon Insulation Services Ltd., Emstar Ltd., Freeman Group plc, Honeywell Controls Ltd., ICI Polyurethanes Group, Keith Young (Insulation Supplies) Ltd., Lin Pac Insulation Products, Pilkington Insulation Ltd., Rockwool Ltd., Sheffield Insulation Group plc, Tarmac Industrial Products Ltd., Thorn Lighting Ltd., Vencel Resi Ltd.

It aims to increase awareness of the benefits of and needs for energy conservation, particularly by lobbying.

Its funds, which amount to about £250,000 annually, come from sponsors and from commissioned research from such organizations as the EEC, CBI, Greenpeace, International Energy Agency, National Power and the World Wide Fund for Nature.

It has published many papers on a variety of subjects, particularly on energy conservation and global warming.

Australian Conservation Foundation (ACF)

Telephone. 03 416 1455 *Fax.* 03 416 0767
Address. 340 Gore Street, Fitzroy, Victoria, Australia. Campaign offices in every State capital and in Canberra
Officials. Peter Garrett (President); Phillip Toyne (Director)

ACF was founded in 1965 and now has 20,000 members and an annual budget of Aust$2 million and more than 40 full-time staff with generous support from volunteers. It is an independent, national, non-profit organization, financed mainly by membership fees, donations and sales of publications and less than 10% of the annual budget from government grants.

It campaigns to overcome environmental problems by positive action to protect the natural environment and to make Australia an ecologically sustainable society. Currently there are three major campaigns dealing with the greenhouse effect, ozone depletion and other global issues; protecting the rich bio-diversity, endangered species, wilderness and native forests; and the proper management of resources by reducing waste, encouraging recycling and minimizing pollution.

It publishes *Habitat Australia* (bi-monthly) and *Conservation News* (monthly).

British Ecological Society (BES)

Telephone. 071 434 2641
Address. Burlington House, Piccadilly, London W1V 0LQ, UK
Officials. P. J. Grubb (President); M. V. Angel, J. P. Grime (Vice-Presidents); A. J. C. Malloch, P. J. Edwards (Hon. Secretaries); R. A. Benton, B. D. Turner (Hon. Treasurers)

The Society, the world's first ecological society, was founded in 1913. Its first president was Sir Arthur Tansley, F.R.S, one of the pioneers of the science of ecology.

It exists to advance and support research in ecology, to disseminate the results of such research and to advance the education of the public. It holds two principal meetings each year and many others organized by its nine specialist groups which cover: production and decomposition ecology; industrial ecology; mathematical ecology; freshwater ecology; mires research; tropical ecology; teaching ecology; forest ecology and ecological genetics.

It publishes four major scientific journals: *Journal of Ecology; Journal of Animal Ecology; Journal of Applied Ecology;* and *Functional Ecology* together with a regular Bulletin to keep in touch with its members. There is also an annual Symposium volume and other, irregular, special issues. Through its Ecological Affairs Committee it becomes involved in political and social issues wherever ecology or ecologists can play a part. Membership is open to anyone who is interested in ecology and currently stands at 5,000, about half of whom live in the UK. The society's income of c. £200,000 a year is mainly from membership subscriptions with some publishing profits.

British Trust for Conservation Volunteers (BTCV)

Telephone. 0491 39766 *Fax.* 0491 39646
Address. 36 St. Mary's Street, Wallingford, Oxon, OX10 0EU, UK
Officials. HRH The Duke of Edinburgh (Patron); The Lord Norrie (President); George MacQuarrie (Chairman); Robert Morley (Director)

The BTCV was founded in 1959 and now has 11,000 members with 50,000 volunteers working with it annually. It works alongside several environment organizations, co-operating in many operations—WWF, NCC, RSNC, NT, RSPB etc.

Its aim is to protect, manage and improve the global, national and local environment by harnessing people's talents, energies and commitment in practical environmental action, in both training and in campaigns.

It organizes natural break conservation working holidays every day of the year in the UK (enjoyed in 1989 by 6,000 people); international working holidays in Luxembourg, Spain and France (1990); a local group network of 560 throughout England, Wales and Northern Ireland; volunteering opportunities during the week and weekend from its 75 offices in the UK.

Its campaigns include the Million Tree campaign; Communities in Conservation fortnight; and Access Footpath fortnight. Members (annual subscription £10) receive quarterly copies of *The Conserver*, a newspaper-type publication, the illustrated Annual Report and many details of the organized activities, natural breaks, training etc., and discounts on BTCV products.

BTCV is a charity which handles the volunteer work and has a trading subsidiary—Conservation Practice Ltd. Overall its turnover is over £9 million of which some £4 million relates to the volunteer work for which there are many sponsors. The major ones are Esso Petroleum Ltd who sponsor the Million Tree campaign, British Petroleum plc who fund the National Break holidays, Barclays Bank who support the Local Groups Development Unit and National Westminster Bank plc, Shell UK Ltd and Cookson. Funds also stem from local and central government, the Countryside Commission, industry, legacies, donations and charitable trusts.

Central Australian Conservation Council (CACC)

Telephone. 089 532988 *Fax.* 089 532988
Address. P.O. Box 2796, Alice Springs, NT 5750, Australia
Other centres. Also operating from the Arid Lands Environment Centre, Gregory Terrace, Alice Springs. *Telephone.* 089 526782
Officials. Mark Stafford Smith (President); Gresley Wakelin-Smith (Vice-President); John Donovan (Secretary)

The CACC, founded in the late 1970s, is a non-profit and community-based voluntary conservation organization, with a special interest in conservation issues in arid lands throughout Australia (covering some 70% of the country) and welcomes members from anywhere who share this interest. Its constitution describes its first object—"to make every effort to ensure that the air, land and waters of central Australia and elsewhere are used with wisdom and foresight, and that competing demands upon them are resolved in the best long-term interests of this nation".

It also fosters the conservation of distinct vegetation and fauna and important natural and archaeological features of central Australia including Aboriginal sacred sites; it acts as a clearing house for the collection, evaluation, dissemination and interchange of information relating the conservation; it co-operates with many other organizations concerned with conservation; in general it promotes conservation.

Currently it is conducting "endangered species" and "recycling" campaigns. It is involved in tourism planning and land-use planning and in running the Arid Lands Environment Centre.

It publishes the *Arid Lands Environment Centre Newsletter, Gardens in the Desert* and the *Alice Springs and Environs Wildlife Guide*; it produces and sells other materials including books, monographs, periodicals, pamphlets, lectures, radio and television programmes and films.

It has an annual budget of about A$50,000 coming from membership (A$20 per annum), Federal government grants, donations and profit from sales.

Conservation Trust (CT)

Telephone. 0734 868442, 0734 869464 *Fax.* 0734 314051
Address. National Environment Education Centre, George Palmer Site, Northumberland Avenue, Reading RG2 7PW, UK
Officials. Colin Hutchinson (Chairman); Peter Richardson (Hon. Treasurer); Peter Berry (Director)

The Trust is a national charity and is totally apolitical. It was originally established in 1970 by The Conservation Society (eventually disbanded in 1987 with all assets transferred to the Trust) to promote greater environmental understanding and awareness among people of all ages. It supports such charitable purposes as are calculated to promote research into and study of population, population growth and the use and development of science and technology in order to establish their effects on human beings, the population of the world or any part thereof, the human environment and the natural resources available to man. There are about 3,000 individual and 500 organization members.

It provides a focus for the collection and dissemination of knowledge relating to the global environment, a forum for the initiation of discussion concerning it and a source of service to other conservation associations. It has one of the largest resource banks of environmental reference and teaching material in the UK and its major data bases include: materials, diary, organizations, journals, articles and general information.

It has published a number of books the latest of which include *Who's Who in the Environment* and a *Guide to Resources in Environmental Education*. It produces much teaching material—briefing notes, study cards and guides, topic cards for seniors and juniors.

It has an annual budget of about £100,000 coming from membership subscriptions (27% in 1989), sales (18%), donations (16%) and grants (31%) from the Department of the Environment, and various sponsors including NCC, ICI, BP, ERT, etc.

Council on Environmental Quality (CEQ)

Address. 722 Jackson Place, NW, Washington, DC 20503, USA

The Council on Environmental Quality was established by the National Environmental Policy Act (NEPA) of 1969 to formulate and recommend national policies to promote the improvement of the quality of the environment. The Council chairman is appointed by the President of the United States with the advice and consent of the Senate. The Council is located within the Executive Office of the President.

CEQ provides expert opinion and policy advice to the President on environmental matters. The Chairman participates in the Domestic Policy Council, the Economic Policy Council and other Cabinet-level meetings. Some of the current issues on which the Council is working include: global change, recycling, pollution prevention, wetlands protection, energy conservation and Soviet–US co-operation.

CEQ has three categories of responsibility: to serve as the President's in-house advisor; to co-ordinate the position of Cabinet departments and independent agencies on environmental issues; and to administer the provisions of the National Environmental Policy Act.

Included within these responsibilities are: (a) advising the President on national and international policies to foster and promote improvement of environmental quality; (b) assisting and advising the President in the preparation of the annual Environmental Quality Report; (c) conducting studies and making recommendations on policy and legislation as requested by the President; (d) providing general leadership and support to the co-ordination of activities of the federal departments and agencies which affect, protect and improve environmental quality; (e) interpreting legal issues related to NEPA, assisting agencies and resolving inter-agency disputes and issuing regulations binding on federal agencies for the assessment of environmental impacts associated with proposals for federal actions; (f) fostering co-operation between federal and local government, the private sector and the environmental community; and (g) administering the President's Award for Excellence in Environmental Education which recognizes teachers who design and implement the most innovative and effective programmes to teach about the environment.

Council for the Protection of Rural England (CPRE)

Telephone. 071 976 6433 *Fax.* 071 976 6373
Address. Warwick House, 25 Buckingham Palace Road, London SW1W 0PP, UK
Officials. HM The Queen (Patron); David Puttnam, CBE (President); David W. Astor (Chairman); Andrew Purkis (Director)

The CPRE was founded in 1926 to protect and enhance the beauty and variety of the English Countryside, its towns and villages.

It now has 44,000 members and relies upon their subscriptions, donations, legacies, trust grants and government funds for specific projects, to meet its annual expenditure of £750,000.

It aims to educate decision-makers at EC, national and local level in the needs of countryside protection and how best to achieve it; and to stimulate public interest and involvement.

It publishes *Countryside Companion* three times per year, an Annual Report and many reports on particular topics.

The CPRE works co-operatively with many other environmental bodies and umbrella voluntary organizations, local and central government and with research teams at universities etc.

Countryside Commission

Telephone. 0242 521 381 *Fax.* 0242 584 270
Address. John Dower House, Crescent Place, Cheltenham, Glos. GL50 3RA, UK
Officials. Sir Derek Barber (Chairman); Adrian Phillips (Director-General)

The Commission was established in 1968 to succeed the National Parks Commission and became an independent Government Agency in 1982. Its task is to promote the conservation and enhancement of the natural beauty of the countryside and to encourage the provision of access to the countryside for informal recreation.

The Commission is the Government's adviser on landscape issues and has special responsibility for designating National Parks and Areas of Outstanding Natural Beauty (AONB), defining heritage coasts and establishing National Trails. Task Force Trees is a special unit set up to repair the damage caused to the landscape by the storm of October 1987. Its work has been extended to help with similar damage in the winter of 1989/90.

The Commission produces a wide range of publications, some priced, some free, details of which can be obtained from Countryside Publications, 19/23 Albert Road, Manchester M19 2EQ.

The Commission is funded by an annual grant from the Department of the Environment of about £22 million.

There are similar organizations in Wales and Scotland (see below).

Countryside Commission—Office for Wales
(Comisiwn Cefn Gwlad—Swyddfa Cymru)

Telephone. 0680 626799 *Fax.* 0686 629556
Address. Ladywell House, Newtown, Powys SY16 1RD, Wales, UK
Officials. Meuric Rees, CBE (Chairman); Martin Fitton (Chief Officer)

The Countryside Commission's committee for Wales has delegated powers for the Commission's work in Wales. It is funded by government grant-in-aid.

It helps to conserve the natural beauty of Wales. It does not own or manage any land but works through partnerships with local authorities and statutory and voluntary bodies by offering advice and providing grants.

It publishes an Annual Review—*The Countryside in Wales*—and leaflets on National Parks, the Welsh countryside and specialist books for farmers and countryside users.

On 1st April 1991 the Commission's and the Nature Conservancy Council's responsibilities in Wales are due to merge to form a new unified agency to care for the Welsh countryside and conservation.

Countryside Commission for Scotland (CCS)

Telephone. 0738 27921 *Fax.* 0738 30583
Address. Battleby, Redgorton, Perth PH1 3EW, Scotland, UK
Official. Duncan Campbell (Director)

The CCS was established under the Countryside (Scotland) Act 1967. It is a non-departmental government body, sponsored by the Scottish Development Department in the Scottish Office, its source of funds of about £6,000,000 per annum.

Its duties are to conserve and enhance the natural beauty of Scottish landscapes; to promote access to and enjoyment of the Scottish countryside; and to have regard to the rural economy.

It provides planning advice to local authorities and the Secretary of State for Scotland; it undertakes research and development; it gives grant aid for landscape and recreational schemes; and promotes understanding and awareness of countryside issues.

It publishes a wide range of free and priced pamphlets and information documents including a quarterly newspaper and an Annual Report. (Lists available, free, from the above address.)

It works with a large number of national, regional and local bodies and with individuals and voluntary groups.

Danmarks Naturfredningsforening (DN)
(The Danish Society for the Conservation of Nature)

Telephone. 33 32 20 21 *Fax.* 33 32 22 02
Address. Nørregade 2, København K., Denmark
Officials. Svend Bichel (President); David Rehling (Managing Director)

The Society was founded in April 1911 and now has 272,000 members.

Its aims are the protection of nature and the environment and concern with physical planning. At the moment it is most active in defending the right to the citizen initiative and the right to appeal. Both these features are unique to Danish society and are important in establishing consensus; both are under attack.

The Society publishes a full-colour, 48 page magazine *Natur og Miljø* four times a year and with a circulation of 300,000. It works closely with the European Environmental Bureau and with IUCN.

Its annual income is DKr 30,000,000 which comes almost entirely (95%) from membership fees.

Defenders of Wildlife

Telephone. 202 659 9510
Address. 1244 Nineteenth Street, NW, Washington, DC 20036, USA
Other centres. Regional offices in California, Montana and Oregon
Officials. M. Rupert Cutler (President); Brenda T. Moorman (Chair, Board of Directors); Dr Bernard Shanks (Vice-chair)

Defenders of Wildlife was founded in 1947 and now has 80,000 members and supporters. It is a non-profit, national, conservation organization, dedicated to protecting wild animals in their natural communities, especially native American endangered or threatened species. These include the grey and the red wolf, the Florida panther, the grizzly bear, the Western yellow-billed cuckoo, the desert tortoise, Kemp's Ridley sea turtle and many others.

It works through litigation, education and advocacy of wise public policies to protect the diversity of wildlife and to preserve the habitats critical to survival. It seeks to enhance and protect the natural abundance of wildlife, to prevent endangerment, to protect key habitats linked by wildlife movement corridors, to improve wildlife protection on public lands and to reduce marine entanglement and plastic pollution.

It publishes the magazine *Defenders* which in 1988 won an Ozzie "award of excellence", an illustrated Annual Report and a quarterly children's newsletter *The Comeback Trial*. Specialist publications, such as the *Oregon Wildlife Viewing Guide*, are also undertaken.

Its annual income (1988) was a little over US$4 million generated mainly from membership subscriptions (39%), contributions (36%) and bequests (18%). The largest items of expenditure were Information and Education (36%) and Wildlife Action (22%). 15% was spent on management, 10% on fundraising and the rest on membership communication and development.

Deutscher Naturschutzring e.V.—Bunderverband fur Umweltschutz (DNR)
(German Federation of Nature Conservation Societies)

Telephone. 49 228 44 15 05
Address. Kalkuhlstrasse 24, D-5300 Bonn 3, Federal Republic of Germany

The umbrella organization for some 90 environmental groups in Germany totalling over three million members,

Dutch Foundation for East European Environmental Contacts

Telephone. 3120 853857 *Fax.* 3120 838955
Address. Postbus 5627, NL-1007 AP Amsterdam, The Netherlands

The Air Pollution Action Network was formed in 1987 (but is no longer active) and in 1989 its Airplan East–West Project became the East–West project of this Dutch Foundation, whose main aim is co-operation with East European environmental NGOs. It has five employees and some 50 volunteers.

It has one general East–West project on environmental networking and campaigning and four bilateral working groups on Poland, Hungary, the GDR and Czechoslovakia.

It publishes newsletters and reports and works with other international groups such as the EEB and Friends of the Earth International.

It is mainly financed by the Dutch Ministry for Public Health and Physical Planning.

Environmental Data Services Ltd (ENDS)

Telephone. 071 278 4745 *Fax.* 071 837 7612
Address. Unit 24, Finsbury Business Centre, 40, Bowling Green Lane, London EC1R 0NE, UK
Official. Marek Mayer (Editor)

The ENDS Report has been published monthly since May 1978 and provides a source of accurate and independent environmental information for business, industrial and government readers. It covers a wide range of environmental issues, particularly with a business perspective, and related information on companies' activities, legislation and products.

It is available only by subscription which covers seven main services: (a) early warning of policy and legislative initiatives in the UK, the EC and other international organizations; (b) interpretation of the business implications of new rules, regulations and legal judgements; (c) analyses of specific problems; (d) case studies of best industrial practice; (e) latest news on developments; (f) details of products and services; and (g) synopses of key national and international studies on pollution and waste management and their market implications.

Environmental Defense Fund (EDF)

Telephone. 212 505 2100 *Fax.* 212 505 2375
Address. 257 Park Avenue, South; 16th Floor, New York, NY 10010, USA
Officials. Frederic D. Krupp (Executive Director); Frank E. Loy (Chairman of the Trustees)

The EDF is a non-profit organization, established in 1967 by a group of volunteer scientists, and now with a membership of 150,000 and a professional staff (52) of environmental scientists, lawyers, economists and computer experts.

It is involved in many projects and campaigns. It was involved with the World Bank in redirecting its funding away from damaging projects to sustainable developments (see Part I, Section 13) and in several domestic successes in changing intended actions and policies. It is working in most of the main areas of interest such as protection of rain forests, the potential damage to plant and animal life from the "ozone hole" over Antarctica and in global warming. It is actively promoting direct contacts and links internationally, particularly with eastern Europe and the USSR.

It publishes details of its work in an annual report and issues a newsletter, *EDF Letter* to members.

The annual expenditure now exceeds US$12 million of which about two-thirds comes from membership dues and contributions and a quarter from foundation grants. It has launched an appeal for a capital fund of $5 million for its project "Program for the Future". (Over $3 million pledged by mid-1990.)

It has regional offices in:

1616 P Street N.W., Washington, DC 20036. *Telephone.* 212 387 3500
5655 College Avenue, Oakland, CA 94618. *Telephone.* 415 658 8008
1405 Arapahoe Avenue, Boulder, CO 80302. *Telephone.* 303 440 4901
1108 East Main Street, Richmond, VA 23219. *Telephone.* 804 708 1297
128 East Hargett Street, Raleigh, NC 27605. *Telephone.* 919 821 7793

A further office in Austin, Texas is due to open in 1990.

Environment Council

Telephone. 071 278 4736 *Fax.* 071 837 9688
Address. 80 York Way, London N1 9AG, UK
Officials. The Earl of Cranbrook (President); Dr Malcolm Aickin (Chairman);
Steve Robinson (Chief executive)

The Council was formed in 1969 and now has 35 members. It is the umbrella body for UK organizations concerned with the environment. Membership is open to non-governmental voluntary and professional organizations, working at national or regional level, and principally concerned with conservation, planning, management or care of some aspect of the environment. It was previously known as CoEnCo—The Council for Environmental Conservation.

It focuses attention on major environmental issues and facilitates co-operation between non-governmental organizations concerned with the environment. It makes authoritative representations to Government and other bodies. It has three main areas of work:

the Council activities, the Business and Environment Programme and the General Programme.

The Council meets four times a year to discuss key environmental issues and examine ways forward. Specialist committees are convened for topics requiring more detailed discussion.

The Business and Environment Programme helps managers realize the opportunities generated by growing environmental pressures on business and appreciate the risks of ignoring them. It promotes the concept that "environmental sense is commercial sense".

The General Programme disseminates environmental information to a wide range of individuals and organizations through publications, the referrals service, conferences and exhibitions.

The Council publishes *Habitat*—a monthly digest of environmental news—and a number of leaflets, guides and directories.

Its annual expenditure is approximately £100,000, met by donations from trusts, sponsorship by companies, membership fees, income from publications and a grant from the UK Department of the Environment.

The present members are:

Airfields Environment Federation
Anglers Co-operative Association
Central Scotland Countryside Trust
Confederation of British Industry
Council for British Archaeology
Council for the Protection of Rural Wales
Countryside Commission
The Environment Foundation
Habitat Scotland
Henry Doubleday Research Foundation English Heritage
The Landscape Institute
National Association of Local Councils
National Council for the Conservation of Plants and Gardens
National Council for Voluntary Organizations
National Society for Clean Air
The National Trust
The National Trust for Scotland
Nature Conservancy Council
The Pedestrians Association
River Thames Society
Royal Forestry Society of England, Wales and Northern Ireland
Royal Society of Arts
The Soil Association
The Tidy Britain Group
Town and Country Planning Association
Ulster Society for the Preservation of the Countryside
Universities Federation for Animal Welfare
Vincent Wildlife Trust
World Wide Fund for Nature—UK
Youth Hostels Association (England and Wales)

Field Studies Council (FSC)

Telephone. 0743 850674, 0743 850997 *Fax.* 0743 850178
Address. Central Services, Preston Montford, Montford Bridge, Shrewsbury SY4 1HW, UK
Other centres. Residential and educational centres in England and Wales
Officials. Ian D. Mercer (President); David J. Stanbury (Chairman); A. D. Thomas (Chief Executive)

In 1943 there was an inaugural meeting of the then Council for the Promotion of Field Studies, which became the Field Studies Council in 1946. It is a charity and its aim and slogan is "Environmental Understanding for All". It now has 5,700 members and provides educational courses to over 30,000 people a year.

The Council manages nine residential centres and one day centre in rich and diverse English and Welsh locations. It services the increasing market for environmental courses for schools, universities, interested amateurs and committed professionals. It provides expert tuition, field equipment, laboratory facilities, library resources and educational sites with long-term data runs. It employs enthusiastic and qualified environmental educators who undertake in-service training, including health and safety. Hundreds of courses are arranged each year and attract wide participation. Many are specifically designed to meet educational criteria, such as GCSE, and "Courses for All" cater for a variety of tastes and interests of older participants.

It also organizes expeditions overseas which, depending on the location, include the study of birds, flowers, butterflies and landscapes as well as painting and photography. In 1990 expeditions, each led by a tutor, are planned to Canada, Kenya, Jamaica, Andulacia, The Scillies, Sarawak, Florida, Morocco, Iceland, Greece, The Alps, Turkey, The Pyrenees, Sicily, Kashmir, Ireland and Swaziland.

The FSC's Research Centre is located at Milford Haven (Director, Dr Clive Morgan) and specializes in environmental impact assessments and monitoring. It offers contract research and consultancy service in biological, chemical and physical environmental sciences, and is widely used by industry, particularly the oil industry, and government agencies to resolve environmental problems.

It publishes the scientific journal *Field Studies* and a number of books and pamphlets relating to specific places or subjects. It also produces the Aidgap Keys (Aids to Identification in Difficult Groups of Animals and Plants).

The FSC works closely with many other bodies in both environmental and educational fields.

Its annual income exceeds £3,000,000, mainly from course fees and contracts and sponsors for specific projects or publications.

Fondation—Hellef Fir D'Natur (HFN)

Telephone. 47 23 69 *Fax.* 47 47 27
Address. BP 709, L-2017 Luxembourg, Luxembourg
Officials. Camille Dimmer (President); Jean-Pierre Schmitz (Secretary)

The foundation was formed in December 1982 with the aim of purchasing rare bio-topes in order to create nature reserves. It now manages nature reserves which cover some 200 hectares in the whole country and carries out biological studies for the Ministry of the Environment.

It publishes leaflets about nature protection. It is funded by private donations. It works with Letzebuerger Natur—a Vulleschutzliga, with whom it shares accommodation, and other similar organizations.

France Nature Environnement
(La Fédération Française des Sociétés de Protection de la Nature, FFSPN)

Telephone. 43 36 79 95 *Telex.* 260921
Address. Maison de Chevreul, 57 rue Cuvier, 75005 Paris, France
Officials. Pierre Delacroix (President)

The Federation was created in 1968 and its domain extends throughout metropolitan France and the departments and territories overseas. It is concerned with the protection of wild plants and animals against the intrusion of such things as roads, nuclear power stations and polluting industries etc. which destroy the environment. There are many national and regional associations in membership which overall total 850,000 persons.

Its aims, under the slogan "we have not inherited the earth from our parents, we borrow it from our children", are to: (a) preserve animal and plant species, especially those that are rare or threatened; (b) safeguard the environment, not only in protected zones but throughout the country; (c) combat all causes of degradation of the living heritage, especially in demanding the carrying out of impact analyses and their application; (d) demand the strict adherence to laws and regulations concerning the protection of the environment; (e) reinforce this legal protection by the preparation and promotion of new legislative proposals; and (f) train the population in the long-term management of natural resources.

It provides information and undertakes specific campaigns, for example on the quality of potable water and on the use of lead in motor spirit; on the protection of Pyrenees bears, the re-introduction of the lynx and the saving of the elephant.

The federation publishes books and brochures and a monthly *La Lettre du Herisson*.

It has an annual budget of over FFr 5 million, met by subscriptions and grants from the Ministère de l'Environnement and the EC, and is reliant upon voluntary help.

Fundación Ecuatoriana para la Conservación de la Naturaleza (NATURA)

Telephone. 459 013; 447 341 *Fax.* 593 2 43 44 49 *Telex.* 21211 NATURA ED
Address. Avenida America 5656 y Voz Andes, Quito, Ecuador
Officials. Rafael Velez (President); Yolanda Kakabadse (Executive Director);
Ruth Elena Ruiz (Technical Director)

The foundation, created in 1978, is a private, non-profit Ecuadorian organization which aims: (a) to promote the conservation and sustainable use of the natural resources of Ecuador, especially through environmental education and the wise planning of development; (b) to preserve Ecuador's biodiversity; and (c) to promote the development and improvement of the lifestyle of its population.

It has a countrywide membership of 6,000 and 100 staff members.

Currently, (a) it has a major programme of environmental education, called EDUNAT III; (b) it supports eight protected natural areas with funds coming from debt swaps; (c) it manages two databases for Amazonia and Pesticides (RAP-AL network); (d) it provides the administration of Pasochoa Protected Forest, a Natural Reserve; (e) it is a data centre for conservation at national level; (f) it has a solid waste management project at national level and an industrial waste management project at local level; and (g) it has a television series about Ecuador's natural resources.

It publishes a magazine (80 pages, full colour) about conservation issues and a Spanish version of the international newspaper *WWF News*. It also publishes a national bulletin about conservation issues and the RAP–AL network bulletin about pesticides. It is affiliated to the WWF and a member of IUCN.

Its annual expenditure is about US$ 100,000, met by members' contributions, government grants and donors such as WWF, USAIS, IUCN and foundations.

Green Movement Organization

Telephone. 285 7187
Address. Novodmitrovskaya, 5A, 125015 Moscow, USSR
Officials. Oleg M. Poptsov (Head of Co-ordinating Board); Lubov B. Rubynchyk (Secretary of the Board); Sergey V. Ryabchuk (Head of Information Service)

The All-Union organization was founded in February 1989 to help prevent possible ecological catastrophes; to resolve eco-cultural problems; and to struggle against monopolism in ecology. It now has over 2,000 members.

It is creating an information service for all ecological organizations in the Soviet Union and undertaking television discussion on topics such as nuclear plant problems. It is in close contact with the Institute for Applied Ecology in Frieburg in the FRG and with more than 200 organizations in the USSR.

It publishes *Land* jointly with the Agricultural Union and is sponsored by the magazine *Selskaya Molodezh* and by the Centre for Social Initiatives and Research of the Academy of Sciences, USSR.

Its annual expenditure is about 15,000 roubles.

Institution of Environmental Sciences (IES)

Telephone. 0252 515511
Address. 14, Princes Gate, Hyde Park, London SW7 1PU, UK
Officials. The Duke of Westminster (President); Prof. J. Rose (Vice President);
Dr M. Romeril (Chairman); Dr J. F. Potter (Hon. Secretary)

A series of meetings held in 1971–72 at the premises of the Royal Society, London, culminated in the establishment of the Institution and its inaugural *conversazione* took place at the House of Lords in January 1973. It now has 650 members plus 100 collective members.

The Institute is a non-profit making, non-governmental organization, registered as a charity. It aims to establish and control an institution for all persons concerned with an interest in environmental sciences; to function as a learned body and to co-ordinate matters of public and professional interest concerning environmental sciences; to promote inter-disciplinary studies and education research; to diffuse information by holding meetings and publishing suitable information; and to bring together into a corporate professional body, all persons possessing responsibilities for environmental affairs.

The scope of its operation covers the full spectrum of the environmental sciences—ecology, education, pollution, public health, urban problems, genetic effects, climatic conditions, effects of technology, transport, etc., both from a fundamental and an applied aspect.

It publishes *The Environmentalist*, an international quarterly journal, an IES News Sheet, six per annum for members only and IES Proceedings at variable intervals and again for members.

It has an annual income of £30,000 from subscriptions.

Institut pour une politique Européenne de l'Environnement (IPEE)

Telephone. 142 22 12 34 *Fax.* 145 44 18 31
Address. 55 rue de Varenne, 75341 Paris Cedex 7, France
Officials. Dr Thierry Lavoux (Director)

The Institute was founded in 1976 to provide a European consultancy on environmental issues. It is sponsored by the French ministries of the Environment, Agriculture and Health and various institutions and has a staff of five persons in Paris.

It is, at present, working on: agriculture and the environment; information system for the Rhine; and the implementation of the European environmental regulations in member states.

It has an annual budget of FFr 2.5 million met by contracts with administrations and industry.

Letzeburger Natur—a Vulleschutzliga (LNVL)
Ligue Luxembourgeoise pour la Protection de la Nature et des Oiseaux

Telephone. 47 23 64 *Fax.* 47 47 27
Address. BP 709, L-2017 Luxembourg, Luxembourg
Officials. Ed. Melchior (President)

The League was founded in 1920 and now has 12,000 members. Its purpose is the protection of nature in Luxembourg. It carries out studies of bird populations and undertakes practical work, for example the planting of hedgerows, in order to protect nature.

It publishes a number of leaflets for public information and a quarterly journal *Regu-*

lus. In 1988 it produced an atlas of *Breeding Birds in Luxembourg* and in 1990 *Vogel Luxemburgs*.

Its income is generated by members' subscriptions and from the sale of stickers, posters, books and pamphlets.

Liechtensteinische Gesellschaft für Umweltschutz (LGU)

Telephone. 25262 *Fax*. 82819
Address. Heiligkreuz 52, 9490 Vaduz, FL (Furstentum Liechtenstein), Liechtenstein
Officials. Dr Peter Goop (President); Wilfried Marxer-Schadler (Secretary)

The Society was founded in 1973 and now has 700 members.

Its aim is simply the protection of the environment. It holds exhibitions, undertakes media work and joins internationally with CIPRA (Commission Internationale pour la Protection des Régions Alpines), NATUROPA etc.

It publishes *Liechtensteiner Umweltbericht* two or three times a year and *LGU-Mitteilungen* quarterly and a series of pamphlets.

It has an annual budget of SFr 120,000 obtained from members' subscriptions, local communities, the government and other sponsors.

Marine Pollution Control Unit (MPCU)

Telephone. 071 405 6911 *Fax*. 071 831 7681 *Telex*. 8812050
Address. Department of Transport, Sunley House, 90–93 High Holborn, London WC1V 6PL, UK
Officials. Capt. W. H. H. McLeod (Director of Marine Emergency Operation)

The MPCU was set up by the UK Department of Transport in 1974 to exercise the responsibility accepted by central Government for counter-pollution operations at sea when spilled oil or other dangerous substances from ships threatens major pollution of the UK coast or is likely to harm important fisheries or important concentrations of sea birds.

The Unit, based in London, maintains a national emergency contingency plan and resources to cover its at-sea clean-up responsibilities. It also provides advice and assistance to local authorities who are primarily responsible for coastal clean-up. Stockpiles of specialist beach cleaning equipment are maintained for deployment; a research programme relating to both at-sea and on-shore clean-up is funded, the results of research are disseminated to interested parties; local authorities and offshore operators are advised on their contingency plans; and assistance is given in training of local authority staff in beach cleaning management and techniques. The Unit also compiles and processes the Government's claims for compensation from polluters or their insurers and follows up reports of possible illegal discharges at seas with a view to initiating prosecutions.

The Unit co-operates closely with many other Government ministries and agencies, both local and national, and with industry bodies. It discharges the UK Government's undertakings under the Bonn Agreement (for Co-operation in dealing with Pollution of the North Sea by Oil and Other Harmful Substances, signed in September 1983 by the coastal states) and participates in the *Mancheplan* with France—a bilateral agreement for co-ordinating resources from both countries in the event of a large incident in the Channel, including search and rescue operations as well as counter pollution measures—and in *Norbritplan*, a similar arrangement with Norway, particularly with respect to oil operations in the Norwegian and UK sectors of the North Sea.

Information notes on the details of response and responsibility are available from the above address.

The Unit has a staff of 13 and an annual budget of £7 million funded by the UK Treasury.

National Audubon Society (Audubon)

Telephone. 212 546 9100
Address. 950 Third Avenue, New York, NY 10022, USA
Capital Office: 801 Pennsylvania Avenue SE, Washington, DC 20003, USA.
Telephone. 202 547 9009 *Fax.* 202 547 9022
National Education Office: Route 4, Box 171, Sharon, Connecticut 06069, USA.
Telephone. 203 364 0520
The Society has regional offices in Anchorage, Alaska; Indianapolis, Indiana; Camp Hill, Pennsylvania; Albany, New York; Boulder, Colorado; Tallahassee, Florida; Austin, Texas; Sacramento, California; Manhattan, Kansas. It has state offices in Honolulu, Hawaii; Minneapolis, Minnesota; Santa Fe, New Mexico; Waisfield, Vermont; and Olympia, Washington.
Officials. Peter A. A. Berle (President); James A. Cunningham (Senior VP Finance and Administration); Les Line (Publications); Susan Parker (Development and Marketing); J. P. Myers (Science and Sanctuaries); Elizabeth Raisbeck (Regional and Govt. Affairs)

The Society was founded in 1905 in New York as the National Association of Audubon Societies for the protection of Birds and Wild Animals, from state Audubon societies. These had grown up mainly to protest over the extensive use of feathers, particularly of wild birds such as plumed wading birds, for the millinery trade. It was originally devoted mainly to the study of bird life, and named after John James Audubon (1785–1851) a French-American ornithologist who initiated the study of bird migrations and completed a large and beautiful collection of paintings of natural history studies. The Society now has 600,000 members organized in over 500 local chapters in North and Central America.

It now has wide interests and believes that all life is interdependent. It sees its role as "advocate for the planet" and has developed its co-ordinated effort in the independent fields of research, education and action. Its research staff include experts in ecology, biology, energy and biotechnology. It has 88 wildlife sanctuaries protecting rare habitats and wildlife and runs nature education centres, and conducts summer ecology camps and workshops. While a passion for birds and wildlife is still the force that most often brings members together, the Society has become involved in the full spectrum of environmental issues, including such global concerns as air and water quality, population, energy policy, climate disruption and the management of wildlife refuges.

The Society publishes the conservation and nature magazine *Audubon*; an ornithological journal *American Birds*; a newsjournal of environmental issues and grassroots activism, *Audubon Activist*; a newsletter as part of the youth education programme, *Audubon*

Adventures and an encyclopaedia of wildlife management programmes, the *Audubon Wildlife Report*. It has made the quarterly, award-winning "World of Audubon Specials" for television which bring the conservation message to millions of people outside the Society's membership.

The Society is a non-profit organization with an annual budget of US$34 million, met by membership dues, gifts and foundation and corporate grants.

National Resources Defense Council, Inc. (NRDC)

Telephone. 212 727 2700 *Fax.* 212 727 1773
Address. 40 West 20th Street, New York, NY 10011, USA
Officials. Adrian W. DeWind (Chairman); John H. Adams (Executive Director)

NRDC was formed in 1970 and now has 139,000 members. Its slogan is "The power of law, the power of science, the power of people, in the defense of the environment". It is a non-profit, tax-exempt membership organization.

It has campaigned against the use of CFCs and other chemicals and has successfully taken several organizations and government departments to court to prevent or compensate for environmental damage. For example it was active in helping persuade the US Government to back a phase-out of CFCs and its Atmospheric Protection Initiative team is now working to write the phase-out into the International Ozone Treaty, now to be revised.

It launched a citizen partnership with the Soviet Academy of Sciences to combat global warming. NRDC and Soviet scientists are developing a series of large-scale energy efficiency projects to show how carbon dioxide pollution can be cut by reducing dependence on fossil fuels.

NRDC has an annual budget of about US$13,500,000 coming from membership dues (about half) and from foundations' contributions, court-awarded fees and contracts.

National Society for Clean Air and Environmental Protection (NSCA)

Telephone. 0273 26313 *Fax.* 0273 735802
Address. 136 North Street, Brighton BN1 1RG, UK
Officials. Sir John Mason (President); Air Commodore John Langston (Secretary-General)

The Society is a non-governmental, non-political organization and charity. Founded in 1899 as The Smoke Abatement Society, its objectives are to secure environmental improvement by promoting clean air through the reduction of air pollution, noise and other contaminants, while having due regard to the other aspects of the environment. NSCA brings together pollution expertise from industry, local and central government, technical, academic and institutional bodies.

The Society publishes a Pollution Handbook and Glossary and many leaflets, reports, teaching packs and conference papers.

It relies upon subscriptions and donations from an extensive membership.

Natural Environment Research Council (NERC)

Telephone. 0793 411500 Fax. 0793 411501
Address. Polaris House, North Star Avenue, Swindon SN2 1EU, UK (also at 22 Henrietta Street London WC2E 8NA *Telephone.* 071 836 6707 *Fax.* 071 497 9061)
Other centres. A number of research establishments around the country.
Officials. Prof. John Knill (Chairman); Dr Eileen Buttle (Secretary)
NERC, established in 1965, has the responsibility for planning, encouraging and carrying out research in the physical and biological sciences which explain the natural processes of the environment. The council is divided into four main areas of study: marine and atmospheric sciences, terrestrial and freshwater sciences, earth sciences and polar sciences, and operates various research establishments and units:

Institute of Oceanographic Science, Deacon Laboratory, Brook Road, Wormley, Godalming, Surrey GU8 5UB. *Telephone.* 142 879 4141 *Fax.* 042 879 3066
Dr J.D. Woods (Director, Marine Sciences); Dr C. P. Summerhayes (Director)
The laboratory's programme is concerned with the study of the oceans and their interaction with the atmosphere and the seabed, with the emphasis on deep ocean physics, chemistry, geology, geophysics and biology, and substantial effort on instrumentation and ocean engineering. It provides the Marine Information and Advisory Service (MIAS).

Plymouth Marine Laboratory, Prospect Place, West Hoe, Plymouth PL1 3DH. *Telephone.* 0753 222772 *Fax.* 0752 670637
Dr B. L. Bayne (Director)
Formed by the merger in 1988 of the Institute for Marine Environmental Research and the Marine Biological Association of the UK. Research is directed at the development of predictive models for estuarine, coastal shelf and oceanic ecosystems.

Proudman Oceanographic Laboratory, Bidston Observatory, Birkenhead, Merseyside L43 7RA. *Telephone.* 051 653 8633 *Fax.* 051 653 6269
Dr B. S. McCartney (Director)
The laboratory co-ordinates the five-year North Sea Community Research Project (CRP) and is involved in numerical modelling and in studies of physical processes including fronts, current profiles and sediment transport.

Dunstaffnage Marine Laboratory, P.O. Box 3, Oban, Argyll PA34 4AD.
Telephone. 0631 72244 *Fax.* 0631 65518
Prof. J. B. L. Matthews (Director)
NERC took over the management of the laboratory from the Scottish Marine Biological Association (SMBA) in April 1989 although the SMBA continues to receive a Grant-in-Aid as a contribution to its own scientific programme. The laboratory's programme is to promote the study of marine science through research and education. The research is mainly concerned with understanding the processes which control the marine ecosystem, particularly in Scottish coastal waters but also in the adjacent parts of the North Atlantic Ocean.

Sea Mammal Research Unit, c/o British Antarctic Survey, High Cross, Madingley Road, Cambridge CB3 0ET. *Telephone.* 0223 311354 *Fax.* 0223 62616
Dr J. Harwood (Head of Unit)
The work of the Unit is designed to investigate the role of seals and whales in the marine ecosystem and, in particular, the effect of management on their populations.

Robert Hooke Institute, Clarendon Laboratory, University of Oxford, Parks Road, Oxford OX1 3PU. *Telephone.* 0865 272200

The unit undertakes collaborative research in atmospheric and associated oceanographic sciences between Oxford University, the Meteorological Office and NERC.

Unit of Aquatic Biochemistry, c/o University of Stirling, Stirling FK9 4LA.
Telephone. 0786 73171
Prof. J. R. Sargent (Head of Unit).

UAB conducts research into basic biochemical processes in marine ecosystems including studies on the exploitation and protection of marine resources.
Dr. P. B. H. Tinker (Director, Terrestrial and Freshwater Sciences).
Institute of Terrestrial Ecology, North. Dr O. W. Heal (Director).
Edinburgh Research Station, Bush Estate, Penicuik, Midlothian EH26 0QB.
Telephone. 031 445 4343/6 *Fax.* 031 445 3943
Dr M. G. R. Cannell (Head of Station)
Merlewood Research Station, Grange-over-Sands, Cumbria LA11 6JU.
Telephone. 05395 32264 *Fax.* 05395 34705
Dr M. Hornung (Head of Station)
Banchory Research Station, Hill of Brathens, Glassel, Banchory, Kincardineshire AB3 4BY. *Telephone.* 03302 3434 *Fax.* 03302 3303
Dr B. W. Staines (Head of Station)

Institute of Terrestrial Ecology, South. Dr T. M. Roberts (Director)
Monks Wood Experimental Station, Abbots Ripton, Huntingdon, Cambridgeshire PE17 2LS. *Telephone.* 04873 381/8 *Fax.* 04873 467
Dr M. D. Hooper (Head of Station)
Bangor Research Station, Penrhos Road, Bangor, Gwynedd LL57 2LQ.
Telephone. 0248 370045 *Fax.* 0248 355365
Dr C. Milder (Head of Station)
Furzebrook Research Station, Wareham, Dorset BH20 5AS. *Telephone* 09295 51518/9 *Fax.* 09295 51087
Dr M. G. Morris (Head of Station)

The ITE studies the factors determining the distribution and abundance of individual plant and animal species and the structure and functioning of terrestrial ecosystems and their interaction with freshwater systems.

Institute of Hydrology, Maclean Building, Crowsmarsh Gifford, Wallingford, Oxon OX10 8BB. *Telephone.* 0491 38800 *Fax.* 0491 32256
Prof. W. B. Wilkinson (Director)

The Institute has a broad programme of both fundamental and applied studies into the movement and behaviour of water in its translation from rainfall into runoff or evaporation.

Institute of Virology and Environmental Microbiology, Mansfield Road, Oxford OX1 3SR.
Telephone. 0865 512361 *Fax.* 0865 59962
Prof. D. H. L. Bishop (Director)

IVEM (renamed in April 1989 from the Institute of Virology) undertakes research on micro-organisms, in particular viruses that cause disease of anthropods and those that are transmitted by anthropods to other organisms, and the ecological importance of naturally occurring viruses both as regulators of populations of insect species in various ecosystems and as potential controllers of insect pests.

Institute of Freshwater Ecology. Prof. J. G. Jones (Director).
Windermere Laboratory, The Ferry House, Far Sawrey, Ambleside, Cumbria LA22 OLP.
Telephone. 09662 2468/9 *Fax.* 09662 6914.

Dr. A. D. Pickering (Head of Northern Division)
The River Laboratory East Stoke, Wareham, Dorset BH20 6BB. *Telephone.* 0929 462314 *Fax.* 0929 462180
Dr A. D. Berrie (Officer in Charge)
Eastern Rivers Group, c/o Monks Wood Experimental Station, Abbots Ripton, Huntingdon, Cambridge PE17 2LS. *Telephone.* 04873 381/9 *Fax.* 04873 467
Dr L. C. V. Pinder (Head of Group)
Scottish Freshwater Group, c/o Bush Estate, Penicuik, Midlothian EH26 0QB. *Telephone.* 031 445 4343/6 *Fax.* 031 445 3943
Dr A. E. Bailey-Watts (Head of Group)

IFE was formed in April 1989 to incorporate the laboratories of the Freshwater Biological Association (FBA) and the Scottish Freshwater Group of ITE. The research programme includes basic chemical and physical studies; biological studies covering taxonomy, community structure, feeding behaviour, population ecology and physiology and their relations with environmental variables both natural and man-induced; and the processes of element cycling and energy transfer.

Unit of Comparative Plant Ecology, Department of Animal and Plant Sciences, University of Sheffield, Sheffield S10 2TN. *Telephone.* 0742 768555 *Fax.* 0742 760159
Prof. J. P. Grime (Director)

UCPE developed from the Grassland Research Unit and studies the interaction of plants with their environment.

Water Resource Systems Research Unit, Department of Civil Engineering, University of Newcastle upon Tyne, Claremont Road, Newcastle upon Tyne NE1 7RU. *Telephone.* 091 232 8511
Prof. P. E. O'Connell (Director)

The Unit undertakes mathematical modelling for predicting the transport and fate of pollutants within the land phase of the hydrological cycle.

Interdisciplinary Research Centre in Population Biology, Imperial College, Silwood Park, Ascot, Berkshire SL5 7PY. *Telephone.* 0990 23911
Prof. J. H. Lawton (Director)

The Centre has been established to develop general principles of population biology and to produce methods of predicting, controlling and manipulating the density and structure of populations.

Prof. J. C. Briden (Director, Earth Sciences).
British Geological Survey, Keyworth, Nottingham NG12 5GG. *Telephone.* 06077 6111 *Fax.* 06077 6602
F. Geoffrey Larminie (Director)

The Survey has offices and directorate around the UK. Its work is centred upon modern geological surveying of the UK landmass, the UK continental shelf and numerous areas overseas and the maintenance of national archives of geological data and specimens.

Antarctic Sciences.
British Antarctic Survey, High Cross, Madingly Road, Cambridge CB3 0ET. *Telephone.* 0223 61188 *Fax.* 0223 62616
Dr. D. J. Drewry (Director)

The establishment by the Royal Navy of "Operation Tabarin" in 1943 marked the beginning of the scientific programme in Antarctica now carried out by BAS. It is responsible for nearly all the British research in the Antarctic, South Georgia and the South Sandwich Islands under the broad headings of Atmospheric, Earth and Life Sciences. It discovered the "Ozone Hole" (see Part I, Sections 2 and 9).

NERC publishes a detailed Annual Report, strategy documents and a newsletter *NERC News*, and many scientific papers. It co-operates with a wide range of similar institutions in the UK and internationally.

Its annual expenditure (1990/1) is about £135 million, of which two-thirds is from government grant-in-aid and one third from commissioned research, again about two-thirds of this from government departments.

Nature Conservancy Council (NCC)

Telephone. 0733 40345 *Fax.* 0733 68834
Address. Northminster House, Peterborough PE1 1UA, UK
Officials. Sir William Wilkinson (Chairman); T. R. Hornsby (Director-General)

The Council was set up under the Nature Conservancy Council Act of 1973. It is the body responsible for advising the government on nature conservation in Great Britain. Its work includes the selection, establishment and management of National Nature Reserves; the selection and management of Marine Nature Reserves; the identification and notification of Sites of Special Scientific Interest (SSSIs); the provision of advice and the dissemination of knowledge about nature conservation; and the support and conduct of research relevant to those functions.

Under the Environmental Protection Bill currently before Parliament (1990), the NCC would be split into three separate bodies, one each for England, Scotland and Wales.

It produces many publications concerned with conservation and a catalogue is available from the Publicity Services Branch at the above address.

It is funded by grant-in-aid from the Department of the Environment and in 1989–90 this amounted to £40.15 million.

Nature Conservation Council

Telephone. 354 1 27855
Address. Hverfisgata 26, 101 Reykjavik, Iceland
Officials. Eythór Einarsson (Chairman); Thoroddur Thoroddsson (Manager)

The Council is a governmental organization working under an act which set it up in 1971. The aim was to encourage the intercourse of man and nature in such a way that life or land be not needlessly wasted, nor sea, fresh water or air polluted. The Act was to ensure as far as possible the course of natural processes according to their own laws, and the protection of exceptional and historical aspects of Icelandic nature. It shall also enhance the nation's access to and familiarity with nature.

The Council receives (in 1990) US$600,000 from the government, it has an income of $200,000 at camp sites in national parks and $100,000 from other funds.

Natuurmonumenten
(The Society for the Preservation of Nature in The Netherlands)

Telephone. 035 62004 *Fax.* 035 63174
Address. Schaep en Burgh, Noordereinde 60, 1243 JJ 's-Graveland, The Netherlands
Officials. Dr P. Winsemius (President); P. J. van Herwerden (Secretary); J. W. Ort (Treasurer)

The Society was formed in Amsterdam in April 1905 and is now the largest independent organization for nature conservation in the Netherlands with a membership of over 300,000.

Its main objective is the conservation and management of nature reserves. It has acquired over 200 sites of natural beauty and interest, totalling over 60,000 hectares. They vary widely in habitat and size and include woodland, heathland and dunes; lakes and marshland; country estates; mudflats; peatlands; and grassland areas. They form the habitats of many species, particularly of breeding waders such as the black-tailed godwit, the purple heron, the spoonbill, cormorants etc., for which the Netherlands are famous.

Natuurmonumenten also preserves many buildings as national monuments including windmills, watermills, castles and farms.

It produces a quarterly magazine *Natuurbehoud* and a handbook which provides details of all the areas of natural beauty in the Netherlands. Books and other information publications are issued regularly.

The Society's annual income is Gld 40 million coming, in equal parts, from exploitation of the reserves, government grants and membership dues.

Norges Naturvernforbund (NNV)
(The Norwegian Society for the Conservation of Nature)

Telephone. 02 71 55 20 *Fax.* 02 71 56 40
Address. PO Box 2113, Grünerløkka, 0505 Oslo 5, Norway (street address: Nedregt. 5, Oslo)
Officials. Dag Hareide (General Secretary); Ragnar Vik (Political leader)

The Society was formed in 1914 and now has over 45,000 members. It has a youth organization, "Nature and Youth".

It works for: (a) the prevention of over-exploitation of natural resources and harmful encroachment or influence on nature; (b) the encouragement of efforts to remedy damage that has already occurred due to industrial encroachment, pollution or over-exploitation; (c) the use of natural resources on the basis of sustained yield and renewal; and (d) the protection of nature's aesthetic, recreational and scientific value and the securing of representative examples of natural topography, cultural sites, unique natural phenomena and species of plants and animals.

Its current activities include a transport campaign; the fishery crisis; air pollution including acid rain, the ozone layer and climate change; sea pollution, energy use and the natural heritage of Norway by taking care of species and of land.

It publishes a magazine *Natur & Miljø* and the *Natur & Miljø Bulletin*.

Annual expenditure amounts to NKr 16 million met mainly from members, but with some support from the Ministry of Environment.

Österreichischer Naturschutzbund (ÖNB)
(Austrian Federation for the Protection of Nature)

Telephone. 0662 75 4 92
Address. Arenbergstrasse 10, A-5020 Salzburg, Austria
Officials. Prof. Dr Eberhard Stüber (President); Hannes Augustin (Secretary)

The alliance was formed in 1913 and its aim is the preservation of nature. It is a federal organization with many autonomous sub-organizations and an overall membership of some 60,000.

Its main activities are the purchase or leasing of land for the preservation of species and habitats and in providing information for the public on environmental problems.

It publishes *Natur und Land*, a periodical dealing with nature protection and landscapes in Austria.

Its income arises from governments, communities and private companies and organizations.

Rachel Carson Council, Inc.,

Telephone. 301 652 1877
Address. 8940 Jones Mill Road, Chevy Chase, MD 20815, USA
Officials. Samuel P. Epstein (President); Claire P. Smith (Vice President); David B. McGrath (Treasurer); Shirley A. Briggs (Secretary)

The Council, formed in 1965 as the Rachel Carson Trust for the Living Environment, Inc., is an association for the integrity of the environment. It was Rachel Carson's wish, expressed before her death in 1964, for an independent, objective information centre on environmental and human health effects of toxic chemical contamination, especially pesticides. It is a non-profit corporation with a worldwide list of sponsors and consulting experts, but is not a membership organization.

With the publication of Rachel Carson's *Silent Spring* people all over the world became aware of environmental problems, particularly the excessive use of chemicals. The new awareness showed itself not only in the hundreds of thousands of people who bought the book and discussed it, but in the floods of correspondence that came to Ms Carson and in the positive action taken to enact legislation, hold meetings, contact the press etc.

The Trust's task is to promote public interest in and knowledge of the environment, encourage enlightened conservation measures, and serve as a clearing house of information for scientists and laymen. Its focus is chemical contamination, especially the pesticides problems explored in *Silent Spring* and their impact on human and environmental health with effects upon the economy, government, agricultural methods and industrial practices.

The Council publishes a number of books and pamphlets (list available from the above address).

The Council is funded by private foundations and individual contributors with no government finance.

Royal Commission on Environmental Pollution (RCEP)

Telephone. 071 276 2080 *Fax.* 071 276 2098
Address. Church House, Great Smith Street, London SW1P 3BL, UK
Officials. Lord Lewis (Chairman); B. Glicksman (Secretary)

The Commission was established by Royal Warrant in 1970. Membership is conferred by Royal Warrant and invitations have been extended, over the years, to many eminent scientists.

It advises on matters, both national and international, concerning the pollution of the environment and on the adequacy of research in this field; and the future possibilities of danger to the environment. It is an independent body and, in its first report (Cmnd 4585, 1971), it noted that, although funded by government it was not constrained by government departmental boundaries and "we have no specific or restricted task. We are authorised to enquire into any matter on which we think that advice is needed and also to enquire into any issues within our terms of reference that are referred to us by any of Her Majesty's Secretaries of State or Ministers". It invites many organizations, government departments and individuals to submit both written and oral evidence when conducting its investigations.

It has published, regularly, reports following its studies (13 altogether), and is currently looking at Fresh Water Quality, whilst it continues to monitor and assess development in all areas of environmental pollution.

Its budget is over £350,000 which is met by the Department of the Environment.

Royal Society for Nature Conservation (RSNC)

Telephone. 0522 752326 *Fax.* 0522 595325
Address. The Green, Nettleham, Lincoln LN2 2NR, UK
Officials. HRH The Prince of Wales (Patron); Dunstan H. Adams (President); Tim S. Cordy (Chief Executive)

The Society for the Promotion of Nature Reserves was formed in 1912 and changed its name in 1976 to The Society for the Promotion of Nature Conservation. It again changed, in 1981, to the Royal Society for Nature Conservation. There is, in most counties of England, a Wildlife Trust, each autonomous, locally owned and run by active citizens, and there is a Trust in Scotland (Scottish Wildlife Trust); there are seven Trusts in Wales and Trusts in Guernsey, the Isle of Man and Ulster. The RSNC is the umbrella association to which they all (48) belong. In all, some 215,000 people belong to the Trusts and, therefore, to the Society.

The Trusts together with 50 Urban Wildlife Groups form a nationwide network of groups and individuals striving to create a better future for wildlife.

The Society aims are: (a) to protect and enhance wildlife habitats, both common and rare, as an investment for the future; it owns and cares for over 1800 sites encompassing more than 52,000 hectares, providing opportunities for all to enjoy wildlife in cities, towns and the wider countryside; (b) to campaign to bring important conservation issues into the public eye and before parliament, seeking to increase commitment to nature conservation in all aspects of environmental and natural resources policy; (c) to promote awareness and appreciation of nature conservation and the need for it; (d) to enable active participation in nature conservation by individuals and community groups; in particular, WATCH, RSNC's Educational Trust for young people, has 30,000 members in 800 local groups and over 1,400 affiliated groups, mainly in schools.

RSNC also provides services, advice, training and undertakes networking, campaigning, fund raising and publicity for its member Trusts. Recent projects have concerned: otters and rivers; pollution; forestry and agriculture; and wetlands.

RSNC publishes *Natural World*, a colourful magazine distributed to all members of Trusts, an annual review and accounts, numerous leaflets and reports to provide information on current wildlife issues. Recent papers have dealt with: Broadleaves Policy of the Forestry Commission; Cardiff Bay Barrage Bill; Derelict Land Management; Privatization of National Nature Reserves, etc. It also publishes *WATCHWORD* three times a year for its junior membership.

The annual expenditure of the RSNC amounts to about £2 million which is met from private companies, public appeals, charitable trusts, individuals, the public sector and sales from RSNC (Mail Order) Ltd. The RSNC's British Wildlife Appeal continues towards its target of £10 million by the end of 1990.

Royal Society for the Protection of Birds (RSPB)

Telephone. 0767 680551 *Fax.* 0767 692365 *Telex.* 82469
Address. The Lodge, Sandy, Bedfordshire SG19 2DL, UK
Officials. Magnus Magnusson (President); Ian Prestt (Director-General)

The RSPB was founded in 1889 by a small group of dedicated women to fight the slaughter of millions of wild birds whose plumage was used in the fashion trade. It now has, a century later, over 680,000 members. It received its Royal Charter in 1904. Its symbol, adopted in 1955, is the avocet.

The RSPB exists to conserve wild birds and the environment in which they live and breed. Its main aim is to maintain the richness of Britain's heritage of wild birds—including bird numbers, diversity and geographical distribution—and to increase this richness where desirable. It considers that conserving habitats is the most important means of protecting wild birds and this is achieved by both acquiring and managing land as nature reserves and by influencing what happens to the rest of the countryside.

The RSPB takes action for birds where and whenever their populations come under threat. Current activities include: (a) scientific research into the distribution and requirements of birds; (b) buying and managing land as nature reserves—it now has 116; (c) influencing land use policy and practices for the benefit of birds and wildlife; (d) advising landowners on managing land with wildlife considerations; (e) surveying and protecting the nests of rare birds and wildlife law enforcement (the best known project has been the return of nesting ospreys to Britain, first at Loch Garten); (f) affecting international policy and implementation of foreign projects to protect British birds overseas; and (g) creating a favourable climate of public opinion about birds and conservation matters.

The RSPB publishes a quarterly magazine *Birds* and a bi-monthly magazine for the junior membership *Bird Life*. It also publishes an annual Conservation Review and many books, educational material for schools, leaflets, posters etc., covering a wide range of information.

Its total income (1989) was over £13 million, coming from members' subscriptions (£5.3 million) legacies (£3.4 million); £1.5 million from appeals and about the same from fund raising activities. The greatest item of expenditure was the management of nature reserves (£2.2 million) and £1.5 million was spent on the acquisition of new nature reserves and extensions to existing reserves. The balance sheet shows total assets are now nearly £27 million, the bulk of which is in nature reserves, recorded at historical cost, but regarded by many, in conservation terms, as priceless.

Schweizer Arbeitsgemeinschaft für Umweltforschung (SAGUF)
(Swiss Association for Environmental Research)

Address. (President) Institute ETH, Zurichbergstrasse 38, CH- 8044 Zurich, Switzerland. *Telephone.* 01 256 45 88. (Secretary) c/o UNA, Moserstrasse 22, CH- 3014 Bern, Switzerland. *Telephone.* 031 40 04 24
Officials. Prof. Dr Frank Kloetzli (President); Ch. Hedinger (Secretary)

The Association was born out of activities at ETH-Zurich (Swiss Federal Institute of Technology) including symposia on environmental problems in 1970, and the Universities of Zurich, Bern and St. Gallen. It now has 243 members.

Its aims include the co-ordination and information on environmental research, evaluation of social projects, and support for interdisciplinary and applied research on the socio-political and/or scientific levels and branches.

It takes an overview of environmental research in Switzerland. It develops new concepts on national environmental research, co-ordination and information problems and organizes symposia on environmental problems. It examines current criteria for present ecological research and seeks early detection of environmental problems.

It has close links with the Swiss Academy of Sciences and other scientific organizations and federal offices. The president and other officers hold offices in related organizations such as the Swiss Federal Commission on Environmental Observation.

The Association publishes the proceedings of its symposia and it is compiling, for publication, a catalogue of the treatments for environmental problems.

It is funded by members' subscriptions and sponsored by the Swiss Academy of Sciences.

Schweizerische Gesellschaft für Umweltschutz (SGU)
Société suisse pour la protection de l'environnement (SPE)
(Swiss Association for Environmental Protection)

Telephone. 01 251 28 26 *Fax.* 01 251 29 41
Address. Merkurstrasse 45, Postfach 124A, CH-8032 Zurich, Switzerland
Officials. Dr Bernhard Wehrli (President)

The Association was formed in 1971 and now has 5,600 members. Its aim is the realization of effective environment protection and enforcement of the "polluter pays" principle. Its present activities are centred on the measures to be undertaken for an ecological agriculture in Switzerland and a revision of the laws governing water protection.

Its activities are limited to Switzerland where it co-operates with other national, nature and environmental organizations.

It publishes the *Bulletin de Schweitzerischen Gesellschaft für Umweltschutz* and several information sheets and reports (only in German).

Schweizer Heimatschutz
Ligue Suisse du Patrimoine National
Lega svizzera per la salvaguardia del patrimonio nazionale
Lia svizzra per la protecziun de la patria
(Swiss League for the Preservation of National Heritage)

Telephone. 01 252 26 60 *Fax.* 01 252 28 70
Address. Merkurstrasse 45, CH-8032 Zurich, Switzerland
Officials. Ronald Grisard (President); Hans Gattiker (Secretary-General)

The League was formed in 1905 and now has 23,500 members.

It is concerned with the preservation of the environment, historical sites and monuments against alteration and destruction. It intervenes to maintain an harmonious environment.

It publishes a review magazine *Heimatschutz/Sauvegarde*, four times a year, in a bilingual edition in German and French.

Its annual expenditure amounts to SFr 1,100,000 and this is met by members' subscriptions, legacies, donations, sales and a subsidy from the Swiss government.

Sierra Club

Telephone. 415 776 2211 *Fax.* 415 776 0350
Address. 730 Polk Street, San Francisco, California 94109, USA
Other Centres. The Club has offices in Washington, DC; Saratoga Springs, NY; Annapolis, MD; Knoxville, North Palm Beach, FL; Madison, WI; Sheridan, WY; Dallas, TX; Boulder, CO; Phoenix, AZ; Salt Lake City, UT; Los Angeles, CA; Oakland, CA; Seattle, WA; Anchorage, AK.
Officials. Richard Cellarius (President); Susan Merrow (Vice-President); Ruth Frear (Secretary); Robert Howard (Treasurer); J. Michael McCloskey (Chairman); Michael L. Fischer (Executive Director)

The Club was founded in San Francisco in 1892 by John Muir, who became its first President, to help preserve the pristine beauty of the Sierra Nevada range. It is a non-profit making, member-supported, public-interest organization that promotes conservation of the natural environment by influencing public policy decisions—legislative, administrative, legal and electoral.

It now has well over half a million members in 57 chapters, divided into 370 groups throughout the USA, whose purpose is to explore, enjoy and protect the wild places of the earth; to practise and promote the responsible use of the earth's ecosystem and resources; to educate and enlist humanity to protect and restore the quality of the natural and human environment; and to use lawful means to carry out these objectives.

It has an impressive history of achievements in its one hundred years and is currently working on many conservation issues. The Directors selected the following seven issues as national conservation campaigns in 1989–90:

(i) Clean Air Act Reauthorisation. The Clean Air Act was passed almost 20 years ago and the Club supports a revised and strengthened act that will impose stricter emission controls on vehicles and industry, a 50% reduction in sulphur dioxide emissions, a significant reduction in nitrogen oxides emissions over the next 10 years and accelerated regulation of toxic air pollutants;

(ii) Arctic National Wildlife Refuge Protection. The Club is urging Congress to reject oil and gas development legislation in the Refuge and instead designate the coastal plain as a protected wilderness area.

(iii) The Bureau of Land Management Wilderness/Desert National Parks. The Club is determined to see that all deserving areas are protected as wilderness. This includes a campaign to support the California Desert Protection Act and the fate of important desert wildlands in Utah, Arizona and other Western states.

(iv) National Forests/National Parks Protection. The Club seeks wilderness status for many national forest lands and the creation of a Tallgrass Prairie Preserve in Oklahoma and a Petroglyphs National Monument in New Mexico. It also seeks improved national forestry management.

(v) Toxics: Resource Conservation and Recovery Act Reauthorisation. The Act is due for renewal in 1989 and the Club believes that it needs improvement. It advocates extending regulations to wastes not currently covered, toughening land-disposal standards for municipal solid wastes, reducing generation on additional toxics and beefing up enforcement.

(vi) Global Warming/Greenhouse Effect. The Club seeks aggressive gains in energy conservation, greater use of renewable energy resources, rapid phase-out of CFCs, constraints of deforestation and hiking automobile efficiency.

(vii) International Development Lending. The Club is working to reform the lending practices of multilateral development banks by increasing their sensitivity to environmental protection and sustainable development.

The Club publishes many books, pamphlets and leaflets on a wide variety of topics. (A literature list is available from the San Francisco address.) It publishes its official magazine *Sierra* six times a year, a *National News Report* about 26 times a year, an *Earth Day Source Book* and many newsletters, particularly by chapters reporting local environmental news and Club events.

Its annual budget (1989) was US$28 million, met primarily by members.

Société nationale de protection de la nature (SNPN)

Telephone. 161 47 07 31 95
Address. BP 405, 57 Rue Cuvier, 75221 Paris Cedex 05, France
Officials. Yves Betolaud (President); Christian Jouanin (Vice-President; Pierre Pfeffer (Secretary-General); Marc Gallois (Director)

The Society was founded in 1854 by Geoffrey St Hilaire under the name "Société impériale zoologique d'acclimatation", changing its name in 1960. It is a non-profit organization and now has some 5,000 members. It is concerned with safeguarding the environment from the many dangers, the protection of the natural flora and fauna in France and to make the living world better known, loved and respected.

The Society owns two national nature reserves in the Carmargue, the Etang de Vaccares situated in the d'Arles and Saintes-Maries districts by the Mediterranean coast, and the other the Lac de Grand-Lieu, south-west of Nantes, on the west coast. It arranges many conferences and campaigns for particular environmental causes both international, for example saving the African elephant, and national.

It publishes a colour magazine *Le Courrier de la Nature* every two months, a prestigious review *La Terre et la Vie—Revue d'Ecologie*, and many books and brochures etc. (in French; a list is available from the above address).

The annual budget amounts to about FFr 450,000 and is met by its members' subscriptions.

Socio-Ecological Union (SEU)

Telephone. 7 095 151 62 70 *Fax.* 7 095 200 22 16, 200 22 17, 200 42 47
Address. Centre for Co-ordination and Information, Krasnoarmeiskaka, 25, 85, Moscow 125319, USSR
Officials. Dr Sviatoslav I. Zabelin (Director)

The Union is an independent, non-governmental, non-party public organization. It was set up in December 1988 as an association of ecological initiative committees, clubs, groups and private citizens on city and regional levels. It now includes more than 150 non-governmental organizations in more than 200 towns and cities in the Soviet Union and its membership includes many professional ecologists and other specialists. It works closely with the Ecological Committee of the Supreme Soviet of the USSR and with Greenpeace USSR.

Its targets include the preservation of the environment, the people's physical and moral health, raising objections to actions and projects damaging to the surroundings and the search for alternatives. It undertakes, as part of its activities, protest demonstrations and collection of signatures to achieve these aims.

Some of its recent activities include: a nationwide protest against the construction of the Volga-Chograi canal; participation in the ecological assessment of the proposed hydro-electric power station on the Katun river in Altai, which led to stopping the project; similarly the building of a water storage basin on the Belaia river in Bashkiria has been stopped; and cessation of the production of single-cell protein from petroleum and an expedition to try to save the cheetah in middle Asia.

Its last conference called for a five-year moratorium on the construction of new nuclear power stations.

It believes that the current climate in the USSR offers excellent opportunities for it to co-operate with international bodies, particularly in the following fields: (a) the safety of populations living in areas polluted by radionucleides as a result of nuclear weapons, nuclear experiments, accidents or waste disposal; (b) the treatment of wastes, both in research effort and the creation of companies to handle the technology; (c) the manufacture of equipment for control of the environment and the quality of foodstuffs; (d) a non-governmental system of monitoring the environment, disseminating information, and checking on enforcement of international agreements; (e) research into alternative energy sources and manufacturing technologies; (f) undertaking non-governmental environmental reviews, including the creation of a list of qualified experts able to judge national and international projects; and (g) better co-operation, with research, in the field of environmental health, particularly of children, with the creation of an international information centre on (*sic*) ecological medicine.

The Union would like to arrange an international festival of Soviet scientific popular films to demonstrate the situation in the USSR and it suggests the establishment of an authoritative international journal, multilingual, for wide dissemination of information on acceptable practices.

The Union makes a plea that, since there are so many difficult problems, international co-operation must be achieved.

It publishes information letters in Russian with, in future, an English translation and publication together with the Natural Resources Defense Council in the USA.

Standing Committee on Urban and Building Climatology

Telephone. 0201 1832734 *Fax.* 0201 1832529 *Telex.* 8579091 unie d
Address. c/o Prof. Dr W. Kuttler, Universitat Essen, Fachbereich 9, Institut für Okologie, Postfach 103 764, D-4300 Essen 1, Federal Republic of Germany
Officials. Prof. Dr A. Bitan (Israel) (Chairman); Prof. Dr. Wilhelm Kuttler (General Secretary)

The Committee was established in 1957 and organizes symposia on the problems of urban building climatology. It now has 66 members and has several working groups concerned with: utilization of IR images in urban climate studies; methods and standardization of measurements and data collecting in urban areas; design guidelines; valuation of the urban climate and effects of urban climate on man; and climate aspects of planning and building of ancient urban settlements and vernacular architecture.

It has published the proceeding of symposia, particularly the Third International Symposium on *Climate—Building—Housing* held in Karlsruhe in 1986 (edited by Dr A. Bitan of Tel-Aviv University).

Stichting Natuur en Milieu

Telephone. 030 331328 *Fax.* 030 331311
Address. Donkerstraat 17, 3511 KB Utrecht, The Netherlands
Officials. P. Nijhoff (Director-General); A. J. M. van den Biggelaar (Director)

The *Stichting* is one of the main non-governmental environmental organizations in the Netherlands. It was established in 1972 and now has 10,000 subscribers and supporters. It is concerned with nature conservation and environmental protection and its goals are clean air, clean water and clean soil. It seeks to preserve nature, natural ecosystems and landscape. It aims for a good system of public transport, sustainable use of natural resources, use of durable energy and environmentally sound agriculture and industry.

It undertakes lobbying to influence political decisions, holds membership of official advisory committees to the government and stimulates public awareness of environmental issues. It initiates legal and administrative juridical procedures and holds monthly press conferences.

Its office consists of a permanent staff of about 35 members and a temporary staff of five to 10 project workers.

It publishes a monthly magazine *Natuur en Milieu*, study reports and books on environmental issues for the general public.

It has formal links with eight national sister organizations, with twelve provincial federations of local action groups and with many foreign environmental organizations.

Its annual expenditure amounts to about Gld 3.4 million which is met by subscriptions, donations and subsidies from the government.

Suomen Luonnonsuojeluiitto ry
(Finnish Association for Nature Conservation)
Telephone. 358 0 642 881 *Fax.* 358 0 622 1815
Address. Perämiehenkatu 11 A 8, SF-00150 Helsinki, Finland
Officials. Esko Joutsamo (Secretary-General)

The Association was founded in May 1938 and now has a membership of about 26,000 in over 200 local associations.

It is a national volunteer citizens' organization dedicated to environmental conservation. This includes conservation of the indigenous nature, animals, plants and valuable natural areas for future generations; the far-sighted use of natural resources and production methods in harmony with the environment; and planning in cities and rural areas on a sound ecological basis.

To achieve these aims the Association publishes informative material about nature and environmental conservation; influences decision-making politicians and officials and takes the initiative, makes proposals and recommendations and takes a stand on current environmental issues; organizes excursions, study courses, demonstrations etc.; and participates in international co-operation, especially with the Scandinavian and Baltic countries. Within Finland it works closely with *Natur och Miljo* (Nature and Environment) a central organization for Swedish-speaking Finns and the junior, nationwide arm of the Association—Luonto-Liitto—the Finnish Youth Association for Environmental Protection.

It publishes *Suomen Luonto* (Nature of Finland) eight times a year and *Luonnonsuojelija* (Conservationist) for members 10 times a year.

Its annual budget (1989) was MKK 13 million, met by membership fees and subscriptions, advertising, sales and royalties (mainly through its own trading company Support for Nature Conservation Ltd.), private contributions, and government subsidy.

Swedish Environmental Protection Agency (SNV/NSEPB)

Telephone. 46 87991000 *Fax.* 46 8292382 *Telex.* 11131 Environ S
Address. (Postal) P.O. Box 1302, S-171 85 Solna, Sweden
Officials. Valfrid Paulsson (President)

The SNV, founded in 1967 is the national government agency for environmental protection and nature conservation. It also promotes and directs environmental research. It monitors the enforcement of existing laws and proposes new legislation to deal better with existing problems or with new problems which it foresees. It has broad responsibilities for pollution control, waste management, protection of nature, forest and wildlife. It is independent and is directed by a board with membership from industry, local government, members of parliament, the workers' educational association (ABF) and the trade unions (LO).

It publishes up to 300 items a year including *Acid Magazine* twice a year which is distributed, free, to a wide, international readership (write to the Information Section at the above address to be put on the list).

It has a staff of 600 and an annual budget of SKr 355 million met from government funds.

Swedish Society for the Conservation of Nature (Naturskyddsföreningen)

Telephone. 08 702 02 65 *Fax.* 08 702 08 55
Address. Box 4510, S-102 65 Stockholm, Sweden
Officials. Anders Wijkman (Secretary-General)

The Society was established in 1909 and is the largest popular organization for nature conservation and environmental protection in Sweden. It has 190,000 members organized in 23 regional and more than 250 local groups. The youth organization, *Faltbiologerna* (The Swedish Youth Association for Environmental Studies and Conservation) has 13,000 members.

It aims to promote public awareness and activity for the protection of the environment and to press decision-makers to respect environmental demands in various fields: agriculture, forestry, industry, transport energy and taxes.

Currently it is focusing on four specific fields: (a) energy, related to the government's goals of phasing out the existing 12 nuclear reactors before the year 2010, protecting the remaining four big rivers and reducing air pollution from the energy sector. The Society has suggested an electricity-efficiency tax, a CO_2 fee on all fossil fuels and efficiency programme and stronger legislation to protect the remaining unexploited rivers; (b) traffic, where the Society has demanded a shift in the national transport policy, a railway tunnel rather than a road bridge across the Oresund sound, emission fees, more investment in railways and the introduction of faster trains, no further small airports in the southern and central parts of Sweden and the introduction of Californian emission standards; (c) agriculture, where the Society demands new regulation, fewer pesticides and fertilizers and economic incentives to support farmers to conserve a variety of biotopes; and (d) *Handla miljövänligt*: a booklet giving advice on "green consumerism" on which the Society has run a campaign to influence the development and use of products and energy-saving habits.

Other important fields of work are the protection of virgin forests, strong conservation demands on Swedish forestry, regulation of bio-technology, improved environmental education and a reform of the environmental laws of the country. It also helps run the Swedish NGO secretariat on acid rain in Gothenburg which co-ordinates campaigns in the rest of Europe aiming to reduce emissions of air pollutants. It has also raised money to start a development programme in Western Samoa to save areas of rain forests with its fauna.

It publishes a bi-monthly member magazine *Sveriges Natur* (Swedish Nature) and a year book, together with a number of books, postcards, brochures, calendars etc.

Its annual budget amounts to about SKr 65 million, mainly covered by individual membership fees and sales of books.

Swiss League for Nature Protection (SLNP)
Ligue Suisse pour la Protection de la Nature (LSPN)
Schweizerischer Bund Fur Naturschutz (SBN)

Telephone. 061 312 74 42 *Fax.* 061 312 74 47
Address. Wartenbergstrasse 22, Postfach CH-4020 Basel, Switzerland
Officials. Maitre Jacques Morier-Genoud (President); Dr Jurg Rohner (General Secretary); Dr Ulrich Halder (Information Officer)

The SLNP started in 1909 as the "Reserves Society" to raise money so that the newly founded Commission for the Protection of Nature could create a National Park, the first in Europe. It now has over 100,000 members (organized in 22 cantonal sections) and has been, and is, heavily involved in many environmental issues both within Switzerland and in international work.

It owns, leases or supports more than 500 reserves, it runs two Field Study Centres (at Aletschwald in the Canton of Valais and at Champ-Pittet in the Canton of Vaud) and publishes many books, pamphlets and posters in both French and German and a periodical, *Schweizer Naturschutz/Protection de la Nature*, eight times a year. It aims to protect species and their habitats and landscapes and is active, politically, in achieving its ends on a wide variety of issues.

Its annual expenditure is over SFr 8 million of which about 40% is spent on nature reserves.

Turkiye Tabiatini Koruma Dernegi
(Turkish Association for the Conservation of Nature and National Resources)

Telephone. 125 19 44
Address. Menekse Sokak 29/4, 06440 Kizilay, Ankara, Turkey
Officials. Hasan Asmaz (President); Dr Osman Taskin (Vice-President); Ekram Y. Demetci (Secretary-General)

The Association was formed in 1955 and now has 2,000 members.

Its annual budget is Tl 30 million.

Uberparteiliche Plattform Gegen Atomgefahren und Zukunftswerkstatt Energie (PLAGE)

Telephone. 0662 882 881
Address. Arenbergstrasse 10, A-5020 Salzburg, Austria
Officials. Heinz Stockinger, Hannes Augustin, Maria Fellner, (Spokespersons); Christine Holzleitner (Secretary)

The Association was originally formed in May 1986 as the *Plattform gegen die WAA Wackersdorf* whose main objective was to stop the nuclear waste reprocessing plant at Wackersdorf, Bavaria in the FRG. It brought about an avalanche of anti-Wackersdorf protests in Austria—a campaign of information and action that culminated in the official objection to the project by the Austrian Minister for Environmental Affairs within the German authorisation procedure in 1988. No doubt this opposition, both "grass roots" and official, from Austria contributed to the abandoning of construction in 1988.

It changed its name and widened its interests. Its aims now include: (a) an overall reduction in the use of nuclear power for civil and military purposes, especially in Austria's neighbouring countries; (b) a reduction of the use of radioactive substances, and thus of radioactive waste, in medicine, research and diverse industries; (c) the promotion of energy conservation and renewable energy development and use; and (d) pressure on official Austrian policy to take a stand, internationally, especially with neighbouring countries, on environmental issues.

Its particular activities recently included the fight against the Czechoslovakian atomic energy programme (especially the power station project at Femelin, only 40 km from the Austrian border) and the control or prevention of various official Austrian activities in the nuclear field in addition to the large-scale energy programme. This would include the production and handling of low- and medium-level nuclear waste, European nuclear fusion research, the Austrian position in case of its entry into the EC and radioactive substances in small items such as watches and alarm clocks.

PLAGE publishes *Platform News* about 10 times a year and a 55-page document *Der Seibersdorfer Atommull* dealing with the handling of low- and medium-level radioactive waste (from industry, research institutions and hospitals) by the Austrian Research Centre at Seibersdorf and of the search for a final waste storage site.

It has a budget of 7–800,000 Austrian Schillings (US$ 70,000) met by donations, sales, fees and subsidies from the city and federal state of Salzburg.

Umweltbundesamt (UBA)

Telephone. 030 89030 *Fax.* 030 89032285 *Telex.* 183 756
Address. Bismarkplatz 1, D I Berlin 33, Federal Republic of Germany
Officials. Dr Heinrich von Lersner (President)

The UBA, the Federal Environment Agency, was founded in June 1974 under the Ministry of the Interior. From 1986, with the creation of the Federal Ministry of Environment, Nature Conservation and Nuclear Safety, its duty is to provide scientific advice to the Minister on all environmental matters except nuclear safety. It incorporated several existing institutions, for example, the air quality measuring system of *Deutsche Forschungsgemeinschaft* and the *Zentralstelle für Abfallbeseitigung* and, later, the *Dokumentationszentrale Wasser*. It now has approximately 500 staff of whom about 40% are professionally qualified.

The Act of 1974 which established Germany's environmental policy and set up the Agency assigned it the following main functions: (a) scientific assistance to the Federal Government in all matters concerning air pollution, noise abatement, waste management, water management and chemical substances affecting the environment with special regard to the preparation of legal and administrative regulations; (b) the preparation and maintenance of an information system for environmental planning; (c) information for the public on environmental issues; and (d) rendering of central services and assistance to the individual departments for their research activities and for the co-ordination of the environmental research work of the Federal authorities.

Since, in Germany, the environmental laws are enforced by the States or Länder governments, the UBA has no direct executive authority, but it does wield extensive influence in formulating the policies and programmes and supplying the evidence on which decisions are taken. It also has adopted a significant campaigning role in many major issues.

Its location in Berlin enables it to work closely with the Federal Health Office, and with the two universities and various institutes, such as that for Materials Testing and the Biological Institute, in Berlin.

It is an independent agency although funded by the Federal Government at an approximate annual cost of DM 75 million.

UK Centre for Economic and Environmental Development (UK CEED)

Telephone. 071 245 6440/1 *Fax.* 071 235 5478
Address. 12 Upper Belgrave Street, London SW1X 8BA, UK
Officials. Sir Arthur Norman (Chairman); David Cope (Executive Director)

UK CEED is an independent charity concerned with promoting a productive partnership between environmental protection and development interests in the UK. It was formed in 1984 on an initiative from the 1983 Conservation and Development Programme for the UK (which was the British response to the IUCN World Conservation Strategy) which recommended the establishment of a centre to help test, promote and monitor those aims.

Its role is to develop policies and initiatives which further the economic well-being of the UK and, at the same time, protect the environment for the future through sustainable use of resources. It advocates economic analysis of the environmental and development problems of the UK by undertaking high-quality research, encouraging debate and providing an information service. It disseminates its own research findings and initiatives taken elsewhere through seminars, conferences and publications programmes.

It publishes a bi-monthly *Bulletin* offering comprehensive coverage of environmental economics and policy and many discussion papers on items of topical interest. Reports and proceedings of conferences are also marketed. It is involved with Queen Mary College, London in the London/Tokyo "World Cities" project. In general it works with experts from many fields in business and industry, central and local government, academia and environmental protection and conservation interests.

It has a small full-time professional staff, several senior research associates and a Board of Directors drawn from leading figures with economic and environmental interests.

It is financially supported by: trusts and charities with environmental interests; commercial and industrial organizations both large and small; and government and private sector agencies responsible for environmental protection. This spread guarantees the independence of UK CEED.

United States Environmental Protection Agency (EPA)

Telephone. 202 382 4355 *Fax.* 202 382 4309
Address. 401 M Street, SW, A-107 Washington, DC 20460, USA
Officials. William K. Reilly (Administrator)

(Although a federal agency of the US Government, the EPA is included in the list of organizations in view of its wide powers and influence in the USA and its reputation and example in other parts of the world.)

The EPA was started in December 1970 and aims to protect and clean up the environment in order to ensure the health and safety of the citizens of the USA.

It is involved in all the major environmental issues and sets rigorous standards for many activities. Amongst the highlights of 1989 are included: (a) Clean Air—comprehensive legislation to reduce air pollution; standards to reduce air pollution from municipal waste incinerators; standards to reduce benzene emissions (by 20,000 tonnes); standards to control radioactive emissions; (b) an innovative project, using bio-remediation to assist in cleaning up Prince William Sound after the Exxon Valdez oil spill; (c) pollution prevention by setting a goal of recycling 25% of all municipal solid waste by 1992 and a ban on asbestos-containing products within the next seven years; (d) phasing out of CFCs and a proposed ban on the export of hazardous waste without adequate safeguards existing in the receiving country; (e) the proposed cancellation of 45 food crop uses for three pesticides and all food uses for a fourth, and a programme to streamline the process for cancelling problem pesticides; (f) the initiation of many clean-up projects and negotiations for more than $1 billion of clean-up work by responsible parties; (g) surveillance of the widespread levels of radon and launch of a campaign to urge comprehensive testing in homes and schools; (h) the instigation of a programme on the proper disposal of medical waste; and (i) the establishment of schedules to end ocean dumping of sewage sludge.

It also has a significant activity in enforcement and referred many civil (364) and criminal (60) cases to the Department of Justice for prosecution. It has issued more than 4,000 administrative orders and 200 binding settlement commitments for clean-up and removal of hazardous wastes.

Watt Committee on Energy

Telephone. 071 379 6875 *Fax.* 071 497 9315
Address. Savoy Hill House, Savoy Hill, London WC2R 0BU, UK
Officials. Dr G. K. C. Pardoe, OBE (Chairman); J. G. Mordue (Secretary)

The Committee was founded in 1976 by the professional institutions in the United Kingdom interested in energy who perceived the need to have a mechanism to address that subject collectively. It now has 60 institutions in membership who, in turn, have a combined membership of some half a million people.

It is a charity run as a voluntary organization, apart from a very small secretariat.

Its objectives are: (a) to promote and assist research and development and other scientific or technical work concerning all aspects of energy; (b) to disseminate knowledge generally concerning energy; (c) to promote the formation of informed opinion on matters concerned with energy; and (d) to encourage constructive analysis on questions concerning energy as an aid to strategic planning for the benefit of the public at large.

Current projects include: the Rational use of Energy in Urban Regeneration; Technological Responses to the Greenhouse Effect; Energy and Risk; and Thermodynamic cycles for Low-Temperature Heat Sources. It is seeking funding for projects on: Energy in the Home; Energy saving in the Mineral Industry; and the Rational Use of Energy: Plans into Action.

The Committee publishes about three reports each year. The most recent include:

Report no. 17: Passive Solar Energy in Buildings.

Report no. 18: Air Pollution, Acid Rain and the Environment.

Report no. 19: The Chernobyl Accident and its Implications for the UK.

Report no. 20: Gasification: Its Role in the Future Technical and Economic Development of the UK.

(Details of reports currently available can be obtained from the above address.)

The Committee works with its members and sponsors and with other corporations and development agencies.

Its annual expenditure (1989) is a little over £100,000, with two-thirds coming from project contributions and one third from general sponsors who include many corporations, utilities, trusts and government agencies.

Wilderness Society (TWS)

Telephone. 002 366 369 *Fax.* 002 23 5112

Address. 130 Davey Stret, Hobart, Tasmania (postcode 7000), Australia (Branches throughout Australia)

Officials. Alistair Graham (Director); Philip Wardle (National Administrator);
Dr Judith Lambert (National Liaison Officer); Bob Burton (Membership/Fundraising Officer)

The Society grew from a state organization, the Tasmanian Wilderness Society, into a national group following successes in campaigns to protect wilderness areas in Tasmania in the late 1970s and early 1980s. Its aims are to preserve the remaining wilderness areas in Australia (and elsewhere when possible) and it runs a number of specific campaigns in all states in Australia, such as an arid lands campaign and one related to the Kakadu National Park (to prevent development there).

It publishes a monthly magazine *Wilderness News* and papers and booklets on various environmental issues. It has some 12,400 members (up from 500 in 1980) and is financed by their membership fees and from sale of goods through TWS shops, raffles, and through National Merchandising (an arm of the Society that produces many of the goods sold in TWS shops and catalogues), leading to an annual income of Aus$ 1.5 million. It organizes many outdoor activities, but two-thirds of its expenditure is devoted to campaign issues.

Wilderness Society

Telephone. 202 842 3400 *Fax.* 202 842 8756
Address. 900 17th Street, NW, Washington DC 20006, USA
Officials. George T. Frampton Jr (President); Alice M. Rivlin (Chair); Thomas A. Barron (Treasurer); Arnold W. Bolle (Secretary)

The Society was founded in 1935 and now has a membership of 350,000. It is a non-profit membership organization devoted to preserving wilderness and wildlife, protecting America's forests, parks, rivers, deserts, wildlife refuges and shorelands and fostering an American land ethic.

Its aims are: (a) to secure the preservation of the American wilderness wherever found, and for this purpose to make or to initiate scientific studies and investigations concerning wilderness areas, their values and uses to the public and the best methods for their protection, preservation and use in the public interest; (b) to enlist the aid and personal services of individuals and of popular and scientific organizations, schools, universities, institutions and government agencies in making these scientific studies and investigations and in protecting and preserving wilderness areas; (c) to educate the pubic concerning the value of wilderness as a national resource and how it may best be used and preserved in the public interest; and (d) to promote nationwide co-operation in resisting the invasion of wilderness by the sights, sounds and other influences of a mechanized civilization.

It currently maintains programmes on national parks, forests and wildlife refuges; Alaska; wilderness area management; and lands administered by the Federal Bureau of Land Management. Analysts are also conducting prototype ecological and economic sustainability studies in the Greater Yellowstone Ecosystem and the Pacific Forest Province. It is developing management options in the Florida Keys, the Everglades and the Maine Woods.

The Society has extensive publications (list available from the above address) covering books papers, handbooks, speeches, editorials and newsletters. It publishes its own magazine *Wilderness*, quarterly.

The Society can receive, hold, convey and transfer real and personal property and receive and accept contributions, gifts, devises, bequests and otherwise raise and obtain money and other property of character whatsoever for the purposes set forth. Its annual expenditure is over US$11 million, met by members' contributions (50%), grants (16%), development contributions (16%) bequests, marketing etc.

Wilderness Watch Inc.

Telephone. 414 743 1238
Address. P.O. Box 782, Sturgeon Bay, WI 54235, USA
Officials. Jerome O. Gandt (President)

Wilderness Watch was established in 1969 and now has over 1,000 members.

Its objective is to sustain the use of America's sylvan lands and waters.

BIBLIOGRAPHY, FURTHER READING AND REFERENCES

PART I: ISSUES

1 ACID DEPOSITION

Batterbee, R. W. *et al. Lake Acidification in the United Kingdom 1800–1986. Evidence from analysis of Lake Sediments* Palaeoecological Research Unit, University College, London (ENSIS 1988)

Brackley, Peter *Acid Deposition and Vehicle Emissions: European Environmental Pressures on Britain* Gower (1987)

Buckley-Golder, D. *Acidity in the Environment* Energy Technology Research Unit, Report no. 23, Harwell (1984)

Cresser, M. & Edwards, A. *Acidification of Freshwaters* Cambridge Environmental Chemistry Series, CIP (1987)

Innes, J. L. *Air Pollution and Forestry* Forestry Commission Bulletin no. 70, HMSO (1987)

Longhurst, J. W. S. (Ed.) *Acid Deposition: sources, effects and controls*. British Library Science Reference and Information Service (Technical Communications Ltd. Vol. I, 1989 Vol. II, 1990)

McCormick, John *Acid Earth: The Global Threat of Acid Pollution*, Earthscan (1989)

Martin, H. C. (Ed.) *Acid Precipitation (Vols. I & II)* D. Reidel (1987)

Mellanby, Kenneth (Ed.) *Air Pollution, Acid Rain and the Environment* Watt Committee on Energy, Report no. 18, Elsevier (1988)

Nilsson, J. (Ed.) *Critical Loads for Nitrogen and Sulphur* Nordic Council Report 1986:11

Acid Rain and Transported Air Pollutants. Implications for Public policy Office of Technology Assessment, New York (1985)

Acidification Today and Tomorrow Environment '82 Committee, Swedish Ministry of Agriculture, Stockholm (1982)

Air Quality Guidelines for Europe World Health Organization, European Series no. 23 (1987)

Annual Report to the President and Congress NAPAP, 1989 Washington

Control of Major Air Pollutants Environmental Monograph, no. 10 (OECD 1987)

Effects of Acid Deposition on the Terrestrial Environment in the UK Terrestrial Effects Review Group, 1st Report, HMSO (1988)

Forest Damage and Air Pollution. Report of the 1987 forest damage survey in Europe, GEMS (1988)

OECD Programme on Long Range Transport of Air Pollutants, OECD (1977)

Acid Magazine (twice yearly) National Environment Protection Board, Solna, Sweden

Acid Precipitation Digest (monthly) Elsevier, New York, NY

Acid Rain News Canadian Coalition on Acid Rain, Ontario, Canada

Monitair Norwegian Institute for Air Research, Lillestrom, Norway

NAPAP Annual Report US National Acid Precipitation Assessment Programme, Washington DC

2 THE ANTARCTIC

The Antarctic 1988 *Oceanus* Vol. 31 (2)

Bonner, W. N. and Lewis Smith, R. I. L. *Conservation Areas in the Antarctic*, Cambridge Scientific Committee on Antarctic Research, 299 pp. (1985)

Fifield, R. (Compiler) *International Research in the Antarctic* Oxford, Scientific Committee on Antarctic Research, 146 pp. (1987)

Parsons, A. (Ed.) *Antarctica: the Next Decade* Cambridge, CUP 164 pp. (1987)

Triggs, G. E. (Ed.) *The Antarctic Treaty Regime* (Law, environment, resources) Cambridge CUP, 239 pp. (1987)

Walton, D. W. H. (Ed.) *Antarctic Science* Cambridge CUP (1987)

3 DEFORESTATION

Caulfield, C. *In the Rainforest* University of Chicago Press, 304 pp. (1984)

Corson, W. H. *Citizens' Guide to Sustainable Development* Global Tomorrow Coalition, 1325 G Street, N.W., Washington D.C., 350 pp. (1989)

Mitchell, A. W. *The Enchanted Canopy* Collins Publishers, London, 256 pp. (1986)

Mitchell, A. W. *A Fragile Paradise* Collins Publishers, London, 256 pp. (1989)

Sutton, S. W., Whitmore, T. C. & Chadwick, A. C. *Tropical Rainforest: Ecology and Management* Special publication no. 2 of the British Ecological Society, Blackwell's Scientific Publications, Oxford, 498 pp. (1983)

World Resources Institute and the International Institute for Environment and Development *World Resources 1988–89* Basic Books, Inc., New York, 372 pp.

4 THE GREENHOUSE EFFECT AND GLOBAL WARMING

Bolin, B., Döös, B., Jäger, J., and Warrick, R. A. *The Greenhouse Effect, Climate Change and Ecosystems* John Wiley (1986)

Everest, David *The Greenhouse Effect: Issues for Policy Makers* Royal Inst. International Affairs (1988)

Gribbin, John & Kelly, Mick *Winds of Change: Living with the Greenhouse Effect* Hodder & Stoughton (1989)

Grubb, Michael *The Greenhouse Effect: Negotiating Targets* Royal Inst. International Affairs (1989)

Grubb, Michael *Energy Policies and the Greenhouse Effect* Royal Inst. International Affairs (1990)

Kellog, W. *The Science of the Greenhouse Effect: an Overview* University of California (1989)

Lashof, D. & Tirpak, D. *Policy Options for Stabilising Global Climate* EPA draft report to Congress (1989)

Pearce, Fred, *Turning up the Heat. Our Perilous Future in the Global Greenhouse* Paladin (1989)

Swart, R. J., De Boois, H. & Rotmans, J. *Targeting Climate Change* International Environmental Affairs, Vol. 1 no. 3 (1989)

Atmospheric Carbon Dioxide and the Global Carbon Cycle US Department of Energy (1986)

Global Change in the Geosphere-Biosphere US Committee on the International Geosphere-Biosphere Programme, National Academy of Sciences (1986)

Report of the International Conference on the Assessment of the Role of Carbon Dioxide and of other Greenhouse Gases in Climate Variations and Associated Impacts Villach, Austria, October 1985, WMO (1986)

5 LAND DEGRADATION AND DESERTIFICATION

Becket, J. *The Stripping of China's Good Earth* The Guardian (1st February 1989)

Currey & Hugo *Famine as a Geographical Phenomenon* D. Reidel (1984)

Cutler, P., & Stephenson, R. *The State of Food Emergency Preparedness in Ethiopia* London Relief and Development Institute (1984)

De Waal, A. *A Famine that Kills* S. C. F. Mimeo (1987)
Glantz & Orlousky, *Desertification: Anatomy of a Complex Environmental Process (1986)*
Gorse & Steeds, *Desertification for the Sahelian and Sudanian Zones of West Africa* World Bank Technical Paper no. 61 (1987)
Grainger, Alan, *Desertification* Earthscan (1982)
Grainger, Alan, *The Threatening Desert: Controlling Desertification* Earthscan (1990)
Haigh, N. *Earthwatch Magazine*, March 1990
Holdgate, Kassas & White *The World Environment 1972–82,* UNEP
Leach & Mearns, *Beyond the Wood Fuel Crisis* Earthscan (1989)
Mabbutt, J. A. *A Review of Progress since the UN Conference on Desertification* Desertification Control Bulletin no. 15 (1987)
Nelson, R. *Dryland Management: The Desertification Problem* World Bank, Environment Department, Working Paper no. 8 (1988)
Walker, P. *Famine Early Warning System: Victims and Destitution* Earthscan (1989)
FAO's Environmental Programmes and Activities—an Overview Rome (1985)
World Resources Report 1987–89

6 THE LOSS OF BIOLOGICAL DIVERSITY

Anderson, I. "Epidemic of bird deformities sweeps US" *New Scientist* (3 September, 1987)
Booth, William, "Monitoring the fate of the forests from space" *Science* 243:1428–1429 (1989)
Collar, N. J. & Andrew, J. *Birds to Watch: the ICBP World Check-list of Threatened Birds* ICBP Technical Publication no. 8, ICBP, Cambridge, UK, 303 pp. (1988)
Connell, J. H. "Diversity in tropical rain forests and coral reefs: High diversity of trees and corals is maintained only in a nonequilibrium state" *Science* 199:1302–1310 (1978)
DeLong, R., Gilmartin, W. G. & Simpson, J. G. "Premature births in California sea lions: Association with high organochlorine pollutant residue levels" *Science* 181:1168–1170 (1973)
Diamond, J. M. "Extant unless proven extinct? Or, extinct unless proven extant?" *Conservation Biology* 1(1):72–76 (1987)
FAO *Tropical Forest Resources* FAO, Rome (1981)
FAO *The Tropical Forestry Action Plan* FAO, Rome, 32 pp. (1986)
Fitter, Richard & Fitter, Maisie *The Road to Extinction* IUCN, Gland, 121 pp (1987)
Frankel, O. H. & Hawkes, J. G. (Eds.) *Plant Genetic Resources for Today and Tomorrow* CUP, London, UK (1974)
Frankel, O. M. & Soulé, Michael E. *Conservation and Evolution* CUP, New York, 327 pp (1981)
Gentry, A. H. "Endemism in tropical versus temperate plant communities" pp. 153–181 in: Michael E. Soule (Ed.) *Conservation Biology: The Science of Scarcity and Diversity* Sinauer, Sunderland, MA (1986)
Graham, N. E. & White, W. B. The El Niño cycle: A natural oscillator of the Pacific Ocean-atmosphere system *Science* 240:1293–1302 (1988)
Holdgate, Martin W. *Managing the Future* IUCN, Gland (1989)
IUCN/UNEP *Review of the Protected Areas System in the Afrotropical Realm* IUCN, Gland, Switzerland (1986)
IUCN/UNEP *Review of the Protected Areas System in the Indo-Malayan Realm* IUCN, Gland, Switzerland (1986)
Leigh, E. G. Jr., Rand, A. S. & Windsor, D. M. (Eds.) *The Ecology of a Tropical Forest: Seasonal Rhythms and Long-Term Changes* Smithsonian Institution Press, Washington, D.C. (1982)
May, R. M. "How many species are there on earth?" *Science* 241:1441–1449 (1988)
Mooney, H. "Lessons from Mediterranean-climate regions" 157–165 pp. in: Wilson, E. O. (Ed.) *Biodiversity* National Academy Press, Washington, D.C. (1988)

Myers, N. "Threatened Biotas: 'Hotspots' in Tropical Forests" *Environmentalist* 8(3):1–20 (1988)
Myers, N. *Deforestation Rates in Tropical Forests and their Climatic Implications* Friends of the Earth, London, (1989)
O'Brien, Stephen, J. & Evermann, J. F. "Interactive influence of infectious disease and genetic diversity in natural populations" *TREE* 3(10):pp. 254–259 (1988)
Plucknett, D. L., Smith, N. J. H., Williams, J. T. & Anishetty, N. M. *Gene Banks and the World's Food* Princeton University Press, Princeton, N.J. (1987)
Pimm, S. L. "Determining the effects of introduced species" *TREE* 2(4):pp. 106–108 (1987)
Polunin, N. V. C. "Marine 'genetic resources' and the potential role of protected areas in conserving them" *Environmental Conservation* 10(1):31–41 (1983)
Rabinowitz, D., Cairnes, S. & Dillon, T. "Seven forms of rarity and their frequency in the flora of the British Isles" 182–204 pp. in: Soulé, M. E. (Ed.) *Conservation Biology: The Science of Scarcity and Diversity* Sinaur Associates, Sunderland, Mass., 584 pp. (1986)
Raup, D. M. "Biological extinction in earth history" *Science* 231:1528–1533 (1986)
Raven, P. H. "Biological resources and global stability" pp. 3–27 in S. Kawano *et al.* (Eds.) *Evolution and Coadaptation in Biotic Communities* University of Tokyo Press, Tokyo (1988)
Ray, G. C. "Ecological diversity in coastal zones and oceans" pp. 36–50 in Wilson, E. O., *Biodiversity* National Academy Press, Washington D.C., (1988)
Ribbink, A. J. *et al.* "A preliminary survey of the cichlid fishes of rocky habitats in Lake Malawi" *South African J. Zoology* 18(3):149–310 (1983)
Savidge, J. A. "Extinction of an island forest avifauna by an introduced snake" *Ecology* 68(3):660–668 (1987)
Scott, J. M., Csuti, B., Jacobi, J. D. & Estes, J. E. "Species richness: a geographic approach to protecting future biological diversity" *BioScience* 37:782–788 (1987)
Soule, Michael & Wilcox, Bruce (Eds.) *Conservation Biology* Sinaur Associations, Sunderland, MA (1980)
Stanton, Nancy L. & Lattin, J. D., "In defense of species" *BioScience* 39(2):67
Vitousek, P. M., Ehrlich, P. R., Ehrlich, A. H. & Matson, P. A., "Human appropriation of the products of photosynthesis" *BioScience* 36:pp. 368–373 (1986)
WCED *Our Common Future* OUP, Oxford, UK (1987)
Whitmore, T. C., Peralta, R., Brown, K. "Total species count in a Costa Rican tropical rain forest" *J. Tropical Ecology* 1:pp. 375–378 (1985)
Whitten, A. J., Bishop, K. D., Nash, S. V. & Clayton, L. "One or more extinctions from Sulawesi, Indonesia?" *Conservation Biology* 1(1):42–48 (1987)
Wilson, E. O. (Ed.) *Biodiversity* National Academy Press, Washington, D.C., (1988)

7 MARINE POLLUTION

Moulder & Williamson (Ed.) "Estuarine and Costal Pollution: Detection, Research and Control" *Water Science and Technology* Vol. 18 nos. 4/5, Pergamon Press (1986)
Newman & Agg (Ed.) *Environmental Protection of the North Sea* Heinemann (1988)
Salomons, W., Byrne, B. L., Duursma, E. K. & Forstner, U. (Eds.) *Pollution of the North Sea: An Assessment* Springer-Verlag (1988)

The Atmospheric Input of Trace Species to the World Oceans GESAMP Reports and Studies, no. 38, WMO (1989)
East Asian Seas Review Ambio, Vol. XVII, no. 3 (1988)
Environmental Capacity: An approach to marine pollution prevention GESAMP Reports and Studies, no. 30, FAO (1986)
Land/Seas Boundary Flux of Contaminants: Contributions from Rivers GESAMP Reports and Studies, no. 32, UNESCO (1987)
Marine Pollution Bulletin
Plastics in the Sea Special Issue of Marine Pollution Bulletin, Vol. 18, no. 6B (1987)

The State of the Marine Environment GESAMP Reports and Studies, no. 39

8 NUCLEAR POWER AND THE ENVIRONMENT

General and safety:

May, J., *The Greenpeace Book of the Nuclear Age* Victor Gollancz, London (1989)

Marshall, W. (Ed.) *Nuclear Power Technology* Clarendon Press, Oxford, 3 vols: Reactor Technology, Fuel Cycle, Nuclear Radiation (1983)

Nero, A. *A Guidebook to Nuclear Reactors* University of California Press, Berkeley (1979)

Patterson, W. C., *Nuclear Power* 2nd Edition, Penguin, Harmondsworth (1983)

Nuclear Power and the Environment Royal Commission on Environmental Pollution, Sixth Report, London, HMSO (1976)

Nuclear Power in the Age of Uncertainty US Congress/Office of Technology Assessment, Washington (1984)

Fuel cycle:

World Nuclear Handbook Nuclear Engineering International, annually, Reed International Publishers, London

Radioactive waste:

Chapman, N. & McKinley, I. G. *The Geological Disposal of Nuclear Waste* John Wiley and Sons, Chichester (1987)

Objectives, Concepts and Strategies for the Management of Radioactive Waste Arising from Nuclear Power Programmes OECD/Nuclear Energy Agency, Paris (1977)

Decommissioning:

Decommissioning of Nuclear Facilities: Feasibility, Needs and Costs OECD/Nuclear Energy Agency, Paris (1986)

Proliferation and security:

Goldblat, J. (Ed.) *Nuclear Proliferation: The why and the wherefore* Sipri, Taylor and Francis London (1985)

Rodgers, P. & Dando, M. *NBC 90: The directory of nuclear, biological and chemical arms and disarmament 1990* Tri-Service Press, London (1990)

Environmental Consequences of Nuclear War Scientific Committee on the Problems of the Environment, International Council of Scientific Union, John Wiley (1986)

9 OZONE DEPLETION

For the general reader:

Gribbin, John *The Hole in the Sky: Man's Threat to the Ozone Layer* Corgi Books (1988)

Protecting the Atmosphere—An International Challenge German Bundestag (Ed.) Bonn, Bonner Universitats-Buckdruckerei (1989)

Stratospheric Ozone United Kingdom Stratospheric Ozone Review Group, London, HMSO (1987)

Stratospheric Ozone 1988 United Kingdom Stratospheric Ozone Review Group, London, HMSO (1988)

Stratospheric Ozone 1990 United Kingdom Stratospheric Ozone Review Group, London, HMSO (1990)

More technical:

Scientific Assessment of Stratospheric Ozone, Vols. 1 & 2 (1989) World Meteorological Organization, Global Ozone Research and Monitoring Project Report no. 20, available from: National Aeronautics and Space Administration; United Kingdom—Department of the

Environment; National Oceanic and Atmospheric Administration; United Nations Environment Program; World Meteorological Organization

The reports of the Environmental Effects Panel, the Technology Review Panel and the Economic Assessment Panel are available from UNEP (United Nations Environmental Programme)

10 RENEWABLE ENERGY

A Single European Market for Energy Science Policy Research Unit and Royal Institute for International Affairs, London, RIIA (1989)

Alferov, Z. "Solar Electricity" in "New and Renewable Sources of Energy" *Impact of Science on Society* no. 147 (1987)

Besant-Jones, J. "The Future Role of Hydropower in Developing Countries" *Industry and Energy Department Working Paper, Energy Series Paper no. 15* (1989)

Braudel, F. *Civilisation and Capitalism 15–18th Century* Vol. I "The Structures of Everyday Life" London, Fontana (1985)

Brinkworth, B. J. "The Challenge of Renewables" in Institute of Energy *Applied Energy Research* Bristol, Hilger (1989)

Carlson, D. E. "Low Cost Power from Thin Film Photovoltaics" in Johansson, T., Bodlund, B. & Williams, R. H. (Eds.) *Electricity—Efficient End-Use and New Generation Technologies and their Planning Implications* Lund, Lund University Press (1989)

Cataldi, R. "World Geothermal Development: the Present Situation and Opportunities for the Future" in *Impact of Science on Society* no. 147 (1987)

Commission of the European Communities *A Community Orientation to Develop New and Renewable Energy Sources* Brussels, Commission of the European Communities (1986)

Commission of the European Communities *Energy and the Environment* Brussels, Commission of the European Communities (1990)

Commission of the European Communities *Energy for a New Century—the European Perspective* Brussels, Commission of the European Communities (1990)

Commission of the European Communities *European Technologies for Energy Management—the Thermie Programme* Brussels, Commission of the European Communities, (1989)

Danish Ministry of Energy *Energy in Denmark* Copenhagen, Ministry of Energy (1987)

Eden, R., Posner, R., Bending, R., Crouch, E. & Stanislaw, J. *Energy Economics—Growth Resources and Policies* Cambridge, CUP (1982)

Energy in Europe, various issues

Energy Technology Support Unit *Background Papers Relevant to the 1986 Appraisal of UK Energy Research Development and Demonstration* London, HMSO (1987)

European Energy Report, various issues

Goddard, S. C., *Proof of Evidence on Comparison of Non-Fossil Options to Hinkley Point C* CEGB 6, Hinkley Point C Power Station Public Inquiry (1988)

Goldemberg, J., Johannson, T. B., Reddy, A. K. N. & Williams, R. H., *Energy for a Sustainable World* New Delhi, Wiley Eastern (1988)

Grubb, M. J. "The Potential For Wind Energy in Britain" *Energy Policy* Vol. 16 no. 6 (December 1988)

International Energy Agency *A Ten Year Review of Collaboration in Energy RD & D 1976–86* Paris, OECD/IEA, (1987)

International Energy Agency *Energy in non-OECD countries—Selected Topics 1988* Paris, OECD/IEA (1988)

International Energy Agency *Energy Policies and Programmes of IEA Countries, 1988 Review* Paris, OECD/IEA (1989)

International Energy Agency *Renewable Sources of Energy* Paris, OECD/IEA, (1987)

Leach, G. & Mearns, R. *Beyond the Woodfuel Crisis* London, Earthscan (1988)

Moore, T. "Thin Films: Expanding the Solar marketplace" *EPRI Journal* Vol. 14, no. 2

Palz, W. & Shock, R. A. *Limiting Emissions: the Importance of New and Renewable Energy Sources* mimeo (1989)

Pearson, P. J. & Steven, P. "The Fuelwood Crisis and the Environment: Problems Policies and Instruments" *Energy Policy* Vol. 17, no. 2 (April 1989)

Rae, John "Global Warming: UK Options and Policy" paper to *Energy Without Frontiers—The Single European Energy Market in an Age of Environmental Awareness* London, IBC (1990)

Review—the Quarterly Journal of Renewable Energy various issues

Shea, C. P. *Renewable Energy: Today's Contribution, Tomorrow's Promise* Washington, The Worldwatch Institute (1988)

Stevens, Y. "Photovoltaics Applications in Rural Areas of Developing Countries: a survey of evidence" *International Journal of Global Energy Issues* Vol. 2, no. 1 (1990)

Stirling, Andrew "The View from the Environmental Movement" paper to *Energy Without Frontiers—The Single European Energy Market in an Age of Environmental Awareness* IBC (1990)

The Engineer, various issues

UK Department of Energy "Renewable Energy in the UK: The Way Forward" *Energy Paper no. 55* HMSO (1988)

UK Department of Energy "The Severn Barrage Project: General Report" *Energy Paper no. 57* HMSO (1989)

UK Department of Energy "An Evaluation of Energy Greenhouse Gas Emissions and Measures to Ameliorate them" *Energy Paper no. 58* London, HMSO (1990)

World Bank *Striking a Balance—the Environmental Challenge of Development* Washington, World Bank (1989)

11 VEHICLE EMISSIONS

Wright, Lawrence J. *Regulation of Air Pollutant Emissions from Motor Vehicles* Washington (1984)

Car Ownership and Use OECD, Paris (1982)

Closing the Gasoline System—Control of Gasoline Emissions from the Distribution System and Vehicle Report 3.90, CONCAWE, Brussels

ENDS (Environmental News Digest) London (monthly)

Environmental Effect of Automotive Transport The OECD Compass Project, OECD, Paris (1988)

Future of the Automobile Counterpoint, London (1985)

JAPCA (Journal of Air Pollution Control and Waste Management Association) Washington (monthly)

Motor Vehicle Emissions Regulations and Fuel Specifications Report 2/90 CONCAWE Brussels (1990)

Volatile Organic Compound Emissions in Western Europe: Control Options and their Cost Effectiveness for Gasoline Vehicles, Distribution and Refining Report 6/87, CONCAWE. Brussels

12 WATER QUALITY

Calow, P. *River Water Quality: An Ecological Approach* British Ecological Society (1990)

Crabtree, R. W. *River Water Quality Modelling in the UK: A Review of Past and Present Use with Recommendations for Future Requirements* Water Research Centre, Frankland Road, Swindon, UK (1986)

Meybeck, M., Chapman, D. V. & Helmer, R. *Global Freshwater Quality: A First Assessment* WHO/UNEP, Blackwell, Oxford, UK (1989)

O'Neill, P. *Environmental Chemistry* George Allen & Unwin, London, UK (1985)

Trudgill, S. T. (Ed.) *Solute Processes* Wiley, Chichester, UK (1986)

World Resources Institute/International Institute for Environment and Development *World Resources, 1988–89* Chs. 8, 9, Basic Books Inc., New York, USA (1988)

13 OTHER ISSUES

Elkington, John & Burke, Tom *The Green Capitalists* Gollancz (1987)
Elkington, John & Hailes, Julia *The Green Consumer Guide* Gollancz (1988)
Elkington, John & Hailes, Julia *The Green Consumer's Supermarket Shopping Guide* Gollancz (1989)
Lovelock, James E. *Gaia: A New Look at Life on Earth* OUP (1979)
Lovelock, James E. *The Ages of Gaia* OUP (1988)

PART II: POLITICS

Bahro, Rudolph *From Red to Green* Verso (1984)
Callenbach, Ernest *Ecotopia* Bantam Books (1977)
Capra, Fritjof *The Turning Point* Wildwood House (1984)
Croall, Stephen & Ramkin, William *Ecology for Beginners* Writers and Readers (1981)
Devall, Bill & Sessions, George *Deep Ecology* Peregrine Smith (1985)
Fenton, James *The Ecology of Environmentalism* ECOS 8(4) (1987)
Foreman, Dave, & Haywood, Bill *Ecodefense: A Field Guide to Monkeywrenching* Ned Ludd Books (1987)
Gruhl, Herbert *A Planet is Plundered* Fischer Verlag (1978)
Illich, Ivan D. *Energy and Equity* Calder & Boyars (1976)
McCormick, John *The Global Environmental Movement* Belhaven (1989)
Meyer *Revolt from the Centre* (Petersen & Sorensen)
Parkin, Sara *Green Parties—An International Guide* Heretic Books (1989)
Poritt, Jonathan *Seeing Green* Blackwell (1984)
Refpin, Jeremy *Entropy: Into the Greenhouse World* Bantam New Age (1989)
Schumacher, Fritz *Small is Beautiful* Abacus (1976)
Schwartz, Walter & Dorothy *Breaking Through* Green Books (1987)
Seed, John *et al. Thinking Like a Mountain* Heretic Books (1988)
Spretnak, Charlene & Capra, Fritjof *Green Politics: The Global Promise* Paladin (1985)
Wall, Derek *Getting There: Steps to a Green Society* Green Print (1980)
Wimmer, Langdon *The Whale and the Reactor: A Search for Limits in our Age of High Technology* Chicago Press (1986)

Blueprint for Survival The Ecologist (1972)
Limits to Growth The Club of Rome, Universe Books (1974)
UK Green Party publications *1990 Budget: The Green Alternative: Don't Let the World Turn Grey*

PART III: CONVENTIONS, REPORTS, DIRECTIVES AND AGREEMENTS

Caroll, John E. (Ed.) *International Environmental Diplomacy* CUP (1988)
Cutrera, Achille (Ed.) *European Environmental Yearbook 1987* International Institute for Environmental Studies
Degenhardt, Henry W. *Maritime Affairs: A World Handbook* Longman (1985)
Degenhardt, Henry W. *Treaties and Alliances of the World* 4th Edition, Longman (1986)

Engali, G., Gijwijt, A. J. & Rhode, B. (Eds.) *Environmental Polices in East and West* Taylor Graham, London (1987)
Grenville, J. A. S. & Wasserstein, Bernard, *Major International Treaties Since 1945* Methuen (1987)
Haigh, Nigel, *EEC Environmental Policy and Britain* 2nd Edition, Longman (1987)
Johnson, Stanley P. *The Pollution Control Policy of the European Communities*, 2nd edition, Graham and Trotman, London (1983)
Shaw, Malcolm N. S. *International Law* Grotius Publications Ltd. (1986)
Wilcher, Marshall E. *Environmental Co-operation in the North Atlantic Area* University Press of America (1980)

UNEP *Register of International Treaties and Other Agreements in the Field of the Environment* Nairobi

PART IV: ORGANIZATIONS

Barker, Michael J. C. *Directory for the Environment: Organisations in Britain and Ireland* Routledge and Kegan Paul, 2nd Edition (1986)
Elkington, John, Burke, Tom & Hailes, Julia *Green Pages Yearbook and Directory* Routledge and Kegan Paul (1988)

Who's Who in the Environment; England The Environment Council (1990)
Who's Who in the Environment; Scotland The Environment Council (1988)
World Directory of Environmental Organizations California Institute of Public Affairs (1989)

GENERAL

Brackley, Peter *Energy and Environmental Terms: A Glossary* Gower (1988)
Hayter, Teresa *Exploited Earth: Britain's Aid and the Environment* Earthscan (1989)
Holdgate, M. W. *A Perspective of Environmental Pollution* CIP (1979)
Leach, Gerald & Mearns, Robin. *Beyond the Woodfuel Crisis* Earthscan (1989)
Nicholson, Max *The New Environmental Age* CUP (1987)
North, Richard *The Real Cost* Chatto & Windus (1986)
Royston, Michael *Pollution Prevention Pays* Pergamon Press (1979)
Shoard, Marion *This Land is Our land: The Struggle for Britain's Countryside* Paladin (1987)
Shoard, Marion *The Theft of the Countryside* Paladin (1980)

Gaia: An Atlas of Planet Management Pan Books (1985)
Our Common Future World Commission on Environment and Development OUP (1987)

INDEX

Abidjan Convention for Co-operation in the Protection and Development of the Marine and Coastal Environment of the West and Central African Region ... 238
Accidents ... 103, 178, 211
Acid deposition ... 3, 227
Acid deposition
  agricultural crops ... 11
  environmental effects ... 9
  human health implications ... 12
  materials degradation ... 12
  monitoring ... 7
  precursors ... 4
  principal agreements ... 229
  stationary source control ... 13
Acid rain ... 3
Acid Rain Information Centre, UK ... 314
Acidic pollution
  transport of ... 6
Advisory Committee on Pollution of the Sea, UK ... 314
AEA Technology: Environment and Energy, UK ... 315
African NGOs Environmental Network ... 294
African Timber Organization ... 231, 294
African Wildlife Foundation ... 295
Agalev, Belgium ... 200, 214
Agalev Parliamentary Group, Belgium ... 214
Agricultural chemicals ... 117
Air pollution
  internal combustion engine ... 16
Alliance to Save Energy, USA ... 315
Alpha particles ... 107
Alternativ Framitid, Norway ... 217
Amenity loss ... 179
American Council for an Energy-Efficient Economy, USA ... 316
American Wilderness Alliance, USA ... 316
American Wildlands, USA ... 316
Ammonia ... 6
Amoco Cadiz ... 178
Antarctic ... 24, 230
Antarctic
  atmospheric science ... 31
  climate ... 24
  earth sciences ... 30
  exploration ... 25
  geography ... 24
  living resources ... 36

marine and life sciences ... 30
medical science ... 31
mineral resource ... 34, 35
principal agreements ... 230
scientific context ... 29
tourism ... 40
waste disposal ... 40
Antarctic and Southern Ocean Coalition ... 295
Antarctic Treaty
parties ... 25, 26
Antarctic Treaty System ... 24, 27, 28
Arab Centre for the Studies of Arid Zones and Dry Lands, Syria ... 296
Aral Sea, USSR ... 161
Arbeitsgemeinschaft fur Umweltfragen e.V., FRG ... 317
Arctic Institute of North America, Canada ... 296
Arctic stratosphere ... 127
Ascension Island
status of selected taxa ... 82
Asia-Pacific People's Environment Network, Malaysia ... 296
Asian Ecological Society, Taiwan ... 297
Asian Environment Society, India ... 297
Asociación pro Conservación de la Pesca Deportiva Costarricense, Costa Rica ... 317
Association for Conservation of Energy, UK ... 317
Atmospheric science
Antarctica ... 31
Audubon Society, USA ... 333
Australia
Green Electoral Movement ... 214
green politics ... 206
Nuclear Disarmament Party ... 214
Rainbow Alliance ... 214
Tasmanian Wilderness Society ... 214
Vallentine Peace Group ... 214
Australian Conservation Foundation ... 318
Austria
United Greens of Austria ... 199
Die Grune Alternative ... 214
Parlamentsklub der Grunen ... 214
Austrian Federation for the Protection of Nature ... 340
Azores
status of selected taxa ... 82

Baltic Marine Environment Protection Committee, Finland ... 297
Banchory Research Station, UK ... 336
Bangor Research Station, UK ... 336
Barcelona Convention on Pollution and the Mediterranean Sea ... 234
Bathing Water Directive
EC ... 247
Belgium
Agalev ... 200, 214
Agalev Parliamentary Group ... 214
Ecolo ... 200, 214
Ecolo Parliamentary Group ... 214
Bequerel ... 107

Beta particles ... 107
Bhopal, India ... 177, 178
Biological diversity ... 79, 233
Biological diversity
  international agreements ... 235
  threats ... 79
Bio-diversity threat
  categories ... 83
  climate change ... 80
  habitat alteration ... 79
  human pressures ... 80
  introduced species ... 80
  overharvesting ... 79
  pollution ... 79
Biomass
  renewable energy ... 136
Brazil
  energy usage ... 57
  Partido Verde ... 214
British Antarctic Survey, UK ... 337
British Ecological Society, UK ... 318
British Geological Survey, UK ... 337
British Trust for Conservation Volunteers, UK ... 319
Bromine cycle ... 126
Bund, FRG ... 186
Bureau of the Convention on Wetlands of International Importance Especially as Waterfowl Habitat, Switzerland ... 256

CAB International, UK ... 256
Canada
  Green Party of Canada ... 215
  Green Party of Quebec ... 215
  Green Party Political Association ... 215
  The Ontario Greens ... 215
  Parti Vert du Canada ... 215
  Parti Vert du Quebec ... 215
Canary Islands
  status of selected taxa ... 82
Carbon dioxide ... 53
Carbon dioxide
  chemical removal ... 59
Carbon monoxide ... 148
Carbon tetrachloride ... 127
Cartagena (Caribbean) Convention ... 234
Cartagena (Colombia) Convention for the Protection and Development of the Marine Environment of the Wider Caribbean ... 239
Catalytic converters ... 17, 150
Central Australian Conservation Council ... 320
Centre for Alternative Technology, UK ... 257
Centre for Economic and Environmental Development, UK ... 352
Centre for Environmental Management and Planning, UK ... 258
Centre for Our Common Future, Switzerland ... 258
CFCs ... 54, 127, 129, 243
Chernobyl, USSR ... 178, 208

China
energy usage ... 57
fossil fuel resources ... 64
reafforestation ... 75
Chipko Information Centre, India ... 216
Chlorine
atmospheric concentrations ... 129
Chlorine monoxide ... 126
Chlorofluorocarbon (CFC) ... 54, 127, 129, 243
Chlorophyll ... 164
Citizens' initiatives ... 197
Club of Rome ... 259
Co-operative Council for the Arab States of the Gulf, Saudi Arabia ... 299
Coal cleaning ... 13
Coal gasification ... 14
Coliforms ... 165
Combatting desertification
World Bank strategies ... 77
Comhaontas Glas, Ireland ... 216
Comité des Constructeurs d'Automobiles du Marché Commun, Belgium ... 298
Comité International de Recherche et d'Etude de Facteurs de l'Ambience, Belgium ... 259
Commission for the Conservation of Antarctic Marine Living Resources, Australia ... 297
Committee of Common Market Automobile Constructors, Belgium ... 298
Committee of International Development Institutions on the Environment, Kenya ... 259
Committees of Correspondence, USA ... 207
CONCAWE, Belgium ... 302
Confederación de los Verdes, Spain ... 218
Conference on Desertification, UN, Kenya ... 232
Conference on Environment and Development, UN, 1992 ... 176
Conference on the Human Environment, UN, Stockholm 1972 ... 4, 105, 223
Conseil Européen des Fédérations de l'Industrie Chimique, Belgium ... 299
Conseil International pour l'Exploration de la Mer, Denmark ... 271
Conservation Trust, UK ... 320
Contract Regarding an Interim Supplement to Tanker Liability for Oil Pollution ... 236
Convention and Resolution on Long-Range Transboundary Air Pollution ... 228
Convention for the Conservation of Antarctic Marine Living Resources ... 28, 32
Convention for the Prevention of Marine Pollution by Dumping from Ships and Aircraft ... 237
Convention for the Prevention of Pollution from Ships ... 237
Convention for the Protection of Birds ... 233
Convention for the Protection of the Ozone Layer ... 243, 244
Convention on Assistance in the case of a Nuclear Accident or Radiological Emergency ... 242
Convention on Long Range Transboundary Air Pollution ... 18
Convention on Nature Protection and Wild Life Preservation in the Western Hemisphere ... 233
Convention on the Early Notification of Nuclear Accidents ... 242
Convention on the Establishment of an International Fund for Compensation for Oil Pollution Damage ... 236
Convention on the Law of the Sea ... 27, 237
Convention on the Prevention of Marine Pollution by Dumping ... 236

Convention on the Protection of the Marine Environment of the Baltic Sea Area ... 237
Convention on the Regulation of Antarctic Mineral Resource Activities ... 28, 33
Costa Rican Sport Fishing Conservation Association ... 317
Council for Environmental Conservation, UK ... 326
Council for the Protection of Rural England, UK ... 322
Council of Europe, France ... 299
Council on Environmental Quality, USA ... 321
Countryside Commission, UK ... 322
Countryside Commission – Office for Wales, UK ... 323
Countryside Commission for Scotland, UK ... 323
Critical level ... 21
Critical load ... 21
Czechoslovakia
  pollution ... 208

Danish Society for the Conservation of Nature ... 324
Danmarks Naturfredingsforening, Denmark ... 324
Danube Circle, Hungary ... 208, 216
Danube dam ... 199
DDT ... 102
De Groenen, Netherlands ... 217
De Groenen–Green Amsterdam, Netherlands ... 217
De Gronne, Denmark ... 215
De Gronne, Norway ... 217
Debt-for-nature swaps ... 176
Deep ecology ... 188
Defenders of Wildlife, USA ... 324
Deforestation ... 42
Deforestation
  agreement ... 231
  effects on coastal waters ... 95
  rates by country ... 86, 87
Dei Greng Alternativ, Luxembourg ... 216
Denmark
  De Gronne ... 215
  green party ... 200
Der Grune Parteio, Switzerland ... 218
Desertification ... 66, 72, 232
Desertification
  definitions ... 67
Deutscher Naturschutzring e.V -Bunderverband fur Umweltschutz, FRG ... 325
Developed countries
  renewable energy usage ... 137
Die Grune Alternative, Austria ... 214
Die Grünen, FRG ... 185, 196, 215
Die Grünen im Bundestag, FRG ... 215
Directive on Air Quality Standards for Nitrogen Dioxide
  EC ... 228
Directive on Major Accident Hazards
  EC ... 250
Directive on Marketing and Use of Certain Dangerous Substances and Preparations
  EC ... 250

Directive on Packaging and Labelling of Dangerous Substances
EC 250
Directive on Pollution caused by Certain Dangerous Substances discharged into the Aquatic Environment of the Community
EC 238
Directive on Prevention and Reduction of Environmental Pollution by Asbestos
EC 250
Directive on the Sulphur Content of Gas oil
EC 228
Disasters 178
Dissolved oxygen 165
Duna Kor, Hungary 216
Dunstaffnage Marine Laboratory, UK 335
Dutch Foundation for East European Environmental Contacts, Netherlands ... 325

Earth First! USA 218
Earth sciences, Antarctica 30
Earthwatch, USA, UK, Australia 260
Eastern Europe
green politics 208
EC Large Combustion Plant Directive 18, 19
Ecoglasnost 208
Ecolo, Belgium 200, 214
Ecolo Parliamentary Group, Belgium 214
Ecological Charter for the Mountains of Northern Europe 234
Ecological Club, Poland 187
Ecological Club & FOW Greece, Greece 215
Ecology 186
Ecology Party, UK 185, 204
Electrical conductivity 164
Emission reductions 62
Endangered species
definition 83
Endangered Species Act, USA 234
Energy and Environment Programme, UK 261
Energy efficiency 58, 62
Energy policies 65
Energy Technology Support Unit, UK 64
Energy usage
national 57
Environment Council, UK 326
Environmental Co-operation Agreement 229
Environmental Data Services, UK 325
Environmental Defense Fund, USA 187, 326
Environmental health 177
Environmental impact assessment
Antarctica 39
Environmental matters
miscellaneous international agreements 251
Environmental Protection Agency, USA 353
Environmentalism 186, 210
Ethiopia
land degradation 71
European Association for the Science of Air Pollution, UK 300
European Atomic Energy Community (Euratom) 242

European Bank for Reconstruction and Development 210
European Community
energy usage 57
European Community
fossil fuel resources 64
European Council of Chemical Manufacturers' Federations, Belgium 299
European Environmental Bureau, Belgium 300
European Green Parties
declaration 218
European Inventory of Existing Commercial Chemical Substances
EC 250
European Monitoring and Evaluation Programme
UN 4
European Parliament 183
European Parliament
elections 184, 205
European Water Charter 247
Eutrophication 166
Extinct species
definition 83
Exxon Valdez 178

Federal Motor Vehicle Central Program, USA 245
Federal Republic of Germany 185
Federal Republic of Germany
Die Grünen 196, 215
Die Grünen im Bundestag 215
energy usage 57
fossil fuel resources 64
Federal Water Pollution Act, USA 247
Federazione delle Liste Verdi, Italy 216
Field Studies Council, UK 328
Finland
Vihrea (Green Party Group) 215
Vihrea Liitto Green Union 215
Finnish Association for Nature Conservation 348
Fish
Antarctica 36
Flue gas desulphurization 15
Fluidised bed combustion 14
Fondation Hellef Fir D'Natur, Luxembourg 328
Food and Agriculture Organization
UN 261
Forest decline 9
Forest inhabitants 43
Forest loss 44
Forest loss
agriculture 46
cattle ranching 47
debt 49
land distribution 47
measurement 44
mining 49
timber 47

Fossil fuel resources
national ... 64
Foundation for Environmental Conservation, Switzerland ... 262
Framtiden i vare hender, Norway ... 217
France
energy usage ... 57
fossil fuel resources ... 64
green politics ... 201
Les Verts ... 215
France Nature Environment ... 329
Friends of the Earth
France ... 201
Italy ... 203
national organizations ... 263–5
Friends of the Earth International ... 263
Fuel switching ... 62
Fundación Ecuatoriana para la Conservación de la Naturaleza, Ecuador ... 329
"Fundis", FRG ... 198
Furzebrook Research Station, UK ... 336

Gaia ... 180
Galapagos
status of selected taxa ... 82
Gamma radiation ... 107
Geothermal
renewable energy ... 136
German Federation of Nature Conservation Societies ... 325
Global temperature rise ... 55
Global warming ... 52, 231
Global warming
sea levels ... 56
temperature rise ... 55
Government departments
environmental ... 308–313
Grass-roots democracy ... 190
Greece
Ecological Club & FOW Greece ... 215
Panhellic Centre for Environmental Studies ... 215
Green Belt Movement, Kenya ... 216
Green Committees of Correspondence Clearinghouse, USA ... 218
Green consumerism ... 210
Green Electoral Movement, Australia ... 214
Green movement
criteria ... 188
ethics ... 189
four principles ... 187
roots ... 187
Green Movement Organization, USSR ... 330
Green parties
voters ... 194
Green Party, FRG ... 185, 196
Green Party, Länder, FRG ... 198
Green Party, UK ... 183, 204, 218

Green Party of Quebec, Canada ... 215
Green Party Political Association of British Columbia, Canada ... 215
Green Platform, Netherlands ... 203
Green policies
  economics ... 191
  future ... 210
  influence ... 195
  nuclear weapons ... 193
  population ... 194
  social issues ... 193
  Third World ... 193
  work ... 192
Green politics ... 183
Greenhouse effect ... 52, 231
Greenpeace ... 186, 211
Greenpeace
  national organizations ... 266
Greenpeace International ... 265
Green Party of Canada ... 215
Ground water acidification ... 10
Group of Experts on the Scientific Aspects of Marine Pollution
  UN ... 93, 266
Grube Partei der Schweiz, Switzerland ... 204
Gruppo Parlamentare Verde, Italy ... 216

Habitat loss
  wetlands ... 91, 95
Habitat loss in Africa ... 89
Habitat loss in Asia ... 90
Habitat range and loss
  selected primates ... 91
Habitats
  threats ... 85
Hainburg dam, Hungary ... 199
Halocarbons ... 125
Halogens
  atmospheric loadings ... 128
Halons ... 127
Hand-arm vibration syndrome ... 178
Hazardous waste ... 175
Health ... 177
Heavy metals ... 167
Helsinki Accord ... 224
Helsinki Commission, Finland ... 297
High Energy Agriculture ... 74
Hungary
  Danube Circle ... 209, 216
  Duna Kor ... 216
  Panos Institute ... 216
  pollution ... 208
Hydrocarbon emissions
  from vehicles ... 149
Hydroelectricity use ... 59

Iceland
Kvennalissstinn ... 216
Men's Green Party ... 216
Incineration at sea ... 96
Indeterminate species
definition ... 83
India
Chipko Information Centre ... 216
energy usage ... 57
soil loss ... 75
Industrial wastes ... 96
Institut pour une politique Europénne de l'Environnement, France ... 331
Institute for European Environmental Policy, FRG ... 300
Institute for Resource Management, USA ... 267
Institute for Social Ecology, USA ... 218
Institute of Freshwater Ecology, UK ... 336
Institute of Hydrology, UK ... 336
Institute of Oceanographical Science, UK ... 335
Institute of Terrestrial Ecology, UK ... 336
Institute of Virology and Environmental Microbiology, UK ... 336
Institution of Environmental Sciences, UK ... 330
Inter-Governmental Maritime Consultative Organization
UN ... 275
Intergovernmental Panel on Climate Change ... 56, 232
International Association for Ecology, USA ... 268
International Association on Water Pollution Research and Control, UK ... 269
International Atomic Energy Agency, Austria ... 242
International Centre for Conservation Education, UK ... 269
International Center for the Solution of Environmental Problems, USA ... 270
International Chamber of Commerce, France ... 270
International Commission on Radiological Protection, UK ... 108
International Committee for Research and Study of Environmental Factors,
Belgium ... 259
International Conference on the Protection of Forests ... 231
International Convention for the Prevention of Pollution by Ships ... 104
International Convention for the Prevention of Pollution of the Sea by Oil ... 236
International Convention on Civil Liability for Oil Pollution ... 236
International Council for the Exploration of the Sea, Denmark ... 271
International Council of Scientific Unions, France ... 272
International Court of Justice, Belgium ... 224, 232
International debt ... 49
International Energy Agency, France ... 272
International Environmental Bureau, Switzerland ... 273
International Geophysical Year ... 26
International Geosphere-Biosphere Programme ... 74
International Institute for Environment and Development, UK ... 273
International Institute for Environment and Safety, FRG ... 289
International Maritime Organization, UK ... 275
International Petroleum Industry Environmental Conservation Association,
UK ... 275
International Professional Association for Environmental Affairs, Belgium ... 276
International Society of Tropical Foresters, USA ... 276
International Solar Energy Society, Australia ... 277
International Tanker Owners Pollution Federation, UK ... 278
International Tropical Timber Agreement ... 231
International Tropical Timber Organization, Japan ... 278

International Union for the Conservation of Nature and Natural Resources, Switzerland ... 281
International Union for the Conservation of Nature and Natural Resources
  land restoration ... 76
  Plant Information Plan ... 82
International Union of Air Pollution Prevention Associations, UK ... 279
International Waterfowl and Wetlands Research Bureau, UK ... 279
International Whaling Commission, UK ... 233, 280
International Youth Federation for Environmental Studies and Conservation, Denmark ... 281
Internationales Institut fur Umwelt und Gesellschaft, FRG ... 289
Ionizing radiation ... 107
Ireland
  Comhaontas Glas ... 216
  green party ... 206
Italy
  energy usage ... 57
  Federazione delle Liste Verdi ... 216
  green politics ... 202
  Gruppo Parlamentare Verde ... 216
IUCN – The World Conservation Union, Switzerland ... 281
Ixtoc 1, Mexico ... 178

Japan
  energy usage ... 57
  fossil fuel resources ... 64
  green politics ... 207
  Midori Green Party ... 216
  Seikatsu Club ... 216
Jedah Convention for the Conservation of the Red Sea and Gulf of Aden Environment ... 238
Juan Fernandez
  status of selected taxa ... 82

Kenya
  Green Belt Movement ... 216
Krill
  Antarctica ... 38
Kuwait Regional Convention ... 238
Kvennalissstinn, Iceland ... 216

La Fédération Française des Sociétés de Protection de la Nature, France ... 329
Lake Manapouri ... 184
Lake Nyos ... 178
Land degradation ... 66, 232
Land degradation
  irrigated croplands ... 72
  mountainous areas ... 70
  restoration ... 74 *et seq.*
  soil loss ... 69
Land restoration
  IUCN guidelines ... 76
Latin American Network of Environmental NGOs, Uruguay ... 304

Law of the Sea
UN ... 237
Le Parti Ecologiste Suisse, Switzerland ... 204
Lead exposure ... 177
League of Conservation Voters, USA ... 207
Lean burn engine systems ... 17
Lega svizzera per la salvaguardia del patrimonio nazionale, Switzerland ... 344
Lego Ambiente, Italy ... 187
Les Verts, France ... 215
Letzeburger Natur – a Vulleschutzliga, Luxembourg ... 331
Lia svizzra per la protecziun de la patria, Switzerland ... 344
Liechtensteinische Gesellschaft für Umweltschutz, Liechtenstein ... 332
Life sciences
Antarctica ... 30
Ligue Luxembourgeoise pour la Protection de la Nature et des Oiseaux, Luxembourg ... 331
Ligue Suisse du Patrimoine National, Switzerland ... 344
Ligue Suisse pour la Protection de la Nature, Switzerland ... 350
Lima Convention for the Protection of the Marine Environment and Coastal Areas of the South-East Pacific ... 239
List of National Parks and Protected Areas
UN/IUCN ... 282
London Dumping Convention ... 104
Lord Howe Island
status of selected taxa ... 82
Los Verdes
Spain ... 218
Love Creek, USA ... 176
Luxembourg
Dei Greng Alternativ ... 216

Madeira
status of selected taxa ... 82
Man and the biosphere ... 284
Marine pollution ... 93, 235
Marine pollution
definition ... 93
inland waters ... 239
metals ... 101
nutrients ... 99
open sea ... 93
petroleum hydrocarbons ... 100
principal agreements ... 240
radioactive substances ... 103
sewage ... 98
shelf and coastal waters ... 94
sources ... 93
synthetic organic compounds ... 102
Marine Pollution Control Unit, UK ... 332
Marine sciences
Antarctica ... 30
Mauritius
status of selected taxa ... 82
McMurdo Station
Antarctica ... 126

Medical science
Antarctica ... 31
Men's Green Party, Iceland ... 216
Merlewood Research Station, UK ... 336
Methane ... 54
Methanol ... 160
Methyl chloroform ... 127
Midori Green Party, Japan ... 216
Miljopariet de Grona, Sweden ... 193, 203, 218
Million tree campaign ... 319
Minamata, Japan ... 178
Mineral resource
terminology ... 34
Mining
forest loss ... 49
Montreal Protocol ... 60, 129
Movimento Democrático, Portugal ... 217

National Ambient Air Quality Standards, USA ... 228
National Audubon Society, USA ... 333
National energy usage ... 57
National Parks and Protected Areas
UN ... 282
National Resources Defense Council, USA ... 207, 334
National Society for Clean Air and Environmental Protection, UK ... 334
National Wildlife Federation, USA ... 207
Natural Environment Research Council, UK ... 335
Nature Conservancy Council, UK ... 338
Nature Conservation Council, Iceland ... 338
Naturskyddsföreningen, Sweden ... 349
Natuurmonumenten, Netherlands ... 339
Netherlands
Die Groenen ... 203, 217
De Groenen (Green Amsterdam) ... 217
energy usage ... 57
fossil fuel resources ... 64
New Zealand ... 184
Nitric acid ... 126
Nitrogen oxides ... 5, 54
Nitrogen oxides
emission limits ... 19
removal or control ... 16, 60
Noise ... 178
Non-Nuclear Weapon States ... 123
Non-violence ... 190
Nordic Council for Ecology, Sweden ... 301
Nordic Council of Ministers, Denmark ... 301
Norfolk Island
status of selected taxa ... 82
Norges Naturvernforbund, Norway ... 339
North American Bioregional Project ... 218
Norway
Alterativ Framitid ... 217
De Gronne ... 217

Framtiden i vare hender ... 217
green party ... 206
Norwegian Society for the Conservation of Nature, Norway ... 339
Nuclear accidents ... 118
Nuclear Disarmament Party, Australia ... 214
Nuclear fuel
military cycle ... 113
reprocessing ... 111
Nuclear fuel cycle ... 109
Nuclear issues ... 241
Nuclear issues
international agreements ... 243
Nuclear Non-Proliferation Treaty ... 123
Nuclear power ... 59, 106
Nuclear power
accident prevention ... 118
decommissioning ... 120
fast breeder ... 120
fusion ... 120
security ... 122
usage ... 112
Nuclear thermal reactors ... 110
Nuclear war
environmental consequences ... 123
Nuclear waste
classification ... 114
management ... 114
Nuclear Weapon States ... 123
Nuclear weapons
green policies ... 193
Nutrients ... 165

Occupational health ... 177
OECD – Environment Committee ... 283
OECD – Nuclear Energy Agency ... 283
Offshore oil exploitation
pollution ... 97
Oil Companies' European Organization for Environmental Health and Protection, Belgium ... 302
Oil pollution
marine ... 100
offshore exploitation ... 97
Ontario Greens, Canada ... 215
Organization of African Unity ... 175
Organization of American States, USA ... 303
Os Verdes, Portugal ... 217
Oslo Commission, UK ... 303
Osterreichjischer Naturschutzbund, Austria ... 340
Oxygen – dissolved ... 165
Ozone ... 54, 125
Ozone depletion ... 125, 243
Ozone hole
Antarctica ... 125

Panhellic Centre for Environmental Studies, Greece 215
Panos Institute, Hungary 216
Paris Commission, UK 304
Paris Convention for the Prevention of Marine Pollution from Land-based
Sources 238
Paris Convention for the Protection of Birds Useful to Agriculture 233
Paris Declaration 220
Parlamentsklub der Grunen, Austria 214
Parti Ecologiste Suisse, Switzerland 218
Parti Vert du Canada, Canada 215
Parti Vert du Québec, Canada 215
Particulate emissions
from vehicles 149
Partido Popular Monárquico, Portugal 217
Partido Verde, Brazil 214
PCBs 102
People Party, UK 185, 204
pH 163
Plastics pollution 96
Plymouth Marine Laboratory, UK 335
Poland
pollution 208
Polski Klub Ekologiczny 217
Wolnosc i Pokoj 217
Polski Klub Ekologiczny, Poland 217
Portugal
Movimento Democrático Portugal 217
Os Verdes 217
Partido Popular Monárquico 217
Programme on Man and the Biosphere 284
Protocol on Co-operation in Pollution Emergencies 239
Protocol on Co-operation in Combatting Pollution in Cases of Emergency ... 238
Protocol on Substances which Deplete the Ozone Layer, Montreal 129
Proudman Oceanographic Laboratory, UK 335

Rachel Carson Council, USA 340
Radiation 106
Radiation dosage 109
Radioactive marine pollution 103
Radioactive waste programme 242
Rainbow Alliance, Australia 214
Rainbow Coalition, Netherlands 203
Rainbow Warrior 178
Rainforest 43
Ramsar Convention 256
Rare species
definition 83
"Realos", FRG 198
Recycling of waste 175
Red Data Books 82, 282
Red Latinoamericana de ONGs Ambientalistas, Uruguay 304
Red mud 249
Regional Organization for the Protection of the Marine Environment,
Kuwait 304

Regional Seas Conventions ... 105
Renewable energy ... 133
Renewable energy
  biomass ... 136
  environmental effects ... 146
  geothermal ... 136
  policies ... 144
  potential ... 140
  research ... 138
  solar ... 135
  usage ... 59, 137
  water ... 135
  wind ... 135
Renewable resources ... 244
Resource Conservation Act, USA ... 248
Rhine pollution ... 177
Robert Hooke Institute, UK ... 335
Rodrigues
  status of selected taxa ... 82
Royal Commission on Environmental Pollution, UK ... 341
Royal Institute of International Affairs, UK ... 261
Royal Society for Nature Conservation, UK ... 341
Royal Society for the Protection of Birds, UK ... 186, 342

St. Helena
  status of selected taxa ... 82
Sandoz ... 178
Schweizer Arbeitsgemeinschaft für Umweltforschung, Switzerland ... 343
Schweizer Heimatschutz, Switzerland ... 344
Schweizerische Gesellschaft für Umweltschutz, Switzerland ... 343
Schweizerischer Bund Fur Naturschutz, Switzerland ... 350
Scientific Committee on Antarctic Research ... 27
Scientific Committee on Problems of the Environment ... 285
Scope
  adhering bodies ... 286
Sea levels
  global warming ... 56
Sea Mammal Research Unit, UK ... 335
Seals
  Antarctica ... 36
Secretariat for the Protection of the Mediterranean Sea, Spain ... 305
Seikatsu Club, Japan ... 216
Sellafield, UK ... 103, 104, 179
Seveso, Italy ... 179
Sewage ... 98
Sewage sludges ... 96
Seychelles
  status of selected taxa ... 82
Shallow ecology ... 189
Sierra Club, USA ... 207, 344
Sievert ... 108
Smoke Abatement Society, UK ... 334
Social responsibility ... 190
Socialist Environment and Resources Association, UK ... 205
Society for the Preservation of Nature in the Netherlands, Netherlands ... 339

Société nationale de protection de la nature, France 345
Société suisse pour la protection de l'environnement, Switzerland 343
Socio-Ecological Union, USSR 346
Socotra
status of selected taxa 82
Soil acidification 9
Soil erosion 69
Soil loss 69
Solar energy
renewable energy 135
South Asia Co-operative Environment Programme 305
South Pacific Regional Environment Programme 306
Spain
Confederación de los Verdes 218
Los Verdes 218
Species diversity 81
Species rarity
forms 84
Squid
Antarctica 37
Standing Committee on Urban and Building Climatology, FRG 347
Status of selected taxa
selected islands 82
Stichting Natuur em Milieu, Netherlands 186, 347
Stockholm Declaration 226
Stratospheric ozone 125
Study Group for Environmental Questions, FRG 317
Sulphur dioxide 5
Sulphur dioxide
emission limits 18
national proposed emission reductions 22
removal after combustion 15
removal during combustion 14
vehicle emissions 149
Suomen Luonnonsuojeluiitto ry, Finland 348
Surface water acidification 10
Suspended sediment 165
Sweden
Miljopartiet de Grona 203, 218
Swedish Action Plan against Air Pollution, Sweden 21
Swedish Environmental Protection Agency, Sweden 349
Swedish Society for the Conservation of Nature, Sweden 349
Swiss Association for Environmental Protection, Switzerland 343
Swiss Association for Environmental Research, Switzerland 343
Swiss League for Nature Protection, Switzerland 350
Swiss League for the Preservation of National Heritage, Switzerland 344
Switzerland 204
Switzerland
Der Grune Parteio 218
Parti Ecologiste Suisse 218
Synthetic organic compounds
marine pollution 102

Tanker Owners' Voluntary Agreement Concerning Liability for Oil Pollution ... 236
Tasmanian Wilderness Society, Australia 214, 354

tbt ... 103
Temperature rise
  global warming ... 53
Terrestrial Effects Review Group, UK ... 9
Third World
  green party attitudes ... 193
Third World development ... 176
Thirty percent club
  membership ... 20
Threatened species
  current status ... 85
Threats to habitats ... 85
Three Mile Island, USA ... 179
Titanium dioxide ... 249
Toronto Conference ... 61
Torrey Canyon ... 179, 235
Total dissolved solids ... 164
Total organic carbon ... 165
Tourism
  Antarctica ... 40
Toxic and hazardous waste ... 248
Toxic Substances Control Act, USA ... 248
Toxic waste ... 175
Toxic Wastes Directive
  EC ... 249
Treaty on the Non-Proliferation of Nuclear Weapons ... 242
Treaty on the Non-Proliferation of Nuclear Weapons in Latin America ... 242
Tropical Forest Action Plan ... 51, 231
Turkish Association for the Conservation of Nature and Natural Resources, Turkey ... 350
Turkiye Tabiatini Koruma Dernegi, Turkey ... 350

Uberparteiliche Plattform Gegen Atomgefahren und Zukunftswerkstatt Energie, Austria ... 351
UK Centre for Economic and Environmental Development UK ... 352
Umweltbundesamt, FRG ... 351
UNEP, Kenya ... 129, 175, 287
UNEP
  regional and other offices ... 288–9
United Greens of Austria ... 199
United Kingdom
  energy usage ... 57
  fossil fuel resources ... 64
  Green Party ... 204, 218
United Nations
  selected articles ... 225
United Nations Environment Programme, Kenya ... 129, 175, 287
United Nations Environment Programme
  regional and other offices ... 288–9
United Nations Economic Commission for Europe, Switzerland ... 306
United States of America
  Earth First! ... 218
  energy usage ... 57
  fossil fuel resources ... 64

Green Committees of Correspondence Clearinghouse 218
green politics 206
Institute for Social Ecology 218
North American Bioregional Project 218
Environmental Protection Agency 353
Uranium 107
USSR
energy usage 57
fossil fuel resources 64

Vallentine Peace Group, Australia 214
Values Party, New Zealand 184
Vehicle emissions 148, 244
Vehicle emissions
controls 149
international agreements 246
legislation 151
legislation on evaporative emissions 158
legislation on lead emissions 157
legislation, Europe 154
legislation, Japan 154
legislation, USA 152, 158
regulation, ECE/EEC 156, 245
sources 148
Vibration 178
Vietnam
reafforestation 75
Vihrea (Green Party Group), Finland 215
Vihrea Liitto Green Union, Finland 215
Volatile organic compound 6
Vulnerable species
definition 83

Waste disposal 175
Waste disposal
Antarctica 40
Water
renewable energy 135
Water Act, USA 247
Water Conference
UN 246
Water quality 161, 246
Water quality
EC Directives 172
international agreements 247
measurement 169
safe limits 172
sources of pollution 171
specification 162
Water Resource Systems Research, UK 337
Watt Committee on Energy, UK 353
Whales
Antarctica 36

Wilderness Society, Australia 354
Wilderness Society, USA 355
Wilderness Watch, USA 355
Wind
  renewable energy 135
Windscale, UK 179
Wissenschaftszentrum Berlin, FRG 289
Wolnosc i Pokoj, Poland 217
World Action for Recycling Materials and Energy from Rubbish, UK 289
World Association of Soil and Water Conservation, USA 290
World Bank
  strategies to combat desertification 77
World Conservation Monitoring Centre, UK 82, 290
World Conservation Strategy
  IUCN 234, 282
World Environment Center, USA 291
World Health Organization
  environmental health 291
World Resources Institute, USA 292
World Wide Fund for Nature, Switzerland 211, 293
World Wildlife Fund, Switzerland 293
WWF, Switzerland 211, 293